PRAISE FOR *THE PRINCIPALSHIP: A LEARNING-CENTERED APPROACH*

"*The Principalship: A Learning-Centered Approach,* coauthored by Frederick C. Lunenburg and Beverly J. Irby, comes at the right time to help leaders navigate the complexities of the school system. Lunenburg and Irby bridge theory and research, combined with practical applications and best practices, to address every facet of the work and leadership needed to support teachers, students, and community members to move toward school improvement. I highly recommend it."
—**Sally J. Zepeda PhD, College of Education, University of Georgia**

"*The Principalship: A Learning-Centered Approach* provides a comprehensive and well-referenced guide to the complexities faced by school leaders. The authors skillfully address all elements of this crucial role, from improving instruction and learning to managing the organization. Particularly timely topics include keeping schools safe and dealing with political concerns, and every chapter contains excellent field-based activities. This informative book will appeal to both practitioners and researchers alike; it should be read by everyone interested in improving the leadership of our nation's schools."
—**Martha M. McCarthy, Presidential Professor, Loyola Marymount University, and Chancellor's Professor Emeritus, Indiana University**

"*The Principalship: A Learning-Centered Approach* is an outstanding book that deftly integrates research and practice. It will be of interest and use to people who work in and study schools. Lunenburg and Irby approach the writing as teachers in the sense that they provide prompts, probing questions, and case studies that compel readers to reflect on their experiences and assumptions while also offering new ways to think about how to improve schools toward excellence, efficiency, and equity. Highly recommended!"
—**Jeffrey S. Brooks, Curtin University School of Education**

"This is a great, inclusive, learner-centered approach to the teaching and practice of the principalship for current times and into the future."
—**Judy A. Alston, director, Department of Doctoral Studies and Advanced Programs, Ashland University, and program chair of AERA Spirituality and Education SIG**

D1607068

THE PRINCIPALSHIP

A Learning-Centered Approach

FREDERICK C. LUNENBURG

Sam Houston State University

BEVERLY J. IRBY

Texas A&M University

ROWMAN & LITTLEFIELD
Lanham • Boulder • New York • London

Acquisitions Editor: Mark Kerr
Acquisitions Assistant: Sarah Rinehart
Sales and Marketing Inquiries: textbooks@rowman.com

Credits and acknowledgments for material borrowed from other sources, and reproduced with permission, appear on the appropriate pages within the text.

Published by Rowman & Littlefield
An imprint of The Rowman & Littlefield Publishing Group, Inc.
4501 Forbes Boulevard, Suite 200, Lanham, Maryland 20706
www.rowman.com

86-90 Paul Street, London EC2A 4NE

British Library Cataloguing in Publication Information Available

Library of Congress Cataloging-in-Publication Data

Names: Lunenburg, Frederick C., author. | Irby, Beverly J., author.
Title: The principalship : a learning-centered approach / Frederick C. Lunenburg, Beverly J. Irby.
Description: Lanham, Maryland : Rowman & Littlefield, 2022. | Includes bibliographical references and index.
Identifiers: LCCN 2022014058 (print) | LCCN 2022014059 (ebook) | ISBN 9781538123942 (cloth) | ISBN 9781538123959 (paperback) | ISBN 9781538123966 (epub)
Subjects: LCSH: School principals—United States. | Educational leadership—United States. | Academic achievement—United States. | School management and organization—United States.
Classification: LCC LB2831.92 .L86 2022 (print) | LCC LB2831.92 (ebook) | DDC 371.2/0120973—dc23/eng/20220510
LC record available at https://lccn.loc.gov/2022014058
LC ebook record available at https://lccn.loc.gov/2022014059

♾️™ The paper used in this publication meets the minimum requirements of American National Standard for Information Sciences—Permanence of Paper for Printed Library Materials, ANSI/NISO Z39.48-1992.

Brief Contents

■ ■ ■

Contents

■ ■ ■

PART II: LEADERSHIP PROCESSES

PART III: MANAGING THE ORGANIZATION

PART IV: ETHICS, POLICY, AND LEGAL ISSUES

xxii ■ Contents

Preface

■ ■ ■

Student learning is the main reason for the school's existence. The focus on results, the focus on student learning, and the focus on students learning at high levels can happen only if teaching and learning become the central focus of the school and the central focus of the principal. The emphasis on student learning (the outcome rather than the process of schooling), coupled with federal legislation to that end, has placed more demands on the role of the principal than ever before in our nation's history.

To address the heightened demands on the principal for greater accountability for student learning, *The Principalship* uses a learning-centered approach, one that emphasizes the role of the principal as the steward of the school's vision: learning for all. The critical aspects of the teaching-learning process are addressed in our text including teaching; learning; student motivation; individual differences; classroom management; assessing student learning; and developing, maintaining, and changing school culture. In addition, we include in our book several topics not found in many other principalship texts. These topics include school safety, special education, gifted education, bilingual education, nontraditional organizational structures, gender-inclusive theories, women and minorities in the principalship, ethics, the political and policy context, human resource management, legal issues, and collective bargaining. Our book is documented extensively throughout and grounded in the latest research and theory with suggestions for applying theory to practice. We believe that our text reflects cutting-edge research and topical issues facing principals in today's schools.

Pedagogical Features
- **Focusing Questions.** Each chapter begins with five or six focusing questions designed to draw the reader's attention to major topics within the chapter.
- **Examples.** Hundreds of examples of real school situations are sprinkled throughout the text. We believe that a well-constructed example can illuminate the most complex concept.
- **Illustrations.** Each chapter contains descriptive figures and tables to visually clarify important concepts covered in the chapter.
- **Summary.** At the end of each chapter, a brief point-by-point summary recaps critical and especially major issues of theory, research, and practice.

- **Field-Based Activities.** At the end of each chapter, activities for discussion are included to help stimulate application of concepts and foster greater understanding of the material.
- **Case Studies.** A case from the world of practice is included at the end of each part of the book.
- **Suggested Readings.** An annotated list of readings on chapter topics is provided at the end of each chapter. These are current and popular readings that principals and prospective principals will find helpful in operating and understanding the operation of schools.
- **Citations.** Our text is documented extensively throughout, so that those who wish to follow up on certain matters and obtain more detail can do so. References appear at the end of the book in American Psychological Association (APA) style. This provides the reader with a quick and easy reference to documented material cited in the text.

Acknowledgments

Getting this book to you was a team effort. It required the highly coordinated efforts of dedicated professionals, faculty reviewers, designers, production specialists, editorial staff, and marketing and sales personnel. Although we cannot possibly thank all of them here, we wish to express our appreciation to all those whose talents made this book a reality.

We acknowledge the many colleagues who read and commented on various portions of the manuscript for this and earlier versions. Their suggestions were invaluable.

Frank Adams, Wayne State University
Anthony Avina, Cal Poly Pomona
Irwin Blumer, Boston College
Janice Buck, Lamar University
Jackson Flanigan, Clemson University
Saul Grossman, Temple University
Jeanette Hagelskamp, University of San Francisco
Christee Jenlink, Northeastern State University
James Mitchell, National University
Wade Nelson, Winona State University
Anthony Normore, Florida International University
Keith Rose, Pennsylvania State University
Pam Salazar, University of Nevada, Las Vegas
Rayton Sianjina, Delaware State University

PART I

Improving Instruction and Learning

1

Cultivating Community, Culture, and Learning

■ ■ ■

FOCUSING QUESTIONS

1. How has the role of the principal changed?
2. What is the appropriate role of the principal today?
3. How can the principal develop a professional learning community that transforms a school from a teaching organization to a learning organization?
4. How can the principal develop a positive school culture that promotes the achievement of *all* students?
5. How can principals assume the role of instructional leader to ensure that school improvement efforts impact teaching and learning?

In this chapter, we address these questions concerning community, culture, and learning. We begin the chapter by discussing a reconceptualization of the role of the principal from a hierarchical, bureaucratic image to one of devolving decision making and school self-determination. Next, we consider the way in which principals develop the capacity of the people within their schools to function as professional learning communities. Four pillars constitute the foundation of a school as a professional learning community: mission, vision, values, and goals. We then examine the elements of school culture that encourage the learning of all students and the professional growth of faculty. Finally, we conclude this chapter with a discussion of the principal's role as instructional leader, the primary focus of which is to promote the learning and success of *all* students.

REFRAMING THE ROLE OF THE PRINCIPAL

Despite some influential work of the effective schools research (Levine & Lezotte, 1990; Lezotte & Snyder, 2010; Lunenburg, 2005; National Center for Effective Schools Research and Development, 2000) and substitutes for leadership (Yukl, 2019), the principalship has historically been defined as position or role based, and hierarchical in nature (Murphy, 2002). This means that those higher in the organizational structure are perceived as more powerful than those below them and that the right to lead is limited to those provided with legitimate authority—that is, superintendent, principal, and so forth.

Why the Principal's Role Must Change

The type of principal needed in today's schools calls for a new approach to leading schools. The principal, faculty, staff, parents, and community work together sharing a vision of how to help all students achieve. Each school is considered a learning organization. Leadership is less hierarchical. Important decisions are made as much by site-level stakeholders as by state- or district-level participants. Decisions about school programs are decentralized to the school level, and leadership is no longer limited to formal organizational positions. Leadership is based on ability rather than role. Leadership activities are dispersed according to competence for required tasks rather than authority. This altered view of the principalship explains the centrality of the empowerment of teachers, parents, and students; the importance of site-based decision making; and the development of professional learning communities.

Central to reframing the role of the principal is a movement from a "power over" approach to a "power to" approach (Berg, 2018; Eckert, 2018; Fullan, 2018; Harris, Jones, & Huffman, 2018; Joyce & Calhoun, 2019; Pankake & Abrego, 2017; Sterrett, 2016). Principals are expected to be change agents and facilitators who improve conditions for learning through the creation of cultures that allow schools to operate as learning organizations (Fisher, Frey, & Pumpian, 2019; Gruenert & Whitaker, 2019; Murphy & Torre, 2014). That is, principals are considered leaders of leaders (Glickman & Burns, 2020). They are expected to bring out the leadership potential of every teacher and employee in the building and to work collaboratively with them, so that the school as a whole ends up making better decisions and is committed to continuous improvement (Bryk, 2020; Murphy, 2016).

Today's effective principals share leadership. They empower teachers to lead school projects and initiatives rather than serving as the chief problem solvers. They lead from the center rather than from the top, and they create an environment where teachers can continually learn and grow (Senge et al., 2012).

In the more successful schools, today's principals clearly defined themselves as at the center of the school's staff rather than at the top. Instead of occupying an authoritative position, they prefer instead to give leadership to others and to guide by example and by indirectly inducing thoughtfulness, rather than by making direct suggestions. In each instance, their role as an authority figure is downplayed and their role as a source of support and assistance is emphasized. These emergent principals believe in delegation, in developing collaborative decision-making processes, and in stepping back from being the chief problem solver in a school, by linking these roles more explicitly to the development of a professional learning community.

PROFESSIONAL LEARNING COMMUNITY

DuFour et al. (2021) define a **professional learning community (PLC)** as "educators committed to working collaboratively in ongoing processes of collective inquiry . . . to achieve better results for the students they serve . . . the key to improved learning for students is continuous, job-embedded learning for educators" (p. xii). Descriptions of a PLC vary (Cranston, 2011; DuFour, DuFour, & Eaker, 2006; DuFour, DuFour, & Eaker, 2008; DuFour et al., 2004, 2010; DuFour, DuFour, Eaker, & Many, 2006; DuFour et al., 2016; DuFour & Eaker, 1998, 2009; Eaker, DuFour, & DuFour, 2002; Eaker, DuFour, & DuFour, 2007; Eaker et al., 2021; Harris & Jones, 2010; Hipp et al., 2008; Hord, 2004; Hord & Sommers, 2008; Huffman & Hipp,

2003; Huffman & Jacobson, 2003; Louis & Marks, 1998; Pirtle & Tobia, 2014; Roberts & Pruitt, 2003; Servage, 2008; Stoll et al., 2006; Stoll & Louis, 2007; Tam, 2015; Vescio, Ross, & Adams, 2008; Wald & Castleberry, 2000). Most descriptions include the following six characteristics:

1. *Shared mission, vision, values, and goals.* The essence of a professional learning community is the educators' focus on and commitment to embracing learning for all students. To achieve this shared purpose, the members of a PLC create and are guided by a clear vision of what their school must become to help all students learn. They make collective commitments that clarify what each member will do to contribute to creating such schools, and they use results-oriented goals to measure their progress. This foundation of mission (purpose), vision (direction), values (collective commitments), and goals (targets) addresses how educators will work to improve their schools.

2. *Collaborative culture.* The basic structure of a PLC is a group of collaborative teams whose members work interdependently to achieve common goals—goals linked to the purpose of learning for all—for which members are held mutually accountable. Individual growth is essential for organizational growth to occur, but it does not guarantee organizational growth. Thus, building a school's capacity to learn is collaborative team learning. School stakeholders who engage in collaborative team learning are able to learn from one another, thus creating momentum to stimulate continued improvement.

   Michael Fullan (1993) stresses the importance of collaborative teams in the improvement process in his classic book *Change Forces*:

   > The ability to collaborate—on both large and small scale—is one of the core requisites of postmodern society. . . . [I]n short, without collaborative skills and relationships it is not possible to learn and to continue to learn as much as you need in order to be an agent of social improvement. (pp. 17–18)

3. *Collective inquiry.* Educators in a PLC engage in collective inquiry including: best practices about teaching and learning; clarification of their current practices; and an assessment of their students' current levels of learning. Collective learning enables team members to develop new skills, experience, and awareness. The increased awareness results in fundamental shifts in attitudes and beliefs enabling team members to make significant changes in the culture of the school.

4. *Action orientation.* Members of PLCs are action oriented. They recognize that learning always occurs in a context of taking action. The very reason teachers work together in teams and engage in collective inquiry is to serve as catalysts for action. Learning by doing develops a deeper and more profound knowledge and greater commitment than passive inaction.

5. *Continuous improvement.* A constant search for a better way to achieve goals and accomplish the purpose of the school are the essence of a PLC. Continuous improvement requires that each member of the school is engaged in an ongoing cycle of: gathering evidence of current levels of student learning; developing strategies to build on strengths and address weaknesses in that learning; implementing the strategies; analyzing the impact of the changes

to discover what was effective and what was not; and applying the new knowledge in the next cycle of continuous improvement. Participation in this process is the responsibility of every member of the school—school leaders, teachers, students, and parents—in the learning process.

6. *Results orientation.* Members of a PLC realize that their efforts to develop a mission, vision, values, and goals, build collaborative teams. engage in collective inquiry, take action, and focus on continuous improvement must be assessed on the basis of results rather than intentions. Purposeful improvement must be subjected to ongoing assessment on the basis of tangible results. Peter Senge (1996) affirms that "the rationale for any strategy for building a learning organization revolves around the premise that such organizations will produce dramatically improved results" (p. 44).

The school as a professional learning community consists of four pillars that constitute the foundation of the school: mission, vision, values, and goals. Each of these pillars takes its form from the answer to a specific question addressed to the stakeholders in the school: *Mission (Why do we exist?), Vision (What do we hope to become?), Values (What attitudes, behaviors, and commitments must we demonstrate to make our vision a reality?),* and *Goals (What specific steps must we take to achieve our objectives?)* (DuFour & Eaker, 1998, 2009).

The First Pillar: Mission

Why do we exist? The **mission** question challenges the faculty to reflect on the fundamental purpose of the school, the reason for its existence. The focus is not on how the faculty can do what it is currently doing better but, rather, why it is doing it in the first place. The aim of the question is to clarify priorities and give direction to all stakeholders in the school.

Mission statements are not new. In fact, mission statements for schools and school districts are commonplace. A review of these statements indicates that they sound much the same. A generic mission statement for North American schools proclaims:

> It is the mission of our school to help each child realize his or her full potential and become a responsible and productive citizen and lifelong learner who is able to use technology effectively and appreciate the multicultural society in which we live. (DuFour, 1997)

The similarity of mission statements is not a cause for concern. What is a cause for concern is the tremendous difference between writing a mission statement and living the mission. Pfeffer and Sutton (2000) found that ineffective organizations often write mission statements to create the illusion of action, substituting writing a mission statement for taking steps to bring a mission to life. They found no evidence that merely drafting and displaying a mission statement impacted how stakeholders in an organization act. Similarly, DuFour et al. (2016) found no correlation between the presence of a written mission statement and the ability of a school to function as a PLC. DuFour and colleagues (2016) wrote in their book *Learning by Doing: A Handbook for Professional Learning Communities at Work,* "The words of a mission statement are not worth the paper they are written on unless people begin to *do* differently" (p. 19). The mission of a school or school district is not revealed by what people say but, rather, by what they do.

Often contained in mission statements is acknowledgment that schools serve a common purpose—to help every child realize their potential and lead a successful and satisfying life. The idea of success for every child is closely linked to another cliché: the belief that all children can learn. It is time for educators—principals and teachers—to embrace the rhetoric of "learning for all" as the fundamental purpose of their schools.

The Every Student Succeeds Act (ESSA) of 2015 and its predecessor, The No Child Left Behind (NCLB) Act of 2001, have removed any doubt concerning the fundamental purpose of schools when they legislated the mission of public schools. The **purpose of schooling** is to help all children learn—to ensure that in every grade, every course, and every unit of instruction, all students acquire the intended knowledge, skills, and dispositions deemed most essential to their success.

More relevant and useful questions to ask when trying to build a shared sense of purpose are: If we believe that all children can learn, (a) What is it that we will expect them to learn? and (b) How do we respond when they do not learn? What would our schools look like if we said our fundamental purpose is to ensure that all students learn? What would people see us doing?

We would clarify what we want students to learn; monitor each student's learning in a timely manner; respond with appropriate interventions when students struggle; and enrich and extend learning for those who are not challenged. We would work together, rather than in isolation, as collaborative teams. We would seek evidence of our effectiveness and use that evidence in an ongoing process to strengthen our skills and understandings of best practices. We would build learning into our decision-making processes and openly examine all of our practices, discarding those that discourage student learning (Ambrose et al., 2010; Borich, 2011; Brookhart, 2011; Earl, 2013; Eby, Herrell, & Jordan, 2010; Kubiszyn & Borich, 2015; Marzano, 2017; Popham, 2020; Ruggiero, 2012).

Other deeper questions that faculty must engage when trying to build a shared sense of purpose include: What does it mean to help students learn how to learn? This goes beyond reading and mathematics to how students organize their time and their materials; How do they work together? A professional learning community involves all stakeholders working together, including students; What kinds of skills do students have for working together (Johnson & Johnson, 2009; Sharan & Sharan, 1999; Slavin, 2011)?; What kinds of skills do they have for understanding themselves, their own learning style (Raynor & Cools, 2011; Zhang & Sternberg, 2006), and being able to evaluate themselves (Dijkstra, Kuyper, van der Werf, Buunk, & van der Zee, 2008)?; How skilled are they at regulating their own learning (Greene, 2017; Paris & Paris, 2001; Pressley & Hilden, 2006; Schunk & Greene, 2018; Zimmerman & Kitsantas, 2005)?; How good are they in applying their learning to other contexts in the school and outside (Craig, Chi, & VanLehn, 2009; De Corte, 2003; Pugh & Bergin, 2005)?; and, How do students use technology and other resources in order to learn on their own (Brush & Saye, 2001; Franzke et al., 2005; Joo, Bong, & Choi, 2000; Kramarski & Zeichner, 2001; Moos & Azevedo, 2009; Scheiter & Gerjets, 2007)?

School principals would be held accountable for focusing on the fundamental purpose of their schools—student learning. This declaration—that the fundamental purpose of the school is to help all students learn the knowledge, skills, and dispositions most essential to their success—is the driving force behind the work of PLCs (Eaker et al., 2021).

The Second Pillar: Vision

What do we hope to become? The terms *mission* and *vision* are often used interchangeably. However, when applying the terms to the foundation of a PLC, they represent distinctly different things. Whereas mission addresses the question of *why* a school exists by establishing its purpose, **vision** addresses the question: *What* must we become to fulfill our purpose and what future do we hope to create for this school? When school stakeholders address the question of vision, they are attempting to describe a realistic future for the school—a future that is better in many ways than existing conditions. According to Bennis and Nanus (1985), a shared vision offers a target that beckons.

Researchers describe the importance of a shared vision in the improvement process and as an essential element of an effective organization (Bryk, 2020; Darling-Hammond et al., 2019; Fullan & Gallagher, 2020; Jackson & Lunenburg, 2010; Leithwood, 2018; Marzano, 2017; Murphy, 2020; Murphy & Bleiberg, 2019; Newmann, Carmichael, & King, 2015), as essential to a successful change process (Fullan, 2018; Hall & Hord, 2010; Murphy & Bleiberg, 2019), and as an absolute requisite for any learning organization (DuFour et al., 2021; Eaker et al., 2021; Senge, 1990, 2006; Senge et al., 2012). The ability to develop and communicate a shared vision has been cited as a critical element of effective leadership (Bryk, 2020; Fullan & Gallagher, 2020; Leithwood, 2018; Murphy, 2020; Northouse, 2021; Reeves, 2021).

Here are some tips for developing a vision for your school that professional learning community advocates recommend. Engage the faculty in a general agreement about what they hope their school will become. Enlist a faculty task force to identify the major findings of research studies on school improvement. Share the research findings with the faculty. Conduct small-group discussion sessions that enable the faculty to review the research and discuss their hopes for the future of the school. Discussions should also include criticisms of the traditional structure and culture of schools.

A traditional obstacle to schools moving forward is the inherent tradition of teacher isolation in schools (Leithwood, 2018; Murphy & Louis, 2018; Sarason, 2004; Senge et al., 2012). This must be addressed and overcome in order for a school to become a professional learning community. At all levels of the system, isolation is seen as the enemy of school improvement. Thus, most day-to-day activities in the school need to be specifically designed to connect teachers, principals, and district administrators with one another and with outside experts with regard to school improvement. Another tradition is that schools are very often run as top-down hierarchies, where faculty are not given a voice in decision making. Faculty need to address these structural and cultural traditions in schools that present obstacles and barriers to substantive improvements.

Using this formula, gradually, the faculty should be able to identify commonalities, a school all stakeholders can endorse. With the vision statement—with the ability to describe the school that all participants are trying to create—the principal then needs to work with students, teachers, parents, and others to discover or invent the structures, policies, and processes that will enable the school to move in that direction.

It should be noted that although the principal remains a valued participant in the development of a vision, vision is embodied by the process rather than by individuals (DuFour et al., 2021; Eaker et al. 2021). Principals must help to keep their colleagues from narrowing their vision and assist the school to maintain "a broader perspective." Excellence is a moving target; therefore, the vision should be revisited periodically to ensure that the vision remains relevant. Principals, in a sense, are keepers of the vision. The principal's modeling and reinforcing of vision-related behaviors appear critical to the success of the professional learning community.

This can be done by keeping the vision and mission at the front and center of all decisions. It means when a principal sits down with a faculty member to talk about a lesson observed, they may bring up the vision and how the lesson connects to that vision. The principal may bring up the vision when the budget is discussed with faculty. When the principal is hiring faculty or making faculty changes, or if the principal is engaged in curriculum changes or implementing new courses, they are always using the vision as the filter. When the principal is doing that, the people involved in the school—students, parents, faculty, and district office administrators—can see, through the principal's behavior and actions, that what is most important is this vision. Thus the principal, as a change agent, helps to create new programs and procedures that evolve from the shared vision and goals.

The Third Pillar: Values
How will we fulfill our purpose and make our vision a reality? Whereas the mission pillar addresses the question "why our school exists" and the vision pillar addresses the question "what we hope the school will become," the **values** question addresses how we will fulfill our purpose and make our desired future (vision) a reality. The values question challenges school stakeholders to identify the attitudes, behaviors, and commitments that they must demonstrate to move the school closer to their vision.

At this point, the members of another faculty task force might begin working with their colleagues to identify shared values—the attitudes, behaviors, and commitments—all teachers would pledge to demonstrate so as to move the school closer to their shared vision. The school board, support staff, administrative team, students, parents, and community members also engage in discussions of the attitudes, behaviors, and commitments the school needs from them to advance the vision. For example, what attitudes, behaviors, and commitments must the school board make to enable the school to achieve the vision statement? What attitudes, behaviors, and commitments must the parents make to become contributors in creating the school described in the vision statement? The process continues until all stakeholders are addressed.

DuFour and Eaker (1998, 2009) recommend a process for developing shared value statements. Each group begins by examining the vision statement and identifying what each group must do to bring it into existence. For example, what can the school board, the superintendent, the principal, the teachers, the parents, and the students do to advance the school toward the vision statement? Each group works in two teams of five. When all the ideas are listed, the five members review each idea. The ideas are shared between the two teams in each group. All ideas generated by each group are then broken down into four, five, or six general themes or categories. The groups do not need to have hundreds of value statements. A handful of value statements is most effective. Throughout this process, it is more powerful to articulate behaviors than beliefs. It is more important for each group to articulate what its members are prepared to do than to state what they believe.

The challenge for each group as it goes through the process is to get the members to understand the need to focus on themselves. They must ask, "What attitudes, behaviors, and commitments are we individually prepared to make in order to move this school forward?" After every group engages in this discussion, each one articulates the commitments it is prepared to make. At this point, the school has reached its first important milestone in the improvement process. Then a school can become more specific about where it goes from there.

The Fourth Pillar: Goals

What steps must we take to achieve our objectives? Goals are the results that a school tries to achieve (Locke & Latham, 2002; Van Soelen, 2021). This definition implies at least three relationships between goals and the principal. First, in terms of laying a foundation for a professional learning community, goals represent the implementation phase of school improvement. The determination of school goals is a primary responsibility of principals. In a professional learning community, faculty are active and valued participants in establishing goals with the principal and other stakeholders. **Goals** become guideposts in defining standards of school improvement efforts. Without clearly stated goals, there is no way to determine if acceptable standards of school improvement have been met (Lunenburg & Irby, 2000).

Second, goals are influenced by the aspirations of a school district's key administrators. For example, the goal of a school to be connected to the Internet; to have a computer lab in every school; to have computers in every classroom; and to provide professional development for faculty assumes that the district has or can obtain adequate resources to achieve the goal and that the school district's top administrators desire the goal (Lunenburg, 2007). This is more likely to happen in a professional learning community because all stakeholders are involved in developing a mission, vision, values, and goals.

Third, goals reflect a desired end result of school actions—what they wish to accomplish. It is important when formulating goals not to confuse means with ends. A powerful goal, and an appropriate one for school improvement, would be as specified following: "Every student in the school will be reading at grade level by third grade." It is direct. It is stating exactly what you want to accomplish. It is measurable. It is an end. It should be noted that because the vision statement is rather broad and tends to point to many different areas in the school, the principal and faculty are not going to be able to attack every area at once. They must make some decisions about which areas will take priority.

The focus may need to be narrowed, and goals help us narrow focus. Principals can provide a faculty with parameters for identifying goals that directly impact teaching and learning. And learning has to be the focus. Reading, writing, mathematics, and helping students learn how to learn are worthy goals. The next step is to plan activities and monitor progress on the stated goals.

Establishing explicit goals benefits all stakeholders by fostering commitment, providing performance standards and targets, and enhancing motivation (Midgley, 2014; Van Soelen, 2021). Each of these benefits will be discussed in turn.

Commitment. Goal statements describe the school's purpose to participants. The process of getting participants to agree to pursue a specific goal gives those individuals a personal stake in the outcome. Thus, goals are helpful in encouraging personal commitment to collective ends.

Standards. Because goals define desired outcomes for the school, they also serve as performance criteria. When appraising performance, principals need goals as an established standard against which they can measure performance. Clearly defined goals enable principals to weigh performance objectively on the basis of accomplishment rather than subjectively on the basis of personality. For example, if a school wishes to increase test scores by 10 percent and the actual increase is 20 percent, the principal and faculty have exceeded the prescribed standard.

Targets. School goals provide principals with specific targets and direct collegial efforts toward given outcomes. People tend to pursue their own ends in the absence of formal organizational goals.

Motivation. In addition to serving as targets, standards, and commitment, goals perform a role in encouraging colleagues to perform at their highest levels. Moreover, goals give principals a rational basis for rewarding performance. If colleagues receive rewards equal to their levels of performance, they should continue to exert high levels of effort (Vroom, 1994).

To make the school's mission, vision, values, and goals something more than words on paper, the principal needs to communicate and model them so that they are embedded in the daily life of the school. The principal is the keeper of the vision and the one who keeps articulating it; when people are at the point where they say they can't go anymore, the principal is the one who comes out and says, "Let me remind you why we can do it." It is the principal's role to repeat such messages, over and over. It is their role to remind people: this is where we started; this is where we are now; and this is where we're headed. The principal does this in a variety of ways—writing about it in the weekly newsletter, talking about it at parent-teacher organizations and faculty meetings—to show the school community that this is the way we do business in this school.

Communication is important, but it is not enough. The thing that is necessary is the day-to-day work. It means when a principal sits down with a faculty member to talk about a lesson observed, they may bring up the vision and how the lesson connects to that vision. The principal may bring up the vision when the budget is discussed with faculty. When the principal is hiring faculty or making faculty changes, or if the principal is engaged in curriculum changes or implementing new courses, they are always using the vision as the filter. When the principal is doing that, the people involved in a professional learning community—students, parents, faculty, district office administrators, and so on—can see, through the principal's behavior and actions, that what is most important is this vision. Thus, the principal, as a change agent, helps to create new programs and procedures that evolve from the shared vision and goals.

A SCHOOL CULTURE: LEARNING FOR ALL

Principals who wish to develop their school's capacity to function as a professional learning community must face the challenge of shaping the school's culture (DuFour

& Eaker, 1998, 2009; DuFour et al., 2021; Eaker et al., 2021). Seymore Sarason (1996) asserts:

> To put it as succinctly as possible, if you want to change and improve the [culture] and outcomes of schooling both for students and teachers, there are features of the school culture that have to be changed, and if they are not changed, your well-intentioned efforts will be defeated. (p. 340)

Regardless of population size or location, wherever people spend a considerable amount of time together, a **culture** emerges—a set of customs, beliefs, values, and norms—that can either create a sense of mutual purpose—mission, vision, values, and goals—or perpetrate discord that precludes even the possibility of any unity or shared meaning. Every school has a culture, whether it is being attended to or not (Deal & Peterson, 2016).

Definition and Characteristics

Culture consists of all the beliefs, feelings, behaviors, and symbols that are characteristic of an organization. More specifically, culture is defined as shared philosophies, ideologies, beliefs, feelings, assumptions, expectations, attitudes, norms, and values (Schein & Schein, 2016). Although there is considerable variation in the definitions of school culture, it appears that most contain the following characteristics.

1. *Observed Behavioral Regularities.* When organizational members interact, they use common language, terminology, and rituals and ceremonies related to deference and demeanor.
2. *Norms.* Standards of behavior evolve in work groups, such as "a fair day's work for a fair day's pay," or "going beyond the call of duty." The impact of work-group behavior, sanctioned by group norms, results in standards and yardsticks.
3. *Dominant Values.* An organization espouses and expects its members to share major values. Typical examples in schools are high performance levels of faculty and students, low absence and dropout rates, and high efficiency and effectiveness.
4. *Philosophy.* Policies guide an organization's beliefs about how employees and clients are to be treated. For example, most school districts and schools have statements of philosophy or mission statements.
5. *Rules.* Guidelines exist for getting along in the organization, or the "ropes" that a newcomer must learn in order to become an accepted member.
6. *Feelings.* This characteristic applies to an overall atmosphere conveyed in an organization by the physical layout as well as the way in which members interact with clients or other outsiders (Schein & Schein, 2016).

None of the aforementioned characteristics by itself represents the essence of culture. However, the characteristics taken collectively reflect and give meaning to the concept of culture. And the culture of a school is interrelated with most other concepts in managing schools, including organizational structures, motivation, leadership, decision making, communication, and change (Lunenburg, 2010b). The challenge for the principal is to create a culture that is advancing the school toward its vision and reinforcing the behaviors that are necessary for moving the school forward. The principal as developer of culture is to be a support and visionary.

In a professional learning community, principals work with all stakeholders to develop the school's culture. Developing culture is a conscious endeavor, and principals must be proactive in doing so. They begin by having people articulate in specific terms the kinds of behaviors and commitments they think are necessary to move their school forward. This is a challenge, for every school faces the issue of developing school culture. In developing a culture for school improvement, the principal can pose the following questions: What is the school trying to become? What is our vision of the school we are trying to create? What attitudes, behaviors, and commitments must we demonstrate for our vision to be realized? What goals should we establish to move closer to the school we desire? Are we clear on what is to be accomplished and the criteria we will use in assessing our efforts? Are the current policies, programs, procedures, and practices of our school congruent with our stated vision and values? What are our plans to reduce discrepancies?

Having defined organizational culture and provided the characteristics thereof, we now turn to examining how organizational cultures are created, maintained, and changed. The following questions arise: How is an organizational culture created? How is an organizational culture maintained? Can organizational culture be changed? Although there are similarities, the process of creating, maintaining, and changing school cultures is complex. Each process will be discussed in turn.

CREATING SCHOOL CULTURE

Terrence Deal and Allan Kennedy (1984) published one of the first books on organizational culture titled *Corporate Cultures*. Deal and Kennedy identified four dimensions of organizational culture: values, heroes, rites and rituals, and communication networks. These four dimensions play a key role in developing school cultures.

Values

What are values, and how do they affect behavior? **Values** are general criteria, standards, or principles that guide the behavior of organization members (Jones, 2013). There are two kinds of values: terminal and instrumental. A **terminal value** is a desired outcome that organization members seek to achieve (George & Jones, 2012). Schools typically adopt any of the following as terminal values: quality, excellence, and success. An **instrumental value** is a desired mode of behavior. Modes of behavior that most schools advocate include working hard, providing excellent teaching, respecting student diversity, being creative, teamwork, and maintaining high standards (Bulach & Lunenburg, 2016a).

Thus, a school's culture consists of outcomes that the school seeks to achieve (its terminal values) and the modes of behavior the school encourages (its instrumental values). Ideally, instrumental values help the school achieve its terminal values. For example, a school/school district whose culture emphasizes the terminal value of high achievement for all students might attain this outcome by encouraging instrumental values like working hard to reach all students. This combination of terminal and instrumental values leads to school/school district success.

Schools are able to achieve success only when shared values exist among group members (Bulach & Lunenburg, 2016b). Shared values can provide a strong school identity, enhance collective commitment, provide a stable social system, and reduce the need for bureaucratic controls. The following guidelines are recommended to achieve shared values (Uhl-Bien, Schmerhorn, & Osborn, 2016):

- A widely shared understanding of what the school stands for, often embodied in slogans
- A concern for individuals over rules, policies, procedures, and adherence to job duties
- A well-understood sense of the informal rules and expectations so that group members and administrators understand what is expected of them
- A belief that what group members and administrators do is important, and that it is important to share information and ideas
- A recognition of heroes, whose actions illustrate the organization's shared philosophy and concerns
- A belief in rites and rituals as important to organization members as well as to building a common identity.

(pp. 372–273)

Heroes and Heroines

Most successful schools have their heroes and heroines. Heroes and heroines are born and created. The born hero or heroine is the visionary institution builder like Henry Ford, founder of the Ford Motor Company, Walt Disney, creator of Disney Studios and theme parks, and Mary Kay Ash, founder of Mary Kay Cosmetics. Created heroes and heroines, on the other hand, are those the institution has made by noticing and celebrating memorable moments that occur in the day-to-day life of the organization. Thomas Watson, former head of IBM, is an example of a situation hero. Other well-known heroes include Lee Iacocca at Chrysler, Sam Walton at Wal-Mart, and Vince Lombardi, the legendary coach of the Green Bay Packers. Heroes and heroines perpetuate the organization's underlying values, provide role models, symbolize the organization to others, and set performance standards that motivate participant achievement.

In many schools, local heroes and heroines—exemplars of core values—provide models of what everyone should be striving for. These deeply committed staff come in early, are always willing to meet with students, and are constantly upgrading their skills.

Rites and Rituals

Another key aspect in developing school cultures are the everyday activities and celebrations that characterize the organization. Most successful organizations feel that these rituals and symbolic actions should be managed. Through rites and rituals, recognition of achievement is possible. The Teacher of the Year Award and National Merit Schools are examples. Similarly, a number of ceremonial rituals may accompany the appointment of a new superintendent of schools, including press and other announcements, banquets, meetings, and speeches.

Some organizations have even created their own reward rituals. At Hollibrook Elementary School in Spring Branch, Texas, rites and rituals reinforce student learning. Under the leadership of the principal and faculty, and supported through ties to the Accelerated Schools Model, the school developed numerous traditions to create a powerful professional culture and foster increased student success. For example, faculty meetings became a hotbed of professional dialogue and discussion of practice and published research. "Fabulous Friday" was created to provide students with a wide assortment of courses and activities. A "Parent University" furnishes courses and materials while building trust between the school and the largely Hispanic community. Norms of collegiality, improvement, and connection reinforce and symbolize what the school is about.

Communication Networks

Stories or myths of heroes are transmitted by means of the communications network. This network is characterized by various individuals who play a role in the culture of the organization (Deal & Kennedy, 1984). Each institution has *storytellers* who interpret what is going on in the organization. Their interpretation of the information influences the perceptions of others. *Priests* are the worriers of the organization and the guardians of the culture's values. These individuals always have time to listen and provide alternative solutions to problems. *Whisperers* are the powers behind the throne because they have the boss's ear. Anyone who wants something done will go to the whisperer. *Gossips* carry the trivial day-to-day activities of the organization through the communications network. Gossips are very important in building and maintaining heroes. They embellish the heroes' past feats and exaggerate their latest accomplishments. And, finally, *spies* are buddies in the woodwork. They keep everyone well informed about what is going on in the organization. Each of these individuals plays a key role in building and maintaining an organization's culture. It should be noted that the names used here are those ascribed by Deal and Kennedy (1984) to emphasize the importance of communication networks in developing an institution's organizational culture.

MAINTAINING SCHOOL CULTURE

Once a school's culture is developed, a number of mechanisms help solidify the acceptance of the values and ensure that the culture is maintained or reinforced (organizational socialization). These mechanisms are described in the following steps for socializing employees (Pascale, 1985).

Step 1: Hiring Staff

The socialization process starts with the careful selection of employees. Trained recruiters use standardized procedures and focus on values that are important in the culture. Those candidates whose personal values do not fit with the underlying values of the school are given ample opportunity to opt out (deselect).

Step 2: Orientation

After the chosen candidate is hired, considerable training ensues to expose the person to the culture. Many forms of orientation are also provided to incoming students to a school, for example, transitions from elementary school to middle school and transitions from middle school to high school.

Step 3: Job Mastery

Whereas step 2 is intended to foster cultural learning, step 3 is designed to develop the employee's technological knowledge. As employees move along a career path, the organization assesses their performance and assigns other responsibilities on the basis of their progress.

Step 4: Reward and Control Systems

The school pays meticulous attention to measuring results and to rewarding individual performance. Reward systems are comprehensive, consistent, and focus on those aspects of the school that are tied to success and the values of the culture. For example, a school will specify the factors that are considered important for success. Operational measures are used to assess these factors, and performance appraisals of employees are tied to the accomplishment of these factors.

Promotion and merit pay are determined by success on each of the predetermined critical factors. For example, teachers who do not fit the school's culture are either transferred to another school or dismissed. It should be noted that collective bargaining agreements may stipulate procedures for teacher transfer or grounds for dismissal (American Arbitration Association, 2022; Lunenburg, 2000).

Step 5: Adherence to Values

As personnel continue to work for the school, their behavior closely matches the underlying values of the culture. Identification with underlying values helps employees reconcile personal sacrifices caused by their membership in the school. Personnel learn to accept the school's values and place their trust in the school not to hurt them.

For instance, teachers work long hours on a multiplicity of fragmented tasks, for which they sometimes receive little recognition from their superiors, subordinates, and community. They sometimes endure ineffective school board members and supervisors and job assignments that are undesirable and inconvenient. Identification with the common values of the school allows these teachers to justify such personal sacrifices.

Step 6: Reinforcing Folklore

Throughout the socialization process, the school exposes its members to rites and rituals, stories or myths, and heroes that portray and reinforce the culture. For example, in one educational institution, the story is told of a principal who was fired because of his harsh handling of teachers. The principal had incorrectly believed a myth that being "tough" with his teachers would enhance his image in the eyes of his superiors. The school district deemed such leadership behavior to be inconsistent with its school district philosophy of cultivating good interpersonal relationships and high levels of morale and job satisfaction among all its employees.

Step 7: Consistent Role Models

Those individuals who have performed well in the school serve as role models to newcomers to the school. By identifying these teachers as symbolizing success, the school encourages others to do likewise. Role models in strong-culture schools can be thought of as one type of ongoing staff development for all teachers.

CHANGING SCHOOL CULTURE

To this point, we have discussed how school culture is developed and maintained. Sometimes an organization determines that its culture needs to be changed. The change cycle has the following components (Pascale, 1985; Schein & Schein, 2016).

External Enabling Conditions

Enabling conditions, if they exist, indicate that the environment will be supportive of culture change. Such conditions are in the external environment and impact the organization. In a school setting, examples include scarcity or abundance of students, stability or instability of the external environment, and resource concentration or dispersion. In combination, these external enabling conditions determine the degree of threat to the organization's input sources (information, people, and materials).

Internal Permitting Conditions

To increase the likelihood of organizational culture change, four internal permitting conditions must exist: (a) a surplus of change resources (administrative time and energy, financial resources, and the like that are available to the system beyond those needed for normal operating); (b) system readiness (willingness of most members to live with the anxiety that comes with anticipated uncertainty that is characteristic of change); (c) minimal coupling (coordination and integration of system components); and (d) change-agent power and leadership (the ability of administrators to envision alternative organizational futures).

Precipitating Pressures

Four factors that precipitate organizational culture change include (a) atypical performance; (b) pressure exerted by stakeholders; (c) organizational growth or decrement in size, membership heterogeneity, or structural complexity; and (d) real or perceived crises associated with environmental uncertainty.

Triggering Events

Culture change usually begins in response to one or more triggering events. Examples include (a) environmental calamities or opportunities such as natural disasters, economic recession, innovations, or the discovery of new markets; (b) administrative crises such as a major shakeup of top administration, an inappropriate strategic decision, or a foolish expenditure; (c) external revolution such as mandated desegregation, PL101-476, Title IX, or the No Child Left Behind Act of 2001 and its successor, the Every Student Succeeds Act of 2015; and (d) internal revolution such as the installation of a new administrative team within the organization.

Cultural Visioning

Creating a vision of a new, more preferred organizational culture is a necessary step toward that culture's formation. Leaders survey the beliefs, values, assumptions, and behaviors of the organization's existing culture. They then seek to anticipate future conditions and create an image of the organization within that future.

Culture Change Strategy

Once a new cultural vision exists, an organization needs a strategy to achieve that culture. Such a strategy outlines the general process of transforming the present culture into the new one.

Culture Change Action Plans

A series of explicit action plans for the inducement, administration, and stabilization of change make a change strategy known. Inducement action planning involves stimulating organizational members to a change or countering resistance to change. Administrative action planning involves outlining interventions and mobilizing change agents. Stabilization action planning focuses on the institutionalization of culture change—that is, establishing the existence of the new culture as an accepted fact.

Implementation of Interventions and Reformulation of Culture

An organization selects culture change interventions based on the ecology of a particular organization for each action-plan phase and the change agent's competencies in implementing them. When implemented, the intervention plans result in a reformulated culture.

In a professional learning community, principals work with all stakeholders to develop, maintain, and/or change the school's culture that is advancing the school toward its mission, vision, values, and goals. Throughout this process, student achievement must be paramount (Bulach & Lunenburg, 2016a). A school should be a place where students come to learn, grow, and improve. Principals can make that happen by functioning as instructional leaders.

THE PRINCIPAL AS INSTRUCTIONAL LEADER

Demands for greater accountability, especially appeals for the use of more outcome-based measures, require the principal to be instruction oriented. Are the students learning? If the students are not learning, what are we going to do about it? The focus on results, the focus on student achievement, the focus on students learning at high levels can happen only if teaching and learning become the central focus of the school and the central focus of the principal.

How can principals help teachers to clarify instructional goals and work collaboratively to improve teaching and learning to meet those goals? Principals need to help teachers shift their focus from what they are teaching to what students are learning. We cannot continue to accept the teachers' premise that "I taught it; they just didn't learn it." The role of instructional leader helps the school to maintain a focus on why the school exists, and that is to help all students learn. Principals in this role *lead learning by leading instruction and curriculum.*

Shifting the focus of instruction from teaching to learning, forming collaborative structures and processes for faculty to work together to improve instruction, and ensuring that professional development is ongoing and focused toward school goals are among the key tasks that principals must perform to be effective instructional leaders (Darling-Hammond & Oakes, 2019; Zepeda, 2019). This will require districtwide leadership, as well as school leadership focused directly on learning. School principals can accomplish this goal by: (a) focusing on learning; (b) encouraging collaboration; (c) providing support; (d) aligning curriculum, instruction, and assessment; and (e) analyzing results. Taken together, these five dimensions provide a compelling framework for accomplishing sustained districtwide success for all children (Lunenburg, 2019).

Focusing on Learning

Principals can help shift the focus from teaching to learning if they insist that certain critical questions are being considered in the school, and principals are in a key position to pose those questions. What do we want our students to know and be able to do? The focus in a professional learning community is not, "Are you teaching?" but, rather, "Are the students learning?" How will you know if the students are learning? And that question points to student progress. How will we respond when students do not learn? What criteria will we use to evaluate student progress? How can we more effectively use the time and resources available to help students learn? How can we engage parents in helping our students learn? Have we established systematic collaboration as the norm in our school?

In their study of improving teaching for rigorous learning, which involved a sample of 1,500 schools, Newmann, Carmichael, and King (2015) found that successful classrooms focused on "authentic" pedagogy (teaching that requires students to think, to develop an in-depth understanding, and to apply academic learning to important realistic problems) and student learning. They achieved this in two ways: greater organizational capacity and greater external support.

The most successful schools, according to Newmann et al. (2015) were those that functioned as learning communities. That is, they found a way to channel staff and student efforts toward a clear, commonly shared purpose for learning. Moreover, they found that external agencies helped schools to focus on student learning and to enhance organizational capacity through three strategies: setting standards for learning of high intellectual quality; providing sustained schoolwide professional development; and using deregulation to increase school autonomy. In short, dynamic internal learning communities and their relationships with external networks made the difference. Evidence on the critical combination of internal and external learning is mounting.

In research recently completed at the Mid-continent Research for Education and Learning (McREL) Institute, Robert Marzano (2017) identified classroom practices that generally increase student achievement: identifying similarities and differences; summarizing and note taking; receiving reinforcement for effort and recognition for achievement; doing homework and practicing; using nonlinguistic representations; learning cooperatively; setting objectives and testing hypotheses; and using cues, questions, and advance organizers. Regardless of whether or not teachers teach to standards, these classroom practices work well.

In addition, Frederick Lunenburg and Beverly Irby (2011) provide long-standing, proven instructional strategies that can improve teaching and learning including: anticipatory set, stimulus variation, closure, reinforcement, recognizing attending behavior, silence and nonverbal cues, cueing, use of examples, planned repetition, questioning skills (fluency of questioning, probing questions, higher-order questions, divergent questions, etc.), the use of multiple frames of reference, and race, class, and gender equity.

Encouraging Collaboration

A key task for principals is to create a collective expectation among teachers concerning student performance—that is, principals need to raise the collective sense of teachers about student learning (Murphy & Louis, 2018). Then principals must work to ensure that teacher expectations are aligned with the school's instructional goals (Murphy, 2016). Furthermore, principals need to eliminate teacher isolation so that discussions about student learning become a collective mission of the school (Leithwood, 2018; Murphy & Louis, 2018; Sarason, 2004; Senge et al., 2012).

Principals must develop and sustain school structures and cultures that foster individual and group learning (Deal & Peterson, 2016; Fisher, Frey, & Pumpian, 2019; Gruenert & Whitaker, 2019; Murphy & Torre, 2014; Senge, 1990, 2006; Senge et al., 2012). Specifically, principals must stimulate an environment in which new information and practices are eagerly incorporated into the system. Teachers are more likely to pursue their group and individual learning when the school provides supportive conditions, such as particularly effective leadership (Costa, Garmston, & Zimmerman, 2014; Fullan, 2018; Glickman & Burns, 2020; Murphy, 2020; Murphy & Bleiberg, 2019; Northouse, 2021). Schools where teachers collaborate in discussing issues related to student learning are more likely to be able to take advantage of internally and externally generated information. Teachers can become willing recipients of research information if they are embedded in a setting where meaningful and sustained interaction with researchers occurs in an egalitarian context.

"The key to student growth is educator growth" (Murphy & Louis, 2016). In a collaborative learning environment, teachers become generators of professional knowledge rather than simply consumers of innovations. Innovations are built around the system rather than using prepackaged school improvement models. Changing mental models replaces training educators in new behaviors (Senge, 1990, 2006). Continuous instruction-embedded professional development replaces one-shot, non-instruction-specific professional development events (Zepeda, 2015). Single-loop, linear learning that monitors whether a system is reaching its goals is replaced by double-loop learning where systems are able to revisit whether goals are still appropriate and then recycle as needed (Argyris, 2007).

One popular collaboration structure is teacher teams. Schools are recognizing that teachers should be working together in teams as opposed to working individually in isolation in their classrooms. High-performing teams will accomplish four different things (Lunenburg & Lunenburg, 2015): (a) they will clarify exactly what students should know and be able to do as a result of each unit of instruction (because we know that if teachers are clear on the intended results of instruction, they will be more effective); (b) they will then design curriculum and share instructional strategies to achieve those outcomes; (c) they will develop valid assessment strategies that measure how well students are performing; and (d) then they will analyze those results and work together to come up with new ideas for improving those results. Regular assessment and analysis of student learning are key parts of the team's process.

Providing Support

Teachers need to be provided with the training, teaching tools, and support they need to help all students reach high performance levels. Specifically, teachers need access to curriculum guides, textbooks, or specific training connected to the school curriculum. They need access to lessons or teaching units that match curriculum goals. They need training on using assessment results to diagnose learning gaps (Lunenburg & Irby, 2000; Murphy, 2010; Popham, 2020). Teachers must know how each student performed on every multiple-choice item and other questions on the assessment measure. And training must be in the teachers' subject areas. Only then can teachers be prepared to help students achieve at high levels.

In addition to professional development for teachers, all schools need an intervention and support system for students who lag behind in learning the curriculum. Schools need to provide additional help—either in school, after school, on weekends, or during the summer—to students who lag behind in core subjects (Timar & Maxwell-Jolly, 2012). School boards and school superintendents need to supply the financial resources to fulfill this mandate (Lunenburg, 2007). This involves acquiring materials, information, or technology; manipulating schedules or release time to create opportunities for teachers to learn; facilitating professional networks; and creating an environment that supports school improvement efforts.

Higher state standards usually mean changes in curriculum, instruction, and assessment—that is, changes in teaching. The history of school reform indicates that innovations in teaching and learning seldom penetrate more than a few schools and seldom endure when they do (Bodilly, 2011; Cuban, 2020; Elmore, 2004; Evans, 2011; Fink, 2000; Lunenburg, 2011a; Murphy, 2020; Murphy & Bleiberg, 2019; Nehring, 2010). Innovations frequently fail because the individuals who make it happen—those closest to the firing line, the classroom teachers—may not be committed to the effort or may not have the skills to grapple with the basic challenge being posed (Fullan, 2018). Principals need to ensure that teachers have the skills to help all students perform at high levels (Darling-Hammond et al., 2019; Leithwood, 2018; Leithwood, Sun, & Pollock, 2017; Murphy, 2016a, 2016b; Stronge, 2018; Zacarian & Silverstone, 2020).

Aligning Curriculum, Instruction, and Assessment

School principals need to ensure that assessment of student learning is aligned with both the school's curriculum and the teachers' instruction (English, 2011). When they are well constructed and implemented, assessments can change the nature of teaching and learning. They can lead to a richer, more challenging curriculum; foster discussion and collaboration among teachers within and across schools; create more productive conversations among teachers and parents; and focus stakeholders' attention on increasing student achievement (Popham, 2010, 2020).

For curriculum goals to have an impact on what happens in classrooms, they must be clear. When school districts, principals, and students are held accountable for results, more specificity is needed in implementing the curriculum (Glatthorn et al., 2018). In a high-stakes accountability environment, teachers require that the curriculum contain enough detail and precision to allow them to know what the students need to learn.

Most states are attempting to align their assessments with their standards. School principals need to consider three principles in this endeavor (Glandel & Vranek, 2001). First, assessments not based on the curriculum are neither fair nor helpful to parents or students. Schools that have developed their own assessment measures have done a good job of ensuring that the content of the assessment can be found in the curriculum—that is, children will not be assessed on knowledge and skills they have not been taught. This is what Fenwick English and Betty Steffy (2001) refer to as "the doctrine of no surprises."

However, the same is not true when schools use generic, off-the-shelf standardized tests. Such tests cannot measure the breadth and depth of the school's curriculum. Second, when the curriculum is rich and rigorous, the assessments must be as well. Assessments must tap both the breadth and depth of the content and skills in the curriculum. Third, assessments must become more challenging in each successive grade. The solid foundation of knowledge and skills developed in the early grades should evolve into more complex skills in the later grades. The work of educators at all levels is being shaped by national accountability standards designed to improve the performance of all students on state-mandated tests.

Critics argue that many state-mandated tests require students to recall obscure factual knowledge, which limits the time teachers have available to focus on critical thinking skills (Lunenburg, 2013a; McNeil, 2000). Other scholars (Au, 2007; Berliner, 2011; Berliner & Glass, 2014; Center on Education Policy, 2008; Jennings & Rentner, 2006; Jones, 2007; McMurrer, 2007; Nichols & Berliner, 2007) indicate that high-stakes testing has resulted in a narrowing of the curriculum. If one accepts the premise that assessment drives curriculum and instruction, perhaps the best way to improve instruction and increase student achievement is to construct better tests. According to Yeh (2001, 2006), it is possible to design force-choice items (multiple-choice items) that test reasoning and critical thinking. Such assessments could require students to *use* facts rather than *recall* them. And questions could elicit content knowledge that is worth learning.

To prepare students to think critically, teachers could teach children to identify what is significant. Teachers could model the critical thinking process in the classroom, during instruction, through assignments, in preparing for assessments, and in the content of the assessment itself. By aligning content with worthwhile questions in core subject areas, it may be possible to rescue assessment and instruction from the current focus on the recall of trivial factual knowledge and a narrowing of the curriculum. Assessment items could be created for a range of subjects and levels of difficulty. Then there would be little incentive for teachers to drill students on factual knowledge.

Analyzing Results

How can schools gauge their progress in achieving student learning? Three factors can increase a school's progress in achieving learning for all students (Sclafani, 2001). The primary factor is the availability of performance data connected to each student. Performance data need to be broken down by specific objectives and target levels in the school curriculum. Then the school is able to connect what is taught to what is learned. The curriculum goals should be clear enough to specify what each teacher should teach. And an assessment measure, aligned with the curriculum, will indicate what students have learned (English & Steffy, 2001). Also, teachers need access to longitudinal data on each student in their classroom. With such data, teachers are able to develop individual and small-group education plans to ensure mastery of areas of weakness from previous years while also moving students forward in the school curriculum.

The second factor is the public nature of the assessment system. Annually, the school district should publish a matrix of schools and honor those schools that have performed at high levels. This activity provides role models for other schools to emulate. At the school and classroom levels, it provides a blueprint of those areas where teachers should focus their individual education plans (IEPs) and where grade levels or schools should focus the school's professional development plans. The public nature of the data from the accountability system makes clear where schools are. Data should be disaggregated by race/ethnicity, socioeconomic status, English language proficiency, and disability. Performance of each subgroup of students on assessment measures makes the school community aware of which students are well served and which students are not well served by the school's curriculum and instruction.

The third factor in gauging progress toward achieving student learning is the specifically targeted assistance provided to schools that are performing at low levels. Before the advent of accountability systems, it was not evident which schools and students needed help. The first step is to target the schools in need of help based on student performance data. Each targeted school is paired with a team of principals, curriculum specialists/instructional coaches, and researchers to observe current practices, discuss student performance data with staff, and assist in the development and implementation of an improvement plan. The targeted schools learn how to align their program of professional development with the weaknesses identified by the data. They learn how to develop an improvement plan to guide their activities and monitor the outcomes of the activities, all of which are designed to raise student performance levels.

Next, once a team of teachers has worked together and identified students who are having difficulty, the school faces the challenge of how the teachers are going to respond to the students who are not learning. The challenge is not simply reteaching in the same way that the teachers taught before but, rather, in providing support for teachers to expand their repertoire of skills and providing support and time for students to get the additional assistance they need in order to master those skills. When students are not learning, principals must ensure not only that professional development programs are in place to give additional support to teachers but also that intervention strategies are in place to give additional support to students.

The new framework for school improvement that we have described here provides a powerful and useful model for achieving school success. Sustained districtwide school improvement is not possible without a strong connection across levels of organization (school, school district, community, and state). Internal school development is necessary from principals, teachers, and parents; but school improvement cannot occur unless each school is supported by a strong external infrastructure; stable political environments; and resources outside the school, including leadership from superintendent and school board as well as leadership from the state.

SUMMARY

1. The role of the principal has changed over time from a hierarchical, bureaucratic image to one of devolved decision making and school self-determination.
2. Principals foster a school's improvement, enhance its overall effectiveness, and promote student learning and success by developing the capacity of staff to function as a professional learning community.

3. Developing and maintaining a positive school culture cultivates a professional learning community, the learning and success of all students, and the professional growth of all school stakeholders.
4. The instructional leadership of the principal is a critical factor in the success of a school's improvement initiatives and the overall effectiveness of the school. The principal's primary responsibility is to promote the learning and success of *all* students.

KEY TERMS

professional learning community
mission
purpose of schooling
vision
values
goals
commitment
standards
targets
motivation
culture
observed behavioral regularities
norms
dominant values
philosophy

rules
feelings
values
terminal value
instrumental value
heroes and heroines
rites and rituals
communication networks
focusing on learning
encouraging collaboration
providing support
aligning curriculum, instruction, and
     assessment
analyzing results

FIELD-BASED ACTIVITIES

1. Get a copy of your school district's District Improvement Plan (DIP) or strategic plan. Analyze the content of the DIP as to (a) content, including vision, mission, values, and goals; and (b) participation of stakeholders in development of the DIP, including administrators, teachers, students, parents, and community. Discuss your findings.
2. Get a copy of your school's Campus Improvement Plan (CIP). Examine the CIP as to (a) content, including vision, mission, values, and goals; (b) participation of stakeholders in development of the CIP, including principals, teachers, staff, students, parents; and (c) whether the CIP content is based on the DIP. Discuss your findings.
3. Interview a school board member, a district administrator, your building principal, a teacher in your school, and the president of the Student Association to determine each person's perception of the culture that exists in your school district and in your school. Note any similarities and differences between your school district's culture and your individual school's culture. Discuss the implications of these findings.

SUGGESTED READINGS

Cuban, L. (2020). *Chasing success and confronting failure in American public schools*. Cambridge, MA: Harvard Education Press. Larry Cuban provides a thorough examination of, and challenges to, past and present definitions of what constitutes educational success in the US.

Darling-Hammond, L., & Oakes, J. (2019). *Preparing teachers for deeper learning*. Cambridge, MA: Harvard Education Press. Linda Darling-Hammond and Jeannie Oakes answer an urgent call for teachers who educate children from diverse backgrounds to meet the demands of a changing world.

Eaker, R., Hagadone, M., Keating, J., & Rhodes, M. (2021). *Leading professional learning communities at work districtwide: From board room to classroom*. Indianapolis, IN: Solution Tree Press. With this book as a guide, you will learn how to align the work of every PLC team within your school district, inspire PLCs to achieve continuous improvement and a guaranteed and viable curriculum for every student.

Fullan, M., & Gallagher, M. J. (2020). *The devil is in the details: System solutions for equity, excellence, and student well-being*. Thousand Oaks, CA: Corwin Press. Michael Fullan and Mary Jean Gallagher provide detailed cases and analyses of successful systems ideas for how leaders at all levels—local, middle, and top—can take steps to begin action and strategies for addressing equity, excellence, and well-being through education.

Glickman, C. D., & Burns, R. W. (2020). *Leadership for learning: How to bring out the best in every teacher* (2nd ed.). Alexandria, VA: ASCD. Carl Glickman and Rebecca West Burns synthesize their decades of experience in teacher education and supervision into a comprehensive guide to supporting teacher growth and student learning.

Murphy, J. (2020). *Bottling fog: Essential lessons in leadership*. New York, NY: Teachers College Press. Joseph Murphy provides the culmination of fifty years of work to capture the core ingredients of leadership.

2

Creating a Vision for Learning

■ ■ ■

FOCUSING QUESTIONS

1. Why is it important to focus on the future when establishing a vision?
2. Why is it important to have a vision?
3. What is a systemic vision?
4. How are visions created?
5. How are visions shared and articulated?
6. How can principals implement a vision?
7. How do principals shepherd their vision?
8. How is a mission developed?
9. What are belief statements?
10. How do goals align with the vision, mission, and beliefs?

In this chapter, we respond to these questions by focusing on the principal's mission to create a vision for learning. We begin by first considering the future of society to gain a perspective on the potential constitution of the school's vision. We explore the creation of the vision; the articulation of the vision; the implementation of the vision; the guidance of the vision to maintain it; the development of a mission statement that leads to the vision; the assessment of beliefs; and the development of goals to achieve the mission and vision.

GAINING A PERSPECTIVE ON THE VISION

Einstein was criticized for saying $E = mc^2$. Einstein's vision of matter and energy, and space and time, bound together in a four-dimensional universe, was published in 1905; however, it was not until fourteen years into the future that his vision would be realized when technology would catch up to his imagination and when astronomers would be able to record, during a solar eclipse, the path of light (curved) in relation to the sun's gravitational force. Gorbachev was condemned for mentioning capitalism; however, Gorbachev's vision of Soviet reform led to the future dismantling of the Soviet Union. DeKlerk was chastised for saying apartheid must end. DeKlerk's vision of a multiethnic government and anti-apartheid was begun when he was elected president of South Africa in 1989. His vision was realized five years later, in 1994, when Nelson Mandela assumed the presidency.

Others were criticized for envisioning a new future. Admonished for educational experiences being too structured and an educational environment being too prepared or stilted, Montessori focused on "the pupil's liberty as the basis for developing independence, his freedom to work when and for as long as he wants to on a given task and to progress at his own rate" (Kramer, 1988, pp. 295–296). This method is now used in more than seven thousand certified schools internationally, with thousands more using Montessori concepts. When she opened her first school in the slums of Rome, she dreamed of helping children who were mentally challenged but never realized that, a century later, her method would be central in educating not only children with special needs but also those who are special in that they are gifted, second language learners, or from low and high socioeconomic status. Furthermore, Piaget was ridiculed for his research techniques of observation, description, and analysis of child behavior that began in the early 1950s; however, his research was the foundation of his vision for the future of education for children. Developed from his research was his theory of cognitive development. Approximately twenty years later, this theory, alone, has altered not only the way in which teachers and curriculum developers create curriculum and instructional strategies within US classrooms, beginning in the mid-1970s, but also the way in which observational research was viewed. The groundswell of acceptance for Piaget's work has added to the base support for qualitative research that has reached an all-time high in publications over a half century later. Lev Vygotsky (1896–1934) lived during the Stalinist period when psychology was heavily influenced by Pavlovian theory. His own theory, which promoted the quality, as well as quantity, of social relationships, and which influenced cognitive functioning or development, was denigrated. Vygotsky's vision of cognition continued to be advanced and influenced the thinking of Bandura in his theory of social learning. Much of Vygotsky's vision began to be taken seriously in child development and language and literacy development only in the latter part of the twentieth century.

Though criticized, all of these individuals had gained a perspective on their vision, had taken risks, and had considered the future. They were visionaries and were able to (a) reflect on what *was* in order to gain a perspective on what *could be*, (b) provide a perspective on their visions through clear articulation of them, (c) share their visions though criticisms emerged, and (d) consider the impact of their visions on the future.

What then does it mean for a school principal to gain a perspective on his or her vision while considering the future? To gain a perspective on a vision requires imagination and consequential and critical thinking. When considering vision, it is just as Einstein stated: "Imagination is more important than knowledge." In a sense, a vision comes out of a vivid imagination and dreams that consider future implications and consequences of that pictured vision. The vision that the principal develops expresses the ideals of standards for future judgment and educational conduct that ultimately impact the advancement of the society.

The Global Society

Society is considered to be a global society, characterized by diversity in cultures, religions, languages, and people. With technology, our world has become virtually borderless. Teachers and students are able to access people and information in a matter of minutes. With immediacy, our students are able to witness events from every point on the globe and also in the universe when science and engineering take us there. With this view of the world and beyond in their living rooms, our students are able to observe wonders, disappointments, civility, incivility, inequities, and exclusions at home and abroad. The United Nations' *Millennium Development Goals Report 2015* and the US Census Bureau's data from 2002 illustrated such globalization and inequities. Some people on earth lived in extreme poverty, 10 percent in 2015; however, according to the World Bank (2018) that number had declined to a less than 10 percent total ending 2018; however, those numbers do not appear to be the target of less than 3 percent worldwide by 2030. A total of 38.1 million people were classified as poor in 2018, indicating a 9 percent increase in the number of people living in poverty (US Census Bureau, 2018; Poverty USA, 2019).

- According to the World Food Program (2019), in 2019, there were 821 million chronically undernourished people worldwide, which showed an increase of 10 million since 2018.
- Primary school enrollments rose worldwide, from 80 percent in 1990 to 84 percent in 1998 (Millennium Development Goals, 2003) and to 90 percent in 2018; this latter number represents similar percentages since 2007 (UNICEF, 2019). Children from the poorest 20 percent of the population are less likely to attend school than those who are more affluent (UNICEF, 2019). Though numbers of primary age children have declined by approximately 50 percent since 2000, there are still 59 million school-age children who were still not in school by 2018, 55 percent of them were girls—a number that has not declined but has remained the same over time—and there is an increase in out-of-school rates as age levels increase (UNICEF, 2019). According to Global Partnerships in Education (2019), worldwide, nine in ten girls completed primary school; however, only three out of four girls completed lower secondary school.
- In 2017, worldwide, 71 percent of people used safely managed drinking-water services (located on premises and free from contamination); however, that leaves 29 percent or another almost 2 billion without safe water services on premises (World Health Organizations, 2019).
- The world's twenty-six richest billionaires own as many assets as the 3.8 billion people who make up the poorest half of the planet's population (Oxfam, 2019).
- In 2018, approximately 6.2 million of the world's children died of preventable diseases (World Health Organization, 2019).

To many who have not witnessed firsthand such conditions or lived those as previously described, it is hard to comprehend. However, we do live in this global society where students from our schools are exposed to the difficult circumstances of the world on television or media daily or, in some instances, live these daily; therefore, it behooves principals to address issues of learning related to such events within our global society.

The Principal's Challenges for Learning

As fast as the world is changing, so too is the United States. At current rates of immigration, minorities will make up almost half of the US population by the middle of this century. According to the 2018 estimates by the US Census Bureau (2018), the number of people who identified their races was (in rounded percentages): 60 percent Whites, 13 percent African Americans, 6 percent Asians, 1 percent American Indians and Alaskan Natives, 2 percent Hawaiians and other Pacific Islanders, 18 percent Hispanic/Latino, and 2 percent two or more races. According to the National Center for Education Statistics (2019a), by 2027, it is projected that there will be 29 percent Hispanic students, denoting a continuous increase. The numbers of Blacks/African Americans are expected to be at 15 percent, while Asian/Pacific Islander are projected to increase to 6 percent, and the number of those indicating two or more races is expected to be at 4 percent. The number of White students is projected to decrease to 45 percent. With Hispanics being the largest ethnic majority and with a native language of Spanish, there is increased awareness of the continued growth in numbers of English learners (EL).

These changing demographic figures present an intricate picture of education in the United States with the challenge of needing teachers who understand the various ethnic or racial groups with which they work. The changes in the demographics contrast with the number of teachers that serve these ethnically, racially, and linguistically diverse students. Nationally, per the National Center of Education Statistics (2019b) between 2000 and 2016, the shortage of teachers of color represented a discrepancy with the student population demographics, with the percentage of teachers who were White declining from 84 to 80 percent and the number of teachers who were Black declining from 8 to 7 percent. The percentage of teachers who were Hispanic increased from 6 to 9 percent, but the student population was approximately 40 percent diverse. Principals, as leaders of student learning, should be intentional in pointing diverse students to the teaching profession and in recruiting a more diverse teaching force. This point is critical to student learning with evidence being presented in areas of impact in student achievement (Clotfelter et al., 2007; Dee, 2004; Egalite et al., 2015; Goldhaber & Hansen, 2010) and in related disciplinary areas for students (Lindsey & Hart, 2016).

There are discouraging achievement findings among racial groups. For example, results from the National Assessment Educational Progress (NAEP, 2019) show that both African American and Latino students perform significantly lower than White students in reading and math at both the fourth- and the eighth-grade levels. The challenge for principals herein is to ensure that minority children receive an equitable education and will be prepared to compete economically in this ever-changing world.

Many more factors, in addition to minority teacher shortages and the apparent achievement gaps, enter into the nation's global society that may perpetuate the exclusion of certain groups. Specifically, in 2015, there were more than 44 million children (64 percent) under the age of eighteen living in economically challenged conditions (National Center for Children in Poverty, 2019) and 4.3 million children under the age of nineteen without health insurance in 2018 (Berchick & Mykyta, 2019). Poverty leads to social exclusion and also generates a lack of requisite knowledge to get work. According to Reardon et al. (2019), poverty has been identified as a main contributor to the achievement gap among racial/ethnic groups.

The American Institutes for Research and National Center on Family Homelessness (2019) indicated that one in every thirty children in the United States is homeless. This presents a challenge to principals in terms of providing as much support as possible to increase the learning capability of these children while they are in school.

Another challenge to principals in the learning situation is children who face abuse and/or neglect. An estimated 683,000 children in the United States were victims of abuse or neglect in 2015 (National Children's Alliance, 2015). Furthermore, it was determined by the National Center on Drug Use and Health (Lipari & Van Horn, 2017), from combined data from 2009 to 2014, that an annual average of 7.5 million (alcohol) and 8.7 million (drugs) children younger than seventeen lived with at least one parent who abused or was dependent on alcohol or an illicit drug.

Not only do the homelife conditions of children present challenges to principals who care about their students' learning but the conditions of the world, at large, do so as well. We suggest several challenges related to what is learned outside the school—for learning cannot be equated to that which is only obtained within the walls of a school. Today, the situation is much broader, and leaders have to consider the society in which the learners in their care reside. Information is very accessible even to the youngest of us via breakneck speed media sources. McDonald (2015) has suggested that teachers may need to become knowledge brokers as knowledge becomes more accessible and prolific. As a result, there are many choices for an education and more on the horizon. Even in 1995, Dias de Figueiredo suggested that traditional schools are badly equipped to face challenges of interactivity, mobility, convertibility, connectivity, ubiquity, and globalization. This means that principals must think nontraditionally—outside the box. Also, according to Research and Markets (2019), the artificial intelligence (AI) market in the US education arena is forecasted to grow at a compound annual growth rate of 47.77 percent during the period of 2018 to 2022. It will offer educational assistance to teachers and students in, hopefully, a supportive manner such as tutoring and coaching, personalized learning, and feedback. Though AI can convey specified content, it is the human element that will, however, transmit culture, conscience, and civility. As one of the most prominent twenty-first-century tools, AI will present new challenges and opportunities, as well as introduce potential threats, to principals and their schools.

Other challenges in schools that may be considered are: stress levels of teachers; emotional intelligence; terrorism; planetary sustainability with resource scarcity; abilities to think critically, research, and discern truth; applicable skills; and ethical dispositions. Certainly, the challenges in education are many for principals as they plan an educational vision for schools full of children and youth under their care. Principals must reflect on broader social issues and where they find themselves in the present, in order to build a vision that is socially responsible for the future. A socially responsible vision challenges principals to educate and assess all children who bring with them their diverse needs through the schoolhouse doors, which also open in the opposite direction, outward, into a myriad of diverse situations and needs within the society at large.

Bringing the Vision Home to the School Culture

The No Child Left Behind (NCLB) Act of 2001 admonished principals to hold all students accountable to high academic standards. The 2001 legislation expanded the federal role in public education by: (a) requiring schools to be accountable to student achievement, in that all students must meet state standards by 2014, and all gaps be closed: (b) mandating schools to hire highly qualified teachers; and (c) emphasizing that schools put into place programs and strategies with demonstrated effectiveness based upon research. In effect, data-driven decision making regarding program implementation in schools was mandated through NCLB.

The Every Student Succeeds Act (ESSA) of 2015, its replacement, is more flexible, allowing for states to set their own goals for student achievement while working within the law's framework and with the states holding schools accountable for student achievement. States had to adopt, just as in the NCLB, challenging academic standards in reading, mathematics, and science, and the federal government could not (and cannot) influence state decisions regarding those standards. Also, when states evaluate schools, they must consider more than just test scores. In fact, there are four academic factors—reading and mathematics test scores, English language proficiency test scores, high school graduation rates, and state-chosen academic measures for elementary and middle schools—that must be used. States can also choose a fifth factor that impacts school quality (e.g., kindergarten readiness, access to and completion of advanced coursework, college readiness, school climate and safety, and chronic absenteeism).

For the NCLB, states had to bring all student to the "proficient" level on standardized tests as well as set targets for adequate yearly progress; if the schools and school districts did not meet those targets, they could be required to fire the staff and face federal penalties. With ESSA, states must set achievement targets for students in schools, and instead of penalizing struggling schools, such schools receive more funding and plans for improvement. NCLB prescribed a specific set of actions for subgroups of students who were struggling, but ESSA gives decision making power to the states and districts as long as decisions are evidenced-based. ESSA also funds a literacy grant program to states and schools, and encourages states to expand personalized learning for students.

ESSA requires states to include input from parents and families in the creation of their educational plans, whereas NCLB did not. ESSA indicates that states may have an opt-out law for parents regarding their children's participation in standardized tests. In terms of funding, states may reserve up to 3 percent of Title II funds for programs to improve principal and school leader capacity. Though ESSA allows much greater flexibility for school and campus improvement plans to respond to locally identified needs and approaches, you should check with your state department of education to determine state-specific requirements such as required personnel, approved providers, mandatory state-provided technical assistance, and so on. At a minimum, schools identified for support and improvement *must* conduct a comprehensive needs assessment and develop an improvement plan utilizing at least one evidence-based intervention.

We recommend that all school principals lead the development of a strategic plan (school improvement plan) and create visions that rethink the structure, organization, and delivery of education in their schools. One of the first steps to rethinking the structure and establishing the vision for the restructured school is the consideration of several aspects of the school culture. School culture, as defined by Schein and Schein (2016), is the transmitted patterns of meaning including understood norms, values, beliefs, ceremonies, rituals, traditions, and myths. They suggested that cultural understanding often shapes what people think and how they act. According to

Deal and Peterson (2016), a vision determines the values and beliefs that will guide policy and practice on a school campus. They say that the creation of a vision is not a static event, because the vision must change as culture changes, and the principal who can develop a vision related to the new challenges society brings will be more successful in building strong school cultures.

Considering challenges as previously described, while couching them in the context of the lived culture (the community, the place, the present one finds oneself in), Browder (2001) aptly shares a story of a high school principal.

> With thoughts of the definition of moral poverty in her head, the principal concludes that she feels a better sense of understanding a complex shift in American society, one that unfortunately leaves a growing number of children-on-their-own. She senses that the best way to deal with this phenomenon is to focus the school's resources for involving parents and engaging teachers and students. She believes it will be necessary for her to assume a leadership role as a moving force and cheerleader for establishing the school's institutional attitude—a positive one anchored in academic achievement and a firm sense of right and wrong. While this approach seems very traditional and may not work well today, the principal senses that, for her community, it is perhaps the most appropriate choice.
>
> Meanwhile, more study will be necessary on determining ways of injecting "contagious" moral attitudes into adolescent peer groups. She realizes it is far easier to offer such a prescription than it is to do so. It is our obligation, however, to try, thinks the principal. (p. 258)

The principal that Browder portrays considers her culture and sees herself as the facilitator to move the vision, with many stakeholders involved, and to include very human and moral factors that are obviously neglected within her setting. Because she is about to embark on a collective venture with parents and teachers, she is setting out to create relationships while promoting her vision. Wheatley (1994) states:

> To live in a quantum world, to wave here and there with ease and grace, we will need to change what we do. We will need to stop describing tasks and instead facilitate process. We will need to become savvy about how to build relationships. . . . The quantum world has demolished the concept of the unconnected individual. More and more relationships are in store for us, out there in the vast web of universal connections. (p. 38)

THE SYSTEMIC VISION

Figure 2.1 depicts a **systemic vision** that is placed within the context of the school that, of course, is within the district. It is not only contextual, but also dependent upon relationships. The systemic vision includes relationships between and among the following factors: (a) the district's vision, mission, and goals; (b) the school's vision, mission, and goals; (c) the school's strategic action plan; and (d) the considered values of the principal, teachers, staff, and community. Each factor is grounded in professional relationships, because such relationships are established as teachers, administrators, support staff, and other stakeholders together develop and understand each factor. Systemically and cyclically, these relational factors lead to the accomplishment of the mission and goals. The process of the systemic vision in the development of the factors leads to outgrowths of motivated students, better

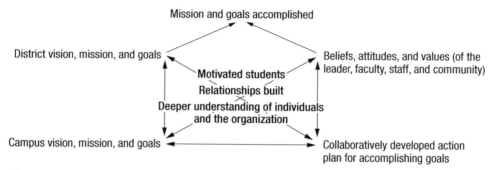

Figure 2.1 Systemic Vision and Its Connection to Context and Relationships

person-to-person relationships among faculty, administrators, and community, and a more sensitive or deeper understanding of each individual in the organization, the organization itself, the vision, the mission, and the goals.

CREATING A VISION

A **vision** statement for a school is a convincing description of how students are improved in a variety of ways through numerous school services. Every principal has the capacity to facilitate the creation of a vision and, in that, to be a visionary. Just as Einstein and others did, the principal, too, can recognize a need or opportunity for his or her students and school and, regardless of critics or cynics, can do something about it. Vision is the portrait the principal paints as he or she creates the future by acting in the present. Another way of considering vision is to think of it like a compass—it is the guiding direction to get us to where we want to go.

The Principal's Vision

For a principal to create a vision or even to facilitate the school community to create a vision, the first step is reflection; the principal must carve out ample reflective time to consider (a) where the school has been, (b) where it is presently, and (c) where he or she wants it to be or to become. This reflective activity is critical to developing a more effective school.

Where the school has been.   Review a history of the school. Take into account the community and how it has changed over time—economically, demographically, culturally. Has the school population increased/decreased? What have been the success stories told in the community? What has the "talk" about the school focused on—on students, faculty, sports, curriculum? What types of leaders (principals and teachers) has the school had?

Where the school is presently.   Review current achievement reports in relation to past achievement. Review current demographics of the school's students, teachers, and community. What are the leader's current behaviors/styles? What is the current focus of the school and what led to that focus? How are teachers and other stakeholders currently involved in making decisions about the school? How are decisions made—upon what are they based?

What the school is to become.   Dream big; dream outside the box; get on top of the box and dance; dream with students at the center. Imagine, with no boundaries and

Table 2.1 Conditions to Grow the Vision

The Principal's Necessary Conditions to Grow a Vision
The principal must be able to know what they believe and value.
The principal and the stakeholders must value students' diverse backgrounds.
The vision must be centered in the needs of the students.
There must be a genuine personal commitment from the principal.
The principal must be able to clearly articulate the vision.
Continuous and repetitive dialogue and actions focusing on the vision are crucial to the life of the vision.

based on the data analyzed, just what the school could become—this is the seed of the vision.

For the vision to grow. We suggest that for the school leader's vision to grow and become established in the school, there are six necessary conditions as outlined in table 2.1. The first necessary condition involves the understanding of self—the principal must know themselves in terms of beliefs, values, and philosophy. Secondly, because of the changing society that was discussed extensively earlier in the chapter, the principal must value students' diverse backgrounds and understand and embrace them. (This is so critical to formulating a vision and moving it forward, it will be discussed extensively later in the chapter.) Third, since our students are diverse and because schools are places for students to grow and learn, the vision must always be centered on the students and their needs. The fourth condition is that principals must be perceived as authentic and must exude a genuine commitment to the vision and, ultimately, to the mission and goals, which leads to the fifth condition—the principal must be able to effectively articulate the vision to all the stakeholders. The principal must, at all times, keep the vision in the forefront of the stakeholders. The dialogue and the message the principal states should always be centered in the vision. When he or she talks to parents, to the clubs and organizations in town, to the superintendent, the custodial staff, to the businesses and industry executives, to members of the church, mosque, or synagogue—wherever the principal is and whatever he or she says related to school business—the vision should be the focal point. Then, *all* will know in which direction the school is headed, and the vision can stay alive in their minds and in their conversation.

Beliefs, Values, and Attitudes

Why is it important for the principal to know their own beliefs and values and how they are portrayed in their attitude? Senge (1990, 2006) strongly urges that the vision be aligned with the values and daily lives of the people involved; if not, the vision would fail, would not foster enthusiasm, and would actually spawn cynicism. He illustrated the importance of knowing personal beliefs and values, and values of the school community.

Why is it important to know the beliefs and values of the school community? The beliefs of the individuals or stakeholders within the school organization are manifested in its actions and decisions. The principal must determine how those beliefs and values are reflected in their organization and exhibited in behaviors of the faculty and staff within the school culture. It is critical for the principal to assess whether their personal beliefs and values are aligned or misaligned with their organization.

You may have seen a set of values a school has printed, framed, and mounted on the office wall and in every classroom. Is there alignment of what is espoused and what is actually valued? The principal must be astute and aware of the alignment between the way the faculty and staff behave and what is printed and framed. Following, is an example of visible awareness of such an alignment.

We recall seeing a stated value of "Respect for all" in a public Montessori pre-kindergarten school recently. We observed on several visits to see if we saw respect from the front office, through the hallways, and to the classroom. What we saw was an amazing alignment of this behavior. It was exhibited, for example, in the cleanliness and orderliness of the building from the hallways, the bathrooms, and the classrooms, in the front office staff as they greeted and assisted parents, in the hallways and classrooms as teachers used quiet and understanding voices with children as they taught or provided corrective feedback, in the library as the librarian demonstrated with the children the respect for books and reading, and in the principal's office as she met with the assistant principal to provide corrective feedback on paperwork. Adults and children were respected, things were respected, and conflict was handled within the classrooms with teachers teaching children how to respect each other. This was an amazing display of alignment of behavior of an entire campus, from the principal to the students, with a value of "respect." This Montessori school's belief statements follow:

- All students can be successful learners.
- Students are capable of learning all material.
- Parents are an important part of our school.
- Respect is key on our campus—respect for all.
- We believe in continuous learning.

Another situation we have all recently observed is the misalignment of the value of "trust" shown in the demise of a major energy corporation. In that corporation, the value of "trust" was underserved and not exhibited by the leaders. The leaders' values were not aligned with the values of the members of this organization. Ultimately, this basic core value was violated and demonstrated in actions that led to illegal, unethical, and destructive behaviors, and, ultimately, the system failed.

Alignment of values between the principal and teachers produces a fruitful yield of trust and open communication at all levels and is seen in quality decisions, motivated teachers, enthusiasm, respect, an ethic of care and social responsibility, development of strategic alliances, openness to change, accountability for mistakes, and a focus on quality (Bryk, 2020).

The Leadership Framework

Alignment of the principal's values and those of the organization (or the teachers within it) is one of the keys to a successful and quality school. To accomplish this alignment, according to Irby and Brown (2000), the principal must first assess his or her own beliefs through the development of a leadership framework. Irby and Brown (2000) describe the **leadership framework** as "a comprehensive analysis of primary beliefs and attitudes regarding students, teachers, schools, learning, and leadership" (p. 18). Further, they iterate that a personal leadership framework helps in clarifying who we are as leaders not only to ourselves but also to our employees. The principal's actions are predicated on his or her beliefs and values; therefore, it is important to know himself or herself well and to express his or her beliefs clearly in writing. The leadership framework compels a principal to reflect on his or her philosophy of leaders, learning, and teaching and offers opportunities for personal and professional growth and prepares the leader for sharing his or her belief system. This step must be done before a leader can move forward in developing and creating a shared vision. The components of the leadership framework are as follows:

1. *Philosophy of Education.* The initial component provides insights into basic beliefs about the purposes of education and the importance of schools to society from the leader's perspective—forming the foundation not only for the principal's practice but also for subsequent components of the framework.
2. *Philosophy of Leadership.* What the individual believes about effective leadership and its impact is stated here. Students address such questions as: What constitutes effective, purposeful leadership? How is effective, purposeful leadership sustained? How do principals lead from the heart as well as from the mind?
3. *Vision for Learners.* An in-depth analysis of what the principal believes about how children or adolescents learn and about his or her role in promoting learning is essential to the development of this component.
4. *Vision for Teachers.* Here individuals examine and share views on teachers—that is, what it means to be a teacher, what a teacher's role is in the lives of children in the classroom and within the campus community, as well as how teachers should relate to students and others. Principals include how they will empower teachers to develop and use their talents to be productive team members.
5. *Vision for the Organization.* A discussion of the principal's visions for their organization or school campus is important because this provides an image of how they think the campus "should be or could be." Within this component, the principal should reflect and comment on:

   • climate
   • community
   • collaboration
   • communication

   Additionally, the principal should address how to implement one's vision for fostering spirit within the workplace. Here principals may discuss commitment to quality and equality, valuing diversity, connectedness, the spirit of service ethic and integrity, compassion, and stewardship to the community.
6. *Vision for Professional Growth.* This component addresses how the way the principal perceives professional growth impacts student achievement and effective schools. Here, the principal discusses personal views on the significance of professional development as well as disclosing how professional growth needs will be determined and addressed.

7. *Method of Vision Attainment.* All visions are merely cryptic illusions without a strategy for attaining the vision. In discussing how to move the organization toward the vision, the principal will need to address the following:

- decision making
- encouragement, initiation, and facilitation of change
- support during change
- development of a shared mission
- how the students will work with others to achieve a school's mission and goals.

(Brown, Irby, & Fisher, 2001; pp. 128–129)

Benefits of Articulating the Vision

The principal, as leader, must effectively articulate and communicate the vision for the school. With such a clearly communicated and future focused vision that is attuned to the whole system of the school and community, the principal will be able to facilitate interest, buy-in, and commitment from the stakeholders and to create a sense of shared vision that will enable the school to realize the benefits associated with a strong sense of vision. Teachers are more likely to support a school vision when it emanates from authentic dialogue among principal, teachers, and other stakeholders—in which trust is built (Fisher, Frey, & Pumpian, 2019; Fullan, 2018; Fullan & Gallagher, 2020; Gruenert & Whitaker, 2019; Leithwood, 2018; Leithwood, Sun, & Pollock, 2017).

The long-term benefits of developing a clear, shared vision include:

- value and respect for human diversity and the breakdown of prejudices through the analysis of personal values in the context of the school community and the global society;
- definition of the values of the school and its stakeholders;
- guidance of the behavior of the stakeholders;
- a productive and efficient school;
- consequential, reflective, and critical thinkers, going beyond what is to what could be;
- a continuity and a focus to planning efforts;
- direction and purpose of the school;
- an alertness of stakeholders to needed changes;
- open communication;
- creativity and imagination in problem solving;
- encouragement and confidence enhancement among stakeholders; and
- ownership and loyalty through continuous involvement.

The principal is, ultimately, accountable for the vision but, as indicated, is not the individual solely responsible for or the singular authority driving it; though, based on some recent reviews of campus improvement plans, this is still happening. However, when the principal can give up the power and share it with teachers and others within the school community, the vision is more likely to be accomplished.

SHEPHERDING THE VISION

The principal must be the shepherd of the vision and the one who facilitates development of it, the mission, and the goals for accomplishing the mission. There are some points to maintain the vision that the principal can remember as they go about the shepherding process and some detractors to consider along the way.

Vision Detractors

The following are **vision detractors** that can impede progress of the school. Beware of vision detractors and consider what can be done to avoid them.

Beware of tradition. Tradition and cultural mores will raise their heads at times and attempt to keep the principal off the path of the vision. Be prepared to question tradition, such as the traditional structure and culture of the school. On the other hand, consider how to use tradition and culture to benefit the vision.

Beware of scorn. Some may ridicule the vision. Stay focused. Keep repeating the vision and the mission of the school. That is part of the focus—to stay focused!

Beware of naysayers. Naysayers will say things cannot change, and then they will proceed to tell the principal how they cannot change and how the principal, themself, cannot get things changed. Stay focused on the vision.

Beware of complacency. The principal must keep the stakeholders motivated toward the vision by keeping the vision and mission front and center of all decisions.

Beware of weariness. Keep focused on the dream, the vision. Envision the future; envision success. When you are weary, focusing on the vision will lift your spirits.

Beware of short-range thinking. Short ranges yield little; sites set too low or too short are very limiting and stifling. Sites must be set long for far-reaching results, allowing room for mistakes and corrections.

Vision Maintainers

Stay centered on **vision maintainers**. These will assist the principal in leading the way for the vision to be realized and success to be celebrated.

Build ownership in the vision. The principal must be able to articulate the vision well and must be able to bring the faculty together to support the vision. Building ownership means talking about the vision and involving teachers in developing the mission and goals to attain the vision. The more they are involved, the more they will own the vision. Keeping the vision in the dialogue, keeping them focused and talking about the vision, and sending them out into the community to share the vision helps in building ownership.

Think of the long-term benefits. Think about how the vision will ultimately benefit the students. An example of one principal's vision was to create a climate of care where everyone is valued and where everyone can succeed. Imagine how that vision led to many wonderful outcomes for students, teachers, custodians, and parents. Just think of all the benefits that could branch out of such a vision.

Seek input from stakeholders on how to achieve the vision. Seek input. The old adage of "two heads are better than one" is true. Ask teachers, parents, and students how the vision can be accomplished. This, again, is a way to build ownership in the vision. As Sarason (2004) indicates, isolation, particularly of teachers, may hinder moving forward with the vision. Address isolation by designing activities that will connect teachers to teachers, and teachers to administrators.

Build confidence in the stakeholders that the vision can be accomplished. The principal has to be the mainstay. The principal must keep the vision alive by continuously encouraging others regarding attainment of the vision.

Stay with the vision—it will keep all decisions focused and will provide direction and purpose. As all decisions are made, the principal must be the one to keep the focus on the vision. Bring the vision into all decisions. The decisions, then, will have a purpose and be guided by the vision.

Stay focused; let all conversations related to public speaking focus on the vision and mission of the school. It is just as candidates in a public campaign do—they stay focused on their platform. Good campaigners keep the platform in front of the voters in every stump speech and every public appearance. This is the job of the principal—be a good campaigner for the vision.

Keep stakeholders alert to any changes that are needed. If unforeseen circumstances arise that would deter you from your vision, alert all stakeholders. Open communication is important to maintaining the vision.

Demonstrate how the focus has resulted in efficiency, effectiveness, and productive teachers, administrators, and students. At the end of the year, provide all stakeholders with a formative progress report. Measure progress made toward attaining the vision and share what was been accomplished. Share this with the superintendent and the community, as well. Excellence is a moving target; therefore, once the progress has been checked, determine how to continue in forward motion and what remains relevant.

MISSION STATEMENTS

While the vision statement projects the school into the future and shares the desire of the stakeholders related to the direction of the school, the mission statement is different. It is, of course, related to the vision; in a sense it is the "why" of the vision. The **mission** is a brief description of the purpose of the school.

The brief mission statement should, like the vision, guide the decision-making process for the school. It should be aligned with not only the vision but also the core values or principles of the school. When this alignment occurs, stability ensues. Actions and resources should be assessed for alignment with the mission. The mission allows teachers, administrators, and other members of the school community to assess their personal actions with respect to the core values and purpose of the school. It depicts an image to the public regarding the purpose of the school and focuses all of the school community toward that purpose.

The Christa McAuliffe Elementary School's mission is "to ensure all students are empowered and inspired to learn and achieve academic success" (Christa McAuliffe Elementary, 2017). The mission enables the teachers and school community to stay focused and serves also as the purpose of the school.

The vision statement of McAuliffe Elementary is "all students future ready." It is easy to see the connection, yet the differences between the vision and mission of this school. This school further delineates its vision and mission with a statement of core beliefs or values as follows: "Reach for the Stars, Be Kind and Respectful, Be Safe and Responsible, Be Your Best."

An example of a school mission statement that depicts the two parts is from the Frost Elementary: "Frost Elementary School's staff, parents, and community are dedicated to the intellectual, personal, social, and physical growth of students. Our highly qualified staff recognizes the value of professional development in order to rigorously challenge students. Our teaching practices are both reflective and responsive to the needs of our students. Through diversified experiences, our students discover their potential, achieve readiness for college and careers, and succeed in a safe and caring environment." Frost Elementary has a vision as stated, "The vision at Frost Elementary School is to prepare and motivate our students for a rapidly changing world by instilling in them critical thinking skills, a global perspective, and a respect for core values of honesty, loyalty, perseverance, and compassion. Students will have success for today and be prepared for tomorrow. and belief statement" (Frost Elementary, 2019). You will note that the vision and mission statement from Frost is longer and more involved than that of McAuliffe Elementary. It appears that Frost also includes much of their beliefs into the two statements.

To write a mission statement, principals should ask the following questions of the teachers in collaborative group settings. They need to have time to discuss these questions and share their thoughts:

- What is the vision, and is our purpose aligned with where we want to be?
- What is our purpose?
- What is important about our purpose?
- What is the most critical point of our purpose in this school?
- Will what we do help us realize our vision?

We would like to suggest that, in addition, belief statements be turned into belief action statements. For example, the previous belief statement, "All learners can have successful and satisfying experiences through active participation in the educational process," might be reconsidered as a belief action statement in this way: "We will provide interesting lessons with satisfying experiences that engage the learners in the educational process."

GOAL STATEMENTS

Once vision, mission, and belief action statements have been articulated, a plan is needed to move the organization forward. Goals statements can assist in that movement. The more specific and measurable the goals, the more promising they are as a strategy to improve schools. **Goals** should yield results that a school or school district tries to achieve (Locke & Latham, 2002; Van Soelen, 2021). Goals equal the vision and mission, with measurable outcomes and a timetable for implementation. Goals are outcomes that the school tries to accomplish and are aligned to the vision and mission.

Hierarchy of Goals
According to O'Neill (2000), there are process-oriented and results-oriented goals. Principals should consider **process-oriented goals** related to activities, programs, and instructional methods. O'Neill provides principals with examples of process-oriented goals such as: (a) developing a balanced literacy program for primary students, (b) implementing an integrated math/science curriculum for incoming freshmen, and (c) adopting a zero-tolerance policy toward violence. She suggests that such

goals fit nicely into methods or strategies sections of action plans. Alternatively, she indicates that **results-oriented goals** provide better feedback on how well teachers help students learn. A test score, a rubric system, or some other quantifiable tool or method evidences results-oriented goals. She provides examples of results-oriented goals such as (a) increasing numbers of students who are reading by the end of third grade, (b) reducing failure rate of incoming freshmen, and (c) eliminating violent behavioral incidents.

Schools may have multiple goals, that is, to: increase test scores, decrease the dropout rate, develop people, and improve community relations. There may be a hierarchy of goals. That refers to the interrelationships that exist between general, overall goals and specific instructional objectives, or between upper and lower organizational units.

The starting point in the task of managing a school, for example, is reviewing the definition of the overall goals of the school district. This definition is the first critical activity of strategic planning. All other planning, organizing, leading, and monitoring that is done should implement the school district's goals for the school year and should align with the school's vision and mission. Long-range goals can be set for multiple school years as well. Unless goals are set, agreed on, and performed on all levels of operating the school district, there will be little basis for measuring the effectiveness of the school and school district outcomes.

A means-end analysis, or developing a **hierarchy of goals,** is the process of translating school system goals into contributing subsidiary goals and objectives for central office administrators, principals, and teachers within the school district (Lemaine, Levernier, & Richardson, 2018; McChesney et al., 2021; Van Soelen, 2021; Wootton & Horne, 2021). Figure 2.2 depicts how school system, various central office, school goals, and classroom instructional objectives form a hierarchy. The hierarchy of goals can be viewed as means that contribute to a single end—the school system's outcomes.

As figure 2.2 indicates, each school is an end for that building; it is also a means to achieve the school district's goals. The school system goals suggest a framework within which the hierarchy of contributing subsidiary goals and instructional objectives can be set. The responsibility for setting overall goals rests with the board of education and superintendent of schools. Assistant superintendents, in turn, generate subsidiary goals. School principals have responsibility for identifying the performance goals for their schools but, again, with the input of teachers, staff, and stakeholders, and with the analysis of data for development of such goals. Finally, department heads, team leaders, and teachers within the grade levels or content areas in the schools produce instructional objectives collaboratively.

Applying the concept at all levels of the school district achieves the benefits derived from developing a hierarchy of goals on a means-ends chain. For example, if the board of education and the superintendent set a goal "to increase the number of students reading on grade level," all efforts of district personnel will be exerted in that direction. Assistant superintendents, directors, building principals, assistant principals, library media specialists, department heads, and teachers will set and synchronize goals and instructional objectives with those of the board of education.

School districts need a comprehensive, long-range blueprint for their total operation. The goal-objective hierarchy allows them to become systematic in design and operation. There is a logical sequence of development of goals and objectives from

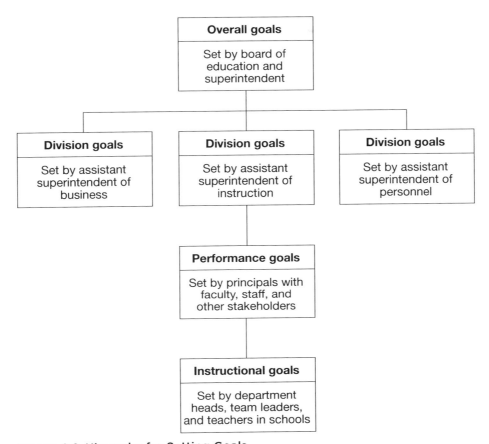

Figure 2.2 Hierarchy for Setting Goals

school district goals to instructional objectives as follows (Glatthorn et al., 2018; Ornstein & Hunkins, 2017):

- Teachers, administrators, students, and lay people can realize a sense of direction.
  - Teachers and administrators are able to sense a common purpose and understand how each person is helping achieve the goals of the total school district. Responsibility for the goals, competencies, and objectives is determined.
  - With the goal-objective hierarchy, articulation between and among the organization levels is highly probable.
- A sense of unity of working as a total group toward a common purpose becomes apparent.
  - Systematic decision making based on how well those decisions will assist in accomplishing the goals and objectives is potentially greater.
  - The goal-objective hierarchy makes the direction for evaluating the curriculum much clearer and exact. Evaluation becomes an ongoing practice

rather than a piecemeal effort. As a consequence, curriculum revision should not have to be radical or upsetting to personnel.

Criteria for Effective Goals

In order to ensure goal-setting benefits for the school district, certain characteristics and guidelines need to be met. In most applications, a criterion holds true regardless of the environment in which the goal is actually being set. For example, goals determined for a teacher may be completely different than those set for a principal—yet they both must meet the same criteria (performance on the job) in order to be effective. Components for principals to effectively set goals are as follows (Locke & Latham, 2002; Van Soelen, 2021).

Clarity and specificity. Whenever possible, principals should express goals in quantifiable terms, such as increasing student achievement on standardized tests by 5 percent, decreasing dropouts by 10 percent, or increasing average daily attendance by 4 percent. Clear and specific goals make it known to all employees where their efforts should lead them. Unclear and nonspecific goals create confusion and conflict among employees.

Time frame. Goals should have time frames within which they will be accomplished. A time frame usually is a deadline specifying the date on which goal attainment will be measured. A goal of increasing average daily attendance could have a deadline such as the end of the school year. If a goal involves a two- to three-year time period, specific dates for achieving parts of it can be developed. For example, reading improvement goals could be established on a three-year time period: (1) 50 percent of students will be reading at grade level in year one, (2) 55 percent of students will be reading at grade level in year two, and (3) 60 percent of students will be reading at grade level in year three. Within a school building or classroom, goals may be set for shorter time frames including daily, weekly, monthly, and yearly.

Key areas. Goals cannot be derived for every aspect of teacher and staff behavior or for each facet of school performance. Instead, principals should identify a few critical success areas, not to exceed four or five, for the school, department, or job. For example, a high school might specify four goals for a given school year: 5 percent increase in standardized test scores, 10 percent decrease in student dropouts, 4 percent increase in average daily attendance, and 20 percent decrease in discipline referrals to the office. The principal is the leader in the process of goal setting so that the number of goals set can feasibly be attained. Goals reached equals increased motivation for teacher, staff, students, and community. Therefore, it is helpful to limit goals to four categories (Van Soelen, 2021): (1) *professional skill goals*, which are clearly defined statements describing critical aspects of administrative or teaching performance; (2) *problem-solving goals*, which are designed to correct areas in which performance is below standard; (3) *innovative goals*, which pertain to improvement projects; and (4) *personal development goals*, which are designed for the purpose of projecting an annual program for personal growth and development.

Challenging but realistic. Although goals should be made challenging, they should be realistic enough to accomplish. Easily attainable goals may lead to complacency. Goals that are too difficult may create frustration. Moreover, with two given employees of equal talent and ability, a given goal might be viewed as entirely possible by one and utterly impossible by the other. One value of limiting goals to professional skill, problem-solving, innovative, and personal development goals is that these offer special challenges to a variety of employees.

Linked to rewards. People who attain goals should be rewarded. Rewards give significance to goals and help energize employees to achieve goals. However, failure to achieve goals may be due to factors outside the employee's control. For example, failure of a school to attain a goal regarding student achievement on standardized tests may be associated with the socioeconomic status of the student body, or population shifts in school attendance areas, or some other phenomena. During such changes, the principal and faculty should be anticipating changes, planning for changes, and setting subgoals in response, even though factors may be outside their control regarding the overarching goal. A positive reward would be appropriate as employees reach subgoals. Celebrate the small wins, along with the big wins.

Principals must ensure that goals are communicated to all members of the school district. Organization members should understand how their performance goals relate to the overall school district goals. Goals should not be so numerous or complex that they confuse rather than direct organization members, and the principal must be prepared to periodically refine goals, or even replace them with new ones. As the school and the environment in which it operates change, goals may require adjustments to reflect these changes.

Educational goals should be as changeable as the social conditions and the groups that formulate them. Panels and commissions are often organized for purposes of formulating goals. They may operate at various government and educational levels. Ornstein (1986) recommends that task forces formulate educational goals and that principals include the following as representatives:

- *Students.* Most secondary students are sufficiently mature and responsible to provide appropriate input in developing educational goals; moreover, they have the most at stake and thus deserve to be represented.
- *Parents.* In addition to providing the students and taxes that support schools, recent movement toward school-based management necessitates their involvement.
- *Educators.* Teachers and administrators must assume major responsibility in developing educational goals. To relinquish this responsibility is to surrender one's professional role.
- *Research community.* Researchers and social scientists must provide objective data concerning trends and issues; they should not, however, serve in the role of advocate.
- *Community members.* Citizens and taxpayers, regardless of whether they have children in school, have a civic responsibility to provide input in school matters. Their support is crucial because they vote on school and fiscal matters.
- *Business community.* Business personnel are natural allies of school people; they should be aggressively enlisted in school affairs because of their economic and political influence and stake in the outcomes of schooling in terms of industrial output.
- *Government officials.* Political officials are also natural allies of schools; they, too, should be enlisted because of their political and economic influence. Indeed, educational policy and politics go hand in hand, as do school finance and governance.

- *Pressure groups.* People have the greatest impact by organizing into groups to promote special interests. The operation of such groups is clearly valid within the democratic process, but extreme views must be tempered.
- *Professional organizations.* The input of professional organizations is important in terms of obtaining support from the educational establishment. The professional roles and responsibilities of the members warrant that what is good for schools should prevail.
- *Governing bodies.* Representatives from governing and legislative groups—at the federal, state, and/or local levels—should be included because they have the power and authority to enact legislation (including the recommendations or policy statements) of commissions or panels designed to formulate educational goals.

It is motivational to involve many and varied stakeholders in the establishment of goals, just as it is when working through your vision, mission, and belief action statements. The activity is motivational because its participatory goal setting and feedback components can enhance the employees' and the school community's motivation. It is also an integral part of the *performance-appraisal* method the school uses: teachers and employees are evaluated on the basis of how well they accomplish the jointly set goals and outcomes of the school and school district. Goal setting is also a *monitoring* technique because the jointly set goals become monitoring standards.

The Goal-Setting Process

Although there are many variations of the **goal-setting process**, the cyclical process consists of four main steps: setting goals, developing action plans, monitoring performance, and evaluating results. Figure 2.3 illustrates these steps as they apply to a districtwide goal-setting program.

Step 1: Setting Goals.   Goal setting begins at the top administrative level—the superintendent and board of education meet and develop the long-range goals and plans for the school district, frequently with input from lower levels. An example of a goal they might set would be to increase student performance on standardized achievement tests. Then, each successive level in the school district develops its own set of goals and instructional objectives that dovetail with school district goals. At all points in the process, a check for alignment with the district vision and mission and the school vision and mission are necessary—this keeps the goals focused on the purpose. Discussions at each level among the administrators and the stakeholders result in an agreed-on set of goals. These goals should be written and measurable.

Step 2: Developing Action Plans.   Once goals are agreed on, individuals at each level of the district develop collaborative action plans. Action plans identify how ends are to be achieved. This includes identifying the activities necessary to accomplish the goal, establishing the critical relationships among these activities, assigning responsibility for each activity, estimating the time requirement for each activity, and determining the resources required to complete each activity.

Step 3: Monitoring Performance.   As members of the school district work toward goal attainment, attention turns to monitoring performance. If the goals are established for a one-year interval, goal-setting advocates recommend that the supervisor and subordinate meet quarterly to review progress to date. It may be necessary to revise goals, especially if districtwide goals have changed, or if essential resources are

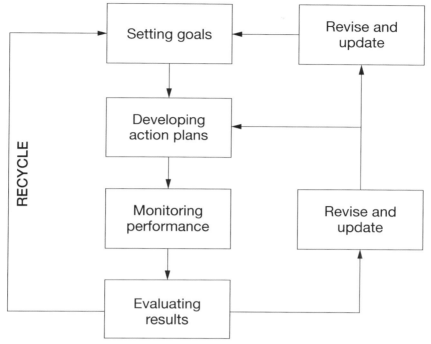

Figure 2.3 The Goal-Setting Process

unavailable. Otherwise, progress toward valid goals is assessed. Periodic reviews give administrators the opportunity to give subordinates feedback on their performance.

Step 4: Evaluating Results.   During the year, the principal and the superintendent or the assistant superintendent should hold formative evaluation meetings to mark progress toward the goals. At the end of one complete goal-setting cycle (usually one year), the principal and the superintendent hold another face-to-face meeting to evaluate the ultimate degree of goal attainment. They discuss which goals the principal was able to meet and which were not met. Principals are rewarded for goal attainment, and future corrective action is planned for goals that were not met during the goal-setting cycle. The emphasis should be constructive and directed toward how to improve future performance rather than dwelling on deficiencies. Finally, a new set of goals is established for the next cycle. The same process should be conducted on the school campus between the principal and the teachers.

Problems with Goal Setting

Goal setting has been used in schools for many years. Despite its widespread use, many principals seem to have difficulty implementing goal setting in their schools. Several predictable problems prevent goal-setting programs from achieving maximum results (Lindsey et al., 2016).

Lack of top-management support. Sometimes central administrators, including the superintendent, do not set overall goals for the system; rather, they delegate the responsibility for goal setting to principals, directors, and coordinators. This limits the program's effectiveness, because the goals set at each lower level of the organization may be incongruent with the actual goals of the central administration, as well as the board. This results in confusion and a lack of common direction for all of the school's members.

Time-consuming. The goal-setting process can be very time-consuming, especially during the first cycle. Principals who are unsure of the new system need to request meetings with their direct supervisors to clarify issues. The quarterly monitoring reviews and end-of-cycle evaluations also take time, especially for principals or directors who have large schools or areas of control.

Excessive paperwork. Goal setting sometimes results in a great deal of paperwork and record keeping. Often, the central administrators allow principals to function largely on their own in determining how goals will be achieved and do not meet during formative stages of the evaluation. For these reasons, many supervisors attempt to stay abreast of what is going on by having principals submit volumes of data, reports, and other performance indicators.

Overemphasis on quantitative goals. The need for specific, measurable goals results in a built-in emphasis on quantifiable outcomes such as achievement test scores, numbers of dropouts, attendance figures, costs, and the like. Factors such as school-community relations, union-management relations, student attitudes, and employee job satisfaction—being difficult to quantify—often are omitted in setting goals. This tends to displace work efforts toward limited and sometimes inappropriate ends.

Administrative style. Goal setting is easily stalled by authoritarian administrators and inflexible, bureaucratic policies and procedures. For many administrators, both at the central level and the campus level, goal setting requires a 180-degree turn from their current ways of thinking and doing things. In many instances, superintendents have relegated, have suggested, or even have assigned goals to principals in the past. Under goal setting, principals are to have input, and garner faculty and stakeholder input, in establishing school goals jointly with their supervisors.

Prepackaged programs. External consultants who follow standard models used in other organizations frequently implement goal setting in schools. This practice spreads the mechanization of goal setting. Any goal-setting package usually requires substantial modification to fit the unique needs of a school campus organization.

Making Goal Setting Effective

Although there are many problems with goal setting, it can be an effective administrative technique if properly used and if it is incorporated into the system. Goals must be part of a total system for them to be effective. Because many principals encounter some type of formal goal-setting program in their school districts, we examine some of the elements required for goal setting effectiveness (Berg et al., 2018; Eckert, 2018; Harris, Jones, & Huffman, 2018; McChesney et al., 2021; Van Soelen, 2021).

Develop a participative organization structure. The formal organization structure must be compatible with the goal-setting process. For example, school districts that emphasize bureaucratic or mechanistic systems—with rigid hierarchies, high degrees of functional specialization, many written rules and procedures, and impersonal human relationships—respond inadequately to goal setting. New organizational structures that are flexible and adaptive are needed, as are systems that both require and allow greater commitment and use of the creative talent of all employees within the system.

Create a positive leadership climate. The leadership climate experienced by a particular work group or hierarchical level in a school district is determined primarily by the leadership behavior of echelons above it. Moreover, the behavior of the leaders at the very top echelon (superintendent and their cabinet) exerts, by far, the greatest influence on lower levels of the organization. In specific terms, the values, attitudes, and perceptions of leaders at the top of the school district hierarchy act as either constraining or adapting forces affecting the successful implementation of goal setting and affecting the systemic outcomes of goals of the district and those of the school campuses.

Maintain the means-ends chain of goals. Goal setting needs to be structured in an interlocking network of means-ends chains to the organization's overall purpose and strategy. In so doing, every member at every level in the school district is a key link in the goal-setting process. Organization members link goals at one level (i.e., the means) to those at the next higher level (i.e., the ends). This ensures that the various levels within the school district have a common direction that is centered in the vision and mission of both the district and the campus.

Train principals. For goal setting to succeed, principals and teachers must understand and be fully committed to it. They must be trained concerning the procedures and advantages of the program, the skills required, and the benefits goal setting provides individuals and the organization. Particularly, if the principal, as leader, is resistant, a goal-setting program is doomed to failure.

Emphasize periodic feedback sessions. The essence of goal setting is regular task-relevant communication among members of the school organization. This includes giving each member feedback on actual performance as compared with planned performance (goals). If goal setting is to work, this must occur throughout the organization—over and over again. The manner in which feedback is given is also important. If it is hostile, performance may actually be reduced. Feedback should not be used to degrade the individual but instead should focus on constructive ways to improve performance.

Collaboration may create the conditions necessary for improving employee productivity. Collaboration in schools has been identified as the key schooling process variable for increasing the norms of student achievement (Berg et al., 2018; Eckert, 2018; Harris, Jones, & Huffman, 2018; Pankake & Abrego, 2017; Sterrett, 2016).

Snyder, Krieger, and McCormick (1984) engaged their faculty in soliciting consensus for school achievement goals and developed a methodology called the **Delphi Dialog Technique** for principals. We advocate that this technique is easy to implement and should be considered by principals. An example is noted in table 2.2. The four-step process is designed to foster faculty dialog about substantive issues through a series of individual and small-group tasks.

The Delphi Dialog Technique: A Goal-Setting Process.

In **Round 1**, the faculty members present relevant data to each other relating to pressures for school improvement. Using the data, the entire faculty engage in a series of small- and large-group activities until consensus is reached regarding the general direction for school improvement.

In **Round 2**, each faculty member reflects on the selected directions, identifying his own concerns and making recommendations for the dimensions of the improvement effort (a goal). Each faculty member is assigned to a group (four to eight

Table 2.2 The Delphi Dialog Technique: A Goal-Setting Process

ROUND 1	ROUND 2	ROUND 3	ROUND 4
The School Community Dialog	*Individual Reflection Delphi*	*Team Reflection Dialog*	*Student Council Reflection Dialog*
Group wishing each goal subsystem	State a concern for goal recommendations	Organize individual recommendations	Organization team goal by subsystem
Group reflection: our school	State a goal for each subsystem	Analyze goal themes	Analyze goal themes
Selection: most promising goal subsystems		Synthesize goal themes into inconclusive goal recommendations	Synthesize goal themes into inconclusive goal recommendations
OUTCOME I	OUTCOME II	OUTCOME III	OUTCOME IV
Recommended areas for school improvement	Goal statements from each school member	A team goal recommendation for each goal subsystem	Council recommendations for school goals

Source: Syder, Kreiger, & Mccormick (1983).

persons) for Round 3. The task in **Round 3** is to listen to individual recommendations and to formulate one team recommendation for each direction that reflects individual faculty member concerns.

In **Round 4**, a representative from each team and a principal form a council. Their task is to listen to each group recommendation and to formulate one council recommendation for each direction that represents all concerns. Rounds 2, 3, and 4 are repeated until faculty consensus (not majority vote) on the improvement efforts for the year is achieved.

DEVELOPING PLANS FOR ATTAINING GOALS

Once organizational goals have been established, the next step is to develop plans for meeting goals. Goals mean little if organization members do not plan how to attain them. In this section, several commonly used plans are discussed: strategic plans, tactical plans, operational plans, standing plans, and single-use plans. As shown in figure 2.4, these plans can be described in terms of different levels of scope and different time frames.

Strategic Plans

Strategic plans are the means by which the goals of the school district are to be attained (Lemaine, Levernier, & Richardson, 2018; Valcik, 2017; Wootton & Horne, 2021). As shown in figure 2.4, they are broad in scope, cover a relatively long time frame, and are developed by top-level administrators and policymakers (superintendent with the school board). The purpose of the strategic plan is to turn school district goals into a reality during a given time frame. The key components of the strategy define the school district activities and resources—money, personnel, space, and facilities—required for meeting the district's goals. For example, if a school district's goal is to improve student performance in mathematics and science, the strategic plan may prescribe in-service training for math and science teachers, identification

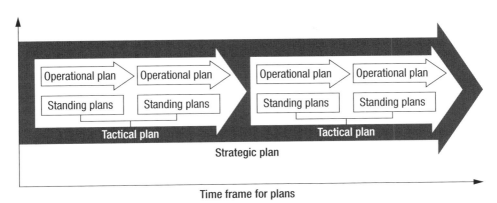

Figure 2.4 Types of Plans

of instructional technology needed, and allocation of resources for supporting an instructional program to meet the needs of all students. The strategic plan provides the basis for more detailed plans at middle and lower school district levels.

Tactical Plans

Tactical plans are designed to help execute strategic plans and to accomplish a specific part of the school district's strategy (Lemaine, Levernier, & Richardson, 2018; Valcik, 2017; Wootton & Horne, 2021). Tactical plans typically have a shorter time frame and a more moderate scope than strategic plans. The term *tactical* derives from the military. Although single battles may be won or lost due to tactical plans, wars are guided by an overall strategic plan. For example, General Norman Schwarzkopf deployed strategic weapons systems, such as intercontinental ballistic missiles (ICBMs) and B1 bombers, to deliver major blows to the enemy during the Persian Gulf War. Strategic weapon systems reflect the country's overall strategic plans. Tactical weapon systems, such as fighter planes, tanks, and infantry soldiers, were used to achieve just one part of the overall strategic plan. In a school system, new teaching techniques may be a part of the strategic plan to increase student performance in math and science, but the use of one piece of media production equipment is part of the tactical plan.

Principals use tactical plans to allocate school district resources and to coordinate their system's internal subdivisions or building units. These plans, therefore, are associated with the organizational responsibility of middle managers, such as building principals. Planning at this level—resource allocation, integrating the visions of top-level administrators with the day-to-day activities of classroom teachers—reflects tactical planning. Although strategic and tactical planning are different, both should be integrated into an overall system designed to accomplish school district goals and outcomes.

Operational Plans

Operational plans are developed at the lower levels of the school district to specify the means toward achieving operational goals and supporting tactical planning activities (Lemaine, Levernier, & Richardson, 2018; Valcik, 2017; Wootton & Horne, 2021). These plans are associated with the organizational responsibilities of department heads or team leaders. Operational planning frequently is the outcome of a goal-setting system; it specifies plans for supervisors, department heads, and classroom teachers.

As shown in figure 2.4, operational plans have a narrower focus and shorter time frame than tactical plans. Schedules are an important component of operational plans. Schedules define precise time frames for the completion of each goal required for the school district's tactical and strategic goals.

Standing Plans

Schools and school districts face similar or identical situations repeatedly. Examples include student tardiness and absenteeism, smoking in the school building, requests by outside groups to use school facilities, and the like. **Standing plans** are predetermined statements that help decision makers handle repetitive situations in a consistent manner. These plans, once established, continue to apply until they are modified or abandoned. The major types of standing plans are policies, procedures, and rules (Lemaine, Levernier, & Richardson, 2018; Valcik, 2017; Wootton & Horne, 2021).

Policies. The broadest and most fundamental type of standing plans, *policies*, serve as guides to administrative decision making or to supervising the actions of subordinates. Sometimes policies are formally determined by the board of education; they may also be informally set by the superintendent, building principals, or classroom teachers. They may be written or unwritten, spoken or unspoken. They may be initiated at any level of the school district.

There are many types of policies—instructional policies, financial policies, personnel policies, to name a few. Within each of these areas, more specific policies are developed. For example, personnel policies may include selection, recruitment, promotion, retirement, collective bargaining, and training and development policies. Instructional policies may encompass policies on class size, grouping for instruction, school hours, grading, and so on.

Procedures. There is a relationship between policies and procedures. *Procedures* indicate how policies are to be carried out. Procedures specify a chronological sequence of steps that must be taken to accomplish a particular task. For example, universities have procedures for registering, for adding and dropping courses, for applying to graduate school, and the like. The essential purpose of procedures is to ensure consistent action. Moreover, they enable administrators to "manage by exception"—that is, to establish policies and procedures to handle recurring problems and to take other action only when exceptional or extraordinary events occur.

Rules. The simplest though usually the most detailed of all standing plans, *rules*, specifically state what can and cannot be done under a given set of circumstances. Rules, unlike procedures, do not specify a time sequence. Rules do not allow for deviations. Unlike policies, rules limit discretion; people use judgment in applying policies. The only choice a rule leaves is whether or not to apply it to a particular situation. Some examples of rules include the following: no smoking permitted on school grounds; no drugs permitted on the premises; a student may enroll in no more than seven courses in a given semester.

Single-Use Plans

Standing plans, in the form of policies, procedures, and rules, provide continued guidelines to the actions of school district members. School districts also use other types of plans, **single-use plans**, which are predetermined courses of action developed for relatively unique, nonrepetitive situations. The major types of single-use plans are programs, projects, and budgets (Lemaine, Levernier, & Richardson, 2018; Valcik, 2017; Wootton & Horne, 2021).

Programs. A *program* is a mixture of goals, strategies, policies, rules, and job assignments, as well as the fiscal, physical, and human resources required to implement them. The program typically specifies the goals, major steps necessary to achieve the goals, individuals' or departments' responsibility for each step, the sequence of the various steps, and the resources to be employed. Programs may be as large in scope as landing a person on the moon or as small as improving the reading level of fourth grade students in a school district, or improving teacher morale in a particular school.

Projects. A *project* is a single-use plan that is a component of a program and is usually more limited in scope. In a university, business administration students speak of being in the finance, industrial relations, or management "program." Each of these programs stipulate a sequence of courses that must be taken to fulfill the requirements of the major. However, as part of the course requirements, students may have to complete "projects" in specific courses. The time horizons for projects may be lengthy or short.

Budgets. A *budget* is a single-use plan, expressed in numerical terms, that specifies in detail the resources or funds assigned to a particular program, project, division, or school building. Although budgets are normally expressed in monetary terms, they can be used to plan allocations of personnel, space, and facilities. Developing budgets is clearly a planning process, because it takes strategic goals into account in deciding in advance how to allocate resources among alternative activities. Budgets, then, serve two major purposes: planning and control. In the planning phase, budgets force principals to evaluate programs and activities in relation to cost effectiveness. In the control phase, budgets let principals know how well operations are conforming to plan, the vision, and the mission.

USING GOAL SETTING TO IMPROVE STUDENT ACHIEVEMENT

Alford and Sampson (2016) have found, in their study across two states, that leaders who are successful in goal setting and school improvement build upon assets of the faculty, community, and students, in fostering school improvement for increased student learning. Those principals with a sustained focus on academic goals within a positive environment characterized by high expectations, mutual respect, and cultural appreciation, can help the school attain students' learning needs.

In another landmark study (Johnson, 1998), the Charles A. Dana Center at the University of Texas studied ten medium-to-large districts in which more than one-third of the high-poverty schools had earned "recognized" or "exemplary" ratings according to the state criteria for rating schools. A finding was that these districts make academic success a nonnegotiable goal. These districts have established clear, tangible, measurable, and challenging academic goals, and they have insisted that the campuses develop believable plans for attaining those goals. They regularly used data to maintain focus on progress made toward meeting academic goals. Another finding was that the leaders, the superintendent and the principals, kept a focus on improving teaching and learning—the primary purpose or mission. In these schools, there was evidence of strong support from the central administration and a strong relationship with the community of each school. The schools also were able to focus state and federal policy and resources toward the attainment of their goals.

Johnson (1998) reported another Dana Center study that occurred in 1996. Similar results were found. The following seven themes emerged from the 1996 study:

1. *Strong focus on ensuring the academic success of each student.* The twenty-six schools in the study established measurable goals that focused on student achievement. The focus was on what was best for the students.
2. *A "no excuses" attitude.* The teachers believed that any student could be successful, and no excuses were allowed for low student performances. There was no blaming of parents, economic status, or any other issue surrounding the student.
3. *A variety of instructional strategies.* The same instructional approaches that had been used in the past and had been unsuccessful were reevaluated for use. Experimentation with a variety of approaches was encouraged.
4. *A community of responsible adults.* These schools solicited assistance from many responsible adults to reach the goal. They utilized many volunteers. The teachers of various subject areas or special subjects and the support staff, all, maintained important roles in working with the students. A systemic approach was used with school personnel, as well as parent and community volunteers. The approach was welcoming to all who came to the school to assist with students' academic improvement.
5. *An environment of family.* These schools tended to act more like families and less like institutions. People involved felt valued and respected. Diversity was celebrated.
6. *Openness, honesty, and trust.* Teachers and staff felt comfortable sharing concerns, ideas, and accomplishments. Principals planned sharing and meeting times, formal and informal.
7. *Passion for continuous improvement, professional growth, and learning.* These schools not only celebrated when success was the result, they also challenged themselves with higher goals.

SUMMARY

1. Vision is critical to the success and future of the school.
2. A mission defines the purpose of the school.
3. The belief, values, and attitudes of the principal, as leader, and the stakeholders are important to ascertain an alignment with the vision and mission.
4. Goals are the starting point for any school district and schools. In addition to providing direction for the school district, they also serve as standards by which individual performance and district outcomes can be measured. Finally, they serve as motivators for organizational members who are given clear aims for which to strive.

5. Goals within the school are defined in a hierarchical fashion, beginning with strategic goals followed by subsidiary goals, performance goals, and instructional objectives.

6. Some criteria for evaluating the effectiveness of goals are clarity and specificity, time frames, key areas, challenging and realistic, and linkage to rewards.

7. One useful technique for systematizing system goals is the goal-setting process. The basic steps in the goal-setting process are setting goals, developing action plans, monitoring performance, and evaluating results.

8. Many goal-setting programs fail due to a lack of top leadership support, time involved, excessive paperwork, overemphasis on quantitative goals, inappropriate management style, and the use of prepackaged programs.

9. Developing a participative organizational structure, creating a positive leadership climate, maintaining the means-ends chain of goals, and emphasizing periodic feedback should increase the likelihood of success of a goal-setting program.

10. Several types of plans for meeting goals include strategic plans, tactical plans, operational plans, standing plans, and single-use plans.

11. Strategic plans focus on what the school will do in the future and involve the determination of strategic goals, adaptation of courses of action, and the allocation of resources necessary to achieve these objectives.

12. Tactical plans are much narrower in scope; their primary purpose is determining how the activities specified by strategic plans are to be accomplished.

13. Operational plans are developed at lower levels of the school district to specify the means toward achieving operational goals and supporting tactical planning activities.

14. Standing plans provide standardized responses for recurring situations; they include policies, procedures, and rules.

15. Single-use plans are established for unique situations; they include programs, projects, and budgets.

KEY TERMS

systemic vision
vision
leadership framework
vision detractors
vision maintainers
mission
goals
process-oriented goals
results-oriented goals

hierarchy of goals
goal-setting process
Delphi Dialog Technique
strategic plans
tactical plans
operational plans
standing plans
single-use plans

FIELD-BASED ACTIVITIES

1. Analyze your school's vision, mission, beliefs, and goals. Are they aligned? Take field notes for one week and observe: (a) the demonstrations within the school of the vision, mission, and beliefs; and (b) the principal's actions as to how he or she is focused on the vision and mission.
2. Write your own leadership framework. It should be single-spaced, 12-point font and about one page in length. Have two other teachers review your leadership framework. Ask them to tell you how they have observed you demonstrating those beliefs and values you have written.
3. Interview the principal. Determine how goals are set on the campus and how those goals are assessed. Determine which strategic goal plan best aligns with what the principal does to set goals.

SUGGESTED READINGS

Glickman, C., & Mette, I. M. (2020). *The essential renewal of America's schools: A leadership guide for democratizing schools from the inside out.* New York, NY: Teachers College Press. Carl Glickman and Ian Mette provide a framework that replaces dependence on top-down state and federal regulations, focusing instead on the creation of locally guided initiatives to address local goals.

Howard, T. K. (2020). *Why race and culture matter in schools: Closing the achievement gap in America's classrooms* (2nd ed.). New York, NY: Teachers College Press. Tyrone Howard identifies innovative programs with evidence-based results on eliminating disparities in student outcomes and includes strategies to help school leaders create more equitable learning environments.

Kariya, T., & Rappleye, J. (2020). *Education, equality, and meritocracy in a global age: The Japanese approach.* New York, NY: Teachers College Press. Takehiko Kariya and Jeremy Rappleye show how the Japanese experience can inform global approaches to educational reform and policymaking—and how this kind of exploration can invigorate a more rigorous discussion of meritocracy, equality, and education.

Kundu, A. (2020). *The power of student agency: Looking beyond grit to close the opportunity gap.* New York, NY: Teachers College Press. Anindya Kundu argues that we can fight against deeply rooted inequalities in the American educational system by harnessing student agency—each person's unique capacity for positive change.

Teranishi, R. T., Nguyen, B. M. D., Alcantar, C. M., & Curammeng, E. R. (2020). *Measuring race: Why disaggregating data matters for addressing educational inequality.* New York, NY: Teachers College Press. The authors provide new ways to critically analyze evidence-based strategies that remove racial and ethnic barriers to achieving greater equity and equality.

Zhoa, Y., Emler, T. E., Snethen, A., & Yin, D. (2020). *An education crisis is a terrible thing to waste: How radical changes can spark student excitement and success.* New York, NY: Teachers College Press. The authors offer a vision of what a modern education could be.

3

Curriculum Development and Implementation

■ ■ ■

FOCUSING QUESTIONS

1. How can we define curriculum?
2. What are the major components of curriculum?
3. What are good criteria to use in selecting content and learning experiences?
4. How are content, learning experiences, and behavioral objectives related in developing and implementing curriculum?
5. Why are curriculum development models behaviorist in nature?
6. How is the principal a curriculum and instructional leader?

In this chapter, we address these questions concerning the principal's role in curriculum development and implementation. We begin the chapter by defining curriculum and examining the major components of curriculum: content, learning experiences, and behavioral objectives. Then we discuss the framework for structuring knowledge and its relationship to curriculum development and implementation: knowledge as facts; the explosion of knowledge; essential knowledge; a return to the liberal arts; computer knowledge and technology; and moral knowledge. Next, we examine several curriculum models useful in developing and implementing curriculum: classical model, systems model, applicative model, managerial model, behavioral/aesthetic model, curriculum overview model, and systemic-integrated model. Finally, we conclude the chapter with a discussion of the principal's role as curriculum and instructional leader.

COMPONENTS OF CURRICULUM

What is curriculum? How does it affect students, teachers, and principals? Some curriculum leaders define curriculum as a formal course of study, emphasizing content or subject matter. Others define curriculum as the totality of experiences of each learner, stressing how subject matter is learned or the process of instruction. Still others point out the importance of statements of expected learning outcomes or behavioral objectives. Behavioral objectives are typically identified within some framework such as the subjects offered in the school program. And some describe the curriculum as a framework for structuring knowledge.

Our own analysis of the components of curriculum embodies all of the afore-mentioned definitions. Each one will be discussed in turn.

Content or Subject Matter

Over the years and currently, the dominant component of curriculum is that of content or subject matter taught by teachers and learned by students. For example, Philip Phenix (1962) defines the curriculum as *what* is studied, the "content" or "subject matter" of instruction.

According to Phenix the **content** includes the whole range of matters in which the student is expected to gain some knowledge and competence. There are the obvious academic subjects that are customarily associated with the idea of curriculum, such as language and literature, mathematics, the natural and social sciences, and the fine arts. These are primarily intellectual in nature. The curriculum may also include the practical studies that develop skills in the industrial arts, either for personal enjoyment or for vocational purposes. Other studies combine the practical and intellectual in preparation for the professions, such as law, medicine, or teaching. Still another group of subjects that are neither primarily intellectual or practical may best be described as personal in orientation. In this category are provisions for physical and mental health education, for sex and drug education, for development of mature human relationships, and for growth of desirable attitudes and values.

Criteria for Selecting Content. Curriculum planners should apply criteria in choosing curriculum content. Although the following criteria are neutral and can fit into any curriculum approach or model, various philosophical camps might place greater emphasis on particular criteria. For example, Hilda Taba (1962), in a classic text on curriculum, maintains that content should include the following functions.

1. *Four Levels of Knowledge.* These include specific facts, skills, and processes; basic ideas such as generalizations, principles, and causal relationships within the subject matter; concepts dealing with abstract ideas, complex systems, multiple causations, and interdependence; and thought systems or methods of problem solving, inquiry, and discovery.
2. *New Fundamentals to Master.* The content in many subjects becomes increasingly obsolete, especially in light of the explosion of knowledge. The curriculum must be periodically updated to include new content to be learned.
3. *Scope.* Scope is the breadth, depth, and variety of the content and includes the coverage of boundaries of the subject.
4. *Sequence.* By sequencing, there is recognition of and need for differentiating levels of knowledge, that learning is based on prior knowledge, and that the curriculum should be cumulative and continuous.
5. *Integration.* Integration emphasizes the relationships among various content themes, topics, or units; it helps explain how content in one subject is related to content in another subject.

A more recent text (Ornstein & Hunkins, 2017) establishes seven additional criteria to consider when selecting and organizing content. Whereas Taba stresses cognitive learning theory for her five criteria, Ornstein and Hunkin's seven criteria combine cognitive and humanistic psychology:

1. *Self-Sufficiency.* A guiding principle for content selection is that it helps learners attain learning skills and self-sufficiency in learning (economy of the teacher's effort and time in instruction and economy of students' efforts and time in learning).
2. *Significance.* Content should contribute to learning particular concepts, skills, or values; it should be significant in terms of what knowledge needs to be transmitted to students.
3. *Validity.* As new knowledge is discovered, old knowledge that is less relevant, misleading, or incorrect must be pruned. Only relevant and accurate knowledge should be a part of the curriculum content. The content should also be sound in relation to stated goals and objectives.
4. *Interest.* Content is easier to learn when it is meaningful. The interest criterion is a progressive concept, but all content should be selected, in part, on the basis of students' interests.
5. *Utility.* Content should be useful in and out of school. What is considered useful will also reflect philosophy.
6. *Learnability.* The content must be within the experiences and understanding of the learner; content should be selected and arranged on the basis that it makes learning easy or, at least, less difficult for students.
7. *Feasibility.* The content must be considered in terms of time allotted, personnel and resources available, and, sometimes, existing legislation, political climate, and money. Although some educators may like to think that they have an entire world of content from which to choose, they do have limitations on their actions.

(Ornstein & Hunkins, 2017)

Learning Experiences

The conception of curriculum as the experiences of the learner, complemented by organized content or subject matter, was introduced by many curriculum scholars. Selecting the content, with accompanying learning experiences, is one of the central decisions in curriculum making and, therefore, a rational method of going about it is a matter of great concern according to Hilda Taba (1962).

Taba asserts that to develop criteria for rational priorities in selecting learning experiences, it is necessary to clarify some significant issues. She points out the importance of understanding that curriculum consists of three different things: the content (the subject matter), the learning experiences (the mental operations that students employ in learning subject matter), and behavioral objectives (linked to content and learning experiences). Although, in the actual learning act, content and learning experiences are in constant interaction; one cannot deal with content without having a learning experience. Nevertheless, content and learning experiences need to be distinguished. According to Taba (1962), it is possible to deal with significant content in a manner that results in inadequate teaching, or to apply fruitful learning processes to content that in itself is not worth knowing. One can speak of effective learning then as consisting of both content and processes that are fruitful and significant.

Taba (1962) further asserts that the failure to make this distinction has caused many misunderstandings in the discussion of curriculum theories. Many reasonable criteria for selecting and organizing curricula have been misapplied or misunderstood by critics, because what was intended as a criterion for selecting learning experiences was also used as a criterion for selecting curriculum content or even for organizing the entire curriculum. For example, the discussion of the role of subjects as a meaning for training in disciplined thought has been obscured because of the assumption that disciplined thought is the direct function of the content rather than of the mental operations employed while learning it. Taba argues that it is possible to learn mathematics by rote memorization, and to learn welding by analyzing and applying some basic principles. In other words, depending on the nature of learning experiences, any subject can be reduced to *learning about something* or become the means for the learning of the *how* of disciplined thinking. A clearer distinction between the content of the curriculum and the **learning experiences** (or the processes that students employ in dealing with content) would be helpful in classifying such problems of selection as determining which criteria apply to which aspect of curriculum—content or learning experiences.

The discussions of behavioral objectives, according to Taba (1962), also shows that some educational objectives are served by the content, whereas others are best implemented by certain learning experiences. On one hand, the objectives described as acquisition of knowledge—the concepts, ideas, and values—cannot be implemented by selection and organization of content alone. To attain them, students need to undergo certain experiences that give them an opportunity to practice the desired behavior. If curriculum is a plan for learning, and if objectives determine what learning is important, then it follows that adequate curriculum planning involves selecting and organizing both the content and learning experiences. Mary Durkin (1993) provides an implementation of Taba's philosophy as applied to the classroom in her book *Thinking Through Class Discussion: The Hilda Taba Approach.*

Criteria for Selecting Learning Experiences. Tyler (1949), in his classic text on curriculum, outlines five general principles in selecting learning experiences. These **learning experiences** can take place in the classroom, outside the classroom (in the schoolyard, auditorium, or laboratory), or outside the school (on a field trip, in the library or a museum, etc.).

1. *Learners must have experiences that give them opportunity to practice the behavior(s) implied by the objective(s).* If the objective is to develop problem-solving skills, then students must have ample opportunity to solve problems. In other words, there must be experiences for students to practice what they are required to learn.
2. *Students must obtain satisfaction in carrying out or performing the learning experiences.* Students need satisfying experiences to develop and maintain interest in learning; unsatisfying experiences hinder learning.
3. *Learning experiences must be appropriate to the student's present attainments.* This basically means that the teacher must begin where the student is and that prior knowledge is the starting point in learning new knowledge.
4. *Several experiences can attain the same objective.* There are many ways for learning the same thing; as long as they are effective and meaningful, a wide range of experiences is better for learning than a limited range. Capitalize on the various interests of students.

5. *The same learning experience usually results in several outcomes.* While students are acquiring knowledge of one subject or idea, they often develop ideas and attitudes in other subjects and certain attitudes toward the original subject.

(Tyler, 1949)

More recently, the criteria for selecting learning experiences have been stated in the form of a question: Will the learning experience do what we wish it to do in light of the overall aims and goals of the program and specific objectives of the curriculum? The following are specific extensions of this question. Are the experiences:

- valid in light of the ways in which knowledge and skills will be applied in out-of-school situations?
- feasible in terms of time, staff expertise, facilities available within and outside of the school, and community expectations?
- optimal in terms of students' learning the content?
- capable of allowing students to develop their thinking and problem-solving skills?
- capable of stimulating in students greater understanding of their own existence as individuals and as members of groups?
- capable of fostering an openness to new experiences and a tolerance for diversity?
- such that they will facilitate learning and motivate students to continue learning?
- capable of allowing students to address their needs?
- such that students can broaden their interests?
- such that they will foster the total development of students in cognitive, affective, psychomotor, social, and spiritual domains?

(Doll, 1996)

Balance in Determining Content and Learning Experiences in the Curriculum. The need for a **balanced curriculum** with appropriate emphasis on content and learning experiences to ensure a proper weight and broad range to each aspect of the curriculum is obvious, but not easy to achieve given competing philosophies, ideologies, and views of teaching and learning. John Goodlad (1963) maintains that the curriculum should be balanced in terms of subject matter and learning. He further asserts that balance needs to be incorporated into the curriculum to "impose floors and ceilings," a proper range of required knowledge, skills, concepts, and learning experiences that considers the "interests, abilities, and backgrounds" of students (p. 29).

For Doll (1996), a balanced curriculum fits the learner in terms of educational needs, abilities, and growth pertaining to the learner's development. Within the classroom and school, the student should receive content and learning experiences of two sorts: those suitable for the whole group and those specifically designed for the individual student—his or her personal needs and abilities. It takes a highly effective teacher to meet the needs, abilities, and interests of the whole group, while serving the needs, abilities, and interests of individuals. It is much easier to teach toward the average—some "mystical mean." The result is that high-achieving students are often bored, and low-achieving students are often frustrated as the teacher teaches toward the "average" student in the class.

As curriculum planners strive for balanced content and learning experiences, they must consider the pulls and tugs of traditional and contemporary philosophies, conservative and liberal politics, and changing state standards. It behooves curriculum leaders to consider the elements of balance—the mix of philosophy and politics, as well as the various schools of thought on teaching and learning—in developing curriculum. The question arises, What should be an appropriate emphasis? To be sure, the concept of balance invokes several competing forces and variables, and a great deal of controversy in some schools and very little controversy in other schools. On a practical level, supervisors and principals need to compromise on differences and reach consensus on the following program concerns, philosophical and social issues, and moral questions:

1. Needs of society vs. learner
2. Excellence vs. equality
3. Standard-based vs. individualized education
4. Cognitive, affective, psychomotor, and moral domains of learning
5. Behavioral vs. nonbehavioral objectives
6. Technological/computerized vs. humanistic/artistic focus
7. Subject-centered vs. student-centered curriculum
8. General vs. specialized content
9. Breadth vs. depth in content
10. Content vs. process
11. Essential (core) knowledge vs. abstract (problem-solving) methods
12. Traditional vs. progressive ideas (and authors)
13. National vs. global (Western vs. non-Western and industrialized vs. emerging nations) history and culture
14. Academic, business, vocational, and technical tracks
15. Gifted, talented, average, and academically challenged learners
16. Advanced placement, required, and elective subjects
17. Whole language vs. phonetics
18. Classroom, lab activities vs. community, field-based activities
19. Homogenous vs. heterogeneous grouping
20. Whole-group, small-group, and individualized instruction

Behavioral Objectives

Past and present efforts at curriculum improvement have made much use of goals and objectives as bases for curriculum planning. Noteworthy is the work of a group of scholars, under the direction of Benjamin Bloom, who attempt to devise some means that permit greater precision of communication with respect to educational objectives. The taxonomy is this means.

The **taxonomy** is a scheme for classifying educational objectives into categories descriptive of the kinds of behavior that educators seek from students in schools. The taxonomy is based on the assumption that the educational program can be conceived of as an attempt to change the behavior of students with respect to some subject matter. When we describe the behavior and subject matter, we construct a behavioral objective. For instance: the student should be able to recall the major features of Japanese culture; he should be able to recognize form and pattern in literary works. The two parts of the objective, the subject matter and what is to be done with respect to the subject matter by the student, are both categorizable. It is, however, the latter, what is to be *done* with the subject matter, that constitutes the categories of the taxonomy.

The taxonomy is divided into three domains: cognitive, affective, and psychomotor. The **cognitive domain** includes those objectives having to do with thinking, knowing, and problem solving (Bloom, 1956). The **affective domain** includes those objectives dealing with attitudes, values, interest, and appreciations (Krathwohl, Bloom, & Masia, 1964). The **psychomotor domain** covers objectives having to do with manual and motor skills (Harrow, 1972).

The classification scheme in each of the three domains is hierarchical in nature—that is, each category is assumed to involve behavior that is more complex and abstract than the previous category. Thus, the categories are arranged from simple to more complex behavior, and from concrete to more abstract behavior.

According to Bloom and his associates, there are at least four values of using the taxonomy for curriculum making. First, the taxonomy provides a basis for working with objectives with a specificity and precision that is not generally typical of such statements. Second, the specificity and precision in the description of a student behavior make it easier to select the kinds of learning experiences that are appropriate to developing the desired behavior. Third, the hierarchical nature of the taxonomy facilitates scope and sequence in curriculum planning. And, finally, the taxonomy may be useful in evaluating teaching. Specifically, the content of norm-referenced and criterion-referenced tests, in addition to educational experiences and innovations in teaching, can be analyzed using the taxonomy as a framework, which may reveal an over- or underemphasis on particular objectives.

The movement toward process-product research complements and builds on the pioneering work of Bloom and his associates. Program goals, classroom objectives, and learning outcomes are integrated with teaching strategies that focus on higher order thinking skills in Bloom's taxonomy and the use of authentic assessment procedures, including constructed response, standardized testing, and portfolios.

Curriculum Goals and Behavioral Objectives. What are the bases of curriculum goals and behavioral objectives? Curriculum goals are derived from three sources: studies of society, studies of learners, and suggestions of subject-matter specialists. From studies of society, the curriculum developer derives information about the needs of contemporary life, tradition, enduring values, and aspirations. From studies of the learner, the curriculum maker learns about needs, interests, ability levels, and learning styles. From subject-matter specialists, the curriculum worker learns what knowledge is of greatest importance (see Ralph Tyler's behavioral model discussed later in this chapter).

Curriculum goals are broad and general statements helpful in the development of programs of instruction or for general goals toward which several years of education might be aimed, such as elementary, middle, and high school courses of study. Examples of curriculum goals are statements such as the following:

- to understand the rights and duties of citizens in American society
- to attain an appreciation for literature, art, music, and nature

- to develop skills in reading, writing, speaking, and listening
- to learn to respect and get along with people of different cultures

In contrast to broad and general goal statements, **behavioral objectives** are precise statements that indicate what students will be able to do as a result of instruction. Examples of behavioral objectives are statements such as the following:

- Shown the letters of the alphabet in random order (in both upper- and lowercase form), the student will be able to say the name of each letter with 100 percent accuracy.
- Given twenty sentences containing a variety of mistakes in capitalization, the student will be able to, with at least 90 percent accuracy, identify and rewrite correctly each word that has a mistake in capitalization.
- Given a twelve-bar Autoharp and the score (including the chord symbols in the form of letters) of a familiar sixteen-measure melody harmonized with two chords, the student will be able to provide accompaniment to group singing of the melody by locating by letter and playing correctly the required cords ("correctly" being defined as the proper channel sounded with rhythmic accuracy).
- Given the stylistic category of Romanticism, together with at least one example each of the musical, literary, and architectural achievements of the period, the student will be able—within one-half hour, without the use of verbal reference sources—to write a two-hundred-word essay comparing and contrasting, in terms of style, the given examples.

Well-written behavioral objectives identify three important elements about learner behavior:

1. The *performance* that is required of the learner
2. The *conditions* under which the behavior will be performed
3. The *extent* or level of performance

Stated in one sentence, a well-written behavioral objective should specify under what conditions and to what extent a certain kind of student performance can be expected to transpire.

For example, look at the first behavioral objective again: shown the letters of the alphabet in random order in both upper- and lowercase form (condition), the student will be able to say the name of each letter (performance) with 100 percent accuracy (extent). The three elements about learner behavior are incorporated in this behavioral objective. You may now wish to identify the three important elements about learner behavior in each of the subsequent instructional objectives.

Classifying Objectives.   Considerable effort has been devoted to the study of cognitive, affective, and psychomotor processes for the purpose of developing behavioral objectives and assessing learner outcomes. One of the most systematic approaches has been the development of three separate taxonomies of educational objectives. The taxonomies are depicted in figure 3.1.

As shown in figure 3.1, the *cognitive processes* are classified in a hierarchical order, from simple to complex levels of thinking: (1) knowledge, (2) comprehension,

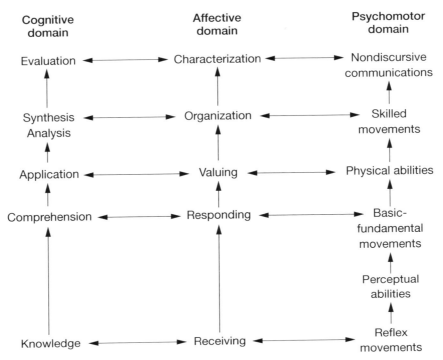

Figure 3.1 Relationships Among Cognitive, Affective, and Psychomotor Domains

(3) application, (4) analysis, (5) synthesis, and (6) evaluation. In the life of the student, the affective processes—interests, attitudes, appreciations, and values—are inseparable from the cognitive processes. The *affective processes* are classified in hierarchical order, from simple to complex levels of feeling: (1) receiving, (2) responding, (3) valuing, (4) organization, and (5) characterization. Integrally related to the cognitive and affective processes are the psychomotor processes. From lowest to highest levels of the schema are the (1) reflex movements, (2) basic-fundamental movements, (3) perceptual abilities, (4) physical abilities, (5) skilled movements, and (6) nondiscursive communication.

The higher *psychomotor processes*, perceptual and physical abilities, skilled movements, and nondiscursive communication operate cooperatively with the cognitive and affective processes. For instance, whether students are concerned with learning handwriting, improving their swimming strokes, learning a new art technique, playing a musical instrument, developing interpretive movements in ballet, or learning a surgical technique, the cognitive and affective processes are interdependent with the psychomotor processes.

Relationship of Objectives and Content. Objectives are usually stated in terms of expected outcomes. For example, a high school science teacher might develop a chronological list of topics to be covered: functions of human organisms, use of plant and animal resources, evolution and development, and the like. This type of list shows what the science teacher intends to teach but not what the expected outcomes of instruction will be. The content outline is useful for the teacher in planning and guiding instruction, but it is insufficient for the statement of behavioral objectives. To be useful in teaching, behavioral objectives must be linked to content.

The real contribution of stating objectives for learning is to think of how each objective can be achieved by students through the content or subject matter they learn. Tyler (1949) has devised a two-dimensional chart for specifying varied types of objectives according to the subject-matter content and the behavioral aspects of the objectives (see table 3.1).

As shown in table 3.1, seven types of behavior are aimed at in the biological science course. The first type of behavior is to develop understanding of important facts and principles; the second type is to develop familiarity with dependable sources of information; the third type of behavior is to develop the ability to interpret data; the fourth type is to develop ability to apply principles that are taught in biological science to concrete biological problems in life; the fifth type of behavior is to develop the ability to study and report the results of the investigation; the sixth is to develop broad and mature interests as they relate to biological science; and the seventh is to develop social attitudes.

However, the listing of the behavioral aspects is not a sufficient formulation of objectives to be most useful in teaching. Hence, table 3.1 also includes a statement of the content aspects of the objectives. Note that the course is viewed as developing these seven behaviors in relation to the nutrition of human organisms, digestion, circulation, respirating, and reproduction. Moreover, note that the course deals with the use of plant and animal growth, heredity and genetics, and land utilization, Finally, note that the behavioral objectives relate to evolution and development.

The formulation of the content aspects of the objectives have served still further to clarify the job to be done by the biological science course. Furthermore, the table indicates the relationship of the two aspects of the objectives: behavioral and content. The intersections of the behavioral columns and the content rows are marked with X's when it is implied that the behavioral aspect applies to a particular area of content.

Relationship of Objectives to Learning Experiences.   In his classic text on curriculum, Tyler defines the term *learning experiences*:

> The term "learning experience" is not the same as the content with which a course deals nor the activities performed by the teacher. The term "learning experience" refers to the interaction between the learner and the external conditions in the environment to which he can react. Learning takes place through the active behavior of the student. (p. 63)

Returning to the objectives of the biological science course, we illustrate several learning experiences that will help the high school science teacher achieve the first behavioral objective.

Objective Number 1: After studying the functions of human organisms, the students will be able to understand the important facts and principles of nutrition.

Learning Experiences:

1. Students study nutrition by classifying foods into four basic groups.
2. Students discuss the properties and nutritional values inherent in each grouping.

Table 3.1 Two-Dimensional Chart for Stating Objectives for a High School Course in Biological Science

Content Aspects of the Objectives	Behavioral Aspects of the Objectives						
	1. Understanding of important facts and principles	2. Familiarity with dependable sources of information	3. Ability to interpret	4. Ability to apply principles	5. Ability to study and report results of study	6. Broad and mature interests	7. Social attitudes
A. Functions of human organisms:							
1. Nutrition	X	X	X	X	X	X	X
2. Digestion	X		X	X	X	X	
3. Circulation	X		X	X	X	X	
4. Respiration	X		X	X	X	X	
5. Reproduction	X	X	X	X	X	X	X
B. Use of plant and animal resources:							
1. Energy relationships	X		X	X	X	X	X
2. Environmental factors conditioning plant and animal growth	X	X	X	X	X	X	X
3. Heredity and genetics	X	X	X	X	X	X	X
4. Land utilization	X	X	X	X	X	X	X
C. Evolution and development	X	X	X	X	X	X	X

3. Students view a film on nutrition.
4. Students read research reports on the relation between nutrition and health.
5. Students write an essay relating the effects of poor nutrition and the incidence of various common diseases.
6. Students chart relationships between principles of nutrition and good health.
7. Students evaluate the many causes of health problems in America.

As noted earlier, content and learning experiences are interrelated. If students are engaged in some learning experience in classrooms, such as reading a book, they are combining that learning experience with content. Students cannot engage in learning without experiencing some activity and content. Likewise, students cannot deal with content without being engaged in some experience or some learning activity.

To be useful in teaching, behavioral objectives must be linked to content. Teachers select learning experiences that will foster active involvement in learning content, in order for students to accomplish the expected learning outcomes specified in the behavioral objectives. Content, learning experiences, and behavioral objectives comprise curriculum unity. The curriculum collectively forms the **framework for structuring knowledge**.

FRAMEWORK FOR STRUCTURING KNOWLEDGE

What knowledge is of most value? This section deals with knowledge as facts, the explosion of knowledge, essential knowledge, knowledge as a return to the liberal arts, computer knowledge and technology, and moral knowledge. Each one will be discussed in turn.

Knowledge as Facts

There is little difference between facts and some aspects of knowledge. In a well-accepted classification of thinking and problem solving by Benjamin Bloom (1956), knowledge is ranked as the lowest form of cognitive learning. However, Bloom points out that the acquisition of knowledge (facts) is often the most common educational objective; that teachers tend to emphasize it in the classroom; and test makers tend to emphasize it on tests. To help clarify Bloom (1956): knowledge as facts by itself has limited value and should be used as a basis or foundation for more advanced thinking, what he calls "problem solving." Basic knowledge has some practical or functional value, but it only serves as the rudiment of more theoretical or abstract thinking. The goal is to encourage advanced thinking—what the Greeks called "contemplation" (Plato, 375 BC), what John Dewey (1933) called "rational" and "reflective thinking," what Jerome Bruner (1960, 1966) and Joseph Schwab (1970) called "structure," what Mortimer Adler (1961, 1982) and Theodore Sizer (1984) called "ideas," what Jeanne Chall (1996) and E. D. Hirsch (1987) called "deep understanding," and what learning theorists today call "critical thinking" and "higher-order thinking."

The point is that knowledge of facts is of little value if it cannot be used in new situations and for more complex learning; the learner (and teacher) need to make use of knowledge—as a base or tool for the pursuit of higher forms of cognition—often called problem solving by progressive educators (John Dewey, 1959 and Ralph Tyler, 1949)—inquiry-based or discovery learning (David Ausubel, 2000 and Jerome

Bruner, 1960, 1966), formal operations (Jean Piaget, 1983 and Lev Vygotsky, 1986), critical thinking (Robert Marzano, 2017 or Robert Sternberg, 2013, 2021), and life-long learning (Elliott Seif, 2021).

Explosion of Knowledge

Since the 1950s, many educators have continued to call attention to the explosion of knowledge. Every fifteen years or so, our significant knowledge doubles. Although it cannot continue indefinitely to double in the future, the explosion of knowledge—especially in health, science, and technology—makes it important to continuously reappraise and revise existing curricula. "It can be affirmed unequivocally," says Bentley Glass (1980), "that the amount of scientific knowledge available at the end of one's life will be almost one hundred times what it was when he was born." (p. 76) Moreover, 95 percent of all scientists who ever lived are alive today. (See also, Edward Teller's [2001] book *A Twentieth-Century Journey in Science and Politics*.)

Although Glass published these remarks more than forty years ago, they still are true; in fact, it can be inferred that half of what a graduate engineer or computer specialist studies today will be obsolete in ten years. Half or more of what we need to know to function in scientific or technical jobs by the year 2035 is not even known today, by anyone.

The idea that knowledge is increasing exponentially or geometrically obscures the fact that the development of knowledge in many fields—especially science, technology and medicine—is more typically related to "branching"—that is, the creation of several subdivisions or specialties within fields, not just simple growth. Each advance in a particular field has the potential for creating another branch (in education, one can find some indicators of proliferation of several fields of study or branches, sometimes identified by departments, programs, and core courses or minors) and within each field or branch, several specializations of knowledge and job titles.

With this increase of knowledge come new professional journals, papers, and speeches, all adding to the proliferation of knowledge. The almost incredible explosion of knowledge threatens to overwhelm us unless we can find ways to deal with the new and growing wealth of information; new knowledge must be constantly introduced into each field of study, while less important material is diminished or deleted. In assessing the ongoing rush of knowledge, Alvin Toffler (1984a, 1984b) asserts that knowledge taught should be related to the future.

Essential Knowledge

E. D. Hirsch (1987) maintains that there is a body of knowledge essential to learn for **cultural literacy** (what he calls "functional literacy") and "effective communication for our nation's populace." Shared information is necessary for true literacy. Hirsch (2006) also stresses the importance of scientific information at all levels of schooling; moreover, he has written a series of follow-up books on essential knowledge for every grade level. Knowing the facts, for him and a growing number of present-day essentialists (Bennett, 1995, 1999; Finn, 2014, 2020; Ravitch, 1995, 2020), increases the students' capacity to comprehend what they read, see, hear, and discuss. The need for background knowledge is judged important for future communication and specialization. Finally, Hirsch argues that we have overlooked content and have stressed process—or thinking skills—with little regard for subject matter. The outcome has been a decline in national literacy. We have a need for a knowledge base and an academic core, to be taught to all students.

What knowledge is essential for the workforce in an increasingly global and high-tech society? For many business and government leaders, this means more mathematics and science and deeper understanding of problem-solving and computer skills. Measuring such subjects and skills will require assessment instruments more sophisticated than multiple-choice tests. This is no easy task, given the high-stakes testing and standards movement, which puts emphasis on short-answer items. Concern among other critics is the growing indifference toward the liberal arts or, even worse, that the virtues and value of the arts (and social studies, history, geography, etc.) will be dismissed as irrelevant or reactionary (Basken, 2008; Cohen, 2016; Newmann, 2008).

Knowledge as a Return to the Liberal Arts

Allan Bloom (1987), in *The Closing of the American Mind*, voices concern about the quality of American education. According to Bloom, deprived of a serious liberal arts and science education, avoiding an engagement with great works and great ideas of the past, our youth lack educational depth. Harry Lewis (2007), former dean at Harvard, finds American institutions "soulless," deprived of high ideals and moral virtues for future American leaders. In a multicultural and global world, universities need to educate students about liberal and democratic ideals. Both Bloom and Lewis have noted the absence of a core curriculum based on common values, grade inflation as a common practice, and professors who teach what they want—based on their own interests (not on the needs of students), and a curriculum that consists of a group of "a la carte" courses—that lack coherence and democratic ideals.

Allan Bloom (1987) and Harry Lewis (2007), as did Robert Hutchins (1954) and Mortimer Adler (1961) more than sixty years ago, seek to reestablish the idea of an educated person along the lines of the great books and great thinkers and to reestablish the virtues of a liberal education.

The great books approach, then, is what Robert Hutchins (former president and chancellor of the University of Chicago) calls the "liberal arts," what Jeanne Chall (Harvard reading specialist) calls "world knowledge," what E. D. Hirsch calls "essential knowledge" and "cultural literacy," and what Allan Bloom (and also Mortimer Adler) call the "great books."

The liberal arts are excluded, at times, because of constraints brought by high-stakes testing. Adding other relevant material discourages educators from exploring rich material that would not only benefit the student but also add cultural enrichment (M. Conway, 2015; Ravitch, 2016). Adding to the decline of the liberal arts are efforts to move in the direction of engineering, technology, and science. Not to diminish the importance of these fields, but efforts made by school leaders and policies affect, at times, the liberal arts in a negative way (Cohen, 2016; Strauss, 2017).

Computer Knowledge and Technology

Computers provide the potential to transform teaching and learning. Certainly, the use of computers offers the ability to help students and teachers organize and present information in a variety of formats, and the Internet can connect people and information sources. Do students learn more with computers? There is no simple answer to that question. Technology-based instruction is not a solution for increasing student achievement, because the learning variables are numerous and the teaching interactions between teachers and students are complex.

As you think about technology resources, consider ways in which the technology might support the learning environment in your classroom. When considering using technology to support learning, the Internet is important to instructional design.

Much has been written about the Internet and education over the past ten years (Internet Society, 2017). Lessons have been learned from experience with different technologies and services in countries with different educational systems. Five broad themes have emerged, from experience to date, as priorities for school policymakers today: infrastructure and access, vision and policy, inclusion, capacity, and content and devices.

Infrastructure and Access. Schools need computers, tablets, and other information and communication technology (ICT) devices that are integrated in a smart fashion in the educational environment to make the best use of Internet-enabled learning. These need to be maintained, upgraded, and cybersecure. They also need reliable electric power. The total costs of ownership—capital and operational—should be factored into budgets, and the importance of financial constraints should not be underestimated. School buildings may need to be redesigned to make effective use of Internet-enabled learning. These, too, are important aspects of enabling access.

Vision and Policy. Policies for Internet access and use should encompass the entire education system—from preschool and primary education, through secondary and tertiary education, to lifelong learning, reskilling, and retraining. The aim should be to improve the digital literacy and skills of everyone throughout society, adults as well as children.

Inclusion. Policies should promote greater equality in access to learning resources for disadvantaged groups within societies, such as those living in rural areas or in poverty, ethnic minorities and speakers of minority languages, and those with disabilities.

Capacity. Success in the digital age requires digital skills. As they enter the world of work, individuals should be able to make use of computers and other digital equipment. Digital literacy—the ability to use online applications, find information online, assess its quality and value, and make use of it in daily life—is crucial to living in the digital world, particularly for the growing number who will work in ICT-intensive industries. School students and adults alike need to learn how to use the Internet to undertake transactions and how to protect themselves against cybercrime. Ways to develop these skills should be included in curricula.

Content and Devices. One of the most dramatic differences the Internet can make lies in opening access to a wider range of content for teaching and learning—content that is explicitly educational in purpose and the much wider range of online content that can supplement curricula. Instead of relying primarily on textbooks, teachers can direct students to many different sources, and students can develop research skills by exploring online content on their own.

Using Technology to Enhance Learning

"Learning is the measure of teaching" (McCown, Driscoll, & Roop, 1996, p. xxiii). No matter what instructional methods a teacher uses, the measure of how well that teacher has taught will be how well students have learned.

Regardless of what students learn or how they learn, there are two common requirements: (a) students must think for themselves—that is, they must construct their own understanding—and (b) students must have ways to test their thinking by sharing with others. The cognitive constructivist seeks to find tools to help the child actively construct conceptual understandings and relationships of ideas. The social constructivist looks for tools that help the child share ideas and findings in a community of peers. Both are necessary (Snowman & McCown, 2015).

Enhancing Understanding and Sharing. How would a teacher incorporate technology into their instruction to enhance their students' understanding and provide them with the opportunity to share their ideas with others? One way to consider technologically enhanced instruction is to examine how instructional technology has evolved. Following is a brief overview of the how the three versions of the Internet contribute to students' understanding and sharing with others (Allen, 2013):

- *Web 1.0: The growth of the search engine.* Allows students to find more information more quickly. Students no longer have to go to the library. This helps students with understanding but not with sharing.
- *Web 2.0: The advent of social interaction.* Allows students to engage others across time and place. Interactions can be both interpersonal and international. Helps with both understanding and sharing.
- *Web 3.0: The development of personalized search results.* Allows students to find more personalized information more quickly. Using analytics, technology can suggest information that students might find helpful. Helps understanding but has not yet advanced sharing beyond 2.0 levels.

The potential contributions that technology can make to students' understanding and sharing are impressive; however, there are some disadvantages. One disadvantage is that while information may be more easily obtained, there is no guarantee to the quality of that information. It may be more convenient to share ideas with others, but there is no guarantee that the sharing will be beneficial. Technology will continue to evolve and contribute to both understanding and sharing. However, teachers will still need to mediate the process of understanding and sharing what students must do, in order for them to learn.

Moral Knowledge

It is possible to provide instruction in *moral knowledge* and ethics. We can discuss philosophers such as Socrates, Plato, and Aristotle who examined the good society and the good person; the more controversial works of Immanuel Kant, Franz Kafka, and Jean-Paul Sartre; religious leaders such as Moses, Jesus, and Confucius; and political leaders such as Abraham Lincoln, Mohandas Gandhi, and Martin Luther King Jr. Through the study of the writings and principles of these moral people, students can learn about moral knowledge. Teaching Johnny or Jane to read by assigning "Dick and Jane" workbooks or "cat and mouse" readers alone is inadequate; the idea is to encourage good reading (which has social and moral messages) at an early age—and which teaches self-respect, tolerance of others, and social good.

The teaching of morality starts in the first grade with folktales such as "Aesop's Fables," "Jack and the Beanstalk," "Guinea Fowl and Rabbit Get Justice," and the stories and fables of the Grimm Brothers, Robert Louis Stevenson, and Langston

Table 3.2 Twenty-Five Recommended Works to Be Read by Eighth Grade

1. Maya Angelou, "The Graduation"
2. Pearl Buck, *The Good Earth*
3. Truman Capote, "Miriam"
4. James Fenimore Cooper, *The Last of the Mohicans*
5. Charles Dickens, *Great Expectations*
6. Anne Frank, *The Diary of a Young Girl*
7. William Faulkner, *Brer Tiger and the Big Wind*
8. William Golding, *Lord of the Flies*
9. John Kennedy, *Profiles in Courage*
10. Martin Luther King Jr., *Why We Can't Wait*
11. Rudyard Kipling, "Letting in the Jungle"
12. Harper Lee, *To Kill a Mockingbird*
13. Jack London, *The Call of the Wild*
14. Herman Melville, *Billy Budd*
15. George Orwell, *Animal Farm*
16. Tomas Rivera, "Zoo Island"
17. J. K. Rowling, *Harry Potter* series
18. William Saroyan, "The Summer of the Beautiful White Horse"
19. John Steinbeck, *Of Mice and Men*
20. Robert Louis Stevenson, *Dr. Jekyll and Mr. Hyde*
21. William Still, *The Underground Railroad*
22. Ivan Turgenev, *The Watch*
23. Mark Twain, *The Adventures of Huckleberry Finn*
24. John Updike, *The Alligators*
25. H. G. Wells, *The Time Machine*
26. Elie Wiesel, *Night*

Hughes. For older children, there are *Sadako and the Thousand Paper Cranes*, *Up from Slavery*, and *The Diary of Anne Frank*. And for adolescents, there are *Of Mice and Men*, *A Man for all Seasons*, *Lord of the Flies*, and *Death of a Salesman*. By the ninth grade, assuming average or above average reading ability, students should be able to read the authors (and books) listed in table 3.2. This list of twenty-six recommended titles exemplifies literature rich in social and moral messages.

As students move up in grade levels and their reading improves, greater variety and options among authors are available to them. Of course, community mores will influence the book selection process. Here we are dealing with issues of whose morality. Whose values? The assumption is that there are agreed-upon virtues such as hard work, honesty, patriotism, integrity, civility, and caring that represent local consensus, if not an American consensus. All we, as educators, need is sufficient conviction to find core commonalities.

The works suggested in table 3.2 can be read in traditional history and English courses or in an integrated course such as Junior Great Books, World Studies, or American Studies. Harry Broudy et al. (1964) refer to this type of content as a *broad fields approach* to curriculum; they organize the high school curriculum into five categories, including "moral problems," that address social and moral issues. Mortimer Adler (1982) divides the curriculum into organized knowledge, intellectual skills, and understanding of ideas and values. The latter deals with discussion of "good books" (his term), and not textbooks, and the Socratic method of questioning. Theodore Sizer (1984, 1992) organizes the high school curriculum into four broad areas, including "History and Philosophy" and "Literature and the Arts."

The content of moral knowledge, according to Phillip Phenix (1964), covers five main areas: (1) *human rights*, involving conditions of life that ought to prevail; (2) *ethics*, concerning family relations and sex; (3) *social relationships*, dealing with class, racial, ethnic, and religious groups; (4) *economic life*, involving wealth and poverty; and (5) *political life*, involving justice, equity, and power. The way we translate moral content into moral conduct defines the kind of people we are. It is not our moral knowledge that counts; rather, it is our moral behavior in everyday affairs that is important.

CURRICULUM DEVELOPMENT

The various components of the curriculum have been reflected in theories of curriculum development. In its most simplified form, **curriculum development** is the process of planning, implementing, and evaluating curriculum that ultimately results in a curriculum plan. We present here a brief description of some selected models of the curriculum development process: behavioral model, systems model, applicative model, managerial model, systemic-dimensional model, curriculum overview model, and the systemic-integrated model. Each one will be discussed in turn.

Tyler: Behavioral Model
Probably the most frequently quoted theoretical formulation in the field of curriculum has been that published by Ralph Tyler in 1949. Tyler states his curriculum rationale in terms of four questions that, he argues, must be answered in developing any curriculum and plan of instruction:

1. What educational purposes should the school seek to attain?
2. What educational experiences can be provided that are likely to attain these purposes?
3. How can these educational experiences be effectively organized?
4. How can we determine whether these purposes are being attained?

These questions may be reformulated into a four-step process: stating objectives, selecting learning experiences, organizing learning experiences, and evaluating the curriculum. The Tyler rationale is essentially an explication of these steps.

Figure 3.2 outlines Tyler's conceptual framework. He proposes that educational objectives originate from three sources: studies of society, studies of learners, and

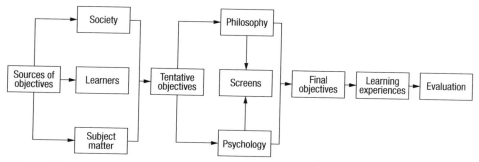

Figure 3.2 Designing the Curriculum

subject-matter specialists. These data systematically collected and analyzed form the basis of initial objectives to be tested for their attainability and their efforts in real curriculum situations. The tentative objectives from the three sources are filtered through two screens: the school's educational philosophy and knowledge of the psychology of learning, which results in a final set of educational objectives.

Once the first step of stating and refining objectives is accomplished, the rationale proceeds through the steps of selecting and organization of learning experiences as the means for achieving outcomes, and, finally, evaluating in terms of those learning outcomes. Tyler recognizes a problem in connection with the selection of learning experiences by a teacher or curriculum designer. The problem is that, by definition, a learning experience is the interaction between a student and her environment—that is, a learning experience is to some degree a function of the perceptions, interests, and previous experiences of the student. Thus, a learning experience is not totally within the power of the teacher to select. Nevertheless, Tyler maintains that the teacher can control the learning experience through the manipulation of the environment, which results in stimulating situations sufficient to evoke the kind of learning outcomes desired.

The final step in Tyler's rationale, evaluation, is the process of determining to what extent the educational objectives are being realized by the curriculum. Stated another way, the statement of objectives not only serves as the basis for selecting and organizing the learning experiences, but also serves as a standard against which the program of curriculum and instruction is appraised. Thus, according to Tyler, curriculum evaluation is the process of matching initial expectations in the form of behavioral objectives with outcomes achieved by the learner.

Beauchamp: Systems Model

George Beauchamp (1981) recognizes the following procedures for curriculum development described by Tyler: the process of determining objectives, selecting and organizing learning experiences, and evaluating the program of curriculum and instruction. Two additional ingredients are included in Beauchamp's design model: a set of rules designating how the curriculum is to be used and an evaluation scheme outlining how the curriculum is to be evaluated. The essential dimensions of his position on curriculum development are shown in figure 3.3.

According to Beauchamp, a curriculum possesses five properties or characteristics: (1) it is a written document; (2) it contains statements outlining the goals for the school for which the curriculum was designed; (3) it contains a body of culture content or subject matter that tentatively has the potential for the realization of the school's goals; (4) it contains a statement of intention for used of the document to guide and direct the planning of instructional strategies; and (5) it contains an evaluation scheme. Thus, by definition, a curriculum is a written plan depicting the scope and arrangement of the projected educational program for a school.

As shown in figure 3.3, provision is made for a statement of goals, or purposes, for the school. Beauchamp argues that at the level of curriculum planning, it is recommended that these goal statements be phrased in general terms, whereas the preparation of specific behavioral objectives should be left to the level of instructional planning.

A large part of a curriculum would consist of the organization of the culture content. Beauchamp designates the realms of culture content as languages,

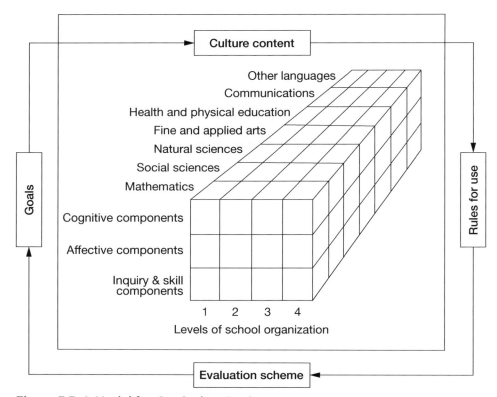

Figure 3.3 A Model for Curriculum Design

communications, health, and physical education, fine and applied arts, natural sciences, social sciences, and mathematics. The culture content is also identified in terms of characteristics other than school subjects. These he refers to as cognitive components, affective components, and inquiry and skill components consistent with Bloom's and others' taxonomy domains. These characteristic components are included so that culture content may be more specifically related to goals and ultimately to behavioral objectives during the instructional planning stage.

Across the bottom of the model four levels of school organization are shown. Typically, these would be labeled in terms of the administrative organization of the school district or individual school, such as grade levels (primary, elementary, middle, or high school), or ordinal years. This three-way organization of the culture content would require decision makers and curriculum planners to be cognizant of such design characteristics as scope, sequence, and vertical and horizontal articulation.

Two additional components are included in Beauchamp's model. One is a set of rules or statements designating how the curriculum is to be used and how it is to be modified based on experience in using the curriculum. An evaluation scheme constitutes the final component of the model. The evaluation scheme is designed to provide feedback data for the products and processes of the curriculum system and the instructional system. Outputs immediately lead back to the curriculum system and the instruction system, thus providing a dynamic cycle of feedback and correction to the fundamental processes of schooling: curriculum and instruction.

Taba: Applicative Model

Hilda Taba (1962) reverses the commonly accepted procedure for curriculum development by suggesting that instead of developing a general plan for the school program, as Tyler and Beauchamp did, it would be more profitable to begin with the planning of teaching-learning units. In such a system, teaching-learning units would provide the basis for the curriculum design. Thus, the curriculum could emerge from the instructional strategies.

Taba (1971) develops a social studies curriculum for grades one through eight organized around teaching-learning units. In the process, a curriculum model evolved that is applicable to many types of curricula and that can be used in a variety of school settings and school levels: elementary, middle, and high school.

The model includes an organization of, and relationships among, five mutually interactive elements—objectives, content, learning activities, and evaluative measures—so that a system of teaching and learning is represented. The model is depicted in figure 3.4.

Taba's model contains within it a number of innovative aspects: specificity in determining objectives and content, learning activities selected and organized in accordance with specified criteria, teaching strategies that specify a variety of methods and technology, and an elaborate array of evaluative procedures and measures. Factors external to the model that may affect its internal components are also represented. Such factors include: (1) the nature of the community in which the school is located—its pressures, values, and resources; (2) the policies of the school district;

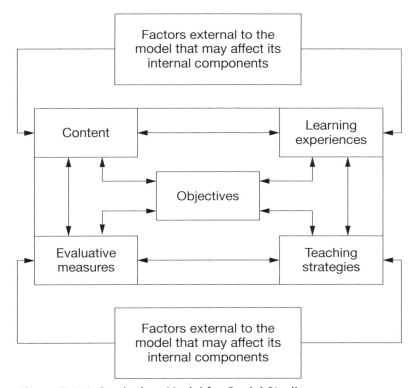

Figure 3.4 A Curriculum Model for Social Studies

(3) the nature of a particular school—its goals, resources, and administrative structure; (4) the personal styles and characteristics of the teachers involved; and (5) the
nature of the student population.

Objectives help to provide a consistent focus for the curriculum, to establish
criteria for the selection of content and learning experiences, and to guide and direct
evaluation of learning outcomes. At the same time that objectives, content, and
learning experiences are being selected and organized, teaching strategies must also
be planned and developed.

The process of determining objectives begins with the development of overall
goals, originating from a variety of sources (for example, the demands of society,
the needs of students, and the social science disciplines); is broken down into behavioral statements, classified in terms of the kinds if student outcomes expected (for
example, the development of thinking skills, the acquisition understanding and use
of important elements of knowledge, and the like); and justified on the basis of a
clearly thought out rationale.

The content for each grade level in the curriculum is contained within a number
of teaching-learning units, all emphasizing to some degree a yearly theme. Each unit
consists of three kinds of knowledge: key concepts (for example, interdependence,
cooperation, cultural change, social control), main ideas (that is, generalizations
derived from key concepts), and specific facts (that is, content samples chosen to
illustrate, explain, and develop the main ideas).

The content contained in the units within a year's work is incorporated into
learning experiences selected and organized in accordance with clearly specified criteria (for example, justifiability, transferability, variety of function, open-minded-
ness, etc.). Care is taken to ensure that the learning experiences develop multiple
objectives: thinking, attitudes, knowledge, and skills.

Especially designed teaching strategies that identify specific procedures that
teachers may use are included within the curriculum. (This makes Taba's model
unique.) Some have been designed to encourage students to examine their individual
attitudes and values. Particularly innovative are certain strategies that promote the
development of children's cognitive skills, such as, comparing and contrasting, conceptualizing, generalizing, and applying previously learned relationships to new and
different situations.

A variety of objective format devices have been prepared to measure the effectiveness of the curriculum in helping students to explain or recognize casual relationships, apply in new settings important generalizations developed in the curriculum,
and to interpret social science data. Several open-ended devices have been designed
to measure the quality of students' generalizations, the flexibility and variety of students' conceptualizations, and the variety and nature of the content that students use
in response to open-ended questions. A coding scheme has been developed and used
to analyze teacher-student discussions as to the levels of thinking that they exhibit,
similar to Benjamin Bloom and others' taxonomies.

Saylor et al.: Managerial Model

Galen Saylor and his associates (1981) adopt a managerial approach to curriculum
development. They describe and analyze curriculum plans in terms of the relations of
ends and means, the attention to pertinent facts and data, and the flow of activities

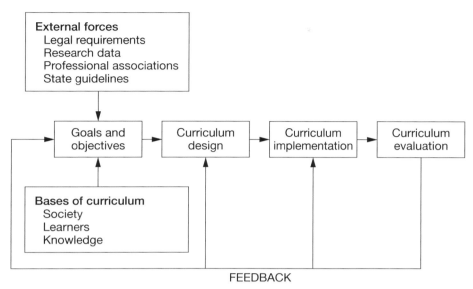

Figure 3.5 Elements of the Curriculum System

or procedures from beginning to end. Figure 3.5 depicts their conceptual model of the curriculum development process.

As shown in figure 3.5, the selection of educational *goals and objectives* is influenced by (1) external forces, including legal requirements, research data, professional associations, and state guidelines, and (2) bases of curriculum, such as society, learners, and knowledge. (Note the similarity to Tyler's and Taba's sources.) Curriculum developers then choose the combinations of curriculum design, implementations, strategies, and evaluation procedures that are calculated to maximize the attainment of goals; review feedback from the plan in effect through instruction; and replan the elements of the curriculum as indicated by the data.

Curriculum design involves decisions made by the responsible curriculum planning group(s) for a particular school center and student population. Having collected and analyzed essential data and identified goals and objectives, curriculum planners create or select a general pattern—a curriculum design—for the learning opportunities to be provided to students. Among their alternatives is a subject design utilizing specific students in the specified curriculum area, a scope and sequence plan built around a selection of persistent topics or themes, an analysis of the essential skills necessary for knowledge and competence in the subject area, and a selection of problems (in cooperation with students) related to the area of study. The design plan ultimately anticipates the entire range of learning opportunities for a specified population.

Curriculum implementation involves decisions regarding instruction. Various teaching strategies are included in the curriculum plan so that teachers have options. Instruction is thus the implementation of the curriculum plan. There would be no reason for developing curriculum plans if there were no instruction. Curriculum plans, by their very nature, are efforts to guide and direct the nature and character of learning opportunities in which students participate. All curriculum planning is worthless unless it influences the things that students do in school. Saylor argues that curriculum planners must see instruction and teaching as the summation of their efforts.

Curriculum evaluation involves the process of evaluating expected learning outcomes and the entire curriculum plan. Saylor and his colleagues recognize both formative and summative evaluation. Formative procedures are the feedback arrangements that enable the curriculum planners to make adjustments and improvements at every step of the curriculum development process: goals and objectives, curriculum development, and curriculum implementation. The summative evaluation comes at the end of the process and deals with the evaluation of the total curriculum plan. This evaluation becomes feedback for curriculum developers to use in deciding whether to continue, modify, or eliminate the curriculum plan with another student population. The provision for systematic feedback during each step in the curriculum system—and from students in each instructional situation—constitutes a major contribution to Saylor's systems model of curriculum development

Eisner: Systemic-Dimensional Model

Elliot W. Eisner (1991) offers a systemic and dimensional view of curriculum, as depicted in figure 3.6, that incorporates a postmodern view of curriculum while maintaining balance with evaluation of it. He indicates that if America is going to have the kind of schools it needs, it needs to pursue the following five dimensions.

The intentional. This refers to the serious, studied examination of what really matters in schools. To realize our intentions, we will need to address the characteristics of our curriculum, the features of our teaching, the forms of our evaluative practices, and the nature of our workplace.

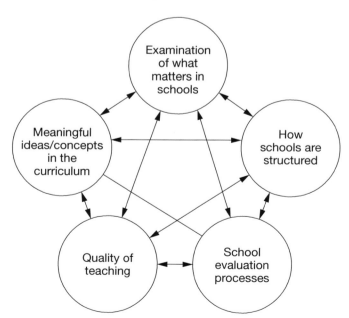

Figure 3.6 Eisner's Systemic and Dimensional Model of Curriculum

The structural. This dimension refers to how schools are structured, how roles are defined, and how time is allocated. All are important in facilitating and constraining educational opportunities. According to Eisner, the structural organization of schools has not changed much in the past one hundred years. We start school in September and end in June; school lasts twelve years with a prescribed curriculum for every one; thirty students per class are taught by a single teacher; grades are given several times a year; and students are promoted to the next grade. Such a structure is restrictive.

The curriculum. The significance of ideas in a curriculum is of great importance. We need to think about those ideas more deeply, and about the means through which students will engage them. The design of curriculum includes attention to ideas that matter, skills that count, and the ways in which students and programs interact.

The pedagogical. Whatever the virtues of a school's curriculum, the quality of teaching ought to be a primary concern of school improvement. To treat teaching as an art requires a level of scrutiny, assistance, and support that any performing art deserves. Schools need to be places that serve teachers, so that teachers can serve students.

The evaluative. School evaluation practices operationally define what really matters for students and teachers. Schools need to approach evaluation not simply as a way of scoring students, but as a way of finding out how well we and our students are doing in order to determine better ways of doing what we do.

Ornstein: Curriculum Overview Model

Allan C. Ornstein (2004) provides a systemic curriculum model that takes into account society and schools today. Figure 3.7 presents an overview of the procedures and steps to consider for planning, developing, and evaluating the curriculum. The model is based on a behavioral/managerial model, rooted in the Tyler-Taba (behavioral, applicative) and Saylor et al. (managerial) approaches.

Overall, the model reflects a *traditional* approach because decisions and actions take place within a formal organization that has a prescribed and expected way of doing things. In joining the school (or school district), participants accept an authority relationship and understand certain roles, limits, and expectations of behavior, and certain policies and procedures for communication, collegiality, and change (the three Cs).

As part of *curriculum planning,* the political forces (category 1) are considered, the situation as it "really is"—or, more precisely, as it appears to the participants. National, state, and local issues and opinion in general will reflect in the aims, goals, and objectives of the curriculum, but they will change over time. (Aims and goals are sometimes used interchangeably at the federal and state levels.) Standards are expressed at the federal and state level—and imposed on the local or district/school level. Specialists, consultants, and experts can provide knowledge or expertise (category 2) for modifying the school district's or school's goals and objectives. These people will most likely be subject, learning, technological, or testing specialists. In determining what to teach, external groups (category 3) play a major role in influencing curriculum participants, organizational norms and policies, and criteria for the selection of content. Major external groups are from the testing industry, textbook companies, professional associations, and colleges. The connection between the external forces and individual participants is virtually "one way"—that is, external

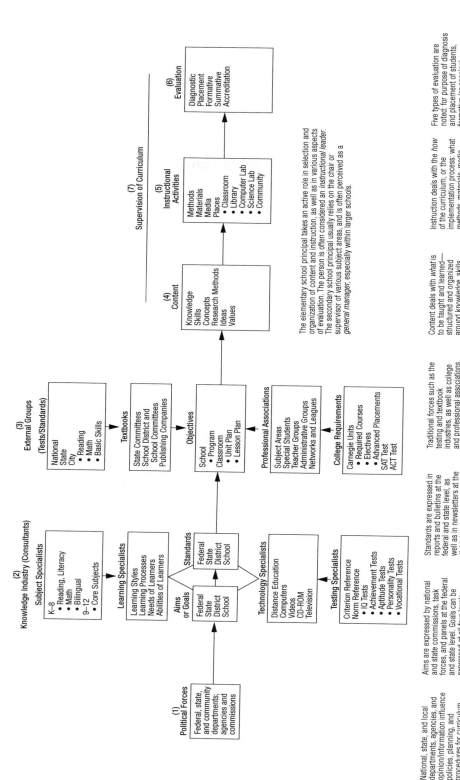

(2)
Knowledge Industry (Consultants)

Subject Specialists

K–8
• Reading, Literacy
• Math
• Bilingual
9–12
• Core Subjects

Learning Specialists

Learning Styles
Learning Processes
Needs of Learners
Abilities of Learners

Standards
Federal
State
District
School

Aims
or Goals
Federal
State
District
School

Technology Specialists

Distance Education
Computers
Videos
CD-ROM
Television

Testing Specialists

Criterion Reference
Norm Reference
• IQ Tests
• Achievement Tests
• Aptitude Tests
• Personality Tests
• Vocational Tests

(3)
External Groups
(Tests/Standards)

National
State
City
• Reading
• Math
• Basic Skills

Textbooks

State Committees
School District and
School Committees
Publishing Companies

Objectives

School
• Program
Classroom
• Unit Plan
• Lesson Plan

Professional Associations

Subject Areas
Special Students
Teacher Groups
Administrative Groups
Networks and Leagues

College Requirements

Carnegie Units
• Required Courses
• Electives
• Advanced Placements
SAT Test
ACT Test

(4)
Content

Knowledge
Skills
Concepts
Research Methods
Ideas
Values

(7)
Supervision of Curriculum

(5)
Instructional
Activities

Methods
Materials
Media
Places
• Classroom
• Library
• Computer Lab
• Science Lab
• Community

(6)
Evaluation

Diagnostic
Placement
Formative
Summative
Accreditation

(1)
Political Forces

Federal, state,
and community
departments, agencies and
commissions

National, state, and local
departments, agencies, and
opinion/information influence
policies, planning, and
procedures for curriculum.

Aims are expressed by national
and state commissions, task
forces, and panels at the federal
and state level. Goals can be
expressed at all four levels:
federal, state, district, and school.

Standards are expressed in
reports and bulletins at the
federal and state level, as
well as in newsletters at the
district and school level.

Traditional forces such as the
testing and textbook
industries, as well as college
and professional associations
and professional associations
curriculum objectives.

The elementary school principal takes an active role in selection and
organization of content and instruction, as well as in various aspects
of evaluation. The person is often considered an *instructional leader.*
The secondary school principal usually relies on the chair or
supervisor of various subject areas, and is often perceived as a
general manager, especially within larger schools.

Content deals with *what is*
to be taught and learned—
structured and organized
around knowledge, skills,
research methods, ideas,
and values.

Instruction deals with the *how*
of the curriculum, or the
implementation process: what
methods, materials, media,
and places of instruction the
teacher plans.

Five types of evaluation are
noted: for purpose of diagnosis
and placement of students,
formative (or ongoing),
summative (or reporting), and
accreditation.

Figure 3.7 Planning and Developing the Curriculum

groups influence participants' decisions and actions, but the reverse influence is almost nonexistent or slight. Viewed as "experts," those involved in determining the content of tests (and now standards), the content of textbooks, college requirements (or Carnegie units), and/or establishing standards and policies of professional associations transmit, from one generation to the next, many of the major ideas of objectives and subsequent content.

"Experts" from external groups may see the world quite differently than teachers and principals, but the latter have little influence in determining the content domain (category 4); basically, their job is to implement the curriculum. *Curriculum implementation* involves the what and how of curriculum. The content is the *what*, sometimes called the heart of the curriculum, and the instructional activities represent the *how*. Content is divided into knowledge, skills, concepts, research methods, ideas, and values. (Knowledge and skills have been delineated elsewhere by Adler, Taba, and Tyler; concepts and relationships are best represented by the theories of Bruner, Dewey, and Ausubel; research methods are expressed by Bruner, Dewey, and Tyler; ideas are described by Adler, Bruner, and Taba; and values are delineated by Adler, Dewey, and Tyler).

Instructional activities (category 5)—methods, materials, and media—usually take place in the classroom (although they can take place in the local and larger community) and represent the processes through which the teacher delivers the content. Activities are part of the implementation process. Although most activities are well entrenched by tradition, different methods, materials, and media evolve and replace traditional modes of instruction. The tension between traditional and progressive ideas of education is clearly depicted in Dewey's compact book, *Education and Experience* (1938). The term *instructional activities* (category 5) closely resembles what Dewey calls "techniques and practices," what Kilpatrick calls "purposeful methods," what Taba and Tyler refer to as "experiences," and what Bruner terms "processes." In short, instruction deals with ways in which content (subject matter) is taught by the teacher and learned by the student—that is, the *how* of implementation.

Curriculum evaluation provides information for the purpose of making judgments and decisions about students, teachers, and programs—or whether to postpone, modify, continue, or maintain the curriculum. Such decisions can be made at the classroom, school, and school district level. The role of the curriculum leader— resource teacher, program director, supervisor or chair, principal, or superintendent in charge of curriculum—is crucial at this stage. The person in charge, the curriculum leader, provides direction, oversees content and instruction, and then based on some form of evaluation makes recommendations and decisions for maintaining, improving, or terminating the program. Five purposes and forms of evaluation (category 6) are listed: diagnosing problems; placement of students; formative—that is, during the implementation stage; summative, or at the end of the program; and accreditation, the whole program is assessed.

Finally, curriculum leaders at the school level include program directors, coordinators, chairs, and principals. They are responsible for overseeing curriculum, instruction, and evaluation. In figure 3.7, this is represented by the term *supervision of curriculum* (category 7). At the district level, the curriculum leader is usually called a director or an assistant or associate superintendent.

Irby and Lunenburg: Systemic-Integrated Model

Beverly Irby and Frederick Lunenburg contend that, with high-stakes testing domi-nating national and state agendas, the curriculum that is emerging must also include connected and aligned content objectives. Careful attention to the types of objec-tives written and the instructional delivery mode can take into account the issues brought forth by current curriculum planners. Our view for principals is that a sys-temic-integrated curriculum must be: (a) led by the principal and developed collab-oratively with teachers and community members; (b) considerate of the community; (c) responsive to the needs of the students related to academic needs, language needs, and social needs; (d) connected to the vision and mission of the school, which is usually focused on increased academic advancement of the students; (e) reflective of the needs of a global society; (f) able to be assessed in terms of how well the students are performing based on standards of performance; and (g) integrated systemically into the "whole" of the campus culture, programs, and instruction. The model is presented in figure 3.8.

Principal acts as leader of curriculum efforts. There is a strong relationship between the level of the building principal's leadership in curriculum project efforts and the success of both teachers and students. March and Peters (2002) have studied the results of the Ohio Proficiency Test in six school districts. In one of those districts, on all but one subtest, the proportion of students passing in one elementary building, where the principal was heavily involved leading curriculum efforts, exceeded by 5 to 15 percent the proportion of students who passed in a neighboring building where the principal provided limited leadership. It is the principal's primary role to focus the entire staff on curriculum development, revision, or reform, and to empower them in their work.

According to Allen (1995a), one strategy for empowering teachers is to provide a "highly interrelated set of three resource elements to support teachers as curriculum constructors" (p. 2). Such resources include (a) guiding frameworks (representative of various sources of input), (b) examples of other teachers' and schools' curricular practice, and (c) formal, collaborative protocols that provide for teacher discussion, reflection, and critique. Allen (1995b) provides the example of the *tuning protocol*

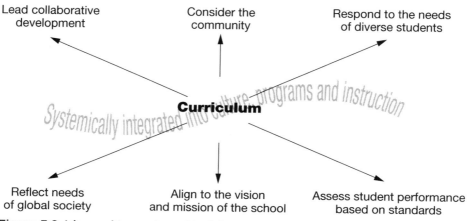

Figure 3.8 Irby and Lunenburg Model of Curriculum

to represent the third type of resource. The tuning protocol helps structure teacher feedback and asks teachers to be "critical friends" to one another, to be their own best guides to reform. The protocol provides a safe, focused process for looking at students' and teachers' work and providing informed feedback on it (Allen, 1995b). The principal or lead teacher can facilitate a discussion within the parameters of preset norms.

Wasley, Hampel, and Clark (1996) claim that if a faculty can develop skills of rigorous self-analysis, they will have added a valuable critical tool to their repertoire of curriculum change. Furthermore, they suggested that schools need to develop habits of "civil discourse"—that is, new norms of conversation. Reflection about practice and about the curriculum is beneficial to teacher growth. The principal who engages faculty in this practice can improve the climate of the school, and it will *become* more professional, less subversive, and more respectful of real intellectual dialogue that fosters the development of shared understandings and more coherent action. As the principal facilitates critical self-reflection and analysis with colleagues, both the capacity for self-analysis among teachers and ways of critiquing each other's work presume a primary responsibility and knowledge on the part of teachers to carry (with assistance from the principal) the work of school improvement. The principal's primary goal in leading the curriculum is to empower teachers regarding curriculum development or school improvement.

As principals lead critical reflection, it is also their responsibility to encourage teachers to seriously examine curriculum that exists in the form of textbooks or other standards frameworks from the state or school district. Sleeter (2002) provides an example of critical examination of the History-Social Science Framework for California Public Schools, first adopted by the California State Board of Education in 1987 and then readopted in 1994, 1998, and 2001, with only minor revisions. The examples follow and are self-revealing as to why it is of utmost importance to critically examine such documents.

> By claiming to tell a multicultural story, the framework masks the ideology of its own story. One way to identify whose experiences center a narrative is to examine the people who appear in it. I counted people who were named for study in the framework's course descriptions. Of the ninety-six named Americans, 82 percent were male and 18 percent were female. They were 77 percent White, 18 percent African American, 4 percent Native American, 1 percent Latino, and 0 percent Asian American. All of the Latino and all but one of the Native American names appeared at the elementary level. At the secondary level, 79 percent of the named people were White, mostly either US residents or famous artists and authors. This analysis suggests that the narrative is centered on experiences of White men.
>
> Another way to identify whose experiences center a narrative is to examine the main topics and ask to whom they most closely relate. For the study of US history, the progression of topics in the framework traces the movement of Europeans and Euro-Americans west, and the expansion of the political boundaries of the United States. People of color and women appear throughout, but within a storyline framed by this westward movement. Urging teachers to tell the stories of multiple groups within a structure of topics that is based on Euro-American experiences, and especially those of English descent, masks the fact that multiple groups' stories are not being told.
>
> Consider, for example, how Indigenous People appear. In third grade, students study local history, beginning with local topography and landforms, then briefly

Indigenous People of the past, and then move on. In fourth grade, students study the history of California, and in that context, briefly study American Indian nations in California's past. In fifth grade, students begin to study US history, starting with a unit devoted to pre-Columbian Indigenous People. After that unit, Indigenous People appear only sporadically, in relationship to the story of the westward movement of Euro-Americans. Even when events such as the Trail of Tears are described as a tragedy, the basic cause of the displacement of Indigenous People is not seriously problematized. (Sleeter, 2002, p. 8)

Curriculum is considerate of the community. As curriculum is developed or reformed, principals must indicate to teachers that community is taken into consideration on several counts. First, the community should be taken into consideration when considering subject matter. For example, in the curriculum needs assessment, the community can be surveyed on several items generated by the teachers. An example would be work transfer skills needed in the community. Those skills would then become important in the curriculum planning. Another example here would be community interests in terms of "service learning" projects, which is an authentic curriculum and a concern that the community be involved in the learning itself. What community partners would best support significant "service learning" projects or community learning projects for the students?

Second, community members need to be included in the curriculum planning itself. Perhaps community members, including parents, may not be in on all the specific writing of the curriculum, but certainly they should be included in the assessment of it. Third, the type of community and needs must be considered. For example, Fiore (2022) indicates it is unlikely that curriculum change in a rural secondary school, closely integrated with community interests, is explained in the same way as change in a suburban school with a cosmopolitan orientation and a heavy investment in college preparatory programs. Conversely, urban schools might deal with funding, access, or safety as basic needs that will need to be addressed in the curriculum. Fiore further indicated that consideration of varying contexts has current significance, in that modern society is tending to become more diversified. Because curriculum and instructional strategies will likely differ from community to community, curriculum actions must be viewed within the context of a community, and such an activity demands that community members be involved.

Curriculum responds to the needs of the students. Considering students' needs and interests presents a challenge to principals as they lead their faculty in curriculum reform. Consideration of student needs encourages more shared inquiry about special needs, such as inquiry about needs of students with disabilities and how to best serve them, students who are classified as gifted, students who are a language minority, students who are economically challenged, and students from other cultures (no classification is mutually exclusive from the others). The curriculum must be inclusive of cultures. The curriculum must also consider more shared inquiry between teachers and students, as opposed to fitting the program to the students. Choice in the curriculum must be considered as student interests are considered. Within the curriculum, the principal must note how students will be assessed and evaluated. Principals must keep in mind that curriculum needs to meet the students' needs, but it must also conform to some reasonably consistent guidelines and goals for what students should know.

Curriculum is connected to the school's vision and mission. Principals must keep the curriculum focused on the vision and mission of the school. They must always ask teachers how the curriculum is moving the school toward the vision and how it is accomplishing the mission. Principals, in a sense, are keepers of the vision. The principal's modeling and reinforcing of vision-related behaviors appear critical to the success of a professional learning community.

This can be done by keeping the vision and mission at the front and center of all decisions. It means when a principal sits down with a faculty member to talk about a lesson observed, she may bring up the vision and how the lesson connects to that vision. The principal may bring up the vision when the budget is discussed with faculty. When the principal is hiring faculty or making faculty changes, or if the principal is engaged in curriculum changes or implementing new courses, she is always using the vision as the filter. When the principal is doing that, the people involved in the school—students, parents, faculty, district office administrators—can see, through the principal's behavior and actions, that what is most important is this vision. Thus, the principal, as a change agent helps to create new programs and procedures that evolve from the shared vision and goals.

Curriculum reflects the needs of a global society. The principal must not only promote the needs of the immediate community but also be attuned to and share the reflections of the global society. He or she can do so by: (a) promoting authentic curriculum; (b) including service learning projects; (c) incorporating and obtaining access to technology and its advances in hardware and knowledge generation; (d) advancing critical thinking; (e) problem finding and problem solving; (f) bringing in cooperative learning; (g) encouraging democratic, responsible, and politically and culturally aware citizenship; and (h) incorporating multiple languages—or at least two, one native and one international.

Curriculum can be assessed based on academic performance standards. The principal promotes an aligned curriculum with the skills and content to be tested as well as a curriculum map or sequence of skills necessary for success at each proximate grade level. The standards-based assessments are grounded in basic academic skills across all populations. They provide for a clear and uniform benchmark for what all children (based locally, by state or in the nation) should know and be able to do at specified points in their academic development. Principals who maintain a standards-based curriculum address societal expectations, focusing on how students will be judged by the state and the nation beyond the classroom and the school district. Alternative assessments can provide valuable insights into student progress in the curriculum.

There is systemic integration of culture, programs, and instruction. The principal is responsible for synthesizing the total of the six components and ensuring that (a) they run through all programs and (b) they are observable in instruction. Additionally, the culture of the school should reflect these components from the curriculum, and all programs should be connected through the curriculum. No program should be an "isolationist" program on the campus. The principal should be able to articulate to the teachers, parents, central administration, and the community the path analysis of how one program relates to the other and how they are tied together by the curriculum of the campus.

THE CURRICULUM-INSTRUCTIONAL ROLE OF THE PRINCIPAL

Regardless of how we view the relationship among content, learning experiences, behavioral objectives, and environment, the center of curriculum development continues to be the local school, which in turn is related to the abilities and performance of the school principal and assistants. The key to curriculum leadership is not the school superintendent, whose responsibilities are more concerned with financial, political, and managerial decisions; it is the school principal who is the instructional leader of the school.

The problem is, however, that many school superintendents are not clear about delegating authority concerning curriculum matters to the school principal, especially at the elementary school level. The superintendent is usually much clearer about delegating responsibility at the centralized level—to the business manager or director of public information—than about delegating it to the principal. In these cases, it appears that the superintendent is more concerned about business or community affairs—that is, how the school district appears—than curriculum for students the school district serves.

In large school districts (50,000 or more students), the central office usually houses a curriculum department whose responsibility is to develop curriculum materials and guides while minimizing the role of the teacher and school principal. Curriculum development is centralized and usually rubber-stamped at the school level; what ideas people have at the local level are passed upward but often lost in the paper shuffle at the centralized level.

In small school districts, however, teachers, principals, and even parents are expected to spend substantial time and effort in curriculum making. Under the leadership of the principal, schools are often expected to develop mission statements, a clear understanding of what constitutes learning, the content and experiences to be included in the curriculum, how the curriculum is to be implemented and evaluated, and how the community is to be included (Glatthorn et al., 2018). Many teachers and principals become involved in curriculum development as a matter of professional routine; but they are rarely, if ever, paid for their time after 3 p.m.

Differences also exist between elementary and secondary school principals. Most elementary principals devote more time to curriculum and instructional matters than do their secondary counterparts, and they view themselves more often as curriculum or instructional leaders rather than managers. Secondary school principals usually complain they have little time for curriculum and instruction (although they recognize the importance of such matters) and see themselves more often as general managers (Jacobson, McCarthy, & Pounder, 2015).

Part of the difference is related to school size. Within the same school district, high schools are usually two to four times the size of elementary schools. In high schools that house more than one thousand students (24 percent of US high schools), principals are often engaged with a continual stream of problems that make it difficult for them to leave the office, and they are more concerned about administrative detail and formal structures than with people (Meier, 2006). Another reason for the difference is that in medium-sized secondary schools (750 to 1,000 students) and large secondary schools (1,000-plus students), there are usually chairpersons responsible for specific subject areas who plan with teachers and supervise curriculum and instruction.

Elementary schools do not have chairpersons as part of their staff, and the focus is on the three Rs (not particular subjects). The principal is supposed to provide the curriculum and instructional leadership in this general area of study. Some balance is needed. In large school districts, curriculum leaders at the central level should make it easier for school personnel to become involved in curriculum opportunities. In small school districts, teachers involved in curriculum should be paid for their services or relieved from other duties, so they can devote time to curriculum.

Research Evidence

Although the literature generally agrees on the need for the principal to be a leader in the areas of curriculum and instruction, there is some disagreement, however, on what specific roles and behaviors should be exhibited by the principal and how much time should be devoted to curriculum and instructional matters (Fullan, 2014; Glatthorn, Jailall, & Jailall, 2017; Kaplan & Owings, 2015; Marshall, 2021; Sergiovanni & Green, 2015; Spillane, & Lowenhaupt, 2019; Ubben, Hughes, & Norris, 2017; Williamson & Blackburn, 2016). When principals are surveyed, they often report that the curriculum and instruction aspects of the job are top-priority work areas and that they need to spend more time on the job related to these two technical areas of development (Goldring et al., 2019).

Given the national and state standards movement, and the need to upgrade the curriculum to meet these standards, school principals' attention has increasingly focused on curriculum. Most national standards have been received with approval by business groups but not by all state education agencies or educational administration groups. The standards emphasize specific knowledge, modes of inquiry and thinking, and consider certain subjects more important than others. Through legislation and assessment, they impact school practice, leadership behavior, and teaching practices.

Principals have historically spent little time (15 to 20 percent) (Fullan, 2014; Matthews & Crow, 2010) coordinating activities in curriculum and instruction, and spend much less time (3 to 7 percent) observing teachers in the classroom, complaining that managerial activities take up most of their time (Murphy, 2020; Murphy & Bleiberg, 2019). Dealing with the daily operation of the school and attending meetings tend to take up most of their time. Although the major principal associations (NAEP and NASSP) overwhelmingly envision the principal as a curriculum-instructional leader, and this theme continually appears in their respective journals (which principals read), the realities of the job do not permit emphasis in these twin leadership areas.

In this connection, Joseph Murphy (1990; 1998; 2016a; Murphy & Louis, 2018) has developed six curriculum and instructional roles for the principal:

1. *Promoting Quality Instruction.* Ensuring consistency and coordination of instructional programs and defining recommended methods of instruction.
2. *Supervising and Evaluating Instruction.* Ensuring that school goals are translated into practice at the classroom level and monitoring classroom instruction through numerous classroom observations.
3. *Allocating and Protecting Instructional Time.* Providing teachers with uninterrupted blocks of instructional time and ensuring that basic skills and academic subjects are taught.

4. *Coordinating the Curriculum.* Translating curriculum knowledge into meaningful curriculum programs, matching instructional objectives with curriculum materials and standardized tests, and ensuring curriculum continuity vertically and across grade levels.

5. *Promoting Content Coverage.* Ensuring that content of specific courses is covered in class and extended outside of class by developing and enforcing homework policies.

6. *Monitoring Student Progress.* Using both criterion- and standardized-reference tests to diagnose student problems and evaluate their progress, as well as using test results to set or modify school goals (Murphy, 1990; 1998; 2016a; Murphy & Louis, 2018).

Based on a review of the research, according to Murphy and others, the six major dimensions or roles exemplify an effective principal; moreover, the research of Murphy and others supports the assumption that the distinguishing reason for effective schools is a school principal who exhibits strong curriculum-instructional leadership.

SUMMARY

1. There are three major components of the curriculum: content, learning experiences, and behavioral objectives.
2. To be useful in teaching, objectives must be linked to content. Tyler has devised a two-dimensional chart for specifying varied types of objectives according to the subject-matter content and the behavioral aspects of the objectives.
3. The relationship among content, learning experiences, and behavioral objectives comprise curriculum unity. The curriculum collectively forms the framework for structuring knowledge.
4. The framework for structuring knowledge is concerned with the question: What knowledge is of most value and includes ideas, such as knowledge as facts, the explosion of knowledge, essential knowledge, return to the liberal arts (great books) approach, computer knowledge and technology, and moral knowledge.
5. The curriculum development models we selected include the following: classical, systems, applicative, managerial, behavioral/aesthetic, curriculum overview, and systemic-integrated model. All models have merit for curriculum leaders.
6. Although the principal is the curriculum and instructional leader, decisions on the curriculum must be shared with the teachers and other stakeholders.

KEY TERMS

content
learning experiences
balanced curriculum

taxonomy
cognitive domain
affective domain

psychomotor domain
curriculum goals
behavioral objectives

framework for structuring
knowledge
cultural literacy
curriculum development

FIELD-BASED ACTIVITIES

1. Review the curriculum on your campus. With what model does it most closely align? How does it differ? Present this review and discuss it at the next departmental or team meeting with your colleagues.
2. (a) Perform a curriculum needs assessment on your campus. Analyze your assessment data; discuss this analysis with your principal. How can you use these data to assist in improving the curriculum? Develop a plan and share it with your principal or supervisor. (b) Develop a plan to conduct a curriculum alignment in one area of the curriculum. What are the critical alignment elements you would include? Review your plan with your supervisor or the director of curriculum in the district. Conduct the curriculum alignment.
3. Have this debate with your team or grade-level colleagues. Record your responses.

SUGGESTED READINGS

Boyle, B., & Charles, M. (2016). *Curriculum development*. Thousand Oaks, CA: Sage. Bill Boyle and Marie Charles enable practitioners, scholars, and academics to understand how to redesign or to suggest changes to curriculum structure, shape, and design.

Glatthorn, A. A., Boschee, F. A., Whitehead, B. A., & Boschee, B. F. (2018). *Curriculum leadership: Strategies for development and implementation* (5th ed.). Thousand Oaks, CA: Sage. The authors help administrators, teachers, and curriculum directors restructure, enhance, and implement school K–12 curriculum.

Heineke, A., & McTighe, J. (2018). *Using understanding by design in the culturally and linguistically diverse classroom*. Alexandria, VA: ASCD. Amy Heineke and Jay McTighe provide teachers, whose classrooms are culturally and linguistically diverse, with Understanding by Design (UbD framework) for curriculum design, which emphasizes teaching for understanding, not rote memorization.

Lalor, A. D. (2017). *Ensuring high-quality curriculum: How to design, revise, or adapt curriculum aligned to student success*. Alexandria, VA: ASCD. Angela DiMichele Lalor provides a comprehensive and accessible roadmap to developing a solid foundation for teaching and learning—and better results in the classroom.

Ornstein, A. O., & Hunkins, F. P. (2017). *Curriculum: Foundations, principles, and issues*. Boston, MA: Pearson. Allan Ornstein and Francis Hunkins provide a comprehensive view of the entire field of curriculum, which encourages readers to formulate their own views on curriculum foundations, principles, and issues.

Tyler, R. W. (1949). *Basic Principles of Curriculum and Instruction*. Chicago, IL: University of Chicago Press. Probably the most frequently quoted theoretical formulation in the field of curriculum largely exemplifies a behavioral and rational approach.

4

Teaching and Learning

■ ■ ■

FOCUSING QUESTIONS

1. What teacher behaviors, as well as teaching principles and methods, make a difference regarding student achievement?
2. Are there instructional strategies that can improve learning?
3. What is the effect of school culture on learning?
4. What is the usefulness of the humanistic approach to teaching in terms of student achievement?
5. How can knowledge of psychosocial and cognitive development help teachers design potentially effective lessons?
6. What are the effects of high-stakes testing on student achievement?

In this chapter, we address these questions concerning teaching and learning in schools. We begin the chapter by discussing teacher behaviors, as well as teaching principles and methods, that have positive effects on student achievement. Then we consider several enduring, research-based strategies that can improve learning. Next, we examine the effects of the academic press/social support model on improving student achievement. We then examine the usefulness of the humanistic approach to teaching in terms of student achievement. This is followed by a discussion of psychosocial and cognitive development that help teachers design potentially effective lessons. We conclude the chapter with a discussion of the effects of high-stakes testing on student achievement.

If you ask people why schools exist, they will likely offer some variation of the following response: to help all children acquire the knowledge and skills considered necessary for successful functioning in society. This is, in fact, the primary goal of schools (Lunenburg, 2015). It follows that a teacher's instructional and curriculum decisions should be based on an understanding of how students learn and the possible effect of teacher's instruction on student learning. It is the principal's role, as instructional leader, to help teachers accomplish that goal.

This chapter is devoted to analyzing teaching and learning. More specifically, this chapter deals with concepts and strategies designed to improve teaching and learning. Although some of the concepts and strategies described in this chapter were proposed forty years ago, their relevance is demonstrated by the fact that they continue to be used and recommended by today's educators (e.g., Darling-Hammond &

Oakes, 2019; Fullan & Gallagher, 2020; Glickman & Burns, 2020; Marzano, 2017; Smylie, Murphy, & Louis, 2020a).

Teaching and learning are appreciably connected. All principals understand that learning is the primary goal of education, and that teaching is the vehicle to accomplish that goal. What is the principal's role in the teaching and learning process? The principal's role in the teaching and learning process is (a) to accommodate teachers in their quest for gaining knowledge related to how the diverse student body learns best, (b) to assess the teaching as it relates to the outcome—learning, and (c) to facilitate the instructional planning process. Successful education can occur only if teachers are prepared to meet rigorous learning demands to accommodate different learning strategies, goals, and types of learners (Darling-Hammond & Oakes, 2019). Principals are the key to improving instruction. A large portion of the principal's time is spent in the classrooms observing and providing feedback on instruction; therefore, principals need to know what effective teaching looks like.

From the thousands of studies that have been conducted to identify the behaviors of successful and unsuccessful teachers, we now know how to distinguish between "good" and "poor," or "effective" and "ineffective," teaching, and the magnitude of the effect of these differences on students can be determined (Bryk, 2020; Darling-Hammond et al., 2019; Good & Lavigne, 2018; Leithwood, 2018). They include the kinds of questions teachers ask, the ways teachers respond to students, teachers' expectations of and attitudes toward students, teachers' classroom management techniques, their teaching methods, and their general teaching behaviors (commonly referred to as "classroom environment") all make a difference in student learning. Nevertheless, even if we are convinced that teachers have an effect, we are unable to determine with certainty the influence a teacher has on student performance, because student learning variables are numerous and teacher-student interactions are complex.

TEACHER EFFECTS

It is important for principals to be familiar with methods and principles of effective teaching, specifically, the most recent "process-product research" and share this research with teachers. Applied as a whole, the teacher effects research is a means of helping students attain intended outcomes. The teacher effects research can serve as a useful guide for principals who are working with beginning or experienced teachers; they can serve as a basis for dialogue between the principal and teacher about instruction.

Teacher behavior research has shown that teacher behaviors, as well as specific teaching concepts and strategies, make a difference regarding student achievement. It should be noted, however, that teachers may not be the only variable, or even the major one, in the teaching-learning equation, but they can make a difference, either positive or negative. The foundational studies are shared as follows, as it is important to historically understand teaching and learning.

Teaching Methods and Student Achievement

Nathaniel Gage (1981) analyzed forty-nine process-product studies. He identified four clusters of behaviors that show a strong relationship to student outcomes: (1) *teacher indirectness*, the willingness to accept student ideas and feelings, and the ability to provide a healthy emotional climate; (2) *teacher praise*, support and encouragement, use of humor to release tensions (but not at the expense of others), and attention to students' needs; (3) *teacher acceptance*, clarifying, building, and developing students' ideas; and (4) *teacher criticism*, reprimanding students and justifying authority. The relationship between the last cluster and outcomes was negative—where criticism occurred, student achievement was low. In effect, the four clusters suggest the traditional notion of a democratic or warm teacher (a model emphasized for several decades).

From the evidence on teacher effects upon student achievement in reading and mathematics in the elementary grades, Gage presented successful teaching concepts and strategies that seem relevant for other grades as well. These strategies are summarized below. Note that they are commonsense strategies. They apply to many grade levels, and most experienced teachers are familiar with them. Nevertheless, they provide guidelines for education students or beginning teachers who say, "Just tell me how to teach."

1. Teachers should have a system of rules that allow students to attend to their personal and procedural needs without having to check with the teacher.
2. A teacher should move around the room, monitoring students' work and communicating an awareness of their behavior while also attending to their academic needs.
3. To ensure productive independent work by students, teachers should be sure that the assignments are interesting and worthwhile, yet still easy enough to be completed by each student without teacher direction.
4. Teachers should keep to a minimum such activities as giving directions and organizing the class for instruction. Teachers can do this by writing the daily schedule on the board and establishing general procedures so students know where to go and what to do.
5. In selecting students to respond to questions, teachers should call on volunteers and nonvolunteers by name before asking questions to give all students a chance to answer and to alert the student to be called upon. (We disagree with this item. Most good teachers first ask the question, then call on a student so everyone in the class is required to listen; hence, no one knows who the teacher will call on.)
6. Teachers should always aim at getting less academically oriented students to give some kind of response to a question. Rephrasing, giving cues, or asking leading questions can be useful techniques for bringing forth some answer from a silent student, one who says: "I don't know," or one who answers incorrectly.
7. During reading-group instruction, teachers should give a maximum amount of brief feedback and provide fast-paced activities of the drill type.

Principles of Teaching and Student Learning

Good and Lavigne (2018) have identified several factors related to effective teaching and student learning. They focus on basic principles of teaching, but not teacher behaviors or characteristics, since both researchers contend that teachers today are looking more for principles of teaching than for prescriptions.

1. *Clarity* about instructional goals (objectives)
2. Knowledge about *content* and ways for teaching it
3. *Variety* in the use of teaching methods and media
4. *With-it-ness*, awareness of what is going on, alertness in monitoring classroom activities
5. *Overlapping*, sustaining an activity while doing something else at the same time
6. *Smoothness*, sustaining proper lesson pacing and group momentum, not dwelling on minor points or wasting time dealing with individuals, and focusing on all the students
7. *Seatwork* instructions and management that initiate and focus on productive task engagement
8. Holding students *accountable* for learning; accepting responsibility for student learning
9. *Realistic expectations* in line with student abilities and behaviors
10. *Realistic praise*, not praise for its own sake
11. *Flexibility* in planning and adapting classroom activities
12. *Task orientation* and businesslike behavior in the teacher
13. *Monitoring* of students' understanding; providing appropriate feedback, giving praise, asking questions.
14. Providing student *opportunity to learn* what is to be tested
15. Making comments that help *structure learning* of knowledge and concepts for students; helping students learn how to learn.

(Good & Lavigne, 2018)

Note that many of these behaviors are classroom management techniques and structured learning strategies, which suggests that good discipline is a prerequisite for good teaching.

Teaching Principles and Student Achievement

The Evertson and Emmer (2017) model is similar to that of Good and Lavigne. The models are similar in three ways: (1) Teacher effectiveness is associated with specific teaching concepts and strategies, (2) organization and management of instructional activities is stressed, and (3) findings and conclusions are based primarily on process-product studies.

Nine basic teaching principles represent the core of Evertson and Emmer's work. Effectiveness is identified in terms of raising student achievement scores.

1. *Rules and Procedures.* Rules and procedures are established and enforced and students are monitored for compliance.
2. *Consistency.* Similar expectations are maintained for activities and behavior at all times for all students. Inconsistency causes confusion in students about what is acceptable.
3. *Prompt Management of Inappropriate Behavior.* Inappropriate behavior is attended to quickly to stop it and prevent its spread.
4. *Checking Student Work.* All student work, including seatwork, homework, and papers, is corrected, errors are discussed, and feedback is provided promptly.

5. *Interactive Teaching.* This takes several forms and includes presenting and explaining new materials, question sessions, discussions, checking for student understanding, actively moving among students to correct work, providing feedback, and, if necessary, reteaching materials.

6. *Academic Instruction.* Sometimes referred to as "academic learning time" or "academic engaged time." Attention is focused on the management of student work.

7. *Pacing.* Information is presented at a rate appropriate to the students' ability to comprehend it, not too rapidly or too slowly.

8. *Transitions.* Transitions from one activity to another are made smoothly, with minimal confusion about what to do next.

9. *Clarity.* Lessons are presented logically and sequentially. Clarity is enhanced by the use of instructional objectives and adequate illustrations and by keeping in touch with students.

The Master Teacher

The national interest in student achievement and excellence in teaching has focused considerable attention on teachers and the notion of the **master teacher.** The direct behaviors suggested by Good and Lavigne, and by Evertson and Emmer, correspond with Walter Doyle's (1985, 1992) task-oriented and businesslike description of a master teacher. Such teachers "focus on academic goals, are careful and explicit in structuring activities . . . promote high levels of student academic involvement and content coverage, furnish opportunities for controlled practice with feedback, hold students accountable for work , . . have expectations that they will be successful in helping students learn, [and are] active in explaining concepts and procedures, promoting meaning and purpose for academic work, and monitoring comprehension" (pp. 30, 486–516).

Robert Marzano (2017) identifies nine instructional strategies that have positive effects on student achievement: (1) identifying similarities and differences in content, (2) summarizing and note taking, (3) reinforcing effort and providing recognition, (4) homework and practice, (5) nonlinguistic recommendations, (6) cooperative learning, (7) providing feedback, (8) testing hypotheses, and (9) cues, questions, and advance organizers. These instructional strategies were considered as having "high probability of enhancing student achievement."

RESEARCH-BASED PRACTICES FOR INCREASING STUDENT ACHIEVEMENT

Teaching, because it is an extremely complex process dealing with many variables, has been difficult to analyze. Research on teaching and learning accumulated during the last four decades has provided a variety of teaching techniques that may be utilized effectively by teachers as they interact with, facilitate, and direct students within their classrooms. Ten enduring, research-based instructional strategies have been shown to have positive effects on student learning: anticipatory set, stimulus variation, closure, reinforcement, recognizing attending behavior, questioning, lecturing, planned repetition, establishing appropriate frames of references, and race, class, and gender equity. Each one will be discussed in turn.

It is important for principals to be familiar with these ten enduring, research-based strategies, which cross grade levels and school subjects. Principals need to share these strategies with teachers. Applied as a whole, these strategies are a means of helping students attain intended outcomes. The strategies can serve as a useful guide for principals who are working with beginning or experienced teachers. The strategies can serve as a basis for dialogue between the principal and teacher about classroom instruction.

Anticipatory Set

Observers have noted that teachers usually do not spend much time preparing a class for an activity. They frequently say, "Read this story tonight for homework," or "Watch this demonstration carefully," and expect their classroom to be full of eager students who are anxious to learn as much as possible.

The problem that every teacher faces at least twice during each classroom period is to hit upon those introductory remarks (or procedures) that will produce the maximum payoff in learning—that is, when introducing an activity, what can a teacher say that will produce the maximum pay-off in learning? What words can a teacher use to produce the maximum in subsequent learning?

Anticipatory set was coined by Madeline Hunter in the 1960s. The concept of anticipatory set and the development of the resulting theory come from research on learning. This research appears to indicate that the activities preceding a learning task influence the outcome of that task, and that some instructional sets are superior to others (M. Hunter, 1984; R. Hunter, 2004; Luiten, Ames, & Ackerson, 1980; Marzano, 2017, 2018; Marzano, Pickering, & Pollack, 2001; Townsend & Clarihew, 1989). If some instructional sets are superiors to others, then each teacher is faced with the need to find those types of sets that will be most useful for his or her purposes and then to modify these sets to fit the specific classroom situation.

Let us suppose that the teacher wishes the class to read chapter 3 in their textbook as homework, and chapter 3 is about Andrew Jackson and the changes that took place under the reign of "Andrew I." The "problem" the teacher faces is which remarks or activities will produce the greatest learning for the next day. The teacher could say, "Now class, for tomorrow I want all of you to read chapter 3 in the text." Such a weak set would probably produce the usual response, and the next day the teacher will discover that half of the class has not read the assignment and the remainder claim that they studied but are unable to answer the teacher's discussion questions.

To improve the set, the teacher might say: "For tomorrow, I want you to read chapter 3 in the text and come to class prepared for a discussion." This last sentence is an improvement because it gives the student more information about his goal, that of preparation for a discussion. But despite the obviousness of the addition, the student may need a good deal more help before he or she is able to prepare for the next day's discussion. What will you discuss? What points should be considered as they read? What should they focus on while they read? How should they use their past information? Should they learn facts or principles? Should they compare, contrast, both, or neither? A sufficient set, then, is one which gives the students adequate preparation so that while they go through the activity, they are able to come as close to the lesson goals as the teacher wishes.

Activities for which set induction is appropriate include the following: at the start of a unit; before a discussion; before question-answer recitation; before giving a homework assignment; before hearing a panel discussion; when assigning student reports; before students present reports; before viewing a video; in a discussion after viewing a video; before assigning homework based on the discussion following a video; before a discussion based upon the homework assignment.

The following are a few examples of anticipatory set:

1. Giving models of good book reports before the class writes their book reports. (Such sets act as facilitating sets. Indeed, such sets are usually quite effective in obtaining desired responses.)

2. Giving an assignment of creating a character as a set for noticing character in the reading of short stories.

3. We are going to take a trip to Rome but don't want anyone to discover that we are really Americans. How should we dress, act, and so on? What small things do you think might give us away? Now read . . .

4. Understanding executive, legislative, and judicial branches of government by working through analogies to family, school, and city.

5. Beginning a unit in physics with a demonstration involving a piece of wood overhanging the edge of a desk. The part on the desk is covered with a piece of paper. When the teacher gives a sharp blow to the part of the wood hanging over the edge (because of the air pressure), the paper is undisturbed and the wood snaps.

Stimulus Variation

Stimulus variation deals with both verbal and nonverbal techniques for varying stimuli presented to the students. A variety of techniques can be used by the teacher. The skill is particularly relevant to activities such as direct teaching or teacher-led discussions, in which the teacher's ability to hold the students' attention determines his or her success.

The concept of stimulus variation comes from research on learning concerned with the effects of change and habituation (Obasi, 2019; Remesh, 2013; Wyckoff, 2015). The research that has been done points to the fact that changes, any deviation from the standard, seem to result in higher attention levels.

Teachers should remember that most youngsters have short attention spans. They often lose interest after a certain period of time. Good teachers vary learning activities and their teaching behavior during a classroom session so that students receive new stimuli that will keep them interested. The stimuli constructed by the teacher compete, in a sense, with irrelevant stimuli that might distract the students.

Six behaviors can be used to vary the stimulus: movement, gestures, focusing, interaction styles, pausing, and shifting sensory channels (Obasi, 2019; Remesh, 2013; Wyckoff, 2015). Each one will be discussed in turn.

Movement. **Movement** by the teacher requires visual and aural sensory adjustments from the student. The students do not shift from one primary receptor to another but, rather, they adjust each behavior. We can generalize from theories about attention and state that a high number of these sensory adjustments, per unit of time, will help the teacher keep the students attending to the message of the lesson. The teacher behavior required is that of moving throughout the lesson in a pattern that ensures: (a) that on numerous occasions the teacher is perceived in both the left and right sides of the classroom; (b) that on numerous occasions the teacher is perceived in both the front and back of the teaching space; (c) that occasionally the teacher moves among and/or behind the students. The wireless multimedia presenter used with PowerPoint presentations is useful here.

Gestures. **Gestures** include hand, head, and body movements that are an important part of communication. The oral message alone is not as effective in conveying meaning as an oral message combined with gestural cues. One can think of the effective communications of Marcel Marceau and Harpo Marx as one end of a continuum and the relatively dry and lifeless communication of Ed Sullivan as the other end of the continuum. Maximum communicative effectiveness probably lies somewhere in between.

Focusing. **Focusing** can be produced either through verbal statements, through specific gestural behaviors or by some combination of both. Some examples follow:

1. *Verbal Focusing.* "*Look* at this diagram!" "*Listen* closely to this!" "Now, here's something really important!" "Watch what happens when I connect these two points!"
2. *Gestural Focusing.* Teacher points to object. Teacher bangs the dry-erase board for emphasis.
3. *Combinations of Verbal and Gestural Focusing.* "*Look* at this diagram [teacher points to diagram]!"

Interaction Styles. A teacher can vary the pattern of the lesson by switching to different **interaction styles**. Three examples follow:

1. *Teacher-Group.* The teacher is presenting or demonstrating to *all* students, ask questions of the group at large and is nonspecific in the presentation or demonstration.
2. *Teacher-Student.* Here the teacher tries to make a point with or for *one* student, or asks a particular student a question
3. *Student-Student.* The teacher can take a student's response and direct it to another student for comment or clarification. Another technique is for a teacher to have one student explain something to another student. The goal here is to have the teacher withdraw briefly from the lesson by allowing student-student interactions to occur.

The deliberate patterning of these interaction styles serves to vary the context within which content is covered. This should result in a higher level of attention than would occur if only a single style were utilized (i.e., presenting or demonstrating).

Pausing. The effectiveness of silence as an attention demanding behavior is well known by public speakers and little used by teachers. There is no reason to rush to fill silent space with talk or activity. In fact, there are some interesting events that occur when pauses are deliberately inserted into the lesson. First, it breaks informational segments into easily processed units. Second, it captures attention by reducing the stimulus present (remember, attention is maintained at a high level when stimulus change occurs, not just when stimulus intensity is increased). Third, it probably causes the student to "strain" for cues and direction, since the situation lacks structure. Finally, a distinct pause prepares the students for the next unit of teacher behavior.

Shifting Sensory Channels. By shifting the primary sensory receptors (e.g., ears to eyes) being used by the student, a necessary set of adjustments must be made by him or her to receive the teacher's message. This is not a shift in reception through the same sensory channel as we discussed in the section on movement. In this case, the emphasis is on the adjustments that must be made by switching the primary receptors. This should ensure a higher level of attention. The behaviors the teacher must produce are those that shift the primary mode of information transfer.

Usually, the teacher is conveying oral messages. These might be supplemented by visual messages through the use of PowerPoint slides, dry-erase boards, pictures, objects, and so on. Tactile attention is demanded when the teacher passes around some object or asks students to adjust or manipulate some apparatus.

Combining behaviors during the lesson can be very effective. For example, the teacher might move from one side of the room to the other, saying "Now watch this." She writes on the dry-erase board. She then steps back, points at what she has written, and says nothing more. In this sequence, the teacher has used five behaviors: movement, verbal focusing, gestural focusing, pausing, and oral-visual switching. Each behavior attracts the students' attention.

Closure. The skills of set induction and closure are complementary. Unless the students achieve **closure**—that is, perception of the logical organization of the ideas presented in a lesson—the effect of an otherwise good lesson may be negated. By using closure techniques, the teacher can make sure that students understand the material and its relationship to what they have learned already (Ganske, 2017; Reese, 2014).

Closure is not limited to the completion of a lesson. It is also needed at specific points within the lesson, so that students may know where they are and where they are going. If the planned lesson is not completed, closure can still be attained by drawing attention to what has been accomplished up to the point where the lesson must end.

Closure can be facilitated in at least four ways (Ganske, 2017; Marzano, Pickering, & Pollack, 2001; Reese, 2014):

1. *Drawing attention to the completion of the lesson or part of the lesson.* This can be accomplished in one or more ways: (a) providing consolidation of concepts and elements that were covered before moving to subsequent learning; (b) relating the lesson back to the original organizing principle; (c) reviewing major points using an outline; (d) summarizing the discussion including the major points that were covered by the teacher and class; (e) developing all the elements of the lesson into a new unity; and (f) reviewing the major points throughout the lesson.
2. *Making connections between previously known material, currently presented material, and future learning.* This can be accomplished by: (a) reviewing the sequence that has been followed in moving from known to new material; (b) applying what has been learned to similar examples and cases; and (c) extending material covered to new situations.
3. *Allowing students the opportunity to demonstrate what they have learned.* This can be accomplished as follows: (a) providing for student practice of new learning and (b) providing for student summary of the learning.

4. *Developing unsuspected closure.* This can be accomplished by helping students to take what has been presented and to develop this material into a new, and unsuspected, synthesis.

Reinforcement

Research has indicated that if teachers **reinforce** students both verbally and nonverbally when they participate both in large- and small-group classroom discussions, irrespective of the correctness of their responses, students will participate more often and more actively in classroom discussion (Agran et al., 2001; Maag, 2001; Marzano, 2017; Marzano, Pickering, & Pollack, 2001; Ramesh, 2013). If teachers wish to get students to participate more often and more actively in class, they should discover what is reinforcing for specific students and then reinforce the students when they do participate in class. The more techniques a teacher has at his or her disposal for reinforcing students, the better his or her chance for getting good pupil participation.

For example, when a student makes a particularly good response, the teacher might say, "That's exactly it," and nod his or her head affirmatively as he or she moves toward the student. In this case, the teacher combines one positive verbal reinforcer with two positive nonverbal reinforcers. Such a combination produces a cumulative effect. Examples of positive nonverbal reinforcement include the following: the teacher nods and smiles; the teacher moves toward the student; the teacher keeps her eyes on the student; and the teacher writes the student's response on the dry-erase board. Positive verbal reinforcement includes the use of the words and phrases such as "Good," "Fine," "Excellent," "Correct," and so on, or otherwise verbally indicating pleasure at the student's response. Teacher actions and responses that act as negative reinforcement tend to decrease student participation and should be avoided. Examples follow: the teacher scowls or frowns; the teacher moves away from the student; the teacher fails to maintain eye contact with the student; the teacher responds with "No," "Wrong," and "That's not it"; or the teacher manifests expressions of annoyance or impatience.

Recognizing Attending Behavior

Related literature on student attending behavior indicates that student behavior can be classified as either work-oriented behavior or nonwork-oriented behavior and that these student behaviors can be distinguished from each other. Two important variables that are dimensions of total teacher behavior were reported in the literature as instructional technique and the immediate effect of technique on student attending behavior (Amstuz & Mullet, 2014; Marzano, 2017; Marzano, Pickering, & Pollack, 2001). An inverse relationship has been found between student attending behavior and student disruptive behavior (Algozzine, Daunic, & Smith, 2010; Emmer, 2017; Evertson, 2017).

Suggested criteria for **recognizing attending behavior** include the following: eye contact with the teacher or the teaching media; active engagement in the task assignment (such as reading, writing, or note taking); a positive response to the teaching tasks; and participation in the class activity. Suggested criteria for recognizing nonattending behavior include the following: the student appears bored, without eye contact with the teaching task; the student appears not to be taking part in the class activity; the student appears to be taking part in class activity other than the assigned tasks; and/or the student appears to be responding negatively to the teacher's direction.

Questioning

The use of **questioning** techniques is basic to good teaching. In general, questions can be classified into four broad categories: Initiating, probing, higher order, and divergent (Erdogan & Campbell, 2008; Harvey & Light, 2015; Haynes, 2014; Moore & Rudd, 2002; Wilen, 1987).

Initiating questions elicit an initial response from the student. Once the student has responded, the teacher probes the student's response. Some of the *probing* questions the teacher asks require the students to remember facts or to describe something they see. The teacher also asks *higher order* questions, which require the students to make comparisons, inferences, evaluations, or to relate ideas. *Divergent* questions have no "right" or "wrong" answers. When first asked divergent questions, many students are uncomfortable because there are no "right" answers for them to lean upon. They are reluctant to explore and hypothesize for fear of giving the wrong or foolish answers. As a result, they try to pick up cues from the teacher as to what answer is wanted. If the teacher gives these kinds of cues, however, her questions are not truly divergent. If, on the other hand, the teacher is not giving cues, some students are likely to feel uncomfortable and uncertain. This should be viewed as a favorable, not an unfavorable, sign.

Lecturing

A **formal lecture** (or direct teaching) refers to a verbal presentation of subject matter content formally organized and unsupported by other learning media, extending over a period of time not less than fifteen or twenty minutes (Brown & Race, 2003; Dennick, 2010; Hativa, 2009: Kember & Kwan, 2000; Penson, 2012; Van Klaveren, 2011). An **informal lecture** refers to a presentation involving multimedia (such as PowerPoint, video, or video streaming) and student interruption for questions and clarification. We might define an informal lecture as the teacher being the presenter for 90 percent of the information and the student 10 percent (Brown & Race, 2003; Dennick, 2010; Hativa, 2009; Kember & Kwan, 2000; Penson, 2012; Van Klaveren, 2011).

Given these definitions, there are two main questions that the teacher needs to consider: (a) When is it effective to lecture? and (b) How can the teacher lecture effectively?

Why or When to Use Lecturing.

1. The teacher may have information that is not accessible to the students. For example, an expert in some subject matter field, a scholar, one who has traveled widely, or so forth, will often have information that the student does not have.
2. A second reason for lecturing is to reinforce written work. Before or after students study a topic, the teacher may want to reinforce their learning by lecturing on some of the same material. This procedure will emphasize the main points of the unit. However, the teacher must be sure not to lecture on everything the student learns. The teachers need only lecture on those things that he or she wishes to emphasize.

3. A third reason for lecturing is to create a change of pace or, as we have discussed, to vary the stimulus situation. In this way, we can switch from the question-answer presentation to that of a lecture. Any method used exclusively usually results in a loss of attention and bored students.

4. Economy is an important reason for lecturing. Through a lecture, the teacher can synthesize many sources, although far too often this is not the case with a lecture. If a lecture is well done, it will have synthesized several sources so that all students can get a universal coverage of the subject matter.

5. The lecture can also inform learners of the expected outcomes of learning. For example, the teacher might say, "We are going to make up a particular unit in which we are going to concentrate on . . . and . . . will be expected of the students."

How to Lecture Effectively. The first assumption is that the listening audience, the students, must be verbal enough to respond to the lecture. You can only communicate to students who employ the language that is used by the speaker. For the teacher, this means that he or she needs to consider the vocabulary which he or she uses in the lecture. In the formal lecture, the verbally adept students have a high potential for compressing ideas or synthesizing points of view. But those who are not verbally adept lack these characteristics, which are features required to absorb the points of the lecture. In other words, if the teacher notes that slow learners are not verbal, then in most cases a lecture to them may be very wasteful and destructive to morale. The slow learner cannot respond to the concentrated medium of a formal lecture. Other oral media may be preferable for this group of students—such as the discussion or informal lecturing techniques with lots of visuals.

Another very important consideration to remember is that if the teacher is going to use a lecturing technique, the students need to be prepared for this formal lecturing technique. One of the skills that many students do not have is the skill of listening (Kneen, 2011). The teacher should provide opportunities for the students to listen in practice sessions, teaching them how to listen for main ideas (Dawes, 2011).

Another consideration should be that of note taking. Robert Gagne (1985) argues that research shows that note taking serves no useful purpose. On the other hand, there is some evidence that note taking helps to assimilate ideas (Hewitt, 2008). Students need to be taught how to take notes effectively if note taking is not going to be an obstruction to their learning. They need to be shown how to listen for the main ideas and put them into note form. Early in the lecture a teacher may ask a question such as: "What do you think the main idea is so far?" This is an attempt to involve the students in the lecture or in the learning process rather than have them as passive observers.

Attributes of a Good Lecturer. What are some of the other attributes of a good lecturer? A good lecturer must have audience appeal—warmth, friendliness, and confidence. They must speak in a voice that is clear and easily understood. He or she should have very good control of the English language—syntax, word selection, enunciation, pronunciation, the use of meaningful figures, and so on. Because of a lack of these characteristics, there may be individuals for whom the lecture is not the best means of presentation. Furthermore, lecturing may be completely alien to the personality and style of certain teachers. A beginning teacher must take these things into consideration in deciding if lecturing should play a major part in his or her teaching style. Using PowerPoint and a wireless multimedia presenter can vary the stimulus and provide movement within the classroom space during a lecture (Harasim, 2011; Hativa, 2009).

The Lecture Itself. Let us turn our attention now to the lecture itself. Two essential components of a lecture are planning and pacing.

Planning. Planning is usually the first criterion of the well-developed lecture. The teacher may find planning a very painful experience. The teacher's objectives must be sharply defined. The way the teacher develops his or her main points must also be sharply defined, and the supporting evidence well organized to make the lecture effective. The teacher should avoid unnecessary repetition or misplaced emphasis. Although the technique of repetition can be very effective to highlight important points, a good lecture needs to be clear and well organized. Notice how a newscaster organizes his or her presentation and enhances it with interesting sidelights and human-interest stories. Most newscasters are good models of organization.

Pacing. We have, of course, already discussed pacing under the technical skill of varying the stimulus. This skill also applies to delivery techniques, using different visual materials, lowering or changing the pitch of the voice. All of these things are part of the total idea of pacing. Remember that one of the objectives of the teacher is to pace the students into the lecture rather than overwhelm them.

If you watch newscasters, you will see them using a rapid cadence of words, slowing down, and speeding up. In other words, they are varying the stimulus that they give to their audience. Main ideas should be repeated and highlighted so that students will pick up cues that these are important concepts or ideas pertaining to the lecture.

As we design the presentation of a lecture (this is also related to pacing) there are some guidelines that should be considered. One model is often called the 10-30-10 principle (Hativa, 2009). A teacher who is going to make a fifty-minute lecture, should probably spend about ten minutes telling the students what he or she is going to tell them. This is incorporated into the idea of set induction, which was discussed earlier. Thirty minutes should be spent in telling the students that material, and the last ten minutes should be taken in reviewing, explaining what the teacher already told them.

For secondary school teachers, the informal lecture method is probably far superior to the formal lecture method. The teacher needs to use visuals to enhance the presentation. Participation should be encouraged. If students do not understand points, they should be encouraged to raise their hands and ask questions of the teacher. Often times, the teacher will want to supplement the informal lecture with written hand-outs, PowerPoint presentations, videos, or slides. The main point is the use of technology should complement rather than be a substitute for the presentation (Harasim, 2011; Hativa, 2009).

Planned Repetition

Planned repetition is a skill that requires careful use. On the one hand, the teacher wants to structure situations to encourage overlearning and relearning. On the other hand, the teacher does not want to "beat a dead horse" with constant repetition. Some teachers do not repeat material enough and others bore the students with repetition.

If continuity from lesson to lesson is important, the teacher should be particularly alert to the possibilities of repetition (Stone, 2010a, 2010b, 2010c). In the actual classroom situation, an effective teacher uses the skill in several sessions. In essence, the teacher reviews previous material by repeating, or having students repeat, main ideas. If these ideas have been forgotten, they may be relearned, as a result of repetition.

Establishing Appropriate Frames of Reference

A student's understanding of the material of a lesson can be increased if it is organized and taught from several **appropriate frames of reference**. A single frame of reference provides a structure through which the student can gain an understanding of the material. The use of several frames of reference deepens and broadens the general field of understanding more completely than is possible with only one.

Teachers can be trained to become more powerful teachers as they are taught to identify many possible frames of reference that might be used in instruction, to make judicious selection from among them, and then to present them effectively (Darling-Hammond, 2008; Marzano, Pickering, & Pollack, 2001).

Race, Class, and Gender Equity

There continues to be serious differences between the level of academic achievement for children coming from wealthy and from poor families, and from ethnic-majority and from some ethnic-minority families. Low socioeconomic status and some ethnic-minority groups continue to be overrepresented in the low achievement groups (Barton & Coley, 2010; Darling-Hammond, 2010; Entwisle, Alexander, & Olson, 2010; Howard, 2020; Ladson-Billings, 2006; Murphy, 2010; Nieto, 2002/2003; Paige, 2011; Rothstein, 2004b; Singham, 2003; Sirin, 2005; Teranishi, Nguyen, & Curammeng, 2020; Wiggan, 2007). More than ever, culturally responsive teaching is essential in addressing the needs of today's diverse student population (Agarwal-Rangnath, 2020; Benson & Fiarman, 2020; Darling-Hammond et al., 2019; Gay, 2018; Hess & Noguera, 2021; Horsford, Scott, & Anderson, 2019; Rivera-McCutchen, 2021; Sleeter & Zavala, 2020).

Thomas Good (1987) reviewed the research on teachers' differential treatment of high-achieving students and low-achieving students. He identified seventeen teaching behaviors that are used with different frequencies with the two groups of students. These behaviors define a pattern of diminished expectations for low-achieving students' ability to learn, and perhaps a lower regard for their personal worth as learners. It is important for a principal to be able to understand Good's practices and share these ineffective teaching practices with teachers. The teaching practices are as follows: (a) wait less time for at-risk students to answer questions; (b) give low-achieving students the answer or call on someone else rather than try to improve their responses by giving clues or using other teaching techniques; (c) reward inappropriate behavior or incorrect answers by low-achieving students; (d) criticize low-achieving students more often for failure; (e) praise low-achieving students less frequently than high-achieving students for success; (f) fail to give feedback to the public responses of low-achieving students; (g) pay less attention to low-achieving students or interact with them less frequently; (h) call on low-achieving students less often to respond to questions, or ask them only easier, nonanalytical questions; (i) seat low-achieving students farther away from the teacher; (j) demand less from low-achieving students; (k) interact with low-achieving students more privately than publicly and monitor and structure their activities more closely; (l) grade tests or assignments in a differential manner, so that high-achieving but not low-achieving are given the benefit of the action in borderline cases; (m) have less friendly interaction with low-achieving students including less smiling and less warm and more anxious voice tones; (n) provide briefer and less informative feedback to the questions of low-achieving students, (o) provide less eye contact and other nonverbal communication of attention and responsiveness when interacting with low-achieving students; (p) make less use of effective but time-consuming instructional methods with low-achieving students when time is limited; and (q) evidence less acceptance and use of ideas given by low-achieving students. According to Good, academic achievement is highly correlated with race and social class, which means that low-achieving students are more likely to come from disadvantaged home backgrounds, whereas high-achieving students are likely to come from advantaged home backgrounds. Therefore, the differential teaching behaviors found by Good suggest a pattern of discrimination based on students' race and social class as well as their achievement level.

More recently, scholars reviewed the literature on effective multicultural teacher practices and teacher characteristics (Agarwal-Rangnath, 2020; Garcia & Kleifgen, 2018; Gay, 2018; Gorski, 2018; Han & Laughter, 2019; Hess & Noguera, 2021; Marshall, Gerstl-Pepin, & Johnson, 2020; Noguera & Syeed, 2020; Paris & Alim, 2017; Sleeter & Zavala, 2020; Walker, 2019). They conclude that effective teachers

- have empathy for people from other cultures;
- accurately perceive similarities and differences between a student's culture and their own;
- describe a student's behavior without judging it;
- express respect and positive regard for all students through eye contact, body posture, and voice tone and pitch;
- use multicultural materials in the classroom;
- recognize and accept both the language spoken in the home and the standard language used in the school;
- help students develop pride in and identification with their native cultures;
- praise all students equally and frequently for success;
- give feedback to the public responses of all students equally;
- pay equal attention or interact with all students frequently;
- demand the same from all students;
- interact the same way with all students and monitor and structure their activities equally;
- grade tests and assignments in the same manner, so that all students are given the benefit of the doubt in borderline cases;
- try to improve on students' responses to questions by giving clues or using other teaching techniques; and
- evidence equal acceptance and use of ideas given by all students

These effective teaching practices and teacher characteristics will likely improve student learning, regardless of the teacher's philosophy of multicultural education (Bulach & Lunenburg, 2008, 2011, 2016a, 2016b). What emerges from the list is a teacher who respects all students and who takes responsibility for knowing about their cultural backgrounds and using this knowledge in his or her teaching.

ACADEMIC PRESS AND SOCIAL SUPPORT: EFFECTS ON STUDENT ACHIEVEMENT

Research has shown that the combined effects of **academic press** (i.e., high standards for academic performance) and **social support** (students' perception that their teachers are caring and concerned about them) have resulted in positive student learning outcomes, including less class cutting, less tardiness, less absenteeism, less behavior problems, better preparation for class, and higher achievement gains, especially in economically challenged or high-needs schools. Some refer to social support as that of social emotional learning (SEL). This supports James Comer's (1980, 1996) School Development Program initiated in the early 1980s, and which has been reinforced recently by the work of Darling-Hammond et al. (2019). It is important for principals to understand and share this research with teachers, in an effort for teachers to increase students' academic achievement. The strategies can serve as a basis for dialogue between the principal and teacher about classroom instruction.

Research Evidence

In a sample of approximately seven thousand high school students from the National Educational Longitudinal Study of 1988, Shouse (1996) investigated school differences on academic press and sense of community. Shouse (1996) found that a school culture characterized by both academic press and a sense of community was associated with higher achievement gains, especially in low-socioeconomic status schools. He concluded that the combination of high academic press and high community was protective for low-income students who may not have academic resources to draw on in their homes and communities. Similar findings were reported in a large-scale Texas study (Jackson & Lunenburg, 2010).

Lee and Smith (1999) examined the combined effects of academic press and social support on achievement in a sample of Chicago middle school students. They found that students with more social support learned the most if they also attended schools characterized by high academic press. This finding is significant, because it indicates an interaction between academic press and social support in producing what Bulach and Lunenburg (2008, 2011 2016a, 2016b) and Lunenburg (2013b) term a *high-performing school*.

Using the same national data set (National Education Longitudinal Study of 1988), Gregory and Weinstein (2004) found that student connection (positive regard for teachers) and regulation (behavioral order in the classroom) predicted growth in achievement through the high school years. Specifically, a combination of high teacher connection and high teacher regulation predicted the greatest achievement for low-income adolescents.

In a nationally representative sample of high schools from the High School Effectiveness Study, Pellerin (2005) examined teacher warmth and academic press. Pellerin found that schools high in teacher warmth and academic press had the least amount of class cutting, tardiness, lack of preparation for class, and absenteeism, compared to other schools. This finding extends previous research showing teachers' expectations for student success are related to the development of students' academic self-concept (Lunenburg, 1983b) and achievement over time (Kuklinski & Weinstein, 2001). A similar process is likely to occur at the school level and in relation to positive behavioral outcomes. Further, a culture of high academic expectations could have a socializing effect. That is, students may internalize the academic mission of the school and become more invested in following school rules (Lunenburg, 2005).

Another possible explanatory association between academic press and low incidents of student behavior problems has to do with how staff perceive and react to student misbehavior. Perhaps in schools with high academic expectations, staff may respond less punitively to student misbehavior and successfully reengage misbehaving students in the learning process (using restorative practices) (Losen, 2015), because of their greater emphasis on developing academic talent compared to staff in schools with low academic expectations (Lunenburg, 1991). Or high rates of student misbehavior may result in teachers lowering their expectations (Lunenburg, 1984; Lunenburg & O'Reilly, 1974).

A related issue to the link between school culture and discipline incidents is the attitude of a school's principal toward the type of punishment used. Principals who believe frequent punishments help improve behavior and those who tend to blame behavioral problems on poor parenting and poverty also tend to administer harsher punishments than those principals who strongly believe in enforcing school rules but who regard harsher methods of discipline, such as suspension, as a measure to be used sparingly (Losen, 2015). This evidence suggests that factors other than student behavior (in this case, principals' beliefs) can influence the administration of discipline (Labby, Lunenburg, & Slate, 2014).

In a large-scale, national study of school culture in 195 schools, Bulach and Lunenburg (2008, 2011) found that the *high-performing school* was high in academic press (i.e., high standards for both academic and behavioral performance) and social support (i.e., students perceive their teachers as caring and concerned about them); the *enlightened school* was relatively high in academic press and relatively low in social support; the *permissive school* was higher in social support than academic press; and the *low-performing school* was disengaged, low in both academic press and social support (Bulach & Lunenburg, 2008, 2011, 2016a, 2016b; Lunenburg, 2013).

THE HUMANISTIC APPROACH TO TEACHING

The national discourse about teaching emphasizes cognitive processes. Politicians and business leaders assert that students need to master higher-order thinking skills, so they can acquire more complex and useful knowledge. We see that perspective reflected in such initiatives as Every Student Succeeds Act and the Common Core Standards.

There is nothing wrong with this goal. What does concern learning experts, however, is that these discussions and programs occur within a very narrow framework. The assumption is that improving how students learn can be achieved simply by altering content standards, instructional methods, and curriculum materials. There are powerful noncognitive variables, such as students' needs, emotions, self-perceptions, and values that all play an important role in learning (Snowman & McCown, 2015).

The theoretical perspective that has addressed these types of affective variables is known as the **humanistic approach**. The humanistic approach to teaching is student-centered instruction. It assumes that students will be motivated to learn: when the learning material is personally meaningful to them, when they understand the reasons for their own behavior, and when they believe that the classroom environment supports their efforts to learn (Snowman & McCown, 2015, p. 483). That is, a humanistic approach to teaching helps students better understand themselves and creates a supportive classroom environment that activates the inherent desire we all have to learn (Bulach & Lunenburg, 2008, 2011, 2016a, 2016b; Combs, 1965; Maslow, 1968, 1987; Rogers & Freiberg, 1994; Snowman & McCown, 2015).

We know that learning is as much influenced by how students feel about themselves as by the cognitive skills they have. When students determine that the demands of a task are beyond their level of skill, they are likely to experience emotions of anxiety and fear. Once these emotions surface, the student must divert time and energy away from the task and determine how to deal with the emotions. Some may decide to decrease their efforts and settle for a passing grade. Others may give up entirely: cut class, not complete homework, and not study for tests. An abundance of research has revealed a correlation between positive student-teacher relationships and higher levels of student achievement (Cornelius-White, 2007; Darling-Hammond et al., 2019; Murphy, 2016c; Noddings, 2005a, 2005b; Roorda et al., 2011; Snowman & McCown, 2015; Wentzel, 2010).

Examples of the Humanistic Approach

Examples of the humanistic approach to teaching can be found in the *child-centered* lab school directed by John Dewey at the University of Chicago from 1896 to 1904; the *play-centered* methods and materials introduced by Maria Montessori that were designed to develop the practical, sensory, and formal skills of pre-kindergarten and kindergarten children in the slums of Italy, starting in 1908; and the *activity-centered* practices of William Kilpatrick, who, in the 1920s and 1930s, urged the elementary teachers to organize classrooms around social activities, group enterprises, and group projects, and allow children to say what they think.

Each of the aforementioned progressive approaches to education were highly humanistic and stressed the child's interests, individuality, and creativity—in short, the child's freedom to develop naturally, freedom from teacher domination, and freedom from the weight of rote learning. But progressivism failed because, in the view of Lawrence Cremin (1961), there were not enough good teachers to implement progressive thought in classrooms and schools. It is much easier to stress knowledge, rote learning, and right answers than it is to teach about ideas, to consider the interests and needs of students, and to give them freedom to explore and interact with each other without teacher constraints.

By the end of the twentieth century, the humanistic teacher was depicted by William Glasser's *Schools without Failure* (1969) and Glasser's *The Quality School* (1990), depicting the "positive" and "supportive" teacher who could manage students without coercion and teach without failure. It was also illustrated by Robert Fried's (2001) *The Passionate Teacher* and Vito Perrone's (1998) *Teacher with a Heart*—teachers who live to teach young children and refuse to submit to apathy or criticism that may infect the school in which they work. These teachers are dedicated and caring; they actively engage students in their classrooms and they affirm their identities. The students do not have to ask whether their teacher is interested in them, thinks of them, or knows their interests or concerns.

Good teaching, according to Alfie Kohn (2005), requires that we accept students for who they are rather than what they do or how much they achieve. All children and youth need to know that their parents will accept them unconditionally, but Kohn goes one step further and maintains that unconditional teaching is also important. For their own self-esteem and ego identity, all children and youth need to feel loved, understood, and valued; this idea is based on Carl Rogers's (1961) classic notion of effective teaching and learning, William Glasser's (1969) concept of a successful school, and Abraham Maslow's (1968) notion of personal healthy growth and development. These are basic sociopsychological principles that date back more than a half century—and they are still relevant today. Now all students need support and encouragement from teachers, but lower-achieving students and disadvantaged learners are more in need of support and positive reinforcement from their teachers, as noted in the previous section on the effects of academic press and social support on student achievement. "Unconditional teachers are not afraid to be themselves with students—to act like real human beings rather than controlling authority figures." These are the kind of teachers who act informally "write notes to students, have lunch with them [and] . . . listen carefully to what kids say and remember details about their lives" (Kohn, 2005, p. 29).

The humanistic teacher is also portrayed by Theodore Sizer's (1984) mythical teacher called "Horace," who is dedicated and enjoys teaching, treats learning as a humane enterprise, inspires his students to learn, and encourages them to develop their powers of thought, taste, and character. There is also a humanistic element in Nel Noddings's (2005a, 2005b) ideal teacher who focuses on the nurturing of "competent, caring, loving, and lovable persons." To that end, she describes teaching as a caring profession in which teachers should convey to students the caring way in thinking about one's self, siblings, and strangers, and about animals, plants, and the physical environment. She stresses the affective aspect of teaching: the need to focus on the child's strengths and interests, the need for an individualized curriculum built around the child's abilities and needs, and the need to develop sound character.

Caring, according to Noddings (2002, 2003, 2005a, 2005b, 2007, 2008), cannot be achieved by a formula or checklist. It calls for different behaviors for different situations—from tenderness to tough love. Good teaching, like good parenting, requires continuous effort, trusting relationships, and continuity of purpose—the purpose of caring, appreciating human connections, and respecting people and ideas from a historical, multicultural, and diverse perspective. The teacher is not only concerned about educating students to be proficient in reading and mathematics but also about making classrooms happy places and helping students become happy with life (Noddings, 2003).

Noddings is not alone in her view. Several researchers have written about providing a caring environment for students (Cohen et al., 2021; Comer, 1980; Comer, 1999; Comer, Joyner, & Ben-Avie, 2004; Darling-Hammond, et al., 2019; Fullan & Gallagher, 2020; Kramer, 2021a; Murphy, 2016c; Seif, 2021; Willis, 2021). Furthermore, several researchers have written extensively about the principal's role in establishing a caring environment in schools and classrooms (Glickman & Burns, 2020; Kramer, 2021b; Leithwood, 2018; Smylie, Murphy, & Louis, 2020a, 2020b). An analysis of their work revealed that teachers who showed empathy and warmth (a caring orientation), encouraged higher-order thinking, and used a nondirective teaching approach were more likely than other teachers to have students who had more positive attitudes toward school, had better attendance and behavior in school, and scored significantly higher on reading/language arts and mathematics tests. These students also were more likely to manifest higher levels of class participation, score higher on measures of self-efficacy, and were less likely to drop out of school.

It is important for principals to be familiar with the vast amount of research that is now accumulating with respect to establishing a *caring* and *socially supportive* environment in classrooms and schools. Principals need to share this research with teachers and understand it as a comprehensive approach to teaching. Applied as a whole, the humanistic approach to teaching is a means of helping students attain intended outcomes. The humanistic approach to teaching can serve as a useful guide for principals who are working with beginning or experienced teachers. The principles of humanistic teaching can serve as a basis for dialogue between the principal and teacher about the teacher's classroom instruction.

PSYCHOSOCIAL AND COGNITIVE DEVELOPMENT

Students vary in how they perceive and think about learning. This observation implies that principals and teachers need to be aware of the ways in which students differ from one another to design potentially effective lessons. The best instructional planning and designs are based on the teacher's knowledge of theoretical frames of learning. Theoretical frames, although not prescriptive, are useful to teachers because they make them more aware of how learning takes place and how students acquire, retain, and recall knowledge. Additionally, teachers can use the learning theories as guidelines to help them in instructional planning, specifically in selecting instructional tools, techniques, and strategies to enable students to successfully complete course objectives. This section deals with how students may differ from one another in psychosocial development, cognitive development, and learning style. Principals and teachers will also discover how those differences affect classroom learning.

More precisely, this section focuses on several frameworks to facilitate academic/personal growth and learning: J. P. Guilford's structure of intellect, Jean Piaget's stages of intellectual development, Lawrence Kohlberg's stages of moral development, Nel Noddings's care theory, Carol Gilligan's view of moral development, Rita and Kenneth Dunn's learning styles theory, and Howard Gardner's multiple intelligences. Each one will be discussed in turn. The principles of students' psychosocial development, cognitive development, and learning style can serve as a useful guide for principals who are working with beginning or experienced teachers. They can serve as a basis for dialogue with teachers about instruction.

Guilford: Structure of Intellect

For many years, there has been a tendency to think of the intellect as a generalized entity that functions on a generalized level in all situations. In contrast, J. P. Guilford (1967) identifies three primary mental abilities, broken down into 120 intellectual factors that may be considered necessary to perform well on a particular task. These primary mental abilities are depicted in figure 4.1.

In his **structure of intellect** model, Guilford classifies and organizes the primary mental abilities according to (a) contents or type of information dealt with, (b) the operations to be performed on the information, and (c) the products resulting from the processing of the information. Instructionally, Guilford's second classification

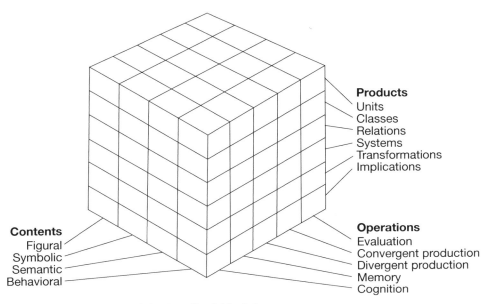

Products
Units
Classes
Relations
Systems
Transformations
Implications

Contents
Figural
Symbolic
Semantic
Behavioral

Operations
Evaluation
Convergent production
Divergent production
Memory
Cognition

Figure 4.1 Structure of the Intellect Model

is probably most useful from the standpoint of principals sharing with teachers, because operations performed on the information refer directly to the major kinds of intellectual processes. The intellectual processes (operations) are as follows:

1. *Cognition.* Intellectual abilities concerned with the discovery or rediscovery of information; these abilities include comprehension and understanding.
2. *Memory.* Intellectual abilities associated with the retention or storage of information cognized.
3. *Divergent thinking.* Intellectual abilities related to the generation of new information from known information, with the emphasis on variety and quantity of information. In this case, thinking goes in varying directions, with no real "right" answer being sought.
4. *Convergent thinking.* Intellectual abilities related to the generation of new information that leads to the right or conventionally accepted answer. In this case, the given or known information usually determines the correct response.
5. *Evaluation.* Intellectual abilities related to the intellectual process by which judgments and decisions are made regarding the goodness, correctness, adequacy, or suitability of information, based on some criterion of consistency or goal satisfaction that resulted from productive thinking.

Guilford's thinking abilities (operations) can be thought of in terms of both their products (units, classes, relations, systems, transformations, and implications) and their content (behavioral, semantic, symbolic, or figural). A major shortcoming in much curriculum planning and instruction is that too much attention is directed toward the products of thinking and not enough to the operations and contents as indicated in the Guilford model. This deficiency needs to be corrected if the precision in planning instructional strategies is to result in predictable behavior changes in students who are exposed to purposeful teaching.

Note in Guilford's model that each of the intellectual processes (operations) is used to deal with processing products in various contents. For instance, students can be taught to comprehend units, classes, relations, systems, transformations, and implications in different content (behavioral, semantic, symbolic, or figural mediums). In the case of comprehending units (segregated items of information that have a single character), the teacher is primarily concerned with informational items or facts. The comprehension of units involves the recognition of visual, auditory, and even emotional units. With respect to instruction, this involves recognizing word structure and knowing the meanings of words in a variety of contexts.

The comprehension of classes (sets of items of information that are grouped by common properties) involves classifying groups of objects or ideas according to a prescribed criterion. At this point, the teacher is concerned with the process of concept formation. At this point, students are in the most critical phase of instructional activity: If students do not learn how to deal intellectually with units and classes, they will be unable to deal effectively with the remaining products (relations, systems, transformations, and implications) depicted in the Guilford model. This appears to be one of the most important keys to ensuring instructional effectiveness and developing basic understanding in pupils at all levels of instruction.

The comprehension of relations (connections between the units of information based on certain points of contact that are applicable to them) involves helping students to discover relationships that exist among objects, symbols, or conceptual material when arranged according to some pattern.

The comprehension of systems (organized complexities of interrelated or interacting items of information) involves the abilities to structurally arrange objects in a given space; to discover patterns or systems among figural, symbolic, semantic, or behavioral elements; and to cognize or structure a problem preparatory to solving it. The comprehension of systems is more involved than the activity suggested in being able to see simple relationships, for it has to do with the organized total of a given structure. Frequently, this involves several simple relationships, fitted together in a conceptual structure that forms the system under consideration.

The comprehension of transformations (changes in existing, known information or in the actual use of information) involves the ability to form a mental image of patterns that would be possible if objects were rearranged in some way. An example is when a player creates a mental projection of a chessboard through several moves. Another ability required in the comprehension of transformations is predictive manipulation of available data to suggest a solution to a future problem. If students are to be taught to deal intellectually with transformations, they must be instructed in the processing of data, the detection of trends, and the development of strategies for theoretical formulation of plausible solutions to problems gleaned from the interpretation of selected data and trends.

The comprehension of implications (extrapolations of information, which can take the form of expectancies, predictions, concomitants, or consequences) involves attempts to plan or predict outcomes that might result from present conditions. In order to deal with implications, pupils must be taught to select the most effective solution to a problem from among a number of alternatives, to validate the process, and to anticipate the likely consequences given a particular situation and a certain arrangement of events.

Knowledge of Guilford's primary mental abilities is potentially useful in analyzing the kinds of instructional activities practiced and planned. In observing classroom activities, a principal can determine whether balanced intellectual development is being encouraged. In analyzing curriculum guides and textbooks, a principal can discover whether balanced intellectual development is an objective, and if it is planned adequately. Of course, this does not imply that intellectual factors should be sought in every teaching unit or daily lesson plan. Nevertheless, awareness of the factors should enable a principal, formally or informally, to analyze curriculum planning and practice.

The teaching of higher-level thinking skills is a topic that appeals to most teachers. These skills include comprehension of text, scientific processes, and problem solving. Although much has been written about the need for students to perform higher-level thinking operations in all subject areas, the teaching of these operations often fails because the instruction is inadequate.

Piaget: Cognitive Development

Jean Piaget (1950), a Swiss psychologist, theorizes that intellective capability undergoes qualitative developmental changes linked to the child's maturation. In this connection, Piaget identifies four developmental stages, each one a necessary condition for subsequent intellective development. Although all children pass through these stages, it is important to recognize that all students in a given classroom will not be at the same cognitive developmental stage. Piaget's **stages of cognitive development** are the following:

1. *Sensory motor stage.* The sensory motor stage, which lasts from birth to about two years, is the prelanguage stage; it is vital to the development of thinking. During this stage, the child learns the rudimentary concepts of space, time, casualty, and intentionality.

2. *Preoperational stage.* True language begins during the preoperational state, which extends between the representative ages of two to six years. During this stage, the child learns to label with words the external world around him and to express his own feelings through language. He learns to adjust to the world through trial and error, to extract concepts from experience, and later to make perceptual and intuitive judgments. However, the child adopts an egocentric orientation, a cognitive state in which the cognizer sees the world from a single point of view only—his own—unaware of the existence of viewpoints or perspectives of others. Instruction during this stage must focus on repeated and forced social interaction with others in order to fortify reflective thought and relinquish the child's egocentric orientation.

3. *Concrete operational stage.* During the concrete operational stage, which occurs between seven and eleven years, the child can move things around and make them fit properly with developed fine motor skills. She can attack physical problems by anticipating consequences perceptually. However, because the student is dependent on personal experience during this time, instruction must be appropriately arranged and must be concrete. For example, the

concept of a rural environment can be understood by an urban student who sees a movie, videotape, or picture depicting farms, tractors, barns, and silos, rather than hearing a verbal description only.

4. *Formal operational stage.* During the formal operational stage, which develops between twelve and sixteen years, the child is no longer tied to concrete reasoning about objects. The child can think hypothetically, reason through the possible process of a logical solution, perform a controlled experiment, and reach some possible conclusion. Instruction can be organized by classifying, seriating, and corresponding. The results of these operations for learners are logical thinking and the intellectual processes of inference, implication, identity, conjunction, and disjunction.

Each successive stage of Piagetian theory requires more abstract thinking, and, therefore, a prime difficulty for the teacher involves selecting subject matter content that is abstract enough to challenge without being so abstract as to frustrate the student. When this is done properly, it is possible to build a spiral curriculum in which basic concepts are structured in such a way that they are used at different levels of abstraction dependent on the age and ability of the students. For example, Hilda Taba (1971) illustrates a hierarchical arrangement of concepts that allows each level to be prerequisite to the subsequent level. Concepts are taught at increasing levels of complexity and abstraction as they thread their way through the curriculum.

Kohlberg: Moral Development

Numerous efforts have been made to examine systematically moral behavior as a developmental process. Lawrence Kohlberg (1969, 1976, 1978), a Harvard psychologist, developed a typological scheme describing general structures of moral thought. Like Piaget's framework, it is a cognitive-developmental theory that proceeds through a series of qualitative distinct stages. In this regard, Kohlberg postulates that the sequence of stages is invariant and that each stage represents a reorganization and displacement of preceding stages. He believes that cognitive conflict is the central condition for reorganization. Unlike Piaget's stages of development, Kohlberg's stages are not strictly linked to ages and extend into the late twenties. However, according to Kohlberg, many people never reach the highest stages of moral development.

Kohlberg (1978) identifies three distinct **levels of moral thinking.** Within each level. There are two stages, thus making a total of six stages that may be considered as separate moral philosophies.

- *Preconventional level.* Although Kohlberg's scheme is not strictly linked to ages, the individual at the preconventional level is typically a preadolescent. To a person at this level, moral value resides in externally imposed cultural rules and labels of good or bad or right and wrong. Thus, the individual interprets moral value in terms of physical or hedonistic consequences of action, such as punishment, reward, exchange of favors; or in terms of the physical power of those who enunciate the rules. The stage 1 individual embraces an *obedience-punishment orientation;* that is, the person has an egocentric deference to superior power and authority, or a trouble-avoiding set. The stage

2 individual has a *naively egoistic orientation*. He or she believes that right action is that which instrumentally satisfies the self's need and occasionally the needs of others. Naive egalitarianism and orientation to exchange the reciprocity along the lines of "you scratch my back and I'll scratch yours" is representative of such a focus.

- *Conventional level*. Chronologically, the individual at the conventional level is an adolescent. To a person at this level, moral value resides in good or right roles, in maintaining and conforming to the conventional order and the expectations of others. The stage 3 individual embraces an *interpersonal concordance orientation* in the good boy–nice girl vein. Thus, the person has an orientation to approval and pleasing and helping others. Conformity to stereotypical images of majority behavior and approval by being "nice" are typical manifestations. The stage 4 individual has an *authority and social-order orientation*. Orientations to authority, fixed rules, "doing duty," and maintaining the social order for its own sake are representative behaviors.
- *Postconventional level*. The individual at the postconventional level is of adult age; however, Kohlberg believes that less than 20 percent of adult society act at the *principled level*, as it is also called. To a person at this level moral values and principles are validated and applied apart from authority or conformity to group membership, though these values and principles are seen as shareable. The stage 5 individual embraces a *contractual-legalistic orientation*. Thus, the person has an awareness of the relativism of personal values and opinions and a corresponding emphasis on procedural rules for reaching consensus. Duty defined in terms of contract, general avoidance, or violation of the will or rights of others, and majority will and welfare are manifestations of such an orientation. The stage 6 individual has a *conscience or principle orientation*. Orientation to principles of choice involving appeal to logical universality and consistency, and to mutual respect and trust with conscience as a directing agent are representative of such a focus.

Many contemporary educators view morality as something as beyond intelligence. Such a perspective creates a schism between the two. Is not an intelligent person a moral being? Dewey (1916) points out that if subject matter is treated merely as knowledge acquisition, then it has only limited technical worth, but when subject matter is engaged in "under conditions where its social significance is realized, it feeds moral interests and develops moral insights" (p. 414).

Some research (Colby, Kohlberg, & DeVries, 1987) has found an association between moral reasoning and measured intelligence. However, Kohlberg asserts that although one has to be cognitively mature to reason morally, one can be intelligent and never reason morally. He connects moral growth with social development, especially the amount of opportunity for role taking.

Kohlberg's (1978) findings suggest implications for teaching. The social life of school and classrooms provide numerous opportunities for moral learning, especially if educators deliberately structure programs that facilitate the movement from one development stage to another. This demands an intimate knowledge of the individual and a program that involves discussion and problem solving.

Gilligan: View of Moral Development

Carol Gilligan (1982, 1988) examines the limitations of Kohlberg's stages of moral development and concludes that Kohlberg's developmental theory has not given adequate attention to the concerns and experience of women. Gilligan argues that Kohlberg's view of moral development more accurately describes what occurs with adolescent males than with adolescent females. In Gilligan's view, Kohlberg's ideas emphasize separation from parental authority and social conventions. Instead of remaining loyal to adult authority, individuals as they mature shift their loyalty to abstract principles (e.g., self-reliance, independence, justice, and fairness). This process allows adolescents to move closer to adulthood.

Gilligan argues that many adolescent females have a different primary concern. They care less about separation and independence and more about remaining loyal to others through expressions of care, responsibility, and relationships. Detachment for these female adolescents is a moral problem rather than a desired developmental stage.

Gilligan's view implies that because females are socialized to value more highly the qualities of care, responsibility, and relationships than that of preserving individual rights, females are more likely to be judged to be at a lower level of moral development than males. Gilligan argues for an expanded conception of adulthood that would result from an integration of the "feminine voice" into developmental theory.

In her book, *In a Different Voice: Psychological Theory and Women's Development* (1982), Gilligan challenges the notion that moral development is the same for girls and boys. For boys, the higher stages of moral development recognize notions of the rights of individuals, and girls tend to view issues in terms of care, responsibility, and relationships. She pinpoints adolescence as a critical time in women's lives. By incorporating gender differences into their work, which Gilligan suggests, researchers can more effectively study adolescent development, prevent psychological suffering, and strengthen women's voices in the world.

Noddings: Care Theory

Nel Noddings (2002, 2003, 2005a, 2005b, 2007, 2008, 2010, 2015), an educational philosopher, has written extensively about establishing a caring environment in classrooms. She describes teaching as a caring profession in which teachers care about students as people and want to help them maximize their learning. She stresses the affective aspect of teaching: the need to focus on the child's strengths and interests, the need for an individualized curriculum built around the child's abilities and needs, and the need to develop sound character.

Caring, according to Noddings (2002, 2003), cannot be achieved by a formula or checklist. It calls for different behaviors for different situations—from tenderness to tough love. According to Noddings, good teaching, like good parenting, requires continuous effort, trusting relationships, and continuity of purpose—the purpose of caring, appreciating human connections, and respecting people and ideas from a historical, multicultural, and diverse perspective. The teacher is not only concerned about educating students to be proficient in reading and mathematics but also about making classrooms happy places and helping students become happy with life. Noddings (2003) asserts that happiness should be an explicit and high-priority goal for educators.

Noddings is supported by other humanistic researchers in her view of caring in schools. Allender and Allender (2008) note that the curriculum should emphasize a student's interests because a student's curiosity will likely lead to high levels of motivation and initial successful learning. Johnson and Thomas (2009) argue that the ideal time to establish a caring environment is in the early grades. Such an environment, according to Johnson and Thomas (2009), promotes a sense of community, safety, learning-oriented values, and positive interpersonal experiences in the later grades. Beverly Falk (2009) comments that children who are in a caring environment develop a sense of self-worth necessary to achieve real learning. More recent research supports the leader's role in facilitating a caring school environment (see, for exmple, Louis & Murphy, 2016; Louis, Murphy, & Smylie, 2016; Smylie, Murphy, & Louis, 2016, 2020a, 2020b).

Dunn and Dunn: Learning Styles

Dr. Paul Witty, one of America's foremost psychologists and educators, once related a story about an experience he had with an elementary school child. After working with the child for several hours, the child still failed to learn a certain task. In frustration, Dr. Witty pushed the materials away and said to the child, "What's wrong with you?" Without a moment's hesitation, the child said, "What's wrong with me? What's wrong with you? You what's wrong!" (Prashnig, 2006). This story describes a feeling that each of us has had. We try everything, and the child still cannot learn, What's wrong with the child? We know that the child is not at fault. We have not found the key as to how this child learns.

Knowing how students learn is of particular interest to teachers. While each student possesses unique ways of learning that have become a part of their personalities, they also share many learning similarities. Being aware of how students learn enables teachers to structure learning experiences in the curriculum (Carter, Bishop, & Kravits, 2014); however, each student will approach these learning experiences in a personal, individualized way.

More than a decade of continuing research on student learning styles has revealed that, when taught through methods that complemented their learning characteristics, students at all levels became increasingly motivated and performed better academically. Essentially, **learning style** can be defined as a consistent pattern of behavior that gives general direction to learning. However, rather than simply looking at learning styles in isolation, teachers need to understand styles as they are exhibited in the classroom, interacting and influencing one another in a variety of ways.

Rita Dunn and Kenneth Dunn (1992; Dunn, Dunn, & Perrin, 1994) identify eighteen elements of learning style that they further subdivide into four stimuli areas: environmental, emotional, sociological, and physical. Each one will be discussed in turn. These four stimuli areas are shown in figure 4.2.

Environmental Elements: Sound, Light, Temperature, and Design. According to Dunn and Dunn (1992), studies have revealed that regardless of age, ability, socioeconomic status, or achievement level, individuals respond uniquely to their immediate environment. For example, some students require absolute silence when concentrating; others do not. Students also respond differently to temperature; some require a cool environment and others prefer to feel comfortably warm. Learners also respond differently to the amount of light available; some require soft light when concentrating and others prefer bright illumination. Finally, some students perform better

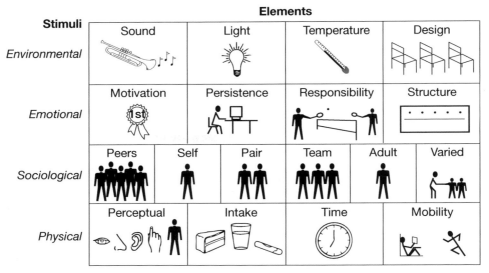

Figure 4.2 Diagnosing Learning Styles

in an informal physical environment (carpeting, lounge chairs, couches) and others achieve better in a formal setting (desks, "hard" chairs, and tables).

Emotional Elements: Motivation, Persistence, Responsibility, and Need for Structure. Motivated, persistent, responsible students need to be told what they are required to learn, what resources to use, how to demonstrate their acquired knowledge, and where to get help if needed. They welcome praise and feedback when the assignment has been completed. The unmotivated, less persistent, less responsible students require short assignments, frequent feedback, a lot of supervision, and praise as they are working.

Structure is another vital element of learning style. Students who require specific directions, sequential tasks, frequent feedback, and continuing support usually achieve well using programmed learning—if they are highly visual or visual-tactual and able to work alone. If youngsters are tactual-kinesthetic and also peer oriented, programmed material may not hold their attention. If they need structure, they are tactual-kinesthetic (but not highly auditory or visual), and find learning difficult, they may do better with multisensory instructional packages.

Learners who tend to be creative, self-structured, or responsive to making choices appear to perform best with Contract Activity Packages (CAPS). Teachers experienced in the effective use of CAPS can decrease the amount of flexibility and the number of options provided, thus making contracts suitable for youngsters who require imposed structure.

Sociological Elements: Working Alone, With Peers, With an Adult, or Some Combination. Some students learn best alone. For them, depending on whether they are auditory, visual, tactual, or kinesthetic, and whether or not they need structure, a Contract Activity Package, a program, and instructional package, or various tactual-kinesthetic resources (task cards, learning circles, or electroboards) should be prescribed.

Other learners achieve best when among their peers: for these Circles of Knowledge, cooperative learning groups, case studies, brainstorming exercises, and other small-group techniques tend to facilitate learning.

Youngsters who require interaction with an adult will benefit from lectures, discussions, or teacher-directed studies. However, it should be determined whether the relationship that is sought is authoritarian or collegial before suggesting whether large or small groups would be more effective.

Physical Elements: Perceptual Strengths, Intake, Time of Day, and Need for Mobility. During the past few years, researchers have found that only between 20 and 30 percent of school-age children appear to be auditory. Approximately 40 percent are visual, and the remaining 30 to 40 percent are either tactual/kinesthetic, visual/tactual, or some combination of these four senses.

Other elements that either permit or inhibit learning is the need to eat or drink, the time of day, and the ability to remain stationary for longer or shorter periods of time. Teachers mistakenly label some students "hyperactive" when they are either light-sensitive or require a great deal of mobility. Many of these students can learn well when they are assigned tasks that require them to move from area to area or when permitted to take frequent breaks.

Most of the eighteen elements of learning style can be accommodated easily by developing students' awareness of their own styles, permitting some flexibility, and then gradually developing the types of resources that complement learning styles.

Gardner: Multiple Intelligences

Howard Gardner (1994, 1999, 2005, 2007), like Guilford, contends that a variety of mental operations are associated with intelligence. First, he states that the theory is an account of human cognition in its fullness. He promotes the intelligences as a new definition of cognitive human nature. He says there are many different types of intelligences, although the society tends to focus on verbal or linguistic factors. He has described human beings as organisms who possess a basic set of seven, eight, or a dozen intelligences (Gardner, 1994, 1999, 2005, 2007).

Gardner (1994) proposes seven relatively independent forms of competence: linguistic, logical-mathematical, spatial, musical, bodily-kinesthetic, interpersonal, and intrapersonal. He later adds an eighth intelligence, the naturalist (Gardner, 1999). Although Sternberg (1994) has noted the lack of empirical support for the theory, Gardner's theory has been widely received by educators and provides a useful framework for understanding the basic skill level of all people as well as the unique strengths of individuals. An individual's uniqueness and cognitive competence are based on a combination of the **multiple intelligences**.

- *Linguistic intelligence* is the capacity to use language, native language and other languages, to express oneself and to understand other people. Poets, writers, orators, speakers, lawyers, or a person for whom language is a strong part of her livelihood demonstrate linguistic intelligence.
- *Logical-mathematical intelligence* is the ability to understand the underlying principles of some kind of a causal system—to manipulate numbers, quantities, and operations, like scientists and mathematicians do.
- *Spatial intelligence* is the ability to represent the spatial world mentally, as when a sailor or pilot navigates large space or when a painter, a sculptor, or an architect envisions a design.
- *Bodily kinesthetic intelligence* is the capacity to use the whole body or parts of the body to solve a problem, make something, or perform. This intelligence

is seen in people who are athletic or who are in the performing arts in dance and theater.

- *Musical intelligence* is the ability to think in music; to hear patterns, recognize them, remember them, and maneuver them.
- *Interpersonal intelligence* is the ability to understand others. People who excel in this intelligence are usually teachers, clinicians, salespersons, and politicians.
- *Intrapersonal intelligence* is having an understanding of yourself; knowing who you are, what you can do, what you want, when you need help, how you respond to events, what to avoid, and what to do.
- *Naturalist intelligence* designates the human ability to differentiate among living things (plants, animals) as well as to demonstrate sensitivity to the natural world (clouds, rock configurations) as seen in farmers, botanists, chefs, or meteorologists. The type of pattern recognition ability respected in some of the sciences may also relate to naturalist intelligence.

(Gardner, 1999)

ACCOUNTABILITY IN EDUCATION: HIGH-STAKES TESTING

What does it mean to be held accountable? The school district and the administrators and teachers who work in it are accountable for student learning. This assertion has strong economic, political, and social appeal; its logic is clear. What teachers teach and students learn is a matter of public inspection and subject to direct measurement (Elmore, 2004).

Accountability for school improvement is a central theme of state policies. Every Student Succeeds Act of 2015 sets demanding accountability standards for schools, school districts, and states, including state testing requirements designed to improve education. For example, the law requires that states develop both content standards in reading, mathematics, and science and tests that are linked to the standards. States must identify adequate yearly progress (AYP) objectives and disaggregate test results for all students and subgroups of students based on socioeconomic status, race/ethnicity, English language proficiency, and disability.

How does the push for accountability affect teachers, principals, and entire school districts? School administrators have always had to deal with bureaucratic accountability—that is, accountability with respect to superordinate-subordinate relationships. For example, the teacher is accountable to the principal; the principal is accountable to the superintendent; and the superintendent is accountable to the school board. However, accountability to constituencies external to the local school board increasingly drives accountability frameworks today. The business community pressures schools to graduate skilled workers for today's economy. Governors and state legislators play key roles in designing accountability plans. The national education plan, titled Every Student Succeeds Act, stipulates specific requirements that states must follow regarding accountability for student achievement.

As accountability has become more prominent at the state and national levels, the focus has shifted from accountability for inputs or transformation processes to accountability for outcomes. This is reflected in state standards and testing. Presently, all fifty states have statewide assessment systems in place, and in nearly half of the states the stakes attached to these outcomes have been gradually increased (Popham,

2010, 2020). The reason for the shift from accountability for inputs and processes to accountability for outcomes can be traced to a growing discontent during the past three decades with the perceived quality of education in America.

In 1983, the National Commission on Excellence in Education published a report titled *A Nation at Risk: The Imperative for Educational Reform*. The report portrayed an overall decline in the quality of education in America. It indicated, for example, that approximately 13 percent of all seventeen-year-olds were found to be functionally illiterate, that standardized test scores had generally declined below levels achieved twenty-five years earlier, and that many seventeen-year-olds were found to be deficient in such higher-order thinking skills as drawing inferences from written material and writing a persuasive essay. To correct these deficiencies, the National Commission on Excellence in Education called for standardized tests to be used as a way of documenting students' achievement and urging educators to focus on raising student achievement in such basic areas as reading, mathematics, and science. Discontent with the performance of students in the United States resulted in two major reform efforts: the No Child Left Behind Act and (its successor, the Every Student Succeeds Act) and the Common Core Standards, each of which uses standardized test scores to hold educators accountable.

Every Student Succeeds Act

On December 10, 2015, President Barack Obama signed into law the Every Student Succeeds Act (ESSA), the most recent reauthorization of the Elementary and Secondary Education Act (ESEA) of 1965, replacing the now defunct No Child Left Behind Act of 2001. The new law builds on key areas of progress made in previous years, including testing of students in reading, mathematics, and science in all public schools. ESSA reaffirms the American ideal—that all children, regardless of race, income, background, or address, deserve the chance to make of their lives whatever they wish. The practice of using the scores from these tests to determine rewards and sanctions (e.g., whether students get promoted, graduate from high school, whether principals, teachers, and schools receive bonuses, whether school districts receive additional state funds or lose accreditation) is commonly referred to as **high-stakes testing**. Principals need to support teachers in the use of ESSA to improve student achievement.

Requirements of ESSA. The Every Student Succeeds Act contains several requirements that states must meet (Every Student Succeeds Act of 2015, Pub L. No. 114-95 Stat. 1177):

Standards. The law provides that states must establish challenging content and achievement standards in reading, mathematics, and science; the legislation leaves it up to each state to decide the meaning of the word *challenging*.

Testing. The law provides that states must test all students in grades three through twelve in reading, mathematics, and science annually; the legislation leaves it up to each state to decide on test format, length, and item type.

Adequate yearly progress (AYP). The law provides that all students must score at least at the "proficient" level defined by each state on their state assessment tests in reading/language arts, mathematics, and science. States must demonstrate each year that a certain additional percentage of all students have met that goal, referred to as adequate yearly progress, or AYP. Adequate yearly progress must be demonstrated by all groups of students, including racial and ethnic minorities, students of low socioeconomic status (SES), English language learners, and students with disabilities. Schools that fail to meet the AYP requirement must use different instructional approaches that are research based.

Reporting. The law provides that states and school districts must issue report cards to parents and the general public that describe how every group of students has performed on the annual assessment.

Accountability system. The law provides that school districts that fail to achieve AYP for two or more consecutive years are subject to sanctions.

(see Every Student Succeeds Act of 2015, Pub L. No. 114-95 Stat. 1177)

Common Core Standards. The impetus for the **Common Core Standards** resulted from allowing states to establish their own content standards and assessment measures under the NCLB legislation. The standards established by the states ranged from weak to rigorous and the tests used to measure the standards varied in quality (Porter et al., 2011; Snowman & McCown, 2015). To remedy this deficiency, the National Governors Association and the Council of Chief State School Officers sponsored a program that would create rigorous tests for reading/language arts, mathematics, and science for grades K–12. The standards were published in 2010. By 2012, most states had adopted the Common Core Standards (Center on Education Policy, 2012; Common Core Standards Initiative, 2012).

With content standards in place, there was a need to have tests that measure how well students learned the standards and the quality of the teacher's instruction. Two groups began developing a testing program: Partnership for Assessment Readiness for College and Careers (PARCC) and the Smarter Balanced Assessment Consortium (SBAC). The items created by these two groups were to be more rigorous than those contained in most state standardized tests (Snowman & McCown, 1015). In recent years, several states have either withdrawn their support or are reconsidering their participation (Crowder, 2014; Eppley, 2015; Kern, 2014; Knoester & Parkinson, 2015; Murphy & Torff, 2016). Criticism of the Common Core Curriculum include the following (Glickman, Gordon, & Ross-Gordon, 2018; Snowman & McCown, 2015): its exclusive focus on preparing students for college and employment, lack of field testing preceding adoption, its one-size-fits-all content, perceived reduction in teachers' capacity for effective teaching, and intrusion into local control of schools.

SUMMARY

1. Teacher behavior research has shown that teacher behaviors, as well as specific teaching principles and strategies, make a difference regarding student achievement. We analyzed the process-product models of Nathaniel Gage, Thomas Good and Alyson Lavigne, Carolyn Evertson and Edmund Emmer, and Walter Doyle. Their research focused on teacher effectiveness and on the products or results of teaching.

2. Teaching, because it is an extremely complex process dealing with many variables, has been difficult to analyze. Research on teaching and learning accumulated during the last four decades has provided a variety of teaching techniques that may be utilized effectively by teachers

as they interact with, facilitate, and direct students within their educational settings. We examined ten durable, research-based instructional strategies: anticipatory set, stimulus variation, closure, reinforcement, recognizing attending behavior, questioning, lecturing, planned repetition, establishing appropriate frames of references, and race, class, and gender equity.

3. A combination of high academic press (i.e., high standards for academic performance) and high social support (i.e., students perceive that teachers care about them) seem to be associated with higher achievement gains, especially for low-income students. This model is supported by research conducted by Shouse (1996), Lee and Smith (1999), Gregory and Weinstein (2004), Pellerin (2005), and Bulach and Lunenburg (2008, 2011).

4. The humanistic approach to teaching is student-centered instruction. Teachers who use a humanistic approach create a classroom environment in which students believe that the teacher's primary goal is to understand the student's cognitive and emotional needs, values, motives, and self-perceptions and to help the student to learn.

5. Students vary in how they perceive and think about learning. This observation implies that teachers need to be aware of the ways in which students differ from one another to design potentially effective lessons. Students may differ from one another in psychosocial development, cognitive development, and learning style. Those differences affect learning.

6. Several frameworks to facilitate academic/personal growth and learning include: Jean Piaget's stages of intellectual development, Lawrence Kohlberg's stages of moral development, Nel Noddings's care theory, Carol Gilligan's view of moral development, Rita and Kenneth Dunn's learning styles theory, and Howard Gardner's multiple intelligences.

7. In 1983, the National Commission on Excellence in Education published a report titled *A Nation at Risk: The Imperative for Educational Reform.* The report portrayed an overall decline in the quality of education in America. This report launched the push for accountability in the United States and subsequently led to the high-stakes testing movement in America's public schools. The federal government became involved in high-stakes testing in 2001 when Congress passed the No Child Left Behind Act (NCLB). The goal of the now defunct NCLB and its replacement Every Student Succeeds Act (ESSA) is to have all students score at least at the proficient level in reading/language arts, mathematics, and science.

8. Allowing states to establish their own content standards and assessment measures under the NCLB legislation was the impetus for the Common Core Standards. The standards established by the states under NCLB ranged from weak to rigorous and the tests used to measure the standards varied in quality. To remedy this deficiency, the National Governors Association and the Council of Chief State School Officers sponsored a program that would create rigorous tests for reading/language arts, mathematics, and science for grades K–12. The

standards were published in 2010. By 2012, most states had adopted the Common Core Standards.

9. With content standards in place, there was a need to have tests that measure how well students learned the standards and the quality of the teacher's instruction. Two groups began developing a testing program: Partnership for Assessment Readiness for College and Careers (PARCC) and the Smarter Balanced Assessment Consortium (SBAC). The items created by these two groups were to be more rigorous than those contained in most state standardized tests. In recent years, several states have either withdrawn their support or are reconsidering their participation. Criticism of the Common Core Curriculum include the following: its exclusive focus on preparing students for college and employment, lack of field testing preceding adoption, its one-size-fits-all content, perceived reduction in teachers' capacity for effective teaching, and intrusion into local control of schools.

KEY TERMS

master teacher
anticipatory set
stimulus variation
closure
reinforcement
recognizing attending behavior
questioning
formal lecture
informal lecture
planned repetition
appropriate frames of reference

academic press
social support
humanistic approach
structure of intellect
stages of cognitive development
levels of moral development
caring
learning styles
multiple intelligences
high-stakes testing
Common Core Standards

FIELD-BASED ACTIVITIES

1. Select a teacher in your building or district whose students achieve high passing rates on the districts' standardized tests. What specific approaches to instruction does the teacher use?

2. Although high-stakes tests are administered in every state and are related to learning standards, there is little evidence about their effects on student achievement. Research the impact of high-stakes testing on student achievement since the enactment of Every Student Succeeds Act of 2015.

3. Discuss the practice of using standardized test scores to determine (a) promotion to the next grade, (b) graduation from high school, (c) receipt or not of additional state funding, (d) job security for teachers and administrators, and (e) school accreditation. Provide reasons for your response.

SUGGESTED READINGS

Brooks, J. G., & Brooks, M. G. (2021). *Schools reimagined: Unifying the science of learning with the art of teaching*. New York, NY: Teachers College Press. The authors provide an approach for putting the intellectual and social-emotional health of students and teachers at center stage.

Darling-Hammond, L., Cook-Harvey, C. M., Flook, L., Gardner, M., & Melnick, H. (2019). *With the whole child in mind: Insights from the Comer School Development Program*. Alexandria, VA: ASCD. Among the many models of school reform that have emerged in the late twentieth and early twenty-first centuries, one that has endured for more than fifty years is James Comer's School development Program (SDP).

McTighe, J., & Ferrara, S. (2021). *Assessing student learning by design: Principles and practices for teachers and school leaders*. New York, NY: Teachers College Press. In a time when high-stakes standardized tests have become the dominant measure of student and teacher success, the authors remind readers that assessment becomes truly valuable as it improves teaching.

Noguera, P. A., Syeed, E. (2020). *City schools and the American dream 2: The enduring promise of public education* (2nd ed.). New York, NY: Teachers College Press. The authors provide concrete examples of innovative strategies and practices employed by urban schools that are succeeding against all odds.

Smylie, M., Murphy, J., & Louis, S. K. (2020). *Caring in school leadership*. Thousand Oaks, CA: Corwin Press. The authors argue for the importance of caring in schools and for the practice of caring leadership as a counterbalance to the emphasis on academic press and accountability.

Tschannen-Moran, M., & Tschannen-Moran, B. (2020). *Evocative coaching: Transforming schools one conversation at a time*. Thousand Oaks, CA: Corwin Press. Evocative coaching is designed to assist teachers to reinvigorate their teaching practices so that students can flourish.

5

Professional Development

■ ■ ■

FOCUSING QUESTIONS

1. What is the principal's mission as it relates to professional development in general?
2. What is the principal's mission as it relates to teachers' professional development?
3. What is the principal's mission for personal professional development?
4. What are the ethics of professional development?

In this chapter, we respond to these questions concerning the importance of professional development and how it relates to student learning. We also examine the concept that schools are places where teachers learn. We begin the chapter with a general discussion of the mission of principals with respect to professional development. This is followed by a more specific discussion of the principal's mission as it relates to teachers' professional development. Next, we examine the principal's mission for her or his own professional development. Finally, we conclude the chapter with a discussion of the ethics of professional development.

THE PRINCIPAL'S MISSION RELATED TO
PROFESSIONAL DEVELOPMENT

Imagine the unveiling of a painting titled "The Ideal Professional Development Situation in a School." What would it look like? Perhaps among the first things to be noticed would be high achievement by the students; high expectations by the principal, the teachers, and the staff; high morale among teachers; and high commitment by the principal, teachers, and staff. You may ask, what underlies this first impression? Come closer; there is a principal who

- is well read, educated in the latest research and best practice; in particular, in leadership;
- defines his or her own personal, professional growth needs according to data received through feedback from teachers, parents, and staff;
- has analyzed his or her impact on the campus;
- is focused on solutions;

- is sensitive to the students and the community;
- thinks forward, and consequentially;
- scans the needs of the teachers, monitors instruction, and disaggregates data on student learning; and
- initiates and implements a collaboratively derived professional development plan for continuous improvement.

The artist's intention is for the onlooker to view the painting of a reformed campus that is a purposefully planned, focused, cohesive, and executed system that yields positive results for all; and there—the focal point, the front and center of the painting—stands the principal.

What is the painter's message? **Professional development** is directly related to improved practice for principals and teachers, yielding subsequent increases in student achievement and overall reform of the school and campus. No reform can take place without a purposeful, coherent, focused, and sustained system that includes professional development. There are *two missions* of the principal related to professional development. First, there is the mission the principal must accomplish as it relates to her teachers' professional growth, and second, there is the mission the principal must attend to as it relates to her own professional growth.

THE PRINCIPAL'S MISSION FOR TEACHERS' PROFESSIONAL DEVELOPMENT

The principal's mission related to his or her teachers' professional development is twofold. The first part of the mission is *to plan*, with teachers, a comprehensive professional development program targeted at identified individual and collective needs. The second part of the mission is *to provide* resources, including time and money, and to include time for teachers to reflect upon and participate in a dialogue about their practice. Darling-Hammond and Oakes (2019) make a strong argument for quality professional development by stating that each dollar spent on improving teachers' qualifications nets greater gains in student learning than any other use of an education dollar.

The National Staff Development Council has called for a shift in the way that principals approach professional development. When the council's recommendations include devoting a full 10 percent of the school budget and 25 percent of teacher time to professional development (Zepeda, 2019), we consider a general gauge for spending education dollars in professional development to be the following. With 80 percent of a school budget being spent on personnel, it appears that a district and/or campus, in the most conservative way, would spend at least 10 percent of the remaining 20 percent on professional development. With either level of funding, principals must monitor the professional development and demand a return on the public's money.

Principals who promote successful professional development experiences for their teachers will, in turn, increase the teachers' interest in and commitment to the profession. Principals should encourage teachers to be the creators of their own professional development, but only when based upon the teachers' critical reflections and self-assessment of their work. When teachers collaborate on and personally plan their own professional development, they have better buy-in to the professional development activities; they see greater relevance in the activities; and, subsequently, they will commit the time required for the activities.

The plan that principals develop with their teachers should be connected to the overall campus improvement plan. Single, disconnected workshops do little to effectively alter instruction and improve learning. Workshops should be ongoing, connected, and embedded in the campus improvement process. The complexity of instruction should be undergirded with inquiry, practice, implementation, reflection, and evaluation. All professional development should be supported by research. Teachers need to have time to make sense of experiences and transform professional knowledge into daily teaching habits (Bransford, Brown, & Cocking, 2021). Without inquiry that imparts the theory and rationale for new instructional techniques or methods, teachers will not understand the "why" of the practice in order to fully embrace it. When teachers (a) understand the practice, (b) have it modeled, and (c) practice it in a risk-free setting with feedback, they can internalize the practice, become comfortable with the practice, and attain the goals of the campus.

HIGH-QUALITY PROFESSIONAL DEVELOPMENT

There is a growing consensus in the literature regarding the elements of effective professional development for principals and teachers. Effective professional development is logically embedded in the reality of schools and teachers' work. It incorporates principles of adult learning (Brookfield, 2013; Knowles, Holton, & Swanson, 2011; Merriam & Baumgartner, 2020; Merriam & Bierema, 2014;): (a) adult learners need to be self-directed; (b) they display readiness to learn when they have a perceived need; and (c) they desire immediate application of new skills and knowledge. Based on adult learning theory, then, principals and teachers would have a need for self-direction, for professional development based on their areas of needed improvement, and for application of what they learn in professional development. Time and created situations during which teachers can dialogue with other teachers, and principals can dialogue with other principals, are critical for effective application of the knowledge gained in professional development sessions.

To be effective, professional development must be internally coherent, rigorous, related to the campus and district vision and mission and the teacher's instructional goals, and sustained over time (Zepeda, 2015). Any professional development that is not sustained and integrated will not be effective to the degree that the principal will desire. Some professional development approaches include university-school partnerships (Darling-Hammond & Oakes, 2019), teacher networks and collaboratives (Martin, Kragler, Quatroche, & Bauserman, 2014), teacher study or inquiry groups (Howell & Saye, 2016; Kroll, 2012), university courses, school district teacher leader cohorts, teacher research, and portfolio development (Martin et al., 2014).

High-quality professional development refers to rigorous and relevant content, strategies, and organizational supports that ensure the preparation and career-long development of teachers and principals whose competence, expectations, and actions influence the teaching and learning environment. The mission of professional development is to prepare and support teachers and principals to help all students achieve to high standards of learning and development. Darling-Hammond et al. (2017; p. v–vi) conducted a comprehensive literature review of thirty-five studies and found seven features of effective professional development. The features are that

Table 5.1 Ten Principles of Effective Professional Development

Effective professional development . . .
1. focuses on teachers as central to student learning, yet includes all other members of the school community;
2. focuses on individual, collegial, and organizational improvement;
3. respects and nurtures the intellectual and leadership capacity of teachers, principals, and others in the school community;
4. reflects best available research and practice in teaching, learning, and leadership;
5. enables teachers to develop further expertise in subject content, teaching strategies, uses of technologies, and other essential elements in teaching to high standards;
6. promotes continuous inquiry and improvement embedded in the daily life of schools;
7. is planned collaboratively by those who will participate in and facilitate that development;
8. requires substantial time and other resources;
9. is driven by a coherent long-term plan; and
10. is evaluated ultimately on the basis of its impact on teacher effectiveness and student learning; and this assessment guides subsequent professional development efforts.

Source: From *The Mission and Principles of Professional Development*, retrieved from http://www.ed.gov/G2K/bridge.html.

the professional development: (a) is content focused on teaching strategies related to curriculum content; (b) engages teachers in active learning where they create and attempt teaching strategies that are not traditional; (c) provides opportunities for teachers to collaborate and share ideas; (d) includes the review of effective practice curriculum and instruction models; (e) provides coaching and expert support to meet teachers' needs; and (f) offers feedback and reflection: Also, principals can provide time and facilitate reflection and soliciting feedback from instructional coaches or peer coaches so that teachers can make changes to their practice and can help them to move toward the expert visions of practice. The ten principles of effective professional development are the following. (See also table 5.1).

Principle 1
Effective professional development focuses on teachers as central to student learning, yet includes all other members of the school community. Many times, professional development is a one-size-fits-all approach; however, effective professional development takes into account the instructional needs of the teacher as they relate *directly to students learning.* As principals consider implementing a systemic approach to professional development on the campus, they will want to consider including support staff (instructional aides, counselors, psychologists, diagnosticians, auxiliary teachers) in those instructional professional development sessions. Instructional aides serve as an extension of teachers while they work with the students; and other support staff should understand what the teacher is trying to accomplish with the students, so that they can strengthen the teacher's instruction in their own fields of support. For example, if a teacher is working on an instructional strategy in reading related to "main idea," other support staff might work on the same topic in their area. The counselor might meet in a group counseling session and support the concept of main idea through an activity. The health and physical education teacher might work with children on main idea through various physical activities.

Principle 2

Effective professional development focuses on individual, collegial, and school improvement. Consider here teachers who might want to expand their knowledge of cooperative learning techniques. While their goal is valid, it becomes relevant only when it is seen in a larger context of school improvement, one that is focused on student learning, driven by data, and nested within school and district curriculum and instructional goals that have been formulated from the vision and mission. In this context, there is an explicit connection between the teachers learning and the results for students.

Principle 3

Effective professional development respects and nurtures the intellectual and leadership capacity of teachers, principals, and others in the school community. Professional development in schools has traditionally consisted of activities such as attending conferences, one-day, one-shot workshops, and make-and-take workshops; or working on curriculum during teacher workshop days. According to Kelleher (2003), such strategies have proved to be inadequate in a number of ways. First, these strategies tend not to help teachers translate new learning into classroom instruction, nor do they nurture the teachers' intellectual capacity. A guest speaker, for example, may be interesting on a personal or professional level, but will the teachers employ the new information in the classroom? Second, these strategies are often not necessarily tied to specific building and district goals for student learning and most often are disconnected from the overall vision and mission of the campus. An example is that if literacy is the campus's top priority, then every workshop should be related to literacy issues. Third, there is usually no assessment mechanism to measure the results of the activities. The principal must, in effect, assess the intellectual capacity of professional development sessions by developing a plan with the teachers. For example, when a teacher attends a conference or a workshop and comes back to the classroom and experiments with the new idea, concepts, or programs, there should be a plan in place to determine how that idea, concept, or program will be assessed as to its effectiveness related to student learning.

The principal, through department, team, or grade-level meetings, inquiry groups, and other forums, can encourage teachers to discuss with colleagues what they have learned and to share materials they have developed through collaboration with peers, workshops, or assessment writing. Principals should keep the focus on connections to student learning by asking the question, "Based on what was learned in this experience, how will instructional practices and student learning change?" Both self-reflection and sharing with colleagues are integral components of professional development itself.

Principle 4

Effective professional development reflects best available research and practice in teaching, learning, and leadership. Some professional development programs have been designed to identify and disseminate scientifically based instructional practices through professional development, resources, and research. Such programs have included (a) identification of scientifically based instructional practices, (b) selection of teams of teachers to attend awareness-level professional development, (c) classroom implementation of scientifically based instructional practice from initial training to quality implementation for all students or specific groups of students, and (d) data

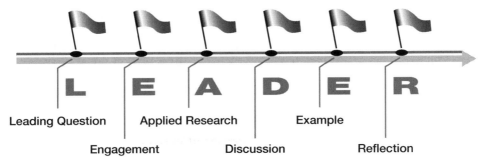

Leading Question **Applied Research** **Example**

Engagement **Discussion** **Reflection**

Figure 5.1 The L.E.A.D.E.R. Five Components for PLCs, VPDs, VPLCs, and VMCs

collection of the results of student learning through traditional and action research methodologies. A principal on a campus could apply such a model, based in research.

Professional development (PD) online has proliferated. PD online with what Irby and colleagues (2020) contextualize as virtual PD (VPD). Within this, they also included the aspect of a professional learning communities (PLC) contextualized as virtual PLCs (VPLCs) which have been supported by a trained virtual mentor-coach (VMC). They built VPD model with Massive Open Online Professional Individualized Learning (MOOPIL) modules (Irby et al., 2017). A MOOPIL VPD is offered on a learning management system as a group process or for individuals. The VPLC with the VMC is a part of the group PD process. Irby and colleagues developed a mentoring and/or coaching process for MOOPIL VPDs that have worked well in practice for either the individual or the VPLC groups. During the VPLCs, VMCs use a process of L.E.A.D.E.R. (Leading Question, Engagement, Applied Research, Discussion, Example(s), and Reflection) and it is shown in figure 5.1. where it is included as the guide for a MOOPIL VPD on the topic of organizational leadership.

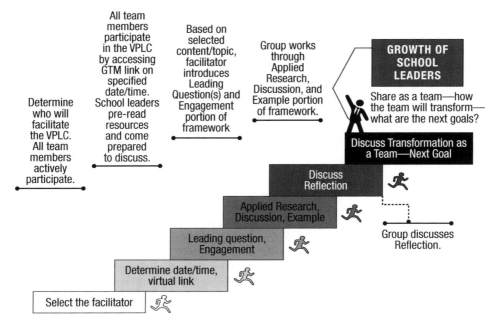

Figure 5.2 VPLC L.E.A.D.E.R. Steps

An example of the L.E.A.D.E.R. is demonstrated in figure 5.2—an applicable example of a VPLC usage in which a VMC leads mentees/coaches and introduces the Leading Question(s) and Engagement portion of the model. Applied Research (information from relevant research studies) is then presented. Next, there is a Discussion that ensues with Examples of the topic of the MOOPIL shared from the teachers' or the leaders' perspectives. Ultimately, there is Reflection that is based on the Brown and Irby (2001) Reflection Cycle which actually ends with the fifth step of Transform. Without transformation of practice based on the new learnings that grow out of the MOOPIL VPDs, there is little to no improved practice. Principals can use these models to increase the teachers' knowledge and improve practice.

Principle 5

Effective professional development enables teachers to develop further expertise in subject content, teaching strategies, uses of technologies, and other essential elements in teaching to high standards. Much of the time, we have seen professional development focused on general topics such as gifted education, self-esteem, communication with parents, or math education. It is hardly ever individualized, planned, and connected to the curriculum or the instructional needs of the teachers, subject matter, or technology needs of the teachers. It rarely connects teachers' reflections on their practice and on their students' achievement to professional development, and often the professional development we see is a one-time shot in the arm. There is no sustained effort to develop instructional knowledge and skills of the teachers that can ultimately lead to changed behaviors. Professional development is key in keeping teachers abreast of current issues in education, assisting them to implement new concepts or innovations, and improving their practice.

Principals should nudge teachers into seeing their subject matter from students' eyes (Darling-Hammond et al., 2019; Garguilo & Metcalf, 2017; Murphy, 2016; Zacarian & Silverstone, 2020). Principals can aid teachers in developing expertise in the content as well as in teaching strategies (Glickman & Burnes, 2020; Joyce, Calhoun, & Weil, 2018). Additionally, when teachers use technology just as students will do in the classroom, then teachers learn that skill to better share with students (Rock, 2019). Becoming a student again is a good way to learn authentically and reexperience one's favorite subject, or to experience the world of technology or other elements related to state or national standards. The national teacher quality grants (former Eisenhower Math and Science grants) provide teachers the opportunity to become students again, learning new subject matter, experiencing firsthand the operation of power plants and waste-water treatment facilities, or testing community water purity levels.

Principle 6

Effective professional development promotes continuous inquiry and improvement embedded in the daily life of schools. Research studies in the area of professional development have supported (a) determining how the newly learned instructional practice is implemented in the classroom, (b) specific guidelines and materials for initial implementation, and (c) ongoing peer coaching (Glickman & Burns, 2020; Joyce & Calhoun, 2019; Rock, 2019; Zepeda, 2018). Incorporating peer coaching into the professional development design dramatically increases the implementation of the training (Tschannen-Moran & Tschannen-Moran, 2020; Zepeda, Goff, &

Steele, 2019). In one of the first and foundational investigations of teachers who participated in professional development workshops but did not receive follow-up peer coaching, it was found that only 10 percent implemented the instructional strategy (Florida Department of Education, 1999).

Action Research. Another way to promote continuous inquiry and improvement is through applied action research, conducted by teachers who want to study their own classroom to improve in their own situation (Congreve, 2015; Shapiro, 2014). In action research, the teacher is the decision maker, data collector, and information source in the research situated in the classroom. **Action research** is a continuous process of planned inquiry to determine the effects of the implementation of an instructional practice on the outcomes of the students in a classroom (Castro Garces & Granada, 2016; Loucks-Horsley et al., 2010). General components of the action research process include: (a) define problems, (b) formulate research questions, (c) plan and implement interventions, (d) collect data, (e) draw conclusions, and (f) make changes accordingly.

Action research, as a professional development experience, can significantly affect teaching and learning. Early in the use of action research, Somekh and Zeichner (2009) reported a meta-analysis of studies of action research activities nationwide, which shows teachers as researchers gaining a new sense of confidence from conducting research, beginning to see themselves as learners, and developing closer relationships with their students and colleagues. Action research involves teachers directly in the selection of immediate and compelling topics to explore with respect to their own practice. Among the many types of teacher research are journaling, video journaling, discussions of practice, data analysis of observations, peer observations, interviews, document analysis, written essays, and/or investigations of specific questions related to student learning and/or teacher practices. The purpose of action research is to improve instruction and learning and impact or change procedures in the classroom, on the campus, or within the district. Action research can ultimately affect policy. Action research continues to be a viable part of professional development that a principal can offer to teachers (Abdullah et al., 2020; Cambereri, 2021; Shanks et al., 2012)

Evaluation Portfolio. Some states, such as Texas, have developed a teacher evaluation and support system (T-TESS), which focuses on providing continuous, timely, and formative feedback to teachers so they can improve their practice. T-TESS is comprised of four domains and sixteen dimensions T-TESS domain and dimension rubrics include specific descriptors of practices and five performance levels: distinguished, accomplished, proficient, developing, and improvement needed. To view the most up-to-date resources and materials for T-TESS, including the rubric, visit teachfortexas.org (Texas Education Agency [TEA], 2021).

Principals can support teacher development by encouraging the inclusion of the teacher evaluation portfolio as an integral component of T-TESS, or other like systems in various states. According to Irby and Brown (2000), by serving as a catalyst for revisions and modifications needed to improve the teacher's pedagogy and subsequent student achievement, the teacher portfolio can (a) provide an organized and systematic vehicle for documentation and reflection in all domains, (b) demonstrate strengths and target areas for needed improvement, and (c) offer teachers' ownership of their own evaluations. The teacher's evaluation portfolio would include items similar to those suggested later for the professional development portfolio.

In addition, the teacher could include artifacts and reflections on peer evaluations, a parent follow-up letter to a conference, or a teaching unit collaboratively developed or singly developed. Other examples might be videotapes of lessons or lesson plans, certificates from workshops or staff development sessions, presentations to colleagues, and class newsletters or other examples that feature student achievement in the classroom or school (Irby & Brown, 2000).

The principal must understand that the key to the teacher portfolio process and teacher growth is the teacher's ability to self-evaluate and reflect upon experiences portrayed by selected artifacts that demonstrate actual teaching practices and that highlight and demonstrate the teacher's knowledge, skills, and attitudes in relation to his work. As teachers reflect on their practice, they are able to critically self-assess the impact of a particular lesson or strategy and clarify future goals and plans for professional development aimed at improved pedagogy. Use of the Reflection Cycle (Irby & Brown, 2000) as described later in this chapter offers the structure for in-depth teacher reflection.

According to Irby and Brown (2000), improvement in the quality of teaching and learning depends largely on the commitment of teachers to continually assess and improve upon their own teaching as measured by student performance and established teaching criterion such as the Texas Teacher Evaluation and Support System (T-TESS). The portfolio should be comprehensive, containing documentation of the many facets of the teacher's work and achievement in relation to the state domains and campus and classroom goals. Artifacts for reflection that may demonstrate strengths or indicate areas for improvement may include: administrator walk-through feedback; observation reports from supervisors and peers; profile sheets on student progress; staff development sessions related to professional goals; implementation of "new learnings" related to professional development goals; and/or feedback from students, parents, and others. Selecting artifacts or samples of work and writing accompanying reflections are beneficial in denoting areas of needed improvement, assisting in maintaining focus, and providing new perspectives and insights.

Using a teacher evaluation portfolio as a part of continuous improvement and professional growth/development is a positive, personal, and individualized approach to appraisal. In portfolio development, teachers must conceptualize their roles and become highly involved in their own evaluation and professional growth. Principals participate in a teacher's appraisal; but, according to Poekert (2012), their assessment simply adds to a teacher's performance portfolio—and, we add, to the teacher's professional development plans.

The portfolio evaluation process encourages collegial interaction among administrators and teachers, providing an avenue for two-way communication (Irby & Brown, 2000). During the final evaluation conference, the teacher, while referring to concrete examples in the portfolio, shares with the principal areas of professional growth over the course of the current school year, reflects on professional development goals that have been accomplished, and offers a proactive plan for new goals for the upcoming year. Additionally, the principal is able to seek clarification, give feedback, and offer suggestions for setting professional growth goals. Through this process, the principal empowers the teachers, who then can assume the major responsibility for their own growth and development. Collectively, the principal and the teachers can assess their evaluations and plan campus-wide needs related to instruction.

Principle 7

Effective professional development is planned collaboratively by those who will participate in and facilitate that development. Kelleher (2003) indicates that certain types of professional development are more likely to have an impact on student learning than others; therefore, it is imperative that the professional development system provides an incentive for teachers to pursue professional development activities that will easily translate into student learning. The principal should develop or offer various professional development strands, based on current research on effective professional development, to prioritize and categorize various pursuits. The four professional development strands are as follows:

1. *Peer collaboration.* This strand should be given the most importance, because it is job embedded and thus should have a bigger impact on student achievement. Teachers collaborate in writing curriculum and assessments, examining student work, working on committees, observing one another's classrooms and coaching, mentoring new teachers, and participating in study groups.
2. *Individualized professional growth.* A teacher participates in activities such as attending a conference, listening to a guest speaker, or taking a course at the college level.
3. *Research and leadership.* Teachers conduct action research and take leadership roles by sharing knowledge and practices through publications and other presentations.
4. *External experiences.* This strand includes many other activities, such as summer externships and visits to other schools.

The principal should help teachers choose among the various strands to ensure a range of appropriate professional development activities. The principal can allocate the budget to encourage teachers to focus heavily on activities related to peer collaboration. There may be some cases in which an activity applies to more than one strand, and in that case the principal (or possibly the assigned peer coach) may assist the teacher in determining which strand best fits his or her learning goals.

Darling-Hammond (2017) provides suggestions for principals and teachers to collaborate in planning professional development as follows. They can (a) examine the current school philosophy regarding teaching and learning; (b) organize study groups to discuss contemporary views of learning and the research on effective instruction for different outcomes, articulating their beliefs about the ways in which learning occurs, and discussing the implications for instructional practice; (c) use the discussions and conclusions of these groups to reach consensus on a collective vision that will provide a philosophical base for the consideration of new curricula and instructional practices; (d) understand principles for effective professional development; (e) examine and discuss current attitudes toward professional development; (f) create a school culture in which teachers feel free to critically assess their own practice; (g) examine the effective learning models and frameworks for designing professional development and discuss conditions in the school or district that facilitate or hinder the use of a variety of professional development strategies; and (h) evaluate the impact and effect of the professional development conducted throughout the school year and make recommendations for improving the professional development for the following year. In conducting the evaluation, the most important point to consider is the impact of professional development—first, on student achievement and, second, on teachers' instructional practices.

Principle 8

Effective professional development requires substantial time and other resources. Principals must devote the time for planning professional development that is systemically connected to the curriculum and instructional needs of the campus as well as to the vision and mission. Principals must advocate for funding to support professional development, and they need to propose that a full 10 percent of the school budget be devoted to professional development. The most effective professional development programs related to time investment are long-term programs, implemented throughout the school year. Such investments of time require funds for hiring consultants, sending teachers to professional development sessions, and/or retaining high-quality substitutes as teachers are in training.

Principle 9

Effective professional development is driven by a coherent long-term plan. Leading an effective professional development program is a complex and comprehensive process, and it promotes change within a system. To achieve desired change, principals must develop a clearly articulated and communicated plan to address commonly identified goals (Fullan & Gallagher, 2020; Fullan & Hargreaves, 2012). In effect, principals create learning organizations where professional development and change become the norm of continuous improvement (Fullan, 2015). According to Fullan (2018), professional development is a goal-oriented and continuous process, supported through mentoring, coaching, and feedback and developed to address the perceived needs of the students.

Principle 10

Effective professional development is evaluated ultimately on the basis of its impact on teacher effectiveness and student learning, and this assessment guides subsequent professional development efforts. According to Kelleher (2003):

> Current research on professional development, which has shown that professional development must be embedded in teachers' daily work to improve student learning, has led school boards and administrators across the country to evaluate the results of their investment in adult learning. The standards movement, along with the push to increase the use of data in educational decision making, has intensified the pressure on school administrators to prove that professional development is showing positive results. (p. 751)

Evaluating the professional development session through a survey at the end of the session is not sufficient. The issue is not how much the teachers liked the session; rather, the issue is what effect the professional development will have on student learning (Pollock, 2007).

The Every Student Succeeds Act (ESSA) of 2015 requires states to have challenging academic standards; to test students annually in grades three through eight and once in high school; and to increase student achievement so that all students reach proficient levels. Some believe there is no link between professional development and student improvements in achievement; and perhaps there are no links in the one-time, shot-in-the-arm professional development strategies. However, when we look across the country and find entire school districts with students in every subgroup (Black, Hispanic, White, and economically disadvantaged) achieving at or above state or district standards in reading and math, we find that it is in those districts where the professional development is ongoing, sustained, and connected to the standards the teachers are trying to accomplish.

A growing body of evidence indicates that teacher effectiveness is not fixed, and that when teachers of all experience levels learn powerful skills and methods to use with students in the classroom, student achievement increases. Linda Darling-Hammond and Jeanie Oakes (2019) suggest that to accomplish this end result, professional development must be (a) grounded in student need in an academic content area; (b) research based; (c) collaborative and ongoing; (d) embedded in the system; (e) built on effective training processes; (f) structured to involve all administrative levels in support and planning; (g) connected to school improvement and aligned with the curriculum standards and assessed needs of the students, as well as the self-assessed needs of the teachers; and (h) monitored (effective professional development is monitored for implementation and results).

DIRECT ASSISTANCE TO TEACHERS

There is considerable evidence that most teachers do not find the evaluation of their teaching helpful to them professionally (Callahan & Sadeghi, 2014; Danielson, 2010/2011; Kowalski & Dolph 2015; Marshall, 2006; Marzano, 2012; Maslow & Kelley, 2012; Toch & Rothman, 2008; Weisberg et al., 2009) For example, in a national survey of teachers, only 26 percent reported that evaluation has been "useful and effective" (Duffett et al., 2008, p. 3).

One conclusion is that teachers' negative perceptions concerning performance evaluations relate more to the way they are conducted than to the function of performance evaluation in general. Teachers might react more positively to a procedure that is responsive to their needs and professional aspirations. Clinical supervision, peer coaching, walk-through observations, and goal setting are examples of this approach to teacher performance evaluation.

Supervision and Evaluation

Teachers, especially beginning teachers, should welcome evaluation as a means of developing professionally. In general, the evaluation a teacher receives takes two forms. Some evaluation teachers receive is formative and some evaluation is summative, just as good student evaluations are of both types. **Formative evaluation,** which places the evaluator in the role of supervisor, is intended to reassure teachers, especially beginning teachers, that they can succeed and can foster student growth. **Summative evaluation,** which places the evaluator in the role of administrator, is intended to help teachers know how they are performing relative to the specific criteria of a school district's evaluation system.

Viewed simplistically, summative evaluation is rating; it is judging the goodness of teaching. Summative evaluation is tough-minded, a quality assurance mechanism, a process, principals and assistant principals carry out to compare one teacher to another and to the school district's standards. Painted in similar broad strokes, formative evaluation is nonjudgmental, reflecting to the teacher the intended and sometimes unintended consequences of her behavior; it is a collegial, humane dialog. Administrators do summative evaluation; supervisors do formative evaluation.

Of course, nothing is ever that simple. Supervision has an important role to play in evaluation. Moreover, supervisors often are called upon to judge, rate, compare, and decide issues such as promotion, tenure, transfer, and dismissal. Four approaches to supervision (formative evaluation) that principals use to improve teacher performance are clinical supervision, peer coaching, walk through observations, and goal setting.

Clinical Supervision

Designed to improve the teacher's classroom performance, **clinical supervision** is a subcategory of instructional supervision. Instructional supervision is defined as all of the activities, functions, maneuvers, and monitoring conditions that a principal performs that are intended to help teachers upgrade their performance. Adding the word *clinical* (as Morris Cogan did in creating the idea as a part of the Harvard Training Program in the early 1960s) indicates that such efforts are based upon data collected in the actual classroom (or other instructional situations), where the teacher is working directly with the learner and the supervisor (principal or assistant principal) is present as a witness, if not a participant. Clinical supervision had its roots in the work of Morris Cogan (1961, 1973) and Robert Goldhammer (1969) at the Harvard School of Education in the early 1960s. Goldhammer, Anderson, and Krajewski (1993), Pajak (2008), and Gall and Acheson (2010) have continued the early, pioneering work of Cogan and Goldhammer.

Basic to the model of clinical supervision is the notion that the clinical supervisor knows more about instruction and learning than the teacher(s) do. Robert Goldhammer and colleagues' clinical supervision model (1993) consists of five stages: (a) pre-observation conference, (b) classroom observation, (c) analysis and strategy, (d) supervision conference, and (e) post-conference analysis. We discuss each of these stages in turn.

Stage 1: Pre-Observation Conference. The principal (or supervisor): obtains information regarding the teacher's lesson objectives, instructional procedures, and criteria of evaluation; establishes a contract between the principal and teacher as to the areas in which the teacher wants feedback; and establishes specific plans for carrying out the observation, such as time limits, instrumentation, and so on.

Stage 2: Classroom Observation. The pre-observation conference leads to the classroom observation. Many methods exist to enable the principal (or supervisor) to collect informative data. Examples of observation methods include (Glickman, Gordon, & Ross-Gordon, 2018; Zepeda, 2017): *checklist* (a standardized form to identify activities or behaviors as present, absent, or in need of improvement); *visual diagramming* (recording behaviors or movement of teachers and students in short time increments); *selected verbatim notes* (recording words, questions, or interactions exactly); *open narrative* (taking anecdotal notes, with or without focus); *teacher-designed instrument* (an instrument to audit certain teaching and learning behaviors); *verbal flow* (detailing who spoke, how often, and when); *class traffic* (tracking the teacher's or students' physical movement); *interaction analysis* (detailing statements made by either the teacher or the students); *on-task* (noting which students appear to be on-task); *audio* (record audio of classroom events and listen to them later); *video* (teacher can review the lesson alone or with a supervisor or peer); and *anecdotal notes* (noting overall what is occurring in the classroom). The supervisor should keep in mind the difference between *descriptions* and *interpretations* of events. The purpose of classroom observation is *description*.

Stage 3: Analysis and Strategy. With observation data collected, analysis and planning a strategy for the post-observation conference are now possible. The principal (or supervisor) examines the recorded pages of observations and analyzes the information. The task might involve counting frequencies, looking for patterns, or isolating a major occurrence. In essence, the supervisor assesses the observed lesson, considers supervisory implications, and develops a strategy for helping the teacher.

Stage 4: Post-Observation Conference. The post-observation conference provides an opportunity for teacher and principal (or supervisor) to talk about the observation data and analysis, interpret the meaning of the data, and develop a plan for instructional improvement. The post-observation conference is more than feedback. The post-observation conference is about the conversations and the opportunities provided to teachers to examine their practices (Cunningham, 2011; Darling-Hammond & McLaughlin, 2011), to build trust between the teacher and supervisor, and to train the teacher in the techniques of reflective practice (Zepeda, 2017).

Stage 5: Post-Observation Conference Analysis. In solitude, the principal (or supervisor) assesses the post-observation conference in relation to their own intentions, supervisory criteria, and the value of the conference to the teacher. It is also an opportunity to analyze the previous four steps concerning format and procedures from pre-conference through post-conference. The principal (or supervisor) may ask himself or herself what was valuable? What was of little value? What changes need to be made during future cycles of clinical supervision?

At its best, clinical supervision is group supervision—that is, two or more supervisors working with the same teacher. Some schools with seasoned teaching teams practice clinical supervision at its finest. The purist would insist that stage 5, post-conference analysis, cannot be done alone. Stage 5 is thought of as the superego of the sequence, the conscience of the clinical process. No matter whether it is conducted by one person or a team, clinical supervision is labor intensive, as the reader can well imagine.

Evaluation takes a somewhat different tack. The rationale behind evaluation is that wise evaluators evaluate only as much as they have to. Whereas clinical supervision puts great stress on teacher behavior in the future, evaluation stresses the here and now. Evaluation is measuring or assessing progress toward predetermined objectives—the teacher performance criteria set as performance standards by the school district or individual school.

The major and continuing difference between supervision and evaluation is that the appraiser in the evaluation process must make performance comparisons, asking and answering these questions: Is this teacher's performance meeting the standards of my school? Is the lesson appropriate for our curriculum and the intended learners? And what can we do together to assure even better teaching and learning in the next cycle? (The last question is where clinical supervision, peer coaching or mentoring, walk-throughs, and goal setting, can come into play.) To do less would not meet the principal's responsibility for quality assurance in that school building and in the school community.

Peer Coaching

Peer Coaching is a technique that a principal can employ with teachers so that they can assist each other in improving instruction and create an environment in which risk taking is appreciated. This process involves a coach who mediates the thinking of the teacher (Costa et al., 2015; Tschannen-Moran & Tschannen-Moran, 2020; Rock, 2019). The coach (a) diagnoses and envisions desired stages for others, (b) constructs and uses clear and precise language in the facilitation of others' cognitive development, (c) devises an overall strategy through which individuals will move themselves toward desired states, (d) maintains faith in the potential for continued movement toward a more harmonious state of mind and behavior, and (e) possesses a belief in her own capacity to serve as an empowering catalyst of another's growth. The coaches are not experts; they are facilitators and mediators.

The coaching model is divided into two parts: planning and reflecting. In the face-to-face planning conference, the coach attempts to assist the teacher to specify the upcoming lesson in as much detail as possible, including student outcomes. The coach helps the teacher to establish goals for the lesson, for assessing the lesson, for teaching the methodology to be used, and for personal growth. The second part of coaching, reflection, begins after the lesson has occurred. The coach will ask the teacher to summarize his impression of the lesson and to provide data to support those impressions. The coach will help the teacher to consider cause-and-effect relationships between himself and the students and between the content and format of the lesson and the results elicited from the students. Again, this type of model provides data for the teacher to include in an annual evaluation portfolio.

Walk-Through Observations

Time is critical for the busy principal, who has to work not only as the instructional leader but also as the school manager. Time management is always a challenge. The walk-through observation can assist the principal in keeping touch with the classroom, being in the classroom, and providing feedback needed for continuous improvement. According to Fink and Resnik (2001), **walk-through observations** are organized observations from the principal, who observes specific instructional practices and subsequent student learning. When combined, all walk-through observations can provide an overall picture of the functioning of instruction within the building, and they can become a part of the evidence for areas of overall school improvement and correlated professional development.

Davidson-Taylor (2002) says that walk-through information can create focus dialogue with teachers about best practices, effective teaching principles, and student learning. The principal should develop a plan for walk-throughs; that is, when, how often, how long (suggested five- to ten-minute snapshots). In addition, the principal should develop a short duplicate feedback form to be completed "on the spot." This technique works best when the principal places the walk-throughs on his or her calendar and honors the time. The principal should train the teachers in the process of walk-throughs, because this will not be a typical classroom observation. During their training, teachers may be informed about what might be observed during walk-throughs. The focus is generally on student work and their behavior, as a result of instruction. At times the principal may choose to share the results of walk-throughs with an entire department, including general observations that are repeatedly recorded in a pattern so that the team can address the issue and improve the teachers' instructional techniques. Grade-level or department meetings can include a time to address the following topics in depth: improving student learning, current research, learning expectations for students, and student performance.

According to Davidson-Taylor (2002), the following are key factors to be observed during a walk-through observation.

1. The principal should attempt to view the classroom from the students' perspective, because they are the recipients of the instruction. Observe the students and converse with them as appropriate about their classwork. Look at what students are doing. Are they actively engaged in learning? Do they understand the teacher's expectations? Can the students articulate what and why they are learning? Do students know the standard of excellence in this classroom? What evidence indicates that students have actually learned the targeted skill(s) or objective(s)? These are questions that need to answered through evidence obtained from discussion with, or observation of, the students.
2. Look at the students' assignments to identify the work they complete. What is the level of thinking? Are students provided with quality samples of work? Are rubrics provided for the achieved criteria of the work completed?
3. Listen to student talk. Are they even allowed to talk? Is the teacher doing all the talking? What is the direction of their conversation? Are students asking questions of the teacher and other classmates? Do the conversations originate with the students as well as the teacher? Are the students talking about learning?
4. Is there evidence of student products in the classroom? Are the products authentic work samples?
5. As principals observe at a specific grade level, are the students, overall, progressing at the usual pace through the curriculum? Are they behind, or too far ahead? Are the curriculum and instructional plan being followed? Is there differentiation at the various grade levels? For example, students should not, with the same purpose, be planting a bean in first grade, again in second, and all the way through fourth grade. Nor should they be reading the same novels in English class in the ninth, tenth, eleventh, or twelve grades. If the curriculum map (scope and sequence) is being followed, then such lack of differentiation should not happen. Is instruction at the appropriate level? Are questions at an appropriate level for the students, and do students model the upper-level taxonomic questions?
6. Are technology standards integrated in instruction? These would have been integrated in the curriculum and the instructional plans; therefore, they should be observed during walk-throughs. Look for signs of how technology is being implemented in the classroom. Are students engaged in Web research, Microsoft PowerPoint presentations, and Web design?
7. What evidence is there that preassessments were given to determine prior knowledge so that skill development can be at the appropriate level? Do teachers reteach needed skills?
8. Are students recognized for their superior work? Is work displayed?

Walk-throughs can change the focus of faculty meetings from administrative issues (can be shared in e-mails, bulletins, or memos) to issues of teaching and learning and discuss curriculum, new research, and best practices in instruction.

Goal Setting

Another popular technique for evaluating teachers is *goal setting* (Locke & Latham, 2002, 2006). **Goal setting** defines job performance based on accomplishing specific task goals, such as student achievement, student growth, skill acquisition, or attitude change. Instead of being evaluated on observed teaching behaviors, teachers are evaluated on what they have accomplished.

The goal-setting approach includes two major elements. First, at some point in the appraisal process, the principal (or supervisor) and teacher meet to determine jointly the teacher's performance goals over some specified time period. Second, the principal and teacher meet to appraise the teacher's performance in relation to the previously established goals. Individual teacher goals evolve at least in part from the school district's goals, which are established by the school and superintendent (Lunenburg, 2011f).

Goal setting as a performance appraisal technique has both strengths and weaknesses. Strengths of goal setting are that it stresses results rather than personality or personal traits, improves motivation due to knowledge of results, minimizes judgment errors, and improves commitment through participation. Major weaknesses of goal setting are that it emphasizes quantitative goals at the expense of qualitative goals, creates too much paperwork, lacks uniformity in performance measurements, and requires constant attention and administrative support (Latham & Locke, 2006).

Overall, for evaluating teacher performance, the approaches of goal setting, clinical supervision, and peer coaching and walk-throughs are particularly well suited to result in better teaching; this is due mainly to the motivational and participative aspects of such programs. Used in the proper way, these techniques are interactive rather than directive, democratic rather than authoritarian, and teacher centered rather than principal centered.

Improving Teacher Evaluations

Conducting teacher evaluations is a difficult task. Principals cannot shirk their responsibility to conduct an accurate appraisal of their teachers. Teacher appraisal is an essential element in a principal's attempt to improve his or her school's instructional program. The following suggestions for improving teacher evaluation may help to improve the process (Glickman, Gordon, & Ross-Gordon, 2018; Sergiovanni, Starratt, & Cho, 2013; Sullivan & Glanz, 2013; Zepeda, 2017):

1. *Principals need to read union contracts and board policies and abide by them.* Contracts can place specific limitations on a principal's conduct of teacher evaluations, including the number of classroom observations, use of evaluation instruments, and the like.
2. *Principals need to ask teachers for self-evaluations.* A self-evaluation serves at least two purposes: first, if teachers rate themselves higher in an area than the principal thinks they deserve, they are prepared for a potential conflict before conducting post-evaluation conferences with those teachers. Second, teachers may identify problems of which the principal is not aware. Their honesty allows the principal to provide assistance that they might not otherwise have offered.

3. *Principals need to plan classroom visits wisely.* Observing a teacher in the classroom is the heart of any successful evaluation, but only if it is done correctly. The authors recommend that principals observe all teachers at least three times a year, and marginal and beginning teachers as many times as needed.

4. *Principals need to make their observations correctly.* Principals need to spend at least a full class period on one of the annual observations in order to identify a teacher's work habits. Observations should be scheduled for different times of the day.

5. *Principals need to take accurate notes.* The wise principal takes detailed notes, including names, dates, times, places, and a narrative account of what happens in the classroom. Such records are invaluable, should a teacher be considered for termination in the future.

6. *Principals need to consider video-recording teachers.* A principal's comments make more sense when teachers can see themselves in action. However, video-recording may be restricted by contract. In many cases, written permission from the teacher is needed as a prior condition to video-recording.

7. *Principals should not limit themselves to ratings.* An evaluation approach that is limited to a 1-to-5 scale is ambiguous and misleading. A more informative evaluation uses a narrative approach. For example, "The teacher repeatedly demonstrated the ability to provide students with feedback by answering their questions and praising and correcting their performance."

8. *Principals need to make sure post-observation conferences mean something.* Principals should use the post-observation conference to discuss possible solutions to any problems cited in the evaluation. Compliment strengths also.

9. *Principals need to offer teachers a chance for rebuttal.* Discussion of the performance appraisal between the principal and teacher can often lead to compromise and changes in the evaluation that are mutually satisfactory. In any case, teachers should be allowed the opportunity to provide a rebuttal to the principal's report.

10. *Principals need to demonstrate that they take evaluations seriously.* There are at least two ways a principal can show he or she takes the evaluation seriously: (a) put all recommendations in writing and (b) hire substitute teachers to free teachers for post-observation conferences during school hours.

11. *Principals need to have the teacher sign the evaluation report.* The signatures of both the observer and the teacher on the evaluation report, and the date, prove that the evaluation actually occurred. An explanatory sentence should appear below the signature line, stating that the teacher's signature does not indicate agreement with the evaluation, but signifies that the teacher received a copy of the evaluation and that the contents were discussed.

Orientation and Induction of the Beginning Teacher

What are the general needs of the beginning teacher? Most schools plan for teacher orientation, but despite efforts to help teachers succeed, many still encounter adjustment problems. A review of the research on problems of beginning teachers shows that feelings of isolation; poor understanding of what is expected of them; workload and extra assignments that they were unprepared to handle; lack of supplies, materials, or equipment; poor physical facilities; and lack of support or help from experienced teachers or supervisors contribute to their feelings of frustration and failure (Kemmis et al., 2014). The result is that many potentially talented and creative teachers find teaching unrewarding and difficult, especially in inner-city schools; and nearly 16 percent of newly hired teachers leave the profession within five years (National Center for Education Statistics, 2018).

There is recognition that the induction period, the first two or three years of teaching, is critical in developing teachers' capabilities, and that beginning teachers should not be left to sink or swim. Several state education agencies have recently developed internship programs for new teachers, while other states have increased professional development activities (Bullough, 2012). However, most important for the professional development of new teachers are the internal support systems and strategies that the schools adopt (that is, the daily support activities and continual learning opportunities).

In general, having to learn by trial and error without support and supervision has been the most common problem faced by new teachers. Expecting teachers to function without support is based on the false assumptions that: teachers are well prepared for their initial classroom and school experiences; teachers can develop professional expertise on their own; and teaching can be mastered in a relatively short period of time. Researchers find there is little attempt to lighten the class load and limit extra-class assignments to make the beginning teacher's job easier. In the few schools that do limit these activities, teachers have reported that they have had the opportunity to "learn to teach" (Birkeland & Feiman-Nemser, 2012).

Unquestionably, new teachers need the feedback and encouragement that experienced teachers can provide. Peer coaching or mentoring is gaining support as an effective supervision tool. *Peer coaching or mentoring* takes place when classroom teachers observe one another, provide feedback concerning their teaching, and together develop instructional plans. An experienced teacher who acts as a peer coach or mentor teacher for an inexperienced teacher performs five functions: (a) *companionship*, discussing ideas, problems, and successes; (b) *technical feedback*, especially related to lesson planning and classroom observations; (c) *analysis of application*, integrating what happens or what works as part of the beginning teacher's repertoire; (d) *adaptation*, helping the beginning teacher adapt to particular situations; and (e) *personal facilitation*, helping the teacher feel good about himself or herself after trying new strategies (Mathur, Gehrke, & Kim, 2013). Others suggest that the main features of a successful mentoring program include the following: proximity, grade equivalence (at the elementary level), subject equivalence (at the secondary level), and compatibility regarding personality, experiences, and educational philosophy (Kearney, 2014).

Perhaps the most important ingredient for a peer coach, mentor, or resource teacher is to allow new teachers to reflect, not react or defend. An integral part of any good program for helping novice teachers is for them to observe experienced teachers on a regular basis and then for experienced teachers to observe novice teachers. With both observational formats, there is need to discuss what facilitated or hindered the teaching-learning process and precisely what steps or recommendations are needed for improving instruction. The peer coach or mentor needs to serve as a friend and confidante (function in a nonevaluative role). The term **peer sharing and caring** among colleagues best describes the new spirit of collegial openness and learning advocated here.

Guidelines for Improving Support for Beginning Teachers. Whatever the existing policies regarding the induction period for beginning teachers, there is the need to improve provisions for their continued professional development, to make the job easier, to make them feel more confident in the classroom and school, to reduce the isolation of their work settings, and to enhance interaction with colleagues. Here are some recommendations that school principals can implement for achieving these goals (Gujarati, 2012; Haynes, Maddock, & Goldrick, 2014; Klinge, 2015):

1. Principals need to schedule beginning teacher orientation in addition to regular teacher orientation. Beginning teachers need to attend both sessions.
2. Principals need to appoint someone to help beginning teachers set up their rooms.
3. Principals need to provide beginning teachers with a proper mix of courses, students, and facilities (not all leftovers). If possible, lighten their load for the first year.
4. Principals need to assign extra-class duties of moderate difficulty and requiring moderate amounts of time, duties that will not become too demanding for the beginning teacher.
5. Principals need to pair beginning teachers with master teachers to meet regularly to identify general problems before they become serious.
6. Principals need to provide coaching groups, tutor groups, or collaborative problem-solving groups for all beginning teachers to attend; they need to encourage beginning teachers to teach each other.
7. Principals need to provide for joint planning, team teaching, committee assignments, and other cooperative arrangements between new and experienced teachers.
8. Principals need to issue newsletters that report on accomplishments of all teachers, especially beginning teachers.
9. Principals need to schedule reinforcing events involving beginning and experienced teachers; examples are mentor-mentee luncheons, parties, and awards.
10. Principals need to provide regular (monthly) meetings between the beginning teacher and supervisor (mentor) to identify problems as soon as possible and to make recommendations for improvement.
11. Principals need to plan special and continuing professional development activities with topics directly related to the needs and interests of beginning teachers. Eventually, beginning professional development activities should be integrated with regular professional development activities.
12. Principals need to carry on regular evaluation of beginning teachers; evaluate strengths and weaknesses, present new information, demonstrate new skills, and provide opportunities for practice and feedback.

THE PRINCIPAL'S MISSION FOR PERSONAL PROFESSIONAL DEVELOPMENT

The second mission that principals have regarding professional development relates to their own professional growth. This mission is for principals to work with their supervisors to develop a personal, professional development plan including the resources, money, and time required. They should establish time for meetings with the supervisor and other principals that will allow for reflection on their leadership practice.

Principals can engage in their own long-term, ongoing professional development and become role models for their teaching staff. According to Brown and Irby (2002), one way that principals can effectively engage in their own improvement and serve as a model for their teachers is by producing a Professional Development Portfolio. The authors indicated that such a portfolio provides an excellent vehicle for organizing and documenting professional development experiences and subsequent improvement.

The Professional Development Portfolio

Brown and Irby (2000) defined the **Professional Development Portfolio** as a collection of thoughtfully selected exhibits or artifacts and reflections indicative of an individual's progress toward and/or attainment of established goals or criteria. In the process of developing a Professional Development Portfolio, principals can focus on

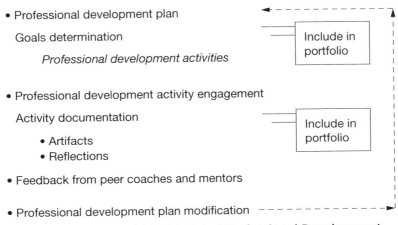

Figure 5.3 Brown and Irby Model of Professional Development

the documentation, through concrete examples (artifacts and reflections), of progress toward goals related to assessment results and their growth as leaders. The portfolio not only offers an effective system for organizing evidence of progress but also promotes self-assessment skills. As principals learn these skills, they can also assist their teachers in doing the same. When principals choose artifacts and write reflections for the portfolio, they become more reflective, more critical, and more able to determine their own strengths and weaknesses.

Brown and Irby (2002) offer a model for implementing the Professional Development Portfolio process over a five-year period. Figure 5.3 depicts the model that principals can use to improve their practice by considering multiple leadership assessment data, including self-assessment; by planning specific activities to enhance growth in targeted areas; and by reflecting on professional growth associated with those activities (Brown & Irby, 2000). This same model could be adapted by principals for use with teachers on their campuses.

Using the Professional Development Portfolio

Brown and Irby (2002) indicate that the Professional Development Portfolio Model facilitates continuous learning. Although assessment results reflect the performance of the individual at a specific point in time, the **Professional Development Portfolio Model** depicts assessment as occurring not only at certain points in time, but as continuous. The authors said that although portfolios are highly individualized, with specific contents usually determined by the individual or the district, the Professional Development Portfolio typically includes a table of contents, an introduction, assessment data, a current résumé, a leadership framework, a professional development plan based on assessment data, and artifacts and reflections related to professional development activities (organized by goals or standards). See figure 5.4.

Table of Contents, Introduction, and Résumé. The *table of contents* should indicate clearly how the portfolio is organized, so that review of the portfolio is easily accomplished. The *introduction* briefly needs to (a) explain the purpose of the portfolio and (b) outline the results of the assessment. Including an updated *résumé* provides an opportunity for the principal to add recent accomplishments and the

---

Contents of the portfolio

- Table of contents
- Introduction
- Assessment data
- Résumé
- Leadership framework
- Professional development
  - Goals
  - Plans
  - Activities
- Artifacts
- Reflections

Figure 5.4 Contents of the Professional Development Portfolio

latest professional development experiences to the résumé. The résumé should also include a listing of certifications or endorsements, education, experience, areas of concentration, and strengths.

Leadership Framework. All actions are predicated on personal beliefs and values; therefore, it is important to express those clearly and concisely in writing. The **leadership framework** (Brown & Irby, 2001), a written statement of primary beliefs and attitudes regarding leadership, assists principals in analyzing why they do what they do as leaders; it also helps clarify who they are as leaders to others, including faculty, colleagues, community, and board. Because it compels principals to reflect on their philosophies of leadership, learning, and teaching, this self-analysis offers opportunities for personal and professional growth. Principals address seven important components as they develop their leadership framework: philosophy of education, philosophy of leadership, vision for learners, vision for teachers, vision for the organization, vision for professional development, and method of vision attainment.

The Professional Development Plan. The **professional development plan,** viewed in figure 5.5, provides direction for specific professional development goals based on assessment results. The principal then can align those goals with the state's principal standards and can select professional development activities accordingly. Although professional development experiences should be planned in advance, modifications should be made as new experiences become available. Next, timelines should be developed as well as brief notes related to securing appropriate artifacts from the experiences. Finally, feedback from colleagues, mentors, peer coaches, or supervisors regarding improvement in targeted areas may be included as further evidence of growth.

Related Professional Development Activity: Artifacts and Reflection. The artifacts and reflections are the heart of the Professional Development Portfolio. Principals who have developed portfolios report that the processes of selecting viable samples of their experiences and writing accompanying reflections are beneficial in maintaining focus on goals, in providing new perspectives and creative insights, and in developing satisfaction that specific goals related to improved leadership are being accomplished.

Name: _____

Prioritized standards/ indicators	Professional goals	Professional development experiences	Timeline	Documentation (artifacts and reflections)	Feedback requested/ from whom

Figure 5.5 Brown and Irby Professional Development Plan

> • Leadership workshop
> • Group-leading skills training
> • Inquiry group on teacher research and improvement
> • Curriculum development
> • Readings in school law
> • Observations when conducting a group meeting
> • Conflict resolution training

Figure 5.6

The artifacts and their accompanying reflections may be organized in the portfolio either by standard or by professional development goal. Figure 5.6 provides examples of artifacts related to professional development experiences.

Much of the current literature on successful leadership emphasizes the importance of self-assessment for growth. The greatest benefit of portfolio development is realized through the process of reflection, as the leader assesses the effectiveness and impact of his leadership beliefs, style, and practices. The reflection inherent in the portfolio development process (a) provides insights into strengths and weaknesses, (b) encourages planning for professional growth, (c) leads to improved practice by the principal, and (d) ultimately, enhances school and teacher effectiveness and improves student learning.

Our research and our work with administrators has indicated the need for a structure for writing reflections. The Reflection Cycle (referred to here as the cycle) (Brown & Irby, 2001) provides such a structure. The five steps of the cycle offer critical prompts. Steps 1 and 2 of the cycle focus on selecting the artifact and describing the circumstances surrounding it. (It is the selected artifact in the Professional Development Portfolio that serves as concrete evidence of the principal's professional development experiences.) Step 3 asks the principal to analyze the experience illustrated by the artifact and the relation of it to issues, expectations, goals, and practice. Step 4 is appraisal of the experience. Here the principal interprets events surrounding the experience; determines her impact or the impact the experiences had on her leadership; determines effectiveness of decisions made; and/or ascertains relationships to her philosophy, values, and/or goals. Step 5 requires the principal to use the interpreted data and develop projections for further improvement and future goals. The Reflection Cycle should also be taught to teachers; however, it is best if the principal is using the cycle to reflect on their practice and can share how they have used it to improve.

ETHICS OF PROFESSIONAL DEVELOPMENT

The National Staff Development Council (2020) adopted a code of ethics and divided the responsibilities into two categories: staff development leader and staff development provider. The council considers professional development leaders as the individuals within a school, school district, university, state education agency, or other educational organization who plan, implement, coordinate, and/or evaluate staff development efforts. They include but are not limited to directors of staff development, superintendents, school board members, principals, curriculum coordinators, and teacher leaders. Staff or professional development providers use their knowledge and skills to promote adult learning or to assist groups and organizations to perform more effectively. They include trainers, facilitators, consultants, mentors, and instructional and leadership specialists or coaches. The most critical person related to professional development on a campus is the principal. It is the principal who has a vantage point of the whole school's needs and who can facilitate, collaboratively with teachers, the professional development that addresses those needs.

Based on the National Staff Development Council's (2020) ethical code, the principal should have the following responsibilities: (a) be committed to achieving school goals, particularly those addressing high levels of learning and performance for all students and teachers; (b) select professional development content and processes that are research based and proven in practice after examining various types of information about student and educator learning needs; (c) improve his work through the ongoing evaluation of professional development's effectiveness in achieving school system and school goals for student learning; (d) improve his own knowledge and skills; (e) ensure an equitable distribution of resources to accomplish school goals for student learning; (f) advocate for policies and practices that ensure the continuous learning of all students and teachers; and (g) conduct himself or herself in a manner that avoids conflict of interest or the appearance of such conflict.

SUMMARY

1. The principal's mission related to her teachers' professional development is twofold. First, the mission is *to plan*, with teachers, a comprehensive professional development program targeted at identified individual and collective needs; and second, the mission is *to provide* resources, including time and money, and to include time for teachers to reflect upon and participate in dialogue about their practice.
2. There is a positive connection between professional development and student learning; therefore, it is important to include in the budget funds for sustained professional development.
3. The best professional development is connected to the needs of the students and the teachers' related instructional concerns.
4. Principals who promote successful professional development experiences for their teachers will, in turn, increase the teachers' interest in and commitment to the profession.
5. Professional development should consider the data gathered related to student achievement and the types of professional development conducted throughout the school year. With these data, a principal and the teachers can plan more effective and sustained professional development programs.
6. Effective professional development is logically embedded in the reality of schools and teachers' work.
7. Principals can engage in their own long-term, ongoing professional development and become role models for their teaching staff.
8. Portfolios provide a means for self-assessment and evaluation. The reflection inherent in the portfolio development process (a) provides insights into strengths and weaknesses, (b) encourages planning for

professional growth, (c) leads to improved practice by the principal, and (d) ultimately, enhances school and teacher effectiveness and improves student learning.

9. The principal has ethical responsibilities toward professional development.

KEY TERMS

professional development
high-quality professional
  development
action research
formative evaluation
summative evaluation
clinical supervision
peer coaching
walk-through observations

goal setting
mission of professional development
professional development portfolio
professional development model
peer sharing and caring
professional development portfolio
professional development model
leadership framework
professional development plan

FIELD-BASED ACTIVITIES

1. Determine, with your principal, the percentage of the school budget that is spent on professional development of administrators, faculty, and staff. Determine, with your business manager in the district, what percentage of the budget is spent on professional development throughout the district.
2. Based on the 10 principles of effective professional development, assess the professional development activities on your campus. Do they meet these standards?
3. Develop a professional development portfolio. Use the components to build your portfolio as suggested in the text.

SUGGESTED READINGS

Brown, G., & Irby, B. J. (2001). *The principal portfolio* (2nd ed.). Thousand Oaks, CA: Corwin Press. This book, in its first edition (1999), was the first to introduce four types of portfolios for principals: (a) Professional Development Portfolio, (b) Evaluation Portfolio, (c) Career Advancement Portfolio, and (d) Academic Portfolio. Benefits of each and how to develop each type of portfolio are included in the book.

Danielson, C. (2016). *Talk about teaching! Leading professional conversations.* Thousand Oaks, CA: Corwin Press. Charlotte Danielson provides school leaders with an understanding of the value of reflective informal professional conversations in promoting a positive environment of inquiry support and teacher development.

Martin, L. E., Kragler, S., Quatroche, D. J., & Bauserman, K. L. (eds.). (2014). *Handbook of professional development in education: Successful models and practices, pre-k–12*. New York, NY: Guilford Publications. This comprehensive handbook provides the best current knowledge on teacher professional development (PD) and addresses practical issues in implementation.

Rock, M. (2019). *The e coaching continuum for educators: Using technology to enrich professional development and improve student outcomes*. Alexandria, VA: ASCD. Marcia Rock offers a blueprint for professional development that maximizes teacher and student growth.

Tschannen-Moran, M., & Tschannen-Moran, B. (2020). *Evocative coaching: Transforming schools one conversation at a time*. Thousand Oaks, CA: Corwin Press. Evocative coaching is designed to assist teachers to reinvigorate their teaching practices so that students can flourish.

Zepeda, S., Goff, L. R., & Steele, S. W. (2019). *C.R.A.F.T. conversations for teacher growth: How to build bridges and cultivate expertise*. Alexandria, VA: ASCD. The authors explore the acronym C.R.A.F.T. to describe the kind of conversations—clear, realistic, appropriate, flexible, and timely—that help educators grow their practice. They then introduce the four cornerstones of C.R.A.F.T. conversations: building capacity, invoking change, promoting collaboration, and prioritizing celebration.

6

Student Services and Special Programs

■ ■ ■

FOCUSING QUESTIONS

1. Why is it important to provide guidance and counseling services in schools?
2. How do student attendance and record keeping support the overall function of the student services department?
3. Could the modern school operate effectively without some means of evaluating student progress?
4. What methods can be used to report student progress to parents/families?
5. What role does the extracurricular activities program play in relation to the overall goals of the school?
6. What are the special education services provided for exceptional children in today's schools? Why is it important for schools to offer such services?
7. What should principals know about gifted education in order to serve all learners?
8. What should principals know about bilingual/English as a second language (ESL) education in order to serve all children?

In this chapter, we respond to these questions concerning student services. We begin our discussion by examining the aims, services, and evaluation of guidance and counseling programs. Then we look at how student attendance and record-keeping support the overall function of the student services department. Measuring and reporting student progress to parents/families are discussed next. Then we examine the role of extracurricular activities in relation to the overall mission of the school. Next, we discuss special education and explore some of the provisions of the reauthorization of the Individuals with Disabilities Act (IDEA). Finally, we examine how gifted education and bilingual education programs benefit students with special needs.

GUIDANCE AND COUNSELING SERVICES

One function of education is to provide opportunities for each student to reach his full potential in the areas of educational, vocational, personal, and emotional development. With continuous societal pressures upon students, the principal must ensure that guidance is an integral part of education and that it is centered *directly* on this function. Guidance and counseling services prepare students to assume increasing responsibility for their decisions and grow in their ability to understand and accept the results of their choices (American School Counselor Association, 2022; Erford, 2018a; Guindon & Lane, 2019; Kolbert et al., 2016; Thompson, 2012). Like other abilities, the ability to make such intelligent choices is not innate but must be developed. In this section, we examine the aims of guidance and counseling programs, major guidance and counseling services, methods of counseling, and evaluation of guidance programs. It is critical for principals to understand the basic concepts of guidance and counseling so that they can work with the counselor on their campuses to ensure quality services.

Aims of Guidance and Counseling Programs

The aims of guidance and counseling programs are similar to the purposes of education in general: to assist the student in fulfilling basic physiological needs, understanding themselves and displaying acceptance of others, developing associations with peers, balancing between permissiveness and controls in the educational setting, realizing successful achievement, and providing opportunities to gain independence (Brigman, Villares, & Webb, 2017; Dimmitt, Carey, & Hatch, 2007; Hatch, 2013; Hatch, Duarte, & Degregorio, 2018; Hatch et al., 2019). The purposes of guidance and counseling are to provide emphasis and strength to the educational program. Some specific aims of the school guidance and counseling program follow:

1. *To provide for the realization of student potentialities*. To all students, the school offers a wide choice of courses and co-curricular activities. A significant function of education is to help students identify and develop their potentialities. The counselor's role is to assist students to distribute their energies into the many learning opportunities available to them. Every student needs help in planning his major course of study and pattern of co-curricular activities.

2. *To help children with developing problems*. Even those students who have chosen an appropriate educational program for themselves may have problems that require help. A teacher may need to spend from one-fifth to one-third of his time with a few students who require a great deal of help, which deprives the rest of the class from the teacher's full attention to their needs. The counselor, by helping these youngsters to resolve their difficulties, frees the classroom teacher to use his time more efficiently.

3. *To contribute to the development of the school's curriculum*. Counselors, in working with individual students, know their personal problems and aspirations, their talents and abilities as well as the social pressures confronting them. Counselors, therefore, can provide data that serve as a basis for curriculum development, and they can help curriculum developers shape courses of study that more accurately reflect the needs of students. Too often, counselors are not included in curriculum development efforts.

4. *To provide teachers with technical assistance*. Pre-service teacher training institutions typically provide very limited experience with the more technical aspects of guidance work. Thus, a need exists in most schools for assistance with guidance and counseling functions essential to the educational program.

Specifically, the guidance counselor is qualified to assist teachers with selecting, administering, and interpreting tests; selecting and using cumulative, anecdotal, and other types of records; providing help and suggestions relative to counseling techniques, which teachers can use in counseling their students; and displaying leadership in designing and conducting professional development of teachers in guidance functions.

5. *To contribute to the mutual adjustment of students and the school.* The guidance program has a responsibility for developing and maintaining a cooperative relationship between students and the school. Teachers and counselors must be cognizant of students' needs. Students also must make adjustments to the school. They have a responsibility to contribute something to the school. A major contribution of students is that of making appropriate use of the school's resources and working toward accomplishments. Such mutual adjustment of students and school is facilitated by providing suggestions for program improvements, conducting research for educational improvements, contributing to students' adjustment through counseling, and fostering wholesome school-home attitudes.

The Role of the Counselor

The major goals of counseling are to promote personal growth and to prepare students to become motivated workers and responsible citizens. Educators recognize that in addition to intellectual challenges, students encounter personal/social, educational, and career challenges. School guidance and counseling programs need to address these challenges and to promote educational success.

The guidance and counseling program is an integral part of a school's total educational program; it is developmental by design, focusing on needs, interests, and issues related to various stages of student growth. The developmental guidance and counseling program in today's school has a broad scope that includes these components:

- *Personal/social.* In addition to providing guidance services for all students, counselors are expected to do personal and crisis counseling. Problems such as dropping out, substance abuse, suicide, irresponsible sexual behavior, eating disorders, and pregnancy must be addressed.
- *Educational.* Students must develop skills that will assist them as they learn. The counselor, through classroom guidance activities and individual and group counseling, can assist students in applying effective study skills, setting goals, learning effectively, and gaining test-taking skills. Counselors also may focus on helping students learn approaches to note taking, time management, memory techniques, relaxation techniques, overcoming test anxiety, and developing listening skills.
- *Career.* Planning for the future, combating career stereotyping, and analyzing skills and interests are some goals students must develop in school. Career information must be available to students, and representatives from business and industry must work closely with the school and the counselor in preparing students for the world of work.

(Couch, 2019; Erford, 2018a, 2018b; 2019a, 2019b; Erford, Byrd, & Byrd, 2013; Goodman-Scott, Betters-Bubon, & Donohue, 2019; Sklare, 2014)

Major Guidance and Counseling Services

The primary mission of a school's guidance and counseling program is to provide a broad spectrum of personnel services to the students. These services include student assessment, the information service, placement and follow-up, and counseling assistance. These four areas should constitute the core of any guidance program and should be organized to facilitate the growth and development of all students from kindergarten through post–high school experiences

Assessment. The **assessment** service is designed to collect, analyze, and use a variety of objective and subjective personal, psychological, and social data about each student. Its purpose is to help the individual to better understand herself. Conferences with students and parents, standardized test scores, academic records, anecdotal records, personal data forms, case studies, and portfolios are included. The school counselor interprets this information to students, parents, teachers, administrators, and other professionals. Students with special needs and abilities are thus identified.

Information. The **information** service is designed to provide accurate and current information in order that the students may make an intelligent choice of an educational program, an occupation, or a social activity. Essentially, the aim is that with such information students will make better choices and will engage in better planning in and out of the school setting. Students not only must be exposed to such information but also must have an opportunity to react to it in a meaningful way with others.

Placement and Follow-up. The school assists the student in selecting and utilizing opportunities within the school as well as in the outside labor market. Counselors assist students in making appropriate choices of courses of study and in making transitions from one school level to another, from one school to another, and from school to employment. **Placement** thereby involves student assessment, informational services, and counseling assistance appropriate to the student's choices of school subjects, co-curricular activities, and employment. **Follow-up** is concerned with the development of a systematic plan for maintaining contact with former students. The data obtained from the follow-up studies aid the school in evaluating the school's curricular and guidance programs.

Counseling. The **counseling** service is designed to facilitate self-understanding and development through dyadic or small-group relationships. The aim of such relationships tends to be focused on personal development and decision making that is based on self-understanding and knowledge of the environment. The counselor: (a) assists the student to understand and accept himself or herself, thereby clarifying his or her ideas, perceptions, attitudes, and goals; (b) furnishes personal and environmental information to the student, as required, regarding his or her plans, choices, or problems; and (c) seeks to develop in the student the ability to cope with and solve problems and increased competence in making decisions and plans for the future. Counseling is generally accepted as the heart of the guidance service (American School Counselor Association, 2022; Erford, 2018a, 2018b; 2019a, 2019b; Guindon & Lane, 2019; Kolbert, Williams, Morgan, & Crothers, 2016; Thompson, 2012).

Methods of Counseling

Counseling students is a basic function of the school guidance program. Counseling skills are needed by school principals, teachers, teacher-advisors, athletic coaches, and club sponsors as well as by professional counselors. Although counseling of serious emotional problems is best handled by professional counselors, teachers and other faculty personnel find themselves in situations daily where counseling is necessary. Acquaintance with counseling methods and points of view is useful to them.

Counseling methods and points of view have developed from research and theories about how individuals grow and develop, change their behavior, and interact with their environment. These counseling methods are generally classified into three broad types or schools of thought: directive, nondirective, and eclectic (American School Counselor Association, 2019; Erford, 2018a, 2018b; 2019a, 2019b; Guindon & Lane, 2019; Kolbert et al., 2016; Thompson, 2012). One of the most fundamental philosophical and theoretical questions that confronts the counselor in the course of her training and professional practice is which method to select in counseling students.

Directive Counseling.   The directive counselor is said to be more interested in the problem than he is in the counselee. This belief is an exaggeration. The student and her problem cannot be separated. All service professions are, by their very nature, concerned with the person to be helped. All teaching, for example, is student centered, even when a teacher has thirty students in a class. The directive counselor, however, focuses attention on identifying and analyzing the problem and finding an appropriate solution to it. He or she tends to make use of test data, school records, and reports, and is more disposed to giving advice and information based on such data. **Directive counseling** is the method most commonly used by counselors in school settings.

Directive counseling seems to be most successful when the counselee is relatively well adjusted; the problem is in an intellectual area; a lack of information constituted the problem; the counselee has little insight into the problem; inner conflict is absent; and the client suffers from anxiety, insecurity, or impatience.

Nondirective Counseling.   The nondirective approach is more effective in the treatment of many types of emotional problems. However, many students who come to the counselor have few if any such emotional problems. Many cases merely call for information or some other routine assistance.

Although there are many proponents of nondirective counseling, Carl Rogers is best known because he started the movement and has given it leadership for more than six decades (Rogers, 1942). The aim of **nondirective counseling** is, according to Rogers, to help the student "to become a better organized person, oriented around healthy goals which [he] has clearly seen and definitely chosen" (p. 227). It aims to provide the student with a united purpose, with the courage to meet life and the obstacles it presents. Consequently, the client takes from his counseling contacts not necessarily a neat solution for each of his problems, but the ability to meet his problems in a constructive way. Rogers defines effective counseling as a definitely structured, permissive relationship that allows the client to gain an understanding of himself of herself to a degree that enables him or her to take positive steps in the light of his new orientation. This hypothesis has a natural corollary—that all the techniques used should aim toward developing this free and permissive relationship, this understanding of self in the counseling and other relationships, and this tendency toward positive, self-initiated action (Rogers, 1942).

Possibly the greatest contribution of the nondirective technique has been its influence in personalizing counseling. Nevertheless, even though this approach may be more effective in certain counseling situations, it is unlikely to be used in most schools because of the extensive training essential to its application in the counseling process.

Eclectic Counseling.   **Eclectic counseling** is the result of selecting concepts from both directive and nondirective approaches. Thus, the eclectic counselor uses whatever approach seems best suited to the situation. Real help given to most students in schools would be located between the highly directive and the eclectic views rather than client centered. The eclectic counselor's effectiveness will depend more on the relationship existing between the students and their counselors than on the method they choose and how well they perform within the method they employ.

Evaluation of Guidance and Counseling Programs

Evaluation consists of making systematic judgments of the relative effectiveness with which goals are attained in relation to specified standards. In evaluating a function like guidance and counseling services, we attempt to determine to what extent the objectives of the service have been attained. The major objectives of guidance are to assist individuals in developing the ability to understand themselves, to solve their own problems, and to make appropriate adjustments to their environment as the situation dictates (Erford, 2018a; Guindon & Lane, 2019). Evaluation is the means by which school personnel can better judge the extent to which these objectives are being met. The following ten characteristics provide criteria for evaluating the effectiveness of a school's guidance and counseling services (Erford, 2020; Jackson-Cherry & Erford, 2018).

1. *Student needs.* Effective guidance programs are based on student needs. Some needs are typical among students of a given age; others are specific to certain individuals in particular regions or schools. In effective guidance programs, teachers, counselors, and principals listen carefully to what students say, because they know the students are expressing either personal or situational inadequacies.

2. *Cooperation.* The staff of effective guidance programs work cooperatively. Cooperation is exhibited in the degree of active interest, mutual help, and collaboration among teachers, counselors, and principals.

3. *Process and product.* Effective guidance programs are concerned with both process and product. The questions "How well is the program operating?" and "What are the outcomes?" guide the focus in effective guidance programs. The most important outcome of a guidance program is desirable change in the behavior of students, such as improved school attendance, better study habits, better scholastic achievement, fewer scholastic failures, lower dropout rate, better educational planning, and better home-school relations.

4. *Balance.* Effective guidance programs balance corrective, preventive, and developmental functions. Personnel in such programs know when to extricate students from potentially harmful situations, when to anticipate student difficulties, and when to provide assistance necessary to a student's maximum development.

5. *Stability.* The ability to adjust to loss of personnel without loss of effectiveness is associated with program quality. Stability requires that the system be able to fill vacant positions quickly and satisfactorily.

6. *Flexibility.* Effective guidance programs manifest flexibility. Flexibility enables the program to expand or contract as the situation demands without significant loss of effectiveness.

7. *Qualified counselors.* Counselors hold a graduate degree in counseling and are fully certified by the state in which they practice.

8. *Adequate counselor-student ratio.* Most accrediting agencies (for example, the Southern Association and the North Central Association) require a counselor-student ratio of one full-time counselor for 250 to 300 students. A caseload of this magnitude is satisfactory if counselors are to have adequate time not only to counsel students individually and in small groups but also to consult with faculty, principals, and parents.

9. *Physical facilities.* Are the facilities for guidance work sufficient for an effective program? Physical facilities that are well planned and provide for adequate space, privacy, accessibility, and the like are characteristic of quality guidance programs.

10. *Records.* Appropriate records are maintained on each student, including achievement test scores as well as information supplied by teachers, principals, parents, employers, and other professional personnel.

Although many of these ten characteristics are useful, they should not be accepted unquestioningly. To some extent, each guidance program is unique to its particular setting and consequently would either add other characteristics to the list or stress those cited previously in varying degrees.

ATTENDANCE AND STUDENT RECORDS

Student accounting is the oldest area of student services. Its beginnings can be traced to enforcement of compulsory attendance in the Massachusetts law of 1642; much later, in 1852, Massachusetts enacted the first compulsory attendance law in the United States. From the beginning, this service was primarily an administrative one aimed at keeping students in school (Guindon & Lane, 2019).

Student accounting has gradually enlarged its administrative emphasis to one of understanding child behavior. In recent years attendance officers have brought about a separation of enforcement and correction, so that truancy is being treated as a symptom of some underlying difficulty. Counselors and principals are working together to determine the causes of nonattendance. School clerks handle routine aspects of truancy, and special cases are referred to personnel workers who have time to deal with them as guidance rather than as administrative problems. Thus, nonattendance is becoming an essential part of personnel work, and its occurrences are viewed as opportunities to discover students who need special help (Evertson & Emmer, 2017; Good & Lavigne, 2018; Marzano, 2017, 2018).

It is the aim of the compulsory attendance laws that have been passed by each of the fifty states that all children shall receive certain minimum essentials as their educational preparation for life. Teachers, principals, and counselors share responsibility for helping all children to secure these essentials. To assist in this process, careful records must be kept.

The Cumulative Record

What are some of the recorded data needed to develop a better educational program for each child? The following information is recommended for inclusion in a student's cumulative record (AACROA, 2019; Cheung, Clements, & Pechman, 2000):

1. *Personal data sheet.* Such a form will provide pertinent and up-to-date information about the child. This information, most of which can be utilized by the teacher, should include family history (parents, siblings, home conditions), health history (diseases, illnesses, injuries), and school-related history (courses, grades, excused and unexcused absences, failures, activities).

2. *Parent's report.* The record should contain a brief report from the parents. This report might include a bit more information about the child's background, including what their problems in school might be, what sort of person they are at home, and any information that might help the teacher do a better job.

3. *Child's self-concept.* This information may be in the form of answers to standardized tests, such as interests and personality tests. The folder should also contain an autobiographical sketch. The following can be solicited from English teachers as part of a writing assignment: free writing or a discussion of specific areas, such as ideas about life at home, life at school, outside activities, and other things of importance to the student.

4. *Sociogram.* The record should contain a sociogram to show the degree of acceptance of the student by his or her peers, also referred to as "belongingness." This provides valuable information to the teacher regarding peer group acceptance or rejection.

5. *Behavior reports.* The student's record folder should contain periodic, objective reports of his or her behavior. In the elementary school, most of these reports would come from one teacher, whereas in the secondary school, they would be compiled by many teachers. These reports should never be used against the child, but instead should always be used for the child's benefit.

6. *Standardized test data.* A major part of the cumulative record is data collected as part of the school testing program—intelligence, personality and adjustment, interests, aptitude, achievement, and the like, and interpretation of test results and recommendations for adjustments and remedial work (AACROA, 2019; Cheung et al., 2000). Such information may help the teacher to better understand each of his or her students, and it may alert him or her to some of the difficulties students may experience in the future.

The Use of Assessment Data to Improve Learning

Many schools have increased the value of their cumulative record by providing careful instructions for their maintenance and use. What outcomes may be reasonably expected from the use of these records? The following five are suggested (Abdul-Hamid, Saraogi, & Mintz, 2017; Bernhardt, 2013):

1. A clearer understanding that the master teacher is a teacher of students, not merely of subject matter
2. A more systematic focusing of attention on the needs of individual students in order to help them to become more self-sufficient and independent

3. A better adjustment of the school and the curriculum to the needs and capacities of every student
4. A practical use of the appraisal of children and their needs that may result in the solution of some of their problems in school
5. A better intellectual and social development of each child so that they may maximize their potential

The cumulative record has value for teachers, principals, and other personnel-service professionals. Such data provide a better understanding of the child—his or her needs, aspirations, interests, and potentialities. The cumulative record can help with the child's adjustment in school, in the transition from one school level to another, and in the selection of postsecondary education and vocational plans.

EVALUATING STUDENT PROGRESS

Testing, evaluating, and measuring student progress is a part of every comprehensive student services program. Practically every faculty member in a school is involved in the appraisal service. Teachers spend a great deal of time testing, measuring, and evaluating their students, as do counselors, social workers, and school psychologists. Few people who work in schools would deny that the modern school could operate effectively without some means of measuring and evaluating student progress, particularly in light of the Every Student Succeeds Act (ESSA), which requires schools to meet adequate yearly progress (AYP) standards in reading, mathematics, and science. Those schools failing to meet the standards for several years could undergo "restructuring."

Adequate yearly progress (AYP) standards require schools and districts to have (a) the same high standards of academic achievement for all; (b) statistically valid and reliable tests; (c) continuous and substantial academic improvement for all students; (d) separate, measurable annual objectives for achievement for all students, racial/ethnic groups, economically disadvantaged students, students with disabilities (IDEA, §602), and students with limited English proficiency; and (e) graduation rates for high school and one other indicator for other schools. ESSA 1111(b)(2)(C)(vi) defined the percentage of students who graduate from secondary school with a regular diploma in the standard number of years, and the regulation clarifies that alternate definitions that accurately measure the graduation rate are permissible. For AYP, each group of students must meet or exceed the established statewide annual objective exception: The number below proficient is reduced 10 percent from the prior year, and the subgroup must make progress on other indicators; and for each group, 95 percent of students enrolled participate in the assessments on which AYP is based (see your state's guidelines for AYP). In this section, we examine the purposes of assessment, establishing information criteria, creating effective tests, and the components of a testing program.

Purposes of Assessment

The basic purpose of the assessment service is to help the student in school. More specifically, the six basic purposes of assessment are (a) to help the students understand themselves; (b) to provide information for educational and vocational counseling; (c) to help principals, faculty, and personnel staff to understand the nature of their student population; (d) to evaluate the academic progress and personal development of students; (e) to help the principal staff appraise the educational program; and (f) to facilitate curriculum revision (Brookhart, 2010; Brookhart & McMillan, 2019; Butler & McMunn, 2006; Klenowski & Wyatt-Smith, 2014; Marzano, 2006; Popham, 2003, 2010, 2011, 2020; Suskie, 2018).

Others suggest three basic purposes of testing students: to make instructional management decisions, to make decisions about screening students, and to make program decisions (Kubiszyn & Borich, 2015; Miller et al., 2012; Sindelar, 2015; Stiggins, 2017). (See table 6.1.)

Table 6.1 describes the relationships among general purposes: assessment context, related decisions, necessary data, and appropriate decision makers. For example, diagnosis of student strengths and weaknesses is one of the decision areas listed under "Instructional Management." Because the purpose of testing in this case is to make decisions about individual students, any test that is adopted must provide information about specific skills and/or subject-matter understanding.

Establishing Information Criteria

After determining the purposes of testing students, the next step is to identify the type of information needed to make the desired decisions. The information provided by any testing program can be classified into one or more of three categories or domains: (a) the **affective domain**, which refers to attitudes, feelings, interests, and values (Krathwohl, Bloom, & Masia, 1964); (b) the **psychomotor domain**, which refers to those skills involving neuromuscular coordination such as handwriting skills and athletic skills (Harrow, 1972); and (c) the **cognitive domain**, which is identified in a variety of ways and is usually classified along a continuum. Knowledge (that is, knowledge of facts, rules, and sequences) is viewed as a lower-order cognitive skill; and higher-order skills include the ability to classify, to recognize relationships, to analyze, to synthesize, and to evaluate (Bloom, 1956). Anderson and Krathwohl (2001) revised Bloom's (1956) taxonomy classified along a continuum from lower-order to higher-order cognitive skills as follows: remembering, understanding, applying, analyzing, evaluating, and creating.

For example, if the purpose of testing is to make decisions about placement of students into academic classes of differing ability levels, it will be necessary to collect data that will yield information about how students perform on specific cognitive objectives. However, if a program has explicit affective goals, and the decision is to determine how well those goals have been reached, it will be necessary to develop or purchase measures of student attitudes, feelings, values, or interests. Both teacher-constructed and standardized instruments can be used for this purpose.

Should tests be authentic simulations of how knowledge is tested in adult work and civic settings? Many educators believe so. Performance assessment, then, calls on test makers to be creative designers, not just technicians.

Creating Effective Tests

Some experts in testing (AERA, 2014; Cohen & Swerdlik, 2018; Furr, 2018; Grath-Marnat & Wright, 2016; Kaplan & Saccuzzo, 2017; Kubiszyn & Borich, 2015; Popham, 2014, 2019; Sindelar, 2015) offer the following eight basic design criteria as assistance to test designers.

Table 6.1 Summary of Various Purposes for Testing

Assessment Context	Types of Decisions	Type of Data Needed	Decision Makers					
			Students	Parents	Teachers	Administrators	Counselors	Public
Instructional Management Decisions								
Diagnosis	Decide students' strengths and weaknesses on specific skills	Individual student data on level of development of specific skills	✓		✓			
Placement	Place student into next most appropriate level of instruction	Scores that place students on relevant knowledge or skill continuum			✓	✓	✓	
Guidance and Counseling	Decide probability of success and satisfaction in given program of educational or vocational development	Data reflecting level of educational development of individual student relative to other students	✓	✓				✓
Student Screening Decisions								
Selection	Decide which students to be selected into or out of a program	Data that rank order individual students on relevant knowledge or skill scale			✓	✓	✓	
Certification	Determine mastery or nonmastery of specified body of knowledge or set of skills	Data reflecting individual student mastery of specified body of knowledge or set of skills			✓	✓		✓
Programmatic Decisions								
Survey	Make educational policy decisions; determine educational development of student group	Group achievement data gathered cyclically to show trends				✓		✓
Formative Evaluation	Decide program components in need of modification	Interim and final program outcomes attained and not attained by participating students considered as a group			✓	✓		
Summative Evaluation	Determine if program is to be adopted, expanded, or discontinued	Program outcomes attained and not attained by participating students considered as a group			✓	✓		✓

- Assessment tasks should be, whenever possible, authentic and meaningful—worth mastering.
- The set of tasks should be a valid sample from which apt generalizations about overall performance of complex capacities can be made.
- The scoring criteria should be authentic, with points awarded or taken off for essential successes and errors, not for what is easy to count or observe.
- The performance standards that anchor the scoring should be genuine benchmarks, not arbitrary cut scores or provincial school norms.
- The context of the problems should be rich, realistic, and enticing—with the inevitable constraints on access to time, resources, and advance knowledge of the tasks and standards appropriately minimized.
- The tasks should be validated.
- The scoring should be feasible and reliable.
- Assessment results should be reported and used so that *all* customers for the data are satisfied.

Components of a Testing Program

A comprehensive school-wide testing program begins in kindergarten and ends in the twelfth grade. Tests administered throughout the school years include assessment of emerging reading; general learning readiness; and tests of general intelligence, achievement, and aptitude and interest. A typical testing program in a school district might resemble the one depicted in table 6.2 (AERA, 2014; Cohen & Swerdlik, 2018; Furr, 2018; Grath-Marnat & Wright, 2016; Kaplan & Saccuzzo, 2017; Kubiszyn & Borish, 2015; Popham, 2003, 2010, 2011, 2020; Sindelar, 2015).

In discussing the evaluation of student growth in schools, Popham (2020) refers to three areas of measurement: (a) knowledge and understanding, (b) skills and competence, and (c) attitude and interest. For each of these areas, the author refers to a number of educational objectives and the appropriate means of evaluating them. It

Table 6.2 Comprehensive School-Wide Testing Program

Grade	Type of Test
K	Reading readiness
1 or 2	Learning readiness
	Reading ability
	Mental ability
3, 4, or 5	Achievement battery (language skills, including reading, mathematics, social studies, science)
6, 7, or 8	Mental ability (repeated at entrance to middle school or junior high)
	Multifactor aptitude
9, 10, or 11	Achievement battery
11 or 12	College aptitude
	Interests—personal
	Interests—vocational

would seem, therefore, that every school should have at least the following components in the way of a testing battery:

1. *Emerging reading test.* An **emerging reading test** should be administered in kindergarten or first grade to determine the child's readiness to profit from reading. Examples include the Gates-MacGinitie Reading Tests (Houghton-Mifflin), Lee-Clark Emerging Reading Test (California Test Bureau), and the Murphy-Durrell Emerging Reading Analysis (Harcourt Brace Jovanovich). These tests measure speed and accuracy, vocabulary, comprehension, and recognition of similarities and differences in printed letters.

2. *Learning readiness test.* A **learning readiness test** should be administered in grade one or two to demonstrate the student's ability to mark pictures and letters and to identify words that match given ones. Examples include the Metropolitan Readiness Test (a group test that assesses six important aspects of readiness for formal first-grade instruction: word meaning, listening, visual perception, alphabet, numbers, and copying) and Primary Mental Abilities Test (measures verbal meaning, number facility, reasoning, perceptual speed, and spatial relations).

3. *Intelligence test.* An **intelligence test** should be administered in grade one, again toward the end of the elementary grades, and again early in high school. An individual measure is better than a group measure. There is a wide discrepancy between tests concerning the accurate measurement of a child's intelligence. Among the best-known intelligence tests are the California Short Form Test of Mental Maturity, Lorge-Thorndike Intelligence Test, Otis-Lennon Mental Ability Test, Revised Stanford-Binet Scale, and the Wechsler Intelligence Scales.

4. *Achievement tests.* At a very minimum, an **achievement test** battery including language, reading, mathematics, and social studies should be given periodically during the student's twelve years of public school education. Examples include the Comprehensive Tests of Basic Skills, Iowa Tests of Basic Skills, Sequential Tests of Educational Progress, and Stanford Achievement Tests. Others include state-developed achievement tests. Since NCLB, all fifty states now have developed their own state test aligned with their state curriculum. Generally, these tests measure the capacity to comprehend written material, to think scientifically and analytically, and to display some understanding of the process of history.

5. *Interest and aptitude tests.* Measures of **interests and aptitudes** might be administered periodically to individuals, or groups of students, for purposes of placement or selection. Examples of aptitude measures include the Differential Aptitude Tests, School and College Ability Test, American College Testing Program, and the Scholastic Aptitude Test. Generally, these tests measure basic verbal and mathematical ability and reasoning.

Perhaps the best reference available for a quick summary and review of nearly all tests on the market is *The Twenty-First Mental Measurements Yearbook* (Carlson, Geisinger, & Jonson, 2021). It should be noted, however, that not all of the tests that are published are available for use without the proper training. Many universities provide courses that are concerned with the understanding, interpretation, and use of one specific test.

There may be missing elements in the conceptualization on which standard test theory is based. Those elements are models for just how people know what they know and do what they can do, and the ways in which they increase these capacities. Different models are useful for different purposes; therefore, test experts are proposing broader or alternative student models. For example, three test experts from the organization Educational Testing Service (ETS) consider a variety of directions in which standard test theory might be extended. They discuss the role of test theory in light of recent work in cognitive and educational psychology, test design, student modeling, test analysis, and the integration of assessment and instruction (Rupp & Leighton, 2017).

REPORTING TO PARENTS AND FAMILIES

Principals must ensure a good school-home connection because the educational program of a school is limited by the amount of cooperation received from the home. Students are not educated by removing them from all of their activities for six hours each day and causing them to study English, mathematics, social studies, and science. They are educated as they live. This places a demand on the school to be interested in the whole of students' lives—their interests at home, their interests in the community, and their abilities and talents as demonstrated in school and in all of the interrelated activities of the school community. The more congruent students' school lives, home lives, and community lives, the more nearly students will be to accomplishing the fulfillment of a true education (Miller, 2002). School newspapers, monthly newsletters, parent-teacher conferences, and teacher and principal visits to the home are methods used to inform the home of school activities and student progress. The report card is another method of informing parents of the child's progress in school (Guskey, 2015).

The value of such reports is unquestionable. The time and effort involved in preparing them becomes one of the biggest clerical tasks the teacher must perform. In addition to recording school grades on the report cards, the teacher must devise a student rating system that is fair, accurate, and consistent (Guskey & Brookhart, 2019). In this section, we examine the difficulties in assigning grades and review some methods of reporting student progress.

Difficulties in Grading

Principals must be aware that teachers experience several fundamental difficulties in assigning grades to students. First, there is the variability of these measures from teacher to teacher. Research has shown that teachers vary in their grading of the same test by as much as four grade levels. That is, a sample of teachers rated a high school essay test from A to D. With more careful preparation of examinations and training of examiners, the reliability and validity of grades can be markedly improved (Reeves, 2016).

The grades teachers assign to students not only show great variability but also do not measure the same kind of accomplishment as do standardized achievement tests in the same subject. Teachers' grades are an undefined composite into which enter estimates of effort and attitude. Thus, in addition to recording scholarship, grades usually include the teacher's personal feelings and reactions to the student. Standardized tests, on the other hand, provide a measure of achievement or aptitude not subject to personal bias. By definition, a **standardized achievement test** is a series of questions designed to provide a systematic sample of performance, administered in accordance with uniform (standard) directions, scored according to definite (standard) rules, and interpreted in reference to normative (standard) information. Furthermore, administration and scoring of standardized tests are determined so precisely that the same procedures could be conducted at different times and places. Both standardized tests and teacher grades are of significance in understanding the student, and neither should be eliminated as an appraisal tool.

Another fundamental difficulty in grading is that relatively few schools have a reliable aptitude or IQ score for all of their students. Without this information, it is difficult for teachers to estimate students' achievement in relation to their ability. Appraisals of students must somehow attempt to relate achievement and ability to determine if students are performing up to their potential, or beyond it.

Further, different grading policies appear to be in operation at various educational levels: elementary school, middle school, and high school. For example, at the elementary school level, a child's achievement may be judged based on his or her own ability, whereas in secondary schools a student may be graded on a strictly competitive basis.

Finally, new approaches to educational assessment—in particular, constructed response, performance testing, and portfolio assessment—provide a full range of alternatives to traditional testing methods. These new approaches are useful in all types of large-scale testing programs, including classroom use (AERA, 2014; Cohen & Swerdlik, 2018; Furr, 2018; Grath-Marnat & Wright, 2016; Kaplan & Saccuzzo, 2017; Kubiszyn & Borish, 2015; Popham, 2003, 2010, 2011, 2019; Sindelar, 2015). To implement these new approaches effectively, however, teacher training will be necessary.

Methods of Reporting Student Progress

Over the years, several methods of reporting grades to parents and caregivers have evolved. In view of the aforementioned difficulties existing in various degrees in different communities, grading systems will vary with the situation. A few of the more common methods of measuring school progress follow (Cornue, 2017; Guskey, 2015; Guskey & Brookhart, 2018; Reeves, 2016; Schimmer, 2016; Schumaker, 2018; Vatterat, 2015; Wormeli, 2018).

Percentage Method. The **percentage method** is one of the oldest. Student ratings are based on a scale that ranges from 0 to 100. For example, suppose that a mathematics test contains ten problems. If all problems are answered correctly, the student will receive 100 percent. If half of the problems are performed correctly, the student will receive 50 percent. Each test given during a marking period are averaged to determine an overall percentage grade for the period. The percentage method is difficult to use. There are so many points along the scale when the teacher must make fine discriminations among a class of students.

Letter Method. The **letter method** offers more flexibility in determining a student's grade. A letter grade on a five-point scale is commonly used: A, B, C, D, and F. To make these letters understandable, two practices have arisen. First, the letters are interpreted in terms of percentages, where, for instance, A = 90 to 100, B = 80 to 89, C = 70 to 79, D = 60 to 69, and F = any mark below 60. Second, definite standards are established for each of the five letter grades. For example, standards for an A might be (a) always hands work in on time, (b) completes all work assigned in a creditable manner, (c) completes more than the assigned work, (d) shows some creativity in mastering the work assigned, and (e) has an excellent record of attendance. Successively lower standards can be established for the remaining letter-grade categories.

Descriptive Method.   Letters to or conferences with parents are used in place of percentages or letter grades in the **descriptive method.** Descriptive statements can also be used to supplement the previously mentioned estimates of achievement, providing explanations of grades or other open-ended information.

Percentile Method.   A percentile score of 72 means that 72 percent of all students on whose test scores the scale is based have scores lower than the examinee. The **percentile method** is frequently used in interpreting standardized achievement test scores. The principal reason for using the percentile is that it enables the parent to know just where the child ranks in the group.

Three-Group Method.   The **three-group method** involves reporting the student's achievement as "above average," "average," or "below average." Definition of these terms is based on the percentile technique. If a student rates among the middle 50 percent of his class group, he is considered an average student. This includes all students between the twenty-fifth and seventy-fifth percentiles. "Above average" means, therefore, that the student is in the upper quartile of his or her group. "Below average" means that the student is in the lower fourth of the group.

Rank Method.   The **rank method** indicates whether the student is in first, second, or any other position in his or her group. Most high schools rank their graduating seniors in this way. Some colleges and universities use rank in class as one criterion for admission. Parents of students in a college-bound track often want to know how their child ranks in the group.

T-Score Method.   Like the percentile score, the **T-score method** is difficult to interpret. The T-score represents one-tenth of the standard deviation of the scores for the group considered. The T-score is not based on the class group, nor on a grade group, but instead on a local or national norm for an entire age group. Use of these scores is more prevalent when reporting standardized achievement test data to parents than when reporting school grades.

Each method of reporting student progress to parents and caregivers has merit. A school must decide, in light of all the factors, what type of report to adopt. The best kind of report appears to be the descriptive account, supplemented by quantitative estimates of achievement, aptitude, and personality.

EXTRACURRICULAR ACTIVITIES

Student activities are found at all levels of our school system, especially in secondary schools. The terms **extracurricular activities**, *cocurricular activities*, and *nonclassroom activities* have all been used interchangeably to mean experiences and activities such as debate, athletics, music, drama, school publications, student council, school clubs, contests, and various social events. This multitude of experiences forms a third curriculum—paralleling the required and the elective curricula—and it is well integrated into the daily school program. Generally, extracurricular activities are voluntary, are approved and sponsored by school officials, and carry no academic credit toward graduation (Deutsch, 2017; Foster, 2017; Fretwell, 2018; Kennedy-Phillips, Baldasare, & Christakis, 2015; Theobald, 2015; Wankel & Wankel, 2016). In this section, we discuss the role of extracurricular activities in relation to the overall goals of education and the functions of extracurricular activities.

Goals of Education

Extracurricular activities, by whatever name they are called, are an essential, vital, and extensive part of education in America. Developing skills in group work; cultivating hobbies and interests; producing yearbooks, newspapers, and plays; and participating in interscholastic athletics and intramural sports are some of the many opportunities students have for discovering and developing talents that approximate life in the adult community (Deutsch, 2017).

The legacy of including worthy use of leisure time as a valid part of educational goals is the foundation of the student activities program in American schools. Although the goals of secondary education had been variously stated for many years, one of the first concerted efforts to define the curriculum of secondary schools resulted in the Cardinal Principles of Secondary Education in 1918 (Commission on the Reorganization of Secondary Education). The seven cardinal principles have had a major impact on shaping the goals of education for nearly nine decades.

The importance of these objectives was demonstrated by a redefinition of the curriculum to include all activities that influence the way others think, feel, believe, and act. Social events, athletics, clubs, and all the many leisure activities have become a part of the values and virtues not only of American education but also of democratic life.

Functions of Extracurricular Activities

Extracurricular activities serve the same goals and functions as the required and elective courses in the curriculum. However, they provide experiences that are not included in the formal courses of study. They permit students to apply knowledge acquired in formal courses and to acquire concepts of democratic life. When managed properly, the extracurricular activities program allows for a well-rounded, balanced program by (a) reinforcing learning, (b) supplementing the required and elective curriculum (formal courses of study), (c) integrating knowledge, and (d) carrying out the objectives of democratic life (Deutsch, 2017; Foster, 2017; Fretwell, 2018; Kennedy-Phillips, Baldasare, & Christakis, 2015; Theobald, 2015; Wankel & Wankel, 2016).

Reinforcing Learning.   One function of extracurricular activities is to reinforce the required course of studies. An activity is used to enrich and extend the work in the classroom. Clubs associated with a subject-matter discipline have considerable reinforcement value. The Spanish club may be used as an example of reinforcing learning. The Spanish club extends the time students spend working on the Spanish language. During the course of club activities, specific linguistic lessons are reviewed or extended. The names of articles of clothing, of food, and of eating utensils are used in a natural setting. Mastery of the Spanish language is thus enriched, which is precisely the objective of the Spanish course.

Supplementing Coursework.   Another function of extracurricular activities is to supplement the required and elective courses of study. This function supplements the curriculum with experiences that are not possible in regular classroom settings. Such activities as school dances, student council, chess, publications, and sports add opportunities to the total learning experience as well as worthwhile leisure-time activities to the total learning process. These nonsubject-related activities add to and enrich even the most innovative programs of required and elective courses.

Integrating Knowledge. An important objective of the total learning process is the integration of knowledge. Extracurricular activities are said to be integrative in nature because they tie together many areas of knowledge and experience. They do not provide abstract and isolated pieces of learning but, rather, synthesize many aspects of real-life situations. For example, the school committee commissioned to select a site for the prom must consider such factors as size of the establishment, distance from the school, reputation of the facility, language in the contract, decor, and cost to the student. In the same way, the purchase of a home involves many of the same human, artistic, legal, and economic factors. Through the student activities program, the student learns to deal with many important aspects of a problem.

Democratization. The extracurricular activities program is effective because it carries out, in an especially vital way, the objectives of present-day democratic life. Generally, American schools devote a part of the required curriculum to study of the development, structure, and problems of American democracy. The actual living of a democratic life is seriously restricted within the formal classroom setting. A rich program of student activities can remove such barriers and provide for individual and group interaction in a natural environment.

The extracurricular activities program offers students an opportunity to participate in administration through the student council, teacher-advisory groups, and organized activities. The student council provides opportunities for administrative experience including planning, organizing, initiating, and controlling many aspects of school life. Through teacher-advisory groups, an advisory unit is created that becomes the source from which activities flow. In these groups, the teacher and students establish proper relationships that are somewhat analogous to those of a family, team, or department in an organization. Through the clubs, athletics, and intramural sports that emanate from subject-matter disciplines, students develop teamwork and cooperation—ideals of competitiveness in a democratic society.

SPECIAL EDUCATION SERVICES

Historically, the attitude that prevailed concerning the education of disabled students was that intellectually disabled, learning disabled, emotionally disturbed (emotionally impaired or emotional disorder) hearing impaired, visually impaired, physically disabled, or otherwise disabled children were not the responsibility of the public schools. Consequently, many disabled children were exempted from compulsory school attendance laws either by parental choice or by school district design. For example, the earliest reported case involving a student with a disability was *Watson v. City of Cambridge* (1893) in which the court upheld a student's exemption for being "weak minded" (*Watson v. City of Cambridge*, 32 N.E. 864, Mass. 1893). Nationally, services for the disabled were either nonexistent or nonextensive. Very few school districts provided services; where such services existed, they were inadequate to meet even the minimal needs of this vulnerable minority group.

In recent years, substantial changes in the attitude toward the disabled have occurred. Although disabled students do not comprise any "protected group" (such as race or gender) that is entitled to constitutional guarantees, federal statutes and state special education statutes have been enacted to satisfy their constitutional rights. Lower court decisions and federal and state legislative enactments of the past three decades have mandated that all children, including the disabled, are entitled to admission to a school and placement in a program that meets their special needs. As summarized in the landmark Supreme Court school desegregation case, *Brown v. Board of Education of Topeka* (347 U.S. 483 [1954]), "education . . . is a right which must be made available to all on equal terms" (*Brown v. Board of Education of Topeka*, 347 U.S. 483 [1954]). Although the Brown decision dealt with the constitutional protections afforded minority children, its consent agreement implied a mandate that all students of legal school age must be provided with appropriate school and classroom placement.

Two key court decisions outlined the legal framework for the constitutional protections of disabled children. In *Pennsylvania Association for Retarded Children (PARC) v. Commonwealth*, 348 F. Supp. 279 E.D. Pa. (1972), a federal district court held that retarded children in Pennsylvania were entitled to a free public education and that, whenever possible, disabled children must be educated in regular classrooms and not segregated from other students. In *Mills v. Board of Education of the District of Columbia*, 348 F. Supp. 866 D.D.C. (1972), another federal district court expanded the PARC decision to include all school-age disabled children.

Section 504 of the Rehabilitation Act
Subsequent to the PARC and Mills decisions, Congress passed two landmark pieces of legislation that led to the rapid development of comprehensive, nationwide educational programs for the disabled: Section 504 of the Rehabilitation Act of 1973 (Section 504) (29 U.S.C.A. § 794 a) and the Education for All Handicapped Children Act (20 U.S.C.A. §§ 1400 et seq.). Section 504 is a broad-based federal law that addresses discrimination against the disabled both in the workplace and in schools. The statute stipulates:

> No otherwise qualified individual with handicaps . . . shall solely by reason of her or his handicap, be excluded from participation in, be denied the benefits of, or be subjected to discrimination under any programs or activity receiving Federal financial assistance. (29 U.S.C.A. § 794 a)

Thus, Section 504 would cut off all federal funds from schools that discriminate against the disabled. The statute also provides that all newly constructed public facilities be equipped to allow free access by disabled individuals.

To qualify for protection under Section 504, an individual must be a "handicapped person," which is defined as follows:

• [A]ny person who (i) has a physical or mental impairment which substantially limits one or more major life activities, (ii) has a record of such an impairment, or (iii) is regarded as having such an impairment. (34 C.F.R. § 104.3, 1997)

Other relevant terms are defined as follows:

- "Physical or mental impairment" means (a) any physiological disorder or condition, cosmetic disfigurement, or anatomical loss affecting one or more of the following body systems: neurological; musculoskeletal; special sense organs; respiratory, including speech organs; cardiovascular; reproductive; digestive; genitourinary; hemic and lymphatic; skin; and endocrine; or (b) any mental or psychological disorder, such as mental retardation, organic brain syndrome, emotional or mental illness, and specific learning disabilities.
- "Major life activities" means functions such as caring for one's self, performing manual tasks, walking, seeing, hearing, speaking, breathing, learning, and working.
- "Has a record of such an impairment" means has a history of, or has been misclassified as having, a mental or physical impairment that substantially limits one or more major life activities.
- "Is regarded as having an impairment" means (a) has a physical or mental impairment that does not substantially limit major life activities but that is treated by a recipient as constituting such limitation; (b) has a physical or mental impairment that substantially limits major life activities only as a result of the attitudes of others toward such impairment; or (c) has none of the impairments defined in . . . this section but is treated by a recipient as having such an impairment.

(34 C.F.R. § 104.3, 1997)

Education for All Handicap Children Act (EAHCA)

The EAHCA (Public Law 94-142) ensured the right of all children with disabilities to a public school education.

The need for this law was expressed by Congress:

1. [T]here are more than eight million handicapped children in the United States today;
2. the special educational needs of such children are not being fully met;
3. more than half of the handicapped children in the United States do not receive appropriate educational services which would enable them to have full equality of opportunity;
4. one million of the handicapped children in the United States are excluded entirely from the public school system and will not go through the educational process with their peers;
5. there are many handicapped children throughout the United States participating in regular school programs hose handicaps prevent them from having a successful educational experience because their handicaps are undetected

(20 U.S.C.A. §§ 1400 et seq.)

To ensure children with disabilities basic educational rights, Public L 94-142 incorporated certain tenets: (1) a free, appropriate public education; (2) an individualized education program; (3) special education services; (4) related services; (5) due process procedures; and (6) the least-restrictive environment (LRE) in which to learn (20 U.S.C.A. §§ 1401).

Since its enactment in 1975, the EAHCA has been amended several times—1986, 1990, 1997, and 2004—each time reaffirming the original intent. In 1990, the statute was renamed the Individuals with Disabilities Education Act (IDEA) (For consistency, we refer to the most recent re-authorization of the IDEA).

The IDEA, revised in 1997 and 2004, provide federal funds to school districts that comply with its requirements; the most recent, 2004, version of the IDEA became fully effective on July 1, 2005. The major thrust of these acts was to ensure the right of all disabled children to a public education. Major provisions include a free appropriate public education, an individualized education program, special education services, related services, due process procedures, and the least restrictive learning environment (20 U.S.C.A. §§ 1400 a).

According to IDEA, all disabled children have the right to a "free appropriate public education." An appropriate education for the disabled is defined as special education and related services. Special education refers to specially designed instruction at public expense, including a variety of opportunities on a spectrum from regular classroom instruction and special classes to placement in a private facility. Related services include transportation, physical and occupational therapy, recreation, and counseling and medical diagnosis. A written individualized education program (IEP) is another key element in a free appropriate public education. An IEP includes an assessment of the child's needs, specification of annual goals, strategies (methods, materials, interventions) to achieve the goals, and periodic evaluations of the child's progress. And, finally, a disabled child must be educated in the least restrictive environment. That is, the placement must be tailored to the special needs of the disabled student. In combination with related state laws, these federal statutes provide the guidelines for the education of the disabled.

In addition to the Rehabilitation Act, the disabled are now protected by the Americans with Disabilities Act (ADA) of 1990 (42 U.S.C.A. §§ 12101–12213). "The law prohibits discrimination in employment (and other situations) against any "qualified individual with a disability." Essentially, it amplifies and extends prohibitions of Section 504 of the Rehabilitation Act of 1973. Coverage is not dependent on involvement of federal funds. A "reasonable accommodation" that would permit a qualified individual with a disability to perform the "essential functions" of a position (or other activity) must be provided.

The definition of a disabled person under the ADA is somewhat different from the Rehabilitation Act. Under the newer law, a "qualified individual with a disability" means "an individual with a disability who, with or without reasonable modifications . . . meets the essential eligibility requirements for the receipt of services or the participation in programs or activities provided by a public entity" (42 U.S.C.A. § 12131 2). To prevent conflict between the Rehabilitation Act and ADA, legislation requires that ADA be interpreted consistently with the older law. Thus, court decisions interpreting Section 504 are not affected by the later law. Furthermore, the Rehabilitation Act looks to the terms of the IDEA for resolution of most disputes concerning the education of the disabled; and compliance with IDEA will usually meet the requirements of ADA. Of these three laws, IDEA has had the most significant impact on public schools.

IDEA

On November 19, 2004, Congress passed legislation reauthorizing IDEA and replacing it with the Individuals with Disabilities Education Improvement Act (Public Law 108-446), known as IDEA 2004. President George W. Bush signed this bill into law on December 3, 2004. IDEA 2004 has significantly affected the professional lives of general education teachers and special educators as well as parents of children with disabilities, all of whom encountered new roles and responsibilities as a result of the law.

The Individuals with Disabilities Education Improvement Act of 2004 (New IDEA) increased the focus of special education from simply ensuring access to education to improving the educational performance of students with disabilities and aligning special education services with the larger national school improvement efforts that include standards, assessments, and accountability (Nolet & McLaughlin, 2005).

Following are highlights of some significant issues addressed in this historic document. These provisions provide a framework for individual states to develop their own standards and procedures.

Highly Qualified Special Education Teachers. The language contained in IDEA 2004 concerning who is considered a "highly qualified" special educator is complementary to the standards promulgated in the NCLB. (See table 6.3.)

Individualized Education Program (IEP) Process.

- Short-term objectives and benchmarks will no longer be required except for those pupils who are evaluated via alternate assessments aligned to alternate achievement standards.
- Assessment of the progress that a student is making toward meeting annual goals, which must be written in measurable terms, is still required. Reference, however, to the current requirement of reporting the "extent to which progress is sufficient to enable the child to achieve goals by the end of the year" is eliminated. The IEP will now need to describe how the individual's progress toward achieving annual goals will be measured and when these progress reports will be made.
- A new provision of the legislation allows for members of the IEP team to be excused from participating in all or part of the meeting if the parents and school district agree that attendance is not necessary because the individual's area of curriculum or related service is not being reviewed or modified. The team member will be required, however, to submit written input into the development of the IEP prior to the meeting.
- PL 108-446 allows for alternatives to physical IEP meetings such as video conferencing and conference telephone calls.
- Once an IEP is established, IDEA 2004 will allow for changes to be made via a written plan to modify the document without convening the entire team and redrafting the whole IEP.
- The new legislation deletes references to transition services beginning at age fourteen. Now, transition services are to begin no later than the first IEP in effect when the student turns sixteen (and updated annually). It also establishes a new requirement for postsecondary goals pertaining to appropriate education, training, employment, and independent living skills.
- School districts will be allowed, with parental consent, to develop multiyear IEPs (not to exceed three years).

Table 6.3 Summary of Requirements to Be a Highly Qualified Special Education Teacher

Category of Special Education Teachers	*Requirements under Public Law 108-446 (IDEA)*
All special education teachers	*General Requirements* hold at least a bachelor's degree must obtain full state special education certification or equivalent cannot hold an emergency or temporary certificate
New or veteran *elementary school* teachers teaching *one or more core academic subjects* only to children with disabilities held to alternative academic standards (most severely cognitively disabled)	In addition to the general requirements above, may demonstrate academic subject competence through "a high objective uniform state standard of evaluation" (HOUSSE) process
New or veteran *middle* or *high school* teachers teaching on or more core academic subjects only to children with disabilities held to alternative academic standards (most severely cognitively disabled)	In addition to the general requirements above, may demonstrate "subject matter knowledge appropriate to the level of instruction being provided, as determined by the state, needed to effectively teacher to those standards"
New teachers of *two or more academic subjects* who are highly qualified in either mathematics, language arts, or science	In addition to the general requirements above, has two-year window in which to become highly qualified in the other core academic subjects and may do this through the HOUSSE process
Veteran teachers who teach *two or more core academic subjects* only to children with disabilities	In addition to the general requirements above, may demonstrate academic subject competence through the HOUSSE process (including a single evaluation for all core academic subjects)
Consultative teachers and other special education teachers who do not teach core academic subjects	Must only meet the general requirements above
Other special education teachers teaching core academic subjects	In addition to the general requirements above, must meet relevant NCLB requirements for new elementary school teachers, new middle/high school teachers, or veteran teachers

- The US Department of Education is charged with developing and disseminating model IEP forms and model IFSP (individualized family service plan) forms.

Identifying Students with Specific Learning Disabilities. Under IDEA 1997, when identifying an individual for a possible learning disability, educators typically looked to see if the student exhibited a severe discrepancy between achievement and intellectual ability. This discrepancy provision was removed from IDEA 2004. School districts will now be able, if they so choose, to use a process that determines if the pupil responds to empirically validated, scientifically based interventions a procedure known as Response-to-Intervention (RTI). Under the new guidelines, rather than comparing IQ with performance on standardized achievement tests, general education teachers can offer intensive programs of instructional interventions. If the child fails to make adequate progress, a learning disability is assumed to be present and additional assessment is warranted.

Discipline.

- PL 108-446 stipulates that when a student is removed from his current educational setting, the pupil is to continue to receive those services that enable participation in the general education curriculum and ensure progress toward meeting IEP goals.
- IDEA 1997 allowed school authorities to unilaterally remove a student to an interim alternative educational setting (IASE) for up to forty-five days for offenses involving weapons or drugs. IDEA 2004 now permits school officials to remove any pupil (including those with and without disabilities) to a IASE for up to forty-five days for inflicting "serious bodily injury."
- Removal to an IASE will now be for forty-five school days rather than forty-five calendar days.
- Behavior resulting in disciplinary action still requires a manifestation review; however, language requiring the IEP team to consider whether the pupil's disability impaired his ability to control behavior or comprehend the consequences of his actions has been eliminated. IEP teams now need to ask only two questions: (1) Did the disability cause or have a direct and substantial relationship to the offense? (2) Was the violation a direct result of the school's failure to implement the IEP?
- IDEA 2004 modifies the "stay put" provision enacted during an appeals process. When either the local education agency (LEA) or parent requests an appeal of a manifestation determination or placement decision, the pupil is required to remain in the current IASE until a decision is rendered by the hearing officer or until the time period for the disciplinary violation concludes. A hearing must be held within twenty school days of the date of the appeal.

Due Process.

- Parents will encounter a two-year statute of limitations for filing a due process complaint from the time they knew or should have known that a violation occurred. Alleged violations might involve identification, assessment, or placement issues or the failure to provide an appropriate education.
- A mandatory "resolution session" is now required prior to proceeding with a due process hearing.

(The parents and school district may waive this requirement and proceed to mediation.) School districts must convene a meeting with the parents and IEP team members within fifteen days of receiving a due process complaint. If the complaint is not satisfactorily resolved within thirty days of the filing date, the due process hearing may proceed.

- Under provisions of IDEA 1997, parents who prevailed in due process hearings and/or court cases could seek attorney's fees from the school district.

IDEA 2004 now permits school districts to seek attorney's fees from the parents' attorney (or the parents themselves) if the due process complaint or lawsuit is deemed frivolous, unreasonable, or without foundation, or the attorney continues to litigate despite these circumstances. Reasonable attorney fees can also be awarded by the court if the complaint or lawsuit was filed for an improper purpose such as to harass, cause unnecessary delay, or needlessly increase the cost of litigation.

Funding.   IDEA 2004 continues to be a discretionary program allowing Congress to fund it at whatever level it chooses. When IDEA was initially enacted in 1975 as PL 94-142, Congress authorized the federal government to pay 40 percent of the "excess cost" of educating pupils with disabilities (commonly referred to as "full funding"). Although mandatory full funding was not accomplished with this reauthorization, a sixyear plan or "glide path" for achieving this goal was enacted. Interestingly, only two days after passing this law, Congress appropriated significantly less ($1.7 billion) than it had just promised. While considerable, the federal government currently provides only about 18 percent of the cost of educating students with disabilities.

Evaluation of Students.

- School districts will be required to determine the eligibility of a student to receive a special education and the educational needs of the child within a sixty-day time frame. (This provision does not apply if the state has already established a timeline for accomplishing this task.) The sixty-day rule commences upon receipt of parental permission for evaluation.
- Reevaluation of eligibility for a special education may not occur more than once per year (unless agreed to by the school district and parent); and it must occur at least once every three years unless the parent and school district agree that such a reevaluation is unnecessary.
- IDEA 2004 modifies the provision pertaining to native language and preferred mode of communication. New language in the bill requires that evaluations are to be "provided and administered in the language and form most likely to yield accurate information on what the child knows and can do academically, developmentally, and functionally, unless it is not feasible to so provide or administer."
- School districts are not allowed to seek dispute resolution when parents refuse to give their consent for special education services. If parents refuse to give consent, then the school district is not responsible for providing a free and appropriate public education.

Assessment Participation.   PL 108-446 requires that all students participate in all state- and districtwide assessments (including those required under the NCLB Act), with accommodations or alternative assessments) if necessary, as stipulated in the pupil's IEP. States are permitted to assess up to 1 percent of students with disabilities (generally those pupils with significant cognitive deficits) with alternative assessments aligned with alternative achievement standards. This legislation further requires that assessments adhere to the principles of universal design when feasible.

GIFTED EDUCATION

Appeals to provide the gifted with specialized instruction have received considerable impetus for over four decades. With the advent of space exploration, the need for the trained and creative mind was recognized. With the impact of Gardner's (1994, 1999, 2005, 2007) multiple intelligence theory over the past several years, more inclusive concepts of giftedness have emerged; and principals and teachers increasingly have recognized the need to train giftedness in a variety of areas. This recognition, however, has brought no surge of legislative action. Some experts in gifted education (Kettler, 2016; Plucker & Callahan, 2020; Roberts, Inman, & Robins, 2018; Robins, Jolly, Karnes, & Bean, 2020; Stephans & Karnes, 2015; VanTassel-Baska & Little, 2017) feel that education policy related to students who are gifted and talented is lacking at the federal level. Although there are federal mandates through Public Law (P.L.) 94-142 and the Individuals with Disabilities Education Act (IDEA) for free and appropriate public education for students with other types of exceptionalities, there are no specific federally mandated policies requiring action by states to enforce educational programming at the local level for gifted and talented students (Irby & Lara-Alecio, 2001).

It is critical for principals to note that during the 1970s and 1980s, attention was focused on providing gifted and talented education through what has been referred to as capacity-building policies, not mandated policies. **Capacity-building policies** call for additional funding to enhance local or state efforts in their provision of gifted and talented education. Although the capacity-building policies, P.L. 95-561 and P.L. 100-297, gave special contingencies to children who were designated as gifted and aided significantly in supporting their education, again, neither of these laws were mandates; nor did these laws, themselves, lead to major systemic educational reform (Irby & Lara-Alecio, 2001). P.L. 100-297 continues today in its capacity-building mode, providing support through competitive grants to fund gifted and talented programs that emphasize economically disadvantaged students, English learners (ELs), and students with disabilities who are gifted and talented.

Irby and Lara-Alecio (2001) indicated that because no federally mandated policy exists for programming for students designated as gifted and talented, educational policy at the state level is muddled, at best, in relation to students who are gifted and talented—and who furthermore are codified as minority in some way. Minority groups such as Hispanics, Blacks, and Native Americans are underrepresented by as much as 70 percent in gifted programs (Card & Giuliano, 2015). These same populations were constantly underrepresented in thirty-four of the fifty states. Those who live in rural areas continue to be overlooked and underrepresented, and those who are emergent bilingual students are further exploited.

Mandated programs, in some form, do exist in some states. However, even if a state mandates a policy through law, the mandates may not be funded; and it is a fact that state funding does vary widely from state to state (Plucker & Callahan, 2020).

It is important for the principal to work toward contextual, systemic policy development in gifted education, observing how the policy situated within the district is impacted by the implementation and then by program redesign or policy revision. Policymakers and principals simply are unable to either predict or directly experience the results that policies will produce. However, over time, the most dangerous consequence of not providing appropriate educational experiences as a result of appropriate policy may be to undermine rather than advance the future of up to 25 percent of our population. What is needed is policy development that investigates potential consequences or outcomes based upon data input in the context of the state or district serving the population. What follows is an example of how a principal might work with the superintendent and board toward an equitable gifted education policy.

Policy development and implementation should include an examination of the impact of each of the following components upon each other within a state or school system: (a) the inventory of outcomes or consequences of identification, (b) a model program design that is sensitive to the population being served, (c) type of teacher training, (d) ongoing staff development, (e) parental involvement and training, and (f) needs-based curriculum and instruction. Further systemic examination would initiate model program redesign, which in turn would impact identification procedures and teacher training. This systemic type of policy development would examine the impact of all outcomes of gifted education services, not only for the emergent bilingual student but also for majority students. Principals should investigate policy and its implementation in a systemic manner to become more aware of the outcomes and impact it has on our society as a whole. A model for this systemic policy development plan is depicted in figure 6.1, using as an example a program for gifted emergent bilingual students.

Irby and Lara-Alecio (2001) indicated that policy development and implementation entail at least five components, as suggested by figure 6.1. First is the idea that there is a mandated policy for services to be provided to emergent bilingual students. From that point, state and district personnel can work on implementation. Note that the policy development and implementation process is both cyclical and systemic; therefore, as the system is complete, the outcomes may impact policy development

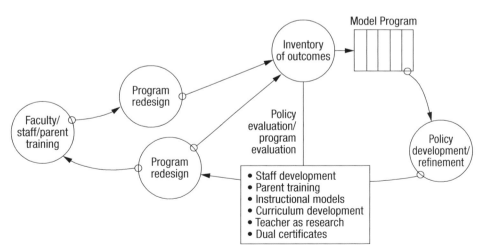

Figure 6.1 Systemic Model for Contextual Policy Development and Implementation for Gifted ELL Students.

Source: Adapted from B. J. Irby & R. Lara-Alecio, "Educational Policy and Gifted/Talented, Linguistically Diverse Students," 2001, in J. A. Castellano & E. Díaz (Eds.), *Reaching New Horizons: Gifted and Talented Education for Culturally and Linguistically Diverse Students* (pp. 265–281). Needham Heights, MA: Allyn & Bacon.

or refinement, which in turn will impact the model used in the schools for service, and so on.

Model design suggests that there is input based on data from professionals who (a) are trained in the particular subject of educating linguistically diverse gifted children and (b) have based decisions on their own investigations. It also suggests that at the state level, model programs for the linguistically diverse gifted should require dual certificates of the teachers. For example, teachers should have a certificate in bilingual education, should speak the language of the child, and should have a certificate in gifted education. This may be made possible through a field-based teacher preparation program in conjunction with area universities, through distance education training programs, or through some type of an effective alternative certification plan. Specialized programs that are sensitive to students' needs require a specialized teaching staff.

In addition, model programs should be based on input from parents who also have received training in supporting and enriching their linguistically diverse children. Parents should receive assistance in a model program for emergent bilingual students because the parents themselves are also linguistically diverse in the society and may need assistance to enhance their children's lives.

Model program design also includes appropriate identification techniques, instructional models for specific populations, and appropriate ethnolinguistic curriculum development. All of these components, along with those mentioned earlier, impact model design.

The developed model further determines the type of faculty, staff, and parental involvement and training from which new discussions, research, and new learnings emerge. This process, in turn, may lead to program *redesign.* Both the program and any redesign should require an evaluation, which should focus on an inventory of outcomes. From the inventory of outcomes, the policy should be analyzed for accuracy, inclusivity, and appropriateness. Then the program is implemented. From the preceding discussion, it is evident that (a) each component affects the others; (b) a systemic policy can determine numbers of students served in a program; and (c) such a program could further access, due to the appropriateness of accompanying training, identification, instruction, curriculum, and program evaluation (Irby & Lara-Alecio, 2001).

Administrative Arrangements for Gifted Education

As the principals work to develop and implement policy for gifted students, there are several general administrative arrangements for service delivery that they, along with the teachers and central office administrators, may consider. Those arrangements and an explanation are given in table 6.4.

Definitions of Giftedness

Principals must be aware of the varied definitions of giftedness. Because we have been discussing policy, as well as state mandates, we will first look at state definitions for gifted. Table 6.5 presents eight definitions that are fairly representative of the definitions from all points of the United States. Some definitions are short; others are extensive. Some use the word *gifted*, and others use the words *gifted and talented*. Many still use the basic Maryland (1971) definition, which dates from the first time the federal government defined *gifted and talented*. It might be noted that four state

Table 6.4 Administrative Arrangement for Gifted Education Service Delivery

Type of Administrative Arrangement for Service Delivery	Description of the Arrangement
Ability Grouping	Students are grouped according to their ability in classes and/or subject area.
Acceleration	Refers to administrative practices designed to allow students to progress through the school grades at a rate faster than the average (e.g., early school entrance, content area acceleration, grade skipping, credit by examination, early graduation).
Advanced Placement	College-level courses provided at the secondary level for which students may receive college credit by examination (administered by the Advanced Placement Program of the College Board).
Alternative School	A school that provides an alternative to the traditional school structure and that is designed to meet the unique instructional needs of some gifted and talented students.
Cluster Grouping	Any classroom with a group of identified gifted and talented students purposefully organized to provide planned differentiated instruction most of the time.
Cluster Classroom	The intentional grouping of the grade level's top intellectually gifted students into a classroom with a teacher who has the desire and expertise to provide a supportive and challenging environment for this population of learners.
Competitions	Organized opportunities for gifted and talented students to enter local, regional, state, or national contests in a variety of subject areas (e.g., Quiz Bowl, Academic Games, Future Problem Solving, Spelling Bees, Science Olympiad).
Community & Business Resources	Continued sharing of resources to increase opportunities for high-ability students
Concurrent or Dual Enrollment	Usually refers to high school students taking some college courses at a nearby college or university before they graduate from high school, but may also refer to students at any level who are allowed to take some classes at the next school level (e.g., elementary/junior high/high school). Also includes correspondence courses.
Convocations, Seminars, Workshops	Special short-term sessions where the student focuses on one area of study (e.g., Young Authors Conference, Science Convocation).
Curriculum Adjustment	Experiences provided in the regular classroom that are additional and/or supplemental to the established curriculum and/or texts and that are purposefully planned with the needs, interests, and capabilities of particular students in mind.
Honors Classes	Courses, usually at the high school level, that are designed for able students.
Independent Study	Individually contracted, in-depth study of a topic.
Interest Groups	Any group organized from one or more classrooms on the basis of interest in a topic; usually of short-term duration.
Internships	Students who demonstrate high ability and need are placed in a professional setting for a specified period to learn skills of that profession.
Individualized Learning	Courses and curricula are altered to meet the specific needs of a high-ability student.

(continued)

Table 6.4 (*continued*)

Type of Administrative Arrangement for Service Delivery	Description of the Arrangement
Local Teacher Consultant Services	The local consultant/helping teacher assists teachers in developing appropriate educational opportunities for high-ability students.
Magnet Schools	Specialized schools for high-ability students, usually with a specific focus (e.g., performing and/or visual arts, math and/or science, aviation school, etc.).
Mentorships	A program that pairs individual students with someone who has advanced skills and experiences in a particular discipline and can serve as a guide, advisor, counselor, and role model.
Ongoing Assessment and Planning	Students' abilities and needs are continually assessed through both formal and informal means designed to discover and nurture talent. The results are used as the basis for appropriate programming decisions.
Pacing	The content and pacing of curriculum and instruction are matched to students' abilities and needs. Students move ahead on the basis of mastery. Differentiation in pacing and/or depth is provided.
Pull-out Programs	A group organized from one or more classrooms that meets regularly to provide experiences beyond the established curriculum. This is enrichment of the regular curriculum.
Recognition	Student achievements are recognized through academic letters, awards, newspapers, and so forth.
Resource Room	Students are released from their regular classroom on a scheduled basis to work with a teacher specializing in education of the gifted in a resource room setting.

legislatures or state education agencies have no definition: Massachusetts, Minnesota, New Hampshire, and South Dakota.

There are, of course, other definitions of giftedness. For example, Sternberg (1985) defined giftedness in terms of intelligence, as do most theorists. He suggested three dimensions to intelligence. "Compotential" intelligence consists of mental mechanisms for processing information. "Experiential" intelligence involves dealing with new tasks or situations and the ability to use mental processes automatically. "Contextual" intelligence is the ability to adapt to, select, and shape the environment.

Gardner (1999) developed his multiple intelligence theory in 1983 by combining studies of the brain with research on the relative aspects of intelligence. He has identified eight different types of intelligence: logical-mathematical, linguistic, visual-spatial, body-kinesthetic, musical, interpersonal, intrapersonal, and naturalistic. Mainly, schools will concentrate on the areas of logical-mathematical and linguistic intelligence.

Renzulli (1985) introduced a definition that denotes an interaction among the three clusters: above average intelligence, creativity, and task commitment. Each factor is important to contributing to giftedness (Renzulli, 1985). Irby and Lara-Alecio (2001) expanded Renzulli's definition in defining bilingual Hispanic students. The combined model can be viewed in figure 6.2. They suggested that there are

Table 6.5 Sample Definitions from States

Florida	1. Gifted. One who has superior intellectual development and is capable of high performance.

2. Criteria for eligibility. A student is eligible for special instruction programs for the gifted if the student meets criteria under (2)(a) or (b) of this rule.

    (a) The student demonstrates: 1. Need for a special program, 2. A majority of characteristics of gifted students according to a standard scale or checklist, and 3. Superior intellectual development as measured by an intelligence quotient of two standard deviations or more above the mean on an individually administered standardized test of intelligence.

    (b) The student is a member of an underrepresented group and meets the criteria specific in an approved school district plan for increasing the participation of underrepresented groups in programs for gifted students.

1. For the purpose of this rule, under-represented groups are defined as groups: (a.) Who are limited English proficient, or (b.) Who are from low socioeconomic status family.

2. The Department of Education is authorized to approve school district plans for increasing the participation of students from under-represented groups in special instructional programs for the gifted. . . .

Procedures for student evaluation. The minimum evaluations for determining eligibility are the following: (a) need for a special instruction program, (b) characteristics of the gifted, (c) intellectual development, and (d) may include those evaluation procedures specified in an approved district plan to increase the participation of students from under-represented groups in programs for the gifted (Fla. Admin. Code Ann. r. 6A-6.03019).

Mississippi	"Gifted children" shall mean children who are found to have an exceptionally high degree of intellect, and/or academic, creative or artistic ability (Miss. Code Ann. §37-23-175).
Virginia	"Gifted students" means those students in public elementary and secondary schools beginning with kindergarten through graduation whose abilities and potential for accomplishment are so outstanding that they require special programs to meet their educational needs. These students will be identified by professionally qualified persons through the use of multiple criteria as having potential or demonstrated abilities and who have evidence of high performance or capabilities, which may include leadership, in one or more of the following areas:

1. Intellectual aptitude or aptitudes. Students with advanced aptitude or conceptualization whose development is accelerated beyond their age peers as demonstrated by advanced skills, concepts and creative expression in multiple general intellectual ability or in specific intellectual abilities.

2. Specific academic aptitude. Students with specific aptitudes in selected academic areas: mathematics; the sciences; or the humanities as demonstrated by advanced skills, concepts, and the creative expression in those areas.

3. Technical and practical arts aptitude. Students with specific aptitudes in selected technical or practical arts as demonstrated by advanced skills and creative expression in those areas to the extent they need and can benefit from specifically planned educational services differentiated from those provided by the general program experience.

Visual or performing arts aptitude. Students with specific aptitudes in selected or visual performing arts as demonstrated by advanced skills and creative expression who excel consistently in the development of a product or performance in any of the visual and performing arts to the extent that they need and can benefit from specifically planned educational services differentiated from those generally provided by the general program experience. (8 Va. Admin. Code §20-40-20)

(continued)

Table 6.5 (*continued*)

Oregon	"Talented and gifted children" means those children who require special educational programs or services, or both, beyond those normally provided by the regular school program in order to realize their contribution to self and society and who demonstrate outstanding ability or potential in one or more of the following areas:

(a) general intellectual ability as commonly measured by measures of intelligence and aptitude;

(b) unusual academic ability in one or more academic areas;

(c) creative ability in using original or nontraditional methods of thinking and producing;

(d) leadership ability in motivating the performance of others either in educational or noneducational settings; and/or

(e) ability in the visual or performing arts, such as dance, music or art.

(Or. Rev. Stat. §343.395)

California   Each district shall use one or more of these categories in identifying students as gifted and talented. In all categories, identification of a student's extraordinary capability shall be in relation to the student's chronological peers.

(a) Intellectual Ability: A student demonstrates extraordinary or potential for extraordinary intellectual development.

(b) Creative Ability: A student characteristically:

(1) Perceives unusual relationships among aspects of the student's environment and among ideas;

(2) Overcomes obstacles to thinking and doing;

(3) Produces unique solutions to problems.

(c) Specific Academic Ability: A student functions at highly advanced academic levels in particular subject areas.

(d) Leadership Ability: A student displays the characteristic behaviors necessary for extraordinary leadership.

(e) High Achievement: A student consistently produces advanced ideas and products and/or attains exceptionally high scores on achievement tests.

(f) Visual and Performing Arts Talent: A student originates, performs, produces, or responds at extraordinarily high levels in the arts.

Any other category which meets the standards set forth in these regulations. (Cal. Code Regs. title 5, §3822)

New York   As used in this article, the term "gifted students" shall mean those students who show evidence of high performance capability and exceptional potential in areas such as general intellectual ability, special academic aptitude and outstanding ability in visual and performing arts. Such definition shall include those students who require educational programs or services beyond those normally provided by the regular school program in order to realize their full potential. (N.Y. Educ. Law §4452)

Ohio   "Gifted" means students who perform or show potential for performing at remarkably high levels of accomplishment when compared to others of their age, experience, or environment and who are identified under division (A), (B), (C), or (D) of section 3324.03 of the revised code. (Ohio Rev. Code Ann. §3324.01)

Kansas   "Gifted" means performing or demonstrating the potential for performing at significantly higher levels of accomplishment in one or more academic fields due to intellectual ability, when compared to others of similar age, experience, and environment. (Kan. Admin. Regs. 91-40-1)

Figure 6.2 Irby and Lara-Alecio's Hispanic Bilingual Definition

socio-cultural-linguistic characteristics that encompass intelligence, creativity, and task commitment.

With the exception of Irby and Lara-Alecio's definition, gifted definitions are predominantly mainstream definitions. Ford and Thomas (1997) warned against definitions that were too narrow and that did not take into account the underachieving gifted student. They provided some advice that principals can heed for reversing a segment of the gifted population:

> Reversing underachievement among gifted minority students requires intensive efforts on the part of teachers and counselors, as well as a partnership with parents and students. For optimal effects, teachers and counselors must tailor interventions to students' needs. Interventions for gifted minority students must consider social-psychological, family, peer, and school factors. Interventions must:
>
> - Ensure that definitions of underachievement are both qualitative and quantitative, and that measures are valid and reliable
> - Enhance self-perceptions, self-esteem, self-concept (academic and social), and racial identity
> - Improve students' skills in studying, time management, organization, and taking tests
> - Involve family members as partners in the educational process
> - Address school-related factors, including providing teachers and counselors with gifted and multicultural training to meet both the academic and affective needs of gifted minority students. This training should include strategies for improving student-teacher relations, teacher expectations, and the classroom climate.
>
> (p. 1)

What Principals Can Do for Gifted Education

Besides ensuring that there is an adequate policy to serve gifted students, some experts in gifted education (Plucker & Callahan, 2020; Robins et al., 2020) suggest the following for principals:

- Understand program expectations.
- Be supportive of the educational model.

- Be an advocate for children to learn at their own level.
- Access appropriate resources to match the curriculum and instruction for the gifted learners.
- Allow for unique delivery of the curriculum that allows children to question, seek answers, and share information.
- Coach staff in a manner that encourages diversity, creativity, and high standards.
- Bridge the gap that can exist between staff and parents.
- Openly celebrate the success of all students.
- Support equity of educational services so that all children's needs are met.
- Modify policies and procedures to support a differentiated classroom.
- Learn the qualities of a high-quality, differentiated classroom.

Principals can help evaluate their gifted programs. VanTassel-Baska and Little (2017) note the importance of understanding the indicators of a quality program for gifted that could be used in evaluating the program. They indicate that the program should include the following:

1. Provides a written philosophy, goals, and anticipated outcomes for students
2. Presents multiple options at and across grade levels
3. Utilizes modified scheduling and differentiated staffing to achieve its goals
4. Utilizes multiple criteria for identification, appropriate instrumentation, and a process for ongoing admissions
5. Is comprehensive across years of schooling
6. Articulates the curriculum across years of schooling
7. Selects teachers according to key characteristics and trains them to work with gifted
8. Uses diverse and multiple resources, including the community, to carry out its goals
9. Uses models that respond to the needs of the students in the particular setting
10. Emphasizes problem solving, higher-level thought processes, inquiry-based discussion, and student-generated, high-quality products
11. Serves as a parent education component and an ongoing school/community awareness component
12. Utilizes curriculum development as an ongoing effort that actively involves teachers in the process
13. Monitors program implementation and revises the context as needed

Curriculum Models for Gifted Education

There are numerous curriculum models for gifted education. We share two that are used primarily at the elementary grade levels: Enrichment Triad Model and Creative Problem Solving. In most cases, the International Baccalaureate and Advanced Placement models are used at the secondary levels.

Enrichment Triad Model.   Renzulli and Reis (1986) created the **enrichment triad model (ETM)** that has three components: Type I enrichment (general exploratory experiences), Type II enrichment (group training activities), and Type III enrichment (individual and small-group investigations of real problems). Organizationally, ETM includes enrichment-planning teams, needs assessments, staff development, materials selection, and program evaluation. ETM also includes lessons to promote development of thinking processes, procedures to modify the regular curriculum, and curriculum compacting. ETM consists of three types of enrichment:

- *Type I—General Interest/Exploratory Activities*. The general interest and exploratory activities are designed to provide students with as wide a range of experiences as possible and include field trips, clubs, interest centers, visiting speakers, and brainstorming sessions.
- *Type II—Group Training Activities/Skills Development*. The group training activities are designed to develop thinking and feeling skills; and students are involved in designing, experimenting, comparing, analyzing, recording, and classifying. Skills development includes creative and critical thinking, learning how to learn, using advanced-level reference materials, and communicating effectively.
- *Type III—Individual and Small Group Investigation of Real Problems*. Students apply the knowledge and skills they have developed while working through Type I and Type II activities. They research real problems and then present the results to a real audience. Activities in Type III include researching, debating, surveying, making a presentation, writing a journal or newspaper article, or producing a book or play.

A significant feature of ETM is that *all* students can work at the first two levels. The activities generated within these levels support the third level. Type III activities are more appropriate for identified gifted students, because they allow for varying degrees of creativity. Type III does not preclude other students from participating, but the products generated should look different for gifted students—more sophisticated at a higher level of thought production.

Creative Problem Solving. The **creative problem-solving** (Parnes, 1992) process is a flexible tool that can be used to examine real problems and issues. There are six stages to the model, providing a structured procedure for identifying challenges, generating ideas and implementing innovative solutions. Future problem solving grew out of this model. Through continued practice and use of the process students can strengthen their creative techniques and learn to generalize in new situations. The six steps are:

1. *Objective (Mess) Finding*—identifying the goal, challenge, and future direction.
2. *Fact Finding*—collecting data about the problem; observing the problem as objectively as possible.
3. *Problem Solving*—examining the various parts of the problem to isolate the major part; stating the problem in an open-ended way.
4. *Idea Finding*—generating as many ideas as possible regarding the problem; brainstorming.
5. *Solution Finding*—choosing the solution that would be most appropriate; developing and selecting criteria to evaluate the alternative solutions.
6. *Acceptance Finding*—creating a plan of action.

Unlike many other problem-solving methods, the creative problem-solving process emphasizes the need to defer judgment on possible ideas and solutions until a final decision is made. In this way, the flow of ideas in the third step is not interrupted, and possible solutions, however, bizarre, are accepted. The teachers' role at this step is important; they are creating an environment in which students can feel comfortable in making suggestions. Quantity of ideas is required in brainstorming, not quality of the initial idea and its solution.

BILINGUAL EDUCATION

The school population is becoming more and more diverse. Projected change in the percentage of school-age children (five through eighteen years of age) for four ethnic groups between 2016 and 2030 are the following: Hispanic Americans will increase from 24.9 percent to 26.5 percent; Asian Americans will increase from 5.2 percent to 6.3 percent; African Americans will increase from 15.1 percent to 15.5 percent; and White (non-Hispanic) Americans will decrease from 51.1 percent to 46.9 percent (Vespa, Armstrong, & Medina, 2018). These figures indicate that the United States is rapidly becoming an even more ethnically diverse nation than ever before, and certain states (e.g., California, New York, Florida, and Texas) already have very large immigrant populations.

According to estimates, nearly one million legal and illegal immigrants come to the United States every year. From 2000 to 2015, 84 percent of legal immigrants to the United States came from non-European countries. Most of these immigrants came from Asia (principally China, the Philippine Islands, and India) and the Americas (principally Mexico, the Caribbean, and South America) and settled in the major cities of California, New York, Florida, and Texas. In the fifteen-year period from 2000 through 2014, more than 14.5 million legal immigrants arrived in the United States, an all-time US immigration record (US Department of Homeland Security, 2015). Many of these immigrants and their children are poor and have limited English proficiency, which places greater demands on educating these students and has increased political debates about bilingual education and testing (Barbian, Gonzales, & Mejia, 2017; Jaumont, 2017).

In seeking to address the educational needs of an ever-increasing Hispanic student population, educators are struggling. Some experts in bilingual education (Barbian, Gonzales, & Mejia, 2017; Echevarria, Vogt, & Short, 2017; Fenner & Snyder, 2017; Garcia, Johnson, & Seltzer, 2016; Gottlieb, 2016; Jaumont, 2017; Sypnieski & Ferlazzo, 2018) are defending bilingual education and are stressing the value of biliteracy, stating that language is at the core of the Hispanic experience in the United States, and it must be at the center of future opportunities. The United States has a mandated policy for service to ELLs under Every Student Succeeds (ESSA) Act. Despite significant research that sound bilingual education programs work, and a federally mandated policy, bilingual education in America continues to be under attack (Suarez-Orozco & Suarez-Orozco, 2010).

Program Descriptions
Several program models have been developed, although nonnative English speakers have been traditionally underserved. The following components should be considered when designing and implementing bilingual and English as a second language

(ESL) programs: (a) state guidelines, (b) student population to be served, and (c) district resources.

Example of State Guidelines. Texas will be used as the example for state guidelines under this section; we use this state because it has large numbers of students who are affected by this policy. It is critical for principals to be familiar with their own state's policy for English learners (EL; what we consider as emergent bilingual students). The statutory authority for services to emergent bilingual students falls under Subchapter BB, issued under Texas Education Code §§29.05–29.064, unless otherwise noted. Texas Education Code §89.1201(a) indicates that every student in the state who has a home language other than English and who is identified as an English leaner shall be provided a full opportunity to participate in a bilingual education or ESL program. To ensure equal educational opportunity as required in Texas Education Code §1.002(a), each school district shall:

1. Identify limited-English-proficient students based on criteria established by the state.
2. Provide bilingual education and English as a second language programs as integral parts of the regular program as described in the Texas Education Code, §4.002.
3. Seek certified teaching personnel to ensure that limited-English-proficient students are afforded full opportunity to master the essential skills and knowledge required by the state.
4. Assess achievement for essential skills and knowledge in accordance with the Texas Education Code, Chapter 39, to ensure accountability for limited-English-proficient students and the schools that serve them.

Furthermore, Texas Education Code §89. 1201(b) promotes the goal of bilingual education programs: to enable limited English proficient (LEP) students to become competent in the comprehension, speaking, reading, and composition of the English language through the development of literacy and academic skills in the primary language and English. Such programs are to emphasize the mastery of English language skills—as well as mathematics, science, and social studies—as integral parts of the academic goals for all students to enable emergent bilingual students (or ELs) to participate equitably in school.

The same policy, Texas Education Code §89.1201(c), addresses the goal of English as a second language, which is to enable emergent bilingual students to become competent in the comprehension, speaking, reading, and composition of the English language through the integrated use of second-language methods. Such programs shall emphasize the mastery of English-language skills—as well as mathematics, science, and social studies—as integral parts of the academic goals for all students to enable EL students to participate equitably in school.

Texas Education Code §89.1201(d) states that bilingual education and ESL programs shall be integral parts of the total school program. Such programs shall use instructional approaches designed to meet the special needs of emergent bilingual students. The basic curriculum content of the programs shall be based on the essential skills and knowledge required by the state.

Texas Education Code §89.1205 requires the implementation of bilingual education and ESL programs. According to this section, a school district that has an enrollment of 20 or more EL students in any language classification in the same grade level district-wide shall offer a bilingual education program for all elementary grade levels, including prekindergarten through fifth, and sixth when it is clustered with elementary grade levels. Cooperative arrangements with other districts may be developed for the provision of services. For bilingual education programs, the Texas Education Code requires the provision of a dual-language program in prekindergarten through the elementary grades, or an approved dual-language program that addresses the affective, linguistic, and cognitive needs of the emergent bilingual students. In addition, school districts are authorized to establish a bilingual education program at grade levels in which the bilingual education program is not required. All emergent bilingual students for whom a district is not required to offer a bilingual education program shall be provided an ESL program. Implementation of this type of program takes place regardless of the student's grade level and home language and the number of such students.

Should a district not be able to establish a bilingual or ESL program, the district may request from the commissioner of education an exception to the programs and an approval to offer an alternative program. Waivers of certification requirements may be requested on an individual basis and are valid only in the school year for which they are negotiated.

Texas Education Code §89.1210(b) indicates that the bilingual education program is to be a full-time program of instruction in which both the student's home language and English are used for instruction. The amount of instruction in each language should be commensurate with the student's level of proficiency in both languages as well as their level of academic achievement. The language proficiency assessment committee (LPAC) designates the student's level of language proficiency and academic achievement. According to Texas Education Code §89.1210(d), instruction in an ESL program may vary from the amount of time accorded to instruction in English language arts in the regular program for non-EL students to total immersion in second-language approaches. In grades six or seven through twelve, instruction in ESL may vary from one-third of the instructional day to total immersion in second-language approaches.

Student Population. Just as the law in Texas indicates that particular student language group populations should be considered when developing a program, all districts should determine the types of emergent bilingual students to be served. Many campuses will find that their populations of language minority students are mobile, while others may be fairly stable. The language groups may be from a variety of language groups, educational levels, and cultural backgrounds. In Texas, most of the immigrants are of the Spanish-speaking language group from Mexico or Central America. The principal must consider the numbers of students from the particular language group, the previous educational levels of the students, and the culture of the students when developing bilingual, dual-language, or ESL programs.

District Resources. Resources for provision of services to English-language learners vary from district to district and from state to state. For example, programs may depend upon geographic location, upsurges in immigrant settlements, district enrollment, physical space, availability of certified teachers, and/or the ability to attract certified teachers through stipends. These resources could significantly influence the types of services the district will provide. Some experts in bilingual education (Echevarria, Vogt, & Short, 2017; Fenner & Snyder, 2017; Sypnieski & Ferlazzo,

2018) suggest that districts and campuses could use specific instructional strategies to develop effective learning environments. Such strategies include (a) small-group instruction, (b) hands-on activities, (c) information exchange among students, (d) computer-based simulations, and (e) Internet-based activities for communication. The authors particularly addressed services that translate text and Web pages from English to other languages, or vice versa, as holding promise for assisting ELs. Specifically, Sypnieski and Ferlazzo (2018) indicate that teachers and principals could use such technology for improving one-to-one communications, both verbally and in writing, with students and parents not only in conferences but also in the classroom and for promoting clarity in classroom assignments.

Administrative Arrangements for Bilingual Education

In this section we present, for a principal's consideration of his or her campus needs, a brief description of potential administrative arrangements that districts may choose in developing and implementing programs in (a) bilingual education and/or (b) English as a second language. When districts consider the type of program arrangement that best suits their population, the following should be taken into account:

- The program should meet the linguistic, academic, and affective needs of students.
- The program should provide students with the instruction necessary to allow them to progress through school at a rate commensurate with their native-English-speaking peers.
- The program should make the best use of district and community resources.

(Sypnieski & Ferlazzo, 2018)

Districts need to have in place the following:

- policies related to language minority students;
- a program design;
- student identification procedures;
- an identified committee that assesses the language proficiency level;
- a means for student assessment;
- a formalized parent authority and responsibility policy, procedure, and plan;
- a plan for staffing and professional development;
- a summer school program; and
- a plan for monitoring and evaluating programs.

(Adapted from *Texas State Plan for Education of Limited English Proficient Students*, ESC §19, 2019)

All of these items should be on file and have documented evidence of implementation for compliance monitoring by the Texas Education Agency and for public consideration; other states have similar compliance components.

Bilingual Education Models

In 1997, the US Department of Education indicated that bilingual education makes certain that children whose native language is other than English receive the necessary grounding in academics while transitioning to all-English classrooms (Barbian, Gonzales, & Mejia, 2017; Jaumont, 2017). The goal of bilingual programs is the acquisition of English skills by language-minority children so they can succeed in mainstream, English-only classrooms (Garcia, Johnson, & Seltzer, 2016; Gottlieb, 2016). A variety of bilingual program models make use of students' primary language while developing English (Echevarria, Vogt, & Short, 2017; Fenner & Snyder, 2017). Following are models that principals can implement on their campuses.

Transitional. **Transitional bilingual programs** have been described as those in which the student's first language and English are used in some combination for instruction, and where the first language serves as a temporary bridge to instruction in English (Bruce et al., 1997; Gersten, 1999; Mora, Wink, & Wink, 2001; Thomas & Collier, 1999). However, there is no single method for helping emergent bilingual students catch up with their peers, and there is no single definition for transitional bilingual education programs. According to Bruce et al. (1997), we must improve our understanding of bilingual education and provide descriptive accuracy. These descriptions should reflect actual instructional practices and be validated through reliable classroom observations.

Early-Exit. **Early-exit bilingual programs** provide some initial instruction, primarily for the introduction of reading, and instruction in the first language is phased out rapidly (Rennie, 1993). Ramirez (1992) describes the early-exit program as one where children receive some instruction in their primary initial reading skills, with all other instruction in English. By the end of second grade, students participating in the early-exit model are expected to be exited from the program and mainstreamed into English-only classrooms (Ramirez, 1992).

The terms *early-exit* and *transitional bilingual education (TBE)* have been used interchangeably to define the model that uses more English instruction at an earlier time in an effort to move children quickly into mainstream English classrooms. In a discussion of the Ramirez study, Thomas (1992) referred to the early-exit program as transitional bilingual education and declared it the most commonly funded type of bilingual program.

Late-Exit. **Late-exit bilingual programs** serve EL students in grades kindergarten through six, and students receive 40 percent of their instructional time in Spanish (Ramirez, 1992). In contrast to students in early-exit programs, the students in late-exit programs receive a minimum of 40 percent of their instructional time in Spanish-language arts, reading, and other content areas such as mathematics, social studies, and/or science (Ramirez, 1992).

English Immersion. Ramirez (1992) describes the **English immersion bilingual program** as one in which instruction is almost exclusively in English. Teachers have specialized training to meet EL students' needs, as well as strong skills in students' receptive language. In an immersion program, English, the target language, is taught in the content areas; and a strong language development component is included in each content lesson. The child's home language is used primarily to clarify English and, on a case-to-case basis, an emergent bilingual student who begins the program in kindergarten is expected to be mainstreamed in two or three years. According to Moran (1993), confusion occurs when the immersion model is misinterpreted, programs are set up, minority children are placed in English-only programs with native English speakers, and the immersion concept is misused on submersion models.

Dual Immersion. **Dual immersion bilingual programs** are those in which non-English-speaking students and native-English-speaking students learn together in the same class. Dual-immersion bilingual programs are a way to help students learn two languages at the same time.

Submersion. **Submersion bilingual programs,** often described as the "sink or swim" approach, calls for placement of EL students in classrooms where only English is spoken. The student's first language is not used for instruction, and no special attempt is made to help overcome language problems (Ovando & Collier, 1998).

Dual Language. Moran (1993) described **dual language bilingual programs** as an adaptation of the French Immersion Model from Canada. In a dual-language bilingual program, native-English-speaking students are immersed in the minority language, Spanish, alongside native Spanish-speaking students. Dual-language bilingual programs are designed to help all participating students become fluent in both English and a second language. English-speaking children are placed in classrooms with non-English speakers, and all instruction is in both languages. As research has shown, the most successful programs begin in prekindergarten and continue through the sixth grade. Students will develop high levels of proficiency in their first and second language. Academic performance will be at or above grade level in both languages, and students will develop greater cross-cultural awareness and knowledge.

Two-Way. **Two-way bilingual programs** (known also as two-way immersion), developmental bilingual, bilingual immersion, and dual-language programs have taken root in schools across the country. These programs integrate two groups of students, language minority and language majority, and provide instruction through the minority students' target language and the majority students' language—English—with the goal of bilingualism for both groups. (In a one-way bilingual program, the minority language group is taught in two languages, with no effort to teach the minority language to others.) Two-way programs cost slightly more than transitional programs to implement (Lara-Alecio et al., 2004), and this is still the case.

English as a Second Language Models

English as a second language (ESL) program models are generally classified as (a) specialized, pull-out ESL programs that focus on linguistics, or (b) English-plus programs, in which the native language may be used in instruction of content areas. English instruction is longer or may represent the entire instructional program (McKeon, 1987).

Pull-Out. Generally used in an elementary setting, **pull-out** is the most expensive of all program models; yet, it is the most common and least effective. The student receives specialized instruction in a separate classroom from her regular classroom during the day. The student is taken from her regular classroom for this special instruction. The teacher may be either stationary on a campus or itinerant (shared between several campuses). Students from different first-language backgrounds may be separated into groups for instruction. In Texas, the teacher must have an endorsement in ESL; however, in other states teachers may or may not be trained in this field. Many ESL teachers are not bilingual or bicultural.

Class Period. The ESL **class period** approach is when ESL instruction is provided during a regular class period, is generally used in a middle or secondary school setting. Students generally receive credit for the course, just as they would for other courses in a departmentalized setting. Students may be grouped according to their level of English proficiency.

Sheltered English or Content-Based Programs. To date, **Sheltered English or Content-Based Programs** have been used primarily with secondary school students. In such programs, ELs from different language groups are placed together in classes where teachers use English as the language of instruction in the content areas of science, social studies, and sometimes mathematics. The language is adapted to the students' proficiency level. Teachers may use gestures and visual aids to help students understand. A teacher certified in ESL offers instruction in this effective program. (The program is effective due to accessibility to a broader curriculum; it is more cost-effective than the pull-out model.) Sheltered English or content-based programs may parallel virtually all mainstream academic curricular offerings, or they may consist of only one or two subjects (Chamot & Stewner-Manzanares, 1985; Ovando & Collier, 1998).

Structured English Immersion. In the **structured English immersion ESL program**, instruction should be provided in the child's home language; but the second language, English, is not used at all until students have a mastery of the first language commensurate with their age and extent of formal schooling. This approach strictly focuses on providing sufficient oral, reading, and writing skills so EL youngsters can eventually transition into mainstream programs (Pardo & Tinajero, 1993). Most students are mainstreamed after being in a structured immersion program for two or three years; however, English-only proponents have misnamed this program model, have left out the native language, and use English only. This program has become a type of ESL content instruction in a self-contained classroom. *Structured* has become equated with highly structured materials that carry students through a step-by-step learning process. Structured immersion models have not proven effective, because the materials did not fit the process of natural second-language acquisition.

High Intensity Language Training (HILT) Programs. **High Intensity Language Training (HILT) ESL Programs** are used primarily at the secondary level. According to McKeon (1987), in the **HILT** design students of various language backgrounds are grouped for a major part of the school day. Students receive intensive ESL instruction, usually for three hours a day in the first year of instruction and less in succeeding years (Chamot & Stewner-Manzanares, 1985). McKeon (1987) indicates that mainstreaming students into regular classrooms is accomplished on a subject-by-subject basis and usually begins with less linguistically demanding classes such as music, physical education, and art. McKeon indicates that some models may include content-based or sheltered English classes. This is an old concept and sometimes this may be seen in newcomer programs where new arrival students are placed. They may be in a HILT-type program a day for beyond the first year. However, that is not always the best program for newcomer students. They should certainly receive support from the ESL program, but they also need to be mainstreamed, particularly at the secondary level. Also, a comprehensive wrap-around program with social, emotional, and health services and parent/caregiver involvement incorporated for these newcomer students. Often these programs are consolidated on specific campuses.

SUMMARY

1. The aims of guidance and counseling programs are to assist individuals to develop the ability to understand themselves, to solve their own problems, and to make appropriate adjustments to their environment.
2. Major guidance services include student appraisal, information giving, placement and follow-up, and counseling.
3. Broadly conceived, two methods of counseling include directive and nondirective approaches. On the one hand, directive counseling focuses attention on identifying and analyzing the problem and finding an appropriate solution to it using all available data. Nondirective counseling, on the other hand, provides the counselee not with a neat solution for her problem, but instead with the ability to meet her problem in a constructive way.
4. Ten criteria are used in evaluating guidance and counseling programs: student needs, cooperation, process and product, balance, flexibility, quality counselors, adequate counselor-student ratio, adequate physical facilities, and appropriate record keeping.
5. The student's cumulative record contains information beneficial to these school officials: principals, counselors, school psychologists, social workers, and teachers. The cumulative record should include the following information: a student's data sheet, parent's report, child's self-concept appraisal, sociogram, behavior reports, and standardized test data.
6. The components of a school's testing battery should include the following tests: emerging reading, learning readiness, intelligence, achievement, and interests and aptitudes.
7. Methods of reporting grades include percentage, letter, descriptive, percentile, three-group, ranking, and T-score. Each method of reporting student progress to parents has merit.
8. Extracurricular activities fulfill the overall goals of education and the curriculum mission of the school. Functions of extracurricular activities include reinforcing learning, supplementing the curriculum, integrating knowledge, and fulfilling the objectives of democracy.
9. Special teaching practices, materials, equipment, and facilities may be required for children with disabilities to achieve their full potential. To that end, Congress has passed four landmark pieces of legislation: Section 504 of the Rehabilitation Act of 1973, the Education for All Handicapped Act of 1975, the Americans with Disabilities Act of 1990 (ADA), and the Individuals with Disabilities Act (IDEA).
10. Of these four laws, IDEA has had the most significant impact on public schools. Congress reauthorized IDEA in 1997, adding new amendments and extending federal funding for special education services.
11. Gifted education programs are not mandated by the federal government. Services to such students must be aligned with the district's definition and identification procedures.

12. Bilingual education has as its goal to successfully prepare all children to transition to English. This goal can be accomplished in a transitional bilingual classroom, a dual-language classroom, or an English as a second language (ESL) classroom.

KEY TERMS

assessment
information
placement
follow-up
counseling
directive counseling
nondirective counseling
eclectic counseling
adequate yearly progress (AYP)
affective domain
psychomotor domain
cognitive domain
emerging reading test
learning readiness test
intelligence test
achievement tests
interest and aptitude tests
standardized achievement test
percentage method
letter method
descriptive method
percentile method
three-group method

rank method
T-score method
extracurricular activities
capacity building policies
enrichment triad model
creative problem-solving model
transitional bilingual programs
early-exit bilingual programs
late-exit bilingual programs
English immersion bilingual
    programs
dual immersion bilingual programs
submersion bilingual programs
dual language bilingual programs
two-way bilingual programs
pull-out bilingual programs
class period bilingual programs
sheltered English bilingual programs
structured English immersion ESL
    program
high-intensity language training
    (HILT) ESL program

FIELD-BASED ACTIVITIES

1. Interview the school counselor on the campus where you work. Determine what methods the counselor uses in counseling students. Review the curriculum the counselor uses in group settings; look for specific skills within the curriculum. Observe the counselor in a group session with students. Review the types of problems the counselor has dealt with over the past month; how did the counselor resolve these problems?

2. Review the district special education procedures. Develop a flowchart from the initiation of an observed problem with a student to placement or non-placement in a special education classroom. Which specific services does the district provide? What tests are used to determine if a student has a disability? Are factors other than test results considered?

3. What are the identification procedures for students being placed in a gifted program or a bilingual program in your district? Is there a district policy on gifted education? What type of program is provided for gifted students at various grade levels? Is the district definition aligned with the identification procedures and with the program type offered? How does gifted education serve students who may also be disabled, or who may be ELL?

SUGGESTED READINGS

Brookhart, S., & McMillan, J. H. (Eds.) (2019). *Classroom assessment and educational measurement: Applications of educational measurement and assessment.* New York, NY: Routledge. Susan Brookhart and James McMillan explore the ways in which the theory and practice of both educational measurement and the assessment of student learning in classroom settings mutually inform one another.

Robins, J., Jolly, J. L., Karnes, F. A., & Bean, S. M. (Eds.) (2020). *Methods and materials for teaching the gifted* (5th ed.). The authors describe various techniques to use in instructing gifted and talented learners.

Erford, B. T. (2018). *Orientation to the counseling profession: Advocacy, ethics, and essential professional foundations* (3rd ed.). Boston, MA: Pearson. Current, innovative, and all encompassing, Bradley Erford provides a wealth of information on the most foundational and emerging issues of the counseling profession.

Garcia, O., & Kleifgen, J. A. (2018). *Educating emergent bilinguals: Policies, programs, and practices for English learners* (2nd ed.). New York, NY: Teachers College Press. This book is an excellent resource for policymakers, researchers, and educators who are interested in taking specific action to improve the education of English learners.

Gross, K. (2020). *Trauma doesn't stop at the school door: Strategies and solutions for educators, Pre–K–College.* New York, NY: Teachers College Press. Karen Gross provides concrete suggestions to assist schools in becoming trauma-responsive environments, including replicable macro- and micro-changes.

Harry, B., & Ocasio-Stoutenburg, L. (2020). *Meeting families where they are: Building equity through advocacy with diverse schools and communities.* This book is a must read for educators committed to meeting the needs of all students regardless of disability, difference, or context.

Overview of Context for Case Studies

■ ■ ■

The case studies are set in a suburban/urban school district. Although the town was once a bedroom community for those who worked in the metropolitan area, in recent years the population has been growing and changing membership. The town has become a city through incorporating several small towns nearby. Students used to be mostly Caucasian. Now the student population of the district is 29.7 percent African American, 29.5 percent Hispanic, 34.7 percent Caucasian, 6 percent Asian/ Pacific Islander, and 0.2 percent Native American. The district has never-ending challenges to build and maintain a vision, and to keep increasing the percentage of students mastering skills as tested on the state exam—whether through curriculum alignment, professional development of teachers, or improving the leadership of the schools. Turnovers in teaching staff and in school and district leadership positions create problems in moving smoothly through the change process.

In the case studies the superintendent, Dr. Petrovsky, has been in place for twenty years. You will find a new principal, Dr. Ted Caruthers, struggling with leadership and management issues. You will find one high school principal, Dr. Alice March, working with professional development and struggling with ethical issues. A second high school principal, Mr. Gary Jones, is dealing with legal issues ranging from theft to sexual harassment. An elementary principal, Glenna Greene, and her colleagues have been working to serve as leaders of change despite little support from the higher administration.

At the end of each case study, questions are raised that relate to the Educational Leadership Constituent Council (ELCC) standard examined in each part of this text (Parts I–IV). Certainly, additional questions may be posed to include more than one standard, and there is flexibility in cases reflecting real-life experiences.

Part I Case Study

A New Role

■ ■ ■

Setting: Eisenhower School District is a fairly large district with two high schools. Three junior high schools feed into each of these schools. Muskie Junior High School is one of the feeder schools for Dover High School. Because this junior high has been a school with an unusually large number of student problems, administrators have come and gone frequently. Teachers with one to five years of experience form 19.8 percent of the staff; those with six to ten years of experience form 32.1 percent of the staff; those with eleven to twenty years form 17.9 percent, and those with more than twenty years of experience form 14.8 percent. The ethnic breakdown for students shows that 39.5 percent are African American, 30.7 percent are Hispanic, and 29.8 percent are White.

Scenario: It is the second day of January in a new year, the day before the staff and teachers return for a workday. Dr. Ted Caruthers, the very recently appointed principal of Muskie Junior High School, is mulling over options for starting his new job effectively. Martha Spieler, one of the assistant principals, finds him reviewing the most recent testing data, staff evaluations from last year, a two-year-old survey on climate at the school, and a three-year-old survey of school needs as perceived by parents and other stakeholders.

"Good morning, Martha," says Dr. Caruthers. "I am trying to get a better understanding of our school. It seems that viewing this school from afar can lead to different conclusions about what's most needed compared to the conclusions I've reached after reviewing this data. I'm not sure how much of this data should be used. Changes have occurred so rapidly around here that even the staff evaluations of last year leave large gaps in the information I need to formulate a plan of action. I know there was at least a 19 percent turnover of staff this last summer. Certainly, that will have changed the climate and the list of school needs that are indicated in these older documents. You've been around here for five years. What do you think the major needs are?"

"Well, I think one of the major needs was met when the superintendent and school board decided you needed to be the principal here," Martha replies. "They all know that you stand for law and order. Your record as the assistant principal at the high school is what got you this job. You are fair, and you respect the students, the teachers, and the parents. That has allowed you to take a strong stance on discipline. We need that here at the junior high, where all three groups of students—White, African American, and Hispanic—are trying to gain control or be top dog. Our teachers and staff really need a boost in morale. Last year the staff tried to take the discipline problems in hand. I tried to help, but our former principal would not make the tough decisions. Now we all suffer the consequences. The students feel as though they are in charge. Teachers are not willing to address discipline problems. We really have no sense of direction in discipline, or in anything else. Every teacher is just trying to make it through the day."

"Are you saying that discipline is the number one issue?" Caruthers asks. "At an even deeper level, are you perhaps saying that with a sense of direction or vision, discipline would fall in place? Am I reading you correctly?"

"Dr. Caruthers, we need a sense of direction, a sense of community, and a sense of order so that we can build a true learning community."

"How would you suggest I start, Martha?"

"First, I think you should ask the staff about their perceptions. Then I would ask some student leaders, some parents, and some community leaders. I know all of this will take time, but I'm afraid if we jump in and make changes too rapidly that we will create more problems. It might be wiser to limp along and gather fresh data as rapidly as possible."

"One thing I do know, Martha. I plan to be very visible and vocal. I am going to address the student body on the first day they return to school. On the teacher workday that's scheduled for tomorrow, I plan to address the faculty and staff. I also plan to start meeting with department groups. I want to have each person list the ten best points of this school and the ten areas needing immediate attention. I'd also like each staff member to prioritize his or her list. That way, I can see if there's a strong pattern for action in one direction or another."

"I think you're going to be surprised at the response, Dr. Caruthers. We were seldom asked what our thoughts were on any topic. I think you may get answers that vary tremendously. Some answers may be facetious. Others will be very serious. You had better be ready to listen and act on what you hear."

"I intend to listen very carefully," Caruthers responds. "Sort all the input, and then call a planning team together. That team will plan for gathering a more extensive, updated set of information, and they'll analyze the information and make recommendations to me about what action needs to be taken. I think it would help to use Stufflebeam's model of context, input, process, and product evaluations (CIPP). We have to understand what needs to be done, and in what order. We also have to understand how these things should be done compared to how they are being done. Finally, we need to learn if our efforts succeed. All this activity must be carefully planned and documented. The entire learning community must understand what's being done, and why it's being done. We're facing a massive task. You and I are just two small pieces in the picture."

"Yes, we are," Martha agrees, "but you as leader have a much greater part than I do. Remember that we have had little direction. We need a leader, and we need a manager too. Unless we have a structured response to the obvious needs such as discipline management, I don't think we'll succeed. Do you think you can persuade the superintendent to give us more help with this effort? After all, we now have a history of changing principals every year, and sometimes even sooner. Those changes haven't helped anyone, as far as I can see. I hang in here because I think that basically, we have a great staff. They just need help in joining together in their efforts. Right now, everyone is acting like the lone ranger."

"Before I ask for any more help, monetarily or otherwise, I need to have a basic plan of action written out—like a position paper that I can use to help anyone see the picture that I see." Caruthers smiles at Martha. "Because we've had a chance to visit about this, I'd like you to review the proposal I am going to draft this afternoon. I plan to use it tomorrow, and in the future too. Of course, I expect my plan to be modified as we gather input and see what successes and/or failures we have. As an assistant principal to Dr. March, I was constantly reflecting and asking myself what I would do if I were in her shoes. Now that I am in the principalship or leadership position, I want you to do much the same. I encourage you to reflect and to share with me as we move along in the process of building a learning team. I hope you feel comfortable enough to do this with me. I will encourage the other assistant to interact with me at the same level, too."

"I can give you some feedback right now," Martha says. "If you mention the CIPP process to others as you did to me, I think it would be better if you used other terms. All that sounds too academic. Even with my basic understanding, I have questions. For one, I want to hear more about how you're going to get input from the community. The parents and some of the business leaders have been very active in this school, helping through the Parent-Teacher Association and the Boosters Club. You will need help in thinking this out."

Questions

1. How is Dr. Caruthers exhibiting leadership?
2. What do you think of Martha's advice to Dr. Caruthers?
3. If you were in Dr. Caruthers's position, what first steps would you take to help your school become a learning community?
4. How would you as a new principal begin to build morale? Shape culture?
5. What evidence, if any, do you see for each of the state or national standards in this case study?

PART II
Leadership Processes

7

Organizational Structure and Design

■ ■ ■

FOCUSING QUESTIONS

1. What are the elements of organizational structure?
2. Why is open systems theory important in understanding how schools function?
3. What are some different approaches to analyzing what principals do in terms of leadership functions, administrative roles, and management skills?
4. Why are some principals more effective than others?
5. How does bureaucracy differ from emerging models of organizational structure?

In this chapter, we address these questions concerning organizational structure in schools. We begin our discussion by defining and describing six basic elements of organizational structure: job specialization, departmentalization, chain of command, span of control, centralization and decentralization, and line and staff positions. Then we discuss the importance of open systems theory in schools. Following that, we examine the learning organization. Then we discuss three approaches to analyzing what principals do: leadership functions, administrative roles, and management skills. We then discuss effective principals in terms of task dimensions, human resource activities, and behavioral profiles of effective versus successful principals. Next, we discuss the characteristics and dysfunctions of bureaucracy. We conclude the chapter by examining five alternatives to the bureaucratic form: mechanistic-organic structures, five structural configurations, System 4 design, four-frame model, and synergistic leadership theory.

Up to this point, we have concentrated on the principal's role as instructional leader. We have examined a host of processes for shaping schools as professional learning communities and have hinted at the implications of these initiatives for school improvement. But managing the school operation is important in addition to instructional leadership (English, 2015; Griffin, Phillips, & Gully, 2019; Hakonsson, Burton, & Obel, 2020; Lunenburg, 2007; Meyer, 2017; Rubin, Baldwin, & Bommer, 2019; Schein & Schein, 2018; Worren, 2018).

We know that when school improvements occur, principals play a central role in: (a) ensuring that resources—money, time, and professional development—align with instructional goals; (b) supporting the professional growth of teachers in a variety of interconnected ways; (c) including teachers in the information loop; (d) cultivating the relationship between the school and community; and (e) managing the day-to-day tasks of running a school. Each of these is viewed as a management task in the sense that it involves daily or weekly attention to problem solving within the school and between the school and its immediate environment.

We think management is a prerequisite to leadership. You can't change something unless it is a viable system in the first place. It has to continue to survive while you take it to the next level. Management of the day-to-day operation of a school is essential. The leadership, though, is in asking: What is the business we are in? What is it we are trying to do? How are we going to make this work better? How are we going to put all of our resources together: to continue to grow; to continue to respond to new needs; to enable schools to be places where engaged teaching and learning occur?

Very often, although good leaders know the management skills, they do not take the time to practice those skills. And part of leadership is in knowing what you do best and using all of the available resources you have. Thus, principals work with students, teachers, parents, and others to set up organizational structures and help to develop other people in the school by delegating and very carefully monitoring the leadership functions in the school, so that effective teaching and learning occurs.

ELEMENTS OF ORGANIZATIONAL STRUCTURE

Think of all the activities employees perform in a school: scheduling classes, ordering supplies, maintaining student records, teaching classes, cleaning classrooms, preparing food, driving buses, typing letters, photocopying, and the like. If you were to make a list, you would probably identify several hundred different tasks. Without some structures, policies, and processes, would all the required tasks be performed efficiently and effectively? Who will teach the classes, clean the classrooms, wash the chalkboards, serve lunch in the cafeteria, drive the buses, or mail student report cards?

The leadership function of **organizational structure** is the process of deploying human and physical resources to carry out tasks and achieve school goals. How do principals manage the day-to-day activities of the school and, at the same time, work toward the school's improvement? They don't do it alone. In this section, we describe six elements of organizational structure: job specialization, departmentalization, chain of command, span of control, centralization and decentralization, and line and staff positions (DuBrin, 2018; Griffin, Phillips, & Gully, 2019; Hitt, Miller, & Colella, 2018; McShane & Von Glinow, 2018; Neck, Houghton, & Murray, 2019; Nelson & Quick, 2019; Robbins & Judge, 2019; Rubin, Baldwin, & Bommer, 2019; Uhl-Bien, Schermerhorn, & Osborn, 2016; Wesson, LePine, & Colquitt, 2016).

Job Specialization

The most basic element of organizational structure is **job specialization**—the degree to which the overall task of the school is broken down and divided into smaller, component parts. For example, a school may employ principals, school psychologists, diagnosticians, social workers, counselors, teachers, and many other support staff including secretaries, food service personnel, maintenance workers, bus drivers, and the like. This specialization of tasks provides an identity for the job and those performing it; and collectively, the tasks add back to the total. That is, the contributions of the individual jobs, including management coordination, equal the original overall job of the school—to educate all children.

Job specialization is a key organizing concept for several reasons. First, repetition improves skill. By performing the same task repeatedly, the employee gains expertise and thus increases productivity. Second, wage economics may also arise through the development of various employee levels. Complex jobs can be staffed with skilled personnel, and simple tasks with unskilled labor. Third, whenever a sufficient volume of routine work is isolated, mechanization becomes a possibility; using computers for office work is an example. Finally, job specialization allows a variety of tasks to be performed simultaneously. For example, in a school, budgeting, counseling, typing, preparing lunch, and teaching can be performed concurrently by different people.

Despite the advantages, however, schools can overdo job specialization. When carried to extremes, job specialization can lead to fatigue, monotony, boredom, and job dissatisfaction, which can result in absenteeism, turnover, and a decrease in the quality of work performed (Wesson, LePine & Colquitt, 2016). To counter these problems, school principals have begun to search for alternatives that will maintain the positive benefits of job specialization.

The three most common alternatives to job specialization are job rotation, job enlargement, and job enrichment (Herzberg, 2009). **Job rotation** involves systematically moving employees from one job to another. In large school districts, principals are often rotated among schools every five years. **Job enlargement** adds breadth to a job by increasing the number and variety of activities performed by an employee. **Job enrichment** adds depth to a job by adding "administrative" activities (decision making, staffing, budgeting, reporting) to a teacher's responsibilities. The latter two alternatives were recommended by school reform advocates as a way to restructure schools through shared governance, participatory management, and site-based decision making, whereby teachers play a more active role in the operation of the school (Bulach & Lunenburg, 2008, 2011; Fullan, 2015; Hess, 1995).

Departmentalization

Once the overall task of a school is divided into specialized jobs, these jobs must be grouped into some logical organizational units such as teams, departments, or divisions—a concept known as **departmentalization**. The most common grouping in schools is by function. Departmentalization by function brings together, in a common organizational unit, people performing similar or closely related activities. For example, common departments in a school are English, social studies, mathematics, and science. Common divisions in school districts are instruction, business, human resources, and research and development. Similar activities are coordinated from a common place in the organizational hierarchy. The instructional division, for example, controls only instructional activities. Each functional unit may be broken down further for coordination and control purposes.

Because of its versatility, **functional departmentalization** is one of the most widely adopted approaches for grouping school district activities. This system can be used in both large and small school districts. It can be used at many different levels in the organizational hierarchy, at the central office level or further down to individual building levels, such as instructional grade-level teams in an elementary school or subject-matter departments within a high school.

Functional departmentalization offers a number of other advantages. Because people who perform similar functions work together, each department can be staffed by experts in that functional area. Decision making and coordination are easier, because division administrators or department heads need to be familiar with only a relatively narrow set of skills. Functional departments at the central office can use a school district's resources more efficiently, because a department's activity does not have to be repeated across several school district divisions. Functional departmentalization has certain disadvantages as well. Personnel can develop overly narrow and technical viewpoints that lose sight of the total system perspective; communication and coordination across departments can be difficult; and conflicts often emerge as each department or unit attempts to protect its own turf.

Chain of Command

The **chain of command** is an unbroken line of authority that extends from the top of the organization down through to the lowest levels in an organization's structure (Robbins & Judge, 2019). It clarifies who reports to whom. It answers questions such as "To whom do I go to if I have a problem?" and "To whom am I responsible?"

The chain of command is associated with two underlying principles: *authority* and *unity of command*. **Authority** refers to the rights inherent in an administrative position to give orders and expect them to be obeyed. The **unity of command** principle helps preserve the concept of an unbroken line of authority. It means that a person has only one supervisor to whom they are directly responsible. Organizations depend on this unbroken line of authority to attain order, control, and predictable performance (Wesson, LePine, & Colquitt, 2016).

Span of Control

Another key element of organizational structure is the **span of control**—the number of subordinates who report directly to a given principal. There is a limit to the number of persons one principal can effectively supervise. Care should be taken to keep the *span of control* within manageable limits.

Although there is agreement that there is a limit to the number of subordinates a principal can effectively supervise or manage, no agreement exists on the precise number. In fact, it is generally acknowledged that the optimum span of control varies greatly, even within the same school. Although principals may directly supervise only three to eight persons, assistant principals and department heads directing subordinates who are performing relatively similar activities may be able to manage much larger numbers efficiently.

Critical factors in determining the appropriate span of control include the following (Griffin, Phillips, & Gully, 2019):

1. *Similarity of functions*. Span of control should increase as the number of different functions to be supervised increases.
2. *Geographic proximity*. Span of control should decrease as the functions to be supervised become more geographically dispersed.
3. *Complexity of functions*. Span of control should be smaller for subordinates performing more complex tasks than for those performing simpler tasks.

4. *Degree of interdependence among units.* The greater the need for coordination of interdependent work units, the smaller the span of control.
5. *Level of motivation of subordinate personnel.* Increased motivation permits a larger span of control, and a larger span of control increases motivation.
6. *Competence of principals.* The ability of principals to delegate authority and responsibility varies. Span of control for those who can delegate more can be much larger than for those who can delegate little authority.

Centralization and Decentralization

Another key element of organizational structure is the degree to which authority within the school or school district is centralized or decentralized. In reality, authority can be centralized or decentralized.

The concept of **decentralization** has to do with the degree to which authority is dispersed or concentrated. Decentralization is the systematic dispersal of power and decision making throughout the school district to middle- and lower-level leaders. Conversely, **centralization** is the systematic concentration of power and authority near the top, or in the head of a school (the principal) or school district (the superintendent) (McShane & Von Glinow, 2018). No organization is completely centralized or decentralized. Rather, these are extremes of a continuum, and school districts fall somewhere in between. The difference is one of relative degree; that is, a school district can be described as decentralized relative to other schools or school districts.

Several characteristics determine how decentralized a school is relative to others (Griffin, Phillips, & Gully, 2019):

1. *Number of decisions made at lower levels.* The greater the number of decisions made by those lower in the organizational hierarchy (staff members), the more decentralized the school.
2. *Importance of decisions made at lower levels.* In a decentralized school, teachers can make decisions involving substantial resources and increased people power, or they can commit the school to a new course of action.
3. *The scope of decisions made at lower levels.* If teachers can make decisions that affect more than one function, the school is probably decentralized.
4. *Amount of checking on school principals.* In a highly decentralized school district, top-level administrators (superintendents) seldom review day-to-day decisions of building principals. The presumption is that these decisions were made correctly. Evaluation is based on overall results of the school.

The advantages of decentralization include the following: unburdening of top-level administrators; improved decision making, because decisions are made closer to the firing line; better training, morale, and initiative at lower levels; and increased flexibility to adjust to changing conditions. These advantages are so compelling that it is tempting to think of decentralization as "good" and centralization as "bad" (Nelson & Quick, 2019).

But total decentralization, with no coordination from the top, would be undesirable. The very purpose of organization—efficient integration of subunits for the good of the whole—would be diminished without some centralized control (Neck, Houghton, & Murray, 2019). Even in very decentralized school districts, top administrators such as superintendents retain a number of decisions, including setting overall goals, strategic planning, school district policy formulation with the school board, collective bargaining with unions, and development of financial and accounting systems. The question for school leaders is not whether a school or school district should be decentralized, but to what extent it should be decentralized.

Decentralization has value only to the extent that it assists a school district or school to achieve its goals effectively. In determining the amount of decentralization appropriate for a school district, the following internal characteristics are usually considered (Hitt, Miller, & Colella, 2018):

1. *The cost and risk associated with the decision.* Principals may be wary of delegating authority for decisions that could have an impact on the performance of their own subunits or the school as a whole. This caution is out of consideration not only for the school's welfare but also for their own, because the responsibility for results remains with the delegator.

2. *A principal's preference for a high degree of involvement and confidence in colleagues.* Some principals pride themselves on their detailed knowledge of everything that happens within their purview of responsibility. This has been referred to as "running a tight ship." Conversely, other principals take pride in confidently delegating everything possible to their colleagues in order to avoid getting bogged down in petty details and to preserve their own expertise with the school's major goal of teaching and learning.

3. *The organizational culture.* The shared norms, values, and beliefs (culture) of members of some schools support tight control at the top. The culture of other schools supports the opposite approach. The history of the school's culture, then, will have some bearing on the amount of decentralization appropriate.

4. *The abilities of staff.* This characteristic is, in part, a circular process. If authority is not delegated, due to lack of confidence in the talents below, the talent will not have an opportunity to develop. Furthermore, the lack of internal training and development will make it more difficult to find and hold talented and ambitious people. This, in turn, will make it more difficult to decentralize.

Line and Staff Positions

An important point in examining the key elements of organizational structure is to distinguish between line and staff positions. **Line positions** are traditionally defined as those forming a part of the main line of authority (or chain of command) that flows throughout the school or school district. **Staff positions** are positions outside the main line of authority or direct chain of command that are primarily advisory or supportive in nature.

Line positions are represented by a solid line in most organizational charts, starting with the superintendent and extending down through the various levels in the hierarchy to the point where the basic activities of the school district—teaching—are carried out. The roles of superintendent, assistant superintendents, directors, principals, and teachers are line positions. Each has goals that derive from and contribute to those of the overall school district. Examples of staff positions are "Assistant to the Superintendent" and "Legal Counsel." These personnel perform specialized functions that are primarily intended to help line administrators. For example, the legal counsel is not expected to contribute to school district outcomes. Instead, they answer questions from and provide advice to the superintendent concerning legal matters that confront the school district. The assistant to the superintendent might be involved in such activities as computer programming, preparing enrollment projections, or conducting special studies that flow to the superintendent requiring information or advice. Staff positions are represented by dashed lines in organizational charts, implying that school district staff personnel communicate and advise line administrators.

The line and staff organization allows much more specialization and flexibility than the line organization alone. However, staff authority sometimes undermines the integrity of line departments and personnel who are accountable for results. Several factors may cause conflicts between and among line and staff departments and personnel (Newstrom, 2016). Due to the nature of this topic, we need to shift our focus to the school district.

1. Staff personnel may exceed their authority and attempt to give orders directly to line personnel.
2. Line personnel may feel that staff specialists do not fully understand line problems and think their advice is not workable.
3. Staff may attempt to take credit for ideas implemented by line; conversely, line may not acknowledge the role staff has played in helping to resolve problems.
4. Because staff is highly specialized, it may use technical terms and language that line cannot understand.
5. Top administration may not have communicated clearly the extent of authority staff has in its relationship with line.
6. Organizationally, staff departments and personnel are placed in relatively high positions close to top administration; lower-level line departments and personnel tend to resent this.

Basically, the line-staff conflict evident in many school districts is impossible to eliminate completely. However, it is possible to create conditions wherein line-staff conflicts are manageable. School districts can reduce the degree of line-staff conflict through the following strategies (Newstrom, 2016):

1. Create a public recognition of the reality of interdependence between the line and staff units and develop a culture that attacks problems in a collaborative manner.
2. Do not allow organizational politics to mask true line-staff contributions. Cross-unit sabotage, backstabbing, spying, and intentional distortion can eliminate any hope of cooperation and lead to internal disintegration.
3. Develop an understanding of the broader organizational vision and goal and an associated recognition of each unit's responsibility to that goal.
4. Foster a climate in which leaders feel free to communicate their concerns, voice their perceptions, and discuss any apprehensions they have concerning actions of the other units.
5. Establish a team-based approach to problem solving that stresses the effective resolution of issues without undue concern over who will get "credit" for the solution.

6. Encourage nontask-related interaction between line and staff administrators to facilitate understanding of the different perspectives, values, needs, and goals held by both groups.

The reduction of line-staff conflict is vital to overall school district performance. The creation of an organizational structure can unintentionally induce or minimize disruptive line-staff relationships.

AN OPEN-SYSTEMS PERSPECTIVE

Schools are social systems in which two or more persons work together in a coordinated manner to attain common goals. This definition is useful, for it specifies several important features of schools: (a) they consist, ultimately, of people; (b) they are goal-directed in nature; (c) they attain their goals through some form of coordinated effort; and (d) they interact with their external environment. Our definition, however, does not elaborate on one important feature of schools deserving special attention: All schools are *open systems*, although the degree of interaction with their environment may vary (Lunenburg, 2010c)

According to **open systems theory**, schools constantly interact with their environments. In fact, they need to structure themselves to deal with forces in the world around them (Norlin, 2009; Scott, 2007). In contrast, **closed systems theory** views schools as sufficiently independent to solve most of their problems through their internal forces, without taking into account forces in the external environment (Miner, 2015). Consider a school closing or realignment of school boundaries, for example. It affects the people in the school and those outside it—in the community it is moving from as well as the one it is moving to. Systems theory works on the inside and outside of the organization, as a way of understanding and anticipating the consequences of any decision.

A **system** can be defined as an interrelated set of elements functioning as an operating unit (Senge, 1990, 2006). As depicted in figure 7.1, an organizational system

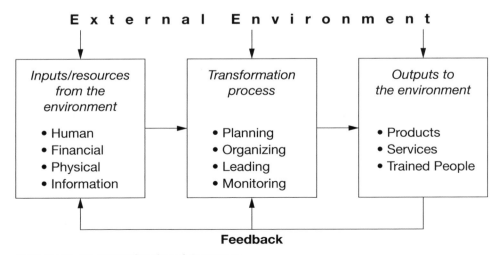

Figure 7.1 An Organizational Structure

consists of five basic elements: inputs, a transformation process, outputs, feedback, and the environment.

Inputs

Systems such as schools use four kinds of **inputs** or resources from the environment: human resources, financial resources, physical resources, and information resources. Human resources include administrative and staff talent, labor, and the like. Financial resources are the capital used by the school or the school district to finance both ongoing and long-term operations.

Physical resources include supplies, materials, facilities, and equipment. Information resources are knowledge, curricula, data, and other kinds of information utilized by the school or the school district.

Transformation Process

The principal's job involves combining and coordinating these various resources to attain the school's goals—learning for all. How do principals accomplish this? They do so by carrying out four basic management functions: planning, organizing, leading, and monitoring. In this way the principal, through the coordinated efforts of all members of the school community, transforms students into graduates. The system adds a value added to the work on process (Shaw, 2006).

This **transformation process** includes the internal operation of the school organization and its system of operational management. Some components of the system of operational management include the technical competence of school administrators and other staff, their plans of operation, and their ability to cope with change. Tasks performed by school administrators within the organization's structure will affect the school/school district's outputs.

Analysis of the school as an open system would be incomplete without an examination of the core technology of schooling—the teaching-learning process. The technical core of the school affects many of the decisions school administrators make concerning structure (Rowan, 1990, 1998; Rowan, Raudenbush, & Cheong, 1993). Although learning is not limited to school, the process of teaching and learning is why schools exist.

Generally speaking, learning occurs when experience produces change in one's knowledge or behavior. Most experts agree that there are three general theories of learning: (a) **behavioral theories** stress observable changes in behavior; (b) **cognitive theories** stress internal mental activities such as thinking memory, and problem solving; and (c) **constructivist theories** stress learners as active in constructing their own knowledge (Woolfolk, 2019). Application of each of these theories of learning has different implications for teaching (see, e.g., Alberto & Troutman, 2009; Bruning, Schraw, & Norby, 2011; Kirschner, Sweller, & Clark, 2006; Windschitl, 2002).

Outputs

It is the principal's job to secure and use inputs to the schools and then transform them through the administrative functions of planning, organizing, leading, and monitoring—while considering external variables—to produce outputs. In social systems, **outputs** are usually labeled *goals* or *objectives* and are represented by the products, results, outcomes, or accomplishments of the system. Although the kinds of outputs will vary with a specific school, they usually include one or more of the following: growth and achievement levels of students and teachers, student dropout rates, employee performance and turnover, school-community relations, and job satisfaction.

Most of these require no elaboration; only the last one is discussed. A school must provide "satisfaction" to members of the school community beyond the physiological needs (salary, working conditions, job security) (Herzberg, 2009). Schools must provide for employees' needs for affiliation, acceptance, esteem, and perhaps even self-actualization if they hope to retain a motivated, committed workforce capable of performing at maximum levels (Maslow, 1998).

Feedback

Finally, the external environment reacts to these outputs and provides **feedback** to the system. Feedback is crucial to the success of the school operation. Negative feedback, for example, can be used to correct deficiencies in the transformation process or the inputs or both, which in turn will have an effect on the school's future outputs.

Environment

The **environment** surrounding the school/school district includes the social, political, and economic forces that impinge on the organization. The environment in the open systems model takes on added significance today in a climate of policy accountability. The social, political, and economic contexts in which school principals work are marked by pressures at the local, state, and federal levels. Thus, school principals today find it necessary to manage and develop "internal" operations while concurrently monitoring the environment and anticipating and responding to "external" demands.

Since the enactment of the Every Student Succeeds Act (ESSA) of 2015 and its immediate predecessor and now defunct No Child Left Behind (NCLB) Act of 2001, education has been near the top of the national political agenda. NCLB and its successor ESSA has nationalized the discussion concerning the well-being of public schooling in America. At the time the report was released, and subsequently, there has been concern with an achievement gap in America (Barton & Coley, 2010; Darling-Hammond, 2010; Entwisle, Alexander, & Olson, 2010; Howard, 2020; Ladson-Billings, 2006; Murphy, 2010; Nieto, 2002/2003; Paige, 2011; Rothstein, 2004; Singham, 2003; Sirin, 2005; Teranishi, Nguyen, & Curammeng, 2020; Wiggan, 2007) and our academic competitiveness with other nations, particularly in mathematics and science (US Department of Education, 2008). These achievement gaps and academic comparisons led many people to conclude that the US public school system was underperforming.

With recognition of an achievement gap and the rise of international educational comparisons, states began to focus their policy on standards, accountability, and the improvement of student academic achievement (Lunenburg, 2015; Ornstein, 2016). Statewide assessment systems were implemented nationwide. Thus, an era of high-stakes testing, complete with rewards and sanctions for low-performing schools, was born.

The social, political, and economic forces that impinge on the school organization are not all state and national, however. Local school principals also face a number of challenges that are exclusively local in nature, such as bond referenda, difficult school boards, and teacher unions. These local political issues can at times confound state-mandated policies. For example, school principals often face mandated programs that do not meet the changing demographics of their student population. Teachers are often bound by union contracts that conflict with the norms of their particular school or school district. Principals are expected to respond to federal mandates even though resources are scarce. Zero-tolerance policies may require expelling a student, even though it may not be in the best interest of the student to miss school for an extended period of time. And educational leaders are faced with ongoing pressures to show good results on standardized achievement tests, while at the same time dealing with a growing number of management duties, such as budgeting, hiring personnel, labor relations, and site committees resulting from school-based management initiatives.

THE LEARNING ORGANIZATION

In recent years, organization theorists have extended the open systems model by adding a "brain" to the "living organization." Today, leaders are reading and hearing a great deal about learning organizations. Peter Senge (1990; 2006), a professor at the Massachusetts Institute of Technology, popularized the concept of "learning organization" in his best-selling book *The Fifth Discipline*.

A **learning organization** is a strategic commitment to capture and share learning in the organization for the benefit of individuals, teams, and the organization. It does this through alignment and the collective capacity to sense and interpret a changing environment; to input new knowledge through continuous learning and change; to embed this knowledge in systems and practices; and to transform this knowledge into outputs.

Senge (2006) defines learning organizations as "organizations where people continually expand their capacity to create the results they truly desire, where new and expansive patterns of thinking are nurtured, where collective aspiration is set free and where people are continually learning how to learn together" (p. 3). Senge describes a model of five interdependent disciplines necessary for an organization to seriously pursue learning. He identifies systems thinking as the "fifth discipline," because he believes that thinking systemically is the pivotal lever in the learning and change process. Brief definitions of Senge's principles are as follows:

- *Systems thinking*. A conceptual framework that sees all parts as interrelated and affecting each other.
- *Personal mastery*. A process of personal commitment to vision, excellence, and lifelong learning.
- *Shared vision*. Sharing an image of the future you want to realize together.
- *Team learning*: The process of learning collectively; the idea that two brains are smarter than one.
- *Mental models*. Deeply ingrained assumptions that influence personal and organizational views and behaviors.

The five disciplines work together to create the learning organization. A metaphor to describe this systems theory–based model would be DNA or a hologram. Each is a complex system of patterns, and the whole is greater than the sum of its parts.

Senge has also coauthored a companion book directly focused on education: *Schools That Learn* (Senge et al. 2012). Senge et al. argue that teachers, administrators, and other school stakeholders must learn how to build their own capacity; that is, they must develop the capacity to learn. From the perspective of Senge et al. (2012), real improvement will occur only if people responsible for implementation design the change itself. They argue that schools can be recreated, made vital, and renewed not by fiat or command, and not by regulation, but by embracing the principles of the learning organization.

Senge et al. make a powerful argument regarding the need for a systems approach and learning orientation. They provide a historical perspective on educational systems. Specifically, they detail "industrial age" assumptions about learning: that children are deficient and schools should fix them, that learning is strictly an intellectual enterprise, that everyone should learn in the same way, that classroom learning is distinctly different from that occurring outside of school, and that some kids are smart while others are not. They further assert that schools are run by specialists who maintain control, that knowledge is inherently fragmented, that schools teach some kind of objective truth, and that learning is primarily individualistic and competition accelerates learning. Senge et al. (2012) suggest that these assumptions about learning and the nature and purpose of schooling reflect deeply embedded cultural beliefs that must be considered, and in many cases directly confronted, if schools are to develop the learning orientation necessary for improvement.

LEADERSHIP FUNCTIONS

Previously, we noted that principals combine and coordinate various kinds of resources by carrying out four basic administrative functions: planning, organizing, leading, and monitoring. Our attention now turns to clarifying these four functions or activities that constitute the work performed by principals. The relationships among these functions are shown in figure 7.2.

Planning

Generally, **planning** defines where the school wants to be in the future and how to get there. Plans and the goals on which they are based give purpose and direction to the school, its subunits, and contributing staff. For example, suppose the principal in

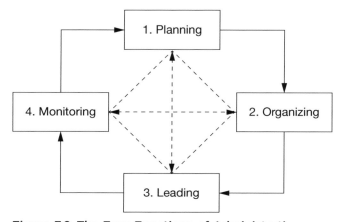

Figure 7.2 The Four Functions of Administration

a large, urban school district decides that the school should attempt to increase the number of students reading at grade level by 20 percent by the year 2025. This goal and the methods needed to attain it would then serve as the planning framework for the school. School counselors, social workers, school psychologists, library media specialists, department heads, and teachers would set and synchronize individual objectives with those of the building principal.

Planning is important because it provides staff with a sense of purpose and direction, outlines the kinds of tasks they will be performing, and explains how their activities are related to the overall goals of the school. Without this information, staff would not know precisely how to use their time and energies efficiently and effectively. Subsequently, they would respond to their job responsibilities randomly, wasting valuable human resources.

Planning is also a prerequisite to other administrative functions. In particular, it becomes the basis for monitoring and evaluating actual performance; that is, plans made during the first step become benchmarks or criteria against which to measure actual performance in the monitoring step. Unless plans are formulated and mutually agreed on, there is relatively little value or basis for measuring the effectiveness of the school outcomes (Lunenburg & Irby, 2000). In addition, comparing planned and actual results provides the principal with a sound basis on which to make necessary adjustments in the school's plan of action.

Since the 1970s, criticisms of traditional planning models have resulted in the development of the strategic planning approach. New ideas have arisen about the nature of educational organizations. Schools have been described as "loosely coupled systems" (Meyer & Rowan, 1977; Rowan, 1990; Weick, 1976) and "organized anarchies" (Cohen, March, & Olsen, 1972). The challenges facing schools have changed significantly as new demands have been placed on them. Their environment has become uncertain and even hostile.

Strategic planning, a subset of the public policy process, could be an ideal technology for shaping the future of education (Lemaine, Levernier, & Richardson, 2018; Wootton & Horne, 2021). Given the contextual constraints on educational policy (social, economic, and political), the challenge for educational strategic planners is to understand the internal and external boundaries and to use this understanding to design policies that could facilitate change in student achievement (Darling-Hammond & Oakes, 2019; Glickman & Burns, 2020) and the very structure of schools (Bryk, 2020; Cuban, 2020; Fullan & Gallagher, 2020).

Organizing

Once principals have developed workable plans and the methods for attaining them, they must design an organization that will successfully implement the plans. **Organizing** involves three essential elements (Anderson, 2018): developing the structure of the organization, acquiring and developing human resources, and establishing common patterns and networks.

In a very basic sense, designing the structure of the organization involves creating the organizational chart for a school. The principal establishes policies and procedures for authority relationships, reporting patterns, the chain of command, departmentalization, and various administrative and subordinate responsibilities (Norton, 2015). Then the principal takes steps to hire competent personnel (Arthur, 2019; Farr & Tippins, 2017; Norton, 2015; Quinn, 2018). When necessary, the principal establishes programs for training new personnel in the skills necessary to carry out their task assignments (Baume & Kahn, 2016; Norton, 2015; Zepeda, 2019). Finally, the principal builds formal communication (Kreps, 2019) and information networks (Graenewagan et al., 2017; Johnson, 2018), including the types of information to be communicated, direction of communication flows, and reductions in barriers to effective communication (Lunenburg, 2010f; Mumby, 2019).

Organizing at the upper levels of an organization usually includes designing the overall framework for the school district (Anderson, 2018; Sinofsky & Iansiti, 2015). At the building level, however, organizing is usually more specific and may involve the following specific activities (Norton, 2015; Rebore, 2014): developing methods to help people understand what portion of the job is their responsibility; coordinating individual efforts through work schedules to avoid unnecessary delay in task accomplishment; designing an efficient system for making day-to-day work assignments should these be necessary; and cross-training personnel or providing for substitute personnel to avoid disruptions in the flow of work caused by absenteeism.

Leading

Once plans are formulated and activities are organized, the next step is leading staff members to achieve the school's goals. Although planning tells principals *what* to do and organizing tells principals *how* to do it, **leading** tells principals *why* the staff member should want to do it. Recently, the leading function is also called *facilitating*, *collaborating*, or *actuating*. No matter what it is called, leading entails guiding and influencing people (Northouse, 2018; Reeves, 2021).

The principal's role has been defined as getting things done by working with all school stakeholders in a professional learning community (DuFour et al., 2021; DuFour & Eaker, 1998, 2009; Eaker et al., 2021). Principals cannot do all of the work in schools alone. They must, therefore, influence the behavior of other people in a certain direction. To influence others, the principal needs to understand something about leadership, motivation, communication, and group dynamics. Leading means communicating goals to staff members and infusing them with the desire to perform at a high level (Kouzes & Posner, 2017). Because schools are composed largely of groups, leading involves motivating entire departments or teams as well as individuals toward the attainment of goals.

Monitoring

When principals compare expected results with actual results and take the necessary corrective action, they are performing the **monitoring** function. Deviations from past plans should be considered when formulating new plans. As shown in figure 7.2, monitoring completes the cycle of leadership functions.

Monitoring is the responsibility of every principal. It may simply consist of walking around the building to see how things are going, talking to students, visiting classrooms, and talking to faculty, or it may involve designing sophisticated information systems to check on the quality of performance, but it must be done if the principal is to be successful.

The success with which principals carry out these functions determines how effectively the school operates. A school is created to perform a set of tasks and achieve a number of stated goals, the most important of which is student learning. It is the principal's job to attain goals by working with all school stakeholders in an atmosphere of a professional learning community. This involves planning, organizing, leading, and monitoring.

LEADERSHIP ROLES

What do principals do? Certain roles are required of all principals, whether they operate elementary, middle, or high schools. A principal does certain things, fulfills certain needs in the school district, has certain responsibilities, and is expected to behave in certain ways.

Thus far, we have described how principals perform four basic functions that help ensure that school resources are used to attain high levels of performance. What do principals actually do to plan, organize, lead, and monitor on an hour-to-hour, day-to-day basis? A number of studies have been conducted in an attempt to describe what principals actually do on the job. Several researchers have followed principals around for long periods of time and recorded all of their activities (Doud, 1989a, 1989b; Fawcett et al., 2001; Ferrandino, 2001; Fullan, 2014; Kaplan & Owings, 2015; Kmetz & Willower, 1982; Marshall, 2021; Martin & Willower, 1981; Sergiovanni & Green, 2015; Spillane & Lowenhaupt, 2019; Ubben, Hughes, & Norris, 2017; Williamson & Blackburn, 2016). The descriptions developed of the principal's actual work can be divided into three general characteristics: heavy workload at a fast pace; variety, fragmentation, and brevity; and oral communication.

Heavy Workload at a Fast Pace

Principals' work is hectic and taxing. On the average, elementary school principals work fifty-one hours a week, from seven to nine hours a day. High school principals average about fifty-three hours a week, dividing forty-two hours during the work day and eleven hours on school-related activities in the evening. The principals observed processed more than thirty pieces of mail a day, attended numerous meetings, and toured their buildings daily. Unexpected disturbances erupted, frequently requiring immediate action and unscheduled meetings. Free time was scarce; and even when time pressure was temporarily relieved, there were previously postponed activities that needed to be completed.

Variety, Fragmentation, and Brevity

Research on principal behavior is consistent in identifying the demands on the administrator as fragmented, rapid fire, voluminous, allowing little time for quiet reflection. The principals engaged in at least 149 different activities per day, half of which took less than five minutes each. This is in sharp contrast to many professional jobs, like engineering or law, which are characterized by long periods of concentration. Principals shift gears rapidly. There is no continuous pattern in their work. Significant crises are interspersed with trivial events in no predictable sequence. Each issue must be decided as quickly as possible.

Oral Communication

Principals spend 70 to 80 percent of their time in interpersonal communication. Personal contacts include colleagues in other schools, senior administrators, staff experts, teachers, and other personnel throughout the school. Effective principals also establish personal contacts outside the school, including principals in other school districts, legislators, state department of education personnel, parents, and people in the community. Most communication is face-to-face and by telephone rather than written. E-mail has added another dimension to the principal's communication patterns. Oral communication is fast and action oriented, and written communication is slow and time consuming. In addition, principals depend heavily on gossip and hearsay, which travel quickly through oral comunication. Finally, oral communication tends to be more personal and satisfies people's needs for social interaction.

An analysis of the roles that principals perform gives a clearer picture of what principals actually do on their jobs than does an analysis of leadership functions. By identifying a specific set of observable principal behaviors, the roles perspective also brings realism to the analysis of what principals do. Principals are the ones who make things happen in the school by doing the planning, organizing, leading, and monitoring that are required for the school to function. What skills are required of principals in order for them to function effectively?

LEADERSHIP SKILLS

Another approach to examining what principals do is based on the types of skills required to perform the job. The necessary skills for planning, organizing, leading, and monitoring have been placed in three categories that are especially important if principals are to perform their functions and roles adequately: conceptual, human, and technical (Katz, 1974). All school administrators must have these skills to be effective, but the amounts differ by hierarchical level (see figure 7.3).

Conceptual Skills

All good school leaders have the ability to view the organization as a whole and solve problems to the benefit of everyone concerned. This is a **conceptual skill** that draws on one's mental abilities to acquire, analyze, and interpret information received from various sources and to make complex decisions that achieve the school's goals. In essence, it concerns the ability to see how the different parts of the school fit together and depend on each other, and how a change in any given part can cause a change in another part.

Conceptual skills are needed by all school leaders; but they are especially important for those at the top of the organization, such as school superintendents. These top-level administrators must perceive the significant elements in a situation and make decisions relevant to broad, conceptual patterns. Because they devote a large

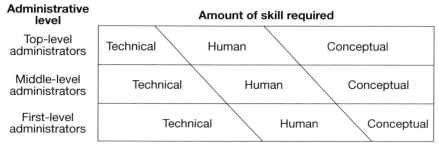

Figure 7.3 Relationship of Skills to Administrative Levels

portion of their time to planning, they draw on conceptual skills to think in terms of relative tendencies, probabilities, patterns, and associations. Conceptual skills provide upper-level administrators with the ability to anticipate changes or to estimate the value of school district strategies. Many of the responsibilities of superintendents, such as decision making, resource allocation, and change, require a broad perspective.

In an era of school-based management, principals were required to further develop their conceptual skills, to think "strategically"—to take a broad, long-term view. This ability enables principals to see what goes on in their work environment and help them to react appropriately and reflectively to situations as they arise (Fullan, 2014; Kaplan & Owings, 2015; Marshall, 2021; Sergiovanni & Green, 2015; Spillane & Lowenhaupt, 2019; Ubben, Hughes, & Norris, 2016; Williamson & Blackburn, 2016). Principals must consider environmental forces, resource flows, staff and administrative talent, school board policies, reform mandates, parent complaints, and organizational change as significant inputs into the internal environment of the school (see figure 7.1).

Human Skills

Principals spend considerable time interacting with people. Recall the researchers' descriptions of how principals spend their time: scheduled and unscheduled meetings, telephone calls, e-mails, hallway and classroom tours, and other face-to-face contacts. All these activities involve other people. For obvious reasons, the principal needs **human skills**: the ability to motivate, facilitate, coordinate, lead, communicate, manage conflict, and get along with others.

Human skills are important to school leaders at all levels. Upper-level administrators (superintendents) must use these skills to deal effectively with school boards, with groups outside of the school district, and with subordinate administrators. Middle-level administrators (principals) need human skills to manage individuals from a wide variety of departments or subject-matter areas and other technical experts (such as counselors, diagnosticians, social workers, school psychologists, and department heads), and to interact productively with upper-level administrators. First-level supervisors (department heads, team leaders) must use human skills to challenge, to motivate, and to coordinate the work of teachers who are responsible for the education of the school district's clients—the students.

In recent years, the awareness of human skills has increased. The phenomenal appeal of such best-selling books as *In Search of Excellence*, *A Passion for Excellence*, *The Fifth Discipline*, *Schools That Learn*, and *Theory Z* attest to that fact. All these books stress the need for leaders at all levels to take care of the human side of the enterprise. Excellent schools and excellent leaders provide warm, nurturing, caring, trusting, and challenging environments. In this view, effective principals are cheerleaders, facilitators, coaches, and nurturers of champions. They build their organizations through people. Effective human skills enable principals to unleash the energy within staff members and students and help them grow, ultimately resulting in maximum performance and goal attainment.

Technical Skills

The ability to use the knowledge, methods, and techniques of a specific discipline or field is referred to as a **technical skill**. Department heads and team leaders in schools are examples of people with technical skills—they are recognized as experts in their disciplines and are presumed to have the ability to supervise others. For the department head or team leader, the nature of technical skills is twofold. First, the supervisor has usually developed some expertise in a discipline or field of study. The department head in a high school, for example, has probably taught the subject they are supervising in an exemplary manner for many years. Second, the supervisor uses skills in the work being done. To successfully run an academic department, the chairperson must know how to teach the subject, how to organize the group, how to acquire resources, how to evaluate performance, and the like.

As shown in figure 7.3, all school leaders need some knowledge of the technical functions they are supervising, although the amount of time they spend performing technical activities decreases as they move up the organizational hierarchy. The first-line supervisor in a school (department head, team leader) will need greater knowledge of the technical parts of the job than will either the superintendent of schools or the building principal. This is because first-line supervisors are closer to the actual work being performed; they often must train and develop teachers and answer questions about work-related problems. Every school district, school, and job has its special technical skill requirements.

Each approach to examining what a principal does looks at the job from a different perspective. Each has its merits. But in the final analysis, a successful principal must: (a) understand the work that is to be performed (leadership functions), (b) understand the behavior needed to perform the job (leadership roles), and (c) master the skills involved in performing his role (leadership skills). Thus, these three approaches to analyzing what a principal does are not mutually exclusive; they are complementary perspectives.

EFFECTIVE PRINCIPALS

At several points in the discussion thus far, the notion of effective principals has been raised. Exactly what is an effective principal? In this section, we examine the notion of effective principals in terms of task dimensions, human resource activities, and behavioral profiles.

Task Dimensions
In analyzing the role of the principal, Marshall Sashkin and Gene Huddle (1987), in their classic study, identify thirteen major task dimensions of the principal's job. They divide these task dimensions into two major categories. One category includes managerial tasks, called "building bureaucratic linkages," normally associated with the role of the principal—creating and enforcing policies, rules, procedures, and authority relationships. The other category, called "building cultural linkages," includes establishing behavioral norms, using symbols, instituting rituals, and telling stories designed to build the cultural foundations of school excellence.

Effective principals create more effective schools by deliberately designing their actions so that those actions build cultural as well as managerial linkages. Table 7.1 shows a number of tasks and related skills for effective management of schools.

Human Resource Activities
Earlier we noted that principals are responsible for getting things done by working with all school stakeholders. The principalship is, above all else, a social process.

Table 7.1 Tasks and Skills for Effective Leadership of Schools

Building Bureaucratic Linkages

1. *Task: Building Sound Relations with the Central Office*

Skills needed: liaison skills and negotiating skills.

2. *Task: Monitoring Organizational Information*

Skills needed: scanning and monitoring information and using information networks.

3. *Task: Coordinating School Activities*

Skills needed: time management, working with groups, and interpersonal skills.

4. *Task: Managing Financial Resources*

Skills needed: developing budgets and mathematical skills.

5. *Task: Maintaining the School Building*

Skills needed: developing maintenance schedules and using general management procedures and practices.

6. *Task: Directing School Support Services*

Skills needed: designing policies, procedures, and rules and developing and monitoring contracts.

7. *Task: Staffing*

Skills needed: use of selection methods, assessment and appraisal skills, and coaching and development skills.

Building Cultural Linkages

8. *Task: Establishing an Atmosphere Conducive to Learning*

Skills needed: organizational communication, interpersonal communication, and using symbols.

9. *Task: Setting High Expectations*

Skills needed: goal setting, interpersonal communication, and interpersonal relationship skills.

10. *Task: Setting School Goals*

Skills needed: goal setting and organizational communication.

11. *Task: Instructional Leadership*

Skills needed: working with groups and committees, observational methods for assessment, and coaching skills.

12. *Task: Organizational Communication*

Skills needed: using teams, committees, and task forces; using internal communication networks; and conflict management skills.

13. *Task: Building Parent and Community Support*

Skills needed: representing the school to the community, public relations skills, and public communications skills.

Principals spend a large portion of their time interacting with others, in face-to-face communication, telephone, and e-mail. Failure to interact well with others may hamper their careers. Recent studies of effective administrators and ineffective administrators emphasize the importance of being able to work effectively with others. In contrast to their effective colleagues, the ineffective administrators were found to have the following shortcomings (Griffin, Phillips, & Gully, 2019; Nelson & Quick,

2019; Reeves, 2021; Robbins & Judge, 2019; Rubin, Baldwin, & Bommer, 2019; Schein & Schein, 2018):

1. Insensitive to others; abrasive, intimidating, bullying style
2. Cold, aloof, arrogant
3. Betrayal of trust (failure to accomplish stated intentions)
4. Overly ambitious: thinking of the next job, playing politics
5. Over-managing: unable to delegate or build a team
6. Unable to staff effectively
7. Unable to plan and organize work
8. Unable to adapt to a superior with a different style
9. Unable to adjust to new and changing conditions
10. Overdependence on an advocate or mentor.

Note that all of these deficiencies are directly related to working effectively with others. People—whether superiors, colleagues, or subordinates—can make or break a principal's career.

Effective and Successful Profiles

Fred Luthans et al. (2015) recently extended the earlier work of Doud (1998a, 1998b, 1998b) and others—Fawcett et al. (2001); Ferrandino (2001); Kmetz and Willower; (1982); and Martin and Willower (1981)—on administrative roles in two significant ways. First, they observed the behavior of 248 administrators at different hierarchical levels in a number of diverse organizations, including schools and universities. This was a much larger and more diverse sample than that used in the earlier research of Doud and others. Second, Luthans and colleagues contrasted the behavior of effective and ineffective administrators and successful and unsuccessful administrators—something not done by Doud and others.

The terms *effective* and *successful* are typically used interchangeably in the literature; therefore, Luthans (2015) makes a clear distinction between the two by operationally defining each term. An administrator's **effectiveness** is measured by subordinates' evaluations of their satisfaction, commitment, and unit performance. Administrative **successfulness** is determined by how fast the administrator has been promoted up the administrative hierarchy. Luthans then ranks the administrators in terms of relative effectiveness and relative successfulness. Less than 10 percent of the administrators in the study were labeled as both effective and successful. In fact, effective and successful administrators turned out to be behavioral opposites.

Results of Luthans's study reveal that effective administrators spent most of their time on task-related communication. Human resource leadership activities were an important part of the effective administrator's day. Successful administrators (those who enjoyed rapid promotions), on the other hand, spent relatively little time on human resource management activities. Instead, they proved to be good at networking (socializing, interacting with outsiders, "politicking"); that is, they were politically savvy and knew how to "play the game."

These conflicting findings may not be surprising to those who say, "It's not *what* you know, but *who* you know." However, Luthans notes that his research has broader implications. He suggests that his findings explain some of the performance problems facing American schools today. He argues that the successful administrators, the politically savvy ones who are being promoted into top-level positions, may not be the effective administrators who have satisfied, committed, and high-performing units. To achieve a more balanced administrative force, those who are both effective and successful, Luthans recommends performance-based evaluation and reward systems that place greater emphasis on human resource leadership activities (communicating, staffing, motivating, managing conflict, and developing staff and students) than on networking and politicking. We believe this is the direction we are headed with greater demands for accountability associated with the Every Student Succeeds Act.

WEBER'S BUREAUCRATIC STRUCTURE

Max Weber's (1947) classic analysis of bureaucracy is the theoretical basis for most contemporary treatments of structure in organizations (Bolman & Deal, 2017; Hall, 2002; Hoy & Miskel, 2013; Hoy & Sweetland, 2000, 2001; Perrow, 1986; Scott, 2007). Weber evolved the concept of bureaucracy as an ideal form of organizational structure.

Weber's characteristics of bureaucracy apply to many large-sized organizations today, including schools. Although few "pure" bureaucracies exist today, almost all organizations have some elements of bureaucracy within their structure: division of labor and specialization, rules and regulations, hierarchy of authority, career orientation, and impersonality in interpersonal relations.

Bureaucratic Characteristics

According to Weber (1947), the ideal **bureaucracy** possesses the following characteristics.

- *Division of labor and specialization.* Divide all tasks into highly specialized jobs. Give each jobholder the authority necessary to perform these duties.
- *Rules and regulations.* Perform each task according to a consistent system of abstract rules. This practice helps ensure that task performance is uniform.
- *Hierarchy of authority.* Arrange all positions according to the principle of hierarchy. Each lower office is under the control of a higher one, and there is a clear chain of command from the top of the organization to the bottom.
- *Career orientation.* Base employment on qualifications and give promotions based on job-related performance. As a corollary, protect employees from arbitrary dismissal, which should result in a high level of loyalty.
- *Impersonality in interpersonal relations.* Maintain an impersonal attitude toward subordinates. This social distance between administrators and staff members helps ensure that rational considerations are the basis for decision making, rather than favoritism or prejudices.

Bureaucratic Dysfunctions

In a period of increasing demands for accountability, demographic changes in population, and economic crisis, most schools are being forced to examine their fundamental structural assumptions. Bureaucracy—the basic infrastructure of organizations in the industrial world—is ill suited to the demands of our postindustrial, demographically diverse information society (Lunenburg, 2017). Bureaucratic characteristics not only are being viewed as less than useful but also are considered to be harmful. Some of these built-in dysfunctions of bureaucracy include the following:

1. *Division of labor and specialization.* A high degree of division of labor can reduce staff initiative. As jobs become narrower in scope and well defined by procedures, individuals sacrifice autonomy and independence. Although specialization can lead to increased productivity and efficiency, it can also create conflict between specialized units, to the detriment of the overall goals of the organization. For example, specialization may impede communication between units. Moreover, overspecialization may result in boredom and routine for some staff, which can lead to dissatisfaction, absenteeism, and turnover.

2. *Reliance on rules and procedures.* Weber (1947) claimed that the use of formal rules and procedures was adopted to help remove the uncertainty in attempting to coordinate a variety of activities in an organization. Reliance on rules can lead to the inability to cope with unique cases that do not conform to normal circumstances. In addition, the emphasis on rules and procedures can produce excessive red tape. The use of rules and procedures is only a limited strategy in trying to achieve coordinated actions. Other strategies may be required. But bureaucracy's approach is to create new rules to cover emerging situations and new contingencies. And, once established, ineffectual rules or procedures in a bureaucracy are difficult to remove.

3. *Emphasis on hierarchy of authority.* The functional attributes of a hierarchy are that it maintains an authority relationship, coordinates activities and personnel, and serves as the formal system of communication. In theory, the hierarchy has both a downward and an upward communication flow. In practice, it usually has only a downward emphasis. Thus, upward communication is impeded, and there is no formal recognition of horizontal communication. This stifles individual initiative and participation in decision making.

4. *Lifelong careers and evaluation.* Weber's (1947) bureaucratic model stresses lifelong careers and evaluations based on merit. Because competence can be difficult to measure in bureaucratic jobs, and because a high degree of specialization enables most employees to master their jobs quickly, there is a tendency to base promotions and salary increments more on seniority and loyalty than on actual skill and performance. Thus, the idea of having the most competent people in positions within the organization is not fully realized. Loyalty is obtained; but this loyalty is toward the protection of one's position, not to the effectiveness of the organization.

5. *Impersonality in interpersonal relations.* The impersonal nature of bureaucracy is probably its most serious shortcoming. Recent critics of bureaucracy attack it as emphasizing rigid, control-oriented structures over people (Bennis, 1966, 1990).

New viewpoints are leading to a decline in the use of bureaucratic structure in modern school organizations (Etzioni-Halevy, 2010, Peters & Waterman, 1982, 2006; Senge, 1990, 2006; Senge et al., 2012). Leaders in the twenty-first century will see a change in some of their duties. One change will be a shift away from simply supervising the work of others to that of contributing directly to the organization's goals.

Instead of shuffling papers and writing reports, the modern school principal may be practicing a craft (Glickman & Burns, 2020).

EMERGENT MODELS OF ORGANIZATIONAL STRUCTURE

What appears to be emerging to replace or extend the bureaucratic structure is a hierarchical model of organization capable of performing collective activities toward the achievement of school goals. Leadership in these hierarchical organizations will need to be considerably different. In particular, significant changes are envisioned in the principalship. Principals will lead from the center rather than from the top. The major focus of leadership will be in supporting teacher success in the classroom (Glickman & Burns, 2020). Change management will be an integral part of the leadership role of the principal. The principal will provide intellectual leadership to support teachers' change efforts (Reeves, 2021). The principal will manage a school culture that supports a professional learning community focused on learning for all (DuFour et al., 2021; Eaker et al., 2021). Whatever their title or formal role definition, it is clear that principals continue to be best positioned to help guide faculty toward new forms of organizational structure (Smylie, Murphy, & Louis, 2020a, 2020b).

Mechanistic-Organic Structures

Some writers have called attention to the incongruency between bureaucratic and professional norms (Crozier & Friedberg, 2010; Etzioni-Halevy, 2010). Specifically, they argue that occupants of hierarchical positions frequently do not have the technical competence to make decisions about issues that involve professional knowledge. That is, there is a basic conflict in educational organizations between authority based on bureaucracy and authority based on professional norms (Abbott & Caracheo, 1988). Others support the notion that bureaucratic orientations and professional attitudes need not conflict if teachers are provided with sufficient autonomy to carry out their jobs (Hoy & Sweetland, 2000, 2001).

We can conclude from this research that most schools have both bureaucratic and professional characteristics that are often incompatible but need not be. Jerald Hage (1965) suggests an axiomatic theory of organizations that provides a framework for defining two ideal types of organizations: **mechanistic** (bureaucratic) and **organic** (professional). His theory identifies eight key variables found in schools and other organizations. These key variables are arranged in a means-ends relationship and are interrelated in seven basic propositions.

Eight Organizational Variables. Complexity, centralization, formalization, and stratification are the four variables that constitute the organizational *means* by which schools are structured to achieve objectives. Adaptiveness, production, efficiency, and job satisfaction are the four variables that represent categories for sorting organizational *ends*. We describe each in turn.

1. *Complexity*, or specialization, refers to the number of occupational specialties included in an organization and the length of training required of each. Person specialization and task specialization distinguish the degree of specialization. A teacher who is an expert in English literature is a person specialist, whereas one who teaches eleventh-grade English is a task specialist. The

greater the number of person specialists and the longer the period of training required to achieve person specialization (or degree held), the more complex the organization.

2. *Centralization*, or hierarchy of authority, refers to the number of role incumbents who participate in decision making and the number of areas in which they participate. The lower the proportion of role incumbents who participate and the fewer the decision areas in which they participate, the more centralized the organization.

3. *Formalization*, or standardization, refers to the proportion of codified jobs and the range of variation that is tolerated within the parameters defining the jobs. The higher the proportion of codified jobs in schools and the lesser range of variation allowed, the more formalized the organization.

4. *Stratification*, or status system, refers to the difference in status between higher and lower levels in the school's hierarchy. Differentials in salary, prestige, privileges, and mobility usually measure this status difference. The greater the disparity in rewards between the top and bottom status levels and the lower the rates of mobility between them, the more stratified the organization.

5. *Adaptiveness*, or flexibility, refers to the use of professional knowledge and techniques in the instruction of students and the ability of a school to respond to environmental demands. The more advanced the knowledge base, instructional techniques, and environmental response, the more adaptive the organization.

6. *Production* refers to the quantity and quality of output. Some schools are more concerned with quantity and less concerned with quality, and vice versa. This variable is difficult to measure because of the dichotomy between quantity and quality. For example, some universities are "degree mills"; that is, they award a large number of degrees each year with little concern for quality. Other institutions are less concerned about increasing the quantity of degrees awarded and more concerned about the quality of the product (the degree recipient). The greater the emphasis on quantity, not quality, of output, the more productive the organization.

7. *Efficiency*, or cost, refers to financial as well as human resources and the amount of idle resources. For example, class size ratios of one teacher to thirty students are more efficient than a one-to-ten ratio. The lower the cost per unit of production, the more efficient the organization.

8. *Job satisfaction*, or morale, refers to the amount of importance a school places on its human resources. Measures of job satisfaction include feelings of well-being, absenteeism, turnover, and the like. The higher the morale and the lower the absenteeism and turnover, the higher the job satisfaction in the organization.

(Hage, 1965)

Seven Organizational Propositions. Central to Hage's axiomatic theory are seven propositions, which have been drawn from the classic works of Weber (1947), Barnard (1964), Perrow (1972, 1986), and Thompson (1961). The major theme permeating Hage's theory is the concept of functional strains, namely that maximizing one organizational-means variable minimizes another. The eight key variables are related in fairly predictable ways. For instance, high centralization results in high production and formalization, high formalization in turn results in high efficiency, high stratification results in low job satisfaction and low adaptiveness and high production, and high complexity results in low centralization. These ideas are expressed in seven propositions:

- The higher the centralization, the higher the production.
- The higher the formalization, the higher the efficiency.
- The higher the centralization, the higher the formalization.
- The higher the stratification, the higher the production.
- The higher the stratification, the lower the job satisfaction.
- The higher the stratification, the lower the adaptiveness.
- The higher the complexity, the lower the centralization.

(Hage, 1965)

Two Ideal Types. The interrelationship of the eight key variables in seven basic propositions was used to define two ideal types of organizations, as table 7.2 shows. Mechanistic and organic concepts are organizational extremes that represent pure types not necessarily found in real life. No school is completely mechanistic (bureaucratic) nor completely organic (professional). Most schools fall somewhere between these two extremes (Lunenburg, 2011b).

Mechanistic (bureaucratic) schools tend to have a hierarchical structure of control, authority, and communication with little shared decision making (high centralization). Each functional role requires precise definitions of rights and obligations and technical methods (high formalization). These schools emphasize status differences between hierarchical levels in the organization (high stratification); and an emphasis on quantity, not quality, of output at least cost is prevalent (high production, high efficiency). There is little emphasis on professional expertise in both subject-matter knowledge and instructional methodology (low complexity). As well, there is little responsiveness to changing needs of students, society, and subject matter (low adaptiveness); and human resources are of little importance (low job satisfaction).

Organic (professional) schools are characterized by high complexity, adaptiveness, and job satisfaction. That is, school principals respect the professional knowledge of teachers, respond readily to the changing needs of the school and society, and consider the intrinsic satisfaction of teachers to be an important school outcome.

Table 7.2 Characteristics of Mechanistic and Organic Structures

Mechanistic Organization (Bureaucratic)	*Organic Organization (Professional)*
Low complexity	High complexity
High centralization	Low centralization
High formalization	Low formalization
High stratification	Low stratification
Low adaptiveness	High adaptiveness
High production	Low production
High efficiency	Low efficiency
Low job satisfaction	High job satisfaction

Furthermore, centralization is low because principals encourage teacher participation in decision making and delegate considerable authority and responsibility to teachers in the operation of the school. A network structure of control, authority, and communication prevails. School principals adjust and continually redefine tasks and avoid always "going by the book." The organization deemphasizes status differences among the occupants of the many positions in the hierarchy and adopts a collegial, egalitarian orientation. Low efficiency and productivity also characterize the ideal professional school. School principals in the professional-type school are not as concerned with the quantity of output as they are with the quality of outcomes. Professional-type schools are probably more expensive to operate than bureaucratic-type schools because professional-school principals tend to deemphasize quantity of output at least cost. Such schools tend to be less efficient but more effective.

Each ideal type of school has advantages and disadvantages. Moreover, there are limits on how much a school leader can emphasize one variable over another. For example, if there is no codification of jobs (formalization), then a condition of normlessness prevails, which will likely result in low job satisfaction among faculty members. If schools do not respond to the knowledge explosion, technological innovations, and the changing needs of students and society, schools are apt to fail in the face of an ever-changing environment. Conversely, too high a change rate is likely to result in increased costs involved in implementing new programs and techniques. Limits exist on each of the eight variables, beyond which a school dare not move. Hage expresses it this way: "Production imposes limits on complexity, centralization, formalization, stratification, adaptiveness, efficiency, and job satisfaction" (Hage, 1965, p. 307). In other words, extremes in any variable result in the loss of production, even in a school that has the means to maximize this end.

All the relationships specified in the seven propositions are curvilinear. For instance, if centralization becomes too high, production drops; if stratification becomes too low, job satisfaction falls. Therefore, exceeding the limits on any variable results in a reversal of the hypothesized relationships specified in the seven propositions. According to Hage, "These represent important qualifications to the axiomatic theory" (1965, p. 307).

Five Structural Configurations

Henry Mintzberg (2009) contends that an organization's strategy determines its environment, technology, and tasks. These variables, coupled with growth rates and power distribution, affect organizational structure. Henry Mintzberg suggests that organizations can be differentiated along three basic dimensions: (a) the key part of the organization, that is, the part of the organization that plays the major role in determining its success or failure; (b) the prime coordinating mechanism, that is, the major method the organization uses to coordinate its activities; and (c) the type of decentralization used, that is, the extent to which the organization involves subordinates in the decision-making process. The key parts of an organization are shown in figure 7.4 and include the following:

- *The strategic apex* is top leadership and its support staff. In school districts, this is the superintendent of schools and the administrative cabinet.
- *The operative core* are the workers who actually carry out the organization's tasks. Teachers constitute the operative core in school districts.

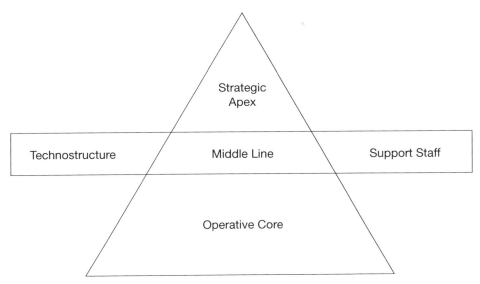

Figure 7.4

- *The middle line* is middle- and lower-level leadership. Principals are the middle-level leaders in school districts.
- *The technostructure* are analysts such as engineers, accountants, planners, researchers, and personnel managers. In school districts, divisions such as instruction, business, personnel, research and development, and the like constitute the technostructure.
- *The support staff* are the people who provide indirect services. In school districts, similar services include maintenance, clerical, food service, legal counsel, and consulting to provide support.

(Mintzberg, 2009)

The second basic dimension of an organization is its prime coordinating mechanism. This includes the following:

- *Direct supervision* means that one individual is responsible for the work of others. This concept refers to the unity of command and scalar principles discussed earlier.
- *Standardization of work process* exists when the content of work is specified or programmed. In school districts, this refers to job descriptions that govern the work performance of educators.
- *Standardization of skills* exists when the kind of training necessary to do the work is specified. In school systems, this refers to state certificates required for the various occupants of a school district's hierarchy.
- *Standardization of output* exists when the results of the work are specified. Because the "raw material" that is processed by the operative core (teachers) consists of people (students), not things, standardization of output is more difficult to measure in schools than in other nonservice organizations. Nevertheless, a movement toward the standardization of output in schools in

recent years has occurred. Examples include competency testing of teachers, state-mandated testing of students, state-mandated curricula, prescriptive
learning objectives, and other efforts toward legislated learning.
- *Mutual adjustment* exists when work is coordinated through informal communication. Mutual adjustment or coordination is the major thrust of Likert's
"linking-pin" concept discussed earlier (Mintzberg, 2009).

The third basic dimension of an organization is the type of decentralization it
employs. The three types of decentralization are the following:

- *Vertical decentralization* is the distribution of power down the chain of command, or shared authority between superordinates and subordinates in any
organization.
- *Horizontal decentralization* is the extent to which nonleaders (including staff)
make decisions, or shared authority between line and staff.
- *Selective decentralization* is the extent to which decision-making power is
delegated to different units within the organization. In school districts, these
units might include instruction, business, personnel, and research and development divisions.

(Mintzberg, 2009)

Using the three basic dimensions—key part of the organization, prime coordinating mechanism, and type of decentralization—Mintzberg suggests that the strategy
an organization adopts and the extent to which it practices that strategy result in
five structural configurations: simple structure, machine bureaucracy, professional
bureaucracy, divisionalized form, and adhocracy. Table 7.3 summarizes the three
basic dimensions associated with each of the five structural configurations. Each
organizational form is discussed in turn (Mintzberg, 1992).

Simple Structure. The **simple structure** has as its key part the strategic apex, uses
direct supervision, and employs vertical and horizontal centralization. Examples of
simple structures are relatively small corporations, new government departments,
medium-sized retail stores, and small elementary school districts. The organization
consists of the top leader and a few workers in the operative core. There is no technostructure, and the support staff is small; workers perform overlapping tasks. For

Table 7.3 Five Structural Configurations

Structural Configuration	Prime Coordinating Mechanism	Key Part of Organization	Type of Decentralization
Simple structure	Direct supervision	Strategic apex	Vertical and horizontal centralization
Machine bureaucracy	Standardization of work processes	Technostructure	Limited horizontal decentralization
Professional bureaucracy	Standardization of skills	Operating core	Vertical and horizontal decentralization
Divisionalized form	Standardization of outputs	Middle line	Limited vertical decentralization
Adhocracy	Mutual adjustment	Support staff	Selective decentralization

example, teachers and principals in small elementary school districts must assume many of the duties that the technostructure and support staff perform in larger districts. Frequently, however, small elementary school districts are members of cooperatives that provide many services (i.e., counselors, social workers) to a number of small school districts in one region of the county or state.

In small school districts, the superintendent may function as both superintendent of the district and principal of a single school. Superintendents in such school districts must be entrepreneurs. Because the organization is small, coordination is informal and maintained through direct supervision. Moreover, this organization can adapt to environmental changes rapidly. Goals stress innovation and long-term survival, although innovation may be difficult for very small rural school districts because of the lack of resources.

Machine Bureaucracy. **Machine bureaucracy** has the technostructure as its key part, uses standardization of work processes as its prime coordinating mechanism, and employs limited horizontal decentralization. Machine bureaucracy has many of the characteristics of Weber's ideal bureaucracy and resembles Hage's mechanistic organization. It has a high degree of formalization and work specialization. Decisions are centralized. The span of management is narrow, and the organization is tall—that is, many levels exist in the chain of command from top management to the bottom of the organization. Little horizontal or lateral coordination is needed. Furthermore, machine bureaucracy has a large technostructure and support staff.

Examples of machine bureaucracy are automobile manufacturers, steel companies, and large government organizations. The environment for a machine bureaucracy is typically stable, and the goal is to achieve internal efficiency. Public schools possess many characteristics of machine bureaucracy, but most schools are not machine bureaucracies in the pure sense. However, large urban school districts (New York, Los Angeles, and Chicago) are closer to machine bureaucracies than other medium-sized or small school districts.

Professional Bureaucracy. The **professional bureaucracy** has the operating core as its key part, uses standardization of skills as its prime coordinating mechanism, and employs vertical and horizontal decentralization. The organization is relatively formalized but decentralized to provide autonomy to professionals. Highly trained professionals provide nonroutine services to clients. Top leadership is small; there are few middle leaders; and the technostructure is generally small. However, the support staff is typically large to provide clerical and maintenance support for the professional operating core. The goals of professional bureaucracies are to innovate and provide high-quality services. Existing in complex but stable environments, they are generally moderate to large in size. Coordination problems are common. Examples of this form of organization include universities, hospitals, and large law firms.

Some public school districts have many characteristics of the professional bureaucracy, particularly its aspects of professionalism, teacher autonomy, and structural looseness. For example, schools are formal organizations, which provide complex services through highly trained professionals in an atmosphere of structural looseness (Bidwell, 1965; Weick, 1976). These characteristics tend to broaden the limits of individual discretion and performance. Like attorneys, physicians, and university professors, teachers perform in classroom settings in relative isolation from colleagues and superiors, while remaining in close contact with their students. Furthermore, teachers are highly trained professionals who provide information to their students in accordance with their own style, and they are usually flexible in the delivery of content even within the constraints of the state- and district-mandated curriculum. Moreover, like some staff administrators, teachers tend to identify more with their professions than with the organization.

Divisionalized Form. The **divisionalized form** has the middle line as its key part, uses standardization of output as its prime coordinating mechanism, and employs limited vertical decentralization. Decision making is decentralized at the divisional level. There is little coordination among the separate divisions. Corporate-level personnel provide some coordination. Thus, each division itself is relatively centralized and tends to resemble a machine bureaucracy. The technostructure is located at corporate headquarters to provide services to all divisions; support staff is located within each division. Large corporations are likely to adopt the divisionalized form.

Most school districts typically do not fit the divisionalized form. The exceptions are those very large school districts that have diversified service divisions distinctly separated into individual units or schools. For example, a school district may resemble the divisionalized form when it has separate schools for the physically handicapped, emotionally disturbed, and learning disabled; a skills center for the potential dropout; a special school for art and music students; and so on. The identifying feature of these school districts is that they have separate schools within a single school district, which have separate administrative staffs, budgets, and so on. Elementary and secondary school districts that have consolidated but retained separate administrative structures with one school board are also examples of the divisionalized form. As might be expected, the primary reason for a school district to adopt this form of structure is service diversity while retaining separate administrative structures.

Adhocracy. The **adhocracy** has the support staff as its key part, uses mutual adjustment as a means of coordination, and maintains selective patterns of decentralization. The structure tends to be low in formalization and decentralization. The technostructure is small because technical specialists are involved in the organization's operative core. The support staff is large to support the complex structure. Adhocracies engage in nonroutine tasks and use sophisticated technology. The primary goal is innovation and rapid adaptation to changing environments. Adhocracies typically are medium sized, must be adaptable, and use resources efficiently. Examples of adhocracies include aerospace and electronics industries, research and development firms, and very innovative school districts. No school districts are pure adhocracies, but medium-sized school districts in very wealthy communities may have some of the characteristics of an adhocracy. The adhocracy is somewhat similar to Hage's organic organization.

Strategy and Structure. The approach began by the work of Alfred Chandler (1962, 2003) and extended by Mintzberg (2009) has laid the groundwork for an understanding of the relationship between an organization's strategy and its structure. The link between strategy and structure is still in its infancy stage. Further research in this area, particularly in service organizations, like schools, will enhance school leaders' understanding of a school's organizational structure and design (Lunenburg, 2011c, 2017). In the meantime, school leaders must recognize that organization strategy and structure are related.

System 4 Design

As the human relations movement emerged, new approaches to organization design were developed (Lunenburg, 2010g). One of the more popular approaches was

Rensis Likert's System 4 design. Likert (1961, 1967, 1979, 1987) argued that the bureaucratic approach to leadership fails to consider the human side of organizations. His work focused less on the rational and mechanistic aspects of organizational structure and more on its social and psychological components.

After studying many organizations, including schools, Likert found that there was a significant relationship between organizational structure and effectiveness. Organizations that hewed to the bureaucratic model tended to be less effective, whereas effective organizations emphasized incorporating individuals and groups into the system as an integral part of leading. Likert developed eight dimensions or processes for use in comparing organizations: leadership processes, motivational processes, communication processes, interaction processes, decision processes, goal-setting processes, control processes, and performance goals.

Using these eight dimensions, Likert observed four design approaches that incorporate these dimensions. At one extreme, Likert identified a form of organization he called System 1. In many ways, a System 1 design is similar to the ideal bureaucracy. In sharp contrast, he described a humanistic, interactive, group-oriented design, which he called System 4 (Likert, 1987). Intermediate designs, Systems 2 and 3, are variants of the two extremes, which have received little attention. Table 7.4 summarizes the characteristics of a System 4 organizational structure and contrasts them with a System 1 approach.

Likert viewed the **System 4 design** as the ideal state toward which principals should try to move their schools. Trust and confidence in the principal are extremely high among System 4 members. A variety of economic, ego, and social factors are used as incentives in motivating participants. Communication flows freely in all directions—upward, downward, and horizontally. Decision making occurs throughout the school and involves all members equally. Cooperative teamwork is encouraged in setting goals, and members are expected to engage in self- and group control. Principals actively seek high performance goals and are committed to professional development.

The System 4 design, according to Likert, rests on the notion of **supportive relationships**. The underlying theory is that if a school is to be highly effective, the leadership and other processes of the school must ensure that, in all interactions between the principal and faculty, each faculty member will perceive the relationship as enhancing their own sense of personal worth and importance in the organization. Furthermore, Likert considered the members of the organization as being brought together through what he called **linking pins**. Every leadership position is linked to two groups of positions: a higher-level group of which the leader is a member and a lower-level group of which the leader is the head. For example, the principal is the leader of school personnel but also a subordinate to a leader at the central office in another group at the next level in the organization. Thus, the principal serves as an important communication link between two levels of organization—school and school district.

Likert's System 4 structure is probably more a prescription for an ideal school or school district than a description of existing organizations. According to Likert, a school's effectiveness increases as it moves from a System 1 to a System 4 design. System 4, then, serves as an ideal organization model toward which principals and other school leaders may aspire. On the other hand, the System 1 design, like the bureaucratic model, was based on the assumption that there is only one best way to structure organizations.

Table 7.4 System 1 and System 4 Designs

System 1 Organization	System 4 Organization
1. *Leadership process* includes no perceived confidence and trust. Subordinates do not feel free to discuss job problems with their superiors, who in turn do not solicit their ideas and opinions.	1. *Leadership process* includes perceived confidence and trust between superiors and subordinates in all matters. Subordinates feel free to discuss job problems with their superiors, who in turn solicit their ideas and opinions.
2. *Motivational process* taps only physical, security, and economic motives through the use of fear and sanctions. Unfavorable attitudes toward the organization prevail among employees.	2. *Motivational process* taps a full range of motives through participatory methods. Attitudes are favorable toward the organization and its goals.
3. *Communication process* is such that information flows downward and tends to be distorted, inaccurate, and viewed with suspicion by subordinates.	3. *Communication process* is such that information flows freely throughout the organization upward, downward, and laterally. The information is accurate and undistorted.
4. *Interaction process* is closed and restricted; subordinates have little effect on departmental goals, methods, and activities.	4. *Interaction process* is open and extensive; both superiors and subordinates are able to affect departmental goals, methods, and activities.
5. *Decision process* occurs only at the top of the organization; it is relatively centralized.	5. *Decision process* occurs at all levels through group processes; it is relatively decentralized.
6. *Goal-setting process* is located at the top of the organization; discourages group participation.	6. *Goal-setting process* encourages group participation in setting high, realistic objectives.
7. *Control process* is centralized and emphasizes fixing of blame for mistakes.	7. *Control process* is dispersed throughout the organization and emphasizes self-control and problem solving.
8. *Performance goals* are low and actively sought by managers who make no commitment to developing the human resources of the organization.	8. *Performance goals* are high and actively sought by superiors, who recognize the necessity for making a full commitment to developing, through training, the human resources of the organization.

Four-Frame Model

Lee Bolman and Terrence Deal (2017) provide a **four-frame model** (see table 7.5) with its view of organizations as factories (*structural frame*), families (*human resource frame*), jungles (*political frame*), and temples (*symbolic frame*). Their distillation of ideas about how organizations work has drawn much from the social sciences—particularly from sociology, psychology, political science, and anthropology. They argue that their *four frames* or major perspectives can help leaders make sense of organizations. Bolman and Deal further assert that the ability to *reframe*—to reconceptualize the same situation using multiple perspectives—is a central capacity for leaders of the twenty-first century.

Structural Frame. Drawing from sociology and management science, the **structural frame** emphasizes goals, specialized roles, and formal relationships. Structures—commonly depicted by organization charts—are designed to fit an organization's

Table 7.5 Four-Frame Model

Frame	Structural	Human Resource	Political	Symbolic
Metaphor for organization	Factory or machine	Family	Jungle	Carnival, temple, theater
Central concepts	Rules, roles, goals, policies, technology, environment	Needs, skills, relationships	Power, conflict, competition, organizational politics	Culture, meaning, metaphor, ritual, ceremony, stories, heroes
Image of leadership	Social architecture	Empowerment	Advocacy	Inspiration
Basic leadership challenge	Attune structure to task, technology, environment	Align organizational and human needs	Develop agenda and power base	Create faith, beauty, meaning

environment and technology. Organizations allocate responsibilities to participants ("division of labor") and create rules, policies, procedures, and hierarchies to coordinate diverse activities. Problems arise when the structure does not fit the situation. At that point, some form of reframing is needed to remedy the mismatch.

Human Resource Frame.   The **human resource frame**, based particularly on ideas from psychology, sees an organization as much like an extended family, inhabited by individuals who have needs, feelings, prejudices, skills, and limitations. They have a great capacity to learn and sometimes an even greater capacity to defend old attitudes and beliefs. From a human resource perspective, the key challenge is to tailor organizations to people—to find a way for individuals to get the job done while feeling good about what they are doing.

Political Frame.   The **political frame** is rooted particularly in the work of political scientists. It sees organizations as arenas, contests, or jungles. Different interests compete for power and scarce resources. Conflict is rampant because of enduring differences in needs, perspectives, and lifestyles among individuals and groups. Bargaining, negotiation, coercion, and compromise are part of everyday life. Coalitions form around specific interests and change as issues come and go. Problems arise when power is concentrated in the wrong places or is so broadly dispersed that nothing gets done. Solutions arise from political skill and acumen in reframing the organization.

Symbolic Frame.   The **symbolic frame**, drawing on social and cultural anthropology, treats organizations as tribes, theaters, or carnivals. It abandons the assumptions of rationality more prominent in the other frames. It sees organizations as cultures that are propelled more by rituals, ceremonies, stories, heroes, and myths than they are by rules, policies, and managerial authority. Organization is also theater: Actors play their roles in the organizational drama while audiences form impressions from what they see onstage. Problems arise when actors play their parts badly, when symbols lose their meaning, when ceremonies and rituals lose their potency. Leaders reframe the expressive or spiritual side of organizations through the use of symbol, myth, and magic

Synergistic Leadership Theory

Modernist theories in leadership were traditionally dominated by masculine incorporation and lacked feminine presence in development and language. The **synergistic leadership theory** (SLT) developed by Irby et al. (2002) seeks to explicate the need for a postmodernist leadership theory by providing an alternative to, and not a replacement for, traditional theories. SLT includes issues concerning diversity and the inclusion of the female voice in the theory. In a tetrahedron model, the theory uses four factors—(1) attitudes, beliefs, and values; (2) leadership behavior; (3) external forces; and (4) organizational structure—to demonstrate not only aspects of leadership, but its effects on various institutions and positions (see figure 7.5)

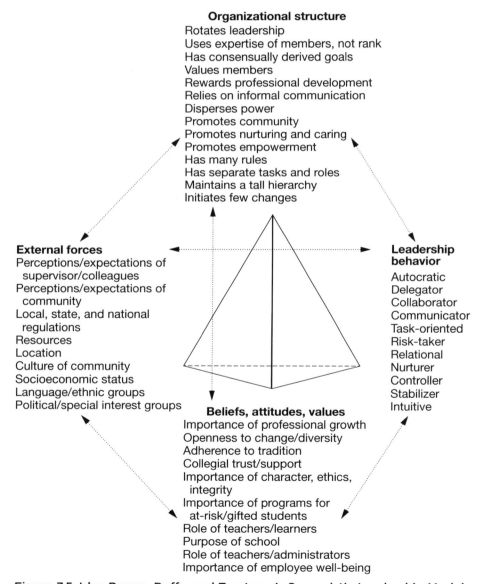

Organizational structure
Rotates leadership
Uses expertise of members, not rank
Has consensually derived goals
Values members
Rewards professional development
Relies on informal communication
Disperses power
Promotes community
Promotes nurturing and caring
Promotes empowerment
Has many rules
Has separate tasks and roles
Maintains a tall hierarchy
Initiates few changes

External forces
Perceptions/expectations of
  supervisor/colleagues
Perceptions/expectations of
  community
Local, state, and national
  regulations
Resources
Location
Culture of community
Socioeconomic status
Language/ethnic groups
Political/special interest groups

Leadership behavior
Autocratic
Delegator
Collaborator
Communicator
Task-oriented
Risk-taker
Relational
Nurturer
Controller
Stabilizer
Intuitive

Beliefs, attitudes, values
Importance of professional growth
Openness to change/diversity
Adherence to tradition
Collegial trust/support
Importance of character, ethics,
  integrity
Importance of programs for
  at-risk/gifted students
Role of teachers/learners
Purpose of school
Role of teachers/administrators
Importance of employee well-being

Figure 7.5 Irby, Brown, Duffy, and Trautman's Synergistic Leadership Model

Factor 1: Attitudes, Beliefs, and Values. As shown in figure 7.5, attitudes, beliefs, and values are depicted as dichotomous, because an individual or group would either adhere or not adhere to specific attitudes, beliefs, or values at a certain time. Some dichotomous examples follow:

  a. believes in the importance of professional growth for all individuals including self / does not believe that professional development is important;
  b. has an openness to change / does not have an openness to change;
  c. values diversity / does not value diversity; and
  d. believes that integrity is important for all involved in schooling / does not value integrity.

Factor 2: Leadership Behavior. The second factor of the theory, leadership behavior, derives directly from the literature on male and female leadership behaviors and is depicted as a range of behaviors from autocratic to nurturer. The range of behaviors include those ascribed to female principals, such as interdependence, cooperation, receptivity, merging acceptance, and being aware of patterns, wholes, and context, as well as those ascribed to male principals, including self-assertion, separation, independence, control, and competition

Factor 3: External Forces. External forces, as depicted in the model, are those influencers outside the control of the school or the principal that interact with the school and the principal and that inherently embody a set of values, attitudes, and beliefs. Significant external influencers or forces relate to local, national, and international community and conditions, governmental regulations, laws, demographics, cultural climate, technological advances, economic situations, political climate, family conditions, and geography. These examples of external forces as well as others, including those listed in the model, interact in significant, nontrivial ways with the other factors in SLT

Factor 4: Organizational Structure. Organizational structure refers to characteristics of the school and how they operate. The SLT model (see figure 7.5) depicts organizational structures as ranging from open, feminist organizations to tightly bureaucratic ones. Bureaucratic organizations include division of labor, rules, hierarchy of authority, impersonality, and competence; whereas feminist organizations are characterized by practices such as participative decision making, systems of rotating leadership, promotion of community and cooperation, and power sharing.

In sum, SLT provides a framework for describing interactions and dynamic tensions of: attitudes, beliefs, and values; leadership behaviors; external forces; and organizational structure. As a result, a principal can analyze and describe particular interactions that may account for tension, conflict, or harmony at specific points in time or over time. If it is discovered that tension exists between even two of the factors, then the effectiveness of the principal or the school itself can be negatively impacted. SLT is not only beneficial in determining "fit" while a principal is employed in a school district but also can be of assistance in job selection. Moreover, SLT can serve to build an understanding of the environment to aid in decisions made by the principal. And SLT fosters a reflective practice approach, because it encourages the leader to engage in self-assessment.

Numerous validation studies of the SLT theory have been conducted to date (Irby, Brown, & Yang, 2009). These empirical tests of the theory have included national and international samples and non-majority populations.

SUMMARY

1. The internal structure of schools differs along a number of dimensions. Among the most important of these are job specialization, departmentalization, chain of command, decentralization, span of control, and line and staff positions.

2. Job specialization, which involves grouping various jobs into units, can either contribute significantly to school effectiveness or create a problem. On the one hand, specialization provides the necessary mechanism for development of job skills and expertise. On the other hand, highly specialized jobs may increase employee boredom, dissatisfaction, absenteeism, and turnover.

3. Departmentalization involves the grouping of jobs according to some logical arrangement. Most schools employ functional departmentalization.

4. Chain of command, the process of establishing a pattern of authority between a leader and a staff member, consists of three basic components: assigning responsibility, granting authority, and creating accountability.

5. At the overall organizational level, the establishment of patterns of authority is called decentralization. Factors influencing the degree of decentralization include cost, risk associated with the decision, leader's preference for involvement, confidence in staff, and organizational culture.

6. Span of control refers to the number of staff members who report directly to a leader. Critical factors in determining the appropriate span of control include similarity of functions, geographic proximity, complexity of function, degree of interdependence, level of motivation of staff, and competence of leaders.

7. Line and staff positions, as opposed to line positions exclusively, can enhance organizational effectiveness. Line positions are those that form a part of the main line of authority that flows throughout the school district. Staff positions are positions outside the main line of authority that are primarily advisory or supportive in nature. Examples in schools include the legal counsel and assistant to the superintendent.

8. The open systems view of schools provides an excellent framework for analyzing the process of education as consisting of the interaction of inputs, a transformation process, outputs, the environment, and feedback loops.

9. Every principal's goal is to ensure high performance of students and faculty in achieving the school's mission. High performance requires the effective use of organizational resources through the management functions of planning, organizing, leading, and monitoring.

10. Just looking at the principal's four leadership functions provides an incomplete picture of the principal's job. Researchers who observed principals on the job identified three characteristics of a principal's

role: principals perform a heavy workload at an unrelenting pace; principals' activities are varied, fragmented, and brief; and principals prefer oral communication.

11. In order to perform these functions and roles, principals need three skills—conceptual, human, and technical. Conceptual skills are more important at the top of the school district's hierarchy; human skills are important at all levels; and technical skills are more important for first-line supervisors, such as department heads and team leaders.

12. Studies of effective principals reveal that the major reason for principal failure is the inability to deal with people. Effective principals have excellent people skills and focus on student learning.

13. There are many dysfunctions of the bureaucratic model, including those dealing with division of labor and specialization, uniform rules and procedures, hierarchy of authority, impersonality in interpersonal relations, and lifelong career and loyalty to the organization. New viewpoints are leading to a decline in the use of bureaucratic structure in schools.

14. Likert's System 4 design grew out of the human relations movement and is the antithesis of the ideal bureaucracy (which Likert calls System 1). An important component of System 4 is the linking-pin concept, relating levels of organization.

15. Other contemporary perspectives on organizational structures in schools, ones that are at the frontier, take several forms. They include Hage's mechanistic-organic structures, Mintzberg's five structural configurations, Bolman and Deal's four-frame model, and Irby et al.s' synergistic leadership theory (SLT).

KEY TERMS

organizational structure
job specialization
job rotation
job enlargement
job enrichment
departmentalization
functional departmentalization
chain of command
authority
unity of command
span of control
decentralization
centralization
line positions
staff positions
open systems theory
inputs
transformation process

outputs
feedback
system
behavioral theories
cognitive theories
constructivist theories
learning organization
systems thinking
personal mastery
shared vision
team learning
mental models
planning
organizing
leading
monitoring
conceptual skills
human skills

technical skills
effective
successfulness
bureaucracy
division of labor and specialization
rules and regulations
hierarchy of authority
career orientation
impersonality and interpersonal
    relations
mechanistic
organic
complexity
centralization
formalization
stratification
adaptiveness

production
efficiency
job satisfaction
simple structure
machine bureaucracy
professional bureaucracy
divisionalized form
adhocracy
System 4 design
supportive relationships
linking pins
four-frame model
structural frame
human resource frame
political frame
symbolic frame
synergistic leadership theory

FIELD-BASED ACTIVITIES

1. Analyze the internal structure of your school in terms of the following six concepts: job specialization, departmentalization, chain of command, decentralization, span of control, and line and staff positions. Describe the evidence of the functioning of each of the six components operating in your school. What can you conclude from your analysis? Be specific.

2. Describe the existing administrative structure in your school using a continuum from bureaucratic, hierarchical management to System 4, contingency organization structures. Take field notes for one week and observe the existence of one or the other administrative structure. What can you conclude from your observations concerning outcomes, such as teacher growth and development, job satisfaction and morale, student success, absenteeism, dropout rate, and so forth?

3. To what extent is your school an open system? Take field notes for one week. Analyze your observations in terms of the interactions of inputs, transformation process, outputs, the environment, and feedback loops. Describe how each component of the open systems model is functioning in your school. Be specific.

SUGGESTED READINGS

Bolman, L. G., & Deal, T. E. (2017). *Reframing organizations: artistry, choice, and leadership* (6th ed.). San Francisco, CA: Jossey-Bass. Rooted in decades of social science research across multiple disciplines, Lee Bolman and Terrence Deal's four-frame model provides time-tested guidance for more effective organizational leadership.

Bryk, A. S. (2020). *Improvement in action: Advancing quality in America's schools*. Cambridge, MA: Harvard Education Press. Anthony Bryk and his colleagues at the Carnegie Foundation for the Advancement of Teaching articulated a set of principles, tools, and processes that educators might use to tackle longstanding inequities in educational outcomes.

Fullan, M. (2015). *The new meaning of educational change*. New York, NY: Teachers College Press. Good leadership is not innate. Leadership today requires the ability to mobilize constituents to do important but difficult work under conditions of constant change, overload, and fragmentation. Fullan offers new and seasoned leaders insight into the dynamics of change and presents a unique and imaginative approach for navigating the intricacies of the change process.

Kouzes, J. M., & Posner, B. Z. (2017). *The leadership challenge: How to make extraordinary things happen in organizations*. New York, NY: Wiley. This best-selling leadership book explores the evolving essence of quality leadership in organizations around the world. This unprecedented resource includes solid research and examples of real leaders in the field.

Northouse, P. G. (2017). *Leadership: Theory and practice* (7th ed.). Thousand Oaks, CA: Sage. Northouse provides an in-depth description and application of many different approaches to leadership. His emphasis is on how theory can inform the practice of leadership. In this book, Northouse describes each theory and then explains how the theory can be used in real situations.

Reeves, D. (2021). *Deep change leadership: A model for renewing and strengthening schools and districts*. Indianapolis, IN: Solution Tree Press. Douglas Reeves highlights engagement, inquiry, and focused action as part of an effective leadership model.

8
Decision Making

■ ■ ■

FOCUSING QUESTIONS

1. Why is decision making such an important activity for principals?
2. How do principals make decisions?
3. What prevents schools from making optimal decisions?
4. What individual influences on decision making can enhance decision making effectiveness?
5. What are the benefits and pitfalls of group decision making?
6. How can knowledge of group dynamics help principals improve decision making in schools?
7. When should a principal involve others in the decision-making process?

In this chapter, we respond to these questions concerning decision making in schools. We begin by defining decision making. Then we describe the major steps in the decision-making process. Next, we discuss the assumptions of rationality and identify factors that limit rational decision making. This is followed by a discussion of the bounded-rationality model. Next, we discuss three individual influences on decision making: decision styles, intuition, and creativity. We then explore the advantages and disadvantages of group decision making followed by a discussion of group dynamics. We conclude the chapter by examining three decision-making models: the decision tree, the pattern-choice continuum, and the synergistic decision-making model.

WHAT IS DECISION MAKING?

Decisions are made at all levels of school organization. The superintendent makes decisions concerning a school district's goals and strategies. Then principals make tactical decisions concerning those goals and strategies to accomplish them in relation to their own buildings. Department heads and team leaders then make curricular and operational decisions to carry out the day-to-day activities of a department or unit. And, finally, classroom teachers make decisions in their classrooms.

Consider the following decisions that need to be made at different organizational levels:

- How much inventory should be carried in the school district warehouse?
- Where should the newly proposed elementary school be located?

- Should the school district renovate the old high school or build a new one?
- How many classes of freshman English should our department offer next semester?
- What textbook series should the mathematics department adopt?
- Should all of our principals attend the conference on the use of technology?
- What minimum rules should I adopt in my classroom?

Questions such as these require an answer. Someone is going to have to do some decision making in order to provide answers.

Decision making is a process of making a choice from a number of alternatives to achieve a desired result (Adair, 2019; van Aken & Berends, 2018; Bowers, Shoho, & Barnett, 2016; Chitpin & Evers, 2015; Genus, 2017; Hruska, 2016; McCabe, 2017; Newton & Burgess, 2017; Preuss, 2017; Rettig, 2017; Shapiro & Stefkovich, 2016; Short, 2018). This definition has three key elements. First, decision making involves making a choice from a number of options—the school district can carry more or less inventory of school supplies, and the math department can choose the Macmillan or McGraw Hill math series. Second, decision making is a process that involves more than simply a final choice from among alternatives—if the school district decides to renovate the existing high school rather than build a new one, we want to know how this decision was reached. Finally, the "desired result" mentioned in the definition involves a purpose or target resulting from the mental activity that the decision maker engages in to reach a final decision—to locate the new elementary school on the east side of town.

Decision making is a way of life for principals (McCabe, 2017). Although everyone in a school makes some decisions, principals are paid to make decisions. Their main responsibility lies in making decisions rather than performing routine operations. The quality of the decisions made is a predominant factor in how the superintendent views a principal's performance. Furthermore, decision making affects the performance of a school or school district and the welfare of its stakeholders: students, teachers, parents, and the community.

Decisions made in schools should result in changes that cause meaningful differences in student academic achievement (Bowers, Shoho, & Barnett, 2015; Newton & Burgess, 2016). Student learning in the complex, multicultural environment of contemporary schools depends on more than a comfortable faculty lounge, ample supplies for teachers, and site-based management that avoids discussion of the real issues associated with teaching and learning.

Now that we have discussed the importance of decision making, we will now consider the matter of how principals go about making decisions. Scientists have considered several different approaches to how individuals make decisions. We will discuss two of the most important models of decision making: the rational model and the bounded rationality model (March, 2010).

THE RATIONAL DECISION-MAKING MODEL

It is useful to conceptualize the decision-making process as a series of steps that a principal might take to solve a problem (van Aken & Berends, 2018). After a problem is identified, alternative solutions to the problem are generated. These are carefully evaluated, and the best alternative is chosen for implementation. The implemented

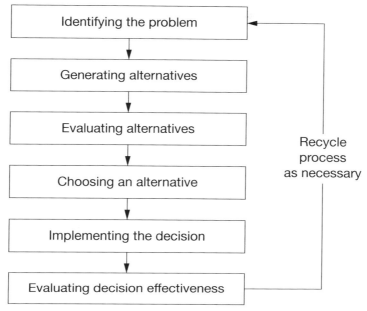

Figure 8.1 The Decision-Making Process

alternative is then evaluated over time to assure its immediate and continued effectiveness. If difficulties arise at any stage in the process, recycling may be required (see figure 8.1).

Thus, we see that decision making is a logical sequence of activities; that is, before alternatives are generated, the problem must be identified, and so on. Furthermore, decision making is an iterative activity. As shown in figure 8.1, decision making is a recurring event, and principals can learn from past decisions. In the following sections, we elaborate on each of these steps and explain their interrelationships (Banasiewicz, 2019; Bowers, Shoho, & Barnett, 2015; Chitpin & Evers, 2015; Datnow & Park, 2014; Newton & Burgess, 2017; Preuss, 2018; Shapiro & Stefkovich, 2016; Short, 2018; Sinofsky & Iansiti, 2016).

Step 1: Identifying the Problem

Schools exist to achieve certain goals, such as educating students. Within the school, each department or subunit has goals, such as increasing test scores, reducing dropouts, and/or developing new approaches to teaching. Establishing these goals becomes the basis for identifying problem areas, deciding on courses of action, and evaluating the decision outcomes. A decision is said to be effective if it helps a principal to achieve a specific objective or set of goals for the school (McCabe, 2017). Failure to achieve a desired goal becomes a problem, and the principal is ultimately responsible for solving it.

Effective decision makers are keenly aware of the importance of properly **identifying the problem** and understanding the problem situation. Kepner and Tregoe (2004) developed a method of problem analysis suggesting that the first step in decision making, identifying the problem, is the most important step. According to these authors, providing a good definition of the problem affects the quality of the decision. Their method suggests that it is often easier to define what the problem is not, rather than what it is. Also, the problem—and its solution—is prioritized with other problems, to clarify its relative importance. The final step is searching for cause-effect relationships. In summary, Kepner and Tregoe's method of problem analysis includes (a) identifying the problem, (b) defining what the problem is and is not, (c) prioritizing the problem, and (d) testing for cause-effect relationships.

The process of identifying problems requires surveillance of the internal and external environment for issues that merit attention. Principals scan the world around them to determine whether the school is progressing satisfactorily toward its goals. For example, principals survey students, teachers, parents, and community members using instruments to measure satisfaction, organizational climate, and the like. Other information may come from formal information systems, such as periodic accounting reports, management information system (MIS) reports, and organizational plans designed to discover problems before they become too serious. Or the information may be gathered informally by talking over the situation and by personal observation. A principal, for example, might discuss a productivity problem with teachers, the superintendent, or other principals to obtain ideas and information. The principal must be plugged into an information system, whether formal or informal, that gathers these data as a means of identifying problems.

In addition to identifying problems, the principal must define the situation, which is partly a matter of determining how a specific problem arose. This is an important stage, because the situation definition plays a major role in subsequent steps. Suppose, for example, that a school has had decreasing test scores for the last two years. One principal might define this situation as the result of a changing student population in the school attendance area and then begin to search for new approaches to teaching these students, who come from lower socioeconomic backgrounds. Another principal might define the situation as a case of an inappropriate match between what is taught and what is measured—that is, placing the blame on the achievement test being used. The problem of declining test scores is the same in both cases, but the two different definitions of the situation call for two different solutions.

Step 2: Generating Alternatives
Once the problem has been identified, the second step in the decision-making process is **generating alternatives** to the problem. In developing these alternative solutions, principals first must specify the goals that they hope to achieve through their decision. Are they trying to reduce the dropout rate, improve the quality of instruction, increase test scores, or something else? Once principals have determined their goals, they can search for alternative means of reaching them. Information must be collected regarding each of the alternatives and their likely consequences. More specifically, the principal must seek to learn as much as possible concerning (a) the likelihood that each alternative will result in the achievement of various outcomes and (b) the extent to which those outcomes will contribute to the achievement of the goals and objectives being sought.

Ideally, the principal should seek to generate as many alternatives as possible and should attempt to ensure that the alternatives are relatively diverse—that is, not highly similar to one another. The extent of the search for alternatives is limited by the importance of the decision, the cost and value of additional information needed to evaluate alternatives, and the number of people affected by the decision (Lemaine, Levernier, & Richardson, 2018; Wootton & Horne, 2021).

The more important the decision, the more attention is directed to developing alternatives. For example, if the decision involves where to build a new, multimillion dollar high school, a great deal of time and effort will be devoted to identifying the best location. On the other hand, if the problem is to select a color to paint the classrooms in the new high school, less time and effort will be devoted to the activity.

The length and thoroughness of the search for alternatives depend on the cost of evaluating additional alternatives. For example, a 2 percent improvement in the solution of a $10 million problem may produce a profit margin of $200,000. However, if the cost of evaluating an additional alternative is $250,000, the evaluation costs $50,000 more than the possible savings. As a rule of thumb, the increase in the improvement of a solution should always be more than the cost of performing the additional evaluation of an alternative. Moreover, the greater the number of people affected by a problem, the more likely the organization will conduct a lengthy and thorough search for alternatives (Narayanan, 2004). However, when dealing with complex school problems affecting numerous people, it is often necessary to compromise on some points. Human benefits cannot be measured in dollars and cents (Chitpin & Evers, 2015).

Step 3: Evaluating Alternatives

The third step in the decision-making process is **evaluating alternatives** generated in step 2. In evaluating an alternative, principals must ask the following three questions: (1) "Is the alternative feasible?"; (2) "Is it a satisfactory alternative?"; and (3) "What impact will it have on people?" (Adair, 2019).

The first question—whether the alternative is feasible—simply means, "Can it be done?" For example, if one alternative requires a general layoff of school faculty but the school district has a collective bargaining agreement that prohibits such layoffs, that alternative is not feasible. Similarly, if a school district has limited capital, alternatives that require large capital outlays are not feasible unless funds can be borrowed to meet the capital outlay requirements.

The second question concerns the extent to which the alternative is satisfactory; that is, the extent to which it addresses the problem. For instance, suppose the principal wants to expand the curriculum by 25 percent. One alternative is to implement a trimester schedule. On closer examination, however, the principal may discover that the plan would expand the curriculum by only 15 percent and that such a modest expansion may also negatively affect the quality of the program. The principal may decide to implement the trimester plan anyway; he will then search for other ways to achieve the remaining 10 percent expansion in the curriculum and find ways to maintain the quality of the program. Or he may decide to drop the alternative from consideration entirely.

The third question addresses the impact of an alternative on school personnel. The alternative that is chosen must be acceptable to those who must live with the consequences of the decision. Failure to meet this condition is the single most likely reason for failure of the decision-making process to solve problems (Rettig, 2017). For this reason, questions of acceptability of a proposed alternative should be of great concern to the principal. On the one hand, even a mediocre solution to the problem may prove effective if it is implemented with enthusiasm and commitment.

On the other hand, a technically correct alternative may fail to succeed if implementation is halfhearted.

Step 4: Choosing an Alternative

Once the principal has evaluated all of the alternatives, he attempts to **choose an alternative**. The evaluation phase will have eliminated some of the alternatives, but in most cases two or more will remain.

How does a principal decide which alternative is the best? One approach is to select the alternative that is feasible, satisfactory, and acceptable to the work group. Because most situations do not lend themselves to sophisticated mathematical analysis, the principal uses this available information in combination with judgment and intuition to make the decision (Davis & Davis, 2003; Klein, 2005). The basis of judgment should be how close the outcomes or consequences of the alternatives come to achieving the desired goals of the school. For example, if the original goal was to decrease the dropout rate as much as possible, regardless of the costs, the principal might choose an alternative that will decrease the dropout rate significantly but that carries a high cost, rather than an alternative that would reduce dropouts only moderately at a minimal cost. However, if the original goal was to reduce the dropout rate by a moderate amount and if that goal is more desirable now, the second alternative might be a better choice.

Finally, the principal may be able to choose several alternatives simultaneously. Suppose, for example, they are hiring an English teacher and has two strong candidates for the position. One frequently used strategy is to offer the position to one candidate and keep the other candidate on hold. Should the first offer be rejected, the principal still has an acceptable alternative to fill position.

Step 5: Implementing the Decision

After choosing an alternative, the principal faces the challenge of *implementing the decision*. A sound decision can fail if implemented poorly. It is useful, therefore, to consider some suggestions for successful implementation (Chitpin & Evers, 2015).

1. *Principals need to make sure that the alternative is clearly understood.* This is accomplished by communicating the decision to all involved staff. Effective communication is necessary for effectively implementing decisions.
2. *Principals need to encourage acceptance of the alternative as a necessary course of action.* Committees can help a principal achieve commitment. If the people who must carry out a decision participate in the process, they are more likely to be enthusiastic about the outcome. Thus the degree to which persons have or have not been involved in prior steps may substantially affect the success of the total decision-making process.
3. *Principals need to provide enough resources to make the alternative succeed.* Principals set up budgets and schedules for the actions they have decided to undertake. Specifically, the decision may require acquiring office space, hiring staff, procuring funds, and the like.
4. *Principals need to establish workable time lines.* The principal now faces a "how much" and "how soon" decision. As part of the process of implementation, he must ask himself whether to move forward step-by-step or whether to take the entire action at once.

5. *Principals need to assign responsibilities clearly.* In other words, what should be done by whom? Because the solution of most administrative problems requires the combined effort of many school members, each person should understand what role they are to play during each phase of the implementation process.

Step 6: Evaluating Decision Effectiveness

The final step in the decision-making process is **evaluating decision effectiveness**. When an implemented decision does not produce the desired results, there are probably a number of causes: incorrect definition of the problem, poor evaluation of alternatives, improper implementation, or any combination of these factors. Among these possible causes, the most common and serious error is an inadequate definition of the problem. When the problem is incorrectly defined, the alternative that is selected and implemented will not produce the desired result.

Evaluation is important because decision making is a continuous process. Decision making does not end when a principal votes yes or no. Evaluation provides principals with information that can precipitate a new decision cycle. The decision alternative may fail, thus generating a new analysis of the problem, evaluation of alternatives, and selection of a new alternative. Some experts (Banasiewicz, 2019; Bowers, Shoho, & Barnett, 2015; Datnow & Park, 2014; Preuss, 2017; Short, 2018) suggest that many large problems are solved by attempting several alternatives in sequence, each providing a modest improvement. Evaluation is the part of the decision-making process that assesses whether a new decision needs to be made.

THE BOUNDED RATIONALITY MODEL

The decision-making process, discussed above, characterizes the decision maker as completely rational; that is, they would have perfect information: know all alternatives, determine every consequence, and establish a complete preference scale. Moreover, the steps in the decision-making process would consistently lead toward selecting the alternative that maximizes the solution to each decision problem.

The following points summarize the assumptions of such a rational decision-making process (Daft, 2016; Nielsen, 2011).

- *Problem clarity.* In rational decision making, the *problem identity* is clear and unambiguous. The principal is assumed to have complete information regarding the problem and the decision situation.
- *Goal orientation.* In rational decision making, there is no conflict concerning the *goal orientation.* Whether the decision involves increasing test scores, reducing dropouts, or developing new approaches to teaching, the principal has a single, well-defined goal that they are trying to reach.
- *Known options.* It is assumed that the principal is creative, can identify all relevant criteria, and can list all the viable alternatives; they *know* all *options.* Further, the principal is aware of all the possible consequences for each alternative.
- *Clear preferences.* Rationality assumes that the criteria and alternatives can be ranked in order of importance, that there are *clear preferences.*

- *Constant preferences.* In addition to a clear goal and preferences, it is assumed that the specific decision criteria are *constant* and the scales or weights assigned to them are stable over time.
- *No time or cost constraints.* The rational principal can obtain full information about criteria and alternatives because it is assumed there are no *time* or *cost constraints.*
- *Maximization.* The rational principal always chooses the alternative that will yield the maximum payoff to the school. It should be noted here that the principal is assumed to be *maximizing* the school's interests, not the interests of the principal.

Rational decision making assumes that decision makers have a tremendous mental capacity both for remembering and storing huge quantities of information and for processing that information in order to choose the optimum solution to each decision problem. Although administrative decision making can follow rational assumptions, most decisions that principals face do not meet all the criteria of complete rationality.

Frequently, school principals are not aware that problems exist. Even when they are, they do not systematically search for all possible alternative solutions. They are limited by time constraints, cost, and the ability to process information. So they generate a partial list of alternative solutions to the problem based on their experience, intuition, advice from others, and perhaps even some creative thought. Rationality is, therefore, limited. Herbert Simon (1982, 1997, 2009) coined the term **bounded rationality** to describe the perspective of the decision maker who would like to make the best decisions but normally settles for less than the optimal. Simon won the Nobel Prize in 1978 for his bounded rationality theory.

In contrast to complete rationality in decision making, bounded rationality implies the following (Nielsen, 2011):

1. Decisions will always be based on an incomplete and, to some degree, inadequate comprehension of the true nature of the problem being faced.
2. Decision makers will never succeed in generating all possible alternative solutions for consideration.
3. Alternatives are always evaluated incompletely because it is impossible to accurately predict all consequences associated with each alternative.
4. The ultimate decision regarding which alternative to choose must be based on some criterion other than maximization or optimization because it is impossible to ever determine which alternative is optimal.
5. Conflicting goals of different stakeholders (e.g., students, teachers and support staff, administrators, parents, community members, and school board) can restrict decisions, forcing a compromising solution.

Satisficing

One version of bounded rationality is the principle of **satisficing**. This approach to decision making involves choosing the first alternative that satisfies minimal standards of acceptability without exploring all possibilities. This is the usual approach taken by decision makers. Simon (2009) expresses it this way: "Most human decision making, whether individual or organizational, is concerned with the discovery and selection of satisfactory alternatives; only in exceptional cases is it concerned with the discovery and selection of optimal alternatives" (p. 57).

A practical example of satisficing is finding a radio station to listen to in your car. You cannot optimize because it is impossible to listen to all the stations simultaneously. Thus, you stop searching for a station when you find one playing a song you like. Another example of satisficing frequently occurs in schools when hiring personnel. Schools begin by listing criteria that an acceptable candidate should meet (such as having an appropriate degree from an accredited college or university, job-related experience, and good references). Then the school will select a candidate who meets the criteria. If schools were to make the optimal hiring decision rather than a satisfactory one, they would have to select the best candidate—the person with the best educational background, prior experience, and references. It would be virtually impossible to do this. The best person may not have applied for the position, so you select a satisfactory candidate from among those who applied for the position.

> Satisficing doesn't necessarily mean that leaders [school principals], have to be satisfied with what alternative pops up first in their minds or in their computers and let it go at that. The level of satisficing can be raised—by personal determination, setting higher individual or organizational standards, and by the use of an increasing range of sophisticated management science and computer-based decision making and problem-solving techniques. . . . You obtain more information about what's feasible and what you can aim at. (Simon, 1997, p. 227)

Contextual and Procedural Rationality

Simon (1997) later proposed two other forms of bounded rationality: contextual rationality and procedural rationality. **Contextual rationality** suggests that a decision maker is embedded in a network of environmental influences that constrain purely rational decision making. Although the principal wants to make optimal decisions, these are mediated by such realities of organizational life as internal and external politics, conflict resolution requirements, distribution of power and authority, and limits of human rationality. Furthermore, schools have vague and ambiguous goals. This, coupled with the lack of clearly defined success criterion, leads to policies and procedures designed to maintain stability and control. Moreover, the objectives of the school as a social institution are to achieve major changes in the student. These changes are not restricted to cognitive behavior (learning), but include a wide range of social, emotional, physical, and, in some cases, moral behavior. Thus, school principals must pursue multiple and often conflicting goals within a network of environmental constraints that restrict the maximization of goal achievement (Lunenburg, 2002).

We noted that bounded rationality, satisficing, and contextual rationality limit perfectly rational decision making. This results in the inability of decision makers to "maximize" outcomes. What, then, can principals do to improve their decisions in view of the constraints on complete rationality implied by the rational decision-making model? Simon (1997) proposes the principle of **procedural rationality**. Instead of focusing on generating and evaluating all possible alternative solutions to a problem and their consequences, decision makers focus on the procedures used in making decisions. Thus, techniques are perfected and used to make the best possible decisions, including operations research, systems analysis, strategic planning, program planning budgeting systems (PPBS), management information systems (MIS), and so on, each prescribed to improve the reliability of decisions. Rational decision-making procedures are not designed to focus on generating and evaluating all available information to solve problems, but they are aimed at adequate acquisition and processing of relevant information.

Heuristics

When principals make satisficing decisions, they may use a set of **heuristics** to guide their decisions. A heuristic is a rule of thumb that can help the decision maker find a solution in a complex and uncertain situation (Lunenburg, 2006; Moustakas, 1990). We use heuristics in our everyday lives. For example, a heuristic rule for dealing with other people is the Golden Rule: "Do unto others as you would have them do unto you." Football coaches use the rule, "When in doubt, punt." In playing chess, we follow the rule of "controlling the center of the board." In blackjack, we follow the rule of "hit on 16, stick on 17." In addition, a heuristic for investors is that if a stock drops 10 percent or more below its purchased price, they should sell.

In management science, many well-known heuristics are used to make a wide variety of decisions: "The customer is always right"; "Treat employees as mature adults"; and Peters and Waterman (2006) advocate: "When in doubt, stick to the business you know best." Management scientists also employ heuristics to aid decisions regarding where to locate warehouses and stockbrokers use heuristics when deciding how to prepare an investment portfolio (Gaethy & Shanteau, 1984). These are all rules that help simplify complex decision-making situations. Applying heuristics often helps principals make satisficing decisions possible. However, the heuristic approach, as with judgment and intuition, has a tendency to oversimplify complex problems or introduce bias—systematic errors in decision making (Tversky & Kahneman, 1974).

Three common rules of thumb are availability heuristics, representativeness heuristics, and anchoring heuristics. The **availability heuristic** reflects the tendency to base decisions on information that is easy to remember (Bazerman & Moore, 2013; Tvershy & Kahnman, 1974). Information is more easily remembered when it involves an event that happened recently and when it elicits strong emotions (e.g., a campus shooting). This heuristic is likely to cause people to overestimate the occurrence of unlikely events such as a school shooting. The availability heuristic also is partially responsible for the primacy/recency effect discussed subsequently.

The **representativeness heuristic** is used when people estimate the probability of an event happening. It reflects the tendency to assess the likelihood of an event occurring based on one's impression about similar occurrences (Hammond, Keeney, & Raiffa, 2006). For example, a person may believe that they can learn a new software package in a very short period of time, because a different type of software was easy to master. However, it may take the person a much longer time to learn the new software, because the new software package involves learning a new programming language.

The **anchoring and adjustment heuristic** is the tendency to make decisions based on adjustments from some initial quantity (or anchor) (Tversky & Kahneman, 1974). Decisions about salary increases typically are made by choosing a percentage increase from a person's current salary. In addition, budget decisions typically are made by deciding whether the current budget should be increased or decreased. In such situations, if the initial amounts are reasonable, then the anchoring and adjustment heuristic might be a good rule of thumb to use. However, if the original amount from which a decision is made is not reasonable, the anchoring and adjustment heuristic will result in biased decision making. That is, if current salary levels are low in comparison to other like positions, even a large percentage increase may leave the employee underpaid. Likewise, if the department's budget is high to begin with, a small percentage decrease will still leave the department's budget too high.

Primacy/Recency Effect
One bias that may decrease the effectiveness of a principal's information search behavior is the **primacy/recency effect**. In the decision-making process, the decision environment is searched for the following purposes: finding problems, identifying decision alternatives, determining consequences, and developing evaluation criteria. Although decision makers may have different strategies for these different purposes, the decision maker is often inordinately influenced by information discovered early in the search process (the primacy effect) or late in the search process (the recency effect). Thus, everything else being equal, the importance attached to information may be affected by its order in the search sequence (Brown & Moberg, 2015).

For example, ideally, performance evaluations should be based on systematic observations of a staff member's performance over an entire rating period (say, six months or a year). Oftentimes, evaluators focus on a staff member's most recent behavior—that is, in an annual evaluation, a principal may give undue consideration to performance during the past two or three months and forget to include important past behaviors. Using only the most recent staff member's behaviors to make evaluations can result in what is called the *recency of events* error (Kreitner & Kinicki, 2016). This practice, if known to employees, leads to a situation whereby employees become visible, motivated, productive, and cooperative just before the formal evaluation occurs. Hence, their performance during the entire evaluation cycle is uneven and inconsistent.

Bolstering the Alternative
Another way in which the search for information is biased and inhibits decision optimization is the phenomenon of **bolstering the alternative** (Bubnicki, 2003). Even before accumulating the information on which to base a decision, the principal may prefer one alternative to all the others; the decision maker, therefore, searches for information that rationalizes the choice. Only information that supports the decision maker's preferred alternative is considered legitimate and acceptable.

A related bias in the search for information is the school administrator's professional training and identification with a particular department that may also bolster the alternative. For example, an assistant superintendent for curriculum may tend to view most problems with a curriculum bias, regardless of their nature, and an assistant superintendent of finance (business manager or chief financial officer) may perceive the same problems in terms of finance. Although such biases are bound to exist, it is important to understand that they can strongly influence a decision maker's ability to make accurate decisions.

Incrementalizing

Another approach to decision making, sometimes referred to as "muddling through," involves making small changes (increments) in the existing situation. Charles Lindblom (1993), its author, distinguishes between completely rational decision making based on the rational model and **incrementalizing,** which is based on successive limited comparisons. The rational approach to decision making involves determining objectives, considering all possible alternative solutions, exploring all conceivable consequences of the alternative solutions, and, finally, choosing the optimal alternative solution that will maximize the achievement of the agreed-on objectives. Incrementalizing, on the other hand, does not require agreement on objectives, an exhaustive search of all possible alternatives and their consequences, or selection of the optimal alternative. Instead, Lindblom argues that no more than small or incremental steps—no more than muddling through—is ordinarily possible. In other words, incrementalizing is a process of successive limited comparisons of alternative courses of action with one another until decision makers arrive at an alternative on which they agree.

The Garbage Can Model

Earlier we noted that while the school principal wants to make optimal decisions, the realities of organizational life—including politics, time constraints, finances, and the inability to process information—limit purely rational decision making. Applying the rational decision-making model is particularly troublesome for schools. The technologies of teaching are varied and not well understood. Moreover, schools have multiple and conflicting goals that are vague and ambiguous. In addition, schools lack clearly defined success criteria. Thus, problems and solutions cannot be translated easily into a logical sequence of steps (rational decision-making model) (Lunenburg, 2002).

In accordance with this view, David Cohen and his associates (Cohen, March, & Olsen, 1972) conceptualize this decision-making process as a **garbage can model.** As members of a school or school district generate problems and alternative solutions to problems, they deposit them into the garbage can. The mixture is seen as a collection of solutions that must be matched to problems. Participants also are deposited into the garbage can. Mixing problems, solutions, and decision participants results in interaction patterns leading to decisions that often do not follow the rational decision-making model sequence.

The garbage can model is an illustration that not all school decisions are made in a step-by-step, systematic way. The high-speed pace of today's schools requires principals to make critical decisions quickly, with incomplete information, and they must involve other stakeholders in the process.

A number of studies in educational administration have specified and tested comparative models of decision making, using the rational and bounded rationality models as one of several. For example, one study found that high schools were more likely to resemble the bounded rationality model than were elementary schools, which more closely resembled the rational model (Firestone & Herriott, 1981). According to the researchers, because high schools were typically departmentalized and had more diverse goals, they could be characterized as more loosely coupled than elementary schools.

Other studies address some of the assumptions of bounded rationality. Research on administrative behavior in schools is consistent in identifying the demands on the principal as fragmented, rapid fire, and difficult to prioritize. For example, one large-scale mixed methods study noted that the fragmented and unpredictable workday of principals was not conducive to rational decision making (Lunenburg & Columba, 1992).

INDIVIDUAL INFLUENCES ON DECISION MAKING

Do all principals go about making decisions in the same way, or are there individual differences in the way principals approach decision making? In general, research has shown that such differences do exist. Three particular, individual influences that can enhance decision making effectiveness will be discussed next: decision-making styles, intuition, and creativity.

Decision-Making Styles

There is a tendency for people to approach the decisions confronting them in different ways. The manner in which people approach decisions confronting them is known as a person's **decision-making style**. A team of researchers developed a model of decision-making styles that is based on the idea that styles vary along two different dimensions: value orientation and tolerance for ambiguity (Rowe & Mason, 1987). **Value orientation** is the extent to which a person focuses on either task and technical concerns or people and social concerns when making decisions. Some people are concerned primarily with achieving success at any cost. Others are more concerned about the effects of their decisions on others. The second dimension pertains to an individual's **tolerance for ambiguity**. This difference indicates the extent to which an individual has a high need for structure or control. Some people desire a lot of structure (a low tolerance for ambiguity) and find ambiguous situations stressful and psychologically uncomfortable. In contrast, others do not have a high need for structure and can thrive in uncertain situations (a high tolerance for ambiguity). The dimensions of value orientation and tolerance for ambiguity, combined, form four styles of decision making: directive, analytical, conceptual, and behavioral (Greenberg, 2014).

Directive. Individuals with a **directive style** have a low tolerance for ambiguity and are oriented toward task and technical concerns when making decisions. They are efficient and systematic in their approach to solving problems. Individuals with the directive style are action oriented and decisive and like to focus on facts. In their pursuit of speed and results, however, these people tend to be autocratic, exercise power and control, and tend to focus on the short run.

Analytical. People with an **analytical style** have a much higher tolerance for ambiguity and are characterized by the tendency to overanalyze a situation. Individuals with the analytical style carefully analyze their decisions using as much data as possible. Such people tend to enjoy solving problems. They want the best possible solutions and are willing to use innovative methods to achieve them. They can often be autocratic.

Conceptual. Individuals with a **conceptual style** have a high tolerance for ambiguity and tend to focus on the people or social aspects of a work situation. Such people tend to consider many broad alternatives when dealing with problems and to solve them creatively. They have a strong future orientation and enjoy initiating new ideas. Individuals with a conceptual style adopt a long-term perspective and rely on intuition and discussions with others to acquire information. They also are willing to take risks and are good at finding creative solutions to problems. However, a conceptual style can foster an idealistic and indecisive approach to decision making.

Behavioral. The **behavioral style** is the most people oriented of the four decision-making styles. People with a behavioral style are concerned deeply about the school/school district in which they work and about the personal development of their coworkers. Individuals with the behavioral style work well with others and enjoy social interactions in which opinions are openly exchanged. People with a behavioral style are supportive, receptive to suggestions, show warmth, and prefer verbal to written information. They tend to rely on meetings for making decisions. However, individuals with the behavioral style have a tendency to avoid conflict and to be too concerned about others. This can lead behavioral style decision makers to adopt a weak approach to decision making and have a difficult time saying no to others and finding it difficult to make hard decisions.

Few people have only one dominant decision-making style. Instead, most principals use many different styles. Those principals who can shift between styles—that is, those who are most flexible in their approaches to decision making—probably have highly complex, individualistic styles of their own. Conflicts often occur between people with different styles. For example, a principal with a highly directive style may have a difficult time accepting the slow, deliberate actions of a staff member with an analytical style. Furthermore, studies reveal that decision-making styles vary by age, occupation, job level, and countries (Rowe & Mason, 1987).

A principal can use knowledge of decision-making styles in three ways. First, knowledge of styles can help you understand yourself. Awareness of your style assists you in identifying your strengths and weaknesses as a decision maker and facilitates the potential for self-improvement. Second, you can increase your ability to influence others by being aware of decision-making styles. For example, if you are interacting with an analytical person, you should provide as much data to support your position as possible. The identical approach is likely to frustrate a directive type. Finally, knowledge of decision-making styles provides you with an awareness of how individuals can take the same information and arrive at different decisions by using a variety of decision-making approaches.

Intuition

Researchers continue to carry on a vigorous debate regarding how executives should make decisions (Mintzberg, 2013). On the one hand, there are those who believe that decision making should be accomplished by using a systematic, step-by-step rational approach. On the other hand, there are those who believe that the very nature of administrative work makes this difficult to achieve in actual practice.

If you think about how decisions are made, undoubtedly you will realize that some, but not all, decisions are made following a systematic, step-by-step rational approach. Decision making is assumed to be rational. By this we mean that principals make decisions under certainty: the problem is clear and unambiguous; a single, well-defined goal is to be achieved; all alternatives and consequences are known; preferences are clear; preferences are constant and stable; no time or cost constraints exist; and the final choice will maximize economic payoff.

The rational explanation of decision making is appealing because there is some logic and system associated with each of these steps. However, rational decision making assumes that decision makers have a tremendous mental capacity both for remembering and storing huge quantities of information and for processing that information, in order to choose the optimum solution to each decision problem. Although decision making can follow rational assumptions, most decisions that principals face do not meet all of the criteria of complete rationality: problem clarity, goal orientation, known options, clear preferences, constant preferences, no time or cost constraints, and maximization.

Frequently, principals are not aware that problems exist. Even when they are, they do not systematically search for all possible alternative solutions. They are limited by time constraints, cost, and the ability to process information. So, they generate a partial list of alternative solutions to the problem based on their experience, advice from others, and intuition. Rationality is, therefore, limited.

The Use of Intuition.   Throughout most of the twentieth century, social scientists believed that leaders' use of intuition was ineffective. That is no longer the case (Anderson, 2000; Burke & Miller, 1999; Khatri & Ng, 2000; Myers, 2002). There is growing evidence that administrators use their intuition to make decisions (Heidegger, 2011; Lunenburg, 2010i; Ruelas, 2011). Henry Mintzberg (1998), in his study of the nature of managerial work, found that, in many instances, executives do not appear to use a rational systematic, step-by-step approach to decision making. Rather, Mintzberg argued that executives make decisions based on "hunches."

Gary Klein (2005), a renowned cognitive psychologist, writes in his book *The Power of Intuition* that skilled decision makers rely on deeply held patterns of learned experience in making quick and efficient decisions. According to Klein, these deeply held patterns of learned experience (templates) represent tacit knowledge that has been implicitly acquired over time. When a template fits or does not fit the current situation, emotions are produced that motivate us to act.

For experts who possess high levels of tacit knowledge, many decisions they face are routine or programmed decisions. For them these decisions become somewhat automatic, because their knowledge allows them to recognize and identify a situation and the course of action that needs to be taken. That is not to say that the decisions are necessarily easy. It simply means that their experience and knowledge allows them to see the problems more easily and recognize and implement solutions more quickly. In short, effective intuition results when people have a certain amount of tacit knowledge.

Malcolm Gladwell (2005) writes in his bestselling book, *Blink: The Power of Thinking without Thinking*, that decisions made very quickly can be every bit as good as decisions made cautiously. With those words, Gladwell summarizes his book's premise on decision making. He begins the book with the story of a rare, ancient, Greek statue, which was under consideration for purchase by the J. Paul Getty Museum in California. All precautionary steps were taken to assure the statue's authenticity. Documents seemed to be in order. Numerous, detailed analyses had been performed by a geologist to confirm the statue's authenticity. After purchasing the statue and publicizing its purchase, the museum began to show it to various art experts. Numerous experts told the museum that there was something wrong with the piece. None of the experts could articulate exactly why they knew it was a fraud. They just knew. These experts were able to come to a conclusion simply based on a quick first impression. The experts turned out to be right. The statue was uncovered to be a fake.

Gladwell goes on to describe numerous experts (doctors, salespeople, marriage experts) who had the ability to take a quick look at a situation (what Gladwell referred to as "thin-slicing") and make judgments and decisions on the basis of what appeared to be limited information. He goes on to say that most of us do not always possess that kind of expertise for the decisions we must make. Halfway through the book, Gladwell switches gears and describes numerous examples in which quick decisions turn out to be ineffective. He goes on to say that most of our first impressions are wrong. This shift in thinking gives the book a duality and a realistic assessment of decision making. On the one hand, some people have the ability to make quick, accurate decisions. On the other hand, many others do not have that ability.

However, the latter is clearly true for some people. Gladwell makes the point that those who have the ability to make immediate and accurate decisions based on "gut feelings" or "hunches" are *experts* on the topic in question. These experts have spent years developing knowledge and skill through practice, repetition, and experience. To the nonexpert, it seems as though these decisions are "snap judgments" or merely "hunches," but in reality, the processing time in gathering pertinent information for these experts has become so automatized that it only seems that way. These experts bring a great deal of explicit and tacit knowledge to the specific situation. Gladwell notes further that frequently these experts cannot verbalize exactly why they make the decisions they do.

Chester Barnard (1938), one of the early influential management researchers, agrees that intuition's main attributes are speed and the inability of the decision maker to determine how the decision was made. Other researchers argue that intuition occurs at an unconscious level, and this is why the decision maker cannot verbalize how the decision was made (Rowan, 1986).

Lee Iacocca (1999), who saved Chrysler from bankruptcy in the 1980s and brought it to profitability, writes in his autobiography, *Iacocca: An Autobiography*: "To a certain extent, I've always operated by gut feelings." Ray Kroc has been described as a legend of intuition on the basis of how he purchased the McDonald's chain from the McDonald brothers: "I'm not a gambler and I didn't have that kind of money, but my funny bone instinct kept urging me on."

Bob Lutz, former president of Chrysler, initiated the Dodge Viper. "It was this subconscious feeling. And it just felt right." Eleanor Friede gambled on a "little nothing book," called *Jonathan Livingston Seagull*, despite rejections of the book by twenty-four publishing houses, including her own: "I felt there were truths in this simple story that would make it an international classic" (Miller & Ireland, 2005). Other researchers have found that intuition was used extensively as a mechanism to evaluate decisions made more rationally (Ehrgott, 2011; Mendel, 2011; Zopounidis, 2011).

Definition of Intuition. **Intuition** has been described variously as follows (Klein, 2005):

- the ability to know when a problem or opportunity exists and to select the best course of action without conscious reasoning (Behling & Eckel, 1991)
- the smooth automatic performance of deeply held patterns of learned experience (Isenberg, 1984)
- a nonconscious process created from distilled experience (Gilovich, Griffin, & Kahneman, 2002)

- the ability to know or recognize quickly and readily the possibilities of a given situation (Agor, 1989).
- emotionally charged judgments that arise through quick, nonconscious, and holistic associations (Dane & Pratt, 2007)
- reliance on mental models—internal representations of the external environment that allow us to anticipate future events from current observations (Sadler-Smith & Shefy, 2004)

These definitions share several common assumptions. First, there seems to be an indication that intuition is quick. Second, intuition is an automatic unconscious analytic process. Third, there seems to be agreement that intuition is based on experience and usually engages emotions. Fourth, intuition offers potential for creativity and innovation.

When relying on intuition, the school principal arrives at a decision without using a rational, step-by-step logical process. The fact that experience contributes to intuition means that principals can learn to become more intuitive in solving many difficult problems. Furthermore, intuition does not necessarily operate in opposition to rational decision making. Rather, the two can complement each other. Principals should attempt to use both when making decisions. For example, rational decision making can be used to verify intuition.

Creativity

Creativity is the ability to produce novel and useful ideas that can be put into action (Amabile, 1988; Perry-Smith & Shalley, 2003). The social and technological changes that schools face require creative decisions. Principals of the future need to develop special competencies to deal with the turbulence of change. One of these important competencies is the ability to promote creativity in schools (Morgan, 1988).

Most people have creative potential. To unleash it, they must escape the psychological blocks that befall many of us and learn how to think about a problem in divergent ways. Three broad categories of blocks are perceptual, cultural, and emotional (Feinstein, 2009; Napier & Nilsson, 2008).

- **Perceptual blocks** include such factors as the failure to use all of the senses in observing, failure to investigate the obvious, difficulty in seeing remote relationships, and failure to distinguish between cause and effect.
- **Cultural blocks** include a desire to conform to established norms, overemphasis on competition or conflict avoidance and smoothing, the drive to be practical and narrowly economical above all else, and a belief that indulging in fancy or other forms of open-ended explorations are a waste of time.
- **Emotional blocks** include the fear of making a mistake, fear and distrust of others, grabbing the first idea that comes along, and so on.

For many schools fostering creativity and innovation is essential to their ability to offer high-quality teaching and learning. We approach creativity in decision making from three perspectives: stages in the creative process, characteristics of creative people, and conditions necessary for creativity.

Stages in the Creative Process. Understanding the stages involved in creativity can help a principal become more creative and better manage creativity in others. The four stages of the creative process are preparation, incubation, illumination, and verification (Wallas, 1926).

Stage 1: Preparation. The preparation stage starts from a base of knowledge. Extensive formal education or many years of relevant experience are needed to develop the expertise required to identify substantive issues and problems. The preparation stage is consistent with Thomas Edison's comment that "Creativity is 90 percent perspiration and 10 percent inspiration." Edison secured more than one thousand patents. The most famous was the 1879 patent for the electric light bulb (Edison, Israel P., 1999).

Stage 2: Incubation. The incubation stage is a process of reflective thought and is often done subconsciously. Distancing oneself or the team from the issue or problem allows the mind to search for possible solutions. Incubation assists **divergent thinking**—finding new ways of looking at an issue or problem, concerned with change and movement. This contrasts with convergent thinking—seeking to find the right answer to a logical problem. The incubation stage can yield fresh ideas and new ways of thinking about the nature of an issue or a problem and alternative solutions.

Stage 3: Illumination. The illumination stage refers to the experience of suddenly becoming aware of a unique idea. What happens is that the mind instantly connects an issue or problem to a solution through a recalled observation or occurrence. Illumination is also called the "aha!" experience. You may recall this happening to you; all of a sudden, something clicks.

Stage 4: Verification. The verification stage involves determining if the solution or idea is valid. This is accomplished by gathering supportive evidence, using logical persuasion, and testing the solution or idea.

Characteristics of Creative People. Several individual variables are associated with creativity. One group of factors involves the cognitive processes that creative people tend to use. One cognitive process is *divergent thinking*. Creative people have the ability to see problems in new ways, to escape the bounds of conventional thinking, and, therefore, generate several potential solutions to a problem (Mumford & Gustafson, 1988). In addition, associational abilities are related to creativity (Poze, 1983). Creative people recognize the significance of small bits of information and are able to connect them. Then they have the capacity to recognize which ideas are worth pursuing and which are not.

Creative people share some other common characteristics such as:

- *Perseverance.* Perseverance drives creative people to continue developing and testing their ideas and solutions. They stay longer attacking problems. This perseverance is based on a high need for achievement and a moderate or high degree of self-confidence (Feist, 1999).
- *Risk-taking propensity.* Creative people take moderate to high risks and stay away from extreme risks.

- *Openness to experience*. Creative people score high on openness to experience. Because creativity is important to leadership, open people are more likely to be effective principals. They also are more comfortable with ambiguity and change than those who score lower on this trait. Therefore, open people cope better with organizational change and are more adaptable to changing contexts (George & Zhou, 2001; LePine, Colquitt, & Erez, 2000).
- *Tolerance for ambiguity*. Creative people can tolerate a lack of structure, some lack of clarity, and not having complete information, data, and answers (Woodman, Sawyer, & Griffin, 1993).

Other traits of creative people, not already mentioned, are independence, internal locus of control, intellectual and artistic values, breadth of interests, high energy, independence of judgment, creative self-image, and desire for recognition (Barron & Harrington, 1981; Woodman, Sawyer, & Griffin, 1993). Exposure to a variety of cultures also can enhance creativity (Leung et al., 2008). People who spend extensive periods of time in other cultures generate more creative solutions to problems (Robbins & Judge, 2018). Taking an international assignment or an international vacation could stimulate the creative process.

Conditions Necessary to Stimulate Creativity. What individual and organizational conditions are necessary to stimulate employee creativity? The most consistent of these conditions include expertise, creative-thinking skills, and intrinsic task motivation (Amabile, 1988, 1997, 2004).

Expertise is the foundation of all creative endeavors. Creativity experts argue that discovering new ideas requires people to have sufficient knowledge and experience in their field of endeavor (Weisberg, 1999). You would expect someone with an abundance of training and experience in programming to be a very creative software engineer.

Creative-thinking skills encompass personality characteristics associated with creativity such as the ability to use analogies (discussed earlier) and the ability to see problems in new ways and escape the bounds of conventional thinking (divergent thinking). Creative people also have the ability to recognize which ideas are worth pursuing and which are not.

Intrinsic task motivation is the desire to work on something because it is interesting, satisfying, and personally challenging. Passion for the task and high intrinsic motivation contribute to a total absorption in the work, which is known as the *experience of flow*. Flow also means being "in the zone." Steve Jobs has been described as one who achieved the experience of flow based on developing a plan for worldwide distribution of a useful product, the Apple computer (Linzmeyer & Linzmeyer, 2004).

Enhancing Creativity. A unifying theme runs through all forms of creativity training and suggestions for enhancing creativity. Creative problem solving requires the ability to see problems in new ways and to escape bounds of conventional thinking and the ability to recognize which ideas are worth pursuing and which are not. In contrast, the concept of conventional thinking refers to a standard way of finding a solution to a problem.

The central task in becoming creative is to break down conventional thinking that blocks new ideas. Overcoming conventional thinking often is characterized as thinking outside the box. A "box" is a category that confines and restricts thinking. Following, we describe several techniques for stimulating employee creativity (DuBrin, 2018).

Brainstorming. Brainstorming is one of the best-known techniques for developing mental flexibility. The brainstorming approach will be discussed later, as one of the techniques for improving group decision making.

Idea quotas. An effective technique for stimulating employee creativity is to demand that organization members generate good ideas. Being creative then becomes a concrete school goal. Thomas Edison used idea quotas, with his personal quota being one minor invention every ten days and a major invention every six months (Israel, 1999). Google's company policy is that company engineers devote a quarter of their time initiating new ideas, even with an uncertain financial payoff. Every Google employee spends a fraction of the workday on research and development.

Heterogeneous groups. Forming heterogeneous groups can enhance creativity, because a diverse group brings various viewpoints to a problem. Key diversity factors include professional discipline, job experiences, and a variety of demographic factors. Diverse groups encourage diverse thinking, which is the essence of creativity (Thompson, 2003). A culturally diverse group can be effective at developing creative marketing ideas to appeal to a particular cultural group. For example, Levi-Strauss has on occasion included an adolescent in a problem-solving group to help understand what type of jeans appeal to members of that age group.

Financial incentives. Numerous studies have concluded that working for external rewards, particularly monetary rewards, does little to enhance creativity (Hennessey & Amabile, 1998). A focus on external rewards may diminish the employee's intrinsic motivation of being creative. However, in work settings, financial rewards are likely to stimulate creative thinking. Such incentives might include paying employees for useful suggestions, paying employees for developing online courses, and paying scientists royalties for patents that become commercially useful. For instance, IBM is consistently one of the leading companies with respect to being awarded patents. IBM employees who are awarded patents are paid cash bonuses.

Architecture and physical layout. Many organizations restructure space to enhance creativity, harness energy, and stimulate the flow of knowledge and ideas. Any configuration of the physical environment that increases the opportunity for physical interaction facilitates the flow of ideas, which in turn facilitates creative thinking (Leonard & Swap, 1999). Another approach to making use of physical layout to enhance creativity is the establishment of *innovation laboratories*. Members of the innovation teamwork in a remote location rather than on traditional company premises.

A classic example of the establishment of an innovation laboratory was the creation of the Apple computer. The next time you use an Apple computer, or see an ad for one of its new products—the iPhone, for example—it is important to recall the history of the original Macintosh. A team created it. The Macintosh team, led by Steve Jobs, co-founder of Apple, was composed of high-achieving members who embarked on an exciting, highly challenging goal. In a separate building removed from corporate bureaucracy flying the Jolly Roger, the team worked ninety-hour workweeks at astonishingly low pay. After three years of labor, the result was the birth of the Mac in 1983. It represented the collective expression of a cohesive, hard-working team. The Mac sold faster than any PC that preceded it and marked a turning point in the history of the PC (Linzmeyer & Linzmeyer, 2004). Product innovation continues to be a hallmark of Apple Computer, Inc. (Cruikshank, 2005).

Creativity Training. A standard approach to stimulating individual and organizational creativity is to offer creativity training to organization members. Much of the training encompasses many of the ideas already covered in this chapter, such as learning to see problems in new ways and to escape bounds of conventional thinking; and learning to recognize which ideas are worth pursuing and which are not. We provide two techniques: de Bono's lateral thinking method, for fostering the development of new ideas, and Osborn's creativity process, to help overcome blockages to creativity (Hellriegel & Slocum, 2015).

De Bono's lateral thinking. The **lateral thinking method** is a set of techniques for generating new ideas by changing a person's or a group's way of perceiving and interpreting information (de Bono, 1970). To better understand the lateral thinking method, Edward de Bono contrasted it with the **vertical thinking method**, which is a logical step-by-step process of developing ideas by proceeding continuously from one bit of information to the next (de Bono, 1970, 1985, 2008). We consider three of the techniques for fostering the development of new ideas: reversal, analogy, and cross-fertilization.

Reversal technique. The **reversal technique** involves examining a problem by turning it completely around, inside out, or upside down. For example, Prudential Insurance Company came up with the idea of "living benefit" life insurance. It pays benefits to people who are terminally ill, "You die before you die."

Analogy technique. The **analogy technique** involves developing a statement about similarities among objects, persons, and situations. Some examples of analogies are "This school operates like a beehive" or "This school operates like a Swiss watch." The technique involves translating the problem into an analogy, refining and developing the analogy, and then retranslating the problem to judge the suitability of the analogy. For a school that is ignoring increased demographic changes, an analogy might be, "We are like a flock of ostriches with our heads buried in the sand."

Cross-fertilization technique. The **cross-fertilization technique** involves asking experts from other fields to view the problem and suggest methods for solving it from their own areas of expertise. For the technique to be effective, these outsiders should be from fields entirely removed from the problem. Each year, Blackboard, the online Internet system, brings to its headquarters fifty or more speakers who might provide fresh ideas to the firm's designers.

Osborn's creativity process. Designed to overcome blockages to creativity, Osborn's (1957) **creativity process** is a three-phase decision-making process that involves fact finding, idea finding, and solution finding. It is intended to stimulate lateral thinking, novel ideas, curiosity, and cooperation that in turn lead to creative decisions.

Fact-finding phase. **Fact finding** involves defining the issue or problem and gathering and analyzing relevant data. The fact finding phase requires that a decision maker make a distinction between a symptom of an issue or problem and the actual issue or problem. For example, a principal might claim that low morale is a problem. A more thorough investigation might reveal that low morale is a symptom of a rankling issue. The issue may be a lack of feedback and rewards to teachers who are performing well.

Idea-finding phase. **Idea finding** begins by generating tentative ideas and possible leads. Then the most likely of these ideas are modified, combined, and expanded. To generate many ideas, Osborn developed seventy-five general questions to use when brainstorming a problem. **Brainstorming** is a technique for creatively generating alternative solutions to a problem (Osborn, 1957). The group or team leader must decide which of the seventy-five questions are most appropriate to the issue or problem being addressed. The following are examples of the type of questions that Osborn (1957) recommends could be used in a brainstorming session:

- How can this issue, idea, or thing be put to other uses?
- How can it be modified?
- How can it be substituted for something else, or can something else be substituted for part of it?
- How could it be reversed?
- How could it be combined with other things?

A brainstorming session should follow four basic rules:

1. *Do not evaluate or discuss alternatives.* Evaluation comes later. Avoid criticism of your own or others' ideas.
2. *Encourage "freewheeling."* Do not consider any idea outlandish. An unusual idea may point the way to a truly creative decision.
3. *Encourage and welcome quantities of ideas.* The greater the number of ideas generated, the greater the number of useful ideas will remain after evaluation.
4. *Encourage "piggybacking."* Group members should try to combine, embellish, or improve on an idea. Consequently, most of the ideas produced will belong to the group and not a single individual.

A brainstorming session should have from five to twelve or so participants in order to generate diverse ideas. This size range permits each member to maintain a sense of identification and involvement with the group. A session should typically run not less than twenty minutes or more than an hour. However, brainstorming could consist of several idea-generating sessions. For example, follow-up sessions could address individually each of the ideas previously generated. Following are guidelines for conducting a traditional brainstorming session (Dharmarajan, 2007; Wilson, 2007).

Basic Facilitator Role:

- Make a brief statement about the four basic rules.
- State the time limit for the session.
- Read the problem and/or related question to be discussed and ask, "What are your ideas?"
- When an idea is given, summarize it by using the speaker's words insofar as possible. Have the idea recorded by a recorder or on an audiotape machine. Number each idea. Follow your summary with the single word, "Next."
- Say little else. Whenever the facilitator participates as a brainstormer, group productivity falls.

- Consider asking participants to spend ten minutes on doping individual brain-storming prior to the start of the session by having them record their initial.
- Consider asking participants to spend ten minutes on doing individual brain-storming prior to the start of the session by having them record their initial ideas on cards that are provided.

Basic Handling Issues during a Brainstorming Session:

- When someone talks too long, wait until they take a breath (everyone must stop to inhale sometime), break into the monologue, summarize what was said for the recorder, point to another participant, and say, "Next."
- When someone becomes judgmental or starts to argue, stop them.
- When the discussion stops, relax and let the silence continue. Say nothing. The pause should be broken by the group and not the facilitator. This period of silence is called the mental pause because it is a change in thinking. All the obvious ideas are exhausted; the participants are now forced to rely on their creativity to produce new ideas.
- When someone states a problem rather than idea, repeat the problem, raise your hand with five fingers extended, and say, "Let's have five ideas on this problem." You may get only one or you may get ten, but you are back in the business of creative thinking.
- Strongly enforce the rule that only one person speaks at a time.
- Provide note cards for people who get ideas while someone else is speaking to minimize production blocking.

Solution-finding phase. **Solution finding** involves generating and evaluating possible courses of action and deciding how to implement the chosen course of action. The solution-finding phase begins when the leader requests the group to identify from one to five of the most important ideas generated thus far. The participants write down these ideas individually on a card and evaluate them. A one to five-point system is used to record the evaluations. A very important idea would receive five points, a moderate idea would receive three points, and an unimportant idea would get one point. The highest combined scores of the group would indicate the ideas to be investigated further.

GROUP DECISION MAKING

Up to this point, our focus on decision making has been primarily on the individual decision maker, the principal. However, groups make many of the decisions in schools (Bonito, 2019). These groups may be called committees, teams, task forces, site-based councils, and the like. But, regardless of what they are called, they make decisions. And, very often, decisions are reached through some kind of consensus process (Corey, Callanan, & Russell, 2015).

It is believed that group decision making results in a number of benefits over individual decision making. Experts advise school districts that a proven method to increase school effectiveness is to involve school employees in the decision-making process (Chitpin & Evers, 2015; Newton & Burgess, 2017). With these generalizations in mind, the benefits of group decision making include the following (Bonito, 2019; Corey, Callanan, & Russell, 2015; Galanes & Adams, 2019; Genus, 2018; Short, 2018).

Advantages of Group Decisions

Greater sum total of knowledge. When many people are involved in decision making, they apply a greater accumulation of information and experience to the decision than that possessed by any one member alone. Gaps in knowledge of one person can be filled by another.

Greater number of approaches to the problem. Most people develop familiar patterns for decision making. If each person has a unique way of searching for information, analyzing problems, and the like, participatory decision processes provide more angles of attack at each stage of the decision-making process.

Greater number of alternatives. Partly because of increased information and the use of varied decision-making patterns, groups typically can identify and evaluate more alternatives than one individual could. In listening to each other's ideas, group members may combine information to develop unique solutions that no single member could conceive.

Increased acceptance of a decision. Group decision making breeds ego involvement. That is, people tend to accept and support the decisions they make rather than those others make. The more people who accept a decision and are committed to it, the more likely the decision is to be implemented.

Better comprehension of a problem and decision. More people understand a decision when it is reached by a group. This factor is particularly important when group members are to be involved in executing the decision.

Group decision making also poses potential problems, which we will be outlining next (Bonito, 2019; Corey, Callanan, & Russell, 2015; Galanes & Adams, 2019; Genus, 2018; Short, 2018).

Disadvantages of Group Decisions

Social pressure toward conformity. This phenomenon, known as *groupthink*, has received considerable attention. Groupthink occurs when the desire for cohesiveness and consensus becomes stronger than the desire to reach the best possible decisions (Janis, 1982). Because individuals fear being labeled uncooperative by other group members, they conform to the direction the group is taking even if they disagree with the group's position.

Individual domination. Often one person will dominate the group because of difference in status or rank from other members, or through force of personality. This can cause resentment among other group members, who are prevented from participating fully. The problem is that what appears to emerge as a group decision may actually be the decision of one person.

Conflicting secondary goals. Many times, participants in group decisions have their own axes to grind or their own turf to protect. Winning an issue becomes more important than making a quality decision. Too much energy is devoted to political maneuvering and infighting, and too little to reaching a quality decision.

Undesirable compromises. Groups often make decisions that are simply compromises resulting from differing viewpoints of individual members. This is likely when a group must make a decision on a controversial issue. Controversial issues, by definition, result in opposing views. After a brief discussion, the group may conclude that a decision favoring either side is unacceptable; so they choose a compromise solution. Such an approach may result in a low-quality decision.

Ambiguous responsibility. Group members share responsibility, but who is actually accountable for the final outcome? In individual decision making, it is clear who is responsible. In a group decision, the responsibility of any single member is diffused across the group participants. Furthermore, research has shown that group decisions are riskier on average than individual decisions. This phenomenon, known as **risky shift** (Stoner, 1968), is somewhat surprising because group pressures tend to inhibit the members. One possible explanation is that people feel less responsible for the outcome of a group decision than they do when acting alone. Risky decisions may be desirable in some situations; in others, the costs of risk may be too high.

Time. Groups often require more time to reach a final decision than do individuals. It takes time to assemble a group, and the interaction that takes place once the group is installed is frequently inefficient. This can limit a principal's ability to act quickly and decisively when necessary. It is also more costly because groups use more human resources.

The arguments for and against shared decision making suggest that choosing this approach requires careful thought. Principals must evaluate whether, for a particular situation, the assets outweigh the liabilities; and whether they can simultaneously take advantage of the assets and control the liabilities. Nevertheless, if principals intend to operate as professional learning communities, they must involve staff in the decision-making process.

GROUP DYNAMICS

We now turn our attention to behavior in groups. Group behavior has been the subject of interest in social psychology for many years, and many different aspects of group behavior have been studied during this time (Foote et al., 2002). We examine two topics relevant to group functioning in schools: stages of group development and characteristics of a mature group.

After its formation, a group goes through predictable stages of development. These stages are forming, storming, norming, performing, and adjourning. If successful, the group emerges as a mature group. A mature group has five distinguishing characteristics: group roles, norms, status, optimal size, and cohesiveness.

Stages of Group Development

The performance of a group depends both on individual learning and on how well the members learn to work together as a unit. One widely cited model of group development assumes that groups pass through as many as five stages of development: (a) forming, (b) storming, (c) norming, (d) performing, and (f) adjourning (Tuckman, 1965; Tuckman & Jensen, 1977). Identifying the stage that a group is in at a specific time can be difficult; nevertheless, it is important to understand the development process. At each stage, group behaviors differ and, as a result, each stage can influence the group's end results. These stages are depicted in figure 8.2.

Forming. The first stage of group development is **forming**. It is characterized by uncertainty and confusion about the purpose, structure, and leadership of the group. Group members tend to focus on efforts to understand and define their objectives,

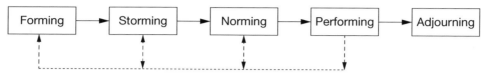

Figure 8.2 Stages of Group Development

roles, and duties within the group. Members share personal information and start to get to know and accept one another. Interaction, among group members, is courteous and cautious. Generally, this stage is complete when individuals begin to view themselves as members of a group.

Storming. The **storming** stage is characterized by conflicts over tasks, relative priorities of goals, roles of group members, and leadership of the group. Coalitions may form to influence the group's goals, means of attainment, and group leadership. Conflict needs to be managed during this stage, not suppressed. The group cannot move into the third stage if group members do not handle conflict effectively. This stage is complete when there is mutual agreement about who will lead the group.

Norming. While the storming stage is characterized by conflict, the **norming** stage is marked by cooperation and collaboration. Roles and responsibilities become clear and accepted. The group develops a sense of cohesion. Members have developed common expectations about how the group's goals should be accomplished. They have developed a feeling of team spirit. The storming stage is complete when group members agree on standards to guide behavior in the group.

Performing. The **performing** stage of group development marks the emergence of a mature, organized, and well-functioning unit. The structure is stable. Group members are ready to focus on accomplishing its key tasks. To accomplish tasks, diversity of viewpoints rather than consensus is supported and encouraged. Groups that encourage diversity in the group tend to be more able to adapt. Groups that are more adaptive tend to be more successful.

Adjourning. The final stage of group development is the **adjourning** stage. Some groups, of course, are permanent and never reach the adjourning stage. For temporary groups, however, such as ad hoc committees, project teams, task forces, and similar groups, this stage involves preparation for disbanding. For example, a group created to examine and report on a specific issue, such as the development of a new faculty evaluation system within six months, has a well-defined point of adjournment. The job is completed; it is now time to move on to other tasks.

Many group members may feel a compelling sense of loss after working so hard to get along with one another and accomplishing something. Adjournment can be eased by rituals, celebrating termination and new beginnings. Parties, award ceremonies, mock funerals, and graduation can provide recognition for participation and achievement. Leaders can take this opportunity to emphasize valuable lessons learned in group dynamics to prepare everyone for future group endeavors.

The five-stage model (forming-norming-storming-performing-adjourning) is intuitively appealing. However, research indicates that not all groups proceed through each of the stages (Mannix, Neale, & Blount-Lyon, 2004). Nor do groups always proceed sequentially from one stage to the next. In fact, some groups may engage in more than one stage at a time, as when groups are storming and performing simultaneously (Peterson & Behfar, 2003; Romanelli & Tushman, 1994). Groups occasionally regress to previous stages. Further research indicates that groups with deadlines for goal accomplishment did not go through a series of developmental stages. Instead, they alternated between periods of inertia in which very little was accomplished and periods of frenzied activity in which the group proceeded rapidly toward its goal (Gersick, 1988, 1989). Research has indicated that groups that proceed through the developmental stages successfully seem to outperform and sustain higher levels of performance when compared to groups that do not (Bushe & Coetzer, 2007).

In sum, the five-stage model should be used as a general framework but not as a perfectly accurate depiction of how groups develop. To accelerate their own development, group members may find it useful to know what characteristics help create successful groups.

Characteristics of Mature Groups

A well-functioning, effective group is a mature group. Such a group has characteristics that shape members' behavior and help explain and predict individual behavior within the group as well as the performance of the group itself. Some of these characteristics are roles, norms, status, size, and cohesiveness (Lunenburg & Lunenburg, 2015).

Group Roles. There is no universally agreed-upon framework of group roles (Aritzeta, Swailes, & Senior, 2007; Manning, Parker, & Pogson, 2006). However, whenever members of a group come together to work on a common task, role differentiation occurs; that is, patterns of behavior for each member develop that tend to become repeated as group activities ensue (Shani et al., 2014). Various roles are necessary to coordinate the group's task and maintain the group's functioning. Some roles can be classified as those that are focused on achieving the tasks of the group (task-oriented roles); other roles build and maintain favorable relationships among group members (relationship-oriented roles); and still others serve individual needs, sometimes at the expense of the group (self-oriented roles). Each group member has the potential of performing each of these roles (Bales, 1950; Klein et al., 2004). This classification forms the foundation of most other models of group member roles (Humphrey, Manor, & Morgeson, 2009; Postrel, 2009).

Task-oriented role. The task-oriented role of a group member involves facilitating and coordinating work-related behaviors and decision making. This role may include:

- *initiating* new ideas or different ways of considering group problems or goals and suggesting solutions to difficulties, including modification of group procedures;
- *seeking information* to clarify suggestions and obtain key facts;
- *giving information* that is relevant to the group's problem, issue, or task;
- *coordinating* and clarifying relationships among ideas and suggestions, pulling ideas and suggestions together, and coordinating members' activities; and
- *evaluating* the group's effectiveness, including questioning the logic, facts, or practicality of other members' suggestions.

(Hellriegel & Slocum, 2015, p. 367)

Relationship-oriented role. The relationship-oriented role of a group member involves fostering group-centered attitudes, behaviors, emotions, and social interactions. This role may include:

- *encouraging* members through praise and acceptance of their ideas as well as indicating warmth and solidarity;
- *harmonizing* and mediating intra-team conflicts and tension;
- encouraging participation of others by saying, "Let's hear from Susan" or "Why not limit the length of contributions so all can react to the problem?" or "Juan, do you agree?";
- *expressing* standards for the group to achieve or apply in evaluating the quality of group processes, raising questions about group goals, and assessing group progress in light of these goals; and/or
- *following* by going along passively or constructively and serving as a friendly member.

(Hellriegel & Slocum, 2015, p. 367)

Self-oriented role. The self-oriented role of a group member involves the person's self-centered attitudes, behaviors, and decisions that are at the expense of the group. This role may include:

- *blocking progress* by being negative, stubborn, and unreasoningly resistant—for example, the person may repeatedly try to bring back an issue that the group had considered carefully and rejected;
- *seeking recognition* by calling attention to oneself, including boasting, reporting on personal achievements, and, in various ways, avoiding being placed in a presumed inferior position;
- *dominating* by asserting authority, manipulating the group or "certain individuals" using flattery or proclaiming superiority to gain attention, and interrupting the contributions of others; and or
- *avoiding* involvement by maintaining distance from others and remaining insulated from interactions.

(Hellriegel & Slocum, 2015, pp. 367–368)

A **role** may be defined as the behavior a person is expected to display in a given context. Effective groups are composed of members who display both task-oriented and relationship-oriented roles. An adept person who manifests behaviors valued by the group likely will have high *status*—status being the rank of a member in a group. A group dominated by individuals who exhibit self-oriented behaviors probably will be ineffective, because they fail to address group goals and the need to collaborate.

Group Norms. Did you ever notice that teachers in one school practically race the students to the exit door the instant the dismissal bell rings, whereas their counterparts in another school seem to be competing to see who can work the latest? These differences are due partly to norms. **Norms** may be defined as the informal rules and shared expectations that groups develop to regulate the behavior of their members (Ehrhart & Naumann, 2004; Hackman, 1992). Some norms become written rules, such as a student attendance policy in a public school or a code of ethics for school administrators. Other norms remain informal, but somehow are known by group members. Furthermore, norms exist only for behaviors that are important to the group (Fehr & Fischbacher, 2004; Feldman, 1984).

A key norm in any group is the performance norm that conveys productivity expectations of group members. For example, a high-performing school sets productivity standards above organizational expectations for students and faculty. A culture evolves concerning performance (Bulach & Lunenburg, 2016a). Average schools set productivity standards based on, and consistent with, organizational expectations. Low productivity schools may set productivity standards below organizational expectations. Other norms are important, also. In order for a department, grade-level team, committee, or task force to function effectively, norms are required. Groups commonly have loyalty norms (e.g., work late, assist other members), appearance norms (e.g., dress codes), and resource allocation norms (e.g., how status symbols, pay, and promotions should be allocated). Groups also commonly have norms concerning how to deal with colleagues, parents, and students, as well as norms establishing guidelines for ethical behaviors expected of school administrators (Irby & Lunenburg, 2014).

Norms are frequently evident in the everyday conversations of people in the workplace. The following examples indicate the types of norms that operate with positive and negative implications for groups and organizations (Allen & Pilnick, 1973; Feldman, 1984; Lawler, 2001; Zander, 1982).

- *Ethics norms*—"We try to make ethical decisions, and we expect others to do the same" (positive); "Don't worry about padding your expense account; everyone does it here" (negative).
- *Organization and person pride norms*—"It's a tradition around here for people to defend the school when others criticize it unfairly" (positive); "In our school, they are always trying to take advantage of us" (negative).
- *High-achievement norms*—"On our team, members always try to work hard (positive); "There is no point in trying harder on our team; nobody else does" (negative).
- *Support and assistance norms*—"People on this committee are good listeners and actively seek out the ideas and opinions of others" (positive); "On this committee, it's dog-eat-dog, and save your own skin" (negative).
- *Improvement and change norms*—"In our department, people are always looking for better ways of doing things" (positive); "Around here, people hang on to the old ways even after they have outlived their usefulness" (negative).
- *Supervisory norms*—"Around here, principals and supervisors really care about people they supervise" (positive); "In our school, it's best to hide your problems and avoid your supervisor" (negative).

(Uhl-Bien, Schermerhorn, & Osborn, 2016, pp. 200–201)

Group Status. **Status** is the relative social position or rank given to an individual, group, or organization by others (Greenberg, 2014). Status functions in group settings, and group members acquire common perceptions for respecting other members on several dimensions, including ability to judge the capabilities of others, professional knowledge, experience, interpersonal skills, and any other attribute valued by the group such as personal appearance, money, or a friendly personality. An overall status that includes a combination of these dimensions is accorded to group members (Shani et al., 2014). Another way of thinking about status is that of credibility (What is my credibility in this group?). Another dimension is acceptability (How acceptable am I in this group?)

Within most organizations, status is conferred upon members through the use of status symbols—objects reflecting the position one holds in the hierarchy. Common examples of symbols include job titles (e.g., principal); perquisites (e.g., reserved parking space); the opportunity to do significant work (e.g., serving on prestigious committees); and luxurious physical space (e.g., large, private office that is lavishly furnished). The aforementioned are examples of formal status symbols. Informal status symbols also exist within groups and organizations. These include symbols accorded to persons with certain characteristics not formally recognized by organizations. Examples include employees who are older and have more seniority in the group or organization may be perceived as having higher status by coworkers. Members who have special skills (such as advanced technology skills) also may be regarded as having higher status than other members.

According Robert Feldman (as cited in Robbins & Judge, 2018, pp. 290–291), status tends to derive from one of three sources:

1. *The power a person has over others.* Because they likely control group resources, people who control the group's outcomes tend to be perceived as high status. For example, many believe that LeBron James has more say concerning player acquisitions than the coach, general manager, or team owner.
2. *A person's ability to contribute to a group's goals.* The more important the task performed by a group or a group's function is, the higher the group's status in the organization. The status of a top leadership team is likely to be very high, because it sets the school's or school district's goals and determines how the goals will be achieved.
3. *An individual's personal characteristics.* One whose personal characteristics are positively valued by the group (physical attractiveness, intelligence, content knowledge, experience, money, or a friendly personality) typically has higher status than someone with fewer valued attributes.

Group Size. The effective size of a group can range from three members to more than twenty (Thompson, 2000). Does the size of a group affect the way group members behave? The answer is: It depends on what dependent variables you examine. According to the results of one meta-analysis, if a group's primary task is fact finding, larger groups should be more effective but smaller groups are more effective at doing something productive with that input (Stewart, 2006). Larger groups have a greater number of resources to accomplish their goals. These resources include the skills, abilities, and knowledge of their members (Kozlowski & Bell, 2003). In addition, larger groups have the benefits of *division of labor*—dividing up assignments to individual group members. When individuals focus on particular tasks, they generally become skilled at performing these tasks. One of the primary reasons groups (as well as total organizations) exist is the benefit of division of labor (George & Jones, 2012).

However, when additional members are added to a group beyond what is necessary to accomplish the task, coordination and communication problems may result. Group members may become less productive because of wasted time and their feeling less accountable for the group's outcomes (Gooding & Wagner, 1985; Markham, Dansereau, & Alutto, 1982). The guidelines regarding group size that Amazon.com's co-founder and CEO, Jeff Bezos, developed for his firm's product development teams is that no team should be larger than two pizzas can feed (Yank, 2006).

Group size and **social loafing**. One of the most important findings concerning the size of a group is the risk of productivity loss due to *social loafing*. Social loafing occurs when group members exert less effort, and usually perform at a lower level, when working collectively than working alone (Comer, 1995; Karau & Williams, 1993; Liden et al., 2004; Murphy, Wayne, Liden, & Erdogan, 2003). Social loafing is most likely to occur in large groups where individual output is difficult to identify (Beyer, & Trice, 1979; Latane, 1986; Latane, Williams, & Harkins, 1979).

Social loafing was first noted by German psychologist Maximilien Ringelmann, who measured individual and group effort on a rope-pulling task (Kravitz & Martin, 1986; Moede, 1927). He hypothesized that three people pulling together should exert three times as much pull on the rope as one person, and eight people pulling together on the rope should exert eight times as much as one person. Ringelmann's findings, however, did not confirm his hypothesis. Specifically, he found that one person pulling on the rope alone exerted an average of 63 kgs of force. In groups of three, the per-person force dropped to 53 kgs. And in groups of eight, it fell to merely 31 kgs per person.

Replications of Ringelmann's research have generally supported his findings (Jassawalla, Sashittal, & Malshe, 2009; Karau & Williams, 1993; Latane et al., 1979; Sheppard, 1993). Group performance increases with group size; however, the addition of new group members results in diminishing returns on productivity. That is, more members in a group may be better, but the individual productivity of each member declines.

Social science researchers have used **social impact theory** (Kerr & Bruum, 1981; Latane & Nida, 1980) to explain the social loafing effect. According to the theory, the impact of any social force acting on a group is dispersed among its members. The larger the size of the group, the lower the impact of its force on any one member. As a result, the more individuals who contribute to a group's output, the less pressure each individual feels to perform well—that is, the responsibility for doing the task is divided among more people. As a result, each group member feels less responsible for producing maximum effort, and social loafing occurs. Another way of understanding the social loafing phenomenon is by recognizing that social loafing occurs because people are more interested in themselves than their fellow group members.

Social loafing is less common when the task is interesting, because people have a higher motivation to perform the task. Moreover, social loafing is less likely to occur when the group's goal is important, because group members feel more pressure from other members to perform well. Finally, social loafing occurs less often among members with strong collectivist values, because they value group membership and believe in working toward group goals (Earley, 1993; Erez & Somech, 1996).

How to reduce social loafing. By understanding the causes of social loafing, principals can identify ways to reduce the problem. Principals can attempt to reduce or eliminate social loafing by: (a) making each group member's individual contribution to group performance identifiable (Gammage, Carron, & Estabrooke, 2001; Jones, 1984; Nordstrom, Lorenzi, & Hall, 1990; Price, 1987; Williams, Harkins, & Latane, 1981); (b) holding each member personally accountable for results (Karakowsky & McBey, 2001; Liden et al., 2004; Mulvey & Klein, 1998; Mulvey, Bowes-Sperry, & Klein, 1998); (c) emphasizing the importance of the task (Bricker, Harkins, & Ostrom, 1986; George, 1992); (d) rewarding individuals for contributing to their group's performance (Albanese & Van Fleet, 1985); (e) controlling the size of groups (Latane, 1986; Latane et al., 1979); (f) selecting members who have high motivation and prefer to work in groups (Stark, Shaw, & Duffy, 2007); and (g) encouraging the development of norms that encourage all members to contribute optimal effort to group goals (Gammage, Carron, & Estabrooke, 2001; Gunnthorsdottir & Rapoport, 2006; Hoigaard, Safvenbom, & Tonnessen, 2006).

Group Cohesiveness. Groups differ in their cohesiveness. The **cohesiveness** of a group is the degree to which members are attracted to the group and motivated to remain part of it. Group members feel cohesiveness when they believe their group will help them achieve not only their need for affiliation or status but also to accomplish a common goal. Accordingly, sociologists have identified two types of group cohesiveness: socio-emotional cohesiveness and instrumental cohesiveness (Tziner, 1982).

Socio-emotional cohesiveness is a feeling of togetherness that evolves when individuals derive emotional satisfaction from group participation. **Instrumental cohesiveness** is a feeling of togetherness that evolves when group members are mutually dependent on one another because they believe they could not achieve the group's goals by acting independently.

Several factors influence group cohesiveness: member interaction, group size, rigorous entry requirements, group success, and external competition and challenges (McShane & Von Glinow, 2018). Cohesiveness tends to be greater the more time group members have spent together. Group cohesiveness is greatest when groups are kept as small as possible, but large enough to accomplish the tasks. Groups tend to be more cohesive when entry to the group is rigorous. Cohesiveness increases with the group's level of success. Group cohesiveness tends to increase when members face external competition or a valued goal that is challenging.

Thus far, we have implied that cohesiveness is a positive attribute. It can be. Members of highly cohesive groups tend to participate more fully in their group's activities; are absent less often; have low turnover; satisfy a broad range of individual needs including emotional and social identity needs; and are sometimes exceptionally productive than members of less cohesive groups (Ellemers, Spears, & Doosie, 2002; George & Bettenhausen, 1990; Sheldon & Bettencourt, 2002).

Whereas, cohesive groups are good for their members, they may or may not be good for the organization. Group cohesiveness tends to foster high levels of motivation and commitment to the group, and as a result, cohesiveness tends to promote higher levels of group performance (Beal et al., 2003; Mullen & Copper, 1994; Podsakoff, MacKenzie, & Ahearne, 1997). But when it comes to organizational performance, group cohesiveness is a double-edged sword: its effects can be both helpful and harmful to the organization (Langfred, 1998).

Members who have a strong desire to remain in a group and personally conform to the group's norms form a highly cohesive group (West, Patera, & Carsten, 2009).

With more conformity to norms, high-cohesive groups perform better than low-cohesive groups. However, the relationship between group norms and performance is a little more complex; as mentioned previously, group cohesiveness tends to foster high levels of motivation and commitment to the group. The effect of cohesiveness on group performance depends on the extent to which group norms are congruent with organizational goals. Cohesive groups will likely have lower performance when group norms are incongruent with organizational goals, because cohesiveness motivates members to perform at a level more consistent with group norms (Gammage et al., 2001).

What causes the incongruence between group norms and organizational goals? In highly cohesive groups, members may try to maintain harmony by striving toward consensus on issues without considering alternative viewpoints. This striving for conformity at the expense of other group perspectives is called *groupthink* and is thought to afflict highly cohesive groups with strong leadership and feelings of over-confidence about the group's capabilities (Janis, 1982).

THE DECISION TREE MODEL

Victor Vroom, Philip Yetton, and Arthur Jago (1988) have developed a model to help principals decide when and to what extent they should involve others in the decision-making process. First, the authors identify characteristics of a given problem situation using a series of seven questions. Second, they isolate five decision-making styles that represent a continuum from authoritarian to participatory decision-making approaches. Finally, they combine the key problem aspects with

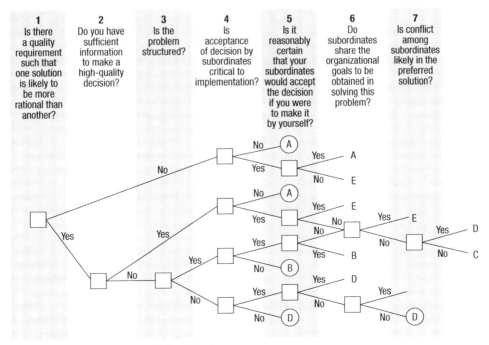

Figure 8.3 Effective Decision Styles

the appropriate decision-making style to determine the optimum decision approach a principal should use in a given situation (see figure 8.3).

Characteristics of a Given Problem Situation

The key characteristics of a decision situation, according to the Vroom-Yetton-Jago model, are as follows:

1. Is there a quality requirement such that one solution is likely to be more rational than others?
2. Does a principal have sufficient information to make a high-quality decision?
3. Is the decision situation structured?
4. Is acceptance of the decision by the principal's subordinates critical to effective implementation of the decision?
5. Is it reasonably certain that the decision would be accepted by subordinates if the principal were to make it alone?
6. Do the principal's subordinates share the organizational goals to be achieved if the problem is solved?
7. Is the preferred solution likely to cause conflict among the subordinates?

In other words, these key variables should determine the extent to which a principal involves others in the decision process or makes the decision alone, without their input.

Decision-Making Styles

Five alternative decision-making styles, from which a principal can choose, include the following:

1. Principals solve the problems or make the decision themselves, using information available at that time.
2. Principals obtain the necessary information from others, then decide on the solution to the problem themselves. They may or may not tell others what the problem is when they request information. The role played by others in making the decision is clearly one of providing the necessary information to principals, rather than generating or evaluating alternative solutions.
3. Principals share the problem with relevant others individually, getting their ideas and suggestions without bringing them together as a group. Then principals make the decision that may or may not reflect others' influence.
4. Principals share the problem with other members as a group, collectively obtaining their ideas and suggestions. Then they make the decision that may or may not reflect others' influence.
5. Principals share a problem with others as a group. Principals and others together generate and evaluate alternatives and attempt to reach agreement [consensus] on a solution. Principals do not try to influence the group to adopt their preferred solution, and they accept and implement any solution that has the support of the entire group.

(Vroom, Yetton, & Yago, 1988)

Choosing the Appropriate Style

Vroom, Yetton, and Jago (1988) match the decision styles to the situation as determined by answers to the seven questions. By answering these questions, the preferred decision style for each type of problem is identified. Figure 8.3 depicts how the Vroom-Yetton-Jago (1988) model works.

The flowchart provides the principal with a step-by-step approach to determining the most appropriate style of decision making under a given set of circumstances. To see how the model works, start at the left-hand side and work toward the right. When you reach a letter, the letter corresponds to the optimum decision-making style to use.

The Vroom-Yetton-Jago model represents an important improvement over rational decision-making theory, with implications for shared decision making. The authors have identified major decision strategies that are commonly used in making decisions, and they have established criteria for evaluating the success of the various strategies in a variety of situations. Moreover, they have developed an applied model for principals to use in selecting decision strategies—one that improves the quality of decisions, increases acceptance of the decisions by others, and minimizes the time consumed in decision making.

DECISION-MAKING STYLE CONTINUUM

Another approach to shared decision making, which specifies under what circumstances participation should be used, was developed by Robert Tannenbaum and Warren Schmidt (1973). These authors posited seven different *decision-making styles*, ranging on a continuum from what they call "boss-centered decision making" to "subordinate-centered decision making" (see figure 8.4).

The theme of this approach is that a wide range of factors determine whether directive decision making, shared decision making, or something in between is best. These factors fall into four broad categories: forces in the leader, forces in the subordinate, forces in the situation, and long-run goals and strategy.

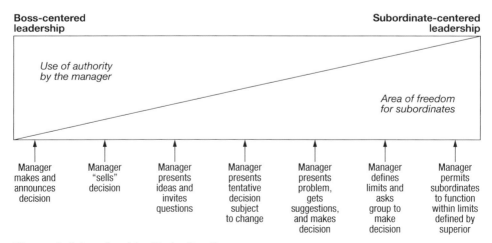

Figure 8.4 Leadership-Style Continuum

Forces in the Leader

Factors operating in the principal's personality influence her choices among the seven decision-making patterns. These factors include the following:

1. *The principal's value system.* How strongly does the principal feel that individuals should have a share in making the decisions that affect them? Or, how convinced is the principal that the official who is paid or chosen to assume responsibility should personally carry the burden of decision making? Also, what relative importance does the principal attach to organizational efficiency and personal growth of staff members?
2. *The principal's confidence in the group members.* Principals differ in the amount of trust they generally have in other people. After considering the knowledge and competence of a group with respect to a problem, a principal may (justifiably or not) have more confidence in his own capabilities than in those of the group members.
3. *The principal's own leadership inclinations.* Principals differ in the manner (e.g., telling or team role) in which they seem to function most comfortably and naturally.
4. *The principal's feelings of security in an uncertain situation.* The principal who releases control over the decision-making process reduces the predictability of the outcome. Principals who have a greater need than others for predictability and stability are more likely to "tell" or "sell" than to "join."

Forces in the Group Members

Before deciding how to lead a certain group, the principal will also want to remember that each member, like themselves, is influenced by many personality variables and expectations. Generally speaking, the principal can permit the group greater freedom if the following essential conditions exist:

1. Members have relatively high needs for independence.
2. Members have readiness to assume responsibility.
3. Members have a relatively high tolerance for ambiguity.
4. Members are interested in the problem and feel that it is important.
5. Members understand and identify with the goals of the school.
6. Members have the necessary knowledge and experience to deal with the problem.
7. Members expect to share in decision making.

Forces in the Situation

Two of the critical environmental pressures on the principal are as follows:

1. *The problem itself.* Do the members have the kind of knowledge that is needed? Does the complexity of the problem require special experience or a one-person solution?
2. *The pressure of time.* The more the principal feels the need for an immediate decision, the more difficult it is to involve other people.

Long-Run Goals and Strategy

As the principal works on daily problems, his choice of a decision-making pattern is usually limited. But he may also begin to regard some of the forces mentioned as variables over which he has some control and to consider such long-range goals as the following:

1. Raising the level of member motivation
2. Improving the quality of all decisions
3. Developing teamwork and morale
4. Furthering the individual development of members
5. Increasing the readiness to accept change

Generally, a fairly high degree of member-centered behavior is more likely to achieve these long-range purposes. But the successful principal can be characterized neither as a strong leader nor as a permissive one. Rather, they are one who is sensitive to the forces that influence her in a given situation and one who can accurately assess those forces that should influence her.

THE SYNERGISTIC DECISION-MAKING MODEL

How can a principal effectively put the resources of a group (or a team) to work on a problem? Getting several people together in one location and using each of their strengths to facilitate decision making are always challenges to a principal. To accomplish this, the group must work smoothly in a team effort and not be dominated by one individual or by factions within the group.

The key to creating the proper environment for shared decision making is shown in figure 8.5, and it is based to a great degree on effective communication skills (Lambert, 2004). We examine how each component of the model relates to each of the others when attempting decision making (see figure 8.5).

Listening

Active listening is not an automatic, easy process, especially when feelings are sensitized and frustration is evident within the group. To effectively accomplish the task, however, a listener should do the following:

- Always respect another's feelings.
- Never interrupt when another person is talking.
- Never prejudge.
- Always be considerate of someone else's remark.
- Never let rank or authority influence a comment.
- Always pay close attention to everything that is said.

Responding

Answering a remark that has been addressed to a group member occasionally requires a high degree of skill and tact. An often-overlooked fact in shared decision making is that an *improper* response (even when it is merely *perceived* that way) can reduce the effects of positive synergism. Accordingly, when responding, an individual should take care to do the following:

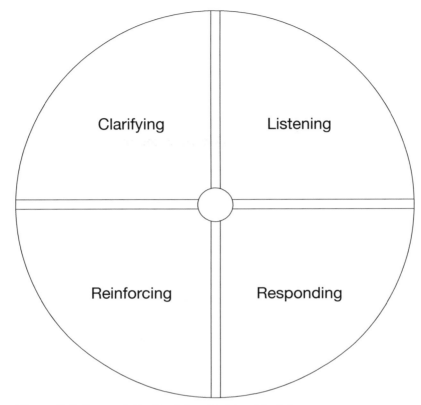

Figure 8.5 Synergistic Decision-Making Model

- Paraphrase the remark, when applicable.
- Never respond in a disparaging manner.
- Keep the other person's feelings in mind at all times.
- Avoid any type of premature judgment.
- Always assume that the other person has spoken with sincerity.
- Avoid having the "final say" in the matter.

Reinforcing

The skill of reinforcing should not be confused with being condescending. The key here is to build on the previous remark(s) so as to encourage more creative thinking for all individuals on the team. To induce the best type of synergistic effect when reinforcing, an individual should do the following:

- Create the proper climate for a nonthreatening dialogue.
- Encourage free discussion by acknowledging appropriate remarks.
- Accept the other person's right to express themselves freely.
- Speak in a noncompetitive manner.
- Build on individual and group ideas.
- Encourage various viewpoints as they arise.

Clarifying

During the course of the decision-making process, a statement or remark made by another person may need clarification. Not to provide that clarification would be a serious mistake. What *is* important to the process is to get every possible confusing or unclear point clarified, so that some type of judgment can be made about it. When attempting to clarify, an individual should always take care to do the following:

- Phrase the question in a neutral way.
- Never imply that a foolish question has been raised.
- Don't show any impatience in either voice tone or body language.
- Deal specifically with the question being addressed.
- Don't generalize about the other person's intentions.
- Don't assume that you always have the answer.

Clearly, a variety of problems can influence decision-making processes. Individuals and groups have various biases and personal goals that may lead to suboptimal decisions. A technique such as the *synergistic decision-making approach* aims to minimize many of these problems by allowing individuals greater freedom of expression, and the group receives far less filtered information with which to make its decision. Thus, although not perfect, this technique can assist principals in need of mechanisms to improve both the quality and the timeliness of decisions made by groups in schools.

SUMMARY

1. Decision making is one of the most important activities in which principals engage daily. The success of a school is critically linked to effective decisions.
2. Decision making is a process involving choices. The process generally consists of several steps: identifying problems, generating alternatives, evaluating alternatives, choosing an alternative, implementing the decision, and evaluating decision effectiveness.
3. Two major approaches to decision making have been identified. The rational model characterizes decision makers as completely searching through perfect information to make optimal decisions. The inherent imperfections of decision makers, and the social and organizational systems in which they are embedded, impose limitations on decision makers' ability to process the information needed to make complex decisions (bounded rationality) and restrict decision makers to finding solutions that are less than optimal.
4. Three major influences on decision making are decision styles, intuition, and creativity. The model of decision-making styles is based on the idea that styles vary along two dimensions: value orientation and tolerance for ambiguity. Combining these two dimensions form four styles of decision making: directive, analytical, conceptual, and behavioral.

5. There is growing evidence that administrators use their intuition to make decisions. Researchers have found that in many instances executives do not appear to use a rational systematic, step-by-step approach to decision making. Rather, they argue that many executives make decisions based on intuition.

6. Creativity is the ability to produce novel and useful ideas that can be put into action. The social and technological changes that schools face require creative decisions. Principals of the future need to develop special competencies to deal with the turbulence of change. One of these important competencies is the ability to promote creativity in schools.

7. Groups such as committees, task forces, project teams, or review panels often play a key role in the decision-making process. Groups offer certain advantages in decision making: greater sum total of knowledge, greater number of approaches, more alternatives, increased acceptance of a decision, and better comprehension of a problem and decision. On the other hand, groups create pressures to conform, can be dominated by one individual, result in conflicting secondary goals and undesirable compromises, cloud responsibility, and take more time. Nevertheless, if a principal wants to maintain a professional learning community, they must involve other stakeholder groups in the decision-making process.

8. Group behavior has been the subject of interest in social psychology for many years, and many different aspects of group behavior have been studied during this time. Two topics relevant to group functioning in schools are stages of group development and characteristics of a mature group. Stages of group development include forming, storming, norming, performing, and adjourning. Characteristics of a mature group include roles, norms, status, size, and cohesiveness.

9. The Vroom-Yetton-Jago model of determining the level of group involvement in the decision-making process requires the principal to diagnose a problem situation and the effect participation will have on the quality of the decision, level of staff members' acceptance, and the time available to make the decision.

10. Another approach to shared decision making, which specifies circumstances under which participation should be used, is the decision-making pattern choice model. The model posits seven different decision-making patterns, on a continuum ranging from "boss-centered decision making" to "subordinate-centered decision making."

11. The synergistic decision-making model is based on a great extent on effective communication skills. The components of the model include listening, responding, reinforcing, and clarifying. It is a technique for increasing the advantages and limiting the disadvantages of shared decision making.

KEY TERMS

decision making

identifying the problem

generating alternatives

evaluating alternatives

choosing an alternative
implementing the decision
evaluating decision effectiveness
bounded rationality
satisficing
contextual rationality
procedural rationality
heuristics
availability heuristic
representative heuristic
anchoring and adjustment heuristic
primacy/recency effect
bolstering the alternative
incrementalizing
garbage can model
decision-making style
value orientation
tolerance for ambiguity
directive style
analytical style
conceptual style
behavioral style
intuition
creativity
perceptual blocks
cultural blocks
emotional blocks
divergent thinking
expertise
creative thinking skills
intrinsic task motivation
brainstorming

idea quotas
heterogeneous groups
financial incentives
architecture and physical layout
lateral thinking method
vertical thinking method
reversal technique
analogy technique
cross-fertilization technique
creativity process
fact finding
idea finding
brainstorming
solution finding
risky shift
forming
storming
norming
performing
adjourning
task-oriented role
relationship-oriented role
self-oriented role
role
norms
status
group size
social loafing
social impact theory
cohesiveness
socio-emotional cohesiveness
instrumental cohesiveness

FIELD-BASED ACTIVITIES

1. Create a scenario that requires an educational decision, and run it through the six steps of the decision-making process: identifying the problem, generating alternatives, evaluating alternatives, choosing an alternative, implementing the decision, and evaluating decision effectiveness. Now reflect on the process. Discuss the advantages of running every important decision through each step in the decision-making process. Write your thoughts in your journal.

2. Examine the three decision-making models described in this book: the decision tree model, the decision-making pattern choice model, and the synergistic decision-making model. Under what circumstances would each of these decision-making models be used? Take field notes for several weeks, and observe the extent to which any or all of the

three models are used in your school or school district. Regardless of the outcome of your observation, how and when would *you* use each of the three models if you were a principal of a school? Be specific.

3. Why is it virtually impossible to use the rational decision-making model? Give some specific examples of how the effects of "bounded rationality" in schools can prevent principals from using purely rational decision making. Take field notes in your school for one week, during which you record reflections from your experience of incidents when bounded rationality was used in making decisions. Use the limits to rationality discussed in your text as a guide: satisficing, heuristics, contextual and procedural rationality, primacy/recency effect, bolstering the alternative, intuition, incrementalizing, and the garbage-can model. Try to find at least one specific school-related incident when each of these limits to rationality has been used in your school or school district.

SUGGESTED READINGS

Epstein, J. L., Sanders, M. G. Simon, B. S., Salinas, K. C., Jansorn, N. R., & Van Voorhis., F. L. (2018). *School, family, and community partnerships: Your handbook for action* (4th ed.) Thousand Oaks, CA: Corwin Press. This book offers a research-based framework that guides state and district leaders, school principals, teachers, parents, and community partners to form Action Teams for Partnerships, and to plan, implement, evaluate, and continually improve family and community involvement.

Gladwell, M. (2005). *Blink: The power of thinking without thinking.* New York, NY: Little, Brown, & Company. Gladwell suggests that intuition, decisions made very quickly, can be every bit as good as decisions made cautiously and deliberately.

Lencioni, P. (2002). *The five dysfunctions of a team.* San Francisco, CA: Jossey-Bass. Lencioni argues that teams face a relatively small number of pitfalls. And unless teams are prepared to face them, they often prove lethal. Five crucial team dysfunctions are absence of trust, fear of conflict, lack of commitment, avoidance of accountability, and inattention to results.

Rubin, H. (2010). *Collaborative Leadership: Developing Effective Partnerships in Communities and Schools* (2nd ed.). Thousand Oaks, CA: Corwin Press. In his provocative book, Rubin empowers school, community, and government leaders with usable, successful models of collaboration that can boost their performance and capacity to propel their missions forward. He illustrates how to cultivate mutually beneficial relationships, including twenty-four specific attributes that foster successful collaboration, twelve phases of collaboration, and the seven essential characteristics of effective collaborative leaders.

Shapiro, J. P., & Stefkovich, J. A. (2016). *Ethical leadership and decision making in education.* Mahwah, NJ: Lawrence Erlbaum. This textbook is designed to fill a gap in instructional materials for teaching the ethics component of the knowledge base that has been established for the profession. The text has several purposes: (a) it demonstrates the application of different ethical paradigms (the ethics of justice, care, critique, and the profession) through discussion and analysis of real-life moral dilemmas that educational leaders face in their schools and communities; (b) it addresses some of the practical, pedagogical, and curricular issues related to the teaching of ethics for educational leaders;

and (c) it emphasizes the importance of ethics instruction from a variety of theoretical approaches.

Surowiecki, J. (2004). *The wisdom of crowds*. New York, NY: Doubleday. Surowiecki argues that under the right conditions, groups of people (or "crowds") make better decisions than the most knowledgeable person in the group could alone. What is surprising is Surowiecki's claim that it is even true in circumstances in which the group is dominated by people who are not particularly well-informed or rational.

9

Communication

■ ■ ■

FOCUSING QUESTIONS

1. What is the importance of communication?
2. What are the major elements in the communication process?
3. What are the main functions of communication?
4. How can nonverbal cues influence communication effectiveness?
5. How does communication flow in school organizations?
6. How has technology influenced communication in schools?
7. What are the common barriers to effective communication?
8. How can principals overcome communication barriers?
9. What are the basics of becoming a more persuasive communicator?

In this chapter, we respond to these questions concerning communication in school organizations. We begin our discussion by defining communication and presenting a model of the communication process. Next, we identify the main functions of communication. Then we discuss how nonverbal cues influence communication effectiveness. We then look at the school district as a whole and consider the direction of communication flow as well as various communication networks. We consider barriers to communication and ways to overcome barriers to effective communication. Finally, we examine the basics for becoming a more persuasive communicator.

THE IMPORTANCE OF COMMUNICATION

Communication is the lifeblood of every school organization (Mumby, 2019). We can say with certainty that every act of communication influences the school in some way. Communication helps to accomplish all the basic leadership functions—planning, organizing, staffing, directing, coordinating, and reviewing (Kreps, 2019). Tasks cannot be accomplished, goals cannot be met, and decisions cannot be implemented without adequate communication.

Given its importance in schools, you may not be surprised to learn that principals spend as much as 70 to 80 percent of their time engaged in one form of communication or another (e.g., writing reports, sending e-mails, talking to others face-to-face, etc.) (Fullan, 2014; Glatthorn, Jailall, & Jailall, 2017; Marshall, 2021; Sergiovanni & Green, 2016; Spillane & Lowenhaupt, 2019; Ubben, Hughes, & Norris, 2017; Williamson & Blackburn, 2016). Communication involves everyone in a school or school district (and outside the school district, in the community as well), from the lowest-level employee to the superintendent of schools.

Not only is communication essential, but also it has been observed that communication is more important in today's school environment than ever before There are several reasons for this (Greenberg, 2014; Lunenburg & Lunenburg, 2015; Von Krogh, Ichijo, & Nonaka, 2000):

- *Technology has increased the pace of work.* As works gets done quicker than ever before, communication must be more effective because there is less time to correct errors or misunderstandings.
- *Teams enhance the need for coordination.* Due to the popularity of teams, people interact with lots of others who perform a wide variety of jobs. This requires coordinating information very carefully.
- *Knowledge and information are keys to success.* For today's schools to be successful, they must not only produce academic success for all students but also stay abreast of rapidly changing pedagogy in the field. This requires information to be accessed and shared in a coordinated fashion among teams.
- *Technology has transformed the way people do their jobs.* In today's electronically sophisticated world, we count on a variety of communication media that have transformed the way people do their jobs.

FUNCTIONS OF COMMUNICATION

In a sense, discussing the functions of communication in schools seems unnecessary because it is so obvious: you must communicate with others to accomplish goals. This is true, but communication serves a much broader range of functions in schools. Communication serves at least nine critical functions in schools. They are the following (Marshall, 2021; Robbins & Judge, 2019; Spillane & Lowenhaupt, 2019; Ubben, Hughes, & Norris, 2017).

Directing Action

Schools have authority hierarchies and formal guidelines that organization members are required to follow. When organization members are required to follow their job descriptions or to comply with school or school district policies, communication between people is necessary to get others to behave in a desired fashion. Principals must communicate with subordinates to tell them what to do, to give them feedback on their performance, to discuss problems with them, to encourage them, and so on.

Linking and Coordinating

For schools to function effectively, individuals and teams must carefully coordinate their efforts and activities, and communication makes this possible. In a school, for example, a teacher teaches the state-prescribed curriculum to students, who are tested using the state-mandated criterion-referenced test. The test is forwarded to the test publisher for scoring. Scores are interpreted for disaggregated student groups. Then academic coaches make recommendations for closing the achievement gaps between subgroups in the student population tested.

Building Relationships

Communication is essential to the development of interpersonal relationships. The work group is the primary source of social interaction for many organization members. The communication within the group is a fundamental mechanism by which members show their satisfaction and frustrations, build friendships, and promote trust. Communication, therefore, provides for the emotional expression of feelings and fulfillment of social needs. Doing so can help create a pleasant environment within the school organization.

Learning Organizational Culture

By communicating with others, organization members come to understand how their school operates, what is valued, and what matters to people. In other words, they learn about the culture of their school. Research on school culture has sought to measure how organization members see their school (Schein & Schein, 2018): Does it encourage teamwork? Does it reward innovation? Does it stifle initiative? Does it emphasize stability or growth? Does it take into consideration the effect of outcomes on people?

Presenting a School's Image

Schools send messages about themselves to stakeholders. For example, schools and school districts publish information about school outcomes to various stakeholder groups. These forms of communication are designed to present certain images of the school or school district to the community.

Generating Ideas

Communication is used to generate ideas and to share them as necessary. In many situations, groups or teams are expected to produce creative or imaginative solutions to organizational problems. In such cases, *brainstorming* often enhances the creative output of the group. Brainstorming can overcome the pressures of conformity that restrict creativity by encouraging any and all alternatives while withholding criticism. When organization members brainstorm with one another, for example, the communication process helps create new ideas.

In a typical **brainstorming** session, six to twelve people sit around a table. The group leader states the problem in a clear manner, so all participants understand. Members then freewheel as many ideas as they can in a given length of time. No criticism is permitted, and all ideas are recorded for future discussion and analysis. One idea stimulates others, and judgments of even the most outrageous suggestions are withheld until later to encourage group members to think as usual. Brainstorming is also accomplished online—participants from different locations enter their suggestions into a computer. Each participant's input appears simultaneously on the screen of the other participants. In this way, no one feels intimidated by the dominant member, and participants think more independently.

Promoting Ideals and Values

Most schools stand for something and have purposes that must be communicated clearly. For example, a stated purpose of the National Organization for Women (NOW) is to help women participate fully in society. Most organizations tend to use numerous slogans as a general practice to promote their ideals and values. Vince Lombardi, the legendary coach of the Green Bay Packers, initiated the slogan, "Winning isn't everything, it's the only thing." Educators tend to use numerous slogans to promote their ideals and values. The Aldine Independent School District in Houston, Texas has perpetuated the slogan, "Keep the main thing, the main thing," to indicate that school and school district discussions need to stay focused on student achievement.

Fostering Motivation
Communication fosters motivation by clarifying to organization members what they must do, how well they are doing, and how to improve performance if it falls below expectations. Research evidence supports the value of goals. We can say that: specific goals increase performance; difficult goals, when accepted, result in higher performance than easy goals; and feedback leads to higher performance than non-feedback (Locke & Latham, 2002). The formation of specific goals, feedback on progress toward the goals, and reward of desired behavior all stimulate motivation and require communication (Van Soelen, 2021).

Providing Information
Communication provides the information organization members need to make decisions. The transmission of data allows organization members to identify and evaluate alternative choices.

None of the nine functions is more important than the others. Communication is vital to ensure that organization members have the direction they need to perform their jobs and achieve their goals, coordinate their activities, build relationships, understand the school's culture, present the school's image, generate ideas, promote ideals and values, and make decision choices. Effective communication also lets teachers know the principal is confident they can perform at high levels and that they will benefit from performing well.

THE COMMUNICATION PROCESS

Communication can be defined as the process of transmitting information and common understanding from one person to another. The word *communication* is derived from the Latin word *communis*, meaning "common." The definition underscores the fact that unless a common understanding results from the exchange of information, there is no communication. Figure 9.1 reflects the definition and identifies the important elements of the communication process (Falkheimer & Heide, 2018; Heath & Winni, 2018; Kreps, 2019; Mumby, 2019; Van der Molen & Gramsbergen-Hoogland, 2018; Wallace & Becker, 2018).

Two common elements in every communication exchange are the sender and the receiver. The *sender* initiates the communication. In a school, the sender is a person who has a need or desire to convey an idea or concept to others. The *receiver* is the individual to whom the message is sent. The sender *encodes* the idea by selecting words, symbols, or gestures with which to compose a message. The *message* is the outcome of the encoding, which takes the form of verbal, nonverbal, or written language. The message is sent through a *medium* or channel, which is the carrier

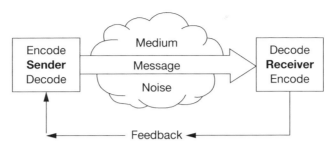

Figure 9.1 The Communication Process

of the communication. The medium can be a face-to-face conversation, telephone call, or written report. The receiver *decodes* the received message into meaningful information. *Noise* is anything that distorts the message. Different perceptions of the message, language barriers, interruptions, emotions, and attitudes are examples of noise. Finally, *feedback* occurs when the receiver responds to the sender's message and returns the message to the sender. Feedback allows the sender to determine whether the message has been received and understood.

Elements of the Communication Process

The elements used in the communication process determine the quality of communication. A problem in any one of these elements can reduce communication effectiveness (Falkheimer & Heide, 2018; Heath & Winni, 2018; Kreps, 2019; Mumby, 2019; Van der Molen & Gramsbergen-Hoogland, 2018; Wallace & Becker, 2018). For example, information must be encoded into a message that can be understood as the sender intended. Selection of the particular medium for transmitting the message can be critical, because there are many choices.

For written media, a principal or other organization member may choose from memos, letters, reports, bulletin boards, handbooks, newsletters, and the like. For verbal media, choices include face-to-face conversations, telephone, computer, public address systems, closed-circuit television, recorded messages, sound or slide shows, e-mail, and so on. Nonverbal gestures, facial expressions, body position, and even clothing can transmit messages (DeVito, 2014). People decode information selectively. Individuals are more likely to perceive information favorably when it conforms to their own beliefs, values, and needs. When feedback does not occur, the communication process is referred to as one-way communication. Two-way communication occurs with feedback and is more desirable.

The most obvious modes of communication are speaking and writing. Words are the main communication symbol used when speaking and writing. A major difficulty is that nearly every common word has several meanings. This difficulty is compounded when people from diverse backgrounds—such as different educational levels, ethnicity, or cultures—attempt to communicate (Ihlen & Heath, 2018). It is no wonder that we have trouble communicating with one another. If words could be simplified, the receiver would understand them more easily. This assumption underlies the idea of readability, which is the process of making speech and writing more understandable (see Lunenburg & Irby, 2008). Following are some suggestions for making your writing more readable.

- Use simple and familiar words. This makes comprehension more likely.
- Use personal pronouns such as "you" and "I" as if you were speaking directly to the reader.
- Use illustrations (figures, tables) and examples. "A picture is worth a thousand words."
- Use short sentences and paragraphs.
- Use active verbs. Active words have impact.
- Use only necessary words.
- Use a structure that resembles an outline, including ample headings and subheadings.
- Use chunking (i.e., lists of key points, accented by numbers or bullets).
- Use techniques of emphasis (e.g., boldface, italics) to accent important ideas.

NONVERBAL COMMUNICATION

Words are not the only way people communicate. Research has indicated that the receiver pays a great deal of attention to the way a message is delivered by the sender—to the sender's tone of voice, stance, facial expressions, emotions, and so forth. All of these factors are used to help interpret the meaning in the message—and the meaning behind it. For example, a principal might say to a teacher, "please complete your grade reports by the end of the day," but the nonverbal cues tell the teacher that the assignment should have been completed already, the principal is angry, and unless the reports are completed by the end of the day there will be big trouble ahead for the teacher. Similarly, when a co-worker slams the door in your face following a recent disagreement, an encoded message is transmitted to you.

We communicate as many messages nonverbally as we do verbally. **Nonverbal communication**—the way we stand, the distance we maintain from another person, the way we walk, the way we fold our arms and wrinkle our brow, our eye contact, being late for a meeting—conveys messages to others (Lunenburg, 2010f). However, we need not perform an act for nonverbal communication to occur. We communicate by our manner of dress and appearance, the automobile we drive, and the office we occupy (Knapp & Hall, 2010).

The four kinds of nonverbal communication are kinesics, proxemics, paralanguage, and chronemics (Birdwhistell, 2013; Burgoon, Guerrero, & Floyd, 2010; Bowden, 2011; DeVito, 2014; Furnham, 2011; Hickson, 2010; Knapp & Hall, 2010; Walters, 2019). They are important topics for school principals attempting to understand the meanings of nonverbal signals from organization members.

Kinesics
Kinesics is the study of body movements, including posture (Birdwhistell, 2013; Bowden, 2011; Hickson, 2010; Walters, 2019). Body movements, or kinesics, include gestures, facial expressions, eye behavior, touching, and any other movement of the limbs and body. Body shape, physique, posture, height, weight, hair, and skin color are the physical characteristics associated with kinesics.

Gestures reveal how people are feeling. People tend to gesture more when they are enthusiastic, excited, and energized. People tend to gesture less when they are demoralized, nervous, or concerned about the impression they are making. Hand gestures, such as frequent movements to express approval and palms spread outward to indicate perplexity, provide meaningful hints to communication.

Facial expressions convey a wealth of information. The particular look on a person's face and movements of the person's head provide reliable cues as to approval, disapproval, or disbelief. When people begin to experience an emotion, their facial muscles are triggered. The six universal expressions that most cultures recognize are happiness, sadness, anger, fear, surprise, and disgust. Smiling, for example, typically represents warmth, happiness, or friendship, whereas frowning conveys dissatisfaction or anger. However, smiling can be real or false, interpreted by differences in the strength and length of the smile, the openness of the eyes, and the symmetry of expression.

Eye contact is a strong nonverbal cue that serves four functions in communication. First, eye contact regulates the flow of communication by signaling the beginning and end of conversation. Second, eye contact facilitates and monitors feedback, because it reflects interest and attention. Third, eye contact conveys emotion. Fourth, eye contact relates to the type of relationship between communicators. One can gauge liking and interest by the frequency and duration of time spent looking. Eye and face contact display one's willingness to listen and acknowledgment of the other person's worth. Eye contact does not necessarily indicate truthfulness, as some people believe. It does show interest in the other person's point of view. Prolonged and intense eye contact usually indicates feelings of hostility, defensiveness, or romantic interest. Lack of interest may be indicated through contractions of the pupils or wandering eyes.

Touching is a powerful vehicle for conveying such emotions as warmth, comfort, agreement, approval, reassurance, and physical attraction. Generally, the amount and frequency of touching demonstrate closeness, familiarity, and degree of liking. A lot of touching usually indicates strong liking for another person. It should be noted that men and women interpret touching differently. Concerns about sexual harassment and sexism have greatly limited the use of touching in the workplace (Lunenburg, 2010d).

Posture is another widely used cue as to a person's attitude. Leaning toward another person suggests a favorable attitude toward the message one is trying to communicate. Leaning backward communicates the opposite. Standing erect is generally interpreted as an indicator of self-confidence, while slouching conveys the opposite. Posture and other nonverbal cues can also affect the impressions we make on others. Interviewers, for example, tend to respond more favorably to job applicants whose nonverbal cues, such as eye contact and erect posture, are positive than to those who display negative nonverbal cues, such as looking down or slouching (Lunenburg, 2012b).

Another nonverbal cue is mode of dress. Much of what we say about ourselves to others comes from the way we dress. Despite the general trend toward casual clothing in the workplace, higher-status people tend to dress more formally than lower-ranking organization members. For example, suppose you joined a new organization (school district, community college, university) and, on your first day, you entered a room full of employees. How would you know which person was the leader? Increasingly, people who specialize in recruiting top executives (such as superintendents and college presidents) are coming to the conclusion that the old adage "clothes make the person" is a particularly good nonverbal clue as to who is in charge. Somehow, the leader is the person who always seems to wear the best tailored suit that flatters their physique, or the nicest shirt or blouse, or the shiniest shoes, and the best-looking briefcase or bag. The payoff is that when you look like a leader, people will often treat you like one and so over time this increases your chances of promotion and success (Navarro, 2011).

Proxemics

Proxemics is the way people perceive and use space, including seating arrangements, physical space, and conversational distance (personal space) (Hall, 1966, 1983: Harrigan, 2009). For example, how close do you stand to someone in normal conversation?

Edward Hall (1983), an anthropologist, suggests that in the United States there are definable personal space zones:

1. *Intimate Zone (0 to 2 ft).* To be this close, we must have an intimate association with the other person or be socially domineering.
2. *Personal Zone (2 to 4 ft).* Within this zone, we should be fairly well acquainted with the other individual.
3. *Social Zone (4 to 12 ft).* In this zone, we are at least minimally acquainted with the other person and have a definite purpose for seeking to communicate. Most behavior in the business world occurs in this zone.
4. *Public Zone (Beyond 12 ft).* When people are more than 12 ft away, we treat them as if they did not exist. We may look at others from this distance, provided our gaze does not develop into a stare.

Related to the notion of personal space zones is the concept of physical space. For example, organization members of higher status have better offices (more spacious, finer carpets and furniture, and more windows) than do employees of lower status. Furthermore, the offices of higher-status employees are better protected than those of lower-status employees. Top executive areas are typically sealed off from intruders by several doors, assistants, and secretaries. Moreover, the higher the employee's status, the easier they find it to invade the physical space of lower-status employees. A superior typically feels free to walk right in on lower-status organization members, whereas lower-status group members are more cautious and ask permission or make an appointment before visiting a superior.

Some organizations are attempting to influence interpersonal communications through the physical environment with the use of feng shui. **Feng shui** is the belief that space needs to be in harmony with the environment. Literally, feng means "wind" and shui means "water." Feng shui was developed thousands of years ago in a village in China. Villagers studied the formations of land and the ways the wind and water worked together to help them survive. Over time, feng shui developed and was used by emperors to ensure their successes. According to feng shui experts, when a harmonious arrangement is created between the wind and water, the individual or organization prospers and the quality of life improves. The ability of feng shui to impact "harmony and energy" has been questioned; nevertheless, its principles for designing buildings and offices, including the placement of furniture and objects, are increasingly being used to varying degrees in Western societies (Tsang, 2004).

A few recommendations for office arrangements related to nonverbal communication based on feng shui include the following: (a) You should have full view of the room's entrance door by merely looking up from your desk. (b) You should be able to see outside while sitting at your desk. If the office does not have a window, brighten up the lighting and use a picture of the outdoors. (c) Your desk should not be placed directly in line with the door. You can place a screen in the space between your desk and the doorway, if necessary. (d) You should have a wall at your back while seated. Presumably, it gives you a "commanding" position (Zeer, 2004). Seating arrangements is another aspect of proxemics. You can seat people in certain positions according to your purpose in communication. To encourage cooperation, you should seat the other person beside you, facing the same direction. To facilitate direct and open communication, seat the other person at right angles from you. This allows for more honest disclosure. When taking a competitive position with someone, seat the person directly across from you. Furthermore, high-ranking people assert their higher status by sitting at the head of rectangular tables, a position that has become associated with importance. It also enables high-ranking administrators to maintain eye contact with those over whom they are responsible.

Paralanguage

Paralanguage consists of variations in speech, such as voice quality, volume, tempo, pitch, non-fluencies (for example, *uh*, *um*, *ah*), or laughing (Jacobi, 2009; Young, 2008). People make attributions about the sender by deciphering paralanguage cues. Aspects of speech such as pitch, volume, voice quality, and speech rate may communicate confidence, nervousness, anger, or enthusiasm. Intelligence is often judged by how people sound. Furthermore, Jeffrey Jacobi, author of *How to Say it with Your Voice* (2009), surveyed one thousand men and women and asked, "Which irritating or unpleasant voice annoys you the most?" Overwhelmingly, the most annoying sound was a *whining*, *complaining*, or *nagging* tone (Jacobi, 2009, p. 27).

Chronemics

Chronemics is concerned with the use of time, such as being late or early, keeping others waiting, and other relationships between time and status (Hickson, 2011). For example, being late for a meeting may convey any number of different messages including carelessness, lack of involvement, and lack of ambition. Yet, at the same time, the late arrival of high-status persons reaffirms their superiority relative to lower-status organization members. Their tardiness symbolizes power or having a busy schedule.

Practical Tips

It is important to have good nonverbal communication skills since they are related to the development of positive interpersonal relationships. One communication expert offers the following advice to improve nonverbal communication skills (Ramsey, 2007):

Positive nonverbal actions that help communication.

- maintaining appropriate eye contact
- occasionally using affirmative nods to indicate agreement
- smiling and showing interest

- leaning forward when someone is speaking to you
- using hand gestures in a relaxed, nontechnical manner
- standing and sitting erect, not slouching or cowering when confronted
- keeping your voice low and relaxed, but audible
- being aware of your facial expressions
- being neat, well groomed, and wearing clean, well-tailored clothes

Negative nonverbal actions to avoid.

- licking your lips or playing with your hair or mustache/beard
- turning away from the person you are communicating with
- closing your eyes and displaying uninterested facial expressions such as yawning
- excessively moving in your chair or tapping your feet
- using an unpleasant tone and speaking too quickly or too slowly
- biting your nails, picking your teeth, and constantly adjusting your glasses

In sum, despite the implications of the information about nonverbal communication, be aware that many nonverbal messages are ambiguous. For example, a smile usually indicates agreement and warmth, but it can also indicate nervousness, contempt, deceit, fear, compliance, resignation—even, on occasion, anger. Nevertheless, nonverbal messages are a rich source of information. Your own nonverbal behavior can be useful in responding to others, making stronger connections with others, and conveying certain impressions about yourself.

As you read this material ask yourself, "What can I do to present myself more favorably to those around me in the workplace? Specifically, what can I do nonverbally to cultivate the impression that I have the qualities to be a good leader?" As we have seen, speaking and writing can enhance your image as a strong leader. Also, there are several things you can do nonverbally that will enhance your leadership image. The aforementioned practical tips may help you to assess your leadership image.

DIRECTION OF COMMUNICATION

The purpose of organizational communication within school districts is to provide the means for transmitting information essential to goal achievement. Much of this **communication flow** is carried in three distinct directions: downward, upward, and horizontal (see figure 9.2). The other major communication flow is the grapevine.

Downward Communication

Hierarchical systems like large school districts tend to use **downward communication,** in which people at higher levels transmit information to people at lower levels within the system. Downward communication is necessary to help clarify the school district's goals, provide a sense of mission, assist in indoctrinating new employees into the system, inform employees about educational changes impacting the district, and provide organization members with data concerning their performance.

Downward communication occurs easily, but it is frequently deficient (Towers Perrin Human Resources Services, 2005). Part of administration's problem may be

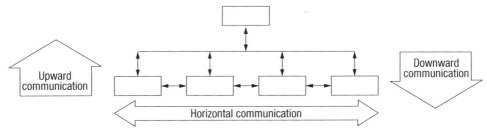

Figure 9.2 Downward, Upward, and Horizontal Communication Flows in School Districts

lack of preparation for effective communication. Often, principals fail to lay a solid foundation for communication.

There are four prerequisites for an effective communication approach (Newstrom, 2016). First, principals need to develop a positive communication attitude. They must realize that communication is an important part of their job responsibilities. Second, principals must continually work to get and keep informed. They need to seek out relevant information of interest to organization members, share it, and help employees feel informed. Third, principals need to consciously plan for communication, and they must do this at the beginning of every course of action. Finally, principals must develop trust. Trust between senders and receivers is important in all communication (Parini-Alemanno & Benoit, 2019). If staff members do not trust their principals, they are not as likely to listen to or believe the principal's messages.

Another problem is that downward communication tends to dominate in mechanistic organizations as opposed to organic systems, which are characterized by more open and multidirectional flows of information (Lunenburg, 2011b; Morgan, 2007; Shafritz, 2011).

Ways for principals to improve downward communication include the following (Mumby, 2019; Van der Molen & Gramsbergen-Hoogland, 2018; Wallace & Becker, 2018):

1. School districts should adopt communication training programs for all administrative personnel. Most school principals could benefit greatly from learning better ways of communicating, as well as developing more effective listening skills.
2. School principals should get out of their offices and talk to employees on the "firing line." One author refers to this technique as "management by wandering around" (MBWA) (Frase, 2003). It allows principals to become more aware of the needs of their organization members.
3. School principals should conduct regular supervisory-employee discussions. Such participative interactions will help principals identify, analyze, and solve problems collaboratively with followers.
4. School principals should explain the reasons why a decision was made. One study indicated that organization members were twice as committed to changes when the reasons behind them were fully explained. Many principals feel they are too busy to explain things or that explanations may lead to more confusion and resistance.

Town hall meetings or open forums are used increasingly in school districts to facilitate downward communication. Tips for conducting such meetings more effectively follow (Levine, 2007; Woodward, 2006):

- Consider using speakers other than your senior executives.
- Schedule meetings in advance and provide notice so all can participate. Video tape the meeting, so absent employees can view the meeting later.
- When making a presentation, take the audience into account. Avoid making presentations too technical.
- Employees should be strongly encouraged to attend, but attendance should not be mandatory.
- The size of the meeting depends on the message being delivered. If you have good news to relate, the meeting can be split into smaller, more intimate groups. If you have bad news to deliver, it is better to have everyone hear it at the same time.

The reluctance to transmit bad news is a phenomenon that frequently occurs in downward communication, which is known as the **MUM effect**. This refers to a person's reluctance to transmit bad news to others (Tesser & Rosen, 1975). For example, a principal may be reluctant to tell a subordinate that they have performed poorly. Thus, the principal may respond in the following ways. Each one is problematic.

- The principal may downplay the seriousness of the problem. Therefore, the organization member may not get a sense of the magnitude of the problem, or even that there is a problem.
- The principal may ask an assistant to transmit the bad news to the employee. However, the assistant is unlikely to be equally familiar with the problem, and furthermore, the assistant's message is not likely to have the same impact as the principal's; thus, the employee may not fully appreciate the problem.
- Finally, the principal may be so reluctant to address the bad news that they say nothing at all to the staff member.

(Heath, 1996)

Failing to overcome the MUM effect can be very problematic. Keeping employees from the corrective feedback that they need will prevent them from taking the steps necessary to improve their work.

Upward Communication

Upward communication also follows the hierarchical chart and transmits information from lower to higher levels in the organization. Upward communication is necessary to provide administrators with feedback on downward communication, monitor decision-making effectiveness, gauge organizational climate, deal with problem areas quickly, and provide needed information to administrators.

An effective school needs upward communication as much as it needs downward communication. One study revealed that, in organizations where upward communication programs were effectively implemented, a majority of administrators improved their performance (Smither et al., 1995). However, for several reasons, upward communication is difficult to achieve (Tourish, 2010).

Upward communication is usually subject to filtering and distortion because organization members do not want their superiors to learn anything that may be potentially damaging to their careers (Lee, 1993). This represents another instance of the MUM effect discussed previously with respect to downward communication. This tendency is likely to increase when organization members do not trust supervisors (Parrini-Alemanno & Benoit, 2019). Furthermore, highly cohesive groups tend to withhold information from superiors that might be damaging to the group as a whole. However, all organization members tend to distort upward communication somewhat less under a participatory management system than under an authoritative system.

Ways for principals to improve upward communication include the following (Molsching & Ryback, 2018; Turner & West, 2018): management by wandering around, climate surveys, 360-degree feedback, participative management, and the union contract.

Management by Wandering Around. An effective procedure to improve upward communication is for principals to get out of their offices and observe firsthand what is happening in the school. This practice has been described as **management by wandering around (MBWA)** (Frase, 2003; Ouchi, 1981; Peters & Waterman, 1982, 2006). According to one communications expert (Dulye, 2006), employees favor MBWA more than e-mails, Web sites, intranet sites, or town hall meetings, even more than the grapevine. According to Dulye, the most effective channel for employees is the informal workplace "walk" around, having their supervisor come to their room and sit and chat about work. Linda Dulye (2006, pp. 100–101) suggests the following tips for conducting MBWA:

1. Dedicate a certain amount of time each week for MBWA.
2. Do not take your cell phone. It is important to stay focused on the person you are speaking with and to avoid distractions
3. Use active listening and do not take the approach that shop talk is the only available topic for discussion. Organization members may enjoy some amount of casual conversation.
4. The experience should be a two-way conversation. Show interest in your faculty's issues and concerns.
5. Do not hesitate to take a notepad and record items requiring follow-up.
6. Thank the person or group for their time and feedback.

Climate Surveys. Climate surveys are useful upward communication devices that have several benefits. A **climate survey**, also known as a morale, opinion, attitude, job satisfaction, or quality of work-life survey is a procedure by which organization members report their feelings toward their jobs and work environment. Individual responses are combined and analyzed.

Climate surveys that are properly planned and administered usually will produce a number of benefits, both general and specific. One benefit of climate surveys is that they provide principals with an indication of general levels of satisfaction in a school. Climate surveys also reveal the specific areas of satisfaction and dissatisfaction (such as guidance and counseling, attendance, and discipline) and the particular groups of organization members (academic departments, new hires, or those approaching retirement). In other words, a climate survey provides information on how organization members feel about their jobs, what parts of their jobs these feelings exist, which departments are specifically affected, and whose feelings are involved (teachers, counselors, social workers, diagnosticians, administrators, or staff). The climate survey is a powerful diagnostic tool for assessing broad organization member problems and positive attitudes.

Climate surveys have many other benefits as well. The *flow of communication* in all directions is improved as people plan the survey, take it, and discuss the results. Climate surveys can serve as a *safety valve*, or emotional release, for people to get things off their chests and afterward feel better. Since organization members are able to report how they feel their principal performs certain aspects of the job, such as providing direction and empowering teachers, *professional development needs* can be identified. Climate surveys also can help principals *plan and monitor new programs*, by receiving feedback on proposed changes in advance before implementation and then conducting a follow-up survey to evaluate the actual response.

360-Degree Feedback. A comprehensive technique for the principal to gather feedback on their performance is **360-degree feedback** (Bradley, Allen, & Filgo, 2006; Brutus & Derayeh, 2002; Dyer, 2001; Lepsinger & Lucia, 2009; Seyforth, 2008; Shinn, 2008), also known as multi-source assessment or full-circle feedback. Initially used in business, 360-degree feedback is now used in a variety of professions and organizations, including schools. The principal using the technique gathers feedback from all groups that they work with, including teachers, students, other administrators, central office administrators, and so forth. By gathering information from multiple sources, information is communicated about areas of performance that may need to be improved. The technique is useful because it allows such information to be collected systematically and from people who are likely to have diverse perspectives on the principal's work. Gathering information from multiple sources makes for a more comprehensive assessment. Ideally, a coach or mentor without line authority over the principal assists the principal throughout the 360-degree assessment.

A number of principles guide the 360-degree feedback process (Glickman, Gordon, & Ross-Gordon, 2018). The feedback should be formative (used for the principal's professional development), not summative (used by the school district to make administrative decisions about the principal). None of the principal's superiors should coordinate the process. The mentor or coach who assists the principal should be committed to the principal's growth and development, have data-gathering and analysis skills, and be willing to openly and honestly critique the principal's performance. In consultation with the mentor or coach, the principal should be allowed to select the groups that will participate in the assessment. The entire process should be confidential, with feedback reviewed only by the principal and mentor or coach.

Participative Management. When a school or school district uses a sufficient number of programs to develop a substantial sense of empowerment among its organization members, it is said to practice **participative management**. These include but are not limited to suggestion programs, quality circles, total quality management, and professional learning communities.

Suggestion programs are formal plans to invite organization members to recommend improvements in functioning. Although many suggestion programs provide useful ideas, they are a limited form of participation that emphasizes individual initiative rather than group problem solving. Few organization members make suggestions in most schools, and the remaining may feel no significant level of involvement in the program. Delays in processing suggestions and rejections of good ideas can cause a backlash. Some principals may have difficulty viewing suggestions constructively and instead view them as criticisms of their own leadership practices.

Quality circles consist of voluntary groups who receive training in statistical analysis and problem solving and then meet to suggest ideas for improving school performance (Bonstingl, 2001). After achieving widespread success in Japan, quality circles expanded rapidly in the United States as an involvement technique. The quality circle approach helps organization members feel they have upward influence in the school. Organization members are committed to the ideas they generate.

Some schools that have used quality circles have experienced problems with them. Not all organization members participate, and when they did, they could not see the impact on the total school. In response to this experience, several school districts have initiated **total quality management** (**TQM**) (Deming, 2000). The TQM approach gets every organization member involved in the process of searching for continuous improvement. Quality of outcome and service is the focus of TQM.

Many schools have implemented professional learning communities as a device for increasing upward communication and school improvement. A **professional learning community** (**PLC**) is a group of people who share a common vision of success for all students. All stakeholders—board of education, superintendent, principal, faculty, and support staff—move together to achieve a shared vision. The principal plays a key role in creating and shepherding a professional learning community. The principal begins by bringing people together to engage in a four-step process: creating a mission statement, developing a vision, developing value statements, and establishing goals (DuFour et al., 2021; Eaker et al., 2021). The Professional Learning Community (PLC) approach was discussed in some detail in chapter 1. All of the aforementioned programs for participation hold promise as substantial programs in participative management.

The Union Contract. A prime objective of the union is to convey to administration the feelings and demands of various employee groups (teachers, professional support staff, office staff, custodians, cooks, bus drivers, etc.). Collective bargaining sessions constitute a legal channel of communication for any aspect of employer-employee relations (Lunenburg, 2000). A typical provision of every union contract is the grievance procedure. It is a mechanism for appeal beyond the authority of the immediate supervisor.

Horizontal Communication

Upward and downward communication flows generally follow the formal hierarchy within the school or school district. However, greater size and complexity of schools and school districts increase the need for communication laterally across the lines of the formal chain of command. This is referred to as **horizontal communication**. These communications are informational too, but in a different way than downward and upward communication. Here, information is basically for coordination—to tie together activities within or across either departments in a single school or divisions in a school district.

Lateral communication takes place between employees at the same hierarchal level. This type of communication is frequently overlooked in the design of most school organizations. Integration and coordination between units in a school organization is facilitated by horizontal communication. At the upper levels of a school district, for example, the assistant superintendents for instruction, business, public relations, and human resources will coordinate their efforts in arriving at an integrated strategic plan for the district. In a high school, meanwhile, the department chairpersons will work together in developing a curriculum for the entire school. Likewise, in a school of education of a large university, it is common to observe departments coordinating their efforts for the purpose of ensuring that all units of the school are working toward the same general goals. This lateral communication is frequently achieved through cross-functional committees or council meetings, groups or liaison positions that tie together units horizontally, and informal interpersonal communication.

Lateral communication falls into one of three categories (Daft, 2016):

1. *Intradepartmental problem solving.* These messages, which take place between members of the same department in a school or division in a school district, concern task accomplishment.
2. *Interdepartmental coordination.* Interdepartmental messages facilitate the accomplishment of joint projects or tasks in a school or divisions in a school district.
3. *Staff advice to line departments.* These messages often go from specialists in academic areas, finance, or computer service to building principals seeking help in these areas.

Many schools and school districts build lateral communications in the form of task forces, committees, liaison personnel, or matrix structures to facilitate coordination. Besides providing task coordination, horizontal communication furnishes emotional and social support among peers. In effect, it serves as a socialization process for the organization. The more interdependent the various functions in the organization, the greater the need to formalize horizontal communication.

Besides being necessary for job coordination, lateral communication is also done because people prefer the informality of horizontal communication rather than the upward-and-downward process of the official hierarchy of authority. Horizontal communication is frequently the dominant pattern within administrative levels.

Organization members who play a major role in horizontal communication are referred to as **boundary spanners**. Boundary spanners have strong communication links within their department, with people in other departments, and frequently with the community (Goldring, 1990; Newstrom, 2016). These connections with other departments or units allow boundary spanners to gather large amounts of information, which they may filter or submit to others. This gives boundary spanners a source of status and potential power.

While boundary spanners acquire their roles through formal task responsibilities, other horizontal communication takes place in less formal ways such as networks. A **network** is a group of people who develop and maintain contact to exchange information formally, usually involving shared interests (Groenewegen et al., 2017; Johnson, 2018). An organization member who becomes active in such a group is said to be networking. Networks can exist within as well as outside a school or school district. Typically, they are built around external interests, such as sports, social clubs, professional associations, career interests, and minority status.

Networks help broaden the interests of staff members, keep them informed about new pedagogical developments, and make them more visible to others. Networks help staff members learn who knows what and who knows who is knowledgeable about a given topic. Thus, a skillful networker can gain access to influential people and centers of power by drawing on common backgrounds, friendships, complementary organizational roles, or community ties. Networking can help organization members obtain job-related information, develop productive relationships, and gain valuable skills, which can help them perform their jobs better.

Another device for improving lateral communication is the use of an ombudsperson. The ombudsperson has been utilized primarily in Scandinavia to provide an outlet for persons who have been treated unfairly or in a depersonalized manner by large, bureaucratic government. More recently, this approach has gained popularity in American state governments, the military, universities, and some business firms. Xerox Corporation inaugurated the position in 1972, and General Electric followed shortly thereafter.

The **ombudsperson** was created to receive and respond to inquiries, complaints, requests for policy clarifications, or allegations of wrongdoing from organization members who feel uncomfortable going through the formal hierarchy. The ombudsperson investigates the matter and intervenes when necessary to correct a wrong and correct the system to prevent future errors. In this way, a streamlined alternative to the formal hierarchy is created, and organization members feel that their problem will receive a fair and impartial hearing. The approach is more common in Europe than in North America and it permits an organization member to receive help from above without relying on the formal chain of command.

According to one study, 85 percent of organization members are satisfied with the nature of horizontal communication (Frank, 1984). Nevertheless, horizontal communication is not without challenges. Horizontal communication is impeded in three ways (Kreitner & Kinicki, 2016): (1) Specialization may cause organization members to work on their tasks and jobs alone. (2) Organization members in different departments may compete against one another for valued organizational resources. As a result, they may exhibit resentment toward one another, substituting an antagonistic, competitive orientation for a friendlier, cooperative one (Rogers & Rogers, 1976). (3) The organizational culture in the school may not promote collaboration and cooperation (Bulach & Lunenburg, 2016a). The three directions of organizational communication flows are shown in figure 9.2.

The Grapevine

Every school needs formal channels of communication to organize, control, and coordinate activity within the building. Coexisting with the formal channels is an informal communication network, commonly referred to as the grapevine. The **grapevine** is simply the informal communication network among people in a school. Grapevines are present and highly active in virtually every school. They flow in all directions—up, down, or horizontally—in unpredictable patterns and are not fixed by any formal organization chart. Moreover, nearly five out of every six messages are carried by the grapevine rather than through official channels (Ivancevich, Konopaske, & Matteson, 2017). And in normal work situations, well over 75 percent of grapevine information is accurate (Newstrom, 2016).

The grapevine serves as an emotional outlet for staff members' fears and anxieties; helps satisfy a natural desire for people to talk about their job, their institution, and their colleagues; gives staff a sense of belonging and a way of gaining social acceptance and recognition; and helps principals to learn how staff members feel about policies and programs.

This has obvious implications for school principals. It means tuning into the grapevine, understanding what it is saying, and knowing and using its sources. Thus, principals can use the energy of the grapevine to supplement formal communication channels. Management by walking around is an excellent way to use the grapevine in a nonthreatening way (Frase et al., 2003).

Although the grapevine offers the aforementioned benefits, information passed through the grapevine often gets exaggerated as it travels from person to person. Furthermore, although 75 percent of grapevine information is accurate (Newstrom, 2016), the grapevine may also be incomplete. It is the remaining 25 percent that is troublesome. The problem is that the inaccurate portions of some messages may alter their overall meaning. For example, a story may be circulating around the school district that someone got passed up for promotion in favor of a lower-ranking staff member, resulting in dissension among the ranks. However, suppose everything is true except that the person declined the promotion. This important fact alters the accuracy of the information transmitted.

Whether positive or negative, the grapevine is an inevitable fact of life in school organizations (Turner & West, 2018). School principals need to view the grapevine as a competitor with formal channels of communication and keep organization members informed before they receive the news through the grapevine. The major problem with the grapevine, and the one that gives the grapevine its poor reputation, is rumor.

Rumor

The word "rumor" sometimes is used as a synonym for "grapevine," but technically the two terms are different. **Rumor** is grapevine information that is communicated without supporting evidence. It is the inaccurate part of the grapevine. It could be accurate by chance, but generally it is inaccurate; therefore, it is presumed to be undesirable.

It is often assumed that rumors begin because they make good gossip. This is not the case. Rumors emerge as a response to situations that are *important* to people, when there is *ambiguity*, and under conditions that arouse *anxiety* (Rosnow & Fine, 1976). Work situations often contain these three elements, which explains why rumors abound in schools. The secrecy and competition that typically exist in large school districts—surrounding the appointment of a new superintendent, the location of new building sites, layoff decisions, or consolidation of school districts—encourage and sustain rumors on the grapevine. A rumor will continue either until the needs and expectations creating the ambiguity are fulfilled or the anxiety has been reduced.

Types of Rumors. Scientists have classified rumors into four distinct categories (Greenberg, 2014; Mishra, 1990). They are as follows:

- **Pipe dreams**. Rumors that reflect people's wishes are known as pipe dreams. These are the most positive rumors; they help to stimulate the creativity of others. Frequently solutions to work problems are a result of employees verbally expressing desire for change. These improvements sometimes increase efficiency for certain departments within a school or divisions within a school district. The downside is when the pipe dreams are inaccurate. For example, suppose a rumor is circulating throughout the school district that bonuses this year will be much larger than usual. This may reflect positive wish fulfillment of those who are spreading the rumor. If the rumor is inaccurate, however, it will eventually lead to disappointment.

- **Bogie rumors.** Rumors that are based on people's fears and anxieties are known as bogie rumors. Such rumors are likely to arise under conditions in which people are uneasy about things, such as when budgets are exceptionally tight. In this case, people verbally express their fears to others. These rumors are sometimes damaging (such as a rumor of possible layoffs). For example, a small rural school district may announce its plans to consolidate with a nearby school district, which may result in laying off vast numbers of its personnel.

- **Wedge drivers.** Rumors in which people go out of their way to spread malicious rumors about someone with the intent of damaging that individual's reputation are known as wedge drivers. This is the most aggressive and damaging type of rumor. It divides groups and destroys loyalties. These rumors are used in an intentionally aggressive fashion. They are divisive and negative rumors. They tend to be demeaning to a school organization or person and can cause damage to the reputation of others. For example, a wedge driver rumor may involve someone at X school district saying that "Mr. Y, the superintendent, was seen the other day alone with Ms. Z, the new teacher. They were in a car together leaving Motel 6."

- **Home-stretchers.** Rumors that are anticipatory of impending decisions are known as home-stretchers. They occur after employees have been waiting a long time for an announcement. There may be just one final piece necessary to complete the puzzle and this, in effect, enhances the ambiguity of the situation. For example, suppose talks have been taking place in your school district about an impending consolidation with another school district. Personnel have been waiting for the announcement, but it has not come yet. Under such circumstances rumors may circulate about the specifics of the consolidation in anticipation of something happening. Given the absence of information from administration to "complete the puzzle," employees try to fill the vacuum by providing bits of information to each other, even if these are based on speculation rather than facts.

Joseph Licata and Walter Hack (1980) examined grapevine structures among principals and report that grapevine linkages differed between elementary and secondary school principals. In elementary schools, where relationships are closer, principals tended to communicate informally; in high schools, where the structure is more formal, principals built the grapevine around professional survival and development.

How to Combat Rumors. As a principal, your first step in dealing with rumors is to make certain you are plugged into the grapevine. You must know what the latest rumor is before you can effectively deal with it. Dealing with rumor can be done formally through official e-mail or announcement during a meeting or informally in a school hallway or lunch conversations with key employees.

Think of the grapevine as one way of taking the pulse of your school (Sims, 2002). It gives principals a feel for the morale of their school and helps them tap into employees' anxieties. This is useful for principals to know, because morale affects employee motivation and job performance.

The principal, therefore, should listen to the grapevine and develop skills in dealing with it. For example, an alert principal might be aware that certain incidents will cause undue anxiety. In this case, the principal should explain immediately why such incidents will take place. When emergencies occur, when changes are introduced, and when new policies are implemented, the principal should explain why and answer all organization members' questions as openly as possible. If the principal does not have all the necessary information available, they should admit this and then try to get all the facts concerning the issue.

Suggestions for reducing the negative consequences of rumors should also be followed (Greenberg, 2014; Hirschhorn, 1983; Newstrom, 2016; Robbins & Judge, 2018; Turner & West, 2018):

1. The grapevine should be viewed as a permanent part of the formal organizational structure and should be used to improve communication within the organization.
2. Principals must be tuned in to what information is being communicated through the grapevine and why that information is being communicated.
3. Principals must seek to keep staff members informed about what is going on in the school. A formal newsletter can help. Inaccurate rumors traveling through the grapevine can be corrected by principals acting promptly by feeding accurate information to primary communicators or "liaison" persons.
4. Rumors are more difficult to correct over time because they "harden"—the details become consistent and the information becomes publicly accepted.
5. Principals need to explain actions and decisions that may appear inconsistent, unfair, or secretive.
6. Principals must refrain from shooting the messenger—rumors are a natural fact of organizational life, so they must respond to them calmly, rationally, and respectfully.
7. Principals need to maintain open communication channels—constantly encourage staff members to come to them with concerns, suggestions, and ideas.
8. If principals gain trust of organization members, those members will share information heard through the grapevine with their principals. With access to this information, principals can then correct or further explain inaccurate information.
9. Principals need to understand that the receptiveness of organization members to rumors is directly related to the quality of the principal's communications and leadership. If staff members believe that their principal is concerned about them and will make every effort to keep them informed, they will tend to disregard rumors and look to the principal for answers to their questions.
10. Finally, the school or school district can conduct training programs for organization members on the negative consequences and disruptive nature of damaging rumors.

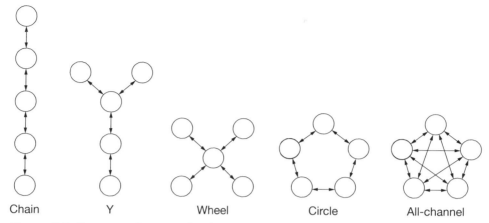

Figure 9.3 Common Communication Networks

Network Patterns

Downward, upward, and lateral communication flows can be combined into a variety of *communication* networks. Five of the most commonly used networks are shown in figure 9.3: the chain, Y, wheel, circle, and all-channel (Groenewegen, Ferguson, Moser, & Borgatti, 2017; Johnson, 2018). An understanding of communication networks can help principals improve their overall communication effectiveness.

Chain Network. The **chain network** represents a five-level vertical hierarchy in which communications can move only upward and downward. In a school district, this type of network would be found in line-authority relations. For example, a teacher reports to the department head, who reports to the principal, who reports to the assistant superintendent, who reports to the superintendent. These five individuals represent a chain network.

Y Network. If we turn the **Y network** upside down, we can see two staff members reporting to a leader, with two levels of authority above the leader. For instance, two high school assistant principals report to the principal, who in turn reports to the assistant superintendent for instruction, who reports to the superintendent. This is, in effect, a four-level hierarchy.

Wheel Network. If we look at the **wheel network** as though we were standing above the diagram, we see that the wheel represents four staff members who report to a leader. For example, four assistant principals in a large high school report to the principal. There is no interaction between the assistant principals. All communications are channeled through the principal.

Circle Network. The **circle network** allows members to interact with adjoining members, but no further. It represents a three-level hierarchy in which there is vertical communication between the leader and staff members and lateral communication only at the lowest level. In a medium-sized high school, the principal communicates with two assistant principals, who communicate separately with two different teachers. The two teachers communicate with each other.

All-Channel Network. Finally, the **all-channel network** allows each of the participants to communicate freely with the other four. Of the networks discussed, it is the least structured. Although it is like the circle in some respects, the all-channel network has no central position, and there are no restrictions; all members are equal. The all-channel network is best illustrated by a committee in which no one member formally or informally assumes a leadership position. All members are free to share their viewpoints.

Effectiveness of different networks. The importance of a communication network lies in its potential effects on such variables as speed, accuracy, morale, leadership, stability, organization, and flexibility. Studies in communication networks show that the network effectiveness depends on situational factors (Groenewegen et al., 2017; Johnson, 2018; Schulz, 2011). For example, centralized networks are more effective in accomplishing simple tasks, whereas decentralized patterns are more effective on complex tasks. In addition, the overall morale of members of decentralized networks is higher than those of centralized networks. This finding makes sense in view of the research indicating that organization members are most satisfied with their jobs when they have participated in decision making about them. Moreover, research shows that a member's position in the network can affect personal satisfaction. Members in more central positions in the network tend to be more satisfied.

Network Analysis

Besides network patterns, another method to help school administrators analyze communication flows and patterns is **network analysis**. In network analysis, communication flows and patterns are analyzed between units and across hierarchical positions. Network analysis uses survey sociometry (Moreno, 1953) rather than controlled laboratory experiments to identify cliques and certain specialized roles of members in the communication structure of real-life school organizations.

To illustrate, consider the communication network for a hypothetical school district (Rogers & Rogers, 1976). Figure 9.4 presents a formal organizational chart showing the hierarchical positions occupied by twenty-two people in three divisions of the school district. The numbers within the boxes represent individuals in the school district. Person 1 at the top of the hierarchy is the superintendent of schools. The three people immediately below person 1 are the assistant superintendents of the three divisions: personnel, instruction, and business. The remaining individuals are employees in each division. This chart represents the formal structure of communications within the school district.

Through network analysis, figure 9.4 shows a communication network and contrasts it with the school district's formal structure. As figure 9.4 shows, Person 1 (the superintendent) frequently communicates with Persons 2, 3, and 4, the assistant superintendents for personnel, instruction, and business, respectively. Person 1's communications with other lower-level members are less frequent or nonexistent. Figure 9.5 also identifies cliques in the communication network of the twenty-two members on the basis of intercommunication patterns among them. The lines indicate patterned communication contacts. Some communication contacts are two-way (←→) and some are one-way (→). Two-way arrows connect Persons 1 and 4, 1 and 2, 1 and 3, and 2 and 4, while one-way communications exist between Persons 2 and 3, 4 and 17, and so on.

There are four cliques in the school district: A, B, C, and D. "A *clique* is a subsystem whose elements interact with each other relatively more frequently than with other members of the communication system." Clique A is composed of Persons 4,

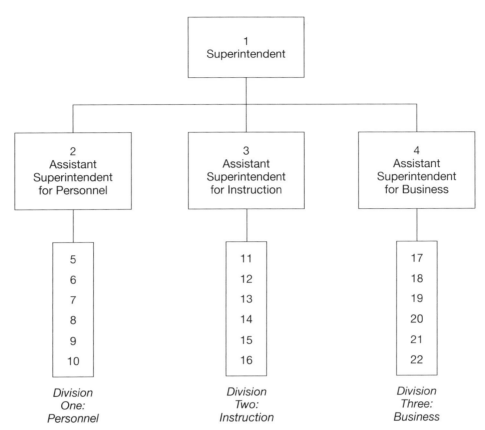

Figure 9.4 Formal Organizational Chart of a Hypothetical School District

17, 18, 19, 20; Clique B is composed of Persons 3, 12, 13, 14, 15, and so on. Most clique members in a network are usually relatively close to each other in the formal hierarchy of the organization. However, a school district's actual communication network can be very different from the pattern of communication established by its formal organizational structure. Four main communication roles have emerged in network analysis: gatekeepers, liaisons, bridges, and isolates.

Person 1, the superintendent, is dependent on Persons 2, 3, and 4, the three assistant superintendents, for access to communication flows. The three assistant superintendents are also *gatekeepers*, having the capacity to control information moving in either direction between the superintendent and the rest of the school district. Person 1 also serves as a *liaison* (an individual who interpersonally connects two or more cliques within the system without himself belonging to any clique) who connects Clique A, Clique B, and Clique D. If this liaison were removed from the network, it would be a much less interconnected system. Person 7 is a *bridge*, a person who is a member of one communication clique and links it, via a communication dyad, with another clique. Thus, Person 7 is a member of Clique D and communicates with Person 9, who is a member of Clique C. Person 11 is an *isolate* (an individual who has few communication contacts with the rest of the system) and is virtually cut off

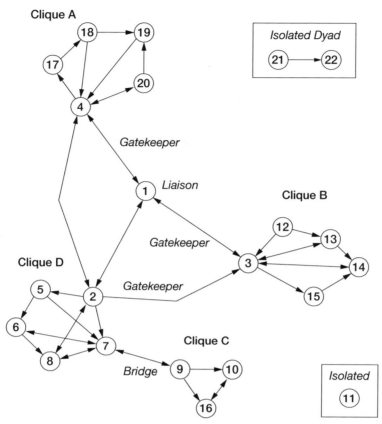

Figure 9.5 Communication Network of a Hypothetical School District

from communication. Person 21 has an in-group relationship in an isolated dyad with Person 22.

Patrick Forsyth and Wayne Hoy (1978) studied communication isolates in five secondary schools. Results indicated that communication isolates tend to be separated from perceived control, the school's control structure, respected colleagues, and sometimes friends. A subsequent study of communication isolates in elementary schools reports similar findings, except that isolation from friends was not related to isolation from formal authority (Zielinski & Hoy, 1983). In another study of communication networks in one high school and five elementary schools, using sociometry and frequency surveys of communication, results indicate more frequent communication contacts in elementary schools as compared with high schools. According to this study, three factors affect horizontal communication patterns in schools: level and size of school, specialization, and proximity (Charters, 1967).

In sum, we have identified and described individuals who have potential influence in the informal communication network and their roles in interpersonal communication in school districts. School administrators entering a school district would be well advised to establish good interpersonal relationships with gatekeepers, liaisons, and bridges. Furthermore, it is vital to be cognizant of the potentially destructive aspect of isolates who often become alienated and exhibit detrimental behaviors dysfunctional to the school district. Knowledge of communication networks can serve as useful interpersonal communication sources. More important, such knowledge can determine the success or failure of a school principal on the job.

ELECTRONIC COMMUNICATION

The primary medium of communication in today's schools is electronic. Electronic communications include e-mail, instant messaging, social networking, voice mail, smartphones, blogs, videoconferencing, and presentation technology.

E-Mail

E-mail uses the internet to send and receive computer-generated text and documents (e.g., graphics, videos, and audio files). E-mail is the most widely used communication tool in organizations (Falkheimer, Heide, & Young, 2018; Schadler, 2009; Sklar & Harris, 2019). Many principals and other school professionals process more than one hundred e-mail messages a day. The main reason for the popularity of e-mail is the freedom it provides people to send and receive messages quickly and efficiently. As a communication tool, e-mail can be distributed to one person, or thousands of people, with a click of a mouse. They can be read at any time by the receiver and organized and stored as well.

E-mail tends to be the preferred means of communicating facts, such as information needed to coordinate efforts between individuals and teams. Brief, well-defined factual messages (e.g., schedule changes) and announcements (e.g., forthcoming events) are effective uses of e-mail. E-mail also has made it easier to soften status barriers between people that often make it difficult to share ideas (Harris & Nelson, 2018; Saunders, Robey, & Vavarek, 1994). For example, whereas one may find it difficult to get a face-to-face meeting with the superintendent of schools of a large school district, it is as easy to send an e-mail message to that person as it is to reach any other organization member, effectively changing the flow of information within a school district. Not surprisingly, many superintendents and building principals rely on e-mail as an effective means of reaching out to everyone in the school district or school.

Problems with E-Mail. Although e-mail has a number of benefits, there are some drawbacks to using e-mail. The following are some of the most significant limitations of e-mail (Falkheimer & Heide, 2018; Freeman, 2012; Greenberg, 2014; McShane & Von Glinow, 2018; Robbins & Judge, 2018; Sklar & Harris, 2019):

- *Misinterpreting the message.* We frequently misinterpret verbal messages, but the potential to misinterpret e-mail messages is even greater. Research indicates that less than 50 percent of users can accurately decode the tone and intent of an e-mail. Furthermore, most people vastly overestimate their ability to send and interpret messages clearly. Misinterpretation is highest when the e-mail comes from the person's superior (Kruger et al., 2008; Taylor, Fieldman, & Altman, 2008). If you are sending an important message, make certain that you reread it for clarity.
- *Sending indiscriminate messages.* A widespread problem with e-mail is that it encourages sending indiscriminate messages, including trivial information,

mass distribution of information of interest to a limited number of people, the relaying of jokes and sports news, and requests for seemingly unimportant information. The explosion of e-mail requires many people to work extra hours to sort through their mail on matters that do not add value to their work.

- *Disinhibiting effect of e-mail.* Some people feel much less inhibited when using e-mail and thus find it far easier to be blunt, overly critical, and insensitive when conveying messages electronically rather than face-to-face. The term **flaming** is used to describe the act of sending an emotionally charged message to others. However, research has indicated that rudeness in electronic communication decreases as team members get to know each other and when organizations establish explicit norms and rules of communication (Hertel, Geister, & Konradt, 2005; Lee, 2005; Lunenburg & Lunenburg, 2015; Molsching & Ryback, 2018).

- *Privacy of e-mail.* There are two privacy concerns with e-mail. First, your e-mails may be, and often are, monitored. You are being watched, so be careful with your e-mail (Zeidner, 2007). In the wake of the Enron scandal, e-mail storage and recordkeeping have become important concerns for many organizations. Nearly all major US companies are now recording and reviewing employees' communications, including e-mail, telephone calls, and Internet connections (Paradis, 2002). You cannot always trust the recipient of your e-mail to keep it confidential. Second, you need to exercise caution in sending e-mail from your school district's e-mail account to a personal, or "public" (e.g., Gmail or Yahoo), e-mail account. These public accounts frequently are not as secure as your school district's accounts, so when sending a school district e-mail to them, you may be violating your school district's policy or unintentionally disclosing confidential information.

- *Unedited, poorly written messages.* E-mails are permanent documents. Once forwarded, an e-mail cannot be taken back. The sender loses all control over who views the message. Therefore, always use correct grammar, spelling, tone, and professional language in preparing and sending messages.

- *Limiting medium for expressing emotions.* People usually find e-mail a highly limiting medium for expressing their emotions. E-mails lack cues like facial expression and tone of voice. Traditional e-mail is restricted to alphanumeric characters and consequently lacks the verbal information that makes face-to-face communication so rich. This results in difficulty for recipients to decode meaning.

- *Time-consuming nature of e-mail.* Many principals and other school professionals process more than one hundred e-mail messages a day. Venture capitalist, billionaire, and Dallas Mavericks owner Mark Cuban receives more than one thousand e-mail messages a day. You probably do not receive that many; however, most people have difficulty keeping up with all e-mail, especially as we advance in our careers (Robbins & Judge, 2018). Moreover, the average organization member checks their e-mail fifty times a day.

The whole field of e-mail courtesy ("netiquette") has emerged, with a set of guidelines to help principals decide how to best proceed via e-mail. The following are sample guidelines for e-mail netiquette (Falkheimer & Heide, 2018; Newstrom, 2016; Sklar & Harris, 2019).

1. Provide your receiver with an informative subject for your message.
2. Indicate the degree of urgency with which you need a response.
3. Be cautious about forwarding messages and replying to them; ensure that the message is sent only to intended recipients.
4. Do not assume that everyone is equally comfortable with e-mail or checks their messages as frequently as you do.
5. Try to respond to all messages requiring a response within twenty-four hours.
6. Be brief.
7. Exercise as much care in spelling and punctuation as you would with a printed message; recipients often judge you on the basis of your care and attention to detail.

Experts (DuBrin, 2018; Robbins & Judge, 2018; Uhl-Bien, Schermerhorn, & Osborn, 2016) suggest the following strategies for more productive use of e-mail:

1. *Check e-mail less often.* Some experts suggest checking e-mail twice a day. Turn off the sound indicating the arrival of new e-mail.
2. *Read e-mail messages once.* Take action immediately to reply, delete, or move to folders.
3. *Clear out your inbox.* A cluttered inbox results in a lot of rereading.
4. *Use mailing lists.* Mailing to an address list saves time. Use "reply to all" only when necessary.
5. *Unsubscribe.* Stop newsletters and other subscriptions that do not offer value to your work.
6. *Use informative subject lines.* Short subject lines avoid full-text messages.
7. *Quote messages.* Include the fragment of the sender's original message for clarification.
8. *Send to fewer people.* The best way to receive lots of e-mail is to send lots of e-mail, so send less.
9. *Be brief.* Shorter e-mails result in shorter responses. A well-written e-mail can be as concise as possible.

Instant Messaging

Instant messaging (IM) allows people who are online to share messages with one another instantaneously, without having to go through an e-mail system. Sending an instant message opens up a small onscreen window into which each party can type messages for the other to read. This makes it possible to exchange written notes in real time, as well as share Web links and files of all types. The use of IM has grown rapidly, because IM is an inexpensive alternative to multiple telephone calls and travel, creates a document trail for future reference, offers integration with voice and video, and provides the capability of carrying on several IM conversations at the same time.

Text messaging is a variant of IM. Text messaging (also called SMS, for short message service), like e-mail but unlike IM, uses portable communication devices. IM is usually sent via desktop or laptop computer, whereas SMS is transmitted via cellphones or handheld devices (Hillebrand, 2011; Sklar & Harris, 2019). IM and SMS are not likely to replace e-mail. E-mail is still a superior device for sending long messages that need to be saved.

Social Networking

Social networking is another emerging form of information technology. A well-known social networking platform is Facebook. Facebook is composed of separate networks based on schools, companies, or regions (Coombs, 2018; Perlman, 2011; Shih, 2011). In addition to Facebook, professional networking sites have entered the marketplace. Companies such as IBM and Microsoft have their own social networks. Public schools and universities are also entering the social networking arena.

Voice Mail

Voice mail is also a widely used communication mode. Some experts believe that voice behavior influences the quality of the work environment (Nelson & Quick, 2019). This has implications for the quality of voice mail as well. Because voice-mail messages are an important aspect of organizational communication, organization members are encouraged to develop the ability to leave concise, professional, and courteous voice-mail messages (Sklar & Harris, 2019). Timely retrieval of messages is important. When using voice mail, it is important to remember that the receiver may not retrieve the messages in a timely manner. Urgent messages must be delivered in person. Experts provide the following best practices for the effective use of voice mail (Falkheimer & Heide, 2018; Sklar & Harris, 2019):

- Before calling, write down the points you want to cover.
- Identify a specific, brief request that can be delivered via voice mail.
- State your name, the time and date, your affiliation, and the purpose of your call.
- Speak a little slower than usual and enunciate clearly.
- Be precise and keep the message simple.
- Say what you would like the receiver to do.
- Give a reason for the request.
- Say "thank you."
- Listen to the message and edit it, if necessary.
- End by stating your name and telephone number again and when you can be reached for a return call.

Personal Digital Assistants and Smartphones

Personal digital assistants (PDAs) and smartphones are perhaps the most widely used communication mode, which permits communication while you are away from the work site. PDAs are small handheld electronic devices that do everything from helping principals stay organized (e.g., manage a calendar, notes, and "to do list") to running popular office software like Microsoft Word and Excel; managing e-mail; and downloading Web pages, data bases, e-books, and Web clippings in real time. Some PDAs also function as phones or global positioning systems (GPSs) (Falkheimer & Heide, 2018; Hartley, 2004; Saranow & Ali, 2006; Sklar & Harris, 2019). The popularity of PDAs has grown substantially since their launch in the mid-1990s.

Fully equipped PDAs, also known as **smartphones**, are perhaps the most widely used communication mode. Smartphones combine the tasks of a PDA, laptop, phone, camera, and MP3 player all in a handheld device. By combining powerful computing entertainment, and business functions, the smartphone allows users to input spreadsheets, show videos, make phone calls, surf the Web, check e-mail, take photographs, play music, and so on. Apple, Hewlett-Packard, and Microsoft are vying for dominance over the next generation of mobile communication (Coombs, 2018; Falkheimer & Heide, 2018; Sklar & Harris, 2019).

Blogs (Web Logs)

Blogs (**Web logs**) are online diaries or journals created by people to express their personal thoughts and to comment on topics of interest to them. The benefits of blogs include the opportunity for people to discuss issues in a casual format. These discussions serve much like chat groups and thus can provide principals with insights from a wide segment of school stakeholders. The two major pitfalls of blogs are the lack of legal guidelines regarding what can be posted online and the potential for employees to say negative things about their employer and the school/school district, as well as to leak confidential information (Adams, 2018; Getgood, 2011; Sklar & Harris, 2019).

Often, organization members post some sensitive and potentially damaging information on a blog. Social networking sites such as Twitter and Facebook are a concern for most employers. On the one hand, employers do not want to suppress what many organization members believe is free and personal expression (Coombs, 2018). On the other hand, superintendents and principals are responsible for looking out for the welfare of their school districts and schools, respectively. They worry about embarrassing posts and loss of goodwill in the community (Adams, 2018). IBM has established some guidelines for posting information on blogs (Coombs, 2018; Falkheimer & Heide, 2018; Sklar & Harris, 2019).

1. Be personally responsible for any content you publish. Do not write anything you would not want your employer to read.
2. Keep in mind that what you publish could be public for a long time.
3. If you are writing about your school or school district, be transparent about your role in the organization.
4. Get approval from the school or school district before posting private or internal conversations.
5. Be ready to correct errors and update previous posts.

Some employees believe that the First Amendment gives them the right to say whatever they want on their personal blogs (Alexander & Alexander, 2019). Thus, many employers now monitor employees' Web sites at work. Some organizations have instituted policies restricting employee blogging activities. If you plan on maintaining a personal blog, be sure to install a work-personal firewall (Sklar & Harris, 2019).

Videoconferencing

Videoconferencing uses video and audio links together with computers to enable individuals in different locations to conduct meetings without getting together face-to-face. In the late 1990s, videoconferencing was conducted from special rooms equipped with television cameras. More recently, cameras and microphones are being attached to an individual's computer monitor, allowing them to participate in long-distance meetings and training sessions without leaving their offices (Raylor, 2011; Cole, 2010).

In sum, some of the electronic communication devices omit many verbal and most nonverbal cues that people use to acquire feedback. Preventing visibility and depersonalization in the workplace are concerns when using information technologies such as e-mail, instant messaging, text messaging, and videoconferencing.

Presentation Technology

Computer-generated slide software, such as **PowerPoint,** is a mode of communication currently being used in classrooms, professional conferences, and faculty meetings. Speakers supplement their talk with computer-generated slides and typically organize their presentation around their slides. Audiences have become accustomed to watching presentations accompanied by an assortment of eye-catching graphics (O'Leary, 2018; Toogood, 2011).

The communication challenge is that during these presentations, the predominant means of connection between sender and receiver should be eye contact, not the screen. The implication for presenters is to find a way to integrate speaking skills with the technology. Following are some suggestions for improving presentations using technology (O'Leary, 2018).

- *Talk to the audience, not the screen.* A problem with computer-generated PowerPoint slides is that the speaker, as well as the audience, tends to focus on the slide. Minimize looking at the slide and spend time looking at the audience. This will make it easier to make eye contact with them.
- *Provide your audience with your PowerPoint slides.* Make three to six slides per page. Some people like to follow the PowerPoint slides on screen. Others prefer to follow the hard copy and take notes. The hard copy also provides the audience with a "take away" from the meeting.
- *Reduce your PowerPoint slides to bulleted items.* A rule of thumb is: include no more than twenty-four words per slide. Use a large enough font size for the slide to be viewed at a distance of at least twenty feet.
- *Keep the slide in view long enough for the audience to comprehend its meaning.* All too often, slide presentations deteriorate into a continual array of flashings on the screen. Synchronize the slides with meaningful comments.
- *Practice learning the content of your talk (or presentation).* If you cannot memorize the content, practice reading the presentation with as much enthusiasm—variation in pitch, tone, and modulation of your voice, as well as periodic eye contact with your audience—as possible. The trick to reading a talk (or presentation) is to appear not to be reading it.
- *During the question portion of your presentation, answer questions completely and succinctly.* When answering the question, maintain eye contact with the questioner while periodically scanning the entire audience. In a large meeting, you might repeat the question for all to hear using a microphone.

In sum, some of the electronic communication devices omit many verbal and most nonverbal cues that people use to acquire feedback. Preventing visibility and depersonalization in the workplace are concerns when using information technologies such as e-mail, instant messaging, text messaging, and videoconferencing.

Choosing an Appropriate Communication Medium

Why do people choose one medium of communication over another—such as a face-to-face meeting instead of a telephone call or e-mail? In this section, we examine how principals can determine the best method or medium to use when communicating across the various formal and informal channels of communication.

Principals can choose from many different types of communication media (face-to-face, videoconference, telephone, instant messaging, e-mail, Web logs, newsletters, formal numerical documents, and so forth. Fortunately, research reveals that principals can improve communication effectiveness through their selection of communication media. If an inappropriate medium is chosen, principal decisions may be based on inaccurate information, important messages may not reach the intended receiver(s), and organization members may become dissatisfied and unproductive.

A critical factor to consider when selecting a communication medium is media richness. **Media richness** refers to the medium's capacity to convey information (Daft, 2016; Daft & Lengel, 1984; Lengel & Daft, 1988). Figure 9.6 depicts various communication channels arranged in a hierarchy of richness. As shown in figure 9.6, face-to-face communication is the richest form of communication. It provides immediate feedback and permits for the observation of multiple language cues such as body language and tone of voice. In contrast, formal numerical documents are *lean media* because feedback is very slow or nonexistent, the channels involve limited visual information, and the information provided is generic and impersonal.

The media richness hierarchy is determined by three factors. First, rich media permit a person to send messages simultaneously in different ways. For example, face-to-face communication is high in richness because it permits people to transmit their messages both verbally and nonverbally at the same time. In contrast, formal numerical documents have low media richness because the message is transmitted

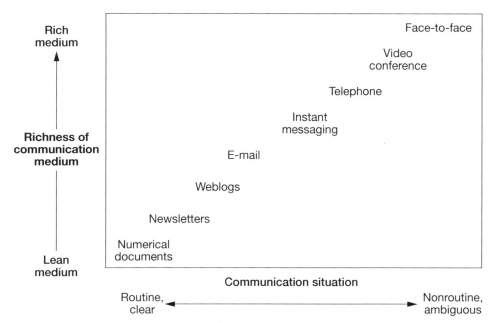

Figure 9.6 Media Richness Hierarchy

only one way (written). Second, rich media permit immediate feedback from receiver to sender, whereas feedback in lean media is slow or nonexistent. For instance, in face-to-face communication, the sender can quickly determine whether the receiver understood the message. In contrast, a person sending a formal numerical report may never know whether the message was received or understood. Third, rich media permit the sender to adapt the message to the receiver. People can easily adjust their face-to-face communication to suit the situation, whereas formal numerical documents have low media richness because everyone receives the same information.

Figure 9.6 also illustrates that rich media are better suited when the communication situation is nonroutine and ambiguous. For example, in nonroutine situations (such as an emergency) the communicator needs to transmit a large volume of information with immediate feedback. In ambiguous situations, rich media is also required because communicators must share large amounts of information with immediate feedback to comprehend possible multiple and conflicting interpretations of their observations (Rice, 1992). In contrast, lean media work best in routine situations and when the message is clear because the sender and receiver share expectations through shared experiences.

BARRIERS TO COMMUNICATION

The sender, the receiver, and the medium are the basic elements of the communication process. But unless a message is interpreted as it was meant, we still do not have communication. Misinterpretation is always possible whenever two individuals interact. The four types of communication barriers are process barriers, physical barriers, semantic barriers, and psychosocial barriers (Falkheimer & Heide, 2018; Harris & Nelson, 2018; Heath & Winni, 2018; Kreps, 2019; Mumby, 2019; Turner & West, 2018; Van der Molen & Gramsbergen-Hoogland, 2018; Wallace & Becker, 2018).

Process Barriers
Every step in the communication process is necessary for effective communication. Blocked steps become barriers. Consider the following situations:

- *Sender barrier.* A new principal with an innovative idea fails to speak up at a meeting, chaired by the superintendent, for fear of criticism.
- *Encoding barrier.* A Spanish-speaking teacher cannot get an English-speaking principal to understand a grievance about working conditions.
- *Medium barrier.* A very upset teacher sends an emotionally charged letter to the principal instead of transmitting her feelings face-to-face.
- *Decoding barrier.* An older principal is not sure what a young department head means when he refers to a teacher as "spaced out."
- *Receiver barrier.* A principal who is absorbed in preparing the annual budget asks a teacher to repeat a statement because they were not listening attentively to the conversation.
- *Feedback barrier.* During a school district meeting, the failure of principals to ask any questions causes the superintendent to wonder if any real understanding has taken place.

Because communication is a complex, give-and-take process, breakdowns anywhere in the cycle can block the transfer of understanding.

Physical Barriers

Any number of physical distractions can interfere with the effectiveness of communication, including a telephone call, drop-in visitors, distances between people, walls, and static on the radio. People often take physical barriers for granted, but sometimes they can be changed. For example, an inconveniently positioned wall can be removed. Interruptions such as telephone calls and drop-in visitors can be decreased by issuing instructions to a secretary. An appropriate choice of media can overcome distance barriers between people.

Semantic Barriers

The words we choose, how we use them, and the meaning we attach to them cause many communication barriers (Arnett, Harden Fritz, & Bell, 2009; Ihlen & Heath, 2018; Karelitz & Budescu, 2004). The problem is with semantics, or the meaning of the words we use. The same word may mean different things to different people. Words and phrases such as *efficiency*, *increased productivity*, *management prerogatives*, and *just cause* may mean one thing to the principal and something entirely different to staff.

Technology also plays a part in semantic barriers to communication (Kreitner & Kinicki, 2016; Ling, 2011; Lunenburg, 2011; McShane & Von Glinow, 2018; Nelson & Quick, 2018; Robbins & Judge, 2019; Sklar & Harris, 2019). Today's complex school districts are highly specialized. Schools have staff and technical experts developing and using specialized terminology—jargon that only other similar staff and technical experts can understand. And if people don't understand the words, they cannot understand the message.

Psychosocial Barriers

Three important concepts are associated with psychological and social barriers: fields of experience, filtering, and psychological distance (Brewer & Westerman, 2017). **Fields of experience** include people's backgrounds, perceptions, values, biases, needs, and expectations. Senders can encode and receivers decode messages only in the context of their fields of experience. When the sender's field of experience overlaps very little with the receiver's, communication becomes difficult. **Filtering** means that more often than not, we see and hear what we are emotionally tuned in to see and hear. Filtering is caused by our own needs and interests, which guide our listening. Psychosocial barriers often involve a **psychological distance** between people that is similar to actual physical distance. For example, the principal talks down to a teacher, who resents this attitude; and this resentment separates them, thereby blocking opportunity for effective communication.

Successful communication by principals is the essence of a productive school. However, as discussed previously, communications do break down. Several communication theorists (Daft, 2016; Molsching & Ryback, 2018; Nelson, 2004; Van der Molen & Gramsbergen-Hoogland, 2018) have focused on the major areas where failures in communication most frequently occur. In schools, communication breakdowns most frequently occur in these areas:

- *Sincerity.* Nearly all communication theorists assert that sincerity is the foundation on which all true communication rests. Without sincerity—honesty, straightforwardness, and authenticity—all attempts at communication are destined to fail.
- *Empathy.* Research shows that lack of empathy is a major obstacle to effective communication. Empathy is the ability to put yourself into another's shoes. The empathetic person is able to see the world through the eyes of the other person.
- *Self-perception.* How we see ourselves affects our ability to communicate effectively. A healthy but realistic self-perception is a necessary ingredient in communicating with others.
- *Role perception.* Unless people know what their role is, the importance of their role, and what is expected of them, they will not know what to communicate, when to communicate, or to whom to communicate.
- *Efforts to distort the message.* Pitfalls in communication often occur in our efforts—both consciously and unconsciously—to distort messages.
- *Images.* Another obstacle to successful communication is the sender's image of the receiver, and vice versa. For example, on the one hand, principals are sometimes viewed as not too well informed about teaching, seen as out of touch with the classroom, and looked on as paper shufflers. On the other hand, some principals view teachers as lazy, inconsiderate of administrative problems, and unrealistic about the strengths and weaknesses of their students. Such views lead to a "we-they" attitude.
- *Vehicle for message.* The vehicle by which we choose to send messages is important in successful communication. In most cases, the vehicle to be used is defined by the situation.
- *Ability to communicate.* Some of the ways we communicate raise barriers by inhibiting discussion or causing others to feel inferior, angry, hostile, dependent, compliant, or subservient.
- *Listening ability.* Frequently, people fail to appreciate the importance of listening, do not care enough to become actively involved with what others are saying, and are not sufficiently motivated to develop the skills necessary to acquire the art of listening.
- *Culture.* Our cultural heritage, biases, and prejudices often serve as barriers to communication. The facts that we are African American or White, young or old, male or female have all proved to be obstacles in communicating effectively.
- *Tradition.* Past practice in a school helps to determine how, when, and what we send and receive. For example, a principal who has an authoritative style may find that their faculty will not share information readily. If a new principal with a collaborative style replaces the authoritarian one, the new principal may find that it takes a while for their colleagues to speak out on important issues.
- *Conditioning.* The manner in which communication is conditioned by the environment influences the accuracy of messages sent and received. If we work for principals who set a climate in which we are encouraged to share information, we soon become conditioned to communicate accordingly.

- *Noise.* A major barrier to communication is what communication experts call noise. Noise consists of the external factors in the channels, and the internal perceptions and experiences within the source and the receiver that affect communication.
- *Feedback.* Faculty and staff tell their leaders that they want feedback. However, feedback improperly given can impede communication rather than improve it. Principals and followers both need more training in how to use feedback more productively.

IMPROVING COMMUNICATION EFFECTIVENESS

Effective communication is a two-way process that requires effort and skill by both sender and receiver. Principals will at times assume each of these roles in the communication process. In this section, we discuss guidelines for improving communication effectiveness, including senders' and receivers' responsibilities, listening, feedback, and nonverbal communication.

Senders' Responsibilities

Several communication theorists (Brewer & Westerman, 2017; Van der Molen & Gramsbergen-Hoogland, 2018) have gleaned ten commandments of good communication that are particularly applicable to the sender. These commandments, together with a basic understanding of the communication process itself, should provide a good foundation for developing and maintaining an effective set of interpersonal communication skills, which principals can use when communicating with various school stakeholders.

1. *Principals need to clarify their ideas before communicating.* The more systematically principals analyze the problem or idea to be communicated, the clearer it becomes. This is the first step toward effective communication. Many communications fail because of inadequate planning. Good planning must consider the goals, attitudes, and needs of those who will receive the communication and those who will be affected by it.
2. *Principals need to examine the true purpose of each communication.* Before principals communicate, they must ask themselves what they really want to accomplish with their message—obtain information, initiate action, or change another person's attitude? Principals need to identify their most important goal and then adapt their language, tone, and total approach to serve that specific objective. Principals should not try to accomplish too much with each communication. The sharper the focus of their message, the greater are its chances of success.
3. *Principals need to consider the total physical and human setting.* Meaning and intent are conveyed by more than words alone; many any other factors influence the overall impact of a communication. Principals must be sensitive to the total setting in which they communicate: the circumstances under which an announcement or decision is made; the physical setting—whether the communication is made in private or otherwise; the social climate that pervades work relationships within the school or department and sets the tone of its communications; and custom and practice—the degree to which

the communication conforms to, or departs from, the expectations of the audience. Principals need to be constantly aware of the total setting in which they communicate. Like all living things, communication must be capable of adapting to its environment.

4. *Principals need to consult with others, when appropriate, in planning communications.* Frequently, it is desirable or necessary to seek the participation of others in planning a communication or in developing the facts on which to base the communication. Such consultation often lends additional insight and objectivity to the message. Moreover, those who have helped plan the communication will give it their active support.

5. *Principals need to be mindful, while communicating, of the overtones as well as the basic content of the message.* The principal's tone of voice, expression, and apparent receptiveness to the responses of others all have tremendous impact on those the principal wishes to reach. Frequently overlooked, these subtleties of communication often affect a listener's reaction to a message even more than its basic content. Similarly, the principal's choice of language—particularly his awareness of the fine shades of meaning and emotion in the words used—predetermine, in large part, the reactions of the listeners.

6. *Principals need to take the opportunity, when it arises, to convey something of help or value to the receiver.* Consideration of the other person's interests and needs—trying to look at things from the other person's point of view—frequently points out opportunities to convey something of immediate benefit or long-range value to the other person. Staff members are most responsive to principals whose messages take staff interests into account.

7. *Principals need to follow up their communication.* A principal's best efforts at communication may be wasted, and they may never know whether they have succeeded in expressing their true meaning and intent if they do not follow up to see how well they have put the message across. A principal can do this by asking questions, by encouraging the receiver to express their reactions, by follow-up contacts and by a subsequent review of performance. A principal needs to make certain that every important communication has feedback, so that complete understanding and appropriate action result.

8. *Principals need to communicate for tomorrow as well as today.* Although communications may be aimed primarily at meeting the demands of an immediate situation, they must be planned with the past in mind if they are to maintain consistency in the receiver's view. Most important, however, is that communications are consistent with long-range interests and goals. For example, it is not easy to communicate frankly on such matters as poor performance or the shortcomings of a loyal teacher, but postponing disagreeable communications makes these matters more difficult in the long run and is actually unfair to the principal's staff and school.

9. *Principals need to be sure that their actions support their communications.* In the final analysis, the most persuasive kind of communication is not what principals say, but what they do. When principals' actions or attitudes contradict their words, others tend to discount what they have said. For every principal, this means that good supervisory practices—such as clear assignment of responsibility and authority, fair rewards for effort, and sound policy enforcement—serve to communicate more than all the gifts of oratory.

10. *Principals need to seek not only to be understood but also to understand—be a good listener.* When a principal starts talking, they often cease to listen, at least in that larger sense of being attuned to the other person's unspoken reactions and attitudes. Even more serious is the occasional inattentiveness a principal may be guilty of when others are attempting to communicate with them. Listening is one of the most important, most difficult, and most neglected skills in communication. For the principal, listening demands that they concentrate not only on the explicit meanings another person is expressing but also on the implicit meanings, unspoken words, and undertones that may be far more significant. Thus, a principal must learn to listen with the inner ear if they are to know the inner person.

Receivers' Responsibilities

Communication depends on the ability not only to send but also to receive messages. The ability to listen effectively thus greatly enhances the communication process; but many of us are not good listeners. Effective listening skills can be developed, however. Summarized, to follow, are ten rules for good listening (Newstrom, 2016):

1. *Stop talking.* You cannot listen if you are talking. As Polonius in *Hamlet* said: "Give every man thine ear, but few thy voice."
2. *Put the talker at ease.* Help a person feel free to talk. This is often called a permissive environment.
3. *Show a talker that you want to listen.* Look and act interested. Do not read your mail while someone talks. Listen to understand rather than to oppose.
4. *Remove distractions.* Don't doodle, tap, or shuffle papers. Will it be quieter if you shut the door?
5. *Empathize with the talker.* Try to help yourself see the other person's point of view.
6. *Be patient.* Allow plenty of time. Do not interrupt a talker. Don't start for the door or walk away.
7. *Hold your temper.* An angry person takes the wrong meaning from words.
8. *Go easy on argument and criticism.* These approaches put people on the defensive, and they may clam up or become angry. Do not argue: even if you win, you lose.
9. *Ask questions.* This encourages a talker and shows that you are listening. It helps to develop points further.
10. *Stop talking.* This rule is first and last, because all others depend on it. You cannot do an effective listening job while you are talking.

Nature gave people two ears but only one tongue, which may be considered a gentle hint that we should listen more than we talk. Listening requires two ears, one for meaning and one for feeling. Principals who do not listen have less information for making sound decisions.

Active Listening

Active listening is a term popularized by the work of Carl Rogers and Richard Farson (n.d.) and advocated by counselors and therapists (Brownell, 2017; Hoppe, 2007). The concept recognizes that a sender's message contains both verbal and nonverbal content as well as a feeling component. The receiver should be aware of both components in order to comprehend the total meaning of the message—for instance, when a school counselor says to the principal, "Next time you ask me to prepare a report, give me some advance notice." The content conveys that the counselor needs time, but the feeling component may indicate resentment for being pressured to meet a deadline with such short notice. The principal, therefore, must recognize this feeling to understand the counselor's message. Here are five guidelines that can help principals to become more active listeners (Rogers & Farson, n.d.):

1. *Listen for message content.* The receiver must try to hear exactly what the sender is saying in the message.
2. *Listen for feelings.* The receiver must try to identify how the sender feels regarding the message content. This can be done by asking, "What are they trying to say?"
3. *Respond to feelings.* The receiver must let the sender know that their feelings as well as the message content are recognized.
4. *Note all cues, verbal and nonverbal.* The receiver must be sensitive to the nonverbal messages as well as the verbal ones. If the receiver identifies mixed messages, they may ask for clarification.
5. *Rephrase the sender's message.* The receiver may restate or paraphrase the verbal and nonverbal messages as feedback to the sender. The receiver can do this by allowing the sender to respond with further information.

The last guideline, one of the most powerful of the active listening techniques, is used regularly by counselors and therapists. It helps the receiver avoid passing judgment or giving advice and encourages the sender to provide more information about what is really the problem.

The Art of Giving Feedback

Feedback is the process of telling other people how you feel about something they did or said (Luthans, Luthans, & Luthans, 2015). There are two types of feedback: responsive feedback and corrective feedback. **Responsive feedback** enables the sender to determine if the message has been correctly interpreted by the receiver. In any kind of oral communication, we can test understanding by asking the receiver to repeat the information. This helps to clarify any misunderstandings immediately.

Corrective feedback is the process of telling other people how you feel about their behavior or performance. Principals regularly give (corrective) feedback to other people. Such feedback is often in the form of performance evaluations or appraisals. There is an art to giving corrective feedback; it must be phrased so that the receiver will accept and use it. Corrective feedback that is poorly given can be threatening and cause resentment instead of corrective behavior change. The following list summarizes some characteristics of effective feedback for staff performance (Luthans, Luthans, & Luthans, 2015):

1. *Intention.* Effective feedback is directed toward improving job performance and making the staff member a more valuable asset. It is not a personal attack and should not compromise the individual's feeling of self-worth or image. Rather, effective feedback is directed toward aspects of the job.

2. *Specificity*. Effective feedback is designed to provide recipients with specific information so that they know what must be done to correct the situation. Ineffective feedback is general and leaves questions in the recipients' minds. For example, telling a staff member that they are doing a poor job is too general and will leave the recipient frustrated in seeking ways to correct the problem.

3. *Description*. Effective feedback can also be characterized as descriptive rather than evaluative. It tells the staff member what they have done in objective terms, rather than presenting a value judgment.

4. *Usefulness*. Effective feedback is information that a staff member can use to improve performance. It serves no purpose to berate staff for their lack of skill if they do not have the ability or training to perform properly. Thus, the guideline is that if the feedback is not related to something the staff member can correct, it is not worth mentioning.

5. *Timeliness*. There are also considerations in timing feedback properly. As a rule, the more immediate the feedback, the better. This way the staff member has a better chance of knowing what the principal is talking about and can take corrective action.

6. *Readiness*. For feedback to be effective, staff must be ready to receive it. When feedback is imposed or forced on staff members, it is much less effective.

7. *Clarity*. Effective feedback must be clearly understood by the recipient. A good way of checking is to ask the recipient to restate the major points of the discussion. Also, principals can observe nonverbal facial expressions as indicators of understanding and acceptance.

8. *Validity*. To be effective, feedback must be reliable and valid. Of course, when the information is incorrect, the staff member will feel that the principal is unnecessarily biased, or the staff member may take corrective action that is inappropriate and only compounds the problem.

PERSUASIVE COMMUNICATION

The more effective principals use a persuasive rather than a directive or autocratic leadership style. All principals must exercise power and influence if they are to ensure staff member performance and achieve results (Lunenburg, 2016). These effective principals are characterized by their use of persuasive communication when influencing others. Specifically, they encourage staff members to achieve results rather than telling them what to do. They avoid highly directive or manipulative behavior in their attempts to influence staff members. Researchers have referred to this approach as the **sleeper or delayed influence** in communication (Kumkale & Albarracin, 2004). The exception to this pattern of communication occurs in emergencies, in which case the principal must be directive and assertive.

A major part of being persuasive involves choosing the right linguistic style. According to Deborah Tannen (1995), linguistic style involves a person's speaking pattern such as the amount of directness used, pacing and pausing, word choice, and the use of such communication devices as jokes, figures of speech, anecdotes, questions, and apologies. Due to the complexity of linguistic style, it is difficult to offer specific prescriptions for using a persuasive linguistic style. Nevertheless, following are several components of a linguistic style that would give power and authority to a leader's communication (Ciadini, 2001; DuBrin, 2018; Tannen, 1995, 1998, 2000):

334 ■ Chapter 9: Communication

- Choose words that show conviction, such as "I'm convinced" or "I'm confident that . . .", and avoid words that convey doubt or hesitancy, such as "I think" or "I hope." Be bold when expressing ideas, without attacking people.
- Intensify your writing with action verbs such as "spearheaded," "expanded," "innovated," and "annihilated."
- Emphasize direct rather than indirect talk, such as saying, "I need your report by 3 p.m. tomorrow." Instead of, "I'm wondering if your report will be available by 3 p.m. tomorrow."
- Frame your statements in a way that increases your listeners' receptivity. For example, when pinpointing a problem that is elusive, use the frame "Let's dig a little deeper." Your purpose is to enlist the help of others in finding the underlying nature of the problem.
- Set the agenda for a conversation, speak at length, make jokes, and laugh. Be prepared to offer solutions to problems, as well as suggest a plan. All of these points are more likely to create a sense of confidence in listeners.
- Minimize the number of questions you ask that imply that you lack information on a topic, such as "What do you mean by RTI, ARD, or IEP?"
- Apologize infrequently and minimize saying, "I'm sorry."
- Take deep breaths to project a firm voice. Most people associate voice with power and conviction.
- Occupy as much space as possible when speaking before a group. Stand with your feet approximately 18 inches apart, and place your hands on your hips occasionally. The triangle you create with arms occupy space, and the hands-on-hips gesture symbolizes power to most people.
- Let others know of your expertise because people tend to defer to experts. Mention how much experience you have had in a particular phase of your profession to get organization members to take your message seriously. A principal might say, "I've brought two schools out of crisis before, and I can do it again for us right now."

Despite the aforementioned suggestions for developing a persuasive linguistic style, Tannen (1995) suggests that there is no one best way to communicate. How to project your power and authority is frequently dependent on the people involved, the organizational culture, and other situational variables. The persuasive linguistic style should be viewed as a general guideline. Another consideration is that you may not want to project a powerful, authoritative image at all. Some principals and other high-ranking professionals may prefer to play a more laid-back, behind-the-scenes role.

SUMMARY

1. Communication is the process of transmitting information and common understanding from one person to another.
2. The elements of the communication process are sending the message, encoding the message, transmitting the message through a medium, receiving the message, decoding the message, feedback, and noise.

3. Communications flow in three directions—downward, upward, laterally.
4. Downward communication consists of policies, rules, and procedures that flow from top administration to lower levels. Upward communication consists of the flow of performance reports, grievances, and other information from lower to higher levels. Horizontal communication is essentially coordinative and occurs between departments or divisions on the same level.
5. Organizational communication also flows through formal network patterns. The five most common networks are the chain, Y, wheel, circle, and all-channel. Besides network patterns, another method to help principals analyze communication flows and patterns is network analysis.
6. Also existing in schools is an informal communication network—the grapevine—that can serve as another important source of information to principals.
7. Many barriers retard effective communication. These can be divided into four categories: process barriers, physical barriers, semantic barriers, and psychosocial barriers.
8. To improve the effectiveness of communications, schools must develop an awareness of the importance of sender and receiver responsibilities, active listening skills, feedback, and nonverbal communication.
9. Principals can choose from many different types of communication media (face-to-face, video conference, telephone, instant messaging, e-mail, Web logs, newsletters, formal numerical documents, and so forth). Fortunately, research reveals that principals can improve communication effectiveness through their selection of communication media. If an inappropriate medium is chosen principal decisions may be based on inaccurate information, important messages may not reach the intended receiver(s), and organization members may become dissatisfied and unproductive.
10. All principals must exercise power and influence if they are to ensure staff member performance and achieve results. These effective principals are characterized by their use of persuasive communication when influencing others. Specifically, they encourage staff members to achieve results rather than telling them what to do. They avoid highly directive or manipulative behavior in their attempts to influence staff members. Researchers have referred to this approach as the sleeper or delayed influence in communication. The exception to this pattern of communication occurs in emergencies, in which case the principal must be directive and assertive.

KEY TERMS

communication
nonverbal communication
kinesics
proxemics

feng shui
paralanguage
chronemics
communication flow

downward communication
MUM effect
upward communication
management by walking around
  (WBWA)
climate surveys
360-degree feedback
participative management
suggestion programs
quality circles
total quality management (TQM)
professional learning community
  (PLC)
horizontal communication
boundary spanners
network
ombudsperson
grapevine
rumor
pipe dreams
bogie rumors
wedge drivers
home-stretchers
chain network
Y network

wheel network
circle network
all-channel network
network analysis
e-mail
flaming
instant messaging (IM)
text messaging
voice mail
personal digital assistants (PDAs)
smart phones
blogs (Web logs)
videoconferencing
presentation technology
PowerPoint
media richness
fields of experience
filtering
psychological distance
active listening
feedback
responsive feedback
corrective feedback
sleeper or delayed influence

FIELD-BASED ACTIVITIES

1. Take field notes for one week and observe the organizational communication flow in your school in four directions: downward, upward, horizontally, and diagonally. Describe how each direction of communication flow is functioning in your school. What can you conclude from your observations? Write your responses in your journal. Be specific.

2. Using this text as your guide, consider the barriers to effective communication that exist in your school: process barriers, physical barriers, semantic barriers, and psychosocial barriers. For each category, discuss barriers to effective communication found in your school. Record your findings in your journal.

3. Imagine that you are the principal of a school. Assuming that communication can always be improved, consider the specific techniques you would use to improve communication in your school relative to (a) awareness of the importance of the sender's and receiver's responsibilities, (b) active listening, (c) feedback, and (d) nonverbal communication. Address each of these areas. Write your communication improvement plan in your journal. Be specific.

SUGGESTED READINGS

Dempster, K., & Robbins, J. (2017). *How to build communication success in your school: A guide for school leaders*. New York, NY: Taylor & Francis. The authors provide a step-by-step guide to achieve best practice communication within schools.

Magette, K. (2018). *The social media imperative: School leadership strategies for success*. Lanham, MD: Rowman & Littlefield. The author provides a practical guide to help school leaders understand how to use live video, social leadership, and effective monitoring to increase, engage, and, ultimately, build trust.

Porterfield, K., & Carnes, M. (2014). *Why school communication matters: Strategies from PR professionals*. Lanham, MD: Rowman & Littlefield. *Why School Communication Matters* is a reference for the communication dilemmas that superintendents, principals, and other school leaders face today as they lead faculty, staff, parents, and students.

Stephenson, K. T. (2016). *School administrators' communication guide: 100 letters and memos you cannot lead without*. Self published. *School Administrators' Communication Guide* is a resource manual consisting of more than one hundred letters and memos used by school leaders to communicate with staff, students, and parents.

Wolter, D. L. (2021). *Restorative literacies: Creating a community of care in schools*. New York, NY: Teachers College Press. Restorative literacies are not just about growing readers and writers, per se. They are about creating a community of care where all students experience racially, culturally, and economically responsive instruction.

Zipke, M. (2021). *Playing with language: Improving elementary reading through metalinguistic awareness*. New York, NY: Teachers College Press. The cognitive skill known as metalinguistic awareness is an important component of reading ability. Marcy Zipke offers suggestions for introducing metalinguistic concepts like phonological, semantic, and syntactic awareness and provides teaching strategies and activities scaled to students' age, linguistic background, and individual strengths and challenges.

10
Organizational Change and Stress Management

■ ■ ■

FOCUSING QUESTIONS

1. What are the forces that bring about the need for change in schools?
2. Why do school employees resist change?
3. What strategies can principals use to overcome resistance to change?
4. What models can principals use to manage change?
5. What professional development techniques can assist in the change process?
6. What are the sources of work stress principals experience on the job?
7. How does job stress affect principal performance?
8. What strategies can principals use to cope with job stress?

In this chapter, we respond to these questions concerning change in school organizations and stress management of principals. We begin our discussion by examining the forces for change, resistance to change, and strategies for overcoming resistance. Next, we examine four models that principals can use to manage change: Lewin's force-field analysis, Kotter's eight-step plan, Harris's five-phase model, and Greiner's six-phase change process. Then we present and analyze eight organizational development techniques designed to plan and implement change. The first set of techniques include process strategies: survey feedback, sensitivity training, behavioral performance management, and quality of work life. The next set of techniques includes structural approaches to change: goal setting, job redesign, strategic planning, and total quality management. Finally, we examine the job stress of principals including sources of stress, stress and performance, and coping strategies.

FORCES FOR CHANGE

The role of the principal is both intense and diverse. Paradoxically, the only constant in the principal's domain of ever-increasing responsibilities is that of change—change in the physical environment; change in the curriculum; change in faculty and staff; change in the student body; unexpected change; and, most importantly, change that can bring about vast improvement in the growth and development of the entire school. The principal must be the primary catalyst in order for change to be both positive and lasting (Fullan & Gallagher, 2020; Reeves, 2021).

In relation to a school building, we define **organizational change** as any modification in one or more elements of the school (Fahey et al., 2019). Practically everything a principal does is in some way concerned with implementing change. Hiring a new teacher (changing the work group), purchasing a computer (changing work methods), and developing curriculum (changing subject-matter content) all require knowledge of how to manage change effectively. Virtually every time a principal makes a decision, some type of change occurs. We discuss six specific forces stimulating change: accountability; changing demographics; staffing shortages; technological changes and knowledge explosion; process and behavior problems; and indicators of declining effectiveness (Andler, 2019; Emery, 2019; Fullan, 2015, 2018; Hodges, 2018, 2019; Hughes, 2018; Lewis, 2019; Noumair & Shani, 2018; Pasmore, Barnes, & Gipson, 2018).

Accountability
School administrators have always had to deal with bureaucratic accountability, that is, accountability with respect to superordinate-subordinate relationships. For example, the teacher is accountable to the principal; the principal is accountable to the superintendent; the superintendent is accountable to the school board. However, accountability to constituencies external to the local school board increasingly drives accountability frameworks today. The business community pressures schools to graduate skilled workers for today's economy. Governors and state legislators play key roles in designing accountability plans. The national education plan, titled Every Student Succeeds Act (ESSA) of 2015, stipulates specific requirements that states must follow regarding student accountability.

As accountability has become more prominent at the state and national levels, the focus has shifted from accountability for inputs to accountability for outcomes. This is reflected in state standards and testing. Presently, all fifty states have statewide assessment systems in place, and in nearly half of the states the stakes attached to these outcomes have been gradually increased (Popham, 2010, 2020). Furthermore, each state is required to implement a statewide system of assessment in reading, mathematics, and science for grades three through twelve.

Another new form of accountability is market accountability. Open enrollment policies, which allow students to choose public schools within and outside their home districts, have become popular (Schneider, 2016). In addition, there has been growing political support for nontraditional methods of funding public schools, such as the expansion of homeschooling, tuition tax credits, charter schools, and school vouchers (Lunenburg, 2015). Such an expansion of public school–choice frameworks has forced some school principals to reallocate their time from internal to external functions, such as marketing and fundraising.

Changing Demographics
Currently, enrollment in public schools is growing. Higher enrollment is generally associated with greater ethnic, racial, and linguistic diversity, a school population that has the greatest level of needs. The National Center for Education Statistics, US Department of Education (2020) reported that the public school enrollment in fall 2018 was 50.7 million students, private school enrollment was 5.7 million students, and charter school enrollment was 3.3 million students. Out of the nation's more than 50 million public school students, 47 percent are White, 15.1 percent

are African American, 27.2 percent are Hispanic, 5.6 percent are Asian or Pacific Islander, and 0.97 percent are American Indian or Alaskan Native (Hussar et al., 2020). Ethnicity is closely related to poverty and dropout rates. For example, 36.2 percent of African American and 33.6 percent of Hispanic families with children lived in poverty in 2014 compared to only 12.5 percent of White families (DeNavas-Walt & Proctor, 2015). And African American and Hispanic students are much more likely to drop out of school than White students.

Immigration is also creating demographic changes in public schools. According to estimates, nearly 1 million legal and illegal immigrants come to the United States every year. From 2000 to 2015, 84 percent of legal immigrants to the United States came from non-European countries. Most of these immigrants came from Asia (principally China, the Philippine Islands, and India) and the Americas (principally Mexico, the Caribbean, and South America) and settled in the major cities of California, New York, Florida, and Texas. In the fifteen-year period from 2000 through 2014, more than 14.5 million legal immigrants arrived in the United States, an all-time US immigration record (US Department of Homeland Security, 2015). Many of these immigrants and their children are poor and have limited English proficiency, which places greater demands on educating these students and has increased political debates about bilingual education and testing (Barbian, Gonzales, & Mejia, 2017; Jaumont, 2017).

These figures indicate that the United States is rapidly becoming an even more ethnically diverse nation than ever before, and certain states (e.g., California, New York, Florida, and Texas) already have very large immigrant populations.

Staffing Shortages
After many years of having a steady stream of qualified teachers and principals, many school districts are facing severe shortages (US Department of Education, 2015). Shortages of teachers and administrators are due largely to retirements, an expanding student population, career changes, and increasing teacher and administrator turnover. Expanding student enrollment, in general, and a growing population of students with special needs may further exacerbate these shortages, especially in areas such as special education and bilingual education (Garcia & Kleifgen, 2018; Graham, Renaud, & Rose, 2020).

Another issue facing school principals is increasing the racial and ethnic diversity of teaching personnel. Although the student population is growing racially and ethnically more diverse, similar demographic shifts have not occurred in the teaching ranks (Cowan, 2010). The teaching force is predominately White (80.1 percent), with the remainder coming from minority groups (19.9 percent) (National Center for Education Statistics, 2018). The student-teacher mismatch often results in considerable cultural and social distance between the middle-class White teachers and students of color. It has been suggested that White educators and school principals do not have a thorough enough understanding of how to deal with students from different cultural backgrounds (Horton, Martin, & Fasching-Varner, 2017). This mismatch may have learning consequences for students of color (Hess & Noguera, 2021). Teacher preparation programs rarely train teacher candidates in strategies for teaching culturally diverse students (Lunenburg, 2013c). The lack of familiarity with students' cultures, learning styles, and communication patterns translates into some teachers holding negative expectations for students (Atay & Toyosaki, 2018). And, often, inappropriate curricula, instructional materials, and assessments are used with these students (Gershon, 2017).

Technological Changes and Knowledge Explosion

Another source of external pressure for change is the technological explosion that all organizations are experiencing. This pressure is due in part to research and development efforts within organizations. For example, many large, urban school districts now have research and development departments as part of their organizational structures. However, a great deal of technological development occurs outside the organization. This development is the result of government-sponsored research efforts and the efforts of numerous educational organizations including the American Association of School Administrators (AASA), National Association of Secondary School Principals (NASSP), National Association of Elementary School Principals (NAESP), Cooperative Program in Educational Administration (CPEA), University Council for Educational Administration (UCEA), International Council of Professors of Educational Leadership (ICPEL), National Academy for School Executives (NASE), Association for Supervision and Curriculum Development (ASCD), National Society for the Study of Education (NSSE), and the American Educational Research Association (AERA).

Concurrent with the development of new technologies is an explosion of knowledge. More people than ever before are attending college, and a large percentage of the population is receiving graduate degrees (Loughead, 2018). Higher education is no longer reserved for the elite few (Lathe, 2018). There is also a growing emphasis on continuing education courses offered on university campuses across the country, and nontraditional students (older students) are returning to community colleges and four-year institutions. New technologies require the development of knowledge to implement the technology. Thus, the interaction of new technology and the knowledge required to generate the technology into the organization compounds the rate of technological change exponentially.

Process and Behavioral Problems

Pressures in the internal environment of the organization that can stimulate change usually can be traced to process and behavioral problems. The process problems include communications, decision making, leadership, and motivational strategies, to name only a few. Breakdowns or problems in any of these processes can create pressures for change. Communications may be inadequate; decisions may be of poor quality; leadership may be inappropriate for the situation; and employee motivation may be nonexistent.

Some symptoms of behavioral problems are poor performance levels of teachers and students (low disaggregated test scores), high absenteeism of teachers or students, high dropout rates of students, high teacher turnover, poor school-community relations, poor management-union relations, and low levels of teacher morale and job satisfaction. A teachers' strike, numerous employee complaints, and the filing of grievances are some tangible signs of problems in the internal environment. These factors provide a signal to school principals that change is necessary. In addition, internal pressures for change occur in response to organizational changes that are designed to deal with forces for change exerted by the external environment.

Indicators of Declining Effectiveness

Schools/school districts have a number of ways of determining how they are doing by looking at indicators from their own or their states' management information systems. A state/school district/school monitors data on disaggregated test scores, attendance, demographics, teacher-pupil ratios, and operating costs. Some schools/school districts also conduct regular climate surveys of their personnel, which may reveal declining trends in personnel morale, commitment, and motivation. Others have systematic methods of obtaining feedback from the community. Other methods of monitoring indicators of effectiveness may involve sampling the opinion of parents the school/school district serves, noting trends in formally registered complaints and grievances, or more informally noting the percentage of time spent off-task in classrooms.

RESISTANCE TO CHANGE

Forces for change are a recurring feature of school life. It is also inevitable that change will be resisted, at least to some extent, by both school leaders and staff. There is a human tendency to resist change, because it forces people to adopt new ways of doing things. To cope with this recurring problem, principals must understand why people resist change. We discuss eight causes of resistance to change: uncertainty, concern over personal loss, group resistance, dependence, trust, organic and mechanistic structures, awareness of weaknesses in the proposal, and collective bargaining agreements (deBiasi, 2018; Emery, 2019; Hodges, 2018, 2019; Hughes, 2018; Jabri, 2018; Lewis, 2019; Pasmore, Barnes, & Gipson, 2018; ten Have & ten Have, 2018).

Uncertainty

Teachers may resist change because they are worried about how their work and lives will be affected by the proposed change. Even if they have some appreciable dissatisfaction with their present jobs, they have learned their range of responsibilities and know how their principal will react to their behavior in certain situations. Any change creates some potential uncertainties.

Concern over Personal Loss

Appropriate change should benefit the school as a whole; but for some teachers, the cost of change in terms of lost power, prestige, salary, quality of work, or other benefits will not be sufficiently offset by the rewards of change. Teachers may feel that change will diminish not only their decision-making authority, accessibility to information, and autonomy, but also the inherent characteristics of the job.

Group Resistance

Groups establish norms of behavior and performance that are communicated to members. This communication establishes the boundaries of expected behaviors. Failure to comply with such norms usually results in sanctions against group members by the group. If principals initiate changes that are viewed as threatening to the staff's norms, they are likely to meet with resistance. The more cohesive the staff is, the greater its resistance to change will be (Lunenburg & Lunenburg, 2015). This may explain partially what causes wildcat strikes by teachers when school districts introduce changes without proper notification and preparation.

Dependence

All humans begin life in a dependent state. Thus, dependence is instilled in all people to a certain extent. Dependency, in and of itself, is not all bad; but if carried to extremes, dependency on others can lead to resistance to change. For instance, staff members who are highly dependent on their principal for feedback on their performance will probably not adopt any new methods or strategies unless the principal personally endorses their behavior and indicates how the proposed changes will improve the teacher's performance.

Trust

Schools vary substantially in the degree to which teachers trust the principal. On the one hand, if a change is proposed when trust is low, a natural first reaction is to resist it. On the other hand, when trust is high, teachers are more likely to support a proposed change (deBiasi, 2018). Further, under conditions of distrust, teachers often resist changes, even when they are understood and they can benefit from them (Parini-Alemanno & Benoit, 2019).

Organic and Mechanistic Structures

Mechanistic structures are more resistant to change. The term **mechanistic structure** is used to describe an organizational structure that is designed to induce organization members to behave in predictable, accountable ways. Tall hierarchies, centralized decision making, and the standardization of behavior through rules and procedures characterize mechanistic structures. In contrast, the term **organic structure** is used to describe an organizational structure that is designed to promote flexibility so that organization members can initiate change and adapt quickly to changing conditions. Organic structures are flat and decentralized and rely on mutual adjustment between people to get the job done (Burns & Stalker, 1961). The extensive use of mutual adjustment and decentralized authority in an organic structure fosters the development of skills that enable organization members to be creative, responsive, and find solutions to new problems (Hage, 1965). Shared work norms and values become the main means through which organization members coordinate their activities to achieve school/school district goals.

Awareness of Weaknesses in the Proposed Change

Teachers may resist change because they are aware of potential problems in the proposed change. If teachers express their reasons for resistance to the principal clearly, along with adequate substantiation, this form of resistance can be beneficial to the school. Principals can use these suggestions to make their change proposals more effective.

Collective Bargaining Agreements

The most pervasive changes in educational policy matters have been brought about by the practice of negotiating formally with the teachers' union and other employee unions in a school district. Agreements between management and union usually impose obligations on participants that can restrain their behaviors. Collective bargaining agreements are a good example—that is, ways of doing things that were once considered management prerogatives may become subject to negotiation and be fixed in the collective bargaining agreement (Lunenburg, 2000). Some examples include salaries, cost-of-living adjustments (COLA), class size, teacher transfer, school calendar, class hours, evaluations, and promotions. Such agreements restrain the behavior of school principals from implementing desired changes in the system.

OVERCOMING RESISTANCE TO CHANGE

Resistance to change may be overcome in several specific ways. We examine seven of the most popular and frequently used approaches (deBiasi, 2018; Emery, 2019; Hodges, 2018, 2019; Hughes, 2018; Jabri, 2018; Lewis, 2019; Pasmore, Barnes, & Gipson, 2018; ten Have & ten Have, 2018).

Education and Communication

Resistance can be reduced when principals communicate with teachers to help them see the need for change as well as the logic behind it. This can be achieved through face-to-face discussions, formal group presentations, and special reports or publications. The approach works, providing that the source of resistance is inadequate communication and that principal-teacher relations are characterized by mutual trust. If trust does not exist, the change is unlikely to succeed

Participation and Involvement

Teachers who participate in planning and implementing a change are less likely to resist it. Before making a change, principals can allow those who oppose the change to express their view on the change, indicate potential problems, and suggest modifications. Such participant involvement can reduce resistance, obtain commitment, and increase the quality of the change decision.

Facilitation and Support

It is important for principals to manifest supportive and facilitative leadership behaviors when change is being implemented. This type of leader behavior includes listening to teachers' ideas, being approachable, and using teachers' ideas that have merit. Supportive principals go out of their way to make the work environment more pleasant and enjoyable. For example, difficult changes may require staff development to acquire new skills necessary to implement the change. Such training will likely diminish resistance to the change.

Negotiation and Agreement

Principals can neutralize potential or actual resistance by providing incentives for cooperation. For example, during collective bargaining between the school board and the teachers' union, certain concessions can be given to teachers in exchange for support of a new program desired by principals. Such concessions may include salary increases, bonuses, or more union representation in decision making (Lunenburg, 2011d). Principals can also use standard rewards such as recognition, increased responsibility, praise, and status symbols.

Manipulation and Co-optation

Manipulation occurs when principals choose to be selective about who gets what information and how much information, how accurate the information is, and when to disseminate the information to increase the chance that change will be successful. **Co-optation** involves giving the leaders of a resistance group (teachers or other staff members who represent their work group) a key role in the change decision. The leaders' advice is sought not to arrive at a better decision, but to get their endorsement. Both manipulation and co-optation are inexpensive ways to influence potential resisters to accept change, but these techniques can back-fire if the targets become aware they are being tricked. Once such tricks are discovered, the principal's credibility may suffer drastically.

Action Learning

When a school introduces a new innovation, teachers and support staff must learn how to adapt their previous behavior patterns to the change. **Action learning** occurs when teachers and support staff, usually in teams, investigate and apply solutions to a problem with immediate relevance to the school/school district (McShane & Von Glinow, 2018). In other words, the task becomes the source of learning. Action learning requires concrete experience with a real organizational problem or opportunity, followed by "learning meetings" in which participants reflect on their observations about that problem and opportunity. Then they develop and test a strategy to solve the problem or realize the opportunity. The process also encourages reflection, so the experience becomes a learning process.

Explicit and Implicit Coercion

When other approaches have failed, coercion can be used as a last resort. Some changes require immediate implementation. And change initiators may have considerable power. Such instances lend themselves more readily to the use of **coercion** to gain compliance to proposed changes. Teachers and other staff can be threatened with job loss, decreased promotional opportunities, salary freeze (this technique is used infrequently in public schools), or a job transfer. There are, however, negative effects of using coercion—including frustration, fear, revenge, and alienation—which in turn may lead to poor performance, dissatisfaction, and turnover.

MANAGING CHANGE

Now we will examine several approaches to managing change: Lewin's three-step model, Kotter's eight-step plan, Harris's five-phase model, and Greiner's six-phase process. Let's review them briefly.

Lewin: Force-Field Analysis

To better understand resistance to change, Kurt Lewin (1951) developed the concept of **force-field analysis**. He looks upon a level of behavior within a school not as a static custom, but as a dynamic balance of forces working in opposite directions within the school. He believes that we should think about any change situation in terms of driving forces or factors acting to change the current condition (forces for change) and resisting forces or factors acting to inhibit change (resistance to change).

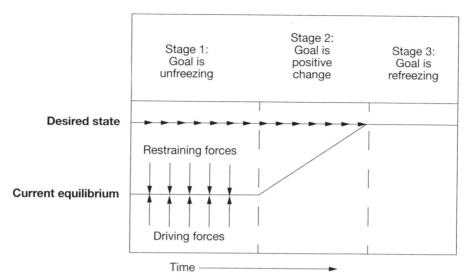

Figure 10.1 Lewin's Force-Field Analysis

These forces may originate in the internal or external environment of the school or in the behavior of the principal (see figure 10.1).

Principals must play an active role in initiating change and in attempting to reduce resistance to change. Principals can think of the current condition in a school as an equilibrium that is the result of driving forces and resisting forces working against each other. Principals must assess the change potential and resistance and then attempt to change the balance of forces so that there will be movement toward a desired condition. There are three ways principals can do this: increasing the driving forces, reducing the resisting forces, or considering new driving forces.

Lewin points out that increasing one set of forces without decreasing the other set of forces will increase tension and conflict in the school. Reducing the other set of forces may reduce the amount of tension. Although increasing driving forces is sometimes effective, it is usually better to reduce the resisting forces because increasing driving forces often tends to be offset by increased resistance. Put another way, when we push people, they are likely to push back. Figure 10.1 illustrates the two sets of forces discussed earlier: forces for change—accountability, changing demographics, staffing shortages, technological changes and knowledge explosion, process and behavioral problems, and indicators of declining effectiveness, and resistance to change—uncertainty, concern over personal loss, group resistance, dependence, trust in the principal, organic and mechanistic structures, awareness of weaknesses in the proposed change, and collective bargaining agreements. These are the types of situations that principals face and must work with on a daily basis when attempting to effect change.

As shown in figure 10.1, change results when an imbalance occurs between the ratio of driving forces and resisting forces. Such an imbalance alters the existing condition—ideally, in the direction planned by the principal—into a new and desired condition. Once the new, desired condition is reached, the opposing forces are again brought into equilibrium. An imbalance may occur through a change in the velocity of any force, a change in the direction of a force, or the introduction of a new force.

Moreover, change involves a sequence of organizational processes that occur over time. Lewin suggests these processes typically require three steps: unfreezing, moving, and refreezing.

Step 1: Unfreezing. This step usually means reducing the forces acting to keep the school in its current condition. **Unfreezing** might be accomplished by introducing new information that points out inadequacies in the current state or by decreasing the strength of current values, attitudes, and behaviors. Crises often stimulate unfreezing. Examples of crises are significant increases in the student dropout rate, dramatic enrollment declines, shifts in population within a school, a sudden increase in teacher or principal turnover, a costly lawsuit, and an unexpected teacher strike. Unfreezing may occur without crises as well. Climate surveys, financial data, and enrollment projections can be used to determine problem areas in a school and initiate change to alleviate problems before crises erupt.

Step 2: Moving. Once the school is unfrozen, it can be changed by **moving**. This step usually involves the development of new values, attitudes, and behaviors through internalization, identification, or change in structure. Some changes may be minor and involve a few members—such as changes in recruitment and selection procedures—and others may be major, involving many participants. Examples of the latter include a new evaluation system, restructuring of jobs and duties performed by staff, or restructuring the school district, which necessitates relocating faculty to different school sites within the system.

Step 3: Refreezing. The final step in the change process involves stabilizing the change at a new quasi-stationary equilibrium, which is called **refreezing**. Changes in school culture, changes in staff norms, changes in school policy, or modifications in school structure often accomplish this. Figure 10.1 illustrates force-field analysis that shows both the pressures for change and resistance to change within a school setting.

Kotter: Eight-Step Plan

Building on Lewin's force field analysis model, John Kotter (1996) of Harvard University developed a more detailed approach for managing change. Kotter begins by listing common errors that administrators make when attempting to initiate change. These include: the inability to create a sense of urgency about the need for change; failure to create a coalition for managing the change process; the absence of a vision for change; failure to effectively communicate that vision; failure to remove obstacles that could impede the achievement of the vision; failure to provide short-term achievable goals; the tendency to declare victory too soon; and failure to anchor the changes into the organization's culture. Based on the errors, Kotter proposes an eight-step process for managing change (see table 10.1).

Note how Kotter's steps build on Lewin's model. Kotter's first four steps represent Lewin's "unfreezing" stage. Steps 5 through 7 represent Lewin's "moving" stage. The final step corresponds to Lewin's "refreezing" stage. Thus, Kotter's contribution provides school principals and change agents with a more detailed guide for managing change successfully.

Table 10.1 Steps in Managing Organizational Change

Step	Description
1. Establish a sense of urgency.	Unfreeze the organization by creating a compelling reason for why change is needed.
2. Create the guiding coalition.	Create a cross-functional, cross-level group of people with enough power to lead the change.
3. Develop a vision and strategy.	Create a vision and strategic plan to guide the change process.
4. Communicate the change vision.	Create and implement a communication strategy that consistently communicates the new vision and strategic plan.
5. Empower broad-based action.	Eliminate barriers to change, and use target elements of change to transform the organization. Encourage risk taking and creative problem solving.
6. Generate short-term wins.	Plan for and create short-term "wins" or improvements. Recognize and reward people who contribute to the wins.
7. Consolidate gains and produce more change.	The guiding coalition uses credibility from short-term wins to create more change. Additional people are brought into the change process as change cascades throughout the organization. Attempts are made to reinvigorate the change process.
8. Anchor new approaches in the culture.	Reinforce the changes by highlighting connections between new behaviors and processes and organizational success. Develop methods to ensure leadership development and succession.

Harris: Five-Phase Model

Ben Harris (1975), formerly of The University of Texas, created a five-stage model for managing change. (See figure 10.2.) He stated that these phases come in a sequential order, but they often overlap one another. Each phase will be discussed briefly.

Phase I: Planning and Initiation.   The purpose of the change is considered, goals are clarified, activities are selected, and resources needed are considered. Interest mounts as individuals involved sense the relationships between the change and its goals and their needs.

Phase II: Momentum.   Goal-directed activities get underway. Resources begin to be used. Interest continues to be high and mounts. Feelings of involvement and personal worth grow. The activities are recognized as potentially satisfying. Leading and organizing processes are most heavily employed in this phase.

Phase III: Problems.   Activities lead to unexpected problems. The plans become increasingly complex. Initial activities lead to a proliferation of still more activities. Certain resources are not readily available. Differences in goal perception among group members become apparent. The demands of other responsibilities produce conflicts. The goal seems more remote and more difficult to attain than before. Some participants fail to live up to expectations. Interest levels out and begins a steep decline. Leadership involvement is crucial during this phase.

Phase IV: Turning Point.   The problem trends described in the previous phase either continue to grow or are overcome and minimized. The momentum the change has gained, the effectiveness of initial planning, and the individuals in the operation are all quite important during this phase. Above all, the amount and quality of leadership continues to be crucial.

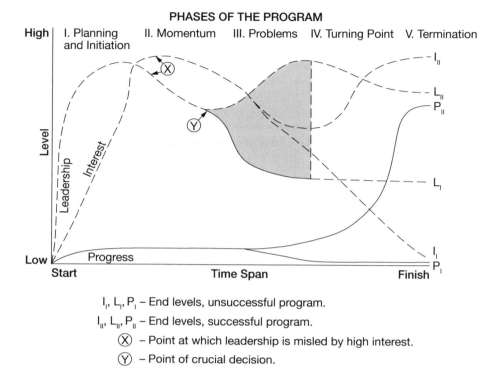

PHASES OF THE PROGRAM

I_I, L_I, P_I – End levels, unsuccessful program.

I_{II}, L_{II}, P_{II} – End levels, successful program.

Ⓧ – Point at which leadership is misled by high interest.

Ⓨ – Point of crucial decision.

▓ – Critical leadership investment.

Figure 10.2 Harris's Five-Phase Change Model

Phase V: Termination.   There can be such expected problems as: the task is too complex; there is a lack of resources; there is pressure of other responsibilities; and interest is waning, and consensus to proceed has still not been reached. This will result in termination of efforts because goal-directed activities will rapidly deteriorate and come to a halt. If, on the other hand, problems are dealt with promptly; the task is analyzed and simplified; new resources are made available; and goals are clarified, then interest gradually mounts again and goal directed activities proceed at an increasing pace. Interest is now based on a sense of anticipated accomplishment and personal worth.

This sequence of events points out the importance of leadership at various phases of the change process. Undoubtedly, this sequence of events will have variations and exceptions depending on the change, activities, and the participants involved.

Greiner: Six-Phase Process

Another well-known and popular model of the change process emphasizes the role of the change agent (Greiner, 1967). A **change agent** is the individual, from inside or outside the school or school district, who takes a leadership role in initiating the change process. In many cases, the change agent is the building principal.

As you study this change process, notice that it must involve two basic ideas for the change to be effective. First, successful change requires a redistribution of power within the existing structure. Successful change is characterized by a greater degree

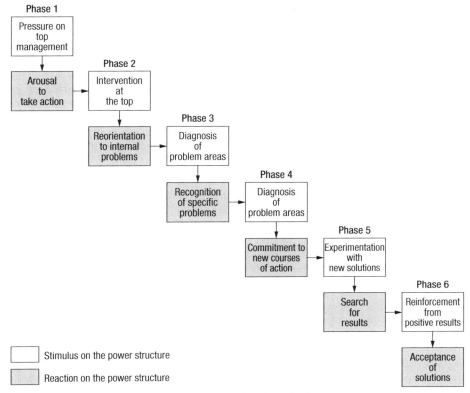

Figure 10.3 Model of Successful Organizational Change

of shared power within the organizational hierarchy. Second, this redistribution of power occurs as a result of a developmental change process. In other words, it is a sequential process rather than a sudden shift.

Figure 10.3 depicts six phases through which change may occur in schools. In this figure, top administration plays a key role as change agent. The potential for change also exists at all levels of leadership and operating responsibilities in the school or school district. Figure 10.3 shows change taking a top-down pattern; it may also occur from bottom-up or middle-outward patterns. In each case, however, school leaders play key change agent roles.

The following list summarizes the activities in each phase of the total developmental process. We will assume that the change process takes place in an individual school, and that the principal assumes the role of top management in the change process.

Phase 1: Pressure and Arousal. The process begins when the principal feels a need or pressure for change. This pressure can be exerted by external factors such as increased competition for students, economic changes, or federal and state mandates. Or it may be felt because of internal factors such as a sharp decline in test scores, reduced teacher productivity, high faculty turnover, increased student dropouts, serious student or teacher unrest, and excessive teacher grievances. The need for change is more readily apparent if there are both external and internal pressures that do not offset each other.

Phase 2: Intervention and Reorientation.   Although school principals may sense the need for change, they may not be able to analyze its problems accurately and thereby make the correct changes. When under severe pressure, principals may rationalize the school's problems by blaming them on another group such as the teachers' union, the federal government, or the state legislature. Principals may be capable of managing the change process if they are perceived as expert and are trusted. If not, an outside consultant or change agent is often brought in to define the problem and begin the process of getting school members to focus on it.

Phase 3: Diagnosis and Recognition.   In the third phase of successful change, the entire school becomes involved in determining the true causes of problems requiring change by gathering relevant information. A shared approach between the principal and staff is common in this stage. The decision-making process has been broadened as the principal shows her willingness to recognize tough problems and to change. Diagnosis of the problem areas leads to recognition of specific problems. This step tends to be avoided in efforts involving unsuccessful change.

Phase 4: Invention and Commitment.   After the problem is recognized, the school moves toward creative solutions to the problems that have been identified. The shared approach again predominates in this phase. If teachers are encouraged to participate in this process, they will probably be more committed to the solutions.

Phase 5: Experimentation and Search.   The solutions developed in phase 4 are usually tested in small-scale pilot programs, and the results are then analyzed. For example, in a high school, one department may try out an idea before it is attempted in the school as a whole. In this way, the principal can work out the bugs before introducing the change on a large scale. Through control mechanisms, the principal determines to what degree the planned change is succeeding in remedying the problem, how well it is being received, and how implementation can be improved.

Phase 6: Reinforcement and Acceptance.   Finally, if the course of action has been tested and found desirable, it should be accepted more willingly. Furthermore, individuals need to be reinforced for making the change successful. The positive feedback coming from the pilot programs in phase 5 adds reinforcement to the change process. Other techniques for reinforcing acceptance include praise, recognition, promotion, salary increases, and continued participation in the change process.

ORGANIZATIONAL DEVELOPMENT

Organizational development (OD) is different from the previously discussed models of change. OD does not involve a structured sequence as proposed by Lewin, Kotter, Harris, and Greiner. OD is much broader in scope than any of the aforementioned models. Specifically, OD constitutes a set of techniques or interventions that are used to implement "planned" organizational change (Cooperrider & Godwin, 2019; Grossman, 2018; Henderson & Boje, 2018; Raina, 2018). For convenience of discussion, we have categorized these techniques into two groups: process strategies and structural strategies.

OD techniques apply to each of the change models discussed previously. For example, OD is used during Lewin's "moving" stage. It also is used during Kotter's steps 1, 3, 5, 6, and 7. Finally, OD is used during Harris's five-phase model as well as Greiner's seven-phase process. We present eight OD techniques (Church &

Vogelsong, 2018; Cooperrider & Godwin, 2019; Grossman, 2018; Henderson & Boje, 2018; Noumair & Shani, 2018; Pasmore, Barnes, & Gipson, 2018; Raina, 2018).

The first set of OD techniques we discuss are **process strategies**. The emphasis of process change strategies is on the *process* to accomplish change. Many of these strategies focus on improving individual and group processes in decision making, problem identification and problem solving, communication, working relationships, and the like. We examine four frequently used process strategies: survey feedback, sensitivity training, behavioral performance management, and quality of work life.

Survey Feedback

Survey feedback is an organizational approach to change that involves collecting data (usually by means of a survey questionnaire) from members of a work group or whole organization, analyzing and summarizing the data into an understandable form, feeding back the date to those who generated it, and using the data to diagnose problems and develop action plans for problem solving (Conlon & Short, 1984).

Survey feedback focuses on the relationships between administrative personnel and their subordinates at all levels of hierarchy. If used properly, attitude surveys can be a powerful tool in school-improvement efforts. Change agents who use survey feedback point out that most attitude surveys are not used properly. At best, most give higher-level school district leaders some data for changing practices or provide a benchmark against which to compare trends. At worst, they are filed away with little consequences for school improvement.

Survey feedback has two major phases. Collecting data is only part of the process; providing appropriate feedback to the organization's members is equally significant. Figure 10.4 outlines the six steps involved in survey feedback, which are described next (Bowers & Franklin, 1977).

Step 1: Preliminary Planning. Organizational members at the top of the hierarchy are involved in the preliminary planning. Surveys used in organizational change efforts are usually constructed around a theoretical model. This allows the user to rate himself or the organization in terms of the theory. When the approach involves a theoretical model, a commitment to the model must be obtained. If top management does not accept the theoretical model undergirding the survey, the approach will likely fail no matter how effective the effort is toward gathering data.

Step 2: Data Gathering. A questionnaire is administered to all organizational members. The best-known survey-feedback instrument is the one developed by the Institute for Social Research (ISR) at the University of Michigan (Taylor & Bowers, 1972). The questionnaire generally asks the respondents' perceptions on such organizational areas as communications, goal emphasis, leadership styles, decision making, coordination between departments, and employee attitudes. The ISR instrument, a standardized questionnaire, permits the additions of questions that may be of interest to the organization under study. However, many organizations, including

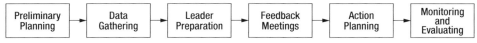

Figure 10.4 Steps Involved in Survey Feedback

schools, develop their own questionnaires that are specific to their individual needs rather than relying on a standardized instrument.

Step 3: Leader Preparation.   Once the data have been obtained from the questionnaire, an external or internal change agent helps school principals understand the data and instructs them on how to present the data to the work group. Data are then fed back to the top administrative team and down through the hierarchy in functional teams.

Step 4: Feedback Meetings.   Each superior conducts group feedback meetings with his subordinates in which the data are discussed and in which subordinates are asked to help interpret the data; plans are made for making constructive changes; and plans are made for introducing the information at the next lower level of subordinates.

For example, the superintendent of schools and the major divisional associate superintendents meet and compare the survey findings for each of the school district's functional areas—such as personnel, business, instruction, and research and development. Each associate superintendent can see the summary data for her division and for the total school district. Problems unique to each division, the implications of the findings, and themes common to the total school district are discussed.

The next feedback meetings occur as each associate superintendent meets with building principals or other subordinates to discuss survey data specific to each. The process continues until department heads discuss with teachers or other school personnel the issues raised in each work group by the survey data.

Step 5: Action Planning.   The fact that a discrepancy exists between the actual state of the school district and the ideal theoretical model does not in and of itself provide sufficient motivation to change. Organization members must be made aware of how the change can be effected. Thus, resources are allocated to implement the changes in accordance with the needs indicated by the group feedback meetings and the systematic diagnosis of the data by the change agent and top-level district administrators.

Step 6: Monitoring and Evaluating.   The change agent helps organization members develop skills that are necessary to move the school district toward its goals. Some of these skills include listening, giving and receiving personal feedback, general leadership techniques, problem solving, goal setting, and diagnosing group processes. Additional questionnaires are administered and analyzed to monitor the change process. Finally, the school district is formally reassessed to evaluate change, again, using questionnaire data.

Sensitivity Training

Lewin was instrumental in the development of **sensitivity training**, also known as laboratory training, encounter groups, or **T-groups** (training groups)—all refer to an early method of changing behavior through unstructured group interaction (Highhouse, 2002). The National Training Laboratories (NTL) developed and refined sensitivity training in a widely used organizational strategy aimed at individual change, which generally takes place in small groups.

Goals of Sensitivity Training.   Based on an extensive review of the literature, two researchers (Campbell & Dunnette, 1968) have outlined six basic objectives common to most laboratory training sessions:

1. To increase understanding, insight, and self-awareness about one's own behavior and its impact on others, including the ways in which others interpret one's behavior.
2. To increase understanding and sensitivity about the behavior of others, including better interpretation of both verbal and nonverbal cues, which increase awareness and understanding of what the other person is thinking and feeling.
3. To improve understanding and awareness of group and intergroup processes, both those that facilitate and those that inhibit group functioning.
4. To improve diagnostic skills in interpersonal and intergroup situations, which is attained by accomplishing the first three objectives.
5. To increase the ability to transform learning into action, so that real-life interventions will be more successful in increasing member effectiveness, satisfaction, or output.
6. To improve an individual's ability to analyze her own interpersonal behavior, as well as to learn how to help self and others with whom they come in contact to achieve more satisfying, rewarding, and effective interpersonal relationships.

These objectives point out that sensitivity training can be a useful strategy for bringing about organizational change. School districts that are experiencing problems with communications, coordination, or excessive and continuing conflict in interpersonal relationships may benefit from sensitivity training as a means of improving individual and organizational effectiveness.

Design of Sensitivity Training. Sensitivity training groups (T-groups) typically consist of ten to fifteen members and a professional trainer. The duration of T-group sessions ranges from a few days to several weeks. The sessions are usually conducted away from the organization, but some occur on university campuses or on the premises of large business organizations. Laboratory training stresses the process rather than the context of training and focuses on attitudinal rather than conceptual training.

The four basic types of training groups are stranger, cousin, brother, and family laboratories. In **stranger T-groups**, members are from different schools or school districts and therefore are unknown to each other before training. An example would be several superintendents from different school districts. **Cousin T-groups** consist of members taken from a diagonal slice of a school district, which cuts across two or three vertical hierarchical levels without a superior and subordinate being in the same group. An example would be the director of secondary education and elementary school principals from the same district. **Brother T-groups** include members who occupy similar horizontal roles in a school district but without superiors and subordinate in the same group. For example, a group of principals from the same school district would be brothers. In the **family T-groups**, all members belong to the same subunit of a school district. The superintendent of a school district and his administrative cabinet or the principal of a school and its department heads are examples of a family training group.

The trainer may structure the content of the laboratory training by using a number of exercises or management games or follow an unstructured format in which the group develops its own agenda. Robert Blake and Jane Mouton (1994) were among the first trainers to modify the unstructured format into an instrumental one.

Stranger T-groups with an unstructured format were the classic form of T-groups used during the early beginnings of sensitivity training. However, the difficulty encountered in applying interpersonal skills acquired away from the organization to the home base organization when participants returned has led to the use of cousin and family T-groups in recent years. In fact, there has been a movement recently away from sensitivity training groups and toward **team building** (Dyer, 1994; Gordon, 2002). This more recent application of T-groups has been exemplified in the work of Chris Argyris (2009), an early proponent of sensitivity training. Thus, sensitivity training is often used today as part of more complex organizational change strategies.

Behavioral Performance Management

Behavioral performance management has its roots in B. F. Skinner's (1974) theory of operant conditioning, which emphasizes the effect of environmental influences on behavior. More recently, a social learning approach has been suggested as a more comprehensive theoretical foundation for applying behavior modification in organizations (Stajkovic & Luthans, 1997, 2003). Thus, organizational behavior modification is a process of changing the behavior of an employee by managing the consequences that follow his work behavior.

Fred Luthans and Robert Kreitner's (1985) S-O-B-C model provides a useful way of viewing the behavior modification process. Based on a social learning approach, the behavior modification process recognizes the interaction of four parts: S (stimulus), O (organism or employee), B (behavior), and C (consequences) (see figure 10.5).

Stimulus. The S in the model refers to stimulus, which includes internal and external factors, mediated by learning, that determine employee behavior. External factors include organizational structure and organizational and administrative processes interacting with the structure: decision making, control, communication, power, and goal setting. Internal factors include planning, personal, goals, self-observation data, stimulus removal, selective stimulus exposure, and self-contracts.

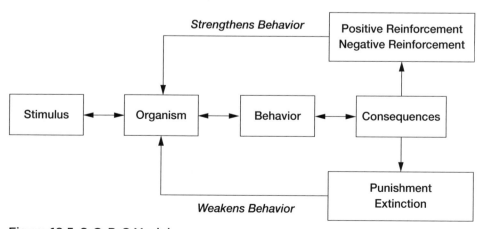

Figure 10.5 S-O-B-C Model

Organism. The O in the model refers to the organism, or school employee. The internal and external factors in the situation constitute the organizational environment in which the school employee operates. School employees can be thought of as consisting of cognitive and psychological processes. For example, motivating behavior with need theories, expectancy theory, equity theory, goal setting, and management by objectives applies to this part of the model.

Behavior. The B in the model represents employee behavior. The study of the organizational environment (S) and the school employee (O) leads to a better understanding of the school employee's behavior—the overt and covert responses to the organizational environment. Behavior includes verbal and nonverbal communication, actions, and the like. In schools, we are specifically interested in work behaviors such as performance, attendance, promptness, participation in committees, superordinate-subordinate relations, interaction among colleagues, or leaving the organization.

Consequences. The C part of the model represents the consequences that result from employee behavior. The study of behavioral consequences can help improve the prediction and control of employee behavior, but this a very simplified generalization. Social learning theorists place more emphasis on internal states and processes when explaining job behavior than the so-called radical behaviorists (Kreitner & Luthans, 1984). However, approaches such as self-management are insufficient in producing a coordinated organizational behavior modification effect. As shown in the model, behavior is a function of internal and external cues and consequences that follow a given behavior. Some types of consequences strengthen behavior while other weaken it.

Contingencies of Reinforcement. Changing interrelationships among organizational environment (S), employee (O), behavior (B), and consequences (C) is referred to as managing the **contingencies of reinforcement** (Skinner, 1991). As figure 10.5 shows, the consequences that strengthen behavior are positive reinforcement and negative reinforcement. The consequences that weaken behavior are extinction and punishment.

Positive reinforcement involves following a desired behavior with the application of a pleasant stimulus, which should increase the probability of the desired behavior. Examples of positive reinforcement in a school setting include promotions, salary increases, merit raises, praise, more desirable work assignments, awards, or simply smiles. All reinforcement strategies, however, are specific to a given individual or situation.

Negative reinforcement involves the removal of an unpleasant stimulus on the appearance of a desired behavior, which should increase the probability of that behavior. For example, a football coach of a major university requires all football players to attend an early Sunday morning practice whenever their performance in a game falls below a minimum level. The players strive for a high performance level in the next game to avoid the unpleasant early Sunday morning practice.

Extinction involves removing a reinforcer that is maintaining some undesired behavior. If the behavior is not reinforced, it should gradually be extinguished. For instance, suppose you have an assistant who enjoys talking about her personal life for fifteen or twenty minutes every time you come into the office. In the past, you have been polite and have listened attentively as they related their personal experiences. In essence, you have been positively reinforcing their behavior. To stop their undesired behavior, you must ignore all conversations after exchanging some brief courtesies, turn around, and walk out of the office. This should dissipate the undesired behavior that is interfering with the performance of their work.

Punishment involves following an unwanted behavior with the application of some unpleasant stimulus. In theory, this should reduce the probability of the undesired behavior. Examples of punishment include oral reprimands, written warnings, suspensions, demotions, and discharge. While punishment may eliminate undesirable employee behavior in the short run, long-term, sustained use of punishment is dysfunctional to the organization (Beyer & Trice, 1984).

Steps in Organizational Behavior Modification. Luthans and Kreitner (1985) suggest five steps for using organizational behavior modification to change employee-behavior patterns. Each one will be discussed in turn.

Step 1: Identify significant performance-related behaviors. The principal and the teachers begin by identifying and describing the changes they desire to make. The analysis includes identification of significant performance-related behaviors that can be observed, counted, and specified precisely. The teacher or the principal can do the identification process. In either case, it requires training to identify behaviors for which reinforcement strategies can be used.

Step 2: Measure performance-related behaviors. Obtain, prior to learning, baseline measurement of the frequency of the desired target behaviors. Use tally sheets and time sampling to gather the data. In a school setting, select for assessment observed classroom performance, work-assignment completions, participation in committees, student achievement, advisement, publications, absences, service to the community, curriculum writing, and complaints. Establish some preliminary period of assessment as a baseline.

Step 3: Analyze the antecedents and consequences of behaviors. The behavior to be changed is often influenced by prior occurrences (antecedents) and has some identifiable consequences. For example, a particularly ineffective teacher may be a case for study. The teacher lacks effective instructional techniques, has poor rapport with students, complains incessantly about administration policies and procedures, and adversely affects the performance and attitudes of colleagues. During this step, the principal identifies existing contingencies of reinforcement to determine when the behaviors occur, what causes them, and what their consequences are. Effective behavior change in the teacher requires replacement or removal of these reinforcing consequences.

Step 4: Implement the change approach. Use positive reinforcements, negative reinforcement, extinction, and punishment to change significant performance-related behaviors of teachers or other employees. In other words, develop an intervention strategy, then apply the strategy using suitable contingencies of reinforcement. Finally, maintain the behaviors with appropriate schedules of reinforcement, including variable ratio, fixed ratio, variable interval, and fixed interval (for more information on schedules of reinforcement, see Luthans, Luthans, & Luthans, 2015).

Step: 5 Evaluate behavior change. Evaluate the effectiveness of behavior modification in four areas: reaction of the teachers to the approach, learning of the concepts programmed, degree of behavior change that occurs, and impact of behavior change on actual performance. In evaluating the success or failure of the behavior modification program, compare the original baseline measurements with outcome measurements of behavior. If it becomes apparent at step 5 that the intervention strategy implemented in step 4 has not resulted in the desired impact, start the process over again at step 1.

Quality of Work Life

There has been growing recognition of the importance of simultaneously improving the value of teachers' psychological experiences at work as well as their productivity. This philosophy is embodied in the quality of work life (QWL) approach to change. Initially used in business, QWL is now applied in a variety of professions and organizations. Such programs are typically broad based and lack the precise definition and focus of survey feedback, sensitivity training, and behavioral performance management.

Quality of work life can be defined as any activity undertaken by a school or school district for the express purpose of improving one or more of the following conditions that affect a staff member's experience with a school or school district: adequate and fair compensation; safe and healthy working conditions; opportunity to use and develop personal capabilities; opportunity to grow and progress in a career; opportunity to participate in decisions; protection from arbitrary and unfair treatment; and opportunity to satisfy social needs (Pasmore, 2011; Pasmore, Barnes, & Gipson, 2018).

One popular approach to improving the quality of work life involves *job redesign*—the process of restructuring the way jobs are performed to make them more interesting. We will be discussing such an approach to job redesign, including *job enrichment* in the next section under structural change strategies. As you will see, this technique is considered an effective way of improving the quality of work life for teachers.

Another approach to improving the quality of work life involves using quality circles. A **quality circle** is a voluntary group of five to ten members, typically from similar jobs or the same school, who meet periodically to identify and solve work-related problems. Each quality circle usually has an appointed group leader; and members are trained in techniques of problem solving and group process by a facilitator, who may be an internal or external change consultant (Bonstingl, 2001).

Groups focus on departmental and organizational goals (e.g., how to reduce vandalism, how to create safer and more comfortable work environments, and how to improve the quality of teaching and learning) and submit proposals for change to the principal. Recently, principals have acted as facilitators of quality circles. A steering committee consisting of members from all levels and areas of the school typically reviews proposals, accepts or rejects them, and allocates resources for implementation. Research has indicated that although quality circles are quite effective at bringing about short-term improvements in quality of work life (i.e., eighteen months), they are less effective at creating more permanent changes (Greenberg, 2014).

Three potential benefits—even if short term—may result from QWL programs. First, increased job satisfaction, organizational commitment, and reduced staff turnover usually occur. A second benefit is increased staff productivity. A final benefit is increased school effectiveness (e.g., goal attainment—including increased learning for all) (Greenberg, 2014).

For success to occur, it is important to incorporate the following key provisions into any QWL program:

- Both administration and staff must cooperate in designing the program. Should either group not be completely committed to the program, it is not likely to succeed.
- The plans agreed to by all concerned stakeholders must be implemented fully. It is easy for action plans developed by QWL groups to be forgotten. To prevent this from happening, organization members at all levels—from the superintendent to the lowest-level employee—must follow through on their parts of the plan.

(Greenberg, 2014)

Successful QWL programs are being used in some of the largest and best-known companies, such as Ford, General Electric, and IBM, as well as many school districts. QWL programs often encompass a wide variety of specific techniques, such as team building, job restructuring, shared decision making, redesign of pay systems, Theory Z, and quality circles. As noted, implementation of these techniques is expected to translate into improved faculty teaching performance and student learning.

We have examined four process OD change strategies: survey feedback, sensitivity training, behavioral performance management, and quality of work life. Our focus now shifts to structural OD change strategies. **Structural change strategies** involve an adjustment in the school's structure to accomplish change goals. Structural adjustment may be the change goal or simply may lead to it. Some strategies focus on changes in the task, whereas others focus on the means of setting goals as well as strategic plans for attaining those goals. Here we discuss the more commonly used structural approaches to change: goal setting, strategic planning, job redesign, and total quality management (TQM) (Church & Vogelsong, 2018; Cooperrider & Godwin, 2019; Grossman, 2018; Henderson & Boje, 2018; Noumair & Shani, 2018; Pasmore, Barnes, & Gipson, 2018; Raina, 2018).

Goal Setting

A major problem confronting large school districts is the lack of identification by the individual staff member with the goals of the district. With specialization so highly developed in schools, many staff members are very much divorced from the direction and purpose of the larger system. **Goal setting** is a method of coordinating individual staff members' efforts toward overall school/school district goals (Van Soelen, 2021). The evidence strongly supports the value of goals in motivating employees (Locke & Latham, 2002). More to the point, the research evidence suggests that: specific goals increase performance; difficult goals, when accepted, result in higher performance than easy goals; and feedback leads to higher performance than does the absence of feedback (Locke & Latham, 2006).

Getting staff to work toward school district goals is not just a matter of informing them what the goals are. Rather, staff members' support for system-wide goals is increased if they participate in the goal-setting process. When the goal-setting process is mutually influenced by leader and staff, the staff are given some control over their work environment (Latham, 2009).

A goal-setting program is systemwide in order to achieve a better fit between individual and system goals. Top leaders (superintendent and their administrative team) set their operating goals, followed by meetings with the second level of administrators (building principals) during which campus goals are mutually set. These principals then meet with their staff to help set their goals, and so on down the hierarchy to the lowest level in the school/school district. In this way, every level is linked with every other level. Short-run goals mesh with long-range goals; broad school district goals mesh with building goals, which in turn mesh with department and instructional objectives (Van Soelen, 2021). This approach increases the chances that the school district will work as a coordinated unit, even in the face of change (Fullan, 2018; Fullan & Gallagher, 2020).

Strategic Planning

Strategic planning is an organizational change process that is very carefully planned and deliberate. We define **strategic planning** as the process of developing, implementing, and evaluating decisions that enable a school/school district to achieve its goals (Lemaine, Levernier, & Richardson, 2018). The process of strategic planning typically follows eight steps (Goodstein, 2011; Wootton & Horne, 2021). Although these steps are not always followed in the exact order specified, they do resemble the way most school districts go about planning strategically (Ewy, 2010). As we describe these steps, you may find it useful to follow along with the steps shown in figure 10.6.

A: Develop a Mission. A strategic plan must begin with a stated goal. Typically, goals involve a school district's outcomes (e.g., to improve student achievement on standardized tests) and/or to improve its organizational culture (e.g., to make the work environment more pleasant). It is important to note that a school district's overall goals must be translated into corresponding goals to be achieved by various school district units. In large school districts, this would include divisions of instruction, finance, research and development, human resources, and so on, as well as individual school buildings and departments within them.

B1: Conduct a Critical Analysis of the Internal Environment. By "internal environment," we are referring to the nature of the school district itself as identified by the unique characteristics which describe the organization. For example, does the organizational structure stimulate or inhibit goal achievement? Does this culture of the school district (or individual school) encourage personnel to be innovative and to make positive changes or does it encourage organization members to maintain the status quo? Are organization members motivated sufficiently to strive for the realization of school district goals? Is there adequate, effective leadership to move the school district forward? Do decision-making practices encourage goal accomplishment? Do people communicate with each other clearly enough to accomplish their goals? Are organization members willing to change in order to improve school district performance?

B2: Conduct a Critical Analysis of the External Environment. School districts (and schools) do not operate in a vacuum. Rather, they function within external environments. For example, local, state, and federal laws impact the internal operation of school districts (and schools). For instance, consider the impact of the Every Student Succeeds Act (ESSA) legislation on the internal operation of public schools throughout the United States.

C: Prepare Planning Assumptions. To clearly understand the nature of your strategic plan, it is important to highlight the assumptions underlying the plan: (a) Is the planning process based on deliberate analyses or based on intuition and informal

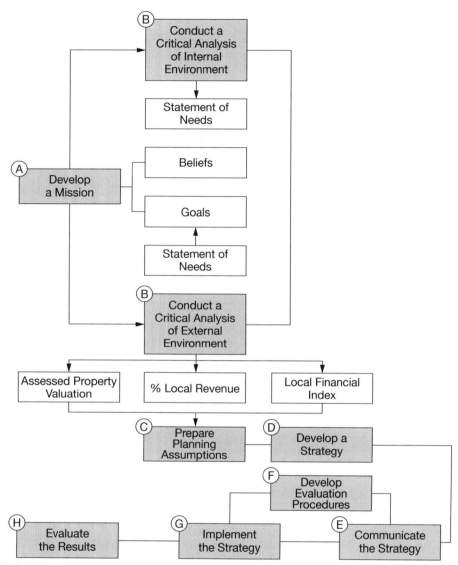

Figure 10.6 Strategic Planning: An Eight-Stage Process

knowledge? (b) Is the strategic plan based on the assumption that radical change is not only possible, but desirable; or instead, will the plan involve only minor incremental adjustments to the current ways of operating? (c) The strategic plan will be made primarily in the interest of which stakeholder groups (community, school board, administrators, teachers, support staff, or students)? Furthermore, what resources does the school district (or school) have available to plan and implement its strategy? The resources include financial, physical, and human resources. The assumptions underlying the strategic planning process are important to the ultimate success of the strategic plan.

D: Develop a Strategy. A strategy is the means by which a school district achieves its goal. Based on a careful assessment of the school district's position on the aforementioned factors or characteristics (e.g., the school district's organizational structure, its culture, motivation of its members, leadership, decision-making strategies used, communication, inclination toward change, and available resources), a decision is made about how to go about achieving its goal.

E: Communicate the Strategy. The strategy must be communicated to stakeholders: individuals or groups in whose interest a school district is run. These are individuals who have a stake in the school district. The most important stakeholders include students, teachers, support staff, administrators, the school board, and community members. It is essential to communicate a school district's strategic plan to stakeholders very clearly so they can contribute to its success, either directly (e.g., organization members who help achieve goals) or indirectly (e.g., school board who set policy, taxpayers who provide local funds, as well as the state and federal government). Unless stakeholders fully understand and accept a school district's strategic plan, it is unlikely to receive the full support it needs to meet its goals.

F: Develop Evaluation Procedures. Evaluation procedures need to be developed prior to *evaluating the results.* These procedures will serve to guide the implementation of the strategy and evaluation of the outcome.

G: Implement the Strategy. Once a strategy has been developed and communicated, the strategy is implemented. When this occurs, there may be some resistance. As we discussed previously, people tend to resist change. School administrators (superintendents and principals) need to apply various techniques to overcome resistance to change, which were discussed earlier.

H: Evaluate the Results. Finally, after a strategy has been implemented, it is important to determine if the goals have been achieved. If so, then new goals are developed. If not, then different goals may be defined, or different strategies for accomplishing the goals may be attempted.

Business has devoted a great deal of attention to strategic planning (Campbell, 2012). Only recently has any emphasis been placed on the study of strategic planning in school settings. In a large-scale study of all 127 school districts in Kentucky, researchers (Basham & Lunenburg, 1989) found relationships between strategic planning and student achievement in reading, language arts, and mathematics at several grade levels. In addition, the researchers found a direct relationship between strategic planning and both school district wealth and per-pupil expenditures—that is, the higher the assessed property value per child and the greater percentage of revenue from local sources supporting education, the more likely the school district was engaged in strategic planning efforts (Basham & Lunenburg, 1989).

Job Redesign

Frederick Herzberg's (2009) motivation-hygiene theory has stimulated programs in job redesign (also known as job enrichment) in many organizations. Herzberg feels that the challenge to organizations is to emphasize motivation factors while ensuring that the hygiene factors are present. He refers to job enrichment as the method for achieving such a condition. **Job enrichment** focuses on achieving organizational change by making jobs more meaningful, interesting, and challenging.

Expanding on the earlier work of Herzberg, Richard Hackman and Greg Oldham (1980) provide an explicit framework for enriching jobs. Based on their own

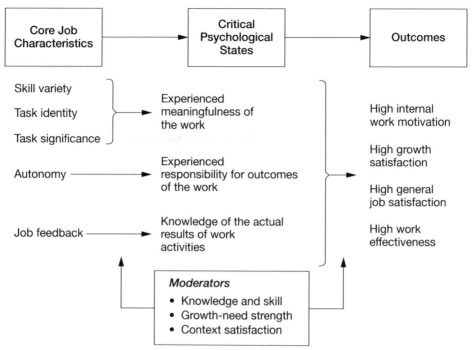

Figure 10.7 Job Enrichment Model

research and the work of others, they developed a job characteristics model (see figure 10.7). As the figure shows, five core job characteristics create three critical psychological states that in turn lead to a number of employee outcomes. The employee's knowledge and skills, growth-need strength, and satisfaction with context factors moderate the linkage among the job characteristics, the psychological states, and the outcomes.

The five job characteristics that are essential to job enrichment are the following:

1. *Skill variety* is the degree to which a job requires a variety of different activities in carrying out the work, which involves the use of a number of different skills and talents of the employee.
2. *Task identity* is the degree to which a job requires completion of a "whole" and identifiable piece of work—that is, doing a job from beginning to end with a visible outcome.
3. *Task significance* is the degree to which the job has a substantial impact on the lives of other people, whether those people are in the immediate organization or in the external environment.
4. *Autonomy* is the degree to which the job provides substantial freedom, independence, and discretion to the individual in scheduling the work and in determining the procedures to be used in doing the work.
5. *Job feedback* is the degree to which carrying out the work activities required by the job provides the individual with direction and clear information about the effectiveness of her performance.

As shown in figure 10.7, skill variety, task identity, and task significance together affect experienced meaningfulness of the work. Autonomy and feedback independently affect the other two psychological states, respectively "experienced responsibility for outcomes of the work" and "knowledge of the actual results of the work activities." And according to Hackman and Oldham, only employees who have job-related knowledge and skills, high growth-need strength, and high satisfaction with context factors (Herzberg's "hygienes") are likely to be affected in the manner specified in the model.

Hackman and Oldham (1975) have developed the job diagnostic survey (JDS) to diagnose the job dimensions in their model (see figure 10.7) and to determine the effect of job changes on employees. Thus, the job dimensions in the job enrichment model can be combined into the following mathematic expression, which explains the relative impact of change in each dimension of the Hackman-Oldham model:

$$\text{MPS} = \left(\frac{\text{Skill variety} + \text{Task identity} + \text{Task significance}}{3} \right) \times \text{Autonomy} \times \text{Feedback}$$

The motivation potential score (MPS) formula sums the score for skill variety, task identity, and task significance and divides the total by three. The combination of these three job characteristics is equally weighted, with autonomy and feedback considered separately. The result is an overall measure of job enrichment.

Total Quality Management (TQM)

Total Quality Management (TQM) is based on the assumption that people want to do their best and that it is the leader's job to enable them to do so by constantly improving the system in which they work (Deming, 2000). TQM is not new. It requires teamwork, training, and extensive collection and analysis of data.

When educators look at TQM principles, they assume that the model applies only to profit-making organizations. Actually, TQM applies as well, to corporations, service organizations, universities, and elementary and secondary schools.

Indeed, the concepts formulated by TQM founder W. Edwards Deming have proved so powerful that educators want to apply TQM to schools. Deming's philosophy provides a framework that can integrate many positive developments in education, such as team teaching, site-based management, cooperative learning, and outcomes-based education.

The problem is that words like *learning* and *curriculum* are not found in Deming's fourteen points. Some of Deming's terminology needs to be translated to schools as well. For example, superintendents and principals can be considered management. Teachers are *employers* or *managers* of students. Students are *employees*, and the knowledge they acquire is the *product*. Parents and society are the *customers*. With these translations made, we can see many applications to schools (Lunenburg, 2010h). The framework for transforming schools using Deming's principles follows.

Create constancy of purpose for improvement of product and service. For schools, the purpose of the system must be clear and shared by all stakeholder groups. Customer needs must be the focus in establishing educational aims. The aims of the system must be to improve the quality of education for all students.

Adopt the new philosophy. Implementation of Deming's second principle requires a rethinking of the school's mission and priorities, with everyone in agreement on them. Existing methods, materials, and environments may be replaced by new teaching and learning strategies where success for every student is the goal. Individual differences among students are addressed. Ultimately, what may be required is a total transformation of the American system of education as we know it.

Cease dependence on inspection to achieve quality. The field of education has recently entered an era that many American corporations have abandoned: inspection at the end of the line (Bonstingl, 2001). In industry this was called "product inspection." According to Deming, it always costs more to fix a problem than to prevent one. Reliance on remediation can be avoided if proper intervention occurs during initial instruction. Furthermore, preventive approaches such as Head Start, Follow Through, Response to Intervention (RTI), and preschool programs can help students to avoid learning problems later.

End the practice of awarding business on the basis of price alone. The lowest bid is rarely the most cost efficient. Schools need to move toward a single supplier for any one item and develop long-term relationships of loyalty and trust with that supplier.

Improve constantly and forever every activity in the company, to improve quality and productivity. The focus of improvement efforts in education, under Deming's approach, are on teaching and learning processes. Based on the latest research findings, the best strategies must be attempted, evaluated, and refined as needed. And, consistent with learning style theories (Dunn & Dunn, 1992; Dunn, Dunn, & Perrin, 1994) and Howard Gardner's (1994, 1999, 2005, 2007) multiple intelligences, educators must redesign the system to provide for a broad range of people—handicapped, learning-disabled, at-risk, special needs students—and find ways to make them all successful in school.

Institute training on the job. Training of educators, called professional development, is needed in three areas. First, there must be training in the new teaching and learning processes that are developed. Second, training must be provided in the use of new assessment strategies. Third, there must be training in the principles of the new management system.

Institute leadership. Deming's seventh principle resembles Peter Senge's (1990, 2006) system thinking. According to both Senge and Deming, improvement of a stable system comes from altering the system itself, and this is primarily the job of management and not those who work within the system. Deming asserts that the primary task of leadership is to narrow the amount of variation within the system, bringing everyone toward the goal of perfection. In schools, this means closing the achievement gap among student subgroups.

Drive out fear. A basic assumption of TQM is that people want to do their best. The focus of improvement efforts then must be on the processes and on the outcomes, not on trying to blame individuals for failures. If quality is absent, the fault is in the system, says Deming. It is management's job to enable people to do their best by constantly improving the system in which they work.

Break down barriers among staff areas. Deming's ninth principle is somewhat related to the first principle: create constancy of purpose for improvement of product and service. In the classroom, this principle applies to interdisciplinary instruction, team teaching, writing across the curriculum, and transfer of learning. Collaboration needs to exist among members of the learning organization so that total quality can be maximized.

Eliminate slogans, exhortations, and targets that demand zero defects and new levels of productivity. Implicit in most slogans, exhortations, and targets is the supposition that staff could do better if they tried harder. This offends rather than inspires the team. It creates adversarial relationships because the many causes of low quality and low productivity in schools are due to the system and not the staff. The system itself may need to be changed. (The authors are not in complete agreement with this item. Educators tend to use numerous slogans as a general practice.)

Eliminate numerical quotas for the staff and goals for management. There are many practices in education that constrain our ability to tap intrinsic motivation and falsely assume the benefits of extrinsic rewards. They include rigorous and systematic teacher evaluation systems, merit pay, management by objectives, grades, and quantitative goals and quotas. These Deming refers to as forces of destruction. Such approaches are counter-productive for several reasons: setting goals leads to marginal performance; merit pay destroys teamwork; and appraisal of individual performance nourishes fear and increases variability in desired performance.

Remove barriers that rob people of pride of workmanship. Most people want to do a good job. Effective communication and the elimination of "demotivators"—such as lack of involvement, poor information, the annual or merit rating, and supervisors who don't care—are critical.

Institute a rigorous program of education and retraining for everyone. The principal and staff must be retrained in new methods of school leadership, including group dynamics, consensus building, and collaborative styles of decision making. All stakeholders on the school's team must realize that improvements in student productivity will create higher levels of responsibility, not less responsibility.

Put everyone in the organization to work to accomplish the transformation. The school board and superintendent must have a clear plan of action to carry out the quality mission. The quality mission must be internalized by all members of the school district. The transformation is everybody's job (Deming, 2000).

JOB STRESS AND ITS MANAGEMENT

Schools have been encountering continuous change since the early 1980s, when *A Nation at Risk* (National Commission on Excellence in Education, 1983) was released. It is argued that the ability to change is a necessary characteristic for an organization to grow and improve its effectiveness (Senge, 1990, 2006; Senge et al., 2012). But what are the costs of change to organization members? Organizational change is a stressful experience for many people because it threatens their self-esteem and creates uncertainty about their future (McShane & Von Glinow, 2018). Don Hellriegel and John Slocum (2015) have indicated that organizational change can be viewed as the greatest source of stress on the job and, perhaps, in an employee's life. This underscores the importance of individual-level effects of organizational change, effects which are often unforeseen by organizations themselves.

Communication, professional development, and employee involvement in organizational change can reduce some of the stressors. However, in general, findings indicate that change increases the probability of increased stress for organization members (Yu, 2009). Overall, these findings call for the need to introduce stress management practices to help employees cope with organizational change (McHugh, 1997). Specifically, stress management minimizes resistance to change by removing some of the direct costs and fear of the unknown of the change process. Stress also drains energy; therefore, minimizing stress potentially increases employee motivation and commitment to support the change process.

Stress is the physiological and psychological response of an individual to the demands, constraints, or opportunities involving uncertainty and important outcomes (Cooper, Dewe, & O'Driscoll, 2002). Prolonged exposure to stress can produce dysfunctional effects that may affect job performance. In particular, in studies of the needs of women leaders, stress management was reported as an important concern (Grogan & Shakeshaft, 2011; Irby & Brown, 1998).

Sources of Stress

Stressors are environmental conditions that have the potential to cause stress. It is important for a principal to recognize stressors because they can induce job-related stress, which may influence work attitudes, behavior, and performance.

Typically, stress is discussed in a negative context (Robbins & Judge, 2018). However, stress is not necessarily all bad. It also can have positive value (Cavanaugh, Boswell, Roehling, & Boudreau, 2000). Stress is an opportunity when it provides potential gain. For example, consider the superior performance an athlete delivers in a "clutch" situation. Such an individual uses stress positively to perform at a maximum level. Also, many professionals thrive on positive stress and see the pressures of a heavy workload and meeting deadlines as challenges that enhance the satisfaction they derive from their work.

Researchers have distinguished between **challenge stressors** ("clutch" situations, heavy workloads, and deadlines) and **hindrance stressors** (red tape, politics, unclear job responsibilities). The evidence suggests that challenge stressors produce less stress than hindrance stressors (Podsakoff, LePine, & LePine, 2007). Furthermore, there is evidence that challenge stress improves job performance in supportive work environments, while hindrance stress reduces job performance in all work environments (Wallace et al., 2009).

We now turn our attention to hindrance stressors. Figure 10.8 depicts three categories of stressors: organizational, personal, and nonorganizational factors. Of the three, organizational factors have the greatest potential to induce job-related stress (Liu, Spector, & Shi, 2007). Factors such as excessively high or low job demands, role conflicts and ambiguities, and poor interpersonal relations can influence the stress level school principals experience. Principals also feel stress in the transition from one career stage to the next, which is due to the uncertainty often associated with new job experiences and expectations (Pink, 2011). A somewhat related factor is career development. A principal can feel stress from underpromotion (failure to advance as rapidly as one desires) or overpromotion (being placed in a job that exceeds one's capabilities) (Ghayer & Churchill, 2013). These organizational factors, independently or in concert, can induce job stress.

Several personal factors are sources of stress for principals in the workplace. Such individual characteristics as need for achievement, aptitudes and skills, task understanding, and personality can influence how individuals experience and react to stress and stressors. For example, personality traits such as authoritarianism, introversion/extroversion, tolerance for ambiguity, locus of control, and self-esteem

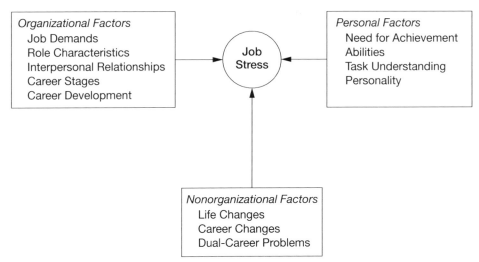

Figure 10.8 Sources of Job Stress

have been found to be related to job stress (Lazarus, 1999). Attention has focused, however, on the Type A personality, which seems to relate to the ways in which individuals experience stress.

Type A Personality.　A person with a **type A personality** is "aggressively involved in a chronic, incessant struggle to achieve more and more in less and less time, and, if required to do so, against the opposing efforts of other things or other persons" (Friedman & Rosenman, 1974, p. 84). In North American culture, such characteristics tend to be highly valued and positively associated with ambition. Characteristics of the type A personality structure include (Friedman & Rosenman, 1974):

- a chronic sense of time urgency
- a constant involvement in multiple projects subject to deadlines
- a neglect of all aspects of life except work
- a highly competitive, aggressive, almost hostile orientation
- an impatience with barriers to goal achievement
- a tendency to measure success by quantity

The time urgency, competitiveness and hostility, multiphasic behavior, and achievement orientation characteristic of type A personalities predispose these individuals to certain physical disorders such as heart attacks (Lovallo, 2005). Much of the stress they feel is of their own making rather than the product of their environment.

Finally, nonorganizational factors can also impact the stress a school principal experiences in the work setting. Such things as life changes (the birth of a child, death of a spouse, divorce), career changes (loss of extra income), and dual careers can influence a person's health and job performance. Dual-career problems typically arise when a married couple attempts to balance two individual careers. Major concerns for couples with dual careers include sharing household chores, child care, and job relocation. Nonorganizational factors can result in a "spillover" of stress, which may influence attitudes, behavior, and job performance.

Time Management.   School principals feel more job pressures and time constraints than ever before. On the average, elementary principals work fifty-two hours a week, from eight to ten hours a day. High school principals average about fifty-five hours a week, dividing forty-three hours during the day and fourteen hours on school-related activities in the evening (Glatthorn, Jailall, & Jailall, 2017; Kaplan & Owings, 2015; Marshall, 2021; Sergiovanni & Green, 2015; Spillane & Lowenhaupt, 2019; Ubben, Hughes, & Norris, 2017; Williamson & Blackburn, 2016).

School principals report that they do not have sufficient time to do everything that needs to be done. The variety of problems principals face and the large spans of control found in most schools make it difficult for them to give all aspects of the school program sufficient attention. Not being able to do all that they would like to do in the time available is a continuing source of stress.

Proper time management is more than a tidy desk and an orderly schedule. It is a career strategy that can help turn any school executive into a high achiever. When school principals allow time to control them, it can result in the kind of stress linked with high blood pressure, heart attacks, excessive irritability, and general anxiety (Claessens et a., 2004). A few of the best-known time-management principles include (a) making daily lists of tasks to be accomplished, (b) prioritizing tasks by importance, (c) scheduling tasks according to priorities, and (d) knowing your daily cycle and handling the most demanding tasks when you are most alert and productive (Lawrence-Ell, 2002; Tracy, 2004).

Stress and Performance

Stress can either help or hinder job performance, depending on the amount of stress (Robbins & Judge, 2018) and type of stress (e.g., challenge stressors or hindrance stressors) (Podsakoff, LePine, & LePine, 2007). Figure 10.9 shows the relationship between stress and job performance. The vertical axis represents the level of performance from low to high. The horizontal axis represents the amount of stress experienced. At very low levels of stress, job challenges are absent, and performance tends to be low. As stress increases, performance tends to increase because stress helps an individual activate physiological and psychological resources to meet job requirements. Eventually, stress reaches a point—the optimum stress level—that corresponds roughly with a person's maximum daily performance capability. Past this point, performance begins to decline. Excessive levels and extended periods of stress can be dysfunctional to the school or school district because stress interferes with performance. Principals, for example, manifest erratic behavior, lose the ability to

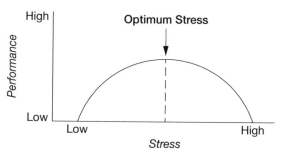

Figure 10.9 Relationship of Stress and Performance

cope, and cannot make decisions. The key is to balance stress so that an optimum level is reached for each school principal.

As noted, schools, by their very nature, are fertile grounds for conflict. The conflicts that occur frequently result in stress for principals, particularly secondary principals. Research on stress in the principalship indicates that much of it is caused by such sources as role conflict, instructional leadership expectations, problem solving, high activity level, time-management demand, and external politics (Lyons, 1990; Quick et al., 2008).

Role Conflict. Principals serve as members of the superintendent's administrative team and are expected to accomplish district goals. Simultaneously, they serve as leader of the school instructional team and its staff. Frequently, the goals, policies, and directives from the central office are incongruent with the goals, wishes, and expectations of staff members. When such conflicts occur, principals may experience stress.

Instructional Leadership Expectations. Most principals know they are expected to be instructional leaders in their schools. However, most secondary school principals find that the management role tends to dominate the instructional leadership role (Goldring et al., 2019). Although principals can delegate management tasks to associate and assistant principals, they are still responsible for overall results. The inability to devote sufficient attention to the instructional leadership role is a source of stress.

Problem Solving. The principal's office is frequently a collection point for problems. The overall effectiveness of the principal hinges on her/his ability to resolve these conflicts. Resolving these problems carries a price. The process is time consuming and stressful.

High Activity Level. The principal's day is busy, rapid-fire, and fragmented with numerous interruptions. There is little time for careful thought, reflection, and long-range planning. The "on-the-spot" interactions require "on-the-spot" answers and decisions. This causes stress.

External Politics. Increased accountability resulting from national and state reform mandates, recent Supreme Court decisions, and issues such as English learners, special education, sex education, drug education, vocational education, and school safety have added to the workload and stress level of principals.

Some suggestions for managing the level of stress follow (Olpin, 2016):

1. Do not allow work problems brought to you to become your problem.
2. Learn to delegate responsibilities and duties.
3. Give careful attention to your role as supervisor.
4. Find and maintain a network of trusted professional and personal friends.
5. Develop some activities that can reduce your anxieties and stress.

Effects of Stress

As noted previously, stress is not all bad. In fact, low-level stress can enhance job performance. High-level, prolonged stress, on the other hand, can be dysfunctional to both the individual's health and organizational performance. The effects of job stress can be manifested physiologically, psychologically, and behaviorally by the individual (Contrada & Baum, 2011).

On the physiological level, all types of stress produce a chemical reaction in the body. These include changes in metabolism, increased heart and breathing rates, increased blood pressure, and increased perspiration, skin temperature, blood glucose level, and blood clotting. If stress persists and is accompanied by these physiological changes, certain annoying and serious health conditions can result. Among them are heart disease, hypertension, increased blood cholesterol levels, ulcers, arthritis, allergies, gastrointestinal problems, and even cancer (Lovallo, 2005; Rice, 1998). It should be noted, however, that stress is not the only cause of these ailments. The genetic predisposition, diet, and lifestyle of an individual can also contribute to various health conditions (Lunenburg & Lunenburg, forthcoming).

While not as much attention has been given to the impact of stress on mental health as on physical health, psychological problems at work can be equally detrimental to job performance. Among the more common psychological outcomes of stress are anxiety, tension, depression, boredom, and mental fatigue (Avison & Gotlib, 2013). The effects of these psychological states on employee job performance are lowered self-esteem and poorer intellectual functioning, including the inability to concentrate and make decisions, irritability, forgetfulness, negativism, apathy, and job dissatisfaction (Conrad, 2011). These outcomes of stress can be costly to a school or school district. For example, there have been an increasing number of workers' compensation awards granted to employees based on job-related psychological stress (Rush, 1999).

The physiological and psychological effects of stress relate to how employees feel, whereas the behavioral effects indicate what employees actually do under stress. Consequently, an analysis of the behavioral effects of job stress may be most helpful to the school principal. Any sudden change in behavioral patterns may suggest that an employee is experiencing a high-level stress. Among the more common indicators are extremes in appetite, drug abuse, impulsive behavior, speech difficulties, accident proneness, higher tardiness and absenteeism, and decreased performance (Horowitz, 1997).

Coping with Stress

As noted earlier, school principals, in particular, are prone to high levels of job stress. Although stress cannot be completely eliminated from their work environments, it can be managed. That is, steps can be taken to minimize its harmful effects not only for themselves but for their employees as well. Several techniques for coping with stress have been proposed. Most fall into two categories: strategies that individuals can apply themselves and procedures that the school/school district can provide to minimize the onset of stress for employees.

Some specific techniques that individuals can use to manage stress are the following: exercise, lifestyle changes, meditation, biofeedback, visualization, networking, and mental health professionals (Allen, 2015; Lunenburg & Lunenburg, forthcoming; Quick et al., 2014; Seaward, 2011).

Exercise. A growing body of research indicates that individuals who exercise regularly are much less prone to heart disease and hypertension than those who do not exercise regularly. Exercise produces chemical responses within the body that diminish many of the physiological symptoms of stress discussed earlier (e.g., heart rate, breathing rate, blood pressure).

Lifestyle Changes. The best way to reduce and prevent stress is to lead a better life. The individual who has a proper diet, gets adequate sleep, exercises regularly, and avoids smoking, alcohol, and illegal drugs is likely to minimize the harmful effects of stress.

Meditation. Some research findings suggest that meditation affects basic bodily functions in a manner equivalent to deep rest. **Meditation** has been described as one of four major states of consciousness: deep rest, the other three are wakefulness, dreaming, and deep sleep. Such relaxation techniques can reduce the symptoms of stress.

Biofeedback. People under medical guidance can learn through electronic machines how to develop an awareness of muscle sensations throughout the body, known as **biofeedback.** With this knowledge, comes the ability to exercise control over their involuntary nervous system, which in turn controls internal processes such as heartbeat, breathing, brain waves, and the like. Thus, biofeedback may be helpful in reducing some undesirable effects of stress.

Visualization. These techniques are frequently used in combination with other stress reduction techniques, such as meditation or biofeedback, but they can also be used effectively alone. Methods of **visualization** can range from concentrating on a soothing color or focusing on a peaceful scene to imagining yourself performing the steps needed to achieve a goal.

Networking. One means of coping with job stress is through **networking**—that is, establishing a network of social support. This would involve building close associations with sympathetic others, especially coworkers and colleagues, who are good listeners and can build confidence.

Mental Health Professionals. Trained professionals such as psychiatrists, psychologists, social workers, or mental health counselors can help reduce feelings of stress and anxiety. A number of major medical centers throughout the country offer formal stress management programs. Most programs emphasize a holistic approach to wellness, teaching stress reduction and relaxation techniques, and offering nutritional counseling.

SUMMARY

1. The following factors create the need for change in schools: changing demographics, staffing shortages, technological changes and knowledge explosion, processes and behavioral problems, and indicators of declining effectiveness.

2. School employees often resist change because of the uncertainty it creates, concern over personal loss, group resistance, need for dependence, lack of trust in the principal, organic and mechanistic structures, awareness of weaknesses in the proposed change, and collective bargaining agreements.

3. Principals also can use specific tactics for overcoming resistance to change, including education and communication, participation and involvement, facilitation and support, negotiation and agreement, manipulation and co-optation, active learning, and explicit and implicit coercion.

4. Principals need to manage change. The most popular models are Kurt Lewin's force-field analysis, John Kotter's eight-step plan, Ben Harris's five-phase model, and Larry Greiner's six-phase process.

5. There are numerous organizational development (OD) techniques designed to plan and implement change. These OD techniques can be divided into two categories: process and structural. Process change strategies include survey feedback, sensitivity training, behavioral performance management, and quality of work life (QWL). Structural change strategies include goal setting, strategic planning, job redesign, and total quality management (TQM). Both process strategies and structural strategies are designed to improve teaching and learning.

6. Several personal factors are sources of stress for principals in the workplace. Such individual characteristics as need for achievement, aptitudes and skills, task understanding, and personality can influence how individuals experience and react to stress and stressors. For example, personality traits such as authoritarianism, introversion/extroversion, tolerance for ambiguity, locus of control, and self-esteem have been found to be related to job stress. Attention has focused, however, on the type A personality, which seems to relate to the ways in which individuals experience stress.

7. School principals feel more job pressures and time constraints than ever before. School principals report that they do not have sufficient time to do everything that needs to be done. The variety of problems principals face and the large spans of control found in most schools make it difficult for them to give all aspects of the school program sufficient attention. Not being able to do all that they would like to do in the time available is a continuing source of stress.

8. Stress can either help or hinder job performance, depending on the amount of stress and type of stress (e.g., challenge stressors or hindrance stressors). At very low levels of stress, job challenges are absent and performance tends to be low. As stress increases, performance tends to increase because stress helps an individual activate physiological and psychological resources to meet job requirements. Eventually, stress reaches a point—the optimum stress level—that corresponds roughly with a person's maximum daily performance capability. Past this point, performance begins to decline. Excessive levels and extended periods of stress can be dysfunctional to the school or school district because stress interferes with performance.

9. School principals, in particular, are prone to high levels of job stress. Although stress cannot be completely eliminated from their work environments, it can be managed. Some specific techniques that principals can use to manage stress are the following: exercise, lifestyle changes, meditation, biofeedback, visualization, networking, and the use of mental health professionals.

KEY TERMS

organizational change	manipulation
mechanistic structure	co-optation
organic structure	action learning

force-field analysis
unfreezing
moving
refreezing
change agent
organizational development (OD)
process strategies
survey feedback
sensitivity training
T-groups
stranger T-groups
cousin T-groups
brother T-groups
family T-groups
team building
behavioral performance
    management
contingencies of reinforcement
positive reinforcement
negative reinforcement

extinction
punishment
process change strategies
quality of work life
quality circle
structural change strategies
goal setting
strategic planning
job enrichment
total quality management (TQM)
stress
stressors
challenge stressors
hindrance stressors
type A personality
meditation
biofeedback
visualization
networking

FIELD-BASED ACTIVITIES

1. What changes have occurred in your school or school district? People often resist change for a variety of reasons: the uncertainty it creates, concern over personal loss, group norms, the need for independence, lack of trust in the principal, organic and mechanistic structures, awareness of weaknesses in the proposed change, and collective bargaining agreements. Observe and reflect on changes that have occurred in your school or school district. Take field notes for one week, during which time you analyze the type(s) of resistance to the change(s) that have occurred. In your journal, record the results of your observations, reflections, and analysis.

2. Principals use specific tactics for overcoming resistance to change: communication, participation, support, negotiation, manipulation and co-optation, active learning, and coercion. Which of these tactics does your principal use? Assuming you were the principal of a school, which tactics for overcoming resistance to change would you use? Write your response in your journal.

3. To accomplish change, principals can use several process change strategies (survey feedback, sensitivity training, behavioral performance management, and quality of work life) and several structural change strategies (goal setting, strategic planning, job redesign, and total quality management). Observe for one or more weeks and reflect on changes that have taken place in your school or school district. What strategies have your principal or central office administrators used to accomplish change in your school or school district? If you were

principal of a school, what strategies would you use to accomplish change in your school? Support your position. Write your responses in your journal. Be specific.

SUGGESTED READINGS

Fahey, K., Breidenstein, A., Ippolito, J., & Hensley, F. (2019). *An uncommon theory of school change*. New York, NY: Teachers College Press. The authors argue that if educators want to create more equitable, socially just, and learner-focused schools, then they need a more robust, transformational theory of school change—an "UnCommon Theory." The authors take a deep dive into the most difficult work that school leaders do: questioning, rethinking, and rein-venting the fundamental assumptions upon which schools are built. The result is a practical book that provides readers with the knowledge and tools needed to do more than just tinker at the edges of school improvement.

Fullan, M. (2015). *The new meaning of educational change* (3rd ed.). New York, NY: Teachers College Press. In 1982, an extraordinary book, *The New Meaning of Educational Change*, revolutionized the way educational reform was regarded. Now, Michael Fullan has greatly revised and expanded the ideas that make this book the definitive up-to-date reference for the educational innovator in the new millennium. It offers powerful insights into the complexity of change and recommends inspiring and practical strategies for lasting improvement.

Lytle, J. H., Lytle, S. L., Johanek, M. C., & Rho, K. J. (2018). *Repositioning educational leadership: Practitioners leading from an inquiry stance*. New York, NY: Teachers College Press. This groundbreaking volume encourages today's edu-cational leaders to reposition the way they think about leadership and its chal-lenges. Experienced school and district leaders reveal how they conceptualize their roles, how they learn by posing and solving problems of practice, and how they cope with increasing expectations and complexity in their work.

Murphy, J. F., & Louis, K. S. (2018). *Positive school leadership: Building capac-ity and strengthening relationships*. New York, NY: Teachers College Press. This landmark book translates asset-based understandings of organizations to develop a powerful model of school leadership that is grounded in research and the complexities of life in schools. The Positive School Leadership (PSL) model draws on the strengths of relationships to create a more inclusive, less "mecha-nistic" approach to leadership.

Sahlberg, P. (2021). *Finnish lessons 3.0: What can the world learn from educa-tional change in Finland?* (3rd ed.). New York, NY: Teachers College Press. This third edition of the Grawemeyer Award Winner includes important new material about teaching children with special needs, the role of play in high-quality edu-cation, and Finland's responses to growing inequality, slipping international test scores, and the global pandemic.

Sarason, Seymour. B. (2002). *Educational reform: A self-scrutinizing memoir*. New York: Teachers College Press. In this "self-scrutinizing memoir," Professor Sarason candidly confronts his "errors of omission and commission, mistakes, and emphases" in his half-century involvement in educational reform. Sharing his thoughts about the future of education, Sarason discusses his thinking on charter schools, productive learning, motivation, high-stakes testing, the impor-tance of working through change, the mistaken idea that we can clone reforms, and much more.

Part II Case Study

The New Math Program

■ ■ ■

Setting: Garfield Elementary School, whose principal is Ms. Glenna Greene, is a feeder school to Johnson Middle School, where Mr. Bill Fripps serves as principal. This middle school feeds into Muskie Junior High School, where Dr. Ted Caruthers is completing his first year as principal. All three principals have been struggling with a mandated change in the teaching of mathematics.

Scenario: Ms. Greene, principal of Garfield Elementary School, isn't sure what Mr. Davis, the new assistant superintendent for curriculum and instruction, wants her to do. In the conference they have just completed, Mr. Davis's message was that the just-released math scores on the state exam are not satisfactory. As he emphasized to Ms. Greene, the school board had told the superintendent that unless each campus met the goal of 90 percent mastery on the math test at each grade level, the board would be requesting weekly progress reports from each principal.

Although Ms. Greene's school has shown an increased percentage of students mastering the exam (from 85 to 87 percent mastery), such a gain, evidently, is not enough. She wonders if the school board members know that changes in programs take a good deal of time to implement. The new math program was initiated just two years ago, after much planning and discussion. Ms. Greene thinks back to the data showing that all grades, one to eight, were lacking a strong program in mathematics. There had been some rather sharp discussions about how to address this need. A review of test results, personnel concerns, teaching strategies, differing philosophies, and more had led to some heated debate. Even some letters from concerned parents had been read during the council meeting. The few teachers who served on the curriculum council voiced their skepticism about how successful a new approach would be, especially with teachers who were experienced and felt they had reasonable success. Nevertheless, after all was said and done, the curriculum council finally recommended that the district adopt a new math textbook and implement new strategies to complement the text. The school board approved that recommendation.

In an unrelated action, the former assistant superintendent for curriculum and instruction had retired. The principals were left to follow up on introducing the new textbook and the accompanying strategies. The new assistant superintendent

377

for curriculum and instruction, Mr. Davis, was hired after the start of the school year. Some of the more accomplished, younger teachers at the three schools favored the new approach and did not mind helping their colleagues; but most of the older teachers resisted adopting the new program. Those teachers would not *really* use the new text and strategies. Ostensibly, they did. When observed, they would have the correct textbook in hand; but they have never fully changed to the new teaching strategies—at least not yet.

Mr. Davis was not familiar with this new approach to mathematics. That left only a few teachers who were comfortable with the change. Teachers at the middle and junior high schools said they felt as though the curriculum council had sold them out. At the time of the vote, the curriculum council was composed of a math teacher from each school, an assistant principal or principal from each campus, and the assistant superintendent for curriculum and instruction. The former assistant superintendent for curriculum and instruction had handpicked the teachers who served on the council. He had sparked the whole move to a new program.

A new curriculum council reviewed the math test scores for last year and found some minimal improvement at the middle school and junior high levels. The elementary level had made the most gains, edging scores upward from 81 to 85 percent mastery in grade three.

Next week, Ms. Greene thinks, the council will review this year's gains. At least her campus has improved again. She is proud of that, of her team, and of their effort to improve. Certainly, she will praise them all and share her pride with the curriculum council.

Ms. Greene wonders about the results at Johnson Middle School and Muskie Junior High School. Just as she is about to pick up the phone and call one of those principals, her phone rings.

"Glenna! Have you heard from our illustrious curriculum leader?" asks Bill Fripps, principal of the middle school. "I'm so mad I could pop! He told me that my campus was a failure, and that I'd better get busy finding out why. Our test results showed that our math scores have not improved substantially again. We did have some improvement, but not enough to please everyone. We moved from 65 percent mastery to 72 percent mastery. I think that's a substantial gain—and pretty good, given the fact that all this change has been imposed on us with no help from the central office. My math teachers are going to be proud of that, not ashamed. I couldn't care less if I have to write another report for the board each week. More paperwork! Another reason I can't become the instructional leader they want me to be. Enough of this. Thanks for letting me blow off steam. How did you do?"

"We improved some, too," Ms. Greene replies. "I'm proud of my staff, just as you are. I think maybe we as principals and instructional leaders need to meet with Mr. Davis and review a few things. What do you think, Bill?"

"You may be on the right track, Glenna. Maybe you don't know that your neighbor at the junior high school is unhappy, too. Have you had a chance to talk to Ted?"

"No, I haven't talked to Ted. What happened with him?"

"His group improved from 77 percent mastery to 80 percent mastery," says Bill. "Still, he hasn't been greeted with congratulations. You know as well as I do that making sure the change went smoothly has really been left to us. We've worked our tails off trying to build a math team on each campus. We all want success for each student, but if you ask me, shooting for 90 percent mastery for all students in two years is too much. I mean, the goal is good; but with a program change like this, we can't expect such huge gains in such a short time."

"Whoops! My secretary is telling me Ted is on the other line. I'll call you back in a few minutes. Will you be there, Bill?"

"Yes. It seems that I have some paperwork to complete. Call me when you finish talking to Ted."

"Hello, Ted," says Glenna, "how can I help you? It's been a busy day. Have you met with Mr. Davis?"

"You bet I have, and he didn't make me very happy. I was just thinking that we should be getting our test results back; and if we succeeded in boosting our scores to 80 percent mastery, I was going to have a faculty party so the teachers could celebrate. Mr. Davis certainly threw cold water on that idea. We did raise our scores to 80 percent mastery, but it seems those results didn't make the central office happy. We've been using this new math textbook for less than two years. My teachers have gone all out, trying to help the students really understand all the tested material. Well, we may have a party anyway, even if I have to throw it off campus or at my home."

"Bill and I were just visiting about this very issue. What do you think of getting together with Mr. Davis soon, before the curriculum council meets? I think we need to explain a few things to him about the background on this, and about all that we and our teachers have done."

"OK. Why don't you try calling him and asking for a meeting before the end of this week? Then, maybe tomorrow, at least the three of us can get together and plan our presentation to him. I have copious notes on what we've done in the last year and a half to support this imposed change. You know, I think perhaps we need to go to the heart of the issue. We need to change the policy about how the curriculum council operates. We need to make certain that membership enables the teachers to have an adequate voice. That's one of my staff's main concerns. They feel that they are professionals and should be given an opportunity to provide input. In this case, only a very few teachers were involved in deciding to make a major change for the district."

"OK, Ted," says Glenna, "I'll set up a meeting for the three of us with Mr. Davis. I agree with you. We need to have more of our teachers involved when we plan such a major change. I'll be in touch with you about the meeting very soon."

Questions

1. What are some of the driving and restraining forces in this case study?
2. What do you think you would have done to support change had you been principal when the new math program was adopted?
3. If you were one of the principals, what assistance would you ask Mr. Davis to provide?
4. How might strategic planning aid in this whole effort?
5. Do you think the test results indicate that some major changes have occurred?
6. As a principal, what evidence would you seek to have in place to substantiate a successful change in the math program?

PART III

Managing the
Organization

11

Budgeting and School Facilities

■ ■ ■

FOCUSING QUESTIONS

1. How are school budgets developed?
2. Why are financial controls necessary in schools?
3. Are zero-base budgeting and planning-programming-budgeting systems, or variations thereof, suitable for schools?
4. What is the average age of schools in your district? What school infrastructure items are most costly in your district?
5. How are principals and other school personnel dealing with environmental hazards in their school buildings?

In this chapter, we address these questions concerning budgeting and school facilities. We begin our discussion with school budgeting, the budgeting process, and financial controls. Then we discuss the pros and cons of two budgeting methods, zero-based budgeting and planning-programming-budgeting systems, as alternatives to line-item budgeting. Next, we discuss school facilities, including school infrastructure costs and financing new construction. We conclude the chapter with a discussion of environmental hazards, including asbestos, radon gas, school lead, indoor air quality, and electromagnetic fields.

SCHOOL BUDGETING

Budgeting is both an executive and legislative function. The executive entity (superintendent/district staff and school principal) proposes, and the legislative entity (school board) enacts. On formal adoption by the school board, the budget becomes a legal document that serves as the basis for annual expenditures, accounting, and auditing. According to school finance experts (Baker, 2018; Born, 2020; Coffin & Cooper, 2017; Odden & Picus, 2020; Owings & Kaplan, 2020; Schilling & Tomal, 2019; Sorenson & Goldsmith, 2018), budgeting involves five major steps: preparation, submission, adoption, execution, and evaluation. The third step, adoption, involves the school board, which appropriates specific amounts for specific categories. The other four steps involve the superintendent, business manager, and/or the principal.

Typically, the **budget** is organized around four major categories: *objects* (e.g., salaries, supplies, travel), *functions* (e.g., instruction, transportation, plant), *programs* (e.g., English, mathematics, gifted education), and *location* (school, groups of schools, or school district). The state usually mandates the items for objects and functions, whereas the school district usually develops the items for programs and locations. The budget may also include other features such as a list of goals, objectives or criteria; projected revenues from all local, state, and federal sources; comparison of expenditures for the previous year by categories; the amount needed to pay the principal and interest for the school bonds maturing during the fiscal year; and a budget summary.

Although the superintendent (with staff assistance) holds the major responsibility for submitting the budget, the principal's role in budgeting may either be limited or substantial. A superintendent who maintains a high centralized administration will most likely limit the principal's responsibilities to completing requisitions, receipts, and disbursements. A decentralized administration will delegate more fiscal decision-making responsibilities to the principal.

Regardless of professional empowerment, the school staff must understand that only 5 to 10 percent of the school district's budget is available for modification. About 65 to 70 percent is earmarked for salaries and benefits; around 20 to 25 percent goes for operating expenses such as utilities, insurance, repairs, and maintenance; and some monies should be committed for reserves and replacement. Although the principal (and staff) may be permitted to make budget recommendations, the school board finalizes the budget.

The principal's budgeting roles can be classified into four major activities: (a) *budget planning*, assisting the superintendent in identifying budget priorities and focusing on school needs at the planning stage; (b) *budget analysis*, dealing with the goals, objectives, and evaluative criteria, suggestions for curriculum materials and instructional equipment, and communicating concerns of the students, parents, teachers, and community about specific expenditures or special purposes; (c) *budget requesting*, involving a review of requests by different groups such as teachers or parents, establishing program priorities, submitting a total budget, and negotiating specific items; and (d) *budget controls,* dealing with inventory expenses, receipts and disbursements, monthly reporting, and balancing the books at the building level (Kaplan & Owings, 2015; Marshall, 2021; Sergiovanni & Green, 2015; Spillane & Lowenhaupt, 2019; Ubben, Hughes, & Norris, 2016; Williamson & Blackburn, 2016). The fourth activity deals with the regular school operation, which involves ongoing paperwork and record keeping.

In large elementary schools, a person (perhaps the assistant principal or a teacher) representing a program area or grade level, and a department head in secondary schools, is usually asked to list and prioritize needs. If cutbacks make it necessary to reduce school budgets, the trimming process usually begins with the low-priority programs or items. Ultimately, the principal submits the budget to the central office. There, it is either approved or modified, with or without negotiation with the principal. Eventually, an approved budget is returned to the principal. Each month, a person at the program or department level may be required to complete requisitions and purchase orders; each month, a budget summary, to date, may be returned by the school district business manager or chief financial officer to the principal and/or school department or program, indicating the amount of money remaining in each account item.

Usually, the principal is required to submit a monthly budget to the central office, which includes several income and expense categories. Depending on the school district's accounting system, the budget items may include receipts, vouchers, bank statements, a method for authorizing expenditures, expenditures paid only by check, a regular audit, and monthly and annual reporting (Baker, 2018; Born, 2020; Coffin & Cooper, 2017; Odden & Picus, 2020; Owings & Kaplan, 2020; Schilling & Tomal, 2019; Sorenson & Goldsmith, 2018).

Budgets translate the school district's education plan into numerical terms (Baker, 2018; Born, 2020; Coffin & Cooper, 2017; Odden & Picus, 2020; Owings & Kaplan, 2020; Schilling & Tomal, 2019; Sorenson & Goldsmith, 2018). Thus, budgets are statements of planned revenue and expenditures by category and period of time. School districts may establish budgets for building units, divisions, or the entire school district. The usual time period for a school district budget is one year.

Expenditures

Education **expenditures** are divided for accounting purposes into current expenses, capital improvement, long-term and short-term debt payment, and interest payment. In addition, the US Department of Education, in conjunction with the Association of School Business Officials (ASBO), has developed a uniform classification system of current expenses that most state departments of education have accepted and are using.

Current Expenses. **Current expenses** include all monies disbursed for the daily operation of schools. They are usually classified in the annual budget under the following four categories: *instruction*, including regular programs (elementary, middle/junior high school, high school), special programs, and adult/continuing education programs; *support services*, including attendance and health services, pupil transportation services, food services and student activities, plant maintenance, instructional staff and support services, and general administration; *community services*, including recreation, civic activities, and nonpublic school services; and *nonprogrammed charges*, including payments to other governmental units.

Capital Outlay. Items that are constructively consumable during a single fiscal year (e.g., salaries, textbooks, and supplies) are listed under current expenses; an item with a life expectancy of more than one year is considered a capital expense. Thus, **capital outlay** includes all permanent additions to existing land, buildings, and equipment. It differs from expenditures for plant maintenance in that capital outlay represents an extension of the existing plant.

Debt Service. **Debt service** includes the payment of short- and long-term loans and revenue payments for the principal as well as interest on these debts. Principal payments are made directly, as in the case of serial bonds, or into a sinking fund for retiring long-term bonds.

If a school district pays for capital extension out of current tax revenues or on a pay-as-you-build basis, there is no need for a budget classification for debt service, except for short-term or floating debts. By law, school districts raise all their own revenue to meet the communities' needs, including capital extension, which sometimes necessitates borrowing funds for that purpose (Alexander & Alexander,

2019; Russo, 2015). The use of credit for plant extension, therefore, represents an additional handicap to school districts, because debt service is a prior budgetary obligation that may carry over from one year's budget to the next until the debt is paid. And the total expense of long-term borrowing for capital extension generally more than doubles the cost of the school plant. *Interest payments* are made as they fall due.

Revenue

Although in the past public schools depended chiefly on local sources of revenue for their support, the relative percentage of local and state contributions has changed greatly over nearly a century. In the 1919–1920 school year, local districts contributed 83.2 percent of the total revenue for the operation of public schools in the United States. State contributions for public education were 16.5 percent. In the 2015–2016 school year, local revenue for public education had declined to 45.0 percent and state appropriations were 46.6 percent nationally. The remaining balance of 8.5 percent was derived from federal funds (National Center for Education Statistics, 2017.) The change has resulted in a better-balanced revenue system generally and, in many cases, better-equalized educational opportunity for all schoolchildren.

Current expenditures and debt payment remain largely dependent on the general property tax. State appropriations are derived primarily from the general property, sales, and income taxes. Regular federal contributions are taken from the general treasury and represent income from all sources of federal taxation. The local school district has comparatively little authority over the methods and sources of financing its schools; this is a state responsibility. The Tenth Amendment to the US Constitution confers on the state the authority not only to regulate and control education but also to devise and implement its own system of taxation.

Thus, the authority of local school districts to raise and collect taxes for schools is a power that the state legislature must confer on them. Furthermore, not all districts have the same taxing power. The legislature can classify school districts and delegate varied financial powers to those dependent on their classification.

Basically, with respect to their power to tax and raise funds for public schools, there are two broad classifications of school districts: fiscally independent school districts and fiscally dependent school districts. The vast majority of the nearly 15,000 public school districts in the nation are fiscally independent.

Fiscally Independent School Districts. The state legislature grants **fiscally independent school districts** legal authority to set the tax rate on real property, within state constitutional and legislative limits; to levy and collect taxes for the support of local schools; and to approve the expenditure of the funds collected. States require local school boards to prepare budgets of proposed expenditures. In fiscally independent school districts, the school boards have a relatively free hand in determining how and where expenditures are to be made, subject to limitations on the total amount by the state's constitution or statute. For example, in Florida, local school authorities levy and collect taxes for school purposes, independent of the local, county, or city governments. However, Florida state law sets a legal limit on the tax rates that can be established by local school boards (Alexander & Alexander, 2019; Russo, 2015). Similarly, in Kentucky, state statutes grant local school boards authority to tax property for the support of public schools (*Kentucky Revised Statutes* Chapter 161.593, 2018).

Fiscally Dependent School Districts. In **fiscally dependent school districts**, the school board prepares and adopts a budget specifying the anticipated expenditures and projected revenue needs. Then a different municipal government may reduce the total budget or eliminate items not required by state law and apportion the school taxes. For example, in Chicago, statutory language authorizes the school tax levy to be a cooperative endeavor, joining the board of education and city officials. Although the local board performs all the preliminary steps in the budget process—preparation, review, and adoption—no school taxes can be forthcoming until the city council adopts an ordinance levying the tax (Alexander & Alexander, 2019; Russo, 2015). Similarly, in Alaska, Maryland, Massachusetts, New Hampshire, New York, and Pennsylvania, school districts are fiscally dependent on the municipal government to apportion taxes for school purposes (Alexander & Alexander, 2019; Russo, 2015).

Challenges to State Finance Schemes

Several states have challenged finance schemes as inequitable. These challenges were advanced using two separate standards: the *educational needs standard* and the *fiscal neutrality standard*. Using the **educational needs standard**, plaintiffs challenged the constitutionality of state finance schemes under the equal protection clause of the Fourteenth Amendment. Additionally, plaintiffs claimed that there were markedly inequitable per-pupil expenditures among school districts in various states. Using the **fiscal neutrality standard**, the US Supreme Court rejected the federal constitutional theory that education is a right under the Constitution. The Court left in the hands of state legislatures the responsibility to remedy any existing inequities in state funding systems. Under the *fiscal neutrality standard*, the quality of a child's education could not be a function of the wealth of the child's local school district but rather must be based on the wealth of the state as a whole.

The fiscal neutrality standard represents an evolutionary step in the judicial expansion of equal rights protection under the federal Constitution regarding public school finance. Litigation in school finance issues continues to flourish. The federal courts have been abandoned as an arena for such litigation. The Supreme Court has made it clear that successful challenges to state finance schemes must be pursued on state constitutional grounds rather than on the provisions of the US Constitution. Plaintiffs continue to pattern their arguments on the fiscal neutrality standard.

THE BUDGETING PROCESS

Traditionally, budgets have been prepared by the school district's chief financial officer (CFO), with the approval of the superintendent, and then imposed on lower-level administrators. Although some school districts may still follow this pattern, many others now allow building principals to participate in the process of formulating the budget. This practice, known as **school-based budgeting**, helps principals to internalize budgets as their own and to use these budgets as operating guides to implement their educational plans (Brimley, Verstegen, & Garfield, 2020; Owings & Kaplan, 2019; Sorenson & Goldsmith, 2018). Although the process could begin in almost any area, school districts usually start with a revenue budget, which is derived from three sources—local, state, and federal revenues—based on projected enrollment figures for the fiscal year. Then, almost simultaneously, building principals prepare their

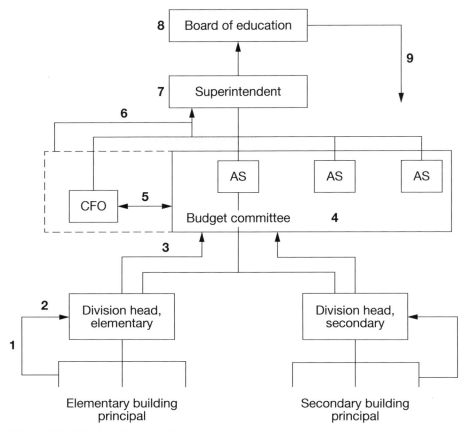

Figure 11.1 The Budgetary Process

own units' expenditure budgets and submit these budgets to upper-level administration for approval. Figure 11.1 illustrates the steps involved in preparing a budget using a school-based budgeting approach.

In step 1, the building principals submit their budget requests to their appropriate division head. The division head takes the various budget requests from the building principals and integrates and consolidates them into one overall division budget request (step 2). Overlapping and/or inconsistent requests are corrected at this stage. For example, two principals might each request $10,000 to buy five computers. The division head knows that an order of ten computers carries a 10 percent discount, so the school district will request $18,000 to buy ten computers. Much interaction between administrators usually takes place as the division head works to integrate and coordinate the budgetary needs of the various building sites.

In step 3, division budget requests are forwarded to a budget committee. The budget committee itself, shown as step 4 in figure 11.1, is composed of top-level administrators with line authority. The committee members are likely to be associate or assistant superintendents (AS). Budget requests from the two divisions are reviewed at this stage and, once again, overlaps and inconsistencies are corrected.

Step 5 of the process involves interaction between the budget committee and the chief financial officer (CFO). This interaction can take a variety of forms. The budgets could pass from the committee to the CFO for further evaluation and approval. Or the CFO could be a member of the budget committee. Or the CFO might evaluate the budget requests before they go to the budget committee.

In step 6, the final budget is sent to the superintendent of schools for approval. After undergoing their scrutiny (step 7), it is passed on to the school board for review (step 8). Final budgets are then passed back down to the division heads and building principals (step 9). As the budget requests pass through these stages, some changes may be made. The budget that each building site ultimately has available may be more than, less than, or the same as what it initially requested.

This school-based budgeting approach is often advocated because it has two primary strengths. First, individual building principals are able to identify resource requirements about which top-level administrators are uninformed. Site leaders (principals) have information on efficiencies and opportunities in their specialized units. Second, school principals are motivated to meet the budget, because they participated in its formulation and therefore feel it is their responsibility (Sorenson & Goldsmith, 2018).

There may be, however, disadvantages to site-based budgeting. Let's look at the advantages and disadvantages of site-based budgeting. The question is, should the building principal have total control of the budget? The school literature on quality supports decentralization of the budget to the site where the product is made or the service is delivered. The thinking behind this recommendation is that those at the site are in a better position to know how to allocate resources in order to meet school goals. In a school setting, site-based budgeting means that the school's administrative team controls all funds necessary for the functioning of the school, including the largest budget category: personnel.

The advantages of site-based budgeting include the following (Brimley, Verstegen, & Garfield, 2020; Owings & Kaplan, 2020; Sorenson & Goldsmith, 2018):

1. Site-based budgeting is an enlightened approach. It empowers the educators at the school site.
2. Principals often feel their hands are tied by bureaucratic regulations originating from the central office.
3. Principals are more able to meet needs if they have control of important variables. Because they are accountable for outcomes of a school, they should have the option of allocating all resources as needed.
4. Only people at the site know exactly what resources are needed. For example, the superintendent has no idea how many teacher aides are needed in a building. The present way of doing things is ineffective.

Here are some disadvantages of site-based budgeting (Brimley, Verstegen, & Garfield, 2020; Owings & Kaplan, 2020; Sorenson & Goldsmith, 2018):

1. Site-based budgeting is inimical to districtwide coordination and quality control. Accountability is diffused and weakened.
2. Policy and regulation, including the teachers' contract, are safeguards that protect most people in the school district from the frivolous behavior of some.
3. People are comfortable with the traditional budgeting paradigm whereby the principal and department chairpersons indicate needs and make requests.

Principals and department chairs would be extremely uncomfortable making all budget decisions and being held accountable for them.

4. Teachers and principals are generally not risk takers. Given full control of a school's budget, they would probably play it safe. They would be unlikely to invest in important but costly new ventures.

Zero-Based Budgeting

In most school districts, the budgeting process begins with the previous year's budget; that is, administrators plan future expenditures as an increase or decrease over the previous year. Under **zero-based budgeting** (**ZBB**), administrators must start the budgeting process at zero every year, and they must substantiate all expenditures—new and continuing (Hammond & Knott, 1980). Thus, the entire expenditures budget must be justified, not merely the adjustments to an existing budget.

Zero-based budgeting was originally developed for use in government organizations as a way to justify budget requests for the coming year. The US Department of Agriculture was the first to use ZBB in the 1960s. Texas Instruments adopted ZBB in 1970, and Jimmy Carter used ZBB while governor of Georgia. Later, as president, Carter ordered ZBB used in the executive branch of the federal government. Since then, many government agencies, business firms, state departments of education, and local school districts have adopted ZBB (or variations thereof).

The ingredients of ZBB are not new. The concept's founders extracted a viable budgetary technique from the following systems: management by objectives, performance budgeting, program budgeting, incremental budgeting, and line-item budgeting. These management techniques were integrated into a budgeting process, ZBB, which involves three steps (Odden & Picus, 2020): (a) identify decision units, (b) develop decision packages, and (c) rank the decision packages.

Identify Decision Units. As a first step, to prevent conflicts and assure complete budgeting for the entire school district, all possible decision units should be identified and the nature of their responsibilities and operation defined. At the district level, decision units might include the superintendent's office, the business office, personnel administration, curriculum and instruction, and the like. At the building level, decision units might include the principal's office, student services, curricular departments, teaching teams, attendance services, and other support service areas.

Develop Decision Packages. A decision package is a document that describes and justifies a specific program or activity in such a way that decision makers can evaluate it and rank it against other activities competing for available resources. Each package must include sufficient information about the program or activity to allow the next level of administration to properly understand and evaluate it. This information includes the following:

1. The purpose or function of the unit
2. Alternative means to carry out unit functions
3. The cost and benefits of each alternative
4. The technical and operational feasibility of each alternative
5. Performance measures to compare past and present productivity
6. The consequences of not funding a particular program or activity

Rank the Decision Packages. The final step in ZBB involves ranking decision packages. The initial ranking occurs at the lowest organizational level, where the packages are developed. In schools, for example, this might involve department chairpersons, head custodians, and building principals. This permits the unit leader to evaluate the importance of her own activities and to rank the decision packages affecting her unit accordingly. Next, the packages would be ranked by each succeeding administrative level (see figure 11.1). Budget revenues are then distributed according to activities ranked as essential to meeting the school district's goals. Some departments or divisions may receive increases, some decreases, and others nothing at all.

On the one hand, ZBB provides a constant reassessment of all the school district's programs and divisions as regards their ongoing contribution to the organization's goals. ZBB facilitates the development of new programs. And it broadens the base of decision making by involving personnel at operating units in the budgeting process. On the other hand, the process of continual justification necessitates more paperwork at every level of administration, and administrators may tend to inflate the benefits of their programs in order to maintain funding.

The application of ZBB in schools is frequently more appropriate in support areas such as research and development, personnel, and finance—where programs are more likely to be discretionary—than in instructional areas. That is, administration can change such programs easily if cost-benefit analysis indicates that such action is warranted. However, ZBB is less applicable in instructional areas, because a prescribed curriculum may be mandated by the state and a core curriculum may be necessary to develop a student's essential and life skills.

Planning-Programming-Budgeting Systems

The planning-programming-budgeting system (PPBS) was pioneered at the RAND (research and development) Corporation in connection with weapons system analysis for the United States Air Force in the 1950s; the Department of Defense implemented the system in 1961. A few years later, in 1965, President Lyndon B. Johnson popularized PPBS by directing all federal agencies to use this budgeting technique (Doh, 1971).

Planning-programming-budgeting systems (PPBS) were developed to provide school leaders with objective information to aid in planning educational programs and for choosing between alternative ways of allocating funds to achieve the school's goals (Odden & Picus, 2020). PPBS is very similar to zero-based budgeting (ZBB), but it does not assume that all programs must be re-justified during each budget cycle.

The essential steps of PPBS include the following: (a) specify goals, (b) search for relevant alternatives, (c) measure the cost of the program for several years, and (d) evaluate the output of each program. Each one will be discussed in turn.

Specify Goals. The process begins by analyzing and specifying the basic goals in each major activity or program area. The starting point of PPBS is to answer such questions as "What is our basic purpose or mission?" and "What, specifically, are we trying to accomplish?" For example, a school district's goal might be to improve management information systems by implementing computer technology districtwide. A school building's goal might be to improve all students' performance on the state-mandated achievement test.

Search for Relevant Alternatives. Through PPBS, school administrators assess as fully as possible the total costs and benefits of various alternatives. Program budgeting is an endeavor to determine the rates of return for programs as well as the rate of return to be forgone when one program is chosen over another. The implementation of a computer network, for example, may be the most efficient way to improve management information systems in the school district.

Measure the Costs of the Program for Several Years. An essential feature of PPBS is long-range planning and budgeting. For example, in budgeting for additional schools, decision makers would need to consider not only the initial costs of construction but also the costs of operating and maintaining the facilities in future years. In addition, long-term enrollment projections must be made to determine the future need for school facilities.

Evaluate the Output of Each Program. PPBS focuses on the outputs of programs, whereas traditional budgeting approaches tend to emphasize expenditure inputs. Program budgeting enables school administrators to compare program proposals, relate them to current activities, evaluate their priority, and then increase or decrease allocations of resources to them. In other words, it is an attempt to answer the question, "How effectively and efficiently are we achieving our goals?"

The planning-programming-budgeting system has great potential benefit in education, where budgeting too often has been regarded as merely a technique for controlling the allocation and expenditure of revenues, rather than as a tool for planning (Baker, 2018; Brimley, Verstegen, & Garfield., 2020; Guthrie et al., 2008). For too many years, public school budgeting has been handled largely on a line-item basis, allocating funds to such accounts as salaries, textbooks, supplies, equipment, and contracted services rather than earmarking money for programs designed to accomplish identifiable program objectives. Furthermore, because program responsibility is often fragmented among various divisions, buildings, or departments, and because most goals are expressed in such general terms as "providing adequate counseling services," budgeting has tended to be an exercise by various divisions of competing and negotiating for funds rather than a unification of effort and support to accomplish specific program goals.

Despite its benefits, for most schools and school districts, PPBS has not been the great tool in practice that its logic would imply. There are several reasons for this. First, many school leaders do not understand the philosophy and theory of the technique. They have tended to provide lower-level administrators, including principals, with directives and forms without really understanding the system. Second, schools have multiple and conflicting goals that are vague and ambiguous. And schools lack clearly defined success criteria. Leaders cannot sensibly program, plan, and budget for an unknown or vague goal that is not easily measurable. Third, in many cases, there is a lack of attention to planning premises: Even with clear program goals, the decision maker needs to have a clear understanding of critical planning concepts. Fourth, schools have a long tradition of doing line-item budgeting, and most school board members, accustomed to this approach, often reject program budgets unless they are presented in a line-item format. Finally, because revenues are dispersed annually for the operation of schools, many school leaders have been reluctant to change from the practice of annual budgets to long-range program budgets.

FINANCIAL CONTROLS

Financial control techniques assist building principals and other school leaders in acquiring, allocating, and evaluating the use of financial resources—cash, accounts receivable, accounts payable, inventories, purchases, and long-term debt. Regardless of their size, school districts must be able to pay short-term obligations and long-term debts. They must also protect the school district's revenue from theft, unlawful conversion, and misuse. Control of financial resources in individual schools and school districts is implemented primarily through two methods: internal control and financial audits (Bragg, 2016).

Internal Control

Internal control is an accounting function and responsibility. Through the efforts of the school district's accounting unit headed by the CFO, policies and procedures are adopted to safeguard assets and verify the accuracy and reliability of accounting data. The following are some characteristics of effective internal control (American Management Association, 2022):

1. Formal organization should be clear. Definitions of job responsibilities must be estimated so as to fix accountability for every aspect of a financial transaction. The organizing function of administration must be the primary source for this important aspect of internal control.
2. Financial accounts must be set up for each division or other unit of administration. When expenses and income are readily traceable to specific administrators, they are more easily controlled. Such communication between accounts and divisions or building units is especially important in both the preparation of budgets and the evaluation phase of the accounting system.
3. Employees who handle assets should not also be responsible for record keeping of those assets. For example, employees who receive and store materials should not also verify the receipt of those materials.
4. No one person should have complete control over all phases of an important transaction. For example, the same individual should not be responsible for preparing purchase orders and for making out the checks in payment of those purchases.
5. The flow of work from employee to employee should not be duplicative, but the work of the second employee should provide a check on the work of the first. For example, the check drawn to pay for supplies and materials should be cosigned by a second employee who verifies the accuracy and legitimacy of the transaction.

Effective internal control procedures can be established for each distinct financial resource. Cash, accounts receivable, interest, inventories, accounts payable, payrolls, and purchases must be safeguarded through procedures that conform to the preceding five characteristics of effective internal control.

Financial Audits

Another major financial control technique is the **financial audit**—an independent appraisal of a school district's accounting, financial, and operational systems. Audits are of two types: external and internal (American Institute of Certified Public Accountants, 2022; Carmichael, 2011; Hooks, 2011; Louwers, 2014; US Government Accountability Office, 2013a, 2013b).

An **external audit** is conducted outside the school district by experts such as bank examiners or certified public accountants (CPA). Their main purpose is not to prepare the school district's financial reports but to verify that the district, in preparing its own financial statements, has followed generally accepted accounting principles and applied them correctly. External audits are so important that some states require all public school districts to have their financial records examined and certified by outside accountants, as assurance to taxpayers that the school district's financial reports are accurate.

An **internal audit** is performed by school district employees who are trained to examine the accuracy of the school district's accounting and financial reports. Large school districts may have an accounting staff assigned to the internal audit function. Like external auditors, internal auditors verify the accuracy of financial and accounting procedures used by the school district. Internal audits also focus on the efficiency and appropriateness of the financial and accounting procedures. Besides appraising the school district's accounting and financial operations, internal audits sometimes involve assessment of operations in general, including policies, procedures, use of authority, quality of management, effectiveness of methods, special problems, and so forth.

Both external and internal audits should be thorough. Following are some of the areas examined by auditors (American Institute of Certified Public Accountants, 2022):

1. *Cash flow*. Confirm bank balances; review cash management procedures.
2. *Accounts receivable*. Obtain verification from vendors concerning amounts owed and anticipated payments; confirm bank balances.
3. *Inventory*. Count physical inventory to verify accuracy of the school district's financial reports.
4. *Fixed assets*. Check physical evidence of fixed assets (buildings, equipment); evaluate depreciation; determine whether insurance is adequate.
5. *Loans*. Review long- and short-term loan agreements; summarize the school district's obligations.
6. *Revenues and expenditures*. Evaluate proper matching; safeguard assets; prevent or detect fraud or theft.

SCHOOL FACILITIES MANAGEMENT

Management of school facilities falls within the key duties of the school principal. Principals need to embrace this responsibility as they gain greater control and are held more accountable. Aging school buildings often create barriers that impede effective teaching and learning. This situation has resulted in escalating school infrastructure costs. A case can be made to renovate or build new facilities that maximize an optimal learning environment. Such a choice will necessitate financing school construction. Moreover, principals need to be cognizant of environmental hazards that can threaten the health and safety of students and staff. In this section, we discuss escalating school infrastructure costs, financing new school construction, and environmental hazards.

School Infrastructure Costs

The nation's school infrastructure is in a state of critical disrepair. By **infrastructure** we mean the physical facilities that underpin the school plant (plumbing, sewer, heat, electric, roof, masonry, carpentry). Schools seem to be deteriorating at a faster rate than they can be repaired and faster than new schools can be built or renovated.

According to a 2008 American Federation of Teachers report, the total school infrastructure need across all fifty states stands at $254.6 billion, with the average state funding need at almost $5.1 billion (Crampton & Thompson, 2008). Harvard professor Lawrence Summers claims that 75 percent of the nation's schools have structural deficiencies, particularly ventilation, sewage, and roof systems problems (Herbert, 2010). In 2017 it was reported by the American Society of Civil Engineers that an estimated amount to improve schools is $2.2 trillion. The president has called for $1 trillion to improve schools infrastructure (American Society of Civil Engineers, 2017; Kominiak, 2017).

Of the fifty states, Vermont has the lowest estimate of infrastructure needs, at $325.7 million; California has the highest need, at $25.4 billion. Between 2011 and 2013, US school districts spent just over $270 billion for school construction. Between 2010 and 2017, more than half the construction dollars went toward additions and renovations. Spending has shifted to almost 75 percent allocated toward new school construction, leaving leaking roofs, faulty wiring, and other deferred expenditures on hold (American Society of Civil Engineers, 2017).

And it is pretty safe to conclude, as does the American Society of Civil Engineers report (2017, p. 18), that "the burden for the funding of school infrastructure . . . will likely . . . result in a zero-sum game whereby existing state and local tax dollars are redirected away from other critical needs. The capacity of states and local communities to fully redress public schools' infrastructure deficiencies, particularly under current economic conditions, is almost certainly insufficient in light of an estimated funding need of $254.6 billion."

The life of a school building has five stages. It has lived its normal life the first twenty to twenty-five years, especially in the Sunbelt where construction is cheaper. When it is twenty-five to thirty years old, frequent equipment replacement is needed. When it is thirty to forty years old, most of the original equipment and materials should have been replaced—especially roofs, lighting fixtures, and heating equipment. Accelerated deterioration takes place when it is forty to fifty years old. A fifty-year-old building is sometimes too new to abandon, especially in the Frostbelt, where construction is usually good; but after sixty years, a number of buildings are usually abandoned, reconstructed, or replaced (Lewis, 1989; Theobald, 2006). That said, a significant number of buildings in big cities, especially in Chicago, Detroit, St. Louis, and Houston are at least seventy-five years old.

Government estimates for the condition of the nation's schools are grim. The top items rated as "inadequate" and in need of repair or replacement in the year 2013 were as follows: (1) heating, air, and ventilation (43 percent); (2) plumbing (13 percent); (3) exterior walls, windows, or doors (24 percent); (4) roofs (19 percent); and (5) electricity (23 percent). As much as 50 percent of the nation's schools had at least one inadequate feature (Digest of Education Statistics, 2017).

Nationwide, 6 percent of schools are considered to be in "poor" condition while 29 percent of all public schools are considered in "fair" condition. 53 percent of all public schools are considered to be in "good" condition while 13 percent are in "excellent" condition. A smaller percentage of schools in the West (5 and 29 percent) and Northeast (3 and 23 percent) are considered either poor or fair, respectively, compared to the Southeast (7 and 30 percent) and Central (2 and 35 percent).

Thirteen percent of schools in the West and 9 percent in the Northeast are in the "excellent" category compared to 13 percent in the Southeast and 8 percent in the West (US Department of Education, 2014). The differences among regions reflect, in part, stagnant enrollments in the Midwest and Northeast and growing enrollments in the Southeast and West.

Small schools (fewer than three hundred students) have an average age of forty-eight years compared to large schools (one thousand or more students) with an average age of thirty-nine years. City schools have a mean age of forty-six years compared to suburban, at forty years, and rural schools, at forty-two years (US Department of Education, 2014). Nationwide, 26 percent of schools were built before 1950. Schools in poorer areas have a greater percentage of newer schools than those in middle-class areas. For example, for schools with less than 20 percent of students eligible for free or reduced-price lunch, 48 percent were built before 1950. In contrast, for schools where 50 percent or more students are eligible for free or reduced-price lunch, 42 percent were built before 1950 (US Department of Education, 2014).

Several factors other than age contribute to the deterioration of school buildings and the costs for repairs and renovation.

1. *Energy prices*. Although energy prices stabilized in the 1990s, they have dramatically increased since 2010. K–12 schools spend more than $8 billion a year on energy costs—or more than $125 per student per year. Most schools, particularly in old, Frostbelt communities, continue to be heated by inefficient boilers. Electrical costs are higher because the school design rarely takes advantage of sunlight. The operating funds devoted to increased energy costs and energy-saving devices have redirected school monies away from repairs and maintenance.

2. *Weather conditions*. In certain parts of the country, the weather is severe, especially in the Frostbelt where the 100- to 120-degree annual temperature range causes considerable contraction and expansion of school buildings, roofs, and pavement. The intense cold makes the water and sewer systems and exterior brick vulnerable to cracks and leaks. In addition, acid rain, common in heavily industrialized or polluted areas, causes deterioration of all structural surfaces.

3. *Density and vandalism*. Big-city schools are usually located in densely populated areas, resulting in concentrated use of and greater demand for facilities. Moreover, many of these schools are located in areas of highly concentrated poverty and service youth populations that are more often involved in property destruction and theft than youth from more affluent areas. All this results not only in higher costs and more frequent repairs but also in higher budgets for security measures. These expenses deplete a system's financial resources and operating funds for repairs and maintenance.

4. *Newer buildings*. Many new schools were constructed during the last twenty-five years, especially in the Sunbelt and suburbs. Many of these schools were constructed hastily to accommodate expanding enrollments. Construction quality suffered, and these buildings are now approaching the end of their life spans. In contrast, the problems with older buildings involve not

only their quality but also their energy efficiency, their failure to meet health and safety codes, and the results of accumulated neglect.

5. *A ticking time bomb*. For the most part, educators and the public, alike, prefer not to discuss the infrastructure time bomb that is ticking in US schools. What catches our attention is student test scores and the need to reform or upgrade the curriculum; the safety and operating efficiency of the schools are not on the minds of the public unless there is a call for new taxes.

Many school board officials are aware of our schools' environmental and structural problems but have left them for the next generation. Ignoring our inadequate school facilities has enormous costs—fiscally and physically—and potentially will lead to inadequate education. The longer the wait, the greater the school districts' costs for future educational services and the more difficult it becomes to sustain long-term educational growth and financial solvency.

Financing School Construction

Public investment in new schools, compared to other public sectors, has been minimal in the last fifteen to twenty years because of prior taxpayer resistance and student-enrollment declines. Where will the money to build new schools come from? Although the states fund about 50 percent of the revenues for school maintenance and operation, they only contribute about 23 percent for construction. According to one study, twenty-seven states use grant programs (equalized, flat, or matching) to finance new schools, twelve states rely on state or local bonds, and two states use fully funded capital programs, but sixteen states provide no state financial assistance (National Association of State Directors of Education Plant Services, 2008).

Building a new school is no simple task. The construction rules are complex, the stakes are high, and the considerations are political. Try these questions: How many students will the school accommodate? Where will the building site be located? How will attendance boundaries be drawn? Have environmental concerns been fully addressed? How will the cost be funded? How will voters react? Which companies will get the contracts? How many minority contractors will be hired? The list of questions, with the potential for vague or controversial answers, is endless.

Is it possible for one school serving the same number of students to be three or four times more expensive than another? Absolutely! Consider different building requirements (local construction codes, insulation factors, space requirements), building designs (open-air or enclosed, horizontal or vertical), land prices, professional fees, labor and material expenses, ease of access to the building site, and a host of other factors. Where you build is important. In 2018 the cost of a school building can run from $150 to $200 a square foot in rural Southern areas to $250 to $500 per square foot in the major cities (and adjacent metropolitan areas).

Square footage is another factor to consider. High schools need about one and a half times more square footage than do elementary schools to adequately serve their clientele. Older students require specialization and additional facilities—larger auditoriums, pools, theatres, cafeterias, indoor gyms, outdoor ball fields, and student parking lots. Schools in cold climates cannot use outdoor areas as effectively as schools in warm climates. In 2018, a typical high school serving one thousand students might comprise one hundred square feet per student (at $150 per square foot) in the rural South. Another high school serving the same number of students might comprise two hundred square feet per student (at $250 per square foot) in the urban Northeast or Midwest. On a national level, the median cost for an elementary school (in 2018) was about $318 per square foot and for a high school was about $304 per square foot (Wang, 2019, 2020). The school's total cost in the urban Northeast or Midwest can run two to three times as high as in rural sites: One school costs $20,000 per student, and the other costs $40,000 per student.

No matter how educators try to defend school building costs, it turns into a political firestorm: it's outlandish to talk about marble or murals in hallways, Olympic-sized pools, or high-tech installations in an era when teachers are being fired, education budgets are being trimmed, and school bonds are being scrutinized by voters around the country. It is hard to defend the idea that children will flourish in a pleasant environment when they are run by the same people who have given us a 50 percent dropout rate in big cities like Los Angeles.

Schools in the future will cost more than current prices because the designs will be more complex and built for varied functions using more sophisticated components and materials. There will probably be more (1) technological equipment, such as computers, videos and satellite dishes; (2) school laboratories; (3) places for small-group and independent study; (4) flexible spaces, module classrooms, and adaptable walls; (5) contrasting or great spaces such as common rooms, atriums, and open courtyards; (6) innovative spaces and materials such as underground structures and new plastic and prefabricated materials; (7) expensive and high-efficient lighting, heating, and communications equipment; (8) energy-conservation controls, solar features, heat pumps, and geothermal heating and cooling systems; (9) earth berms and high-clerestory windows; (10) curved corners and curved furniture, (11) pitched roofs and arches; and (12) centers or wings to house child care, elder care, and community services (Bryk, 2010; Ornstein, 2012). Yesterday's "boxy" classrooms and rectangular buildings will increasingly be replaced by flexible spaces and a variety of exterior designs. "Going green" is now the "in" word and new design feature, despite the additional cost.

Environmental Hazards

In many of America's schools, environmental hazards including asbestos, radon gas, school lead in paint and pipes, poor indoor air quality, and electromagnetic fields pose threats to the health and safety of students and staff. School principals need to be cognizant of these and other environmental hazards.

Asbestos. The US Environmental Protection Agency (EPA) has ordered government and commercial property owners to clean up **asbestos-laden buildings** that have been housing people at work and in school for the last twenty-five to fifty years. Estimated costs to clean up these buildings are hard to come by, although one estimate was $100 billion for government and commercial buildings and $3.5 billion for some 45,000 schools in 31,000 school districts. Another nationwide study puts the estimate at $1.2 billion, or $22,858 per school and $31 per student (US Environmental Protection Agency, 2010a). The cost exceeded $150 per student in 10 percent of the schools, and the Oklahoma City School District had the greatest expenditures—or the dubious distinction of having a $65 million bill and $1,688 cost per student. These costs are based on an estimate of $15 to $20 per linear square foot to remove asbestos, depending on whether this once acclaimed "wonder fiber" is located in the ceilings, walls, floors, or basements. One 132-year-old school in Cortland, Ohio was demolished in 2010, but $800,000 had to be allocated for asbestos removal (US Environmental Protection Agency, 2010a).

Estimates of people on the job who will die from direct exposure to asbestos-containing buildings are extremely low (twenty-five per year) when compared to the ten thousand per year who die due to workplace accidents. The ultimate question is, do we need to spend all this money on asbestos removal? At what level of exposure is asbestos unsafe? If asbestos is intact, not flaking, and out of reach of students and employees, should it be removed? Although airborne asbestos can be deadly (when more than 1 percent is present in the air), the dangers of inert asbestos are minimal in most buildings. Nonetheless, children are considered to be especially vulnerable because their longer life expectancy means that a latent asbestos-related disease has more time to develop.

The federal government has imposed many environmental requirements and regulations on the schools but did not provide funds for compliance. Many school districts delayed in removing the asbestos, while others used funds from their school maintenance budget to comply with federal regulations. However, one EPA study reports that as much as 75 percent of all school cleanup work was done improperly up to 1985 (R. Garratt, staff specialist, Environmental Protection Agency, Region 5, personal communication, April 9, 2010). Rather than mitigating the problem, cleanup efforts may have exacerbated the problem in many cases; indeed, the cure may be worse than the disease, especially with a lot of "rip and skip" court cases in the 2010 news are any indication, that trend still continues. Today, while cleanup efforts are better, around half are still done improperly (Glen I. Earthman, Virginia Tech professor emeritus and facilities expert, personal communication, April 9, 2010).

Be aware that removal of asbestos is not the only form of abatement, although the great majority of school districts have chosen this option. Encapsulation, if done properly, can last for several years (ten or more years, depending on the materials applied and the method used) at an average cost of 10 percent of the removal bill. The savings to be realized by encapsulating are obvious; but in cases where asbestos is loose or crumbling, removal is the best solution for medical reasons (Castleman, 2005; Craighead & Gibbs, 2008). In still other cases, encapsulation is only a stop-gap measure until a school district can raise sufficient money for removal.

Radon Gas. Radon gas may pose as much of a threat to the health and safety of students and staff as asbestos does. **Radon gas** is considered the second leading cause of lung cancer among adults. A 2010 US Environmental Protection Agency (EPA, 2010b) report shows dangerously high levels of this invisible, odorless gas in 54 percent of the 130 schools randomly checked; homes are also affected. In short, many of our children are exposed to a risk equivalent to smoking from half to one and a half packs of cigarettes a day. A 2010 EPA report states that one in five schools nationwide has classrooms with unacceptably high levels of radon gas (2010c, p. 2).

Radon gas (radon-222) seeps into buildings through the foundation from soil and rock as the radium-226 isotope decays. In some cases, well water may be a source of radon. No EPA, federal, or state guidelines exist for containment or abatement of the gas; however, the situation is considered dangerous, and levels are too high in schools to wait for the EPA. Basically, procedures for ascertaining radon levels include (a) testing all school rooms on and below ground level, (b) testing in the cold months of the year, and (c) testing for two days to four weeks depending on the type of test. Screening test results of over 4 pCi/L (picocuries/ liter, or one-trillionth of a unit of radon) are considered dangerous enough to require a lengthy retest (nine to twelve months); levels over 100 pCi/L are considered sufficiently dangerous to call for relocating children (Schneider, 1993).

Average corrective costs per school run from as low as $1,000 if ventilation adjustment works to $10,000 if subventilation is needed. On the other hand, some observers contend that the cost for decontaminating the nation's schools runs into billions of dollars, and since the connection between radon and illness has not been firmly proven, it may not be worth the cost to ventilate schools.

School Lead. The water our children are drinking at home and school may be tainted with lead. Lead accumulates in their brains, blood, and bones. As lead bonds with the oxygen in the blood's hemoglobin molecules, it eventually dulls the mind and causes severe behavior problems and learning disorders.

According to one US government survey, 15 to 16 percent of the nation's children under the age of fourteen years have high enough levels of lead in their blood to cause academic and neurobehavioral problems in school, which eventually lead to school failure (US Agency for Toxic Substances, 2010). The ratios of high lead levels are three times higher for poor White than for middle-class White children, and seven times higher for inner-city Blacks than for suburban Whites; these results are due largely to the differences in air quality and the age of the children's housing (Richardson, 2005).

The federal Centers for Disease Control and Prevention (CDC) maintains that lead poisoning is the nation's number-one preventable child health problem and that proper lead abatement would eventually reduce the cost of child medical care and special education as much as $39 billion annually (CDC, 2010). The CDC has revised its definition of lead poisoning, lowering the level at which lead is now considered dangerous from 25 micrograms (mcg) per deciliter in 1974 to 10 mcg in 1991. The last revision resulted in a tenfold increase in the number of children now considered poisoned by lead—about 1.5 percent, which means lead poisoning now affects 15 percent of all US preschoolers (Markowitz & Rosner, 2013). Moreover, at least twenty recent US and international studies from industrialized nations show that levels of lead in children are associated with measures of low IQ, language and reading incompetency, limited attention span, inability to follow instructions, and behavioral impairment as well as with forty other cognitive, social, psychological, and health problems (Ettinger et al., 2002; Han et al., 2000; Koger & Du Nann, 2010; Landrigan et al., 2002; Winter, 2001a, 2001b).

In another study, one researcher found that first and second graders who had moderate quantities of lead (5.0 mcg or less) in their systems were six times as likely to exhibit reading problems and seven times more likely to drop out of high school when compared with children who were lead free (Lanphear, 2001). Although the lead variable possibly interacts with a social-class variable, the fact remains that lead infects multiple organs of the body.

In short, childhood lead poisoning may be one of the most important and least acknowledged causes of school failure and learning disorders. Given all the rhetoric and funding for school reform, which focuses on curriculum, instruction, teaching, and testing, we may have been myopic and even foolhardy not to realize that part of school failure may be related to the adverse effects of lead.

The major source of lead poisoning is old lead-based paint and the dust produced from it when windows are opened and closed or renovations take place. The problems exist in nearly all schools built before 1978—and that's more than 65 percent of the nation's schools—the year Congress banned lead-based paint. Several layers beneath newer lead-free paint, because of cracking and flaking, the lead-based paint is not always sealed as we might believe; and it can be found in the air teachers and students breathe. Renovations cause bigger problems because these building areas are not properly sealed and monitored with sample air readings, as in the prescribed manner for asbestos removal.

And we have some more bad news. Dangerous traces of lead are sometimes found in the municipal water we drink. Even worse, lead gets into water from lead lines in our older water coolers, faucets (unless they are made from plastic, which most people feel is inferior in quality), and copper pipes (from the lead solder on the joints). Lead also comes from the cities and villages with old plumbing that connects the water main to our schools and homes. Allowing water to run for a couple of minutes before drinking it or using it for cleaning foods can flush out the lead that has collected, but that idea does not always sit well with budget-minded people who pay utility bills.

It costs about $50 to $75 for a laboratory to test each water faucet and cooler in our schools; however, this is not going to happen on a large scale unless schools are forced to budget this item. The National Education Association estimates that $30 million per year is needed for paint and water testing in our schools—a tiny sum for such an important safety measure (National Conference of State Legislatures, 2000). Because the problem is odorless and invisible, and because most parents are not aware the problem even exists, school officials are not under pressure to take appropriate measures.

No testing and reporting procedures are required for lead, and school authorities have been remiss in dealing with the problem. Furthermore, many school officials who are able to do something about it take the position that there is no problem (they believe it went away when lead was outlawed in paints and gasoline); or, they see the solutions as too expensive because, eventually, abatement and not just testing will have to be done in many schools (and other government buildings). The cost of lead abatement is estimated at between $10,000 and $30,000 per 1,000 square feet of lead paint coverage. Most school boards (and owners of property) find the cost too expensive and just leave the problem as is, gambling that if a party files a claim due to lead injury, the school district's insurance will pay for it. Verdicts run as high as $20 million, though most cases are settled in the range of $1,000,000 (Castillo, 2008; Miranda, Dolinoy, & Overstreet, 2002).

EPA or health requirements are needed to ensure adequate compliance. Like the tobacco industry, which fights facts about cigarette smoking and cancer, the lead industry has its spokespeople and lobbyists who obscure the health hazards of lead. The federal government, medical profession, and socially concerned groups need to come together to force cleanups of lead contamination in the same way they have acted to discourage cigarette smoking.

Indoor Air Quality. Some schools suffer from what is known as sick building syndrome (SBS) and other indoor air quality (IAQ) shortcomings due to the trend to increase insulation and tighten schools (and office buildings) to save energy (Bas,

2004; Spengler, Samet, & McCarthy, 2001). The outcome, in extreme cases, is virtually no outside air infiltration.

Everything in a building has some form of toxic emission (Burroughs & Hansen, 2004). The human body exhales carbon dioxide, and it emits body odors, gases, and other *bio-effluents*. Carbon monoxide, also colorless and highly poisonous, results from incomplete combustion of fuel. It can be a problem when auto engines are left running, say, in school parking lots near open windows when parents pick up or drop off their children. Diesel exhaust from parked buses is also common, as drivers keep bus engines running while waiting for students or warm the bus in winter before students board. Carpets, plastics (most furniture and bathroom fixtures contain plastics), and pressed wood emit formaldehyde and other gases. Room dividers and window blinds emit a host of carbon chemicals. Copy machines give off ozone, spirit duplicators give off methyl alcohol, and fluorescent lights give off ultraviolet rays.

Then there is the dilemma of doing battle with pests—fleas, cockroaches, termites, wasps, and rodents. Although chemical pesticides are a critical component of successful pest control, there is the other side of the coin—our concern to limit or even rid schools of pesticides (Levine, 2007). It's one thing to permit weeds to run amok on school playgrounds because of our concern to reduce pesticide exposure, but it's quite another to allow indoor pests to run wild with the likelihood of increasing. Nonetheless, educators and parents are concerned that students are unknowingly breathing in various poisonous chemicals used to kill vermin. As of 2000, thirty-one out of fifty states had school pesticide management policies that were considered "inadequate" or "unsatisfactory" for protecting children from pesticides that are harmful to their central nervous system and have "very profound consequences for human beings" (Matthews, 2006).

Even drywall, paints, and cleaning fluids have various fumes that are dangerous in sufficient quantities. Long-term exposure to chemicals and volatile compounds from art supplies, science labs, shop facilities, and indoor pools is potentially dangerous, and it affects all students because the vapors and dusts enter the heating and cooling systems. Excessive humidity found in locker rooms, pool areas, and school basements can lead to mold and fungus growths that multiply to potentially harmful levels—which they often do, unbeknownst to school authorities (Burroughs & Hansen, 2004).

As schools become more insulated, the toxins from cigarette smoke, chalk dusts, science labs, art rooms, and shop facilities cannot escape and thus are circulated through the ventilation system. In addition, the entire duct system usually has dust or mold that spreads germs throughout the building. If vents are not cleaned regularly, the potential for Legionnaires' disease or other respiratory infections caused by bacteria and/or germs exists (Spengler, Samet, & McCarthy, 2001). The Occupational Safety and Health Administration (OSHA) requires that outside air be circulated into buildings to avoid the constant recirculation of viruses and bacteria.

Roughly one-third of the nation's schools (and offices) are considered to be afflicted with sick building syndrome. We need to follow the amended recommendations of the American Society for Heating, Refrigeration and Air Conditioning Engineers; they raised air circulation standards from five cubic feet per minute to fifteen (National Conference of State Legislatures, 2003; USA Today, 2008). Two problems arise: more energy is consumed; and in some big cities, such as Los Angeles,

Houston, and New York, it is even more damaging to bring in outside air at certain times of the year.

The human symptoms of poor IAQ are eye, nose, throat, or lung irritations. Students (and teachers) are drowsy, exhibit shorter attention spans, or become out of breath when walking up the stairs or playing in the gym. In searching for problems, one important consideration is whether people's symptoms disappear within a few hours after leaving school. Parents whose children suffer from respiratory problems often feel their children are being infected by classmates; such parents fail to consider the strong possibility that the air at school may be the culprit.

Unless symptoms are apparent, educators usually believe the school's IAQ is fine. But many air pollutants, including radon gas, carbon monoxide, asbestos particles, and lead dust, are not easily detectable by sight or smell. Other pollutants are obvious only in high concentrations. Formaldehyde, paint, and cleaning fluid vapors, and mold and fungus, for example, have an odor only at harmful levels.

Obviously, schools need to test air quality regularly and not assume the best-case scenario (Zhang, 2004). But when was the last time your neighborhood school—or the school that your brother, sister, or children attend—tested the air to see whether it was "healthy"? Given the budget constraints of most school districts, the answer is probably, "Not since anyone can remember." So long as parental and public pressure is on improving the curriculum and teaching process, and minimal attention is directed at the air we breathe (which is merely taken for granted), and so long as there is no legislation requiring the testing and improvement of our air, the problem will be ignored. With lack of funds a common school problem, ventilation maintenance is not a top priority; in fact, the maintenance budget is often robbed to pay for curriculum and teaching reform—an unfortunate circumstance that threatens student health and learning conditions.

When the public becomes more aware of the hazards related to indoor pollutants, air quality within school buildings will become the focal point for student rights and litigation. Lack of responsiveness today by school officials can make a seemingly innocuous problem and noncontroversial issue into a serious issue in the future.

Electromagnetic Fields. Electromagnetic fields (EMF) are part of our complicated and growing technology: radio, television, computers, microwaves, fluorescent lights, and so on. The most controversial and visible electromagnetic fields are produced by the existence of transmission lines running through our communities—often near our schools, playgrounds, and homes. Only six states set limits on the strength of EMF around transmission lines. New York State, for example, requires a 350-yard corridor around its lines. The fear seems to coincide with growing research data: children exposed to these power lines suffer from childhood cancer two to three times more frequently (depending on years of exposure) than do children who are not exposed (Van Bladel, 2007).

What about our home appliances and school machines? The higher the strength of the magnetic field (in devices such as microwaves, ovens, stoves, and heaters), as well as the closer the object and the longer the exposure (as with electric blankets, computers, copy machines, televisions, and fluorescent lights), the greater the risk. Actually, objects with electric motors (such as air conditioners, electric clocks, hair dryers, and even telephones) present a possible risk to humans. In theory, because our bodies are often only inches away from them, these household and school objects may be more dangerous than transmission lines are (Shadowitz, 2010).

To get an idea of the emission effects of these household and school objects, copy machines give off 4.0 milligauss (mG) units, computers 10.0 mG, and microwave ovens 15.0 mG (Guru & Hiziroglu, 2004). The problem is, some of us sit at a computer for hours. In general, the research on EMF is highly complex and tentative.

Some scientists claim we are unsure what to measure to determine exposure. For right now, the best precaution is to have children keep their distance from all EMF emitters at home and in school, especially televisions and computers (Bakshi, 2009; Wangsness, 1986). Schools need to enforce this notion of distance and purchase computers and electronic equipment with screens or filters. Because there is little public pressure to spend money on screens or filters, and no legislation requiring schools to take corrective steps, few schools are considering these precautions.

SUMMARY

1. School budgeting involves expressing statements of planned revenue and expenditures for a coming fiscal year in numerical terms.
2. Many school districts now allow school principals to participate in the budgeting process, called school-based budgeting.
3. Financial control techniques, such as internal control and financial audits, assist administrators in acquiring, allocating, and evaluating the efficient and effective use of financial resources.
4. Two alternative methods for developing budgets are zero-based budgeting (ZBB) and planning-programming-budgeting systems (PPBS). ZBB requires that principals start from zero to justify budget needs every year. PPBS, a variation of ZBB, requires that budgets be developed from a program perspective rather than using the traditional line-item approach.
5. A key responsibility of school principals is facilities management. School buildings across the nation are aging and becoming a barrier to optimal learning and teaching. This results in escalating school infrastructure costs. A case can be made to renovate, or to build new facilities that maximize an effective learning environment. This will involve allocating funds for building renovation or new construction.
6. Principals need to be sensitive to environmental hazards, such as asbestos, radon gas, school lead, indoor air quality, and electromagnetic fields that can threaten the health and safety of students and staff.

KEY TERMS

budgeting

budget

expenditures

current expenses

capital outlay

debt service

fiscally independent school districts

fiscally dependent school districts

educational needs standard

fiscal neutrality standard

school-based budgeting

zero-based budgeting (ZBB)

planning-programming-budgeting systems (PPBS)

financial control
internal control
financial audit
external audit
internal audit

infrastructure
asbestos-laden buildings
radon gas
sick building syndrome (SBS)
electromagnetic fields (EMF)

FIELD-BASED ACTIVITIES

1. Many school districts now allow school staff to participate in the budgeting process. Interview your building principal concerning the budgeting process. Does your principal allow staff to participate in the budgeting process? If your principal uses a school-based budgeting process, what procedure do they use to get input from staff concerning both budget development and implementation? Outline the budgeting procedures used in your journal. Interview the chief financial officer (CFO) in your school district. Determine from the interview what the district's philosophy is regarding staff participation in the budgeting process.

2. Interview the school principal, bookkeeper, and all other individuals who handle money in your school. Discuss with them their opinions concerning the importance of using effective financial control techniques, including internal control and external control and financial audits. Record the responses in your journal.

3. Due to the general practice of streamlining budgets, controversy over school infrastructure costs and the abatement of environmental hazards such as asbestos removal and radon gas are likely to continue to affect school expenditures in the future. Interview the superintendent and CFO in your school district, and your building principal, to secure each person's opinion concerning school infrastructure costs and expenditures for the removal of environmental hazards. Record their responses in your journal.

SUGGESTED READINGS

Baker, B. D. (2018). *Educational inequality and school finance: Why money matters for America's students*. Cambridge, MA: Harvard Education Press. In *Educational Inequality and School Finance*, Bruce Baker offers a comprehensive examination of how US public schools receive and spend money. Drawing on extensive longitudinal data and numerous studies of states and school districts, he provides a vivid portrait of the stagnation of state investment in public education and the continuing challenges of achieving equity and adequacy in school funding.

Born, C. (2020). *Making sense of school finance: A practical step-by-step approach*. Lanham, MD: Rowman & Littlefield. Clinton Born thoroughly and clearly describes complex school finance concepts regarding local, state, and federal revenues along with authentic accounting processes for public and charter schools.

Brimley, V., Verstegen, D. A., & Garfield, R. R. (2020). *Financing education in a climate of change* (13th ed.). Boston, MA: Pearson. The authors provide a practical examination of the issues impacting education finance today. The thirteenth edition contains information on classic and current topics, including the economics of education, recent court decisions, fity-state comparison tables, state taxes, and the ongoing debate about school vouchers, tax credits, church-state issues, and charter schools.

Odden, A., & Picus, L. (2020). *School finance: A policy perspective* (6th ed.). New York, NY: McGraw-Hill. Allan Odden and Lawrence Picus provide an evidence-based model for financing the resources, programs, and services needed in K–12 schools with an eye on issues and challenges faced by those at the policy level in school districts and states.

Owings, W. A., & Kaplan, L. S. (2020). *Financing education in a climate of change* (8th ed.). Boston, MA: Pearson. William Owings and Leslie Kaplan cover all current trends of school finance policy and issues, as well as the tools for formulating and managing school budgets.

Schilling, C.A., & Tomal, D. R. (2019). *School finance and business management: Optimizing fiscal, facility, and human resources* (2nd ed.). Lanham, MD: Rowman & Littlefield. Craig Schilling and Daniel Tomal provide a comprehensive treatment on managing school financial resources to increase student performance.

12

Creating Safe Schools

■ ■ ■

FOCUSING QUESTIONS

1. What does the research reveal about school violence and safety in schools?
2. What are the causes of school violence?
3. What measures can principals take to improve school safety?
4. What is the most recent data on adolescent alcohol and drug use?
5. What are some strategies principals can use to reduce school violence and misbehavior?

In this chapter, we respond to these questions concerning the creation of safe schools for all students. We begin our discussion with an overview of the research concerning violence in our schools. Then we look at some of the causes of school violence including access to weapons; media violence; cyber abuse; and school, community, and family environments. Next, we examine measures schools are taking to improve school safety, including physical surveillance, school policies, instructional programs, profiling potentially violent students, and counseling and mediation. We then discuss the most recent data available on alcohol and drug use among adolescents. And, finally, we provide an action plan consisting of seven strategies for reducing school violence and misbehavior: predict school violence, prevent school violence, focus resources on schools, strengthen the system, develop a crisis management plan, create an orderly climate for learning, and implement instructional techniques that enhance student academic engagement.

SCHOOL SAFETY AND VIOLENCE

Many Americans have been concerned about the safety of their children at school for more than a century (Cohen & Espelage, 2020). Numerous incidents of lethal violence at school beginning with the Columbine High School massacre and others confirmed what many had feared—that no school, however privileged and well run, was invulnerable to acts of violence. The apparently random nature of these highly publicized shootings has raised public fears to epidemic proportions. According to the latest PDK Poll, more than 50 percent of parents with children in grades K–12 (PDK Poll, 2020) and 75 percent of secondary school students (Wang et al., 2020) now believe that a school shooting could occur in their community.

Although the situation in some schools and neighborhoods is more serious than in others, creating a safe, disciplined, and drug-free learning environment is a challenge for all school principals. Increasing the graduation rate, improving student achievement in challenging subject matter, and ensuring our students' ability to compete in a world economy and carry out their responsibilities of citizenship will be much more difficult to achieve if our schools and neighborhoods are unsafe for our children (Lunenburg & Irby, 2000).

Understanding School Violence

School violence is youth violence that occurs on school property, on the way to and from school or school-sponsored events, or during a school-sponsored event. A young person can be a victim, a perpetrator, or a witness of school violence. School violence may also involve or impact adults (Centers for Disease Control, Division of Violence Prevention, 2021).

Youth violence includes various behaviors. Some violent acts—such as bullying, pushing, and shoving—can cause more emotional harm than physical harm (Astor & Benbenishty, 2017; Daly, 2018; Klinger & Klinger, 2018). Other forms of violence, such as gang violence and assault (with or without weapons), can lead to serious injury or even death (Kann, McManus, & Harris, 2018; Tahtah, 2021).

Our nation's schools should be safe environments for teaching and learning, free of crime and violence. Instances of crime or violence on school campuses not only affect the individuals involved, but also may disrupt the educational process and affect bystanders, the school itself, and the surrounding community (Brookmeyer, Fanti, & Henrich, 2006; Goldstein, Young, & Boyd, 2008; Schargel, 2014).

Research on School Crime and Violence

Establishing reliable indicators of the current state of school crime and violence across the nation and regularly updating and monitoring these indicators are important in ensuring the safety of our nation's students. This is the aim of the **Crime and Safety Surveys (CSS)** program.

The following statistics are from the *Indicators of School Crime and Safety: 2019* report (Wang et al., 2020), which is designed to provide an annual snapshot of specific crime and safety indicators, covering topics such as victimization, teacher injury, bullying and cyber-bullying, school environments, fights, weapons, availability and student use of drugs and alcohol, and student perceptions of personal safety at school. (Student use of drugs and alcohol will be discussed in a separate section of the chapter.)

The report is the twenty-third in a series of annual publications produced jointly by the National Center for Education Statistics (NCES), the Institute of Education Sciences (IES), in the US Department of Education (DoE), and the Bureau of Justice Statistics (BJS) in the US Department of Justice (DOJ). This report presents the most recent data available on school crime and student safety. The indicators in this report are based on information drawn from a variety of data sources, including national surveys of students, teachers, principals, and postsecondary institutions. Sources include results from the School-Associated Violent Deaths Study, sponsored by the DoE, the DOJ, and the Centers for Disease Control and Prevention (CDC); the National Crime Victimization Survey and School Crime Supplement to that survey, sponsored by BJS and NCES, respectively; the Youth Risk Behavior Survey, sponsored by the CDC; the Schools and Staffing Survey and School Survey on Crime and Safety, both sponsored by NCES; and the Campus Safety and Security Survey, sponsored by DoE.

Violent Deaths at School and Nonfatal Student Victimizations. Between July 1, 2017 and June 30, 2018, there were a total of 47 school-associated violent deaths (homicide, suicide, or legal intervention death) in elementary and secondary schools in the United States. In 2018, among students ages 12–18, there were about 749,400 victimizations (theft and nonfatal violent victimization) at school and 601,300 victimizations away from school.

School Environment–Crime Incidents. During the 2018–2019 school year, 85 percent of public schools recorded that one or more crime incidents had taken place at school, amounting to an estimated 1.9 million crimes. This translates to a rate of 40 crimes per one thousand public school students enrolled in 2017–2018. During the same year, 60 percent of public schools reported a crime incident that occurred at school to the police, amounting to 689,000 crimes—or fifteen crimes per one thousand public school students enrolled.

Bullying. In 2018, about 28 percent of twelve- to eighteen-year-old students reported being bullied at school during the school year. In 2019, approximately 9 percent of students ages twelve to eighteen reported being *cyberbullied* anywhere during the school year.

Disrespect for Teachers. In 2018–2019, about 38 percent of teachers agreed or strongly agreed that student misbehavior interfered with their teaching, and 35 percent reported that student tardiness and class cutting interfered with their teaching.

Gang Activities. During the 2018–2019 school year, 16 percent of public schools reported that gang activities had occurred, and 2 percent reported that cult or extremist activities had occurred during this period.

Fights and Weapons. In 2019, about 33 percent of students in grades nine through twelve reported they had been in a physical fight at least one time during the previous twelve months anywhere, and 12 percent said they had been in a fight on school property during the previous twelve months. Between 1993 and 2018, the percentage of students in grades nine through twelve who reported carrying a *weapon anywhere* on at least one day during the past thirty days declined, from 22 percent to 17 percent, and the percentage who reported carrying a *weapon on school property* on at least one day also declined, from 12 percent to 5 percent.

Fear and Avoidance. Between 1995 and 2019, the percentage of students ages twelve to eighteen who reported being afraid of attack or harm at school decreased from 12 percent to 4 percent.

Discipline, Safety, and Security Measures. During the 2018–2019 school year, 10 percent of public school teachers reported being threatened with injury by a student from their school and 6 percent reported being physically attacked by a student from their school. Also, in 2018–2019, about 37 percent of public schools (about 31,100 schools) took at least one serious disciplinary action against a student for specific offenses. Of the 433,800 serious disciplinary actions taken during the 2018–2019 school year, 74 percent were suspensions for five days or more, 20 percent were transfers to specialized schools, and 6 percent were removals with no services for the remainder of the school year.

CAUSES OF SCHOOL VIOLENCE

School violence is a many-faceted problem, making it difficult for researchers and practitioners to pinpoint its causes. Many school violence statistics, for example, do not match the norms in our larger society. A National Crime Victimization Survey, compiled and maintained by the US DOJ, shows that overall crime rates in US society have fallen (Federal Bureau of Investigation (FBI), 2019). After two consecutive years of increase, the estimated number of violent crimes in the nation decreased 0.2 percent in 2019 when compared with 2018, according to FBI figures. Property crimes dropped 3.0 percent marking the fifteenth consecutive year the collective estimates for these offenses declined. Simultaneously, school-based studies reveal that many violent behaviors have increased among children and adolescents in elementary and secondary schools in the United States (Wang et al. , 2020).

It is important to recognize that a large majority of young people are not violence-prone, do not have criminal attitudes or criminal records, and can be "demonized" by legislators, the media, and the general public. Therefore, while it is critical that schools and communities recognize that school violence needs to be addressed, it is also important that they respect the hopes and rights of the majority of students who are neither perpetrators nor victims of school violence and who want nothing more than to receive a good education in a safe environment (Lunenburg, 2010j).

Most educators, education researchers, and practitioners would agree that school violence arises from a layering of causes and risk factors that include, but are not limited to: access to weapons; media violence; cyber abuse; and the impact of school, community, and family environments (Astor & Benbenishty, 2017; Cohen & Espelage, 2020; Daly, 2018; Fennelly & Perry, 2014; Gunzelmann, 2015; Klinger & Klinger, 2018; Kramen, 2013; Lassiter & Perry, 2013; Madfis, 2014; Scherz & Scherz, 2014; Tahtah, 2021). Each one will be discussed in turn.

Access to Weapons

During the late 1980s and early 1990s, teen gun violence increased dramatically in the United States. More teens began to acquire and carry guns, leading to a sharp increase in gun deaths and injuries. A 2019 report, *Indicators of School Crime and Safety: 2019* (Wang et al., 2020) revealed that forty-seven school-associated deaths occurred in elementary and secondary schools in the United States in 2016–2017. Of these incidents, 100 percent involved firearms.

According to the National Center for Injury Prevention and Control (David-Ferdon et al., 2018), fewer adolescents are carrying guns now, and gun-related murders and suicides have begun to decline. Nevertheless, the National Center for Injury Prevention and Control claims that many adolescents still illegally carry guns and harm others and themselves. Furthermore, studies reveal that teens have easy access to guns in the home; teens can acquire guns in illegal sales (Wang et al., 2020); and mentally ill students can acquire guns as easily as those who are sane. Ian Shapira and Tom Jackman reported in the *Washington Post*, April 17, 2007, that Seung-Hui Cho, a mentally ill student, killed thirty-two people at Virginia Tech, which in 2007, was the deadliest shooting in US history on a school campus. Although Cho purchased his weapons from a licensed gun dealer, his medical records declaring him mentally unstable did not surface during the transaction.

Media Violence

By the time the average American child reaches seventh grade, they will have witnessed 10,000 murders and 200,000 acts of violence on television. Some people say that so much violence on television makes American society—including its children—more violent.

Discussion regarding the impact of the media on youth behavior is not new. Beginning in 1961, and following in 1963, Albert Bandura, D. Ross, and S. A. Ross (1961, 1963) studied the effect of exposure to real-world violence, television violence, and cartoon violence. They divided one hundred preschool children into four groups. Group 1 watched a real person shout insults at an inflatable doll while hitting it with a mallet. Group 2 watched the incident on television. Group 3 watched a cartoon version of the same scene, and group 4 watched nothing. When the same children were later exposed to a frustrating situation, groups 1, 2, and 3 responded with more aggression than did group 4. More recently, Bandura (1994) validated his earlier findings on media effects on behavioral change.

In 2001, Craig Anderson and Brad Bushman conducted a meta-analytic review of more than 130 studies involving more than 130,000 participants around the world. The researchers claim that these studies provide evidence that violent video games can lead to an increase in aggressive behavior, aggressive cognition, aggressive affect, psychological arousal, and prosocial behavior, confirming Bandura, Ross, and Ross's earlier findings.

In 2003, Anderson and others published another study on the influence of media violence on youth. The report published by *Psychological Science in the Public Interest*, a journal of the Psychological Science Institute, claims that extensive research on violent television and films, video games, and music reveals unequivocal evidence that media violence increases the likelihood of aggressive and violent behavior.

According to the aforementioned 2003 study, this new research base is large and consistent in overall findings. The evidence is clearest in research on television and film violence but a growing body of video-game research yields "essentially the same conclusions" that "exposure to these media increases the likelihood of physically and verbally aggressive behavior, thoughts, and emotions." The divergent findings of these studies, conducted over a protracted length of time, underscore the difficulties in quantifying cause factors for youth violence in or out of school. However, many researchers, including the respected expert Jonathan Freedman (2002) of the University of Toronto, Christopher Ferguson (2016) of Texas A & M, and Elson and Ferguson (2014) maintain that the scientific evidence simply does not show that watching violence either produces violence in people, or desensitizes them to it.

Cyber Abuse

Since the 1990s, the Internet, blogging, e-mail, and cell-phone text messaging have grown to play significant roles in the erosion of school safety. Violent, Internet-based video games have also grown in popularity since the 1970s as cyber technology becomes more sophisticated.

Violence in screen entertainment media (i.e., television, film, video games, and the Internet) feature high levels of realistic violence. How do children respond to such screen entertainment media? The Workgroup on Media Violence and Violent Video Games (Anderson, 2017) and colleagues reviewed numerous meta-analyses and other relevant research from the past sixty years. The Workgroup found compelling evidence of short-term harmful effects, as well as evidence of long-term harmful effects. The vast majority of laboratory-based experimental studies have revealed that violent media exposure causes increased aggressive thoughts, angry feelings, physiologic arousal, hostile appraisals, aggressive behavior, and desensitization to violence and decreases prosocial behavior (e.g., helping others) and empathy. Nevertheless, larger-scale studies with more comprehensive and longer-term assessments are needed to fully understand long-term effects of violence in screen entertainment media. Earlier in 2001, communications researcher John Sherry (2001) of Michigan State University conducted a broad-ranged review of research focusing on violent video games and concluded that the overall effect of these games on aggressiveness does not appear great.

Cell-phone text messaging and e-mail provide additional platforms that support a new form of violence—cyberbullying. **Cyberbullying** occurs when young people use electronic media to taunt, insult, or even threaten their peers (Hinduja & Patchin, 2013; Horowitz & Bollinger, 2015).

Environmental Impact

Race and ethnicity, income levels, and other measurable elements have often been identified by public health experts as risk factors contributing to antisocial behavior, from smoking and drinking to violent behavior and suicide (Rosenfeld, 2013). More important, investigators say, are school performance, the nature of friends' behaviors, and family relationships. In short, immediate environments including schools, communities, peer groups, and families can exert a powerful influence on young persons' attitudes and behaviors (Blanchfield & Ladd, 2013).

School Environments. The *Indicators of School Crime and Safety: 2019* report (Wang et al., 2020) revealed that almost 50 percent of all teenagers, regardless of their settings—rural, suburban, or urban—believe that their schools are becoming more violent.

Gangs at schools. In 2018, 24 percent of students ages twelve to eighteen reported that there were gangs at their schools. However, relatively few young people join gangs; even in highly impacted areas, the degree of gang participation rarely exceeds 10 percent and less than 2 percent of juvenile crime is gang-related (Wang et al., 2020).

School size. Wang et al. (2020) found that discipline problems are often related to school enrollment size. Large schools tended to yield more discipline problems than small schools. Thirty-four percent of schools with 1,000 or more students reported student disrespect for or assaults on teachers at least once per week, compared with 21 percent of those at schools with 500 to 999 students, 17 percent of those at schools with 300 to 499 students, and 14 percent of those at schools with fewer than 300 students.

Middle schools. Middle school students are more than twice as likely as high school students to be affected by school violence. Seven percent of eighth graders stay home at least once a month to avoid a bully. Twenty-two percent of urban eleven- and twelve-year-olds know at least one person their age in a gang. The typical victim of an attack or robbery at school is a male in the seventh grade who is assaulted by a boy his own age (Wang et al., 2020).

Studies suggest two reasons for the higher rates of middle school violence (Queen, 2002). First, early adolescence is a difficult age. Young teenagers are often physically hyperactive and have not learned acceptable social behavior. Second, many middle school students have come into contact for the first time with young people from different backgrounds and distant neighborhoods.

Community Environments. As with schools and families, communities can neglect children. If our communities are not responsive to the needs of families and their children, this neglect can develop into school violence. After-school and summer programs are not always available. A child who starts acting violently will often do so during periods of unstructured and unsupervised time.

Juvenile-justice statistics show that, lacking after-school supervision, youth violence rises to above-average rates between 3 and 7 p.m. School violence has also been linked to the transformation of communities. Constantly shifting school demographics often reflect larger upheavals as communities undergo changes in size, economic well-being, and racial and ethnic mix (Rosenfeld, 2013).

Family Environments. Although our culture expects the family to deal with childhood problems, contemporary society makes it difficult for parents to meet all their children's needs. The current economy, for example, often demands that both parents work; more children are raised by single parents, including teenage mothers; and some children are subjected, by their parents, to neglect or physical, sexual, and substance abuse (Rosenfeld, 2013).

Ideally, parents nurture and reinforce positive behavior. When parents fail to do so, children may develop negative—and often violent—behavior patterns. In addition, neglectful or abusive family environments can inhibit the development of communication skills; self-esteem can be seriously damaged (Raine, 2013). In homes where positive behavior is not the norm, exposure to violence through popular culture may have a more profound impact (Preiss et al., 2007).

Parental alcohol abuse, domestic violence, and the presence of guns in the home may encourage a child to follow in their parents' footsteps. Regardless of family and community dependence on schools to educate and discipline their children, most schools have difficulty playing multiple roles as educators, surrogate parents, social services, or law-enforcement agencies (David-Ferdon et al., 2016).

IMPROVING SCHOOL SAFETY

Schools are taking a variety of measures to improve school safety. These include: physical surveillance, including weapons deterrence and the presence of security guards or police officers on campus; school policies designed to prevent violence by punishing those who perpetrate violence; instruction-based programs designed to address the precursors of violence, including bullying; profiling of potentially violent individuals; counseling at-risk students; and conflict mediation and resolution (Astor & Benbenishty, 2017; Centers for Disease Control and Prevention, 2021; Cohen & Espelage, 2020; Daly, 2018; David-Ferdon et al., 2016; Fennelly & Perry, 2014; Gunzelmann, 2015; Klinger & Klinger, 2018; Madfis, 2014; Schargel, 2014; Scherz & Scherz, 2014; Tahtah, 2021).

Physical Surveillance

Among the most common physical surveillance measures currently used in schools are weapons deterrence and the use of campus security and police officers. These strategies are aimed at preventing the most extreme forms of violence.

Weapons Deterrence.   Although bullying is far more prevalent than violence that involves weapons (Wang et al., 2020), one primary goal of improved physical surveillance measures is to prevent youth from bringing weapons to school. Metal detectors and searches of student lockers and book bags are not uncommon, especially in large urban middle and high schools. Indeed, fewer weapons are confiscated with these measures in place than are confiscated without them, implying that students are bringing weapons to school less frequently. Whether metal detectors and searches can prevent a well-planned incident from taking place is less clear (CDC, 2021).

Campus Security and Police Officers.   The presence of security guards and officers employed by the school, district, or local law enforcement on school grounds is gaining popular support. The duties of campus officers vary from patrolling the school and grounds to assisting school personnel with discipline issues. However, little is known about the long-term or concurrent effects that the presence of uniformed officers might have on students' feelings of safety (Bracken et al., 2015; Klinger & Klinger, 2018). For example, although the presence of an officer may provide peace of mind for principals and parents, we cannot presume that students view officers as their allies or defenders. The presence of uniformed officers can, in fact, breed a sense of mistrust among students and hence adversely affect school climate (Blanchfield & Ladd, 2013). Indeed, some preliminary evidence suggests that physical surveillance methods (metal detectors, searches, and security guards) can predict increased disorder.

School Policies

A wide variety of school policies related to student conduct and dress code is enforced in schools across the nation. Rules and regulations that directly target violence are **zero-tolerance policies** in which a single violation results in punishment, often either suspension or expulsion.

Zero tolerance school-discipline policies became popular in the 1980s, fueled by both President George H. W. Bush's war on drugs and the **"broken windows philosophy,"** which holds that cracking down on lesser crimes prevents bigger ones. Also leading to the policies was the 1994 Gun-Free Schools Act, which requires schools to suspend students who bring firearms to school for one year or lose all federal funding.

Zero-tolerance policies were initially intended to address and prevent serious problems involving weapons, violence, and drug and alcohol use in the schools (Kafka, 2012). However, since the Columbine school shootings, legislators and school boards have tightened their zero-tolerance policies to such an extent that school officials are now empowered to punish all offenses severely, no matter how minor.

The disciplinary policies in effect in many schools today apply zero tolerance to public school students in three rigid ways (Blumenson & Nilsen, 2002). First, they are blind to the most basic distinctions between types of offenses. In many schools, dangerousness is irrelevant; the penalties are the same for weapons and alcohol, sale and possession, theft, and disorderly offenses. Offenses that used to be resolved informally with an apology or an after-school detention now lead to formal disciplinary hearings. Second, they require a severe sanction, typically suspension or expulsion, for all of these offenses, regardless of the circumstances of the offense or the intent, history and prospects of the offender. Third, these policies generally mandate some degree of information-sharing with law enforcement. This multiplies the consequences of student misconduct in two directions: out-of-school offenses referred to the child's school may result in suspension or other sanctions, and in-school infractions referred to law enforcement agencies may result in juvenile or criminal prosecution. Suspensions and expulsions can predict a cascade of poor outcomes for kids, including failing a grade, dropping out of school (Bulach & Lunenburg, 2008, 2011; Lunenburg, 1999), or becoming incarcerated (Kim, Losen, & Hewitt, 2010).

In February 2015, New York City's Department of Education, under Chancellor Carmen Fariña, called for an end to principal-led school suspensions without prior approval—a practice that grew in popularity during the Bloomberg years as part of a focus on the "broken windows philosophy." And the Los Angeles Unified School District made a similar move two years ago when it banned suspensions for "willful defiance," punishment that had a disproportionate impact on students of color. These large cities are at the vanguard of a shift away from zero-tolerance school discipline toward less punitive strategies that emphasize talking it out and resolving disputes among students to keep them in school.

To some extent, these massive districts are rejuvenating the "whole-child" approach integral to what's known as "**progressive education**"—a model that was once viewed as incompatible with urban school systems. The contours of this model, which are often vaguely defined as schooling that is "child-centered" and focused on "active learning," are outlined by the educator Tom Little and writer Katherine Ellison (2015) in *Loving Learning: How Progressive Education Can Save America's Schools*. Little (who died in 2014) toured forty-five so-called progressive schools in 2013 and found several consistent features: attention to relationships; the students' freedom, within limits, to follow their interests; and hands-on, creative projects.

But despite the allure of progressive education, Little's findings illustrate the challenge of scaling the model up to districts with large, high-poverty schools. Research has long demonstrated that stringent discipline policies are thriving in high-poverty, urban public schools across America (Lunenburg & Schmidt, 1989; Lunenburg, 1991). UCLA's Center for Civil Rights Remedies makes clear that many of the country's schools are a long way from enjoying the values typical of progressive education. That is particularly true of the second quality identified by Little—student freedom—given that the nation's schools since 2009 have, on average, reported an annual suspension rate of 10 percent, the highest it's ever been (Lunenburg, 2012c). The rate, which started steadily increasing in 1972, is based on US DoE's civil-rights data (Losen, 2011) and pertains to the percentage of individual students who were suspended once or more in any given year; it does not use the total number of suspensions at a school, which could include the same student numerous times.

Nationally, African American students are suspended at three times the rate of their white counterparts, creating a "**discipline gap**," as Daniel Losen (2015), director of UCLA's Center for Civil Rights Remedies, puts it. The term, he said, shows the link between discipline trends and the socioeconomic gap in academic achievement. The discipline gap is so well documented (Gregory, Skiba, & Noguera, 2010; Gregory, Cornell, & Fan, 2011; Losen & Skiba, 2010; Losen, 2011; Lunenburg, 2013b; Skiba & Horner, 2010) that the US DoE and the US DOJ issued a joint "Dear Colleague" letter in January 2015 telling school systems to fix discriminatory punitive practices.

Because numbers vary widely by school district, the prevalence of suspensions appears to correlate more with policy than it does with student behavior. Suspensions have come to serve as a proxy for school climate—and on campus, climate, as anyone who went to school knows, can be warm and embracing or rigid and impersonal, depending on the district, school, and even classroom (Lunenburg, 1983a).

No one really knows for sure if zero-tolerance policies or progressive education is critical to a school's success. The research evidence is mixed. Any positive impacts of rigid, zero-tolerance policies, according to Golann (2015), may be more a result of supplementary features, such as longer school days and intensive tutoring, being implemented in a low-performing school.

But now that large school districts are adopting newer, so-called progressive education practices, clearer evidence is emerging. According to progressive education advocates (Gregory, Cornell, & Fan, 2011; Lunenburg, 2000b, 2015), students learn best when they are being actively engaged in a supportive environment, not when they are worried about getting suspended for any minor incident.

New York City, which with 1.1 million students is the largest school district in the nation, may have looked for inspiration from the second largest school district in the nation: Los Angeles, which saw suspension rates drop by 53 percent for its roughly 700,000 students in the two years since it banned suspensions for subjective offenses such as "willful defiance." Graduation rates in Los Angeles, meanwhile, rose by 12 percent, between the 2012–2013 and 2013–2014 school years (Losen, 2015).

New York City's DoE is slated to allocate $1.2 million toward expanding "**restorative practices**," a term used to describe talk-it-out behavior interventions. In these interventions, students involved in disputes or infractions participate in developing their resolutions, which include peer mediation, restorative circles, and group conferences.

The restorative approach is already well established in some parts of the country—and outcomes suggest that it's working. After Denver Public Schools, for example, implemented a districtwide "restorative justice program" in the early 2000s, suspension rates were cut in half over seven years and the discipline gap between African American and White students shrunk by a third, according to the book *Closing the School Discipline Gap*, edited by Daniel Losen (2015). More recently, Frederick Hess and Pedro Noguera (2021) provide a thoughtful and engaging book, *A Search for Common Ground*, useful for understanding the complex challenges facing schools today and show us how to break through the polarization that too often hampers our progress to create a better system for learning.

Although the secondary school programs are all curriculum-based, they are often implemented much like group counseling sessions and only sometimes are they embedded within the larger context of a school-wide prevention approach. Short-term outcomes for such programs are promising (Allen, Weissberg, & Hawkins, 1989; Dishion & Andrews, 1995; Farrell & Meyer, 1997); however, there are limited data on their long-term effects. A recent long-term follow-up (Dishion, McCord, & Poulin, 1999) shows that repeated interventions that include only problem youth can be counter-effective. Grouping high-risk youth together appears to reinforce negative behavioral patterns in a form of "deviance training," increasing rather than decreasing the risk that they will engage in anti-social behavior subsequently.

Instructional Programs

A program is defined as instructional if it consists of multiple lessons that are implemented by teachers or other adult staff. These programs tend to focus on precursors or antecedents of violent behavior (Hawkins, Farrington, & Catalano, 1998) with the presumption that, by targeting behaviors that predict violence (e.g., bullying and impulsive behavior), more serious manifestations of aggression will be prevented (Elliott, Hamburg, & Williams, 1998). Other programs, such as character education and lessons in social skills, aim to make individuals more socially competent (Henrich, Brown, & Aber, 1999; Samples & Aber, 1998).

Instructional programs vary in their target audience; some are designed for all students and the whole "system," whereas others are developed as special programs for "at-risk" youth. One example of a *systemic* program is the Bully/Victim Program, designed originally by Dan Olweus (1994) in Norway. (This program was selected as the only model program for school-based prevention at the secondary level in the Blueprint Programs by the Center for Prevention of Violence at the University of Colorado at Boulder, along with the CDC and other institutions in 1996).

According to Olweus, the program aims to alter social norms by changing school responses to bullying incidents. In addition to explicit anti-harassment policies, the program is designed to improve the social awareness of staff and students. Instructional materials designed for all students (not only bullies and victims) include a series of exercises that help students see problems from the perspective of the victim of bullying and raise consciousness about the role of bystanders in encouraging the bully. The program provides teacher training and information for parents about the program.

Numerous instructional violence prevention programs are available for elementary schools, including The Good Behavior Game (Tingstrom, Sterling-Turner, & Wilczynski, 2006), Best Foot Forward (Hudley, Graham, & Taylor, 2007), Judicious Discipline (Landau & Gathercoal, 2000), Classroom Check-up (Reinke, Lewis-Palmer, & Merrell, 2008), Positive Peer Reporting (Morrison & Jones, 2007), and Unified Discipline (Algozzine, Daunic, & Smith, 2010; Algozzine & White, 2002).

Profiling Potentially Violent Students

One approach that gained support immediately following the highly publicized school shootings was early identification or profiling of potentially violent students. This approach is based on the assumption that we can predict who will become violent. Although a great deal is known about early warning signs of violent behavior, the truth is that many students fit these "profiles" and only very few will ever commit a violent act. Hence, many students who will never commit violence are labeled as potentially violent. The label itself can lead to stigmatization and, if linked with a segregated group intervention, the labeling can also significantly limit the opportunities of the identified students.

Counseling and Mediation

Other violence prevention efforts rely on counseling students with disciplinary problems and mediating in specific incidents of conflict as needed. These are reactive rather than proactive approaches.

The assumption underlying the counseling approach is that students who repeatedly get into trouble need specific attention and services. Counseling often involves parents and teachers. Mediation of conflicts, on the other hand, is incident rather than person based: the goal is to negotiate and resolve conflicts in a constructive manner as soon as they happen (Hudley, Graham, & Taylor, 2007). Mediation and conflict resolution programs provide opportunities for modeling and rehearsing critical negotiation and resolution tactics (Brown et al., 2004; Selfridge, 2004).

Various school personnel can be in charge of the counseling and mediation. In some schools, the administrators (e.g., assistant principals) who are in charge of discipline problems handle counseling and mediation too. Some schools have trained school psychologists/counselors or "violence prevention coordinators." The professional qualifications of these personnel vary; there are no uniform educational requirements for school violence prevention coordinators. Yet the qualifications and training of personnel might be critical factors, determining the success or failure of these approaches.

Another approach is peer mediation. Although these programs can be effective in elementary schools, some evidence indicates that high school mediators are not well screened (Gottfredson, 1987).

ADOLESCENT DRUG USE

Establishing reliable information of the current state of adolescent drug use across the nation and regularly updating and monitoring this information is important in ensuring the safety of our nation's students. This is the aim of *Monitoring the Future* (MTF) survey of drug use among eighth, tenth, and twelfth graders. *Monitoring the Future: National Survey Results on Drug Use 1975–2019* (Johnston et al., 2020) is the most recent, complete data available on adolescent drug use. (Data collected for the 2020 survey stopped prematurely due to the COVID-19 pandemic. Completed surveys for 2020 represented about 25 percent of the size of a typical year's data collection. Results were gathered from a broad geographic range and were statistically weighted to be nationally represented. However, we used the 2019 national survey results, which were more representative of a typical year's data collection.)

The need for a study such as MTF is clear. Substance use by young people in the US has proven to be a rapidly changing phenomenon, requiring frequent assessments and reassessments. Since the mid-1960s, when it burgeoned in the general youth population, illicit drug use has remained a major concern for the nation. Smoking, drinking, and illicit drug use are leading causes of morbidity and mortality during adolescence as well as later in life (Kann, McManus, & Harris, 2018). How vigorously the nation responds to teenage substance use, how accurately it identifies the emerging substance abuse problems, and how well it comes to understand the effectiveness of policy and intervention efforts largely depend on the ongoing collection of valid and reliable data.

MTF is uniquely designed to generate such data in order to provide an accurate picture of what is happening in this domain of behavior and why. The study has served this function, since its inception in 1975. Policy discussions in the scientific literature and media, in government, education, public health institutions, and elsewhere have been informed by the ready availability of extensive and consistently accurate information from the study relating to a large and ever-growing number of substances. Similarly, MTF findings help to inform organizations and agencies that provide prevention and treatment services.

The 2019 MTF adolescent survey involved about 44,500 students in eighth, tenth, and twelfth grades enrolled in 392 secondary schools nationwide. A summary of the first published results based on the 2019 survey are presented in the following pages. Recent trends in the use of licit and illicit drugs are emphasized.

Vaping

The most important finding to emerge from the 2019 survey is the dramatic increase in vaping by adolescents. **Vaping** involves the use of a battery-powered device to heat a liquid or plant material that releases chemicals in an inhalable aerosol. Examples of vaping devices include e-cigarettes such as the popular brand JUUL and "mods." The aerosol may contain any of the following: nicotine, the active ingredients of marijuana, flavored propylene glycol, and/or flavored vegetable glycerin. Liquids that are vaporized come in hundreds of flavors, many of which are likely to be attractive to teens (e.g., bubble gum and milk chocolate cream).

Vaping is a relatively new phenomenon. Vaping of all substances increased dramatically in 2019. **Nicotine vaping** in the 2019 calendar year increased by 3.4, 8.9, and 10.9 percentage points in eighth, tenth, and twelfth grades. In tenth and twelfth grades these increases are the largest ever recorded for any substance in the forty-five years that MTF has tracked adolescent drug use. Nicotine vaping prevalence rates in 2019 were 11 percent, 25 percent, and 30 percent respectively. Given that nicotine is involved in most vaping, and given that nicotine is a highly addictive substance, this presents a serious threat to all of the progress that we have tracked since the mid-1900s in reducing cigarette smoking among adolescents.

Marijuana vaping also increased substantially in 2019 as this new way of using marijuana becomes more mainstream. In 2019 prevalence or use in the last twelve months increased 1.3., 4.2, and 3.6 percentage points in grades eight, ten, and twelve to levels of 4.4 percent, 12.4 percent, and 13.1 percent, respectively. Vaping *just flavoring* also substantially increased in 2019 to past-year prevalence levels of 15 percent, 25 percent, and 26 percent in grades eight, ten, and twelve.

Adolescents associate little risk of harm with vaping. MTF asks separately about regular use of "e-cigarettes" and also regular vaping of nicotine. Levels of perceived risk for these behaviors rank near the lowest of all substances, with little change in recent years.

Marijuana

Annual *marijuana* prevalence rose by a nonsignificant 0.5 percentage points to 23.9 percent in 2018 based on data from the three grades combined. Prevalence refers to the percent of the study sample that reports using a drug once or more during a given period—that is, in their lifetime, during the past twelve months, during the past thirty days, or daily in the past thirty days. This follows a significant increase in 2017. Annual prevalence stands at 11 percent, 28 percent, and 36 percent in grades eight, ten, and twelve. *Daily marijuana* prevalence changed little in 2019, with rates at 1 percent, 3 percent, and 6 percent, respectively.

Any Illicit Drug

Annual use of **any illicit drug**, which tends to be driven by marijuana—by far the most prevalent of the illicit drugs—also rose nonsignificantly in grades eight and ten, but declined nonsignificantly in twelfth grade. Change in 2019 for the three grades combined also did not reach significance. Since 2006 there has been rather little systematic change in this index.

Any Illicit Drug Other Than Marijuana

The index of **any illicit drug other than marijuana** showed no change in annual prevalence in 2018 for the three grades combined, but has shown a very gradual decline since 2001 when it was 16 percent compared to 2018 when it was 9 percent.

Any Illicit Drug Including Inhalants

The annual prevalence of the index of **any illicit drug including inhalants** changed little in 2019 for the three grades combined, after rising significantly the previous two years. Since 2006 there has been little systematic change in this index.

Illicit Drugs Showing Declines in Use in 2019

Relatively few drugs exhibited a significant decline in use in 2019, although the use of most drugs is well below the peak levels reached in recent years. Annual prevalence for salvia continued its gradual decline in 2019 with a significant drop of 0.2 percentage points to 0.8 percent. It appears that the use of this drug is close to ending. Annual **tranquilizer** prevalence among twelfth graders continued to fall significantly in 2019 by 0.8 percentage points to 3.9 percent—well below the 7.7 percent observed in 2002. There has been little change in the lower grades, however, since 2013.

Illicit Drugs Holding Steady in Use in 2019

There are many classes of drugs tracked in the MTF study, and the majority of them held relatively steady in 2019. These include an *index of any illicit drug other than marijuana, synthetic marijuana, LSD, hallucinogens other than LSD, MDMA* (ecstasy, Molly), *cocaine, crack, bath salts, heroin* (overall, and when used with or without a needle), *narcotics other than heroin* (reported for the twelfth grade only), *OxyContin, Vicodin, amphetamines* (taken as a class), *Ritalin, Adderall, sedatives* (reported at twelfth grade only), *tranquilizers, methamphetamine, crystal methamphetamine,* and *steroids.* While not strictly speaking illicit drugs, over-the-counter *cough and cold medications* used to get high (most of which contain dextromethorphan) also remained level in 2019, with an annual prevalence of 3.2 percent for the three grades combined.

Psychotherapeutic Drugs

Use of **psychotherapeutic drugs** outside of medical supervision warrants special attention, given that they came to make up a substantially larger part of the overall US drug problem in the 2000s. This was in part due to increases in nonmedical use of many prescription drugs over that period, and in part due to the fact that use of many of the street drugs declined substantially after the mid- to late 1990s.

The use of most of these drugs by youth began to decline by the start of the current decade. The proportion of twelfth graders misusing any of these prescription drugs (i.e., amphetamines, sedatives, tranquilizers, or narcotics other than heroin) in the prior year continued its gradual decline in 2019 (-1.1 percent, not significant) to 10 percent, down from a high of 17 percent in 2005, when this index was first calculated. Use of **narcotics other than heroin** without a doctor's orders (reported only for twelfth grade) continued a gradual decline begun after 2009, when annual prevalence was 9.2 percent; it was 3.4 percent after a significant decline of 0.8 percentage points in 2018.

Tobacco

Cigarette smoking continued its long decline in 2019 and is now at or very close to the lowest levels in the history of the forty-four-year survey. For the three grades combined, thirty-day prevalence of cigarette use, which reached its peak in the mid-1990s, has fallen by 84 percent. Daily prevalence has fallen by 88 percent, and current half-pack-a-day prevalence by 91 percent since their peak in the 1990s. Current prevalence of half-a-pack-a-day smoking stands at just 0.3 percent for eighth graders, 0.7 percent for tenth graders, and 1.5 percent for twelfth graders. Thirty-day smoking fell another significant 2.0 percentage points in 2018. Use by 10th graders fell a smaller, nonsignificant, 0.8 percentage points to 4.2 percent. Initiation of **cigarette** use also continues its long-term and extremely important decline in 2019, but only in twelfth grade. Lifetime prevalence declined between 2017 and 2019 in twelfth grade by a significant 2.8 percentage points to 23.8 percent. The fact that fewer young people now initiate cigarette smoking is an important reason for the large declines in their current use. The proportion of students who have ever tried cigarettes has fallen from peak levels reached in 1996 or 1997 by roughly four fifths, three quarters, and three fifths in eighth, tenth, and twelfth grade, respectively.

It seems likely that some of the long-term attitudinal change surrounding cigarettes is attributable to the considerable adverse publicity aimed at the tobacco industry in the 1990s, as well as a reduction in cigarette advertising and an increase in antismoking campaigns reaching youth.

Various other attitudes toward smoking became more unfavorable during that interval as well, though most have since leveled off. For example, among eighth graders, the proportions saying that they "prefer to date people who don't smoke" rose from 71 percent in 1996 to 81 percent by 2004, about where it remained through 2019. Similar changes occurred in tenth and twelfth grades. Thus, at the present time, smoking is likely to make an adolescent less attractive to the great majority of potential romantic age-mates.

In addition to changes in the attitudes and beliefs about smoking, price probably has played a role in the decline in use. Cigarette prices rose appreciably in the late 1990s and early 2000s as cigarette companies tried to cover the cost of the 1998 Master Settlement Agreement, and as many states increased excise taxes on cigarettes. A significant increase in the federal tobacco tax passed in 2009 may have contributed to the continuation of the decline in use since then.

Cigarillos. One consequence of the rise in cigarette prices is that it may have shifted some adolescents to less expensive alternatives, like **cigarillos** (little or small cigars), which are taxed at a lower rate than cigarettes. It does appear, however, that the prevalence of using small cigars is also in decline, with 9 percent of twelfth graders in 2018 reporting any past use, down substantially from 23 percent in 2010.

Hookah. Annual prevalence of smoking tobacco using a **hookah** (water pipe) had been increasing steadily until 2015 among twelfth graders (eighth and tenth graders are not asked about this practice), reaching 23 percent in 2015; but use has been declining steadily since, reaching 8 percent by 2019.

Smokeless Tobacco. From the mid-1990s to the early 2000s, **smokeless tobacco** use declined substantially, but a rebound in use developed from the mid-2000s through 2010. Since 2010, prevalence levels have declined modestly in all three grades. Perceived risk and disapproval appear to have played important roles in the earlier decline in smokeless tobacco use. The decline in smokeless tobacco use from

2010 through 2017 may be attributable, at least in part, to the 2009 increase in federal taxes on tobacco.

Snus. **Snus** is a form of smokeless tobacco. Its annual prevalence has decreased considerably from when it was first measured in 2011 (or 2012 in lower grades), but it showed little change in 2019.

Alcohol

Alcohol remains the substance most widely used by today's adolescents. Despite recent declines, by the end of high school six out of every ten students (59 percent) have consumed alcohol (more than just a few sips) at some time in their lives (after a significant 3 percentage point drop in 2019); and about a quarter (24 percent) have done so by eighth grade. (Only the twelfth grade showed significant change in 2019.)

Alcohol use began a substantial decline in the 1980s. To some degree, alcohol trends have tended to parallel the trends in illicit drug use. These include a modest increase in **binge drinking** (defined as having five or more drinks in a row at least once in the past two weeks) in the early to mid-1990s, though it was a proportionally smaller increase than was seen for cigarettes and most of the illicit drugs. Fortunately, binge drinking rates leveled off in the early 2000s, just about when the illicit drug rates began to turn around, and in 2002, a drop in **drinking** and **drunkenness** resumed in all grades. Gradual declines in thirty-day prevalence continued in the upper grades into 2019, which marked the lowest levels for alcohol use and drunkenness ever recorded by the survey in the three grades combined.

Still, prior to this year lifetime prevalence and annual prevalence for the three grades combined both declined by roughly 40 to 45 percent from the peak levels of use reached in the mid-1990s; thirty-day prevalence was down by about one-half since then; and daily prevalence by three-fourths. These are dramatic declines for such a culturally ingrained behavior and good news to many parents.

APPLYING RESEARCH TO PRACTICE: DEVELOPING AN ACTION PLAN

So far, we have examined the research on school crime and student safety, causes of school crime and violence, improving school safety, and research on alcohol and drug use among adolescents. We now provide an action plan designed to reduce school violence and misbehavior in schools. The action plan consists of seven strategies: (1) predicting school violence, (2) preventing school violence, (3) focusing research on schools, (4) strengthening the system, (5) developing a crisis management plan, (6) creating an orderly climate for learning, and (7) implementing instructional techniques that engage students (Astor & Benbenishty, 2017; Bracken et al., 2015; Cohen & Espelage, 2020; Klinger & Klinger, 2018; Scherz & Scherz, 2014; Tahtah, 2021). We discuss each one in turn.

Strategy 1: Predict School Violence

Interest in **predicting school violence** stems from a desire to prevent it rather than attempt to control it after it occurs. Ideally, if teachers and school principals could determine the conditions that cause violence and the types of students most likely to engage in it, as well as those teachers whose behavior precipitates violence, timely corrective interventions could be initiated to prevent its occurrence. This approach would be far better than waiting for violence to erupt and then having to deploy resources to quell the incident.

Predicting violence in schools is not impossible. In fact, school administrators in the Milwaukee (Wisconsin) Public Schools are using a school-violence tool that has enabled them to reduce attacks against teachers by 75 percent in ten years. The program, entitled "Safe Schools—Better Schools," allows school security officials to identify behavior problems in schools and provide resources immediately to prevent violence from occurring. School security officials in Milwaukee Public Schools are taking a proactive stance. They plan in advance and anticipate problems.

In Milwaukee Public Schools, violence against teachers has decreased from 1,080 cases in 1998–1999 to 275 in 2018–2019. The Safe Schools—Better Schools program has a three-pronged strategy to predict violence: collect and analyze data, identify problem students, and identify problem teachers (National Alliance for Safe Schools, 2020).

Collect and Analyze Data. Information on violence and discipline problems reported by teachers is collected, using standardized incident reporting forms, and analyzed by computer. School principals and central office administrators then look at where incidents are occurring, their frequency, and whether specific schools, teachers, or locations within schools are showing a pattern of repeated incidents. For example, if a particular school building is having difficulty during the beginning of school or at dismissal, then additional security officers can be marshaled to patrol the school during those times.

Identify Problem Students. Milwaukee public school administrators believe that little is accomplished simply by punishing students who are referred frequently to principals for acts of violence or disciplinary problems. Additional resources are provided to these disruptive students, such as counseling, referrals to social agencies, or assignments to alternative school programs. Milwaukee Public Schools provide a variety of alternative programs for weapon-carrying students, for those prone to violence, and for those with other behavior or learning problems.

Identify Problem Teachers. Identifying problem teachers may sound a bit negative, but some teachers actually precipitate student violence. Much assault behavior by students can be diminished with good psychological preparation of teachers and consistent support of school policies and procedures (Brownlie, 2000). Milwaukee public school administrators observe that a disproportionate number of discipline referrals are made by a few teachers in a school. Typically, 3 percent of the faculty is responsible for about 50 percent of the discipline referrals. In response, school principals arrange for teachers with classroom management problems to attend the school district's Professional Development Academy in order to learn how to handle students. On-site follow-up relative to effective classroom management techniques designed for unique populations is also available through the academy.

Another important part of the Safe Schools—Better Schools program is to develop "school teams" consisting of teachers, parents, university professors, and school principals from various school sites. These individuals agree to be part of a team. The team approach helps prevent cases from being thrown out of court due to being improperly prepared. Teams of educators working together can prevent that from happening. Milwaukee public school administrators claim that the

Safe Schools—Better Schools program will work with schools of any size or type: urban, suburban, or rural. The program provides a planning system for administering school security resources.

Strategy 2: Prevent School Violence

After two consecutive years of increase, the estimated number of crimes in the nation decreased 0.2 percent in 2018, when compared with 2017 data, according to Federal Bureau of Investigation (2019) data. Simultaneously, school-based studies reveal that many violent behaviors have increased among children and adolescents in schools (Wang et al., 2020).

Violence in schools is endangering the health, welfare, and safety of students and teachers. Students cannot learn and teachers cannot teach in an atmosphere where fear and anxiety prevail (Schargel, 2014). Two ways of preventing school violence are to toughen weapons laws and to deal with violent students (Kann, McManus, & Harris, 2018).

Toughen Weapons Laws. School principals should advocate for state legislation and school board policies that address violence in schools. Tough measures have already been implemented in most states for dealing with violent behavior, especially regarding possession of weapons and initiation of a parent responsibility law for minors possessing weapons. School principals can be strong advocates of such legislation and school board policies.

Establish weapon-free school zones. School boards might consider making their schools weapon-free zones. Efforts to do so would ideally involve the school, home, community, law enforcement, and health services. Strategies would include apprehension, prevention, intervention, education, counseling, and student and public awareness programs (CDC, 2021; David-Ferdon et al., 2016).

The following is a concise statement suggested by the National School Boards Association (n.d.):

> The School Board determines that possession and/or use of a weapon by a student is detrimental to the welfare and safety of the students and school personnel within the district. Possession and/or use of any dangerous or deadly weapon in any school building on school grounds, in any school vehicle, or at any school-sponsored activity is prohibited. Such weapons include but are not limited to any pistol, revolver, rifle, shotgun, air gun or spring gun; slingshot; bludgeon; brass knuckles or artificial knuckles of any kind; knives having a blade of greater than two inches, any knife the blade of which can be opened by a flick of a button or pressure on the handle, or any pocketknife where the blade is carried in a partially opened position. The possession or use of any such weapon will require that the proceeding for the suspension and or expulsion of the student involved will be initiated immediately by the principal.

In addition to a written school board policy, the following state legislation is recommended to provide for weapon-free schools: make it a felony to knowingly and willfully bring a firearm on school property; make it a felony for any person to knowingly allow a minor to carry a weapon to school; and provide that any person convicted of bringing a firearm on school property will lose his or her driver's license.

Limit access by minors to handguns. To provide for limited access by minors to handguns, the following laws are recommended: make it a misdemeanor for any person to allow a minor to have access to a handgun without the consent and supervision of a parent, guardian, or other responsible adult; and make possession of a handgun by a minor without the consent and supervision of a parent, guardian, or other responsible adult a misdemeanor.

Deal with Violent Students. Students cannot learn when they are in fear of harm from their classmates. Teachers cannot teach in an atmosphere of fear for their own safety, as well as that of their students (Cohen & Espelage, 2020; Klinger & Klinger, 2018). To provide a safe and secure learning atmosphere for children, school districts must be able to expel violent students to alternative schools; require schools to report violent offenders to law enforcement officials; require court counselors to confer with school officials; expand immediate school actions; and take privileges away from students.

Expel violent students. Most state statutes provide that a school board can expel a student, age fourteen or older, only if he has been convicted of a felony *and* if his continued presence in the school constitutes a clear threat to the safety and health of other students or staff. State statutes should be amended so that when the principal and the superintendent can prove a student is a clear threat to the safety and health of other students or employees, the school board has the option of expelling the student, even though no felony has been committed. School officials are encouraged to use long-term suspension and alternative schools or programs in lieu of expulsions.

Transfer violent students to alternative schools. Under compulsory attendance laws, states have a duty to provide an education for all of their children, even those deemed violent by the juvenile justice system. In numerous instances a violent student has been placed in a regular school setting, and the results have been disruptive and even dangerous. To provide a safe and secure setting for all children and teachers, school districts must be able to transfer to another institution the juveniles who have been categorized as violent by the courts, as well as the juveniles whose presence poses a clear threat to others within the school.

Transferring a juvenile to an alternative school for long-term supervision is a viable option to expulsion. The state fulfills its duty to provide an education; the school is made safer by removing the violent juvenile; the community is not burdened by juveniles who have been suspended from school and are roaming the streets; and the juvenile is provided a safe and structured setting in which to continue the educational process. For juveniles awaiting trial for violent acts, this approach would provide a supervised situation while preventing the juvenile's continued presence at a school from becoming disruptive.

Due to the expense of alternative schools, such placement should constitute a last step in a continuum of services for violent students. Placement should be temporary, with the goal being to return the student to the regular school setting at the appropriate time. Although the format of alternative programs varies from small, informal programs similar to homebound instruction in some systems to more formal school settings in larger systems, the focus must be on providing a strong, academic course of study with therapeutic emphasis. Other service agencies such as Public Health, Mental Health, Social Services, Juvenile Justice, and so forth must be an integral part of the team providing the alternative education program. School districts should consider using drug-free school funds, dropout prevention funds, juvenile justice and delinquency prevention funds, community-based alternative funds, in-school suspension funds, average daily membership positions, basic education program positions, and contributions from other agencies to staff alternative programs.

Report violent offenders to law officials. School violence is a community problem, not just a school problem. Violence in the schools will be stopped only when the schools join with local law enforcement, parents, juvenile court counselors, and other agencies to work together to solve the problem (Office of Juvenile Justice and Delinquency Prevention, 2022). To obtain the support of law enforcement in curtailing school violence, principals must report all felonies and misdemeanors involving personal injury, sexual assault, possession or use of weapons, possession or sale of drugs occurring on school property. Schools can appropriately handle misdemeanors—which do not involve violence, sexual assault, weapons use, firearms, or drugs—without calling on law enforcement for help.

Require court counselors to confer with school officials. Juvenile court counselors should be required to confer with school officials, the juvenile, and the juvenile's parents or guardian whenever the minor is ordered to attend school as part of his probation after adjudication of a crime of violence. Juvenile court counselors should be given the resources needed to work more closely with the schools. The state's juvenile code should specify that minors placed on probation and required to attend school must maintain a passing grade.

Expand immediate school actions. School districts should take immediate actions to make school safer. These actions should address a comprehensive approach to prevention, intervention, and crisis management. Use of school security officers, peer mediation, and crisis intervention teams is encouraged, as well as the development of policies and procedures governing student behavior (Astor & Benbenishty, 2017; Bracken et al., 2015; CDC, 2021; Cohen & Espelage, 2020; Daly, 2018; David-Ferdon et al., 2016; Fennelly & Perry, 2014; Gunzelmann, 2015; Klinger & Klinger, 2018; Madfis, 2014; Schargel, 2014; Scherz & Scherz, 2014; Tahtah, 2021). The following recommendations will expand immediate school actions:

1. A student's right to park on school property can be conditioned upon agreeing to have their vehicle searched at any time by school officials.
2. Metal detectors, cameras, lights, handheld radio communications, and other security measures may be installed.
3. Cooperative arrangements with local law enforcement should be arranged to put trained resource officers in schools that need them.
4. Parent training and involvement programs should be established or strengthened.
5. Peer mediation and conflict resolution programs for students and teachers should be established.
6. Rules governing student behavior should be established, communicated, and enforced.
7. Warrants against students who commit violent acts in schools should be sought.
8. Rewards for information leading to the confiscation of weapons, drugs, firearms, and other dangerous items should be offered.
9. Anonymous reporting of weapons or drugs on school property must be encouraged.
10. Taking book bags to lockers should be restricted.

11. Intruder drills and other crisis management drills should be conducted periodically to ensure that students and other school employees are prepared for emergencies.

Take privileges away from students. Principals must have the authority to act immediately in ways that restrict meaningful student privileges. No appeal of these actions should delay implementation of the action. A prompt and meaningful response to student misconduct is an effective way to produce desired conduct.

The department of education in each state needs to adopt procedures that enable principals to:

1. Suspend school bus transportation privileges for students who commit acts of violence
2. Suspend parking privileges on school grounds for students who commit acts of violence
3. Assign to an alternative school those students who commit acts of violence
4. Remove from extracurricular activities (athletic and academic) students who commit acts of violence
5. At extracurricular activities, restrict attendance of students who commit acts of violence

Strategy 3: Focus Resources on Schools

The number of dysfunctional and violence-prone youth in our schools is growing rapidly. These students require special attention. To meet their needs, additional resources may be required, including more assistant principals, guidance counselors, school psychologists, social workers, nurses, and teachers. Providing for the needs of violence-prone students also includes funding the basic education program, teaching violence prevention, and establishing local task forces (David-Ferdon et al., 2016).

Fund the Basic Education Program. Providing smaller class sizes to deal with these special needs students will require the allocation of additional teaching positions in the regular school program. In addition, many schools are now assigning school resource officers to schools to prevent school violence. School districts that utilize these plainclothes police officers report significant reductions in school violence (National Alliance for Safe Schools, 2020). Alternative schools or programs must have additional staff members as well as intensive therapeutic support to serve violence-prone youth. Basic education program funding must be reviewed as "positive prevention," because our failure to serve the special needs population inevitably leads to incarcerations or welfare that will cost the taxpayers much more in the future.

Teach Violence Prevention. State departments of education need to ensure that violence prevention is included in their state's K–12 curriculum. Peer mediation, conflict resolution, multiculturalism, media literacy, and citizenship should be part of that curriculum (see, for example, the *Texas School Law Bulletin*, 2020). Principals need to advocate for the state department of education to encourage teacher training in these areas. In particular, the teaching of citizenship skills needs to be developed more fully in schools. Courses should include personal responsibility, cultural and racial differences, morals and ethics, and problem-solving strategies. However, merely teaching about these topics will not be sufficient; schools must work to develop these skills in students.

There are, of course, many effective classroom-wide and school-wide approaches to managing student behavior. We suggest you read about them. Some examples follow: The Good Behavior Game (Tingstrom, Sterling-Turner, & Wilczynski, 2006), Best Foot Forward (Hudley, Graham, & Taylor, 2007), Judicious Discipline (Landau & Gathercoal, 2000), Classroom Check-up (Reinke, Lewis-Palmer, & Merrell, 2008), Positive Peer Reporting (Morrison & Jones, 2007), Unified Discipline (Algozzine, Daunic, & Smith, 2010; Algozzine & White, 2002; White et al., 2001), Performance Character/Moral Character (Davidson, Khmelkov, & Lickona, 2010; Lickona & Davidson, 2005), and Resolving Conflict Creatively (Lantieri, 1995).

Establish Local Task Forces. Principals need to advocate for each school district to establish a school safety task force consisting of students, parents, teachers, school administrators, law enforcement officials, juvenile court personnel, local government representatives, and community leaders. Task force goals will be (a) to evaluate the extent of violence in the schools and the community and (b) to develop an action plan that includes both prevention and intervention strategies. In addition to these goals, the two most important contributions of the task force will be to develop a vision within the community that violence can be diminished and to model the collaboration among stakeholder groups.

Strategy 4: Strengthen the System

As noted previously, juvenile violence has increased substantially during the past few years. In some states, the juvenile justice system is not adequately dealing with the problem. Improving the state's juvenile code and creating a statewide center for the prevention of school violence may help strengthen the system (Office of Juvenile Justice and Delinquency Prevention, 2022).

Improve the Juvenile Code. School principals can be advocates for an examination of the state's juvenile code and the way its juvenile justice system handles crimes committed by juveniles. The review of issues should include fingerprinting of juveniles for violent crimes; submission of these fingerprints to the State Bureau of Investigation for inclusion in the Automated Fingerprint Identification System; the age at which a juvenile can be bound over to superior court for trial as an adult; and the access by superior court judges to prior juvenile convictions at sentencing.

Create a State Center for the Prevention of School Violence. School principals can be advocates for the governor of each state to establish a state center for the prevention of school violence. The center would function as the state clearinghouse and contact agency for technical assistance and program development. Specifically, the center would perform the following functions: serve as the point of contact for data and information about the number of violent incidents occurring in schools across the state; conduct periodic analysis of school violence trends, and assess the impact of programs initiated and legislation enacted to deal with the problem of violence; and provide direct service to those requesting to establish violence reduction programs in the schools.

Strategy 5: Develop a Crisis Management Plan

As discussed earlier, one of the most serious problems that principals face today is the increasing level of violence in schools. It is essential for principals and their staffs to be prepared for such incidents. Schools need to have a comprehensive crisis management plan. By adhering to the following steps, principals can ensure to the greatest degree possible that their schools are safe for students and staff alike (Astor & Benbenishty, 2017; Bracken et al., 2015; Cohen & Espelage, 2020; David-Ferdon et al., 2016; Dunlap, 2013; Fennelly & Perry, 2014; Klinger & Klinger, 2018; Schargel, 2014; Scherz & Scherz, 2014; Tahtah, 2021).

Form a School-Wide Crisis Management Team. The team should be made up of school staff and parents as well as representatives from social service and mental health agencies, the religious community, recreational organizations, and law enforcement. The charge of the crisis management team is to develop and evaluate a comprehensive plan for school safety.

Conduct an Ongoing, School-Wide Safety Audit. A firm knowledge base has emerged, called Crime Prevention through Environmental Design (CPTED) that examines the design and use of school spaces according to how well they enhance school safety. A CPTED evaluation prescribes changes in the design of the school building, in patterns of building use, and in supervision processes to reduce the likelihood of school crime and violence.

Items addressed in a CPTED analysis would include: the design and location of bathrooms; the height of windows; how entrances and exits to the school are monitored and managed; the use of lighting, natural surveillance capabilities, and obstructions thereof; where locker bays are located and how they are managed; identification of low-traffic areas requiring an increased adult presence; identification of school sites that tend to be inhabited inappropriately by certain groups of students; scheduling procedures that result in large groups of students coming in contact with each other in crowded spaces; how students and other adults who belong in the school are recognized and identified; and procedures that allow students to communicate anonymously their concerns about other students or situations.

Develop Policies and Procedures for Various Emergencies. Specific policies and procedures must be developed to address a wide range of potential problems at the district, school, and classroom levels. These could include a violence prevention policy, a zero-tolerance policy for weapons and drugs, a dress code, and an intruder policy.

It may be helpful if the principal divides policies and procedures into categories like the following:

1. The *people crisis* category could include medical emergencies, intruders, drive-by shootings, student runaways or abductions, deaths of students or staff members, and bomb threats.
2. The *natural disaster* category could include fires, tornados, earthquakes, other severe weather, or floods.
3. The *physical plant* category could include policies that address power outages, nonworking phone lines, gas leaks, hazardous materials, or explosions.

Conduct Safety Drills. Every aspect of the crisis management plan should have at least two people responsible for coordinating each task. Staff members should be assigned to respond to emergency teams, parents, and the press. Each school should carefully consider its physical plant and analyze where students should be directed to go from wherever they are in the school. Upon hearing a predetermined signal or tone, teachers should lock down classrooms. Every room should have two methods for communicating with the office (i.e., a two-way public announcement system and a phone, cell phone, or walkie-talkie).

Develop a School-Wide Discipline Plan. School discipline should be consistent, predictable, and perceived as fair by students in the school. It is essential that every crisis management plan include a carefully developed school-wide discipline plan that has input from teachers, students, parents, administrators, and other adults in the school. The plan should be posted throughout the school with clearly stated rules that govern classroom, cafeteria, playground, gym, and hallway behavior.

Provide a Means for Students to Communicate Information to Staff. A recent report from the CDC (2021) notes that in several instances of school violence or student suicide, some students knew in advance of the activity but did not tell anyone. It is essential in such situations that children be able to communicate their concerns or fears to the staff in a way that maintains confidentiality, respect, and safety.

Teach Students Alternatives to Violence. In any program aimed at averting student violence, it is first necessary to focus attention on students' individual needs and problems. School staff should address such topics as self-esteem, conflict resolution, impulse control, consequences of gang membership, and stress management. Schools also need to foster a sense of belonging among students. One reason students join gangs is that these groups meet their need for belonging. Membership in after-school extracurricular activities and clubs also may help reduce violence.

Evaluate Administrative Practices of the School. How a school is operated can have a strong impact on its relative safety. Academically effective schools, for example, tend to be safer schools. Schools that provide a positive, inclusive climate tend to have less conflict and fewer instances of aggressive, bullying behavior. Schools attended by the number of students for which they were designed tend to have fewer behavioral incidents and problems. Safer schools tend to have clear behavioral and performance expectations for everyone.

Use Resources to Identify Students at Risk for Violent Behavior. School principals can use an excellent resource for identifying troubled youth and responding to their needs. It is called the *Early Warning/Timely Response Guide* for making schools safer and violence free. This guide was jointly developed by the US Attorney General's Office and the US Department of Education. It contains comprehensive guidelines and recommendations for the early profiling of troubled youth and the role that schools, teachers, parents, communities, and peers can play in responding to their problems and meeting their needs. It is a valuable tool for addressing the current crisis of school safety. The guide is a public domain publication, costs nothing, and can be downloaded from the Internet at http://www.ed.gov/about/offices/list/osers/osep/gtss.html. Table 12.1 provides a sample checklist that principals can use to identify violence-prone students.

Strategy 6: Create an Orderly Climate for Learning

Several authors (Algozzine & White, 2002; Algozzine, Daunic, & Smith, 2010; Crawford, 2004; Cushman, 2003; Cushman & Rogers, 2008; Emmer & Evertson, 2017; Emmer & Stough, 2001; Evertson & Emmer, 2017; Kraft, 2010; Levin & Nolan, 2004; Lindberg & Swick, 2006; Ross et al., 2008; Shea & Bauer, 2011; Simonsen et al., 2008; Smith & Bondy, 2007; Weinstein, Romano, & Mignano, 2011; Woolfolk, Hoy, & Weinstein, 2006) suggest ways that schools may be able to reduce student violence by creating an orderly climate conducive to learning. According to these authors, research has indicated two important differences between schools that create an orderly climate for learning and those that fail to do so: goals and rules and procedures. Each one will be discussed in turn.

Table 12.1 Checklist for Identifying Students at Risk for Violent Behavior

Children and adolescents at risk may:

- express self-destructive or homicidal ideation
- have a history of self-destructive behavior
- articulate specific plans to harm self or others
- engage in "bullying" other children
- have difficulty with impulse control
- evidence significant changes in behavior
- engage in substance abuse
- become involved with gangs
- evidence a preoccupation with fighting
- have a history of antisocial behavior
- evidence a low tolerance for frustration
- externalize blame for their difficulties
- evidence a preoccupation with guns and weapons
- have engaged in fire setting
- evidence persistent bed wetting
- appear to be, or acknowledge, feeling depressed
- talk about "not being around"
- express feelings of hopelessness
- give away possessions
- appear withdrawn
- evidence significant changes in mood
- experience sleep and eating disturbances
- have experienced prior trauma or tragedy
- have been, or are, victims of child abuse
- have experienced a significant loss
- evidence a preoccupation with television programs and movies with violent themes
- evidence a preoccupation with games with violent themes
- have harmed small animals
- have access to a firearm
- have brought a weapon to school
- evidence frequent disciplinary problems
- exhibit poor academic performance
- have frequently been truant from school

Establish and Emphasize Goals. In schools that emphasize academic goals, students are more engaged in schoolwork (Anderman & Anderman, 2014; Jackson, 2011; Riggs & Gholar, 2009)—that is, they spend more time on task. Teachers in these schools have higher expectations (Benner & Mistry, 2007; Good & Nichols, 2001; Hinnant, O'Brien, & Ghazarian, 2009; McKown, Gregory, & Weinstein, 2010; Rosenthal, 2002; Spitz, 1999; Tenenbaum & Ruck, 2007; Torff, 2011; Zhao & Qiu, 2009) for their students and tend to have more positive interactions with them. These student and teacher characteristics make it more likely that students invest more time and energy in academic goals rather than in a peer culture (Bulach & Lunenburg, 2016b) that might sanction violence and disruptive behavior (Lunenburg, 2010j). Studies reveal that school violence is much more likely to occur when students feel that grades are punitive or impossible to obtain (Brookhart, 2011; Brookhart & Nitko, 2008; O'Connor, 2009) and if the school curriculum is unimaginative and meaningless to students (Bloomquist & Schnell, 2002; Guerra & Leidy, 2008; Lowry et al., 1995). Also, the level of violence increases with class size, especially for at risk students (Addonizio & Phelps, 2000; ERIC Digest, 2003; Research Points, 2003). Moreover, a higher incidence of aggression against teachers occurs if the class consists largely of students with behavior problems (Algozzine, Daunic, & Smith, 2010; Burke et al., 2011; Evans & Schamberg, 2009; Hamby & Grych, 2013; Tough, 2012), low achievers (Entwisle, Alexander, & Olson, 2010; Ladson-Billings, 2002; Sirin, 2005; Ready & Wright, 2011), or minority students (Banks, 2009, Bennett, 2011; Graham & Hudley, 2005; Losen, 2015; Nieto, 2002–2003, 2012; Robins et al., 2012; Singham, 2003; Wiggan, 2007). This is one of many reasons for the elimination of tracking (Oakes, 2005).

Specific areas of the school program, as related to school violence, that should be evaluated include the curriculum and the instructional setting. For the curriculum, the following questions should be asked: Is the curriculum relevant? Does it meet the needs of all students (Ford, 2014; Oliva & Gordon, 2013; Ornstein & Hunkins, 2017; Ukpokodu, 2010)? Regarding the instructional setting, the following are significant questions: Are the class size and total students manageable for effective teaching (Marzano, 2017)? Are the instructional materials and procedures appropriate (Zepeda, 2017)? Are grades attainable and fair (Brookhart, 2011; Brookhart & Nitko, 2008; O'Connor, 2009)? Are the students tracked by ability or other factors (Glickman, Gordon, & Ross-Gordon, 2018; Ornstein, Pajak, & Ornstein, 2015)?

An effort should be made to improve the achievement of all students in schools (Darling-Hammond & Oakes, 2019; Lunenburg, 2013b; Ornstein, 2016). And schools must expand teaching beyond the basic skills to include citizenship, effective decision making, conflict-resolution skills, cooperation, and courtesy (Brown et al., 2004; Davidson, Khmelkov, & Lickona, 2010; Knoester & Parkinson, 2015; Lickona & Davidson, 2005; Selfridge, 2004). Teachers and students alike should model the art of compromise. Students need to learn that these are acceptable ways to deal with their conflicts and to meet their individual needs (Brown et al., 2004; Lantieri, 1985; Selfridge, 2004).

The need to reach children in the early years is important. Early childhood programs can make a difference in academic, economic, and social arenas (Lunenburg, 2000c). Programs that provide support for young families should be enhanced. Head Start, Follow Through, day care, and after-school care for children of working or student parents should be funded (Lunenburg, 2011g). School districts must become involved in early childhood education by providing facilities and staff. Teachers need to be trained to work with infants, toddlers, and preschoolers. Parents may require assistance in acquiring parenting skills.

Establish Rules and Procedures. Students and teachers feel safe in schools with clear discipline standards that are enforced firmly, fairly, and consistently. This environment can be accomplished by developing a comprehensive student handbook that identifies expectations for student behavior and states the consequences for students who violate the rules. Student handbooks should unambiguously outline student rights and responsibilities. Suspension and expulsion procedures should be carefully explained, and the appeals process fully described. Due to the frequency of gang activity in schools, the handbook should include sections on dress codes, search and seizure, graffiti, and school design (see, for example, *Student Code of Conduct: 2020–2021* and *Student Handbook: 2020–2021*, published by the Cypress-Fairbanks Independent School District, Houston, Texas). We discuss each of these policies in turn.

Establish dress codes. School boards should consider establishing policies regarding dress codes for students and teachers. For example, the Oakland (California) School Board banned clothing and jewelry denoting identification with a gang; expensive jogging suits often worn by drug dealers; and all hats and clothing designating membership in nonschool organizations. Detroit (Michigan) Public Schools have implemented a ban on expensive clothing and jewelry. Baltimore (Maryland) Public Schools are experimenting with school uniforms. The Dallas (Texas) School Board has adopted a policy opposing clothing and grooming that are considered distracting or disruptive. And school principals have been given the discretion to determine what are inappropriate dress and appearance at their school (National School Boards Association, n.d.).

School boards may enact reasonable regulations concerning student appearance in school. Such regulations have focused on male hairstyles and pupil attire (Lunenburg, 2011h). Student challenges to these regulations have relied on First Amendment constitutional freedoms to determine personal appearance. The US Supreme Court has consistently refused to review the decisions of lower courts on these matters (*Karr v. Schmidt*, 401 U.S. 1201, 1972). Generally, courts tend to provide less protection to some forms of expression (e.g., pupil hairstyle and attire) than to others (e.g., symbolic expression and student publications). Nonetheless, awareness of constitutional freedoms places limits on school principals to regulate student dress, excluding special situations (e.g., graduation and physical education classes). Pupil attire can always be regulated to protect student health, safety, and school discipline. In short, the extent to which school principals may control student appearance depends more on different community mores and on "the times" than on strict principles of law.

Use search and seizure cautiously. The introduction of drugs, weapons, and other contraband in schools has placed school principals in the position of searching students' persons or lockers, and students claim that such acts violate their Fourth Amendment guarantees. A student's right to the Fourth Amendment's protection from unreasonable search and seizure must be balanced against the need for school principals to maintain discipline and to provide a safe environment conducive to learning. State and federal courts generally have relied on the doctrine of in loco parentis, reasoning that school principals stand in the place of a parent and are not subject to the constraints of the Fourth Amendment. In *New Jersey v. T.L.O.*, 469 U.S. 325 (1985), the US Supreme Court held that searches by school officials in schools are within the constraints of the Fourteenth Amendment. The Court concluded that the special needs of the school environment justified easing the warrant and probable cause requirement imposed in criminal cases, provided that school searches are based on "reasonable suspicion."

Pay attention to graffiti. Attending to symbols is an important way of controlling misbehavior. Graffiti is a form of vandalism (defacing school property) that frequently serves as gang symbolism. Immediate removal of graffiti sends a message to students of the school principal's opposition to vandalism and gang symbols. It not only prevents conflict over potential gang territory but also tells students and staff alike that the principal cares about personnel safety and is taking appropriate steps to protect everyone's safety.

Reconsider school design. School design and facility use can encourage undesirable behaviors. School policy should restrict student congregation in "blind spots"; recommend random spot checks of problem areas, such as restrooms, locker rooms, and parking lots; and increase physical security with fences, lights, and metal detectors. The least costly security measure is faculty supervision. When principals and teachers are visible throughout the buildings and school grounds, disruptive behavior is less likely to occur.

Strategy 7: Implement Instructional Techniques that Engage Students

To this point, we have examined the role of cultural, academic, cognitive, psychological, psychosocial, and neuropsychological factors in school violence. Such explanations place the responsibility for violent behavior on the individual. Other explanations for violent behavior focus on schools that: do not meet the needs of their students; lack clear goals; do not enforce rules fairly or consistently; use punitive ways to resolve conflicts; and impose poorly delivered instruction that does not engage students in the learning process.

Two important variables that are dimensions of total teacher behavior were reported in the literature as instructional technique and the immediate effect of technique on student engagement in learning (Evertson & Emmer, 2017; Good & Lavigne, 2018). An inverse relationship has been found between student engagement and student disruptive behavior (Algozzine, Daunic, & Smith, 2010; Algozzine & White, 2002; Belvel, 2010; White et al., 2001).

Quality teaching may avert violence and disruptive behavior in classrooms and throughout the school. By making sure that all students are actively engaged in meaningful, challenging learning every day, students are less likely to be disruptive. Furthermore, all teachers and students should be encouraged to treat others with respect at all times (West, Lunenburg, & Hines, 2014). A few examples of evidence-based teaching strategies that keep students engaged in meaningful, challenging learning follow.

In their study of improving teaching for rigorous learning, which involved a sample of 1,500 schools, Newmann, Carmichael, and King (2015) found that successful classrooms focused on "authentic" pedagogy (teaching that requires students to think, to develop an in-depth understanding, and to apply academic learning to important realistic problems) and student learning. They achieved this in two ways: greater organizational capacity and greater external support.

The most successful schools, according to Newmann et al. (2015) were those that functioned as learning communities. That is, they found a way to channel staff and student efforts toward a clear, commonly shared purpose for learning. Moreover, they found that external agencies helped schools to focus on student learning and to enhance organizational capacity through three strategies: setting standards for learning of high intellectual quality; providing sustained schoolwide professional development; and using deregulation to increase school autonomy. In short, dynamic internal learning communities and their relationships with external networks made the difference. Evidence on the critical combination of internal and external learning is mounting.

In research recently completed at the Mid-continent Research for Education and Learning (McREL) Institute, Robert Marzano (2017) identified classroom practices that generally increase student achievement: identifying similarities and differences; summarizing and note taking; receiving reinforcement for effort and recognition for achievement; doing homework and practicing; using nonlinguistic representations; learning cooperatively; setting objectives and testing hypotheses; and using cues, questions, and advance organizers. Regardless of whether or not teachers teach to standards, these classroom practices work well.

In addition, Frederick Lunenburg and Beverly Irby (2011) provide enduring, research-based instructional strategies that can improve teaching and learning including: set induction, stimulus variation, closure, reinforcement, recognizing attending behavior, silence and nonverbal cues, cueing, use of examples, planned repetition, questioning skills (fluency of questioning, probing questions, higher-order questions, divergent questions), the use of multiple frames of reference, and race/class, and gender equity.

There continues to be serious differences between the level of academic achievement for children coming from wealthy and from poor families, and from ethnic-majority and from some ethnic-minority families. Low socioeconomic status and some ethnic-minority groups continue to be overrepresented in the low achievement groups (Barton & Coley, 2010; Darling-Hammond, 2010; Entwisle, Alexander, & Olson, 2010; Howard, 2020; Ladson-Billings, 2006; Lee & Bowen, 2006; Murphy, 2010; Paige, 2011; Rothstein, 2004; Schmidt et al., 2015; Singham, 2005; Siren, 2005; Teranishi, Nguyen, & Curammeng, 2020; Wiggan, 2007). More than ever, culturally responsive teaching is essential in addressing the needs of today's diverse student population (Benson & Fiarman, 2020; Darling-Hammond et al., 2019; Gay, 2018; Scott & Anderson, 2019; West, Lunenburg, & Hines, 2014).

Several scholars reviewed the literature on effective multicultural teacher practices and teacher characteristics (Agarwal-Rangnath, 2020; Darling-Hammond, 2010; Garcia & Kleifgen, 2018; Gay, 2010; Gorski, 2018; Han & Laughter, 2019; Herrera, 2010; Hess & Noguera, 2021; Lara-Alecio, Bass, & Irby, 2001; Lara-Alecio et al., 2004; Marshall, Gerstl-Pepin, & Johnson, 2020; Noguera & Syeed, 2020; Paris & Alim, 2017; Sleeter & Zavala, 2020; Walker, 2019; West, Lunenburg, & Hines, 2014). They concluded that effective teachers:

1. Have empathy for people from other cultures
2. Accurately perceive similarities and differences between a student's culture and their own
3. Describe a student's behavior without judging it
4. Express respect and positive regard for all students through eye contact, body posture, and voice tone and pitch
5. Use multicultural materials in the classroom
6. Recognize and accept both the language spoken in the home and the standard language
7. Help students develop pride in and identification with their native culture
8. Praise all students equally and frequently for success
9. Give feedback to the public responses of all students equally

10. Pay equal attention or interact with all students frequently
11. Demand the same from all students
12. Interact the same way with all students and monitor and structure their activities equally
13. Grade tests and assignments in the same manner, so that all students are given the benefit of the doubt in borderline cases
14. Try to improve on students' responses to questions by giving clues or using other teaching techniques
15. Evidence equal acceptance and use of ideas given by all students.

These effective teaching practices and teacher characteristics will likely improve student learning, regardless of the teacher's philosophy of multicultural education (Bulach & Lunenburg, 2016a, 2016b; Westley, 2011). What emerges from the list is a teacher who respects all students and who takes responsibility for knowing about their cultural backgrounds and using this knowledge in his or her teaching.

SUMMARY

1. Many Americans have been concerned about the safety of their children at school for more than a century. The *Indicators of School Crime and Safety: 2019* report contains the latest statistics on school crime and violence in schools. Between July 1, 2017, and June 30, 2018, there were a total of forty-seven school-associated violent deaths (homicide, suicide, or legal intervention death) in elementary and secondary schools in the United States.

2. In 2018, among students ages twelve through eighteen, there were about 749,400 victimizations (theft and nonfatal violent victimization) at school and 601,300 victimizations away from school.

3. It is important to recognize that a large majority of young people are not violence-prone, do not have criminal attitudes or criminal records and want nothing more than to receive a good education in a safe environment. Nevertheless, it is critical that schools and communities recognize that school violence needs to be addressed.

4. Most educators, education researchers, and practitioners would agree that school violence arises from a layering of causes and risk factors that include, but are not limited to: access to weapons; media violence; cyber abuse; and the impact of school, community, and family environments.

5. Schools are taking a variety of measures to improve school safety. These include: physical surveillance, including weapons deterrence and the presence of security guards or police officers on campus; school policies designed to prevent violence by punishing those who perpetrate violence; instruction-based programs designed to address the precursors of violence, including bullying; profiling of potentially violent individuals; counseling at-risk students; and conflict mediation and resolution.

6. Drugs and alcohol have been widely used by young people in the United States for a very long time. *Monitoring the Future: National Survey Results on Drug Use 1975–2018* (Johnston et al., 2019) is the most recent data available on adolescent drug use. Generally, the use of illicit drugs, cigarette smoking, and alcohol among adolescents has been decreasing since the mid- to late 1990s.

7. In applying research to practice, we developed an action plan consisting of seven strategies: (1) predicting school violence, (2) preventing school violence, (3) focusing resources on schools, (4) strengthening the system, (5) developing a crisis management plan, (6) creating an orderly climate for learning, and (7) providing instructional techniques that enhance student academic engagement.

KEY TERMS

school violence
Crime and Safety Surveys (CSS)
cyberbullying
zero-tolerance policies
broken windows philosophy
progressive education
discipline gap
restorative practices
vaping
nicotine vaping
marijuana vaping
marijuana
any illicit drug
any illicit drug other than marijuana
any illicit drug including inhalants

salvia
tranquilizer
psychotherapeutic drugs
narcotics other than heroine
heroin
cigarette smoking
cigarillos
hookah
smokeless tobacco
snus
alcohol
binge drinking
drinking
drunkenness
predicting school violence

FIELD-BASED ACTIVITIES

1. Take field notes for one week, during which time you will investigate your school's violence prediction strategies and violence prevention strategies. Record these in your journal. Then interview your building principal to determine how the violence prediction and prevention strategies are functioning in your school. If your school has no such strategies, find out if they exist in other schools in your district and/or other school districts in your state or other states—that is, do a survey of effective violence prediction and violence prevention strategies in operation in schools. Record your findings in your journal.

2. Additional resources may be required to meet the needs of violence-prone students. Some strategies are funding the basic education program, teaching violence prevention, and establishing task forces.

What additional resources and strategies exist in your school or school district to meet the needs of violence-prone students? Record these strategies in your journal. Next, interview a state official to learn how your state's juvenile code applies to violence in your state. Record your findings in your journal.

3. Student violence may be reduced in schools by creating an orderly climate conducive to learning. Some strategies are establishing and emphasizing goals, establishing and implementing rules and procedures fairly and consistently, and providing teaching techniques that enhance student academic engagement. Investigate which of the three strategies just mentioned are used successfully in your school to reduce student violence. Record your findings in your journal. Recommend other strategies not described in this text.

SUGGESTED READINGS

Centers for Disease Control and Prevention (CDC) (2019). National Center for Injury Prevention and Control. *Web-based injury statistics query and reporting system (WISQARS)* [online] 2017 www.cdc.gov/injury. The CDC provides an in-depth analysis of violence prevention programs.

Cohen, J., & Espelage, D. L. (Eds.). (2020). *Feeling safe in school: Bullying and violence prevention around the world.* Cambridge, MA: Harvard Educational Publishing Group. The text adds to the understanding of the possibilities for increasing student safety by examining the experiencing of eleven different countries view and definition of what it means to feel safe in school.

Daly, S. E. (2018). *Everyday school violence: An educator's guide to safer schools.* Lanham, MD: Rowman & Littlefield. Sarah Daly discusses small-scale school violence. Many children suffer the effects of everyday violence that affect the learning environment and the sense of safety in schools: bullying, threats, fights, theft, weapon-carrying, and the like.

David-Ferdon, C., Vivola-Kantor, M., Dahlberg, L. L., Marshal, K. J., Rainford, N., & Hall, J. E. (2016). *A comprehensive technical package for the prevention of youth violence and associated risk behaviors.* Atlanta, GA: National Center for Injury Prevention and Control. Centers for Disease Control and Prevention. https://www.cdc.gov/violenceprevention/pdfyvtechnicalpackage.

Klinger, A., & Klinger, A. (2018). *Keeping students safe every day: How to prepare for and respond to school violence, national disasters, and other hazards.* Alexandria, VA: ASCD. In this informative guide, school safety experts address hazards of all kinds: crisis, hurricanes, earthquakes, explosions, an active shooter and offer a plan to deal with hazards of all sorts.

Scherz, J. M., & Scherz, D. (2014). *Catastrophic school violence: A new approach to prevention.* Lamham, MD: Rowman & Littlefield. Jared and Donna Scherz delve deep into school culture and the school shooter. The authors generate a more comprehensive picture of school violence, including personal, interpersonal, and environmental factors that help to generate a school mass killer.

13

Human Resource Management

■ ■ ■

FOCUSING QUESTIONS

1. What are the steps in the human resource management process?
2. How do principals recruit personnel?
3. What steps do principals use in selecting personnel?
4. Why are professional development programs needed?
5. What are the most commonly used professional development methods?
6. Why is teacher evaluation important?
7. How can staff performance be measured? What are some common errors principals make in evaluating personnel?
8. What is the impact of collective bargaining on the principal's role in operating schools?

In this chapter, we respond to these questions concerning human resources administration in schools. We begin our discussion with an overview of the human resource management process. Then we look at recruitment, selection, and professional development of personnel. Next, we examine performance appraisal, including methods, rating errors, and programs specific to teachers. And, finally, we discuss collective bargaining, including the collective bargaining process, bargaining issues, and bargaining tactics used to arrive at a collective bargaining agreement.

Who performs the human resource management function? In many large school districts, human resource management activities are carried out largely by a human resources department. However, not all principals work in school districts that have a human resources department; and even those that do still must be engaged in some human resource management functions. Principals in small- to medium-sized school districts are examples of individuals who must frequently do their hiring without the assistance of a human resources department. But even principals in large school districts are involved in recruiting, reviewing applications, interviewing applicants, developing faculty and staff, and appraising performance. And with the advent of site-based management, principals are becoming more involved in human resource management decisions—involving both certificated and classified employees—than in the past.

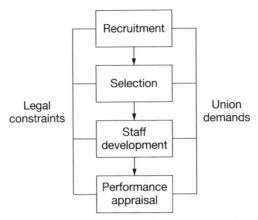

Figure 13.1 Human Resource Management Process

The human resource management process consists of the following steps: recruitment, selection, professional development, and performance appraisal (Arthur, 2019; Norton, 2014; Rebore, 2014; Smith, 2013; Tomal & Schilling, 2018). Figure 13.1 illustrates these steps. The figure also indicates that all of these various activities are affected by legislative constraints and union demands. Legal constraints and union demands are discussed in relation to the preceding four steps.

RECRUITMENT

Recruitment is the process of attracting a pool of qualified applicants to replenish or expand a school's human resources. To effectively recruit applicants, principals must (a) have a thorough analysis of job requirements, (b) know the legal constraints that influence recruiting efforts, and (c) cultivate the sources of potential employees.

Job Analysis

To recruit appropriate personnel to fill vacant positions, the principal must know in detail what tasks are to be performed and the personal characteristics necessary to perform the tasks. These determinations are derived through **job analysis** (US Department of Labor, 2022). The information obtained through job analysis is used in most subsequent personnel decisions, such as selection, professional development, and performance appraisal. But its most immediate use is to prepare job descriptions and job specifications (see figure 13.2).

The *job description* is a written statement of the duties and responsibilities, relationships, and results expected of the job incumbent. It generally includes a job title, the person to whom the job incumbent reports, and a statement of the job goal. The **job specification**, also based on job analysis, specifies the minimum acceptable qualifications that an incumbent must possess to perform the job successfully. It identifies the degree of education required, the desirable amount of previous experience, and the skills, abilities, and physical requirements needed to do the job effectively. Figure 13.2 illustrates the relationships of job analysis to job description and job specification.

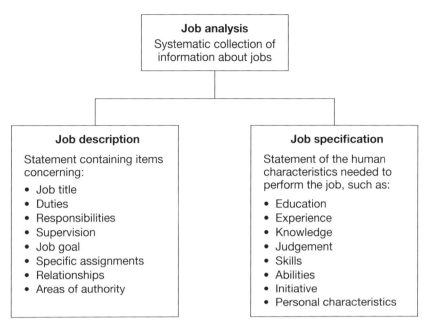

Figure 13.2 A Principal's Guide to Job Requirements

Legal Constraints

Every principal is affected to some extent by federal laws governing the recruitment and selection of employees. The laws governing **equal employment opportunity** (**EEO**) have had an especially long history in the United States; the laws prohibit employment decisions based on race, color, religion, sex, national origin, age, or disability (Cushway, 2018; Gold, 2018; Guerin & Barreiro, 2018; Harper, Estreicher, & Griffith, 2019; McMullen, 2019). This legal environment has increased the need for high-caliber principals who can deal with the complex legal requirements in human resource management (Norton, 2014; Rebore, 2014).

Specific requirements of the most important EEO laws are shown in table 13.1. The laws apply to: recruitment and selection; wages, hours, and working conditions; classification, assignment, transfer, and promotion of employees; training and development; and performance appraisal.

These basic laws have been supplemented by numerous guidelines and regulations issued by the Equal Employment Opportunity Commission (EEOC), the Office of Federal Contract Compliance, and the Department of Labor. The regulations are too numerous and complex to mention here; however, their impact on employment decisions in schools has been significant. For example, job descriptions and job specifications must be written so as not to exclude any race, sex, age, or other factor prohibited by law. Applicant interviewing and testing, which we discuss later, also must be conducted carefully, in order to meet legal requirements. And **affirmative action programs**, designed to increase employment opportunities for women and minority groups, put pressure on principals to ensure that females and other minorities (including veterans, the aged, and the handicapped) are employed in proportion to their actual availability in the area labor market (Weatherspoon, 2018). Courts have ruled that religious schools may use religion as an employment consideration.

Table 13.1 Major Laws Affecting Hiring Practices

Law	Basic Requirements
Title VII of the Civil Rights Act of 1964 (as amended)	Prohibits discrimination in employment on the basis of race, color, religion, gender, or national origin
Age Discrimination in Employment Act of 1968 (as amended)	Prohibits discrimination in employment against any person forties years of age or over Prohibits discrimination in employment against any person
Equal Pay Act of 1963	Prohibits wage discrimination on the basis of gender; requires equal pay for equal work regardless of gender
Rehabilitation Act of 1973	Requires employers to take affirmative action to employ and promote qualified handicapped persons
Pregnancy Discrimination Act of 1978	Requires employers to treat pregnant women and new mothers the same as other employees for all employment-related purposes
Vietnam Era Veterans Readjustment Act of 1974	Requires employers to take affirmative action to employ disabled Vietnam War veterans
Occupational Safety & Health Act (OSHA) of 1970	Established mandatory safety and health standards in organizations

Personnel Sources

School districts have numerous sources available for obtaining personnel. When attempting to fill a position, most principals look within the school district first. Policies for promoting from within are widely used because they tend to increase employee morale and motivation while reducing recruitment costs (Norton, 2014; Rebore, 2014; Smith, 2013).

External sources of potential employees are used when personnel with specialized skills, such as teachers, counselors, social workers, and computer programmers, are required. Some of the most frequently used external sources include college and university placement offices, state employment services, private employment agencies, newspaper and radio advertisements, professional journals, employee referrals, and professional meetings and conventions (Norton, 2014; Rebore, 2014; Smith, 2013).

School districts committed to equal employment opportunities and affirmative action programs typically take additional steps to ensure that available positions are provided the broadest possible publicity. For instance, the district might try: advertising in publications designed specifically for minority candidates; contacting colleges and universities that specialize in educating women or minorities; and contacting employment agencies that specialize in placing women and minority candidates. To reach minorities and women, the district may also contact neighborhood groups or national organizations, such as the Urban League or the National Organization for Women. These organizations, and groups like them, have newsletters or other media for contacting minority and female prospects.

Most school districts hire from a pool of candidates who apply to their individual school systems. Occasionally, someone might notify universities or colleges of the school district's specific needs; but all too often, the search for qualified candidates does not extend beyond the central office applicant file. Sometimes, the candidates are qualified and plentiful. Often, however, personnel doing the hiring find themselves making too many compromises.

As a means of alleviating such recruiting problems, some school districts have formed a teacher recruiting consortium. To expand a school district's applicant pool, the consortium hires a consultant to help the district streamline its application procedure, increase its visibility, and orchestrate the logistics of recruiting for several different school systems.

Teacher Recruitment Consortium

Lindquist and Metzger (2004), working with the National School Boards Association, describe the operation of the teacher recruitment consortium, which works through a consultant. The consultant puts a workable program in place.

1. *The consultant identifies which recruiting fairs the consortium should visit.* They make sure each school district is properly registered for each recruiting fair.
2. *The consultant standardizes the recruiting process.* For example, applicants submit a single application form, credential file, transcripts, criminal clearance (required in some states), and teaching certificate to the consortium.
3. *The consultant trains teams of administrators from different school systems to serve as recruiters.* They develop a standardized process for interviewing and evaluating candidates.
4. *The consultant creates a computerized database of qualified applicants.* The database is updated twice a month, and updated disks are sent out to all school districts in the consortium regularly from April 1 through Labor Day. School districts review information on the disk (a brief biography of the candidate) and then decide which candidates to call for final interviews. The school districts also can review the candidate's complete file, which is kept in the consortium office.

SELECTION

Once applicants have been recruited, the next step is **selection**—the process of determining which candidates best meet the job specifications. Steps in a typical selection process include (a) preliminary screening of credentials, (b) preliminary interview, (c)

Table 13.2 Procedures for Selecting Employees

Steps in the Selection Process	Reasons for Rejection
Preliminary screening from application blank or letter, vita, school records, and so forth	Inadequate educational or experience record for the job specifications
Preliminary interview	Obvious disinterest in and unsuitability for the job
Testing	Failure to meet minimum standards on job-related measures
Reference checks	Unfavorable reports on past performance
In-depth interview	Inadequate ability, ambition, or other job-related qualities
Physical examination	Physically unfit for the job
Hiring decision	Overall inability to fit the job requirements

testing, (d) reference checks, (e) in-depth interview, (f) physical examination, and (g) hiring decision. Table 13.2 lists the specific steps in the selection process and gives sample reasons for rejecting applicants at each stage.

The actual selection process varies with school districts and between hierarchical levels in the same school district. For instance, the in-depth interview for classified staff may be quite perfunctory; instead, heavy emphasis may be placed on the preliminary screening interview or on performance tests. In selecting certificated personnel, like teachers, the interview may be extensive—sometimes lasting an hour or more—and there may be little or no formal testing. Instead of completing an application blank, the candidate for a certificated position may submit a letter of application and/or a resume. Some school districts omit the physical examination. Three techniques often used in the selection process are interviews, testing, and assessment centers.

Interviews

The interview is perhaps the most widely used personnel technique in the selection process (Arthur, 2019; Quinn, 2018). It serves as a two-way exchange that allows both the principal and the applicant to gather information that would otherwise be difficult to secure. Unfortunately, despite its widespread use, the interview is a poor predictor of job performance (Conway, Jako, & Goodman, 1995; McDaniel et al., 1994; Posthuma, Morgeson, & Campion, 2002; Schmidt & Hunter, 1998; Wilk & Cappelli, 2003).

Interviewing Problems. The three major interviewing problems that should be avoided are as follows (Arthur, 2019; Farr & Tippins, 2017; Lunenburg, 2010e; Quinn, 2018):

1. *Unfamiliarity with the job.* Interviewers frequently are unfamiliar with the job. When interviewers do not know what the job entails, they: do not ask the right questions; interpret the obtained information differently; have faulty impressions of the information supplied; and spend time discussing matters irrelevant to the job (Fry, 2011).
2. *Premature decisions.* Interviewers tend to make a decision about an applicant during the first few minutes of the interview, before gathering all the relevant information (Dougherty, Turban, & Callender, 1994). Then they spend the rest of the interview seeking information that confirms their initial impression.
3. *Personal biases.* Some interviewers tend to have preconceptions and prejudices about people. Other biases may reflect negatively against some minority groups or in favor of those candidates who have backgrounds similar to the interviewer(s). Furthermore, some interviewers are overly impressed with surface signs of composure, manner of speech, and physical appearance (Hosoda, Stone-Romero, & Coats, 2003; Luxen & van de Vijver, 2006).

Improving the Interview Process. School organizations will continue to use interviews regardless of the problems. Thus, researchers have identified several techniques for improving the interview process:

1. *Use a structured interview format.* It has been widely suggested that interviews be more structured. In a structured interview, questions are written out in advance, rated on a standardized scale, and asked of all applicants for a

job. The structured interview has three major advantages (Campion, Palmer, & Campion, 1997; Moscoso & Salgado, 2002): it brings consistency to the interview process; it provides an opportunity to develop questions that are relevant to the job; and it allows screening and refinement of questions that may be discriminatory. In addition, the structured interview is more defensible in court (Huffcut & Woehr, 1999). A less-structured method can be used when interviewing administrative personnel (Cohen, 2011). That is, the interview is still carefully planned regarding content areas covered, but it allows the interviewer more flexibility in asking questions.

2. *Train interviewers*. One way to improve the validity and reliability of the interview is to train interviewers. Effective interviewing requires specific skills, including asking questions, probing, listening, observing, recording unbiased information, rating, and the like (Caruth, 2009). Workshops can be specifically designed to teach these skills. A cadre of trained interviewers can then be used to interview job applicants.

3. *Use the interview as one aspect of the selection process*. Avoid using the interview as the sole criterion for selecting applicants. By the same token, the interviewer(s) should not be the sole decision maker(s) concerning who is hired or not hired. Supplement the interview with data from other sources, including biographical information, results of tests, written references, and oral telephone inquiries. Interviewers cannot be privy to the telephone reference checks, which must rest exclusively in the hands of the top executive officer. When these suggestions are implemented, the interview can be a useful source of information in the selection process.

The most important part of the selection process begins and ends with the interview. By including several key components in this process, principals can ensure they will offer contracts to worthy candidates.

Components of a Good Interview Process

Several authors have studied and recommended the following major components of a good interview process (Arthur, 2019; Farr & Tippins, 2017; Lunenburg, 2012b; Quinn, 2018; Williamson & Williams, 2018):

1. *Give interviews to candidates only after checking their references*. This information gives the interviewer(s) some insight into prior experiences that shape the candidate's attitudes and work ethic.

2. *Screen candidates' files to ensure completeness, neatness, and lack of gaps in their employment history*. Experience has shown that an application that is incomplete, sloppy, or missing pieces of past employment is indicative of a candidate's work quality.

3. *Make time an important consideration during the interview*. Candidate interviews should not be scheduled close together, because the candidates may become anxious upon seeing the waiting room filled with other candidates.

4. *Before the interview, mail two or three questions to the candidates*. By getting some questions in advance, the candidates can reflect on their responses before they come in for the interview. This can make the beginning of the interview more productive.

5. *Place a name card in front of each interviewer for easy identification.* A host should greet each candidate before the interview.
6. *Make introductions at the outset.* Each member of the interview committee should be introduced, the position fully explained, and the process and time-line for the selection process outlined.
7. *After the interview, give each candidate an evaluation form regarding the interview experience.* This evaluation, which covers interview team preparation, attention to the process, and listening skills, should be accompanied with a stamped, self-addressed envelope. The evaluation should have room for the candidate to share any ideas for improving the interview process.

Interview Questions: Potential Problem Areas

What questions are permissible and impermissible during interviews? The basic principle in determining the acceptability of any applicant questions is whether the employer can demonstrate a job-related reason for asking the question. In asking the applicant questions, the interviewer should decide whether or not the information is truly necessary in order to evaluate the applicant's qualifications, skills level, and overall competence for the job in question. Problem areas arise with respect to questions, whether direct or indirect, about the applicant's gender, sexual orientation, race, age, national origin, marital or parental status, handicap, or disability.

The following are some broad generalizations regarding permissible and impermissible approaches to a variety of employment questions. Because state and federal laws prohibiting discrimination in the employment arena can be vast and complex, it is imperative for the principal to consult with their legal counsel when reviewing the school district's or school's current employment application or when making changes to the application or questions asked by an interviewer.

To ensure that they are conducting a nonsexist, nonracist interview, interviewers should follow these guidelines (Gold, 2018; Guerin & Barreiro, 2018; Harper, Estreicher, & Griffith, 2019; Weatherspoon, 2018):

- Ask the same general questions and require the same standards of all applicants.
- Treat all applicants with fairness, equality, and consistency.
- Use a structured interview plan that will help achieve fairness in interviewing.

Questions That May Be Asked. The following are some of the questions that may be asked at an interview (Gold, 2018; Guerin & Barreiro, 2018; Harper, Estreicher, & Griffith, 2019; Weatherspoon, 2018):

- Why do you want to teach here?
- What can you bring to the school or department that is uniquely yours?
- What type of grading criteria do you use?
- How do you keep current in your field?
- In the last year, what have you done to develop professionally?
- What is your view of the relationship between faculty and administration?

Questions That May Not Be Asked. A search committee cannot ask an applicant about the following (Gold, 2018; Guerin & Barreiro, 2018; Harper, Estreicher, & Griffith, 2019; Weatherspoon, 2018):

- age, unless it is relevant to the job
- financial condition
- prior wage garnishments
- credit rating and bank accounts
- home ownership
- disabilities
- marital status
- where their spouse works or resides
- pregnancy or medical history concerning pregnancy
- ages of children
- military experience or discharge
- religious observance
- lineage, ancestry, national origin, descent, place of birth, original language, or the national origin of parents or spouse
- how they learned to read, write, or speak a foreign language
- membership in clubs such as country clubs, social clubs, religious clubs, or fraternal orders that would indicate an applicant's race, color, sex, religion, and the like
- names and addresses of relatives other than those working for the school or school district
- how long they intend to work

Testing

A wide range of instruments are available to examine applicants' abilities, skills, knowledge, and attitudes. The best tests assess those factors that the job analysis identifies as necessary for the applicant to perform well on the job. For instance, the three top candidates for a secretarial job could each be given a typing and short-hand test. In the states that use them, scores on the National Teachers Examination (NTE) and/or the Liberal Arts and Science Test (LAST), the Elementary and Secondary Assessment of Teaching Skills (ESATS) and the grade point averages (GPA) of the final candidates for a teaching position could be used as criteria in selecting certificated personnel.

School districts use tests infrequently as an employment device. Conversely, most United States firms give an hour-long test to entry-level, blue-collar employees; and applicants for professional and managerial positions take a battery of tests requiring a day or less. Toyota Motor Corporation in Georgetown, Kentucky, for example, puts applicants for entry-level jobs through fourteen hours of testing. Many human resource experts believe that testing is the best selection device (Arthur, 2019; Barrett & Barrett, 2018; Farr & Tippins, 2017; Tomal & Schilling, 2018). Tests yield more information about an applicant than do preliminary screening of records and letters of recommendation, and they are less subject to bias than interviews (Eysenck, 2018a, 2018b; Highhouse, Doverspike, & Guion, 2015; Kline, 2016; Spielman, 2018; Weiner & Greene, 2017). School districts may need to take a closer look at testing as a valid criterion for selection, based on the evidence from business firms (Lunenburg, 2011i). Many tests are available to school districts for use in the selection process (Barrett & Barrett, 2018; Bryon, 2018; Flanagan & McDonaugh, 2018; Piccadilly, 2018).

There are three major problems with using tests as an employment selection device: they are time-consuming to administer; some require training to administer and score; and tests discriminate against minorities (Biddle, 2017). Ethnic minorities, such as African Americans and Hispanic Americans, may score lower on certain paper-and-pencil tests because of cultural bias. EEOC guidelines and amendments to the Civil Rights Act prohibit employment practices that artificially discriminate against individuals, on the basis of test scores (Weatherspoon, 2018).

The objective of any employment test is to gather information that will help predict the applicant's future job success or performance. To do so, a test must be both valid and reliable. A **valid test** measures what it purports to measure relative to the job specifications (Johnson & Christensen, 2020). Selection of criteria to define job specifications is difficult, and its importance cannot be overemphasized. Obviously, test validity cannot be measured unless satisfactory criteria exist. A **reliable test** yields consistent results over time (Johnson & Christensen, 2020). Scores should remain fairly stable for an individual who takes the test several times.

It may interest you to know that the most widely used test for selecting employees in most occupations is a twelve-minute paper-and-pencil test. It is the Wonderlic Personnel Test, one of the most extensively validated tests used in hiring decisions (Robbins & Judge, 2018). The Wonderlic Personnel Test contains fifty questions; scores range from 0 to 50, with the average about 21/50. Most organizations that use the Wonderlic Personnel Test continue to use other selection devices, such as application forms and interviews.

Performance Simulations

The idea behind performance simulations is to have applicants perform simulations of part or all of the job to determine whether applicants can do the job successfully (Thornton, Mueller-Hanson, & Rupp (2017). One example of a performance simulation is the **NASSP Assessment and Development Center** (National Association of Secondary School Principals, n.d.). A typical NASSP Assessment Center session lasts two days, with groups of six to twelve assessees participating in various administrative exercises. NASSP Assessment Center sessions include two in-basket tests, two leaderless group activities, a fact-finding task, and a personal interview. Candidates are assessed individually by a panel of NASSP-trained assessors on several task-relevant dimensions using a standardized scale. Later, by consensus, a profile of each candidate is devised, and each assessee receives a written and oral report. Assessment centers are also used to help design appropriate training and development programs for high-potential employees interested in the principalship (NASSP, n.d.). The centers are quite valid and reliable, providing NASSP guidelines are followed, and they are fair to women and members of minority groups (NASSP, n.d.).

Pre-Teacher Assessment Program. An extension of the NASSP Assessment and Development Center, designed to assess and develop a candidate's teaching potential, is the **Pre-Teacher Assessment Program**. Developed by a consortium composed of Indiana University of Pennsylvania, Millersville University, and Slippery Rock University more than two decades ago (Millward & Gerlach, 1991), it is a method of predicting future teacher behavior by using behavioral simulations (similar to those at NASSP) that measure a candidate's ability to handle future responsibilities in teaching. Although the Pre-Teacher Assessment Program is discussed here primarily as an aid in selecting teachers, it has been used also in the training and development of pre-service teachers.

Table 13.3 Thirteen Skill Dimensions of the Pre-Teacher Assessment Center

1	Planning and organizing	Establishing a course of action for self or others to achieve a specific goal; planning appropriate time, resources, setting, and sequence of activities for task accomplishment
2	Monitoring	Establishing procedures to monitor classroom activities and student progress
3	Leadership	Setting high standards, communicating a clear philosophy about learning, challenging students, reflecting on teaching
4	Sensitivity	Showing consideration for feelings and needs of others in verbal and nonverbal situations
5	Problem analysis	Identifying issues or problems; securing relevant information; identifying causes of problems; relating, comparing, or quantifying data from various sources
6	Strategic decision making	Developing alternative courses of action, making decisions, and setting goals when time for deliberation is available
7	Tactical decision making	Making appropriate decisions in ongoing situations where time for deliberation is limited and extensive information gathering may be inappropriate
8	Oral communication	Expressing ideas with clarity, style, appropriate volume and rate of speech, and appropriate grammar for classroom use
9	Oral presentation	Presenting ideas in an organized manner with an opening and a closing, while using persuasiveness, enthusiasm, and eye contact
10	Written communication	Expressing ideas clearly in writing (includes grammar, context, syntax)
11	Innovativeness	Generating or recognizing and adopting new or creative instructional approaches, techniques, and materials
12	Tolerance for stress	Performing with stability under pressure or opposition; ability to maintain attention on multiple tasks or activities
13	Initiative	Actively attempting to influence events to achieve goals; taking action beyond what is necessarily called for; self-starting

How are Pre-Teacher Assessment activities developed? Behaviors required for successful job performance are identified; dimensions that represent those behaviors are defined; simulations that require a candidate to exhibit selected dimensions are developed (these activities mirror the work activities of teachers); and scoring techniques that can discriminate between high and low skill acquisition for each dimension are designed. Table 13.3 provides brief descriptions of the thirteen Pre-Teacher Assessment Program dimensions.

Four simulations—classroom vignettes, actual teaching simulations, the educational fair, and the school museum—have been designed to assess the thirteen skill dimensions. A brief description of these simulations follows:

1. *Classroom vignettes.* In this exercise, students view a series of five-minute videotapes portraying different classroom episodes. At selected intervals, students are asked to respond in writing to such questions as, "How would you react to this situation?"

2. *Actual teaching simulations.* In this exercise, students are given a lesson packet with content they will be required to teach. After two hours of preparation, the student teaches the lesson.
3. *The educational fair.* In this two-hour exercise, students are faced with the problem of organizing a districtwide educational fair. Students are given a packet of information that must be analyzed, reviewed, and then organized into an overall plan.
4. *The school museum.* This is another two-hour exercise that requires students to read and analyze data related to a problem. Students are asked to develop an educational museum exhibit that would be relevant for students and be educationally sound.

Following the assessment, each candidate meets with a trained assessor to discuss the assessment report. The report can be used for selection, placement, promotion, compensation, or further development of skills. If the report is used for development, the candidate will have an opportunity to improve these assessed dimensions through work in training modules or through other resources on a university campus.

PROFESSIONAL DEVELOPMENT

Schools recruit and select people who match their job specifications as closely as possible, but the match is seldom perfect. Usually staff at all levels—maintenance, service, clerical, and professional—need to be taught how to apply their abilities to specific job requirements. This instruction, which teaches new employees the skills they need, is known as **training**. **Development** usually refers to teaching experienced professionals how to maintain and even improve those skills.

The training and development of faculty and staff are essentially a four-step process: assessing needs, setting objectives, selecting methods, and evaluating the program (Baume & Kahn, 2016; Bransford, Brown, & Cocking, 2021; Glickman & Burns, 2020; Joyce & Calhoun, 2010, 2019; Lunenburg, 2011d1; Zepeda, 2019). Figure 13.3 presents these steps. Each one will discuss in turn.

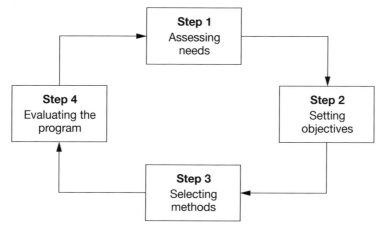

Figure 13.3 Steps in the Staff Development Process

Assessing Professional Development Needs

Before a principal can properly plan professional development activities, they must assess the professional development needs of both the employees and the school. The discrepancy between a job's skill requirements and the employee's job determines the specific training needs. For example, if a secretary lacks basic skills, he should receive computer literacy training. If a teacher lacks proficiency in one or more teaching skills, they should attend a professional development program to improve those skills. Furthermore, professional development must be aimed at the achievement of some school district goal or school objective, such as improved teacher performance, more efficient operating methods, or increased student achievement. A school should commit its resources only to professional development that can help in achieving its objectives.

To determine the professional development needs of individuals in their school, principals can choose from three basic methods (Baume & Kahn, 2016; Zepeda, 2019):

1. *Reviewing performance appraisals.* Employees' work is measured against the performance standards established for the job (using the job description as a guide). If actual performance is significantly below the acceptable standards, a performance deficiency exists. Those employees become candidates for a training and development program.
2. *Conducting organizational analyses.* The effectiveness of the school and its success in achieving its goals are analyzed to determine where discrepancies exist. For example, members of a department or grade-level team with low student achievement scores on a standardized test may require additional staff development.
3. *Surveying human resources.* Interviews with employees, questionnaires, and group discussions can be used to determine staff development needs. Data from these sources can pinpoint areas, skills, or abilities that need improvement.

Setting Professional Development Objectives

Once professional development needs have been identified, objectives must be set for meeting these needs. The objectives should be in writing and be meaningful, concise, and measurable. There are usually three major categories of objectives: transmitting information, changing attitudes, and developing skills (Baume & Kahn, 2016; Zepeda, 2019):

1. *Transmitting information.* This is typically a training objective rather than a development one. It may include a general orientation into the school's policies and procedures. For example, a teacher needs to learn board of education policies, local school policies, the union contract (if there is one), the school and school district's communication structure, and the like.
2. *Changing attitudes.* This is a kind of socialization. It is an attempt to change the employee's ideas about the school and/or the school district and the various jobs within it. Every school has a unique culture, and every employee—maintenance, service, clerical, and professional—at that school must understand its culture to perform effectively in it.

3. *Developing skills.* With the introduction of site-based management, teachers and other staff members need to develop three kinds of skills: human, technical, and conceptual. **Human skills** are essential to increase staff leadership, teamwork, and effective interactions with students, parents, and colleagues. **Technical skills** are essential to performing classroom teaching functions, such as preparing lessons, presenting information, diagnosing learning, reinforcing and correcting students, and evaluating learning. And **conceptual skills** are essential to decision making and strategic planning, that is, thinking about the school and school district as a system of interrelated parts rather than as isolated pieces of an organization (Senge, 1990; 2006; Senge et al, 2012). The development of human, technical, and, particularly, conceptual skills among the faculty and staff should help to facilitate the implementation of site-based management.

Selecting Professional Development Methods

Professional development goals establish a frame of reference for choosing appropriate instructional methods. Table 13.4 presents some of the more widely used professional development methods (Lunenburg, 2011d2).

Selection of a particular method depends on many considerations, but perhaps most important are the goals of the professional development effort. For example,

Table 13.4 Widely Used Professional Development Methods

Methods	Comments
Assigned readings	Readings may or may not be specially prepared for training purposes.
Behavior modeling	A videotaped model displays the correct behavior, then trainees role-play and discuss the correct behavior (used extensively for supervisor training in human relations).
Simulation	Both paper simulations (such as in-basket exercises) and computer-based games teach management skills.
Case discussion	Real or fictitious cases or incidents are discussed in small groups.
Conference	Trainees participate in small-group discussion of selected topics, usually with the trainer as leader.
Lecture	The trainer makes an oral presentation; audience participation is limited.
On the job	This method ranges from trainees receiving no instruction, to casual coaching by more experienced employees, to carefully structured explanation, demonstration, and supervised practice by a qualified trainer.
Programmed instruction	This is a self-paced method using text followed by questions and answers (expensive to develop).
Role playing	Trainees act out roles with other trainees, using scenarios such as "boss giving performance appraisal" and "subordinate reacting to appraisal" to gain experience in human relations.
Sensitivity training	Called T-group and laboratory training, this is an intensive experience in a small group. Individuals try new behaviors and give feedback (promotes trust, open communication, and understanding of group dynamics).
Vestibule training	Trainees participate in supervised practice on manual tasks in a separate work area with emphasis on safety, learning, and feedback.
Online training	Many Web sites are available that can assist in staff development training.

if the goal is for employees to learn about school policies and procedures, then assigned reading, lecture, and programmed learning might be an effective approach. If the goal is to teach professionals how to make decisions effectively, role playing, case discussion, conference, and sensitivity training might work best. If the goal is to teach a physical skill such as operating a new machine, then behavior modeling, vestibule training, or on-the-job training might be the most appropriate method. Other considerations in choosing a professional development method are cost, the time available, the number of persons to be trained, background and skill of the trainees, and whether the training is to be done by in-district personnel or contracted to an outside professional development firm or a university skilled in staff development methods.

Evaluating the Professional Development Program

The final step of the professional development effort is evaluation. Considering the cost investment of professional development programs—costs include training materials, trainer time, and time lost while employees are being trained—principals must make sure that the program goals are met.

Ideally, the best method to use in evaluating the effectiveness of professional development is the controlled experiment. In a controlled experiment, one or more groups that receive professional development (experimental groups) and a group that does not receive professional development (control group) are used. Relevant data—for example, some output variable(s)—should be secured before and after the training in both the experimental group(s) and the control group. Then a comparison is made of the performance of the groups to determine to what extent any change in the relevant variable(s) occurred due to training. One study, which used a quasi-experimental design, found no change in principals' leadership effectiveness before and immediately following situational leadership training, but did discover a change in their effectiveness three years after training (Pascarella & Lunenburg, 1988).

More specifically, four basic categories of professional development outcomes can be measured (Baume & Kahn, 2016; Zepeda, 2019):

1. *Reaction*. How well did the staff like the program?
2. *Learning*. What principles, facts, and concepts were learned in the program?
3. *Behavior*. Did the job behavior of staff members change because of the program?
4. *Results*. What were the results of the program?

The last category is probably the most important one. Staff members may say they enjoyed the professional development program and learned a great deal, but the true test is whether their job performance has improved after the development. For example, if a professional development program is designed to increase the proficiency of secretaries' basic skills, the secretaries' performance should improve after the training. Teachers who participate in many professional development activities and achieve high marks in those activities should improve their performance in the classroom. If these results are not achieved, then, in the final analysis, the professional development program has probably failed.

PERFORMANCE APPRAISAL

After employees have been recruited, selected, and trained, the next step in the human resource management process is **performance appraisal**—the process of evaluating the contribution employees have made toward attaining the school's goals. There are several reasons to evaluate employee performance. First, the school needs evidence to justify the selection techniques used in hiring personnel. Second, performance appraisal provides input for determining both individual and organizational professional development needs and later gauges whether these have been effective. Third, performance evaluation serves as the basis for making decisions about salary and merit increases, promotions, transfers, or terminations. Finally, it is used as a means of communicating to employees how they are performing and suggesting needed changes in behavior, attitudes, skills, or knowledge. Principals can use several different kinds of techniques for performance appraisal (Norton, 2014; Rebore, 2014; Smith, 2013; Tomal & Schilling, 2018).

Appraisal Techniques

Job analysis is the foundation on which employee performance appraisal is based. A job analysis identifies the standards and expectations against which performance is later measured. Principals have two ways of comparing actual to expected performance: nonjudgmental and judgmental methods (Lunenburg, 2011).

Nonjudgmental Methods. Performance indicators that can be counted, seen, touched, and so on, represent **nonjudgmental methods** of performance. No judgment is involved in obtaining these measures. Nonjudgmental methods can be quite useful because numbers are readily understandable, easy to explain, and in some cases may reflect the most important dimensions of an employee's performance. Nonjudgmental factors include indirect measurements such as absenteeism, tardiness, and number of complaints lodged against the employee by others. Direct measures of performance, however, are usually more important and include counts of the employee's actual output: number of pages typed, number of clients seen, or number of errors made. Nonjudgmental measures tend to be objective indicators of performance. In table 13.5, we present some examples of direct, nonjudgmental measures of performance.

Performance measures like those in table 13.5 are easy to obtain. But for most positions, objective measures are neither possible nor accurate. For instance, in some tasks, performance is the combined effort of many individuals. Winning a football game requires a team effort. In other cases, an objective count says nothing about quality of performance. A professor's performance is not judged solely on the number

Table 13.5 Nonjudgmental Performance Measures for Different Positions

Position	Sample Measure
Bus driver	Accident-free miles driven
Custodian	Tasks completed per day and minutes taken per task
Secretary	Lines typed per week
Teacher	Higher- and lower-order questions asked per class period
Counselor	Number of students counseled per week
Principal	Number of teacher observations completed per semester

of books or journal articles published in a year. Such factors as quality must be taken into account. Furthermore, even though different observers are likely to agree on the numbers collected, different principals are likely to disagree on the importance of these measures of performance output. For example, "lines per week" may not be as important to the overall performance of a secretary as the ability to compose a professional-quality business letter. The ability to handle irate parents and to screen principals' calls may be equally important. For these reasons, principals often use judgmental methods to appraise performance rather than, or in addition to, objective methods.

Judgmental Methods. When one person (a supervisor) makes a judgment about the performance of another (the staff member), **judgmental methods** are involved, which include ranking and rating techniques. **Ranking,** as the term implies, requires the supervisor to list all employees in an order of performance from best to worst, usually based on overall performance. Ranking has several limitations. First, because a single, global assessment of performance is used, the various dimensions of behavior are frequently overlooked. Second, when there are a large number of employees, it may be difficult to place them into a simple ranking. Third, by forcing a principal to rank employees as high or low performers, it is possible that the highest performer still falls short of the school's expectations. Conversely, the lowest-ranked employee could be meeting the school's goals quite well, if not as well as those ranked above him. Finally, because this method pits one employee against another, it creates jealousy and competition rather than teamwork.

Rating compares the performance of each employee to an absolute standard instead of to the performance of other employees. Thus, principals rate the degree to which performance meets the standard. The rating scale provides the standard. Figure 13.4 presents an example of a rating scale for judging the performance of teachers. The rater is asked to assess a teacher on several criteria (classroom management and procedure, teacher-pupil relationship, staff relationships, and professional attributes) using some form of rating scale. As shown in figure 13.4, these scales may range from "outstanding" to "unsatisfactory," or from "most desirable" to "least desirable," and the like.

Regardless of the scale used, evaluators are looking for some evidence of the quality of a teacher's performance in all aspects of the role description and the contract. From the many instruments reviewed, the characteristics delineated in figure 13.4 are among the criteria school systems consider important (Educational Research Service, 2004). One problem with such rating scales is that performance criteria are so loosely defined that there is frequently no consistency in rating teachers. "Outstanding," "good," "satisfactory," and the like may mean different things to different principals. Some principals are lenient and others are strict in applying the rating scale.

Common Rating Errors

A major objective in developing performance appraisal systems is to reduce errors and personal biases so that the most accurate portrayal of actual performance emerges. Several common sources of error found in performance appraisal systems that can jeopardize the validity of the rating include strictness or leniency, central tendency, single dimension, halo effect, recency of events, and personal biases and first impressions (Deblieux, 2003; Lunenburg, 2011e).

Teacher_____

School _____

Assignment _____

Classroom Management and Procedure	Outstanding	Good	Satisfactory	Needs improvement	Unsatisfactory	Comments
1. Shows evidence of planning						
2. Demonstrates initiative and adaptability in adjusting to circumstances and individuals						
3. Uses effective teaching techniques						
4. Maintains adequate and accurate pupil records						
Teacher-Pupil Relationship						
1. Encourages pupil participation in classroom activites						
2. Deals with behavior problems						
3. Shows evidence of pupils' respect and confidence						
4. Identifies the special needs of students						
5. Uses appropriate instructional materials						
6. Demonstrates willingness to spend time with students in addition to what is assigned						
Staff Relationships						
1. Cooperates with other members of staff						
2. Demonstrates respect for the opinions and contributions of others						
3. Utilizes services of specialized personnel within the district						
Professional Attributes						
1. Manifests adequate preparation for teaching subject matter						
2. Enhances academic development through continue formal education and inservice activities						
3. Handles reports efficiently						
4. Fulfills obligations related to board policies and building regulations						
5. Uses discretion in releasing information gained from professional activities						

Figure 13.4 Rating Scale for Teachers

Strictness or Leniency. Every evaluator has their own value system that provides a standard against which appraisals are made. In university classrooms, for example, we know of professors who are notoriously tough graders and others who give easy A's. Similar situations exist in K–12 schools, where some principals see most staff as not measuring up to their high standards, whereas other principals see most staff as deserving a high rating. These situations are referred to as **strictness or leniency** rating errors, respectively. The strict rater tends to give ratings that are lower than the average ratings usually given to staff. Conversely, the lenient rater tends to give higher ratings than those usually given. Strictness or leniency errors fail to adequately distinguish between good and poor performers, but instead relegate nearly everyone to the same or related categories.

Central Tendency. This error is similar to that of strictness and leniency, but in this case the principal's ratings cluster together at the middle of the scale. For example, if the rating scale ranges from one to five, many principals will tend to avoid the highs (four and five) and lows (one and two), and put most of their check marks in the three category—satisfactory (see figure13.4). This **central tendency** error means that all staff members are simply rated average. As with strictness and leniency, central tendency errors make it difficult to separate good performers from poor ones. In addition, this error makes it difficult to compare ratings from different principals. For example, a good performer who is evaluated by a principal committing central tendency errors could receive a lower rating than a poor performer who is rated by a principal committing leniency errors.

Single Dimension. An employee's job typically consists of many different tasks. A teacher's job, for example, includes preparing lessons, presenting information, diagnosing learning, reinforcing and correcting students, evaluating learning, and performing other administrative or supervisory duties. If performance on this job were evaluated on a **single dimension**—say, preparing lessons—the result would be a limited appraisal of that job. More important, teachers whose performance appraisal included evaluation solely on this single dimension would likely ignore those other tasks of the job. Similarly, if their superintendent appraised all the principals in a school district solely on their ability to perform management functions, they would likely attend to managerial tasks exclusively and ignore other instructional leadership duties required of today's principal. The point is that when staff are evaluated on a single dimension, and when successful performance in that position requires good performance on a number of dimensions, staff members will emphasize the dimension that is being evaluated to the exclusion of other job-relevant dimensions.

Halo Effect. The **halo effect** occurs when principals allow a single prominent characteristic of an employee to influence their judgment on all of the dimensions or characteristics being assessed. Thus, the staff member who is rated high on quantity of performance will also be rated high on quality, initiative, cooperation, and the like. The result is that employees show no variation in ratings across dimensions—they are rated consistently high, medium, or low on all performance dimensions. The problem created by a halo effect is that it is impossible to identify areas of weakness that need development for staff who are generally strong, and conversely, the areas of strength for staff who are generally weak.

Recency of Events. Ideally, performance appraisals should be based on systematic observations of a staff member's performance over an entire rating period (say, six months or a year). Oftentimes, evaluators focus on a staff member's most recent behavior—that is, in an annual evaluation, a principal may give undue consideration to performance during the past two or three months and forget to include important past behaviors. Using only the most recent evaluatee behaviors to make evaluations can result in what is called the **recency of events** error. This practice, if known to employees, leads to a situation whereby employees become visible, motivated, productive, and cooperative just before the formal evaluation occurs. Hence, their performance during the entire evaluation cycle is uneven and inconsistent.

Personal Biases and First Impressions. Some principals allow their personal biases and first impressions to influence the appraisals they give staff members. The **personal biases** may be gross prejudices concerning not only gender, race, color, or religion but also other personal characteristics such as age, social status, style of dress, or political viewpoint. In addition, principals have permitted **first impressions** to influence later judgments of a staff member. Although first impressions represent only a sample of behavior, people tend to retain these impressions even when confronted with contradictory evidence. Personal biases and first impressions can interfere with the fairness and accuracy of an evaluation.

COLLECTIVE BARGAINING

The final aspect of human resources administration to be discussed is **collective bargaining,** the process of negotiating and administering a collective bargaining agreement or negotiated contract between a union (teachers) and the employing organization (school board). Collective bargaining agreements specify the rights and duties of employees and management with respect to wages, hours, working conditions, and other terms of employment (Dismuke, 2018).

Collective bargaining by teachers emerged as a new factor in human resource management in the early 1960s and has become an increasing concern to teachers, administrators, and school board members. Today, forty states have enacted statutes permitting public school employees to bargain collectively with school boards, and more than 70 percent of the nation's teachers are covered by negotiated agreements (US Department of Labor, 2022).

In addition to professional, certificated employees, non-certificated groups are demanding the right to negotiate with management as well. Thus, many principals today work with employee groups that are represented by unions. (Since teachers make up the largest group of employees in schools, we will limit our discussion to teachers' collective bargaining agreements.)

The Collective Bargaining Process

To bargain collectively, management and the union each select a negotiating team. In small school districts, the superintendent often conducts negotiations with the teachers' union. Experts advise against this practice, however (DeMitchell, 2020; Fossum, 2014; Lunenburg, 2011). In large districts, a full-time administrator (director of employee relations, assistant superintendent, or director of personnel) usually serves as chief negotiator. Still other districts employ an outside negotiator—an attorney or labor relations specialist.

One or more building principals often are included on management's negotiating team. These people live with the contract day to day; they know its weak and strong points; they will administer the new agreement; and they will likely give the contract greater support if they can participate in the changes made in it. The union team generally consists of the local union president and other members of the local membership. Its team may also include an attorney or a labor relations specialist from a regional unit who negotiates for other teachers' unions in the region.

Once each side has selected its negotiating teams, the bargaining process begins. The bargaining takes place in face-to-face meetings between management and union representatives during which numerous proposals and counterproposals concerning bargaining issues are exchanged. Several rounds of negotiations may be needed to reach agreement on all bargaining issues. When the two parties agree on the issues, a new negotiated contract is presented to the union membership and the school board for a ratification vote. If both parties approve the agreement, it goes into effect. If they reject the agreement, each goes back to the bargaining table for another round of negotiations.

An **impasse** is said to exist when both parties are unable to reach agreement on a contract. State procedures vary when the union and the school board are deadlocked in negotiations. Most states have some provision for resolving impasses. Some states have developed a procedure for resolving impasses. The procedure involves the following steps: mediation, fact finding, and arbitration.

Mediation.   The two contending parties meet with a neutral third person who attempts to persuade them to settle the remaining issues through discussion and by proposing compromise provisions to the contract. The mediator acts as a facilitator, however, and has no legal authority to force the parties to accept the suggestions offered.

Fact Finding.   The state appoints a group or committee to investigate and report the facts that are presented by each party. The fact-finding committee's recommendations are generally made public, which places additional pressure on the parties to come to agreement.

Arbitration.   If the parties are still at an impasse, state law may require the union and the school board to submit to arbitration or binding arbitration. Guidelines for teachers' contracts in Wisconsin, for example, stipulate that arbitrators must choose the proposal of either the school board or the teachers' union, but not a compromise solution. This forces the two contending parties to bring their contract proposals closer together (American Arbitration Association, 2022).

Bargaining Issues

Collective bargaining agreements are complex and often lengthy, written contracts that are legally binding on both management and the union(s) representing its employees. Although the specific provisions of collective bargaining agreements vary from state to state and from one school district to another, the collective bargaining process and negotiated agreement generally address the following issues (DeMitchell, 2020; Dismuke, 2018; Fossum, 2014; Lunenburg, 2000; Marietta, d'Entremont, & Kaur, 2017; Moskaw, 2017; Sharp, 2012): management rights, narrow grievance definition, no-strike provision, zipper clause, maintenance of standards, just cause, reduction in force, wages and benefits, and other issues.

Management Rights.   During collective bargaining, unions strive to increase wages, protect job security, and improve the work conditions of employees. On the other hand, management tries to protect and clarify its rights as employer. Any rights not given to the union in the collective bargaining agreement are assumed to belong to management. These are called **management rights**. A common management rights clause includes the right to: supervise all operations; control all property and equipment; determine the size of the workforce; assign work to be done; introduce new methods, programs, or procedures; hire and fire employees; promote, demote, and transfer employees; and, in general, maintain an orderly, effective, and efficient operation.

Narrow Grievance Definition.   The definition of a grievance in a written collective bargaining agreement determines which employee complaints are subject to binding grievance arbitration. A **narrow grievance definition** that limits employee complaints to the specific written agreement is recommended. Such an approach does not preclude other complaint procedures. It does limit what a grievance arbitrator can decide during the written terms of the negotiated agreement in force.

No-Strike Provision. Federal law prohibits strikes by teachers. Most states have passed similar laws. Because teacher strikes occur despite the laws against them, additional protection can be gained through a **no-strike provision** in the collective bargaining agreement. Such a provision puts the union on record against strikes and involves the union in the enforcement of the laws prohibiting them. In addition, a no-strike provision usually permits management to impose monetary damages on teachers who engage in an illegal strike.

Zipper Clause. A **zipper clause**, or waiver provision, stipulates that the written agreement is the complete and full contract between the parties. The purpose of such a provision is to avoid continuing negotiations after the contract has been ratified; when coupled with a strong management rights clause, it limits the role of past practice used by grievance arbitrators. Such a provision, however, does not preclude the parties from negotiating further if both agree.

Maintenance of Standards. Management should avoid a **maintenance of standards** provision. Such a provision is routinely included in most union proposals and incorporates the school district's current practices on a wide range of items, many of which are not mandatory subjects of bargaining. Furthermore, a maintenance of standards provision leaves the district vulnerable to the role of past practice used by grievance arbitrators in settling contract disputes. It is the antithesis of a management rights provision and a zipper clause.

Just Cause. The term **just cause** is found in numerous collective bargaining agreements in public education and is routinely included in most union proposals. There is a danger in using such a term, from management's standpoint, because *just cause* has no clear definition. If a collective bargaining agreement has binding arbitration as the last step in the grievance procedure, then an arbitrator will decide what the term means. The arbitrator's interpretation of the term may be different from what management had intended. The meaning of *just cause* must be spelled out clearly somewhere in the contract or eliminated entirely.

Reduction in Force. Most all collective bargaining agreements have some form of **reduction in force (RIF)** provision. Seniority, or length of continuous service within a certificated field, is the key factor used in employee layoff and recall. Some agreements allow for *bumping*, which means that teachers laid off in one certificated field may replace another teacher in another certificated area who has less seniority in the field than the bumping teacher. Other factors considered are affirmative action and teacher merit. Such provisions are more favorable to management but are opposed by most teachers' unions.

Wages and Benefits. Much time at the bargaining table is devoted to wage increases and fringe-benefit improvements. Wage and salary increases are often stated as across-the-board salary increases for steps on a lockstep salary schedule. Besides salary increases, unions often demand improvements in various fringe benefits such as insurance programs (life, health, and dental); pension plans; merit pay; and sick leave, personal days, and paid religious holidays. It should be noted that compensation costs (wages and benefits) in today's school districts often range from 75 to 85 percent of the total school district budget.

Other Issues. Among other important bargaining issues are grievance arbitration, teacher evaluation, class size, school calendar, and the like. Binding grievance arbitration is not a problem providing the rest of the agreement protects management prerogatives. Likewise, teacher evaluation, class size, and school calendar should not be overly restrictive on the school district.

Bargaining Tactics

Negotiators use a number of tactics to improve their bargaining. Four tactics that are typically used are counterproposals, tradeoffs, the caucus, and costing proposals (Carrell, 2007, 2010; DeMitchell, 2020; Lunenburg, 2000; Neal, 1982).

Counterproposals. Collective bargaining consists of the exchange of proposals and counterproposals in an effort to reach settlement between the negotiating parties. A proposal is an offer presented by one party in negotiations for consideration by the other party. A **counterproposal** is an offer suggested as an alternative to the previous proposal by the other party. The union introduces the majority of proposals. Generally, management responds to the union's demands through counterproposals. There are at least two advantages to this approach for management: (a) the party that moves first on an issue is usually at a disadvantage, for it invariably reveals some information helpful to the other negotiator; and (b) the union, as the initiating party, is forced to work for every concession it gets.

Tradeoffs. Another bargaining tactic is the **tradeoff**, which is giving one issue in return for another. For example, a teachers' union will make a number of proposals, such as fair share, salary increase, increased sick leave, increased personal days, extra holiday(s), hospitalization, life insurance, dental insurance, maternity leave, binding arbitration of grievances, past practice provision, reduction in force procedures, teacher evaluations, class size, school calendar, and the like. Management then responds by stating that it will grant a 5 percent salary increase if the union withdraws its proposals for increased sick leave and personal days, hospitalization, life insurance, and dental insurance. Further, management will grant the past practice clause if the union drops its request for binding arbitration of grievances. All proposals are "packaged" in this manner until the teacher's union and the school board reach a settlement. While neither party wants to give up its item, each may perceive the exchange as a reasonable compromise.

Caucus. A basic principle of negotiating is that only one person speaks at the bargaining table—the chief negotiator. The other members of the bargaining team must remain quiet. Remaining quiet at the bargaining table can be a frustrating demand for the other members of the bargaining team. A **caucus** is a private meeting of a bargaining team to decide what action to take on a particular phase of negotiations. It provides an opportunity to get needed input from other team members and to release built-up tensions that arise during stressful negotiations.

Costing Proposals. All proposals in collective bargaining have direct, hidden, and administrative costs. Management must know the cost of all union proposals. Therefore, **costing proposals** is another important bargaining tactic.

Preparation for this phase of bargaining should be a continual process throughout the school year. Such an approach will avoid errors made in costing proposals hastily during the heat of negotiations. The logical department in a school district to maintain a data bank and generate data for costing proposals is the Office of the Assistant Superintendent for Business (or the Chief Financial Officer). This office can then provide a database to the board's negotiating team at the beginning of the bargaining process.

The following guidelines for costing proposals are recommended (Lunenburg, 2000):

1. *Cost proposals accurately.* Typically, the union will request copies of all cost data that management prepares. Management can expect distribution of part or all of the data supplied. Therefore, prepare cost data carefully. All calculations must withstand the scrutiny of the public, a mediator, a fact-finding committee, or an arbitrator.
2. *Cost proposals separately.* Cost each union proposal separately. For example, the estimated cost of increasing the number of personal leave days must be costed independently of a proposal for increasing the number of sick days. Each must be based on historical data and cost projections.
3. *Cost proposals from management's viewpoint.* Prepare costings from management's point of view. For example, proposals to reduce services must consider either the cost of replacing those services or the economic loss resulting from not having those services performed. In one school district in a midwestern state, a teachers' collective bargaining agreement stipulated that high school English teachers were required to teach only four classes a day (not exceeding twenty-five students in a class) in order to alleviate the heavy load of correcting daily written assignments. All other high school teachers in the district taught five classes a day. Because there were twenty-four high school English teachers in the district at an average salary of $60,000 a year, this provision in the contract cost the school district $288,000 a year ($12,000 × 24).
4. *Cost proposals as of a common date.* Base all costings on data gathered as of a common date. The usual cycle used in school districts is the fiscal year beginning July 1.
5. *Analyze comparable data from neighboring organizations.* The board's chief negotiator must be able to analyze comparable data from neighboring school districts. For instance, cost data from neighboring school districts must not be considered in isolation. Public school financing is tricky business and comprises numerous factors. The personnel practices and curriculum of each situation are different. While the salary schedule in one district may be better than that in another, the work load in the latter district may be less demanding (e.g., see number 3). Or the salaries in the neighboring district may be distributed differently—higher at the top of the scale but lower at the bottom, for example. Therefore, the board's chief negotiator must be thoroughly familiar with the collective bargaining agreements in neighboring districts. It is a natural tendency for the teachers' union to seek the best of both worlds.
6. *Supply specifically requested information only.* Cost data should be pertinent to each proposal. Only management's chief negotiator should be provided with the raw data that was used to prepare summaries. Related data may suggest counterproposals. Never distribute raw data to the union and supply only specifically requested information.
7. *Provide management's negotiating team with a budget projection.* The superintendent must provide management's negotiating team with a budget projection at the start of bargaining. The document can be used to set the tentative limits on the chief negotiator. The budget projections must provide

a minimum and several alternatives, including factors that might influence the final budget.

The following are some important factors that influence a school district's final budget (Lunenburg, 2000). This information should be part of a school district's data bank. Such cost data can assist management's bargaining team in costing proposals.

1. *Salary*
   - salary schedules and placement of teachers
   - average salary of newly hired teachers
   - average base salary of teachers, by school, level, department
   - contract salaries distribution
   - past record of salary schedule improvements (dollar amount and percentage)
   - total cost of past schedule improvements
   - past record of change in the salary schedule (steps and lanes)
   - projected cost: normal increment, $100 on base schedule, 1 percent schedule increase

2. *Fringe Benefits*
   - fringe benefits as percentage of salaries paid
   - cost of fringe benefits per new position
   - leave history: policy and record
   - separation pay: number of individuals, per diem rate, annual rate, average pay
   - sabbatical leave: granted, denials, costs, subsequent separations
   - retirements: mandatory versus actual, reason for retirement

3. *Staffing*
   - number of employees
   - staffing ratios by school, level, department
   - recruitment history: applicants, offers, acceptances
   - separation history: number, reason, scale placement, turnover experience
   - general statistics: age, gender, race, marital status of employees
   - scale placement: academic advancement record, payment for graduate credits, merit pay

4. *Administration*
   - cost of recruitment
   - cost of selection
   - cost of training
   - cost of basic supplies and equipment for new employees
   - cost of negotiations
   - budget history/forecasting
   - expenditure history
   - enrollment history and projections
   - per-pupil cost history
   - reserve trends/forecasting
   - building factors affecting conditions of employment

New Bargaining Strategies

Currently, forty of the fifty states permit teachers to bargain collectively with school boards. Where such bargaining is allowed, almost all school districts employ traditional or adversarial bargaining. In recent years, a new unionism, one that connects teacher participation in educational decisions to taking responsibility for outcomes, has become apparent. Studies of a number of collaborative efforts in union-management relations describe reform initiatives in Rochester, Pittsburgh, Cincinnati, Glenview (IL), Greece (NY), Jefferson County (KY), and other cities (Hannaway & Rotherham. 2006; Marietta, d'Entremont, & Kaur, 2017; Sharp, 2012). This research describes professional unionism and how it contrasts sharply with the beliefs and practices of traditional industrial unionism.

One consequence of professional unionism is the emergence of a new mode of principal leadership. While they vary in personal style, gender, and ethnicity, professional unions share similar management styles. They empower the people with whom they work. They use a hands-on approach. They are entrepreneurs; they gather and redistribute resources and encourage others to do so. They abide by a common realization that one leads best by developing the talent of others and gaining commitment rather than compliance with organizational rules.

Consistent with professional unionism is collaborative bargaining (also known as win-win bargaining). Typically, collaborative bargaining focuses on ongoing problem solving rather than dealing with a buildup of issues presented at the bargaining table. Both management and union keep a "tickler file" of problems encountered in administering the current contract. Joint committees deal with the problems encountered. Then when contract language is finally discussed the parties present specific notes to support their positions. Both parties establish agreed-on ground rules and specific time limits for negotiations, and write trust agreements and memoranda of understanding, and carefully select respected, credible members of negotiating teams. These procedures can help establish trust and a sense of collaboration to solve mutual problems throughout the school year and at the bargaining table.

SUMMARY

1. The human resource management process consists of the following steps: recruitment, selection, professional development, and performance evaluation. Today's principals must work within a growing body of laws regulating the personnel process.

2. Recruitment involves attracting a pool of qualified applicants to replenish or expand a school's human resources. To effectively recruit applicants, principals must know the job, know the legal constraints that influence recruiting efforts, and cultivate the sources of potential employees.

3. Selection involves the process of determining which candidates best meet the job requirements. Preliminary screening of credentials, preliminary interview, testing, reference checks, assessment centers, and in-depth interviews are often used as aids in the selection process.

4. Professional development programs are used to teach new employees the skills they need and to help experienced professionals maintain and

improve those skills. The staff development process involves assessing needs, setting goals, selecting methods, and evaluating the program.

5. Performance appraisal is the process of evaluating the contribution employees have made toward attaining the school's goals. Appraisal techniques include the traditional nonjudgmental and judgmental approaches. Performance appraisal rating errors include strictness or leniency, central tendency, halo effect, and recency of events,

6. Forty states have enacted laws that permit public school employees to bargain collectively with school boards. Collective bargaining is the process of negotiating and administering a collective bargaining agreement or negotiated contract between a union (teachers) and the employing organization (school board). Collective bargaining agreements specify the rights and duties of employees and management with respect to wages, hours, working conditions, and other terms of employment.

KEY TERMS

recruitment
job analysis
job specifications
equal employment opportunity
    (EEO)
affirmative action programs
selection
valid test
reliable test
NASSP Assessment and
    Development Center
Pre-Teacher Assessment Program
training
development
human skills
technical skills
conceptual skills
performance appraisal
nonjudgmental methods
judgmental methods
ranking

rating
strictness or leniency
central tendency
single dimension
halo effect
recency of events
personal biases
first impressions
collective bargaining
impasse
management rights
narrow grievance definition
no-strike provision
zipper clause
maintenance of standards
just cause
reduction in force (RIF)
counterproposal
tradeoff
caucus
costing proposals

FIELD-BASED ACTIVITIES

1. Interview your building principal or the human resources department in your school district to determine what procedures they use to select personnel: administrators, faculty, and staff. Find out the answers to questions like these: What are the contents of preliminary screening of

credentials? Are preliminary interviews held, and with whom? Are testing, reference checks, and assessment centers used? Are in-depth interviews held, and with whom? Describe these procedures in your journal.

2. Interview your building principal or the human resources department in your school district to determine the amount and type of professional development provided in your school and school district for school administrators, faculty, and staff. Report the results of these interviews in your journal.

3. Interview your building principal or other appropriate central office administrator to determine what procedures are used to evaluate school administrators, faculty, and staff. How often are evaluations done of each employee group? What types of instruments are used to evaluate administrators, faculty, and staff? How are the results of evaluations communicated to each employee group? Report your findings in your journal.

SUGGESTED READINGS

Ekelund, B. Z. (2019). *Unleashing the power of diversity: How to open minds for good*. New York, NY: Routledge. Bjorn Ekelund provides a clear tool to create a common language across teams and organizations that reinforces positive identity, builds trust towards people and processes, supports innovation and helps make diversity sustainable.

Norton, M. S. (2014). *The principal as human resources leader: A guide to exemplary practices for personnel administration*. New York, NY: Routledge. Norton emphasizes coverage of selection, professional development, teacher evaluation, school climate, and legal considerations and projects competencies that will be required of future human resource professionals.

Rebore, R. W. (2014). *Human resources administration in education.* Boston, MA: Pearson.. The text is organized around the processes and procedures necessary for implementing effective human resources administration. Treated in separate chapters are the eight essential dimensions of the human resource function: human resource planning, recruitment, selection, placement and induction, professional development, appraisal, rewarding, and collective bargaining.

Seyfarth, J. T. (2010). *Human resource leadership for effective schools* (5th ed.). Boston, MA: Pearson. Many human resource leadership books emphasize only the functions of the area. Seyfarth emphasizes how human resource decisions affect student achievement and provides practical applications for research related to human resource practice.

Smith, R. E. (2013). *Human resources administration: A school-based perspective.* New York, NY: Taylor & Francis. This field-based book provides easy-to-read checklists, sample forms, and summary charts. Topics include strategic human resources planning, recruitment, selection, orientation and induction, supervision and evaluation, assisting the marginal teacher, staff development, collective bargaining, and continuity and legal issues.

Tomal, D. R., & Schilling, C. A. (2018). *Human resource management: Optimizing organizational performance.* Lanham, MD: Rowman & Littlefield. Issues that have been and continue to be the mainstay of the human resource function are examined from both traditional and novel perspectives.

14
Community Relations

■ ■ ■

FOCUSING QUESTIONS

1. What is the role of the principal as "boundary spanner"?
2. How can the principal promote school, community, and family involvement?
3. How can the principal promote effective internal and external public relations?
4. How does a principal develop a public relations plan?

In this chapter, we address these questions that deal with democracy and community. We respond to those questions with suggestions about how principals can involve the community in the functions of improving policy and purposefully educating students.

"**Democratic education** guarantees to all the members of its community the right to share in determining the purposes and policies of education" (Educational Policies Commission, 1940, p. 36). This resounding statement, made more than eighty years ago, is the foundation of community involvement in the schools. Today, principals appreciate and understand not only the learning potential in positive school-community relations but also the interdependence among schools, families, and communities. In addition to acknowledging this interdependence, principals are also beginning to realize that building social capital in the community is necessary. If the community is strengthened, the school is also strengthened for successful education. Principals today have a sense of even larger community issues, conditions, and needed investments such as housing quality, parks and recreation opportunities for after-school activities, employment and training, and law enforcement (Fiore, 2022).

PRINCIPALS AS "BOUNDARY SPANNERS"

Goldring (1990) identifies principals as a bridge between the school and external constituencies and refers to principals in this role as **boundary spanners**. Miller (2008) indicates that principals serve as the individuals who market the school, who interpret the school's program to the parents and community. These authors indicate that principals are being called upon to form partnerships with the business community and to enter the discussion and debate regarding future policy directions for their schools. Moore, Bagin, and Gallagher (2020) indicate that principals must be active and visible in the community and need to communicate with the overall community. This means reaching out or spanning boundaries with different business, religious, political, and service entities. Relationships must be established and nurtured with community leaders. Indeed, in addition to their ever-increasing responsibilities, principals must span the boundaries strengthening the link between the community and the school. Until recently, schools have done little to improve, empower, or revitalize the community or neighborhood (Williamson & Blackburn, 2016).

The school has viewed partnerships as minimally disenfranchising the community; in fact, schools are more likely to think of partnerships as doing crisis intervention with parents rather than sharing power with the community (Noltemeyer, McLaughlin, & McGowan, 2017). The principal is the boundary spanner for ensuring that partnerships go beyond parents to include the community in interagency collaborations that can make decisions about the education of the "whole child." However, because interagency collaboratives—or coordinated service models, in some cases—have viewed some community problems, such as racism, crime, gangs, or poverty, as too difficult to handle, the traditionally empowering strategy of including the community to make decisions in policy and education of students sometimes amounts only to maintaining the status quo (Capper, 1996; Edwards et al., 2019). Principals must respond to community politicization, particularly in the urban areas, that appreciates such elements as market forces, choice, empowerment, enterprise strategies, self-reliance, and development above meeting needs, providing services, offering guidance, helping, involvement, and partnerships (Fiore, 2022). Epstein (2018) argues that although partnerships can improve school programs and school climate, provide family services and support, increase parents' skills and leadership, connect families with others in the school and in the community, and help teachers with their work, their main benefit comes from helping all youngsters succeed in school and in later life.

SCHOOL, FAMILY, AND COMMUNITY INVOLVEMENT

The literature defines most of the community involvement in schools in relation to the parents; however, a broader definition of community involvement is needed. **Community involvement** is defined as volunteerism in the school by community members who devote their time to a variety of school needs. Those community members include local businesspersons, mayor, city council, urban planner, county judge, the media, police, firefighters, medical personnel, and/or clergy. How can these people be involved for a cogent, effective partnership?

In effect, principals must be involved in developing coordinated services, an array of partnered services extending from schools to families, which is a significant broadening of the mission of the public school (Fiore, 2022). Principals can consider many possibilities for spanning the boundaries and coordinating the services of community members; such services may range from volunteering time to providing resources. For example, businesses may adopt a school to fund an event, or to buy paper and pencils for economically disadvantaged students, or to provide coffee for "donuts with Dad" or "morning with Mom." The media, such as the local newspaper, may adopt a school and give the students newspapers once a week for improving their reading. Medical personnel may provide health workshops at the various grade levels for students and their parents. The police and firefighters may share important before- and after-school safety tips with youth. Clergy may assist students and families in a time of crisis at the school.

The coordinated services model is akin to the growing trend of community schools. Although they are a current trend, community schools date back to when Dewey (1966 [1916]) brought the school into the community, indicating that learning within the school should be continuous outside the school, and when Addams (1910) brought the community into the school. Dryfoos (2002, p. 393) describes community schools as follows:

> A **community school**, operating in a public school building, is open to students, families, and the community before, during, and after school, seven days a week, all year long. It is jointly operated and financed through a partnership between the school system and one or more community agencies. Families, young people, principals, teachers, youth workers, neighborhood residents, college faculty members, college students, and businesspeople all work together to design and implement a plan for transforming the school into a child-centered institution. Oriented toward the community, a community school encourages student learning through community service and service learning. A before- and after-school learning component encourages students to build on their classroom experiences, to expand their horizons, to explore their cultural heritage, to engage in sports and recreation, and just to have fun. A family support center helps families with child rearing, employment, housing, and other services. Medical, dental, and mental health services are also available on site.

Even though a district does not particularly house "community schools," the principal can take elements of coordinated services from the community school description by Dryfoos (2002) and incorporate those components into a school community relations plan.

Principals Leading Community Efforts During Catastrophes

In times of catastrophe, schools often become the lifeline to the communities they serve. Noltemeyer, McLaughlin, and McGowan (2017) determined some imperatives for principals following a natural disaster by interviewing principals, assistant principals, crisis intervention specialists, and district coordinators of psychological services one year after Hurricane Andrew, which struck in August 1992. The authors examined how these individuals coped in the aftermath of the hurricane and what they learned in the process. They concluded that principals should rapidly establish a means of communication. Often, when a natural disaster occurs, telephone service is interrupted or destroyed. The authors suggested that a telephone tree be developed before a crisis. They gave the following examples: one Florida principal sat on his roof, calling faculty members on a cellular telephone while others had to drive to locate staff and arrange assistance for them.

Another strategy is to quickly assess the damage and make appropriate accommodations. Principals and teachers can register the damage caused to their school and classrooms. Going through all buildings to determine their usability and safety is essential before students return. If there is structural damage, other accommodations will be needed for classes. Additionally, principals must prioritize needs and establish authority to make site-based decisions. Noltemeyer et al. (2017) reported that after

Hurricane Andrew, tent cities, medical assistance areas, and food distribution tents were established. Thousands of armed personnel and volunteers from all over the country arrived to help. There was a real display of coordinated services, and principals helped to facilitate those services. The military involvement enabled schools to open three weeks after the hurricane struck. Troops moved tons of building remnants, mangled fences, and uprooted trees from school campuses. Site-based decision making helped make areas accessible and reduced potential safely hazards.

Principals must address the emotional and survival needs of faculty, staff, and students after a disaster. Coordinating crisis counseling is imperative and must be provided to all affected schools to help not only students but also teachers, staff, and parents. Noltemeyer et al. (2017) made the point that after Hurricane Andrew, the primary stress was on adults. Small and large group counseling sessions were organized by campus counselors.

Principals must arrange for training and support for mental health caregivers. According to Noltemeyer et al. (2017), the National Organization for Victims Assistance, the American Psychological Association, and the American Red Cross have training programs to assist mental health personnel who work in schools following a disaster. These personnel can benefit from additional training in how to respond to a large-scale crisis specifically related to stress reactions, stress response, issues of loss and grief, coping skills, debriefing techniques, and crisis resolution.

Either the principal or a designee should provide feedback to the news media. This will ensure consistency of shared information, rumor control, and reduced interruptions to staff members. Media control can enlighten others to the impact and needs of the schools following a natural disaster and establish partnerships between citizens and schools. After Hurricane Andrew, schools in Miami were adopted by other schools across the nation.

Principals need to encourage creative instructional methods using lessons learned in the aftermath. Students' emotional needs must be addressed before beginning academic instruction. In interviews with principals, Noltemeyer et al. (2017) found that daily discussions in which everyone relates their experience can create a strong bond and feeling of community among class members. The authors said that in dealing with lessons from disasters, teachers can use real-life examples to teach about math, weather, geology, history, geography, politics, economics, social science, psychology, and English.

Principals must identify and secure all available resources and implement systemic interventions to meet school and community needs. They can assess the needs of their school and help secure resources. Noltemeyer, et al. (2017) reported that one school created a "Teachers Helping Teachers" bulletin board, listing the needs of staff (e.g., food, child care, a place to do laundry, space to store items). A sign-up sheet was also posted, with names of volunteers willing to assist in specific areas. The PTA and the student council provided funds for gift certificates or household items. Donations were obtained from community businesses and schools across the country. The counseling and school psychology staff distributed gifts, thus gaining the opportunity to touch base with members of the school community who were most affected and to offer psychological assistance as needed. Guest speakers addressed parents and teachers on crisis reactions, stress reduction, and coping. The primary benefit of many of these interventions was to establish the school as a source of security and stability in a fearful and anxious community (Noltemeyer et al., 2017).

Principals Leading School, Family, and Community Involvement

Epstein (2018) suggests that there are six types of school, family, and community involvement: (1) parenting, (2) communicating, (3) volunteering, (4) learning at home, (5) decision making, and (6) collaborating with the community. What can principals do to lead in these components? We discuss each type of involvement in turn.

1. *Parenting.* Families must provide for their children's health and safety, and they must maintain a home environment that encourages learning and good behavior in school. Principals must provide training and information to help families understand their children's development and how to support the changes they undergo.
2. *Communicating.* Principals must reach out to families with information about school programs and student progress. This includes encouraging teachers to make the traditional phone calls, send report cards, and hold parent conferences, as well as to send new information on topics such as magnet schools, transition from elementary school to higher grades, and involvement opportunities. Because communication must be in forms that families find understandable and useful, language translations are necessary. For example, principals must hire translators and interpreters to reach parents who do not speak English well.
3. *Volunteering.* Parents can make significant contributions to the environment and functions of a school. Principals can get the most out of this process by creating flexible schedules to enable more parents to participate and by working to match the talents and interests of parents to the needs of students, teachers, and administrators.
4. *Learning at home.* Principals should encourage teachers to train family members to assist the children at home with homework assignments and other school-related activities.
5. *Decision making.* Principals can give parents meaningful roles in the school decision-making process by providing parents with training and information so they can make the most of those opportunities. The opportunity to participate in decision making should be open to all segments of the community as well.
6. *Collaborating with the community.* Akin to the coordinated services model, Epstein's model suggested that principals help families gain access to support services offered by other agencies, such as health care, cultural events, tutoring services, and after-school child-care programs. Principals also can help families and community groups provide services such as recycling programs and food pantries.

Epstein (2018) further addresses the development of *comprehensive partnerships* with the family and community that are linked to school improvement goals. Epstein suggests that as programs develop: (a) many ways should emerge for parents, other family members, community groups, and other citizens to gain and share information about parenting; (b) communication should become clearer with educators and each other about school programs and children's progress; (c) volunteerism at school, at home, or in the community should increase; (d) interactions with children regarding in-class work, homework, and academic decisions such as course choices should be observed in the home; (e) parents should become informed about and involved in school decisions; and (f) connections with organizations, services, and other opportunities in the community should be more apparent. Such partnerships should be reviewed annually and improved from year to year with more parents and community members becoming involved.

Schiller, Clements, and Lara-Alecio (2003) remind principals that *family involvement* is a current, more inclusive term for what has always been referred to as parent involvement. They indicate that *family* is used in place of *parent* because it includes all students, even those living with someone other than their parents.

Family involvement includes family visits to the school for observation purposes, active roles by families in the classroom instruction, family education programs, family support from home, family volunteers, parent boards, family participation in special events, and family partnerships in advocacy for children and youth (Herrera, 2020; Herrera, Porter, & Barko-Alva, 2020; Ishimaru, 2020).

Family Involvement and Student Achievement

The research has been specific to parent involvement in the past; and it has been determined that the more actively involved in their children's educational activities the parents are, the better the children's academic achievement, self-confidence, and attitudes toward school (Beveridge & Jerrams, 1981; Chavkin & Williams, 1989; Comer, 1980, 1999; Comer et al., 2004; Epstein, 1918; Epstein et al., 2018; Harry & Ocasio-Stoutenburg, 2020; Levin, 1987; Lightfoot, 1978; McLaughlin & Shields, 1987; Slavin, 2001; Tizard, Schofield, & Hewison, 1982). Additionally, when parents are actively involved in their children's education, positive cognitive and affective changes in their children can be observed, regardless of the parents' economic, ethnic, or cultural background (Flaxman & Inger, 1991). Researchers continuously have reported that parent participation in their children's education (a) enhances children's self-esteem, (b) improves children's academic achievement, (c) improves parent-child relationships, and (d) helps parents develop positive attitudes toward school and a better understanding of the schooling process (Schiller et al., 2003). However, parents may find it difficult to find the time, resources, or energy to become involved or to coordinate their schedules with school events, particularly in today's engaged society.

Involvement of parents in their children's education, whether at home or at school, whether initiated at preschool age or later, has significant, long-lasting, and positive effects. For example, home-based parental involvement is reported to have a positive, significant effect on achievement (Bermúdez & Padron, 1988; Chavkin & Williams, 1989; Comer, 1986; Dornbusch & Ritter, 1988), particularly for children of low-income parents (Herrera, Porter, & Barko-Alva, 2020; Ishimaru, 2020; McLaughlin & Shields, 1987).

Some parents and families may feel uncomfortable when visiting school because of previously bad experiences or because of a language barrier; however, low-income and poorly educated parents want to become involved in their children's education (Chavkin & Williams, 1989; McLaughlin & Shields, 1987). But no matter how strong their desire, the Hispanic English-language-learning proficient parents are typically not involved for a number of reasons, including low levels of proficiency in English, little understanding of the relationship between home and school, little knowledge of how the school system operates, work schedule demands, negative experiences with schools, and lack of sensitivity and understanding on the part of school personnel (Herrera, Porter, & Barko-Alva, 2020; Ishimaru, 2020). The involvement of language minority parents in their children's education is necessary for the reinforcement of native language development and for the communication of high expectations and emotional support regarding academic achievement (Crawford, 1989).

Because the need to increase the involvement of Hispanic parents in their children's schools is critical (Herrera, Porter, & Barko-Alva, 2020), many administrators and teachers have begun to address these issues by collaboratively developing strategic plans and goals for their campuses (Irby & Brown, 1996; Ishimaru, 2020). They have begun to develop parent resource centers, where parents can review and develop materials to assist them in child rearing (Bermúdez & Márquez, 1996), and they have initiated parent involvement workshops (Edwards et al., 2019). Yet many school district personnel lack the necessary skills to involve language-minority parents effectively (Bermúdez & Márquez, 1996). A modest body of research exists regarding effective parenting or parent involvement strategies of disadvantaged and/or Hispanic students (Edwards et al. 2019; Flaxman & Inger, 1991; Herrera, 2020; Inger, 1992; Ishimaru, 2020; Laosa, 1977, 1978, 1982; Laurea, 1989; Nicolau & Ramos, 1990; Parker et al., 1996). However, Lara-Alecio, Irby, and Ebener (1997) found only one study (Clark, 1988) that investigated effective home practices of minority parents, including Hispanics, of higher-achieving students. Clark found various positive parental practices associated with standards, norms, rules, allowances, and sanctions, such as (a) a wide range of enriching materials during home instructional activities, (b) cooperation of parents with teachers, (c) adult and peer modeling of academic and social behaviors, (d) clear expressions of right and wrong, (e) support of the child's personal worth, and (f) reward and respect.

Principals must first be committed to involving families and parents, but principals must also motivate and encourage teachers to be committed to involving families and parents and to use as many ways as possible to involve the parents. To get parents and families involved, principals and teachers must find ways to increase communication with parents and encourage involvement in children's learning experiences (Brown, 1989; Edwards, 2019; Edwards et al., 2019).

Parent and family involvement may be school-based, including such activities as parent-teacher conferences, class parties, field-trip chaperone, school volunteer, classroom assistant, or parent-teacher organization meetings. Parent involvement may be home-based, focused on things that parents can do with their children at home. Parent involvement may be education-based, with parents attending classes to learn how to (a) improve discipline, (b) encourage children in reading or math improvement, (c) improve their own technology skills, (d) pass a high school equivalency test, or (e) learn to speak English. Such educational programs for parents are planned with flexible scheduling; some programs are held in the early morning, some during the school day, others in the evening, and yet others on Saturdays.

Schiller, Clements, and Lara-Alecio (2003) indicated that communication with families and parents falls into two broad categories—general information that applies to all students (about the school, curriculum, upcoming events, etc.) and specific information about individual students. Both types of communication are important in bringing the school and home together. All communication should be inclusive of the languages spoken at home and at school.

Schiller and colleagues (2003) recommend the following general communication avenues:

1. *Orientation meetings.* Orientation meetings can be held during the semester prior to student enrollment, during the first month of school, or at both times. This meeting provides opportunities for the teacher to communicate school policies and rules, bus schedules, emergency routines, and pick-up and drop-off requirements of families.

2. *Newsletters.* Newsletters allow teachers to stay in contact during the year. They can relay information about upcoming events, specific topics regarding child development, parenting tips, health and safety tips, and changes in procedures. They may describe changes in curriculum and suggest activities in which families and parents can become involved at home or in the community.

3. *School handbook.* The school handbook is a great way to get information to families before the first day of school. Handbooks can be provided during orientation, mailed to students' homes, or put up on the school Web site. Handbooks will include the school calendar, faculty names, programs at the school, school services, and school policies and procedures.

4. *Programs for families.* Family seminars, meetings, and school programs are types of programs for families. Each program offers opportunities to share information with families. Some schools have Saturday programs for families and their children, particularly for those families who are English language learners.

5. *Suggestion box.* Families can make suggestions to school personnel through the use of a suggestion box.

6. *Home visits.* Home visits usually are reserved for the very young child, with the purpose of having the child meet the teacher in familiar surroundings.

7. *Conferences.* Conferences are the most formal way to meet with family members; they are recommended at least twice a year. Of course, for students with special needs, conferences will be required for reviewing their assessment, individual educational plans, placements, and transition-to-work plans. Encourage teachers to begin with successes in any conference and then discuss challenges. If problems are suggested, then offer the family an opportunity be involved in planning the solutions.

8. *Journals.* Principals can encourage teachers to have students take home a journal or a folder for exchanging information with parents or families. Additionally, children's class portfolios may be sent home periodically for review and comment.

9. *Personal notes.* A note to the families sharing their children's accomplishments is a good way to include them in the successes at school. In the secondary school, notes or letters sharing the students' successes are also welcomed.

10. *Phone calls.* Families expect telephone calls for bad news, but a telephone call about good news is an excellent way of staying in touch with parents and families. The principal and teacher can become liaisons for families, directing them to agencies that can assist in making their lives better.

SCHOOL-COMMUNITY RELATIONS AND PUBLIC RELATIONS

As principals engage in building cooperative and working relationships with teachers and the community, they are developing school-community relations. Good school-community relations foster *communications* and a *working relationship* between the school and the community, giving community members greater awareness of the school's purposes and achievements. By fostering involvement of the school and community, the principal can develop joint ventures for the mutual benefit of all parties. The principal will need to develop relationships with businesses, retired persons, human services, governmental agencies, and legislators. School-community relations create an image. It has been said that image is perception, and perception is everything. In public relations, the effort is to transmit and create an image from the school to the community; in school-community relations, there is more emphasis on involvement of community groups and joint development of the image desired with various public sectors (Currie, 2015; Fiore, 2022; Moore, Bagin, & Gallagher, 2020; Williamson & Blackburn, 2016).

The National School Public Relations Association (NSPRA, n.d.) defines school public relations in the following way:

> Educational public relations is a planned and systematic management function to help improve the programs and services of an educational organization. It relies on a comprehensive two-way communications process involving both internal and external publics, with a goal of stimulating a better understanding of the role, objectives, accomplishments, and needs of the organization. Educational public relations programs assist in interpreting public attitudes, identify and help shape policies and procedures in the public interest, and carry on involvement and information activities which earn public understanding and support.

It is crucial for the principal to establish good community and public relations. Campus communication needs have increased dramatically and become more complex. The principal on the campus must either act as the public relations coordinator or assign that role to another individual. In any case, the public relations coordinator not only develops and executes the school's communication plans through print and electronic media as well as face-to-face communication but also handles relations with the multitude of media that call school districts weekly. Languages of parents must be taken into account when establishing communications and collaboration. Principals must realize that education is under attack from taxpayers, business groups, special interest groups, and others (Berliner & Glass, 2014; Lunenburg, 2015; Ravitch, 2020). The campus needs to establish a two-way communication pattern allowing information to flow out about the school as well as allowing feedback to come into the school. Positive news about achievements by students, teachers, and staff as well as new or successful programs are the type of outward-flowing information that promotes positive feelings in the community about the school. Such information aids the principal in being on the offensive rather than the defensive in communications with the public. Principals may get help in promoting information about the school from district public relations, or they may do much of the work themselves. Many public relations persons suggest that principals arrange meetings with realtors, school open houses, or breakfasts with clergy, parents, legislators, city council members, or the Chamber of Commerce to develop an informed and supportive public.

Some districts have an employed public relations person, but not all of the principal's work will be done through the district. The NSPRA (n.d.) suggests the following examples for developing two-way communications and collaboration within the community:

1. Provide public relations counsel, taking a proactive stance. Anticipate problems and provide solutions.
2. Handle all aspects of the school's publications, such as its external and internal newsletters.
3. Write news releases for all local newspapers, TV, and radio; work to get media coverage of school district news. Serve as the media's liaison with the school.
4. Stay closely attuned to the entire budget-making process, and promote community input.
5. Write and develop a communications plan for the campus, detailing how to reach its internal and external publics; write and develop a crisis communications plan of reaching publics, gathering the facts, and dealing with media in a crisis.
6. Conduct formal and informal research to determine public opinion and attitude as a basis for planning and action.
7. Promote the school's strengths and achievements and its solutions to problems.
8. Vigorously publicize student and staff achievement; develop staff and retirement recognition programs.
9. Answer public and new resident requests for information; maintain extensive background files; keep the school's historical and budget passage records; and plan for school anniversary celebrations.
10. Provide public relations training to staff and PTOs in areas such as talking to the media, communicating in a crisis, and recognizing that nonteaching staff are part of the school public relations team.
11. Serve as the school's liaison with community groups such as civic associations and service clubs; help plan and publicize the school's parent, senior citizen, and community service programs. Develop ways to bring the community into the schools.

According to the NSPRA, true communication is a two-way process involving both inflow and outflow of information. The principal, in essence, helps keep both *I*'s of the school open, working to keep the public, in turn, both *I*nformed and *I*nvolved in the schools.

The Politics of Internal and External Publics

Community and public relations begin at home and operate from the inside out; therefore, it is extremely important that the principal identify and communicate effectively with their internal and external publics. Internal publics refer to those groups of people directly associated with the campus or the school district, such as administrators, teachers, students, support staff, or the school board. External publics refer to those people who are outside of the campus or district or who have an indirect relationship with the campus or district; these include such groups as parents, community organizations, churches, government, businesses, or senior citizens.

The principal will want to draw the attention of both internal and external publics toward the school's faculty and student accomplishments as well as its effective programs. No principal can afford to be unmindful of the opinion and attitudes of those publics concerning the campus. The principal must develop a two-way communication system through which they or the teachers will not only inform people of its accomplishments and programs but also study the people's reactions to them. Carefully handled through competent professional techniques and media, a community relations process goes a long way in building a favorable school image and public satisfaction. However, complaints about the school or its personnel must also be handled carefully, through a two-way communication process. It is the principal's responsibility to correctly assess public opinion and reactions to the information being propagated; the principal must then react appropriately and thoughtfully toward public opinion. The faster the principal knows about concerns, the faster they can respond and take corrective actions. It may be wise to devise some early warning networks to monitor public opinion or reaction. Use of technology can aid not only in gathering information from the public but also in disseminating information and providing feedback. The politics of public or community relations basically becomes the ability to present complex issues in a way that makes sense to all publics. The principal must present their school in the best light.

Media and Community Relations

The media is an external public that keeps the remaining external public notified of daily happenings on the campus or in the school district. We are certain that you have repeatedly viewed the following scenario on your television screen. The television reporter sticks a microphone in front of anyone passing by, asking them questions to get the breaking story. The reporter states that the principal was unavailable for comment, or the principal walks by and the reporter catches the principal and pulls them into the report. The principal, unaware of how to deal with the media, says too much. Parents are outraged and come to protest the comments. In another scenario, the district's trained public relations coordinator is immediately on the scene, getting the answers from school officials and parents and seeking out the reporters to respond for the district and the campus.

Unfortunately, not every school system has a district-level media coordinator; this means that principals need to know how to deal with the media. Perhaps part of the crisis plan for the district is to have a district media liaison, particularly during times of crisis. In fact, Brock, Sandoval, and Lewis (2001) recommend that districts have such a person. Larger districts have media liaisons who also are usually the public relations director or coordinator; however, in smaller districts, as indicated, the liaison job falls to the principal.

If a crisis occurs on the campus, news reporters usually want to know who, what, when, where, why, and how. Noltemeyer, McLaughlin, & McGowan (2017) recommend that, if at all possible, when preparing to be interviewed, the principal should try to get a sense of what the topic or focus will be. The authors provide some examples: a print reporter may leave you a message that they are doing a story on empathy or the failure to develop empathy in teenagers for an article that will be printed in two days. They need to speak with you if at all possible before 7:00 p.m. A national news network may tell you that they are doing a piece from 5:30 p.m. to 6:00 p.m. on how crisis counselors respond to grieving children and want to know if you can be available in the studio for a live interview at that time.

Brock and colleagues (2001) provide six suggestions for dealing with news reporters. The authors suggest that the person being interviewed should: (a) display a high energy level, (b) use simple language rather than technical terms and speak in short sentences, (c) be brief, (d) be friendly; (e) be knowledgeable, sincere, and compassionate, and (f) use good nonverbal communication (p. 194).

Noltemeyer and colleagues (2017) stress the importance of remembering that everything you say is on the record and that you should choose your words carefully; anything you say to a reporter may eventually be read by tens of thousands of individuals. Messages to newspaper reporters are usually more complex; therefore, the authors recommend that you check with the reporter to be sure they understood you correctly. Asking the reporter to repeat the information you have delivered can ensure its accuracy. When the news story appears in print, it should be read for accuracy, because it is possible to correct any inaccurate information in later editions (Noltemeyer, McLaughlin, & McGowan, 2017).

Always remember to report only the facts and try not to get into the attorney's job or the detective's job. Try to ensure that the media portray the situations accurately. Always try to emphasize what the school is doing to address the issues in question.

Noltemeyer and colleagues (2017) provide suggestions for avoiding some of the pitfalls presented by media coverage of crisis events. (a) Attempt to clarify the subject matter of the interview. If it appears to be sensationalistic, do not agree to participate. Some interviewers have well-established reputations for providing sensationalistic coverage of tragic events. Consider such reputations before agreeing to an interview. (b) Try to avoid playing the blame game. Placing blame does not give the general public the kind of information it needs on coping with tragedy. (c) Try to avoid participating in interviews that might give undue attention to the perpetrators of violent acts. (d) Establish some ground rules for what you will and will not discuss.

NSPRA Standards for Public Relations Programs

Textbox 14.1 is an excerpt of the standards from the National School Public Relations Association (NSPRA; available at http://www.nspra.org/).

These are the standards by which a principal and teachers could collaboratively develop a public relations program, should one not already exist on the campus or in the district. If a program exists, the principal and a committee would want to review it based on the following standards.

Educational public relations is a planned and systematic management function designed to help improve the programs and services of an educational organization. It relies on a comprehensive two-way communications process involving both internal and external publics, with a goal of stimulating a better understanding of the role, objectives, accomplishments, and needs of the organization. Educational public relations programs assist in interpreting public attitudes, identifying and helping shape policies and procedures in the public interest, and carrying on involvement and information activities that earn public understanding and support.

Textbox 14.1

I. Concept
    A. Policy
        1. The organization shall adopt a clear and concise public relations policy statement.
        2. The policy statement shall be approved through formal action of the organization's governing body, shall be published in its policy manual, and shall be reviewed annually by the governing body.
        3. The policy statement shall express the purposes of the organization's public relations program and shall provide for the delegation of authority to appropriate executives.
    B. Procedures
        1. Management shall clarify the public relations policies through the development of written operational procedures.
        2. The procedures shall outline major components of the public relations program, detail rules and regulations, and specify employee roles and responsibilities.
        3. The procedures shall be distributed to all employees and representatives of key external publics.
II. Resources
    Commitment to the achievement of the purposes of the organization's public relations policy shall be demonstrated through the allocation of adequate human and financial resources to the public relations program.
    A. Staff
        1. The staffing of a public relations program will vary according to an organization's size, needs, and availability of resources. In every situation, however, the responsibility shall be assigned to an individual who reports directly to the chief executive officer and who participates as a full member of the administrative cabinet.
        2. Recognition of public relations as a management function of primary importance shall be demonstrated through the existence of a unit staffed by full-time professional public relations personnel. Staff size shall be sufficient to accomplish the objectives of the organization and to cope with the variety of inherent conditions and problems.
        3. The public relations staff shall meet NSPRA's Standards for Educational Public Relations Professionals.
        4. Provision shall be made for continuous training and development for members of the public relations staff.
    B. Budget
        1. The organization's budget shall include a specific item for public relations staffing, services, and programs.
        2. The amount of the public relations budget will vary according to organizational needs. However, in addition to staff, appropriate provisions shall be made for the following: materials and equipment; facilities; technical services (publications, advertising, audiovisual, radio, television, etc.); involvement activities; professional growth and development; research and evaluation.
        3. Provisions shall be made for appropriate public relations activities in the budgets of each of the organization's major departments and programs.
III. Internal Communications
    The basic foundation of the organization's public relations program shall be a sound and effective system of internal communications.

A. Planning
1. The organization shall develop a written plan which identifies key internal audiences, as well as procedures for determining the kind of information they need and desire.
2. Each major department, program, or unit in the organization shall develop appropriate communications strategies based on the overall plan.

B. Implementation
1. An appropriate variety of communications methods shall be used, including vehicles for encouraging, receiving, analyzing, and using feedback.
2. A continuing public relations training program shall be provided for the entire staff or membership of the organization.

IV. External Communications
The organization shall be committed to continuing and creative efforts to inform and involve external publics.

A. Planning
1. The organization shall develop a written plan which identifies key community individuals and groups, as well as procedures for determining the kind of information they need and desire.
2. Each major department, program, or unit in the organization shall develop appropriate communications strategies based on the overall plan.

B. Implementation
1. An appropriate variety of communications methods shall be used.
2. Special efforts shall be made to encourage, receive, analyze, and use feedback.
3. Strategies shall be developed to identify and involve community resources.

V. Accountability
A. Program Performance
1. The organization shall provide for evaluation of the public relations program based on proposed objectives and the degree to which they have been achieved.
2. The staff or membership of the organization shall be included in any evaluation process.

B. Development
1. The organization shall provide for long-range public relations planning.
2. The organization shall develop a plan for anticipating, preparing for, and dealing with the public relations aspects of unusual or crisis situations.
3. Emphasis shall be given to seeking and developing new and different avenues of communications and relationships.

A School District's Plan

The Tacoma (Washington) Public Schools Public Relation Plan adheres to the standards set forth by the NSPRA. The Tacoma Plan follows:

> The Board of Directors believes it is the responsibility of each Board member, as well as each employee of the District, to actively pursue a two-way communications program that highlights the educational experiences in the city's public schools and promotes effective school/home/community partnerships.

The Board recognizes that citizens have a right to know what is occurring in their public school system; that Board members and all school administrators have an obligation to see that all publics are kept systematically and adequately informed; and that the District will benefit from seeing that citizens get all information, good and bad, directly from the system itself.

The Board affirms the following objectives:

1. To maintain an effective two-way communication system between the District and its various publics which ensures:

   a. Dissemination of accurate, timely information about school policies
   b. programs, procedures, achievements, decisions, critical issues
   c. Interpretation of decisions and action
   d. Elimination of rumors and misinformation
   e. Programs and practices designed to provide an open climate which will elicit ideas, suggestions, reactions from the community and employees alike
   f. An effective working relationship with the news media

2. To maintain a Public Information Office which will coordinate the District's communication efforts.
3. To develop and maintain an organizational environment where all District staff members are aware that they share the responsibility for communication of school policies, programs and activities to parents, members of the educational and other communities.
4. To maintain a written plan of communication policies and guidelines which will be available to employees and to the public upon request.
5. To support the establishment of a Communications Review Committee to review and evaluate District-wide two-way communication efforts.

Board members believe it is essential to the development of excellence in the education of youngsters that the maximum possible knowledge about the goals, achievements, activities and operations of the school district be conveyed to the students, staff and citizens. The Board therefore reaffirms its commitment to openness in relationships with its patrons. The Board further believes that the citizens, as well as the staff and students, should be consulted and involved in the problem-solving and decision-making processes at as early a stage as possible. This involvement should be solicited actively and honestly through a wide variety of means. A principal could model a public relations plan for the campus after the Tacoma Board plan.

PUBLIC RELATIONS PLAN

The NSPRA published a model for establishing a community relations or public relations plan. In it, the NSPRA (n.d.) indicates that the role of school public relations is to maintain mutually beneficial relationships between the school district and the many publics it serves. Each principal will have their own unique way of carrying out this role, but there is one common element of all successful public relations programs: they are planned.

A well-thought-out public relations plan will help ensure that a school district carries out its mission and meets its goals with the support of its staff and community. Where does the principal begin? The NSPRA provides a basic process for developing a district public relations plan; and from that plan, a principal can develop one at the campus level.

Four-Step Public Relations Process
Exemplary public relations programs follow this four-step process:

1. *Research.* The principal conducts an up-front analysis on where the district (campus) stands in regard to all publics it wishes to reach.
2. *Action plan.* The principal develops public relations goals, objectives, and strategies that go hand in hand with the district's (campus's) overall mission and goals.
3. *Communicate.* The principal carries out the tactics that are necessary to meet the objectives and goals.
4. *Evaluate.* The principal reflects on actions taken to determine their effectiveness and to identify what changes are needed in the future.

Public Relations Planning Process
The NSPRA (n.d.) also provides a planning process to assist in developing the public relations plan.

1. *Do variety assessment.* Begin by meeting with the superintendent and school board to discuss their priorities for district public relations objectives. Know the district mission and goals and be prepared to discuss how your program can help achieve those goals.
2. *Develop internal and external research.* Before structuring the plan, you must be aware of where the district stands in the eyes of both staff and the community. There are a variety of questions to answer: Who are our publics? What are our publics' overall perceptions of our schools? What "hot issues" are circulating among staff and community? What issues affecting other school districts may soon be coming our way? . . . the list goes on and on. Base your research on your district mission and goals and use several methods. Tactics to consider: national studies, census data, telephone logs, media reports, interviews with community opinion leaders, focus groups, and written or telephone surveys.
3. *Develop public relations goals and objectives.* Thinking first and foremost about facilitating achievement of district goals, develop short-term and long-term public relations goals to accomplish. It is advisable to develop these with input from a committee representing board, staff, parents, families, and outside community members. Remember, to make the objectives timed and measurable, so that you will know if you achieved them. Example: By the end of the school year, 75 percent of the district's teachers will be involved in projects to improve teacher-parent relations.
4. *Identify target publics.* These "targets" are the groups of people that need to be reached in order to achieve the goals. Primary publics are those most important to achieving goals. In schools, they are often students, staff, and parents. Secondary publics are those who could be reached if money or time permits, or those who are indirectly reached by public relations tactics.

5. *Identify desired behavior of publics.* This is a critical step! For the plan to succeed, you must decide what you want the program to do. Do you want to provide information? Or, do you want to reinforce or change the behavior of certain publics? These questions must be answered before tactics are created.

6. *Identify what is needed to achieve desired behavior.* Using research data, decide what actions must take place to create the behaviors you desire. For example, you could find out by taking attendance that only 50 percent of the parents and families at your school normally attend the fall open house. The desired behavior is to increase this number. A follow-up written survey could help you identify the reasons that 50 percent do not attend. Then you can decide what actions to take to change this percentage.

7. *Create strategies and tactics for reaching publics.* Strategies are overall procedures, like developing a media kit that provides general information about the school district. Tactics are the actions that must be taken to carry out the procedures, like writing the press release or printing the folder for the district media kit.

8. *Put your plan on paper.* This is where you develop the budget, create a timeline, and assign responsibility for all strategies and tactics.

9. *Implement the plan.* After management and board approval, put your plan into action. Keep your committee involved, and prepare to refine the plan along the way.

10. *Evaluate your efforts.* Using the same methods you used in the research phase, evaluate your plan. First, evaluate the planning process itself: What worked and what didn't? Continue to evaluate your program as it is implemented to determine what revisions may need to be made. Finally, measure your goals and objectives to determine whether you have reached them.

SUMMARY

1. Today, principals appreciate and understand the learning potential in positive school-community relations and the interdependence among schools, families, and communities.

2. Principals are also beginning to realize that building social capital in the community is necessary because if the community is strengthened, the school will also be strengthened for successful education.

3. Principals are a bridge between the school and external constituencies, and they are called boundary spanners as they fulfill this role.

4. The principal is the boundary spanner for ensuring that partnerships go beyond parents to include the community in interagency collaborations that can make decisions about the education of the "whole child."

5. A community school, operating in a public school building, is open to students, families, and the community before, during, and after school, seven days a week, all year long. It is jointly operated and financed through a partnership between the school system and one or more community agencies.

6. In times of catastrophe, schools often become a lifeline to the communities they serve.
7. There are six types of school, family, and community involvement: parenting, communicating, volunteering, learning at home, decision making, and collaborating with the community.
8. Principals must first be committed to involving families and parents; but principals must also motivate and encourage teachers to be committed to involving families and parents and to use as many ways as possible to involve the parents.
9. Community and public relations begin at home and work from the inside out; therefore, it is extremely important for the principal to identify and communicate effectively with his or her internal and external publics. Internal publics refer to those groups of people directly associated with the campus or the school district, such as administrators, teachers, students, support staff, or the school board. External publics refer to those people who are outside of the campus or district or who have an indirect relationship with the campus or district, such groups as parents, community organizations, churches, government, businesses, or senior citizens.
10. If a crisis occurs on the campus, news reporters usually want to know who, what, when, where, why, and how.
11. School public relations is a planned and systematic management function performed by the principal and designed to help improve school programs and services.
12. Exemplary public relations programs follow this basic four-step process: research, action plan, communicate, and evaluate.

KEY TERMS

democratic education
boundary spanners
community involvement

community school
educational public relations

FIELD-BASED ACTIVITIES

1. Interview your principal and determine how they incorporate a coordinated services model. If your principal does not use such a model, determine with them how to develop one for the campus.
2. Develop a family involvement plan for the campus. Include on your team other teachers and parents.
3. Develop a four-step public relations plan for your school. What steps will you take in its development? Work with your principal or assistant principal in developing this plan.

SUGGESTED READINGS

Edwards, P. A., Spiro, R. J., Donke, L. M, Castle, A. M., Peltier, M. R., Donohue, T. H., & White, K. L. (2019). *Partnering with families for student success: 24 scenarios for problem solving with parents.* This book helps teachers gain confidence and build sensitivity when interacting with caregivers and families who speak different languages and may come from different cultural, racial, and social backgrounds.

Epstein, J. L. (2018). *School, family, and community partnerships: Preparing educators and improving schools.* Boulder, CO: Westview Press. In *School, Family, and Community Partnerships*, the author offers educators a framework for thinking about, talking about, and then actually building comprehensive programs for school and family partnerships. Epstein offers a framework of six types of involvement for creating partnerships.

Fiore, D. (2022). *School community relations.* New York, NY: Routledge. In this book, the author provides school leaders and other educators with background knowledge about school-community relations and describes practical techniques for improving principals' ability to understand and communicate with the many publics they serve.

Herrera, S. G., Porter, L, & Barko-Alva, K. (2020). *Equity in school-parent partnerships: Cultivating community and family trust in culturally diverse classrooms.* New York, NY: Teachers College Press. Starting from the premise that children learn better when their learning community respects their families and cultures, this thought-provoking resource shows what it means—and what it takes—to include today's diverse parents in their children's learning.

Ishimaru, A. M. (2020). *Just schools: Building equitable collaborations with families and communities.* New York, NY: Teachers College Press. This text examines the challenges and possibilities for building more equitable forms of collaboration among nondominant families, communities, and schools.

Moore, E. H., Bagin, D., & Gallagher, D. R. (2020). *The school and community relations* (12th ed.). New York, NY: Pearson. This book enables school officials to communicate effectively with their staff and the community to improve school quality and student learning. The authors explain not only "why" but "how" to communicate to create a supportive environment in which students learn better.

Part III Case Study

Tough Decisions

■ ■ ■

Setting: Dr. Alice March, principal of Dover High School, is in the process of selecting a new chair for the English department at her school. This position is one of strong influence, because the chair sits on many standing committees in the district. In the past, the chairperson has been a leader on the curriculum council and on the site-based decision-making (SBDM) committee.

Scenario: Dr. March is on the telephone, discussing the situation with Dr. Petrovsky, superintendent of schools.

"I have no idea who will apply for the position, Dr. Petrovsky," says Dr. March. "Yes, I realize that you have given the committee autonomy to decide who will be the next chair of the English Department. I realize how important that role is, and we on the selection team will do our homework."

As she gets off the phone, Dr. March is almost beside herself. Two board members have already called her about this position. Now the superintendent has called to ask who is applying. It has been only an hour since she posted the expected vacancy on the bulletin board in the faculty room.

The principal thinks about which portions of the job description are most important to her: the required qualifications, the desired qualifications, and the performance responsibilities. Required and desired qualifications are valid teaching and supervisory certificates; at least six years of classroom teaching in high school English; experience in planning, developing, and evaluating the English program; and experience in preparing the budget. Performance responsibilities include contributing to a positive atmosphere, maintaining healthy relationships with colleagues, developing positive school-community relations to promote understanding and acceptance of the English program, assisting all English teachers in identifying and solving instructional-related problems, and assuming responsibility for acquiring knowledge, supervisory, and leadership skills necessary for fulfilling all assigned duties.

Dr. March recognizes that performance on the state test for reading and writing at the high school has not improved much in the last three years—except in grade nine. The poor test results certainly contributed to the current department chair's decision to retire.

Within two weeks, Dr. March receives three applications from her current staff. The applicants are all in-district veterans. Mary Worthy has been in the district for twenty years. She earned her master's degree and her certificate for instructional supervision in the year after graduating with her teacher's certificate. She has served as an English teacher for twelve years and as an English and geography teacher for the last eight years. She writes in her application that she "would cherish the opportunity to lead the English teachers." Mary notes that her experience includes curriculum writing; mentoring new teachers; assisting in the budget planning; and of course, teaching English to freshmen, sophomores, juniors, and seniors. Her style is steady and methodical. She prides herself on never failing to get an assignment done on time. She is quite knowledgeable and is well respected in the community.

The second applicant is Tim Cooke, a ten-year veteran whose experience is primarily with ninth-grade students. He is innovative, creative, enthusiastic, a hard worker, and very organized. His student teachers have truly enjoyed his classes. Scores on the state English test for the ninth grade have increased significantly since Tim introduced some new strategies to help all students improve their reading and writing. Teacher colleagues like him and his outgoing, easy manner. He has mentored two student teachers and has helped in the curriculum budget planning. He has just completed his master's degree in instructional supervision.

Dan Olenik, the third applicant, also has ten years of teaching experience at this campus. He has taught English at the sophomore and junior levels. He has some experience in curriculum writing and budgeting. He, too, has mentored two student teachers and has earned a master's in instructional supervision. (In Dr. March's mind, Dan can be somewhat unorganized. She could count on him coming to ask for an extra day to complete some of his lesson plans, particularly when he was working on his master's degree. Yet, to be fair, since then he has responded promptly to all her requests.) The current department chair thinks highly of him. Dan has sponsored the Literary Club, and he has trained debaters for interschool competition. He has done well in both; as a result, he is well known in the community. Of course, having the superintendent as his uncle has not hurt him.

The selection committee is composed of five members—two department chairs, those from social studies and science, plus two English teachers and Dr. March. One of the English teachers serving on the committee has six years of experience, and the other has fifteen years. Both of the women are competent but not outstanding teachers. Dr. March thinks that it will be interesting to hear their comments about the applicants. Dr. Peter Pharr, chair of the social studies department, is the most experienced member of the committee with thirty-two years in education. Phil Blalock, chair of the science department, has twenty-five years of teaching experience.

Dr. March puts the applications aside and proceeds to review her mail for the day. The first letter she picks up is unsigned. It is addressed to her and to members of the selection committee.

Dear Committee Members,

There are a few things I think you ought to know. The teachers are all talking about who will get this job and betting on the side. You-know-who is their first guess for the next chair of the English department because of his connections to the superintendent. I can tell you that this man is not the right choice. His professors never caught his plagiarism in papers written during his master's program; but as a fellow student, he boasted to me about it. His moral standing is questionable not only because of this but also because of his cheating on his wife. She does not know, but I have seen him several times in a hotel with another woman late at night. If you want someone with integrity, and one who can help with public relations, I would not select this person. I believe I have completed my duty in notifying you.

[No Name]

Normally, Dr. March thinks, I would pay no attention to an unsigned letter. Dr. Petrovsky knows this, too. Do I ignore it this time—especially because it refers to the superintendent's nephew? I wonder if this letter was sent to the other committee members. She does not have long to wonder, for at that moment her secretary appears in the doorway and says, "Dr. Pharr and Phil Blalock would like to see you. What shall I tell them?"

Dr. March meets with the department chairs and, after that, with the two English teachers on the selection committee. The men say they have no problem with ignoring the letter; but both women say they can easily believe what the letter revealed and are not comfortable with selecting Dan as chair. Dr. March asks that the selection committee not pass judgment based on such an unfounded rumor. She explains her practice of ignoring unsigned mail. After more discussion, they also agree to proceed with the interviews as scheduled.

Before conducting the team interviews, committee members rate each applicant using a paper review. During the interviews, applicants are rated again based on the responses to ten questions. All the applicants do well in the interview session, particularly Dan Olenik. His answers are outstanding. When all scores are tallied, Dan has scored a couple more points than either of the other two applicants have. Mary Worthy is ranked second, and Tim Cooke is rated last by only one point.

The results surprise Dr. March, but she has said that she is open to working and supervising any one of the three candidates. Just as the session is about to end, the two female teachers mention that they are afraid of what the superintendent might do if they do not select his nephew. Also, the women say, they are uncomfortable with the information in the unsigned letter and wish to state that they are upset because they have been pressured to proceed as if they had not received the letter.

Now Dr. March is not sure what to do. She did persuade the teachers to proceed as if they had not received the letter. Did they think she was pressuring them? Dr. March believes that ignoring any unsigned letters, in line with her consistent practice, has eliminated the possibility of subterfuge from someone with an invalid complaint. She is uncomfortable with the timing of the teachers' objection. Should she take the unsigned letter to the superintendent now, and use that as a tool to move Dan out of consideration? What is the right thing to do?

Questions

1. How can Dr. March remove any suspicion of a forced persuasion? Could she have acted earlier? If so, how?
2. If Dan were selected now, what effect might that have on committee members and ultimately on the department? How would you feel if you had been one of the members?

3. Is Dr. March putting loyalty above what might be truth? What can she say or do now to be perceived as an ethical leader?
4. Could the superintendent and board members be perceived as being unethical because of their phone calls to Dr. March? Explain your answer.

PART IV
Ethics, Policy, and Legal Issues

15

The Principal and Ethics

■ ■ ■

FOCUSING QUESTIONS

1. How is the ethical principal defined?
2. What are the philosophical concepts of ethics that the principal must consider on the job?
3. How does the principal promote ethical behavior in schools?
4. What are some examples of national and state codes of ethics for principals?
5. How have the new PSEL and NELP standards guided the preparation and practice of school principals?

In this chapter, we respond to these questions concerning the principal and ethics. We begin the chapter with a discussion of several general definitions of the ethical principal. Then we examine several philosophical concepts of ethics that principals must consider on the job. This is followed by a discussion of how the principal promotes ethical behavior of all stakeholders in the school. Then we examine some examples of national and state codes of ethics for principals. Finally, we conclude the chapter by providing a description of the PSEL and NELP standards and compare these new standards with their predecessors the ISLLC and ELCC standards respectively.

The unparalleled events at the turn of the twenty-first century cry out for ethical leaders worldwide. Some of those events have revealed leadership full of hate that has annihilated thousands with no remorse, leadership full of greed that has wrecked families with no guilt, leadership full of infidelity that has undermined the public's faith with no shame, and leadership full of desire for power that has stirred fear among innocents with no retraction.

When this type of leadership is witnessed 24/7 on the television, what greater calling is there for a school principal than to step forward and lead future generations to a better life, a better world? Starratt (2004) reminded principals of the importance for their leadership to demonstrate ethical behavior as a life's work in progress and action when he indicated that ethical education is a lifelong education. Society today is screaming for leaders who demonstrate integrity; who model ethical, moral, and caring behavior; and who can help others along their own life's journey. Although the cry is for ethical leadership, there is a paucity of research regarding whether principals, in particular, exhibit such ethical behavior (Hughes, 2005; Johnson, 2017; Ubben, Hughes, & Norris, 2017).

THE ETHICAL PRINCIPAL

How is an ethical principal defined? The ethical principal is one who, in the face of adversity, ambiguity, and challenge, reflects on what is right by some set standard or code and acts in a rational and caring manner to resolve problems and conduct business. An ethical principal must know her own values and goals and how those are aligned with the campus and district's vision, mission, and goals. Additionally, an ethical principal will have already asked himself, "What is important? What is the purpose of my being here? What do I stand for?" The answers from the principal during a challenging situation, and during these uncertain times in our world, can help in providing stability to students and their parents, teachers, and the community.

The ethical principal acts in genuine ways and is not ostentatious. The ethical principal must face decisions head on when they are made, and they must be able to stand firm during such confrontations while remaining true to her moral compass. What controls the moral compass in the face of ethical dilemmas are the moral principles instilled by the principal's family; principals are not guided exclusively by school policies or professional codes but must be trained in ethics in order to confront the issues of poverty, racism, sexism, and inequities (Levinson & Fay, 2016; Strike, 2007; Strike, Haller & Soltis, 2005). The development of values is necessary but not sufficient for ethical growth. Practice is needed for growth to occur (Ciulla, 2014; Martin & Ruitenberg, 2018).

Ethics defines the way we participate in the community around us. Yet it is also a deeply personal construct, developing powerful standards and practices in each of us (Wagner & Simpson, 2009). How one thinks and what one believes about leadership are translated into institutional values and practices (Cherkowski, Walker, & Kutsyruba, 2015; Gross & Shapiro, 2004).

Ethical principals must be able to motivate followers to use many of their innate talents in pursuing the school goals and mission. Principals as "moral leaders train, educate, and coach followers, provide motivation, involve them in appropriate networks, and then free them from situational constraints that may hamper their growth or transformation toward full effectiveness. They endow followers with the capacity to lead themselves in accomplishing the organization's ends" (Houston, Blankenship, & Cole, 2008, p. 57). Rebore (2014) captured the essence of the **ethical principal** by stating, "the ethical administrator is a person who makes decisions with the dignity of each person in mind, who empowers others, who has a sense of solidarity with at-risk students, who promotes equality in all aspects of education, and who is a responsible steward of school-districts assets" (p. 275).

PRINCIPALS AND PHILOSOPHICAL CONCEPTS OF ETHICS

According to Beckner (2004, pp. 25–40), ethical principals must be concerned with the following six philosophical concepts: (a) rights, (b) freedom, (c) responsibility, (d) duty, (e) justice, and (f) equity. The American Association of School Administrators (AASA) (2020) listed several other practical concepts related to ethics for principals: (a) authority, (b) caring, (c) character, (d) commitment, (e) conflict of interest, (f) formality, (g) loyalty, and (h) prudence. Shapiro and Stefkovich (2016) noted four paradigms: (1) justice, (2) critique, (3) care, and (4) the profession.

We add a moral imperative to these lists. All of these principles, concepts, or paradigms reflect personal character traits, behaviors, and incidences involving ethical decision making. Shapiro and Stefkovich (2016) suggested that principals can become more aware of their own perspectives, and with such principles or paradigms they can be better equipped to solve the daily, complex dilemmas they encounter on their campuses.

Rights

Ethical principals have a responsibility to respect the rights of others, as moral decision makers and as role models. But disagreement occurs about what rights should apply, in a given situation, or what constitutes violation of another person's rights. Those are **rights**

> which God and nature have established, and are therefore called natural rights, such as are life, and liberty, need not the bid of human laws to be more effectual than they are . . . no human legislature has power to abridge or destroy them, unless their owner shall himself commit some act that amounts to forfeiture. (Blackstone, 1941, p. 21)

Absolute rights of individuals have withstood the test of time; and rights related to principals would include those indicated by Blackstone (1941) of personal security, personal liberty, and private property. The principal is responsible to all individuals on the campus to ensure the right of personal security. An example of personal security responsibility was published in September 2004 in the report, *Preparedness in America's Schools: A Comprehensive Look at Terrorism Preparedness in America's Twenty Largest School Districts*. In that report, Phinney (2004) equated principals as public officials who are accountable and responsible for the security of our children. Phinney stated that "in light of the conclusions of the 9/11 Commission, it benefits none of us if we mince words about how the nation's school officials are fulfilling, or not fulfilling, their responsibility to protect our children from another terrorist attack" (p. 4).

Beckner (2004) recognized that absolute rights prevail in all circumstances; however, he indicated that if justified by circumstances, prima facie rights—such as the right to freedom of speech within the classroom or freedom of dress on the campus—may be overridden. Personal liberty is seen as an absolute right; but in the case of schools, it may become a prima facie right because it would be overridden if within the personal liberty there is potential for harm or harassment to others or for endangerment of the equal rights of others. Because "school" is a public property, the personal liberty of individuals is subject to the scrutiny of the law. The function of civil law is to protect the natural liberty of individuals, not to punish them for their sins.

Another right indicated by Beckner (2004) as an essential concern of principals is *negative rights*. This concept extends the right to be left alone, to not be interfered with when one wants to do something (i.e., teachers moonlighting after contract hours). Negative rights also relate to safety issues to which the principal must attend in the school; these issues are within the arenas of counseling, curriculum, and crisis management. For example, Wellman (2019) stated that an example of negative rights would be "one's right not to be killed, which imposes a duty upon others not to kill one" (p. 24).

Beckner (2004) related that *positive rights* require others to assist in their exercise, usually through some governmental entity (i.e., equal opportunity through affirmative action). These rights operate in a positive sense, in that they declare the right of an individual to have something (e.g., a humane standard of living; the right to an appropriate education). In order to protect positive rights, the state must do or give something to improve the individual's life; therefore, it is the principal's ethical duty to ensure that each child is educated in the best possible way (Shapiro & Stefkovich, 2016; Stefkovich, 2006; Stefkovich & Begley, 2007)

Another set of rights that Beckner (2004) included were *human rights*, which are obtained because one is human. Negative human rights are life, physical property, due process, privacy, autonomy, freedom of thought and expression; positive human rights include food, adequate housing, competent medical care, employment at a living wage, and education. Finally, Beckner reported that "particular rights" are dependent upon specific circumstances; for example, a person who is promised a specific thing has the right to receive it. If a child who has a learning deficit that must be addressed by a variety of instructional techniques is promised an education—meaning, in the basic sense, the ability to read, write, and do arithmetic—then the principal could be called into question regarding her responsibility and ethical obligation to protect and ensure the child's particular rights if the child cannot function at a basic level of education.

Freedom

Beckner (2004) suggested that the concept of **freedom** is related closely to that of rights, and it is aligned in Americans' minds with the notions of liberty, independence, and individuality. The *Washington Times* published an article that is related to freedom and how principals must engage in ensuring the freedom of all students. The article described the Civic Mission of Schools, a study from the Carnegie Corporation of New York and the University of Maryland's Center for Information and Research on Civic Learning and Engagement, which revealed that most formal civic education today comprises only a single course on government, with little emphasis on the rights and responsibilities of citizens and ways that they could work together and relate to government. However, the report cited research that children start to develop social responsibility and interest in politics before the age of nine.

These are critical teaching and learning principles for school principals to consider when dialoguing with their teachers. For example, the same *Washington Times* article reported increased class discussions and debates in some schools on the justification for forcibly disarming Saddam Hussein. Some principals have had to warn teachers to ensure that all sides are given equal opportunity to be heard.

Despite the fact that freedom of speech in class debates has to be pointed out to teachers, the newspaper reported, the teaching of our constitutional history has been sorely lacking. The newspaper reported that Charles Haynes, a senior scholar at the Freedom Forum First Amendment Center, said that this generation has been called upon to defend freedom at home and around the world. Our task is to ensure that they understand what they are defending and why ("Bringing the Constitution to Life," 2003). Infusing an understanding of various freedoms into the curriculum and establishing such an understanding with the teachers and students are the ethical responsibility of the principal.

Responsibility and Authority

Rights and freedom carry with them responsibility. There is responsibility for the consequences of actions that may result from exercising various rights and freedoms. One major freedom enjoyed by all US citizens is the freedom of speech. In relation to that freedom, the principal must consider consequences involving this right. Consequently, the principal's role in freedom of speech issues is one that has been scrutinized, such as in the following cases. Branson and Gross (2014) stated that principals are often viewed as public figures and as such both enjoy and suffer from their status. They reported that the Georgia Supreme Court determined that high school principals were not public officials and as such did not need to prove malice on the part of a defendant in a libel suit. In Maryland and Mississippi, principals are held to be public officials, whereas the law in Illinois grants principals the same protections that private citizens enjoy. In general, principals do not stand in a confidential relationship with others, as do a husband and wife or attorney and client. Thus, principals have the responsibility to limit their negative comments about students and staff members to those they have personally observed. Also, principals should report any statements that are possibly defamatory only to those who have a need to know.

The AASA (2020) indicates that **responsibility** has two dimensions: (1) objective responsibility and (2) subjective responsibility. *Objective responsibility* arises from legal, organizational, and societal demands upon our role as public administrator. *Subjective responsibility* is rooted in experience like loyalty, conscience, and identification. We feel inclined, or even compelled, to act in a particular way, not because we are required to do so by a supervisor or the law but because of an inner drive.

Related to responsibility is authority. The AASA (2020) defined **authority** as the power to influence the behavior of others. He said that excess in the arbitrary use of authority and the failure to exercise authority effectively both represent failure to meet acceptable ethical standards.

Duty

According to Beckner (2004), sometimes duty and responsibility are thought of as synonymous; however, **duty** tends to regard demands that override other values. The principal must perform duties that come with rules and regulations. Some of the prima facie duties are (a) fidelity, (b) reparation, (c) gratitude, (d) justice, (e) beneficence, (f) self-improvement, and (g) non-maleficence. Other duties that may take precedence in the school arena over the prima facie duties are (a) duty to students, (b) duty to colleagues, (c) duty to discipline, (d) duty to the school team, (e) duty to the profession, (f) duty to funding sources, (g) duty to parents, and (h) duty to community.

Justice

There are concerns for principals in dealing with justice—one concern is the equal treatment of non-equals or the unequal treatment of equals. Shapiro and Stefkovich (2016) indicated that the ethic of justice "focuses on rights and law and is part of a liberal democratic tradition" (p. 11). Many have defined justice; but more recently, Beckner (2004) defined **justice** using the term *fairness*, which implies that individuals could be just and fair if they would see clearly and think rationally and act in an uninterested and benevolent manner. Beckner shared from the literature five types of justice: (1) **procedural justice**—treatment people should receive in connection with the application of rules; (2) **substantive justice**—examines the "rightness" of rules and procedures and protects ownership of property, compensation for work, freedom, privacy, bodily safety, truth telling, citizenship, and copyright; (3) **retributive justice**—involves punishment for wrongdoing; (4) **remedial justice** or compensatory justice—involves wrongdoing in relation to the victim, not the perpetrator, and involves making amends; and (5) **distributive justice**—does not necessarily deal with a wrongdoing, but relates to benefits and burdens shared equally among people.

Equity

The words *justice* and *equity* are sometimes used interchangeably. **Equity** refers to the bending of rules to fit a situation. This implies treating equals equally and nonequals unequally to level the playing fields, but not to the point of being unfair. Beckner (2004) provides an excellent example: Applying the same standardized test score requirements for admission to a university or consideration for scholarships may be unfair to one whose native language is not English or to one whose cultural background is different from that on which the test is based. To do so may also create inaccurate results (prediction of academic success). Therefore, certain individuals would not have an equal opportunity to succeed in life. Recently, a large university changed its rules of providing extra points on its admissions criteria to those whose parents attended the university. This may not have been a popular decision to former students, but it was a decision in favor of justice and equity.

Recently, several researchers (Agarwal-Rangnath, 2020; Brooks & Brooks, 2021; Harry & Ocasio-Stoutenburg, 2020; Hess & Noguera, 2021; Howard, 2020; Ishimaru, 2020; Kundu, 2020; Noguera & Syeed, 2020; Sleeter & Zavala, 2020; Teranishi et al., 2020) have spoken of a renewed interest in the need to prepare educational leaders to deal with equity issues due to the substantial demographic changes occurring in the United States. Specifically, as school principals seek to discover fundamental ways to deal with rapidly changing populations of students, they find themselves confronted with fundamental questions of about equity, rights, freedom, character, justice, caring, and the like.

Caring

Noddings (2005) notes that "an ethic of care starts with a study of relation. It is fundamentally concerned with how human beings meet and treat one another" (p. 45). A **caring** principal develops meaningful relationships while inspiring others to excellence. Being thoughtful and sensitive, such principals recognize diversity and individualism in people. Whereas bureaucrats emphasize compliance with rules and regulations, caring principals above all else are uncritical, collegial, and supportive (Smylie, Murphy, & Louis, 2020a, 2020b). The AASA (2022) suggests that caring includes such actions as commitment, patience, knowledge of the needs and wants of others, tolerance, trust, hope, courage, and the ability to listen. Smylie, Murphy, and Louis (2020a, 2020b) assert that a caring school is where everyone counts, where all are heard, and where the principal works to ensure the personal growth and development of all.

Character, Commitment, and Formality

According to Palmour (1986), Aristotle defined good **character** as the life of right conduct—right conduct in relation to other persons and in relation to one's self.

Character is closely associated with caring; if a principal is perceived to have a good character, then he has exhibited behavior such as honesty, courage, dependability, generosity, and acceptable motivations. The principal should be of honorable repute in the eyes of the teachers and community (AASA, 2020).

Commitment is related to character in that the principal must be committed to doing the right thing. Commitment is related to dependability. For example, if the principal is constantly late to meetings with the teachers, who always arrive on time, then her commitment as well as her dependability come into question. The teachers begin to question the principal's ethics. If the principal is not faithful or committed in little, then teachers begin to question her commitment in much.

Formality relates to commitment and, according to AASA (2020), refers to being in compliance with accepted norms of behavior and ceremonies. **Formality** includes keeping personal appointments, promptness, courtesy, language, manners, and attention to individuals or ceremonies. Public display of professional, ethical behavior is at the center of formality.

Conflict of Interest

A **conflict of interest** is a situation in which the principal would have a competing professional or personal interest that would make it difficult to fulfill his duties fairly. In cases of a conflict of interest, the principal should recuse himself from the matter—not take part in, or influence in any way, the process. For example, if the principal's wife is hired and the principal is the evaluator who may or may not recommend her for a merit raise or job security, then the principal should recuse himself to avoid a conflict of interest.

At times, principals may be involved in situations with companies or private interests that promote student learning. An example situation occurs with the Channel One news program for teenagers, as described by Stark (2001). Stark states that principals who engage in Channel One, which advertises commercial products, have put themselves into a kind of conflict of interest. Considering that principals and teachers are public officials, it stands to reason that teachers should make their official decisions—including those about allocating curricular time and classroom space—on their merits, according to the public interest, and not based on the school's need for private support. The Channel One example is not the most serious kind of conflict of interest. That would be the case when an official has the capacity to use her public role to benefit a private company in return for a personal payment. Instead, the Channel One arrangement resembles the milder form of conflict (but one still statutorily regulated at the federal level) in which officials take something of value from a private company not for themselves personally, but to help serve the purposes of their cash-strapped public school (Stark, 2001, p. 59).

The following are the most common forms of conflicts of interests:

1. Self-dealing, in which public and private interests collide; for example, issues involving family or privately held business interests
2. Outside employment, in which the interests of one job contradicts another
3. Accepting of benefits, including bribes and other gifts accepted to curry favor
4. Influence peddling—using one's position to influence other realms
5. Use of government, corporate, or legal property for personal reasons
6. Unauthorized distribution of confidential information

There are two kinds of conflicts of interests. In a *real conflict*, which is the type mentioned earlier, the competing interests are exploited for personal gain. In an *apparent conflict*, the parties involved acknowledge the conflict of interests and deal with it accordingly (*World History Encyclopedia*, 2004).

Loyalty

Loyalty generally refers to faithfulness, devotion, and allegiance to a leader, person, group, ideal, cause, or duty. A supervisor may ask the school principal to do something that the principal believes to be unethical. For example, the principal may be asked to place the superintendent's son in the gifted education program when, in fact, the child does not meet the criteria for placement. Of course, blind loyalty is extreme and produces negative results leading to unethical behavior. Principals who have blind loyalty may be viewed as "yes people."

Loyalty runs in both directions—to the supervisors as well as the supervised. Loyalty is developed and earned over time. Is whistle-blowing an act of disloyalty? According to AASA (2020), whether a whistle-blower acts from personal interest or from moral conscience, the principal must see that justice is done and consider the reported wrong, regardless of the source. Loyalty also implies openness and the feeling that one can share with the principal any serious violations that are observed.

Prudence

Prudence refers to the exercise of good judgment, common sense, and even caution, especially in the conduct of practical matters. Principals must remember that their actions have influence on people (AASA, 2020). Prudence implies consequential thinking by the principal. If the principal does not think with prudence or consequentially, then the result may be harmful to the students and teachers. For example, during the budgeting process a principal may ask the superintendent for only one additional faculty member when, in fact, three faculty members are needed to handle the foreseen increase in students. If the principal is thus granted one faculty member, the principal will have to hire uncertified long-term substitutes to cover two classrooms. This outcome is ultimately injurious not only to student learning but also to continuous school improvement, due to the lack of permanent faculty members to plan and develop programs and carry out the mission and goals of the school.

Critique

According to Shapiro and Stefkovich (2016), "the ethic of **critique** is based on critical theory, which has, at its heart, an analysis of social class and its inequities," and it is "linked to critical pedagogy" (p. 14). They further claim that critique is

> aimed at awakening educators to inequities in society and, in particular, in the schools. This ethic asks educators to deal with the hard questions regarding social class, race, gender, and other areas of difference, such as: Who makes the laws? Who benefits from the law, rule, or policy? Who has the power? Who are the silenced voices? This approach to ethical dilemmas then asks educators to go beyond questioning and critical analysis to examine and grapple with those possibilities that could enable all children, whatever their social class, race, or gender to have opportunities to grow, learn, and achieve. Such a process should lead to the development of options related to important concepts such as oppression, power, privilege, authority, voice, language, and empowerment. (p. 15)

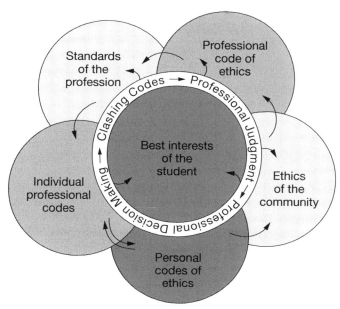

Figure 15.1

Profession

Shapiro and Stefkovich (2016) describe a paradigm for the profession. The ethic of their **profession** requires that principals develop and examine their own professional codes of ethics, which consider their own "individual personal codes of ethics, as well as standards set forth by the profession, and then calls on them to place students at the center of the ethical decision-making process" (p. 23). The authors state that the ethic of the profession is "dynamic—not static—and multidimensional, recognizing the complexities of being an educational leader in today's society" (p. 23). In their model (figure 15.1) for the ethic of the profession, Shapiro and Stefkovich (2016) demonstrate that all factors converge to create the professional paradigm. The circles depict (a) standards of the profession, (b) professional code of ethics, (c) ethics of the community, (d) personal codes of ethics, (e) individual professional codes, and (f) best interests of the student. The figure also demonstrates that the ethic is affected by other factors, like clashing codes, professional judgment, and professional decision making. The authors' ethic of the profession raises questions to the principal posed by the other ethical paradigms or principles, but the principal must move further and "ask what the profession would expect and what is in the best interests of the students taking into account the fact that they may represent highly diverse populations" (p. 25).

Moral Imperative

The moral imperative is an outward demonstration of morality that includes making hard choices when public opinion may be opposite, disturbing the status quo, and self-discipline. The worse situations become in schools, the greater the need for principals to exhibit this moral imperative. Moral leadership is not only about ethical decision making; it is about elements of the moral leadership process that are not directly covered in decision making (Shapiro & Gross, 2013). The moral decision making and actions of a principal are strongly influenced by her values (Begley & Johansson, 2003; Furman, 2003; Irby et al., 2002).

Sergiovanni (1992) also notes the influence of values, by including more characteristics of moral leadership that are akin to the spirit. He indicates that principals must appeal to their followers' sense of righteousness, obligation, and goodness as motivations for action and work. Additionally, principals must possess a personal sense of righteousness, obligation, and goodness. If the principal does not demonstrate these qualities, the question is, how could his followers be motivated to follow a moral path? Therefore, Sergiovanni says that the principal must have a moral position—a moral imperative.

PRINCIPALS AND ETHICAL BEHAVIOR IN SCHOOLS

In the following section, we outline some of the most controversial ethical components principals have to deal with in schools. We also describe some specific school situations in which principals model and promote ethical behavior.

Principals Promoting Ethical Behavior in Athletic Programs

Conn and Gerdes (1998) state that "the ethical standards or principles are immutable, regardless of the environment or circumstance in which they are implemented. As such, ethical decisions shape the nature of the sport experience for all participants, to include administrators, coaches, athletes, and parents" (p. 121). The community looks to high school and junior high school principals to monitor the ethical behavior of the coaches and players on their campuses. Principals as well as assistant principals pull duty for the games, where they monitor ethical behavior not only in the game but also on the sidelines and in the stands from the fans.

Why do campus principals need to monitor ethical behavior in athletics? According to Conn and Foshee (1993), there are coaches who (a) have students playing who are not eligible, (b) conduct out-of-season practices, (c) illegally recruit out-of-district players, (d) play injured players in order to win "championships," (e) leave players stranded on buses in a desert, (f) molest players, and (g) improperly desensitize (moderating the intense emotions and actions of competition) athletes post-contest and then re-socialize them back into the mainstream.

Several ethics principles are undeniably linked to numerous core values upon which sports were founded several thousand years ago. Such principles are connected to character development or sportsmanship and not so much to the number of wins. Specific principles identified and linked to modern sports are that (a) athletes must always be considered ends and not means (Merriman & Hill, 1992); (b) the competition must be fair (Jones, Wells, Peters, & Johnson, 1988); (c) participation, leadership, resources, and rewards must be based on achievement rather than ascribed characteristics (Coakley, 2021); and (d) the activity must provide for the relative safety of the participants (Conn & Gerdes, 1998). Each principal sustains the inherent and traditional values of sport, reinforcing the "goodness" of the sports experience for players and coaches alike.

The National Federation of State High School Associations (NFHS, 2022) posts on its Web site an established code of ethics that is a valuable tool for principals and coaches. This code of ethics establishes mutually beneficial systems of conduct among members of the sport community such as coaches, players, spectators (fans), and vendors. Moreover, the code of ethics provides a publicly acceptable justification for actions and policies and serves as a benchmark for principals in assessing the actions and decision-making behavior of the coaches. The National Federation's code is based on the following statement: Each student-athlete should be treated as though they were the coaches' own, and their welfare should be uppermost at all times.

The principal can influence the coach; and discussing the principles of the code is as critical as observing what is happening in the coach's classroom. As the code indicates, the coach has a tremendous influence, for either good or ill, on the student-athletes' education and thus must never value winning above instilling the highest ideals of character. Coaches have great influence not only on athletes but on the entire student body. In all personal contact with student-athletes, officials, athletic directors, school administrators, the state high school athletic association, the media, and the public, the coach must strive to set an example of the highest ethical and moral conduct (NFHS, 2022).

Principals Promoting Ethical Behavior through Character Education

Principals have encouraged **character education** for three reasons. According to Lickona (2010), good character helps people become fully human and more capable of work and love by building strength of mind, heart, and will. Next, schools are better places "when they are civil and caring human communities that promulgate, teach, celebrate and hold students and staff accountable to the values on which good character is based" (p. 93). Finally, teaching character education is essential to the task of building a moral society.

Principals can promote such activities within the curriculum that could enhance ethical behavior among teachers, staff, and students. Principals who facilitate parents, students, and community organizations make character education an integral part of the education process and teach students methods of critical reflection about situations and other moral dilemmas.

It is important to recognize that over the past two decades, character education has undergone some criticism. For example, Kohn (2005) states, "What goes by the name of character education nowadays is, for the most part, a collection of exhortations and extrinsic inducements designed to make children work harder and do what they're told" (p. 24). Furthermore, Lockwood (2014) advises that "any program that intends to promote good behavior by teaching values rests on a shaky foundation" (p. 73). As for Kohn's attack on character education, Lickona (2010) indicates that it is not complex enough to be justified to guide the field, because it does not thoroughly discuss theories and accurately describe character education in schools.

Character education is a key feature of the Every Student Succeeds Act of 2015, the landmark education reform law designed to change the culture of America's schools by closing the achievement gap, offering more flexibility, giving parents more options, and teaching students based on what works. Under the act's strong accountability provisions, states must describe how they will close the achievement gap and ensure that all students, including those who are disadvantaged, achieve academic proficiency. In addition, states must produce annual state and school district report cards informing parents and communities about state and school progress. Schools that do not make progress must provide supplemental services such as free tutoring or after-school assistance, take corrective actions, and, if still not making adequate yearly progress after five years, dramatically change the way their school is run.

As indicated by legislation in the early 2000s, the now defunct No Child Left Behind Act of 2001, replaced by Every Student Succeeds Act of 2015, character education had become a prominent curriculum concern. For example, the *Character Education Manifesto*, in 2003, was the first document of its kind to define character education and to present to administrators, teachers, and parents seven guiding principles for school reform and to build character education (Center for the Advancement of Ethics and Character Education, 2003). The *Character Education Manifesto* principles could serve as a guide or map for principals and teachers to develop a campus manifesto on character education.

- *Principle 1: Education is an inescapable moral enterprise.* Education in its fullest sense is inescapably a moral enterprise—a continuous and conscious effort to guide students to know and pursue what is good and what is worthwhile.
- *Principle 2: Parents.* Parents [are] the primary moral educators of their children and schools should build a partnership with the home. . . . [A]ll schools have the obligation to foster in their students personal and civic virtues such as integrity, courage, responsibility, diligence, service, and respect for the dignity of all persons.
- *Principle 3: Virtue.* Character education is about developing virtues—good habits and dispositions which lead students to responsible and mature adulthood.
- *Principle 4: Teachers, principals, staff.* The teacher and the school principal are central to this enterprise and must be educated, selected, and encouraged with this mission in mind. In truth, all of the adults in the school must embody and reflect the moral authority which has been invested in them by the parents and the community.
- *Principle 5: Community.* Character education is not a single course, a quick-fix program, or a slogan posted on the wall; it is an integral part of school life. The school must become a community of virtue in which responsibility, hard work, honesty, and kindness are modeled, taught, expected, celebrated, and continually practiced. From the classroom to the playground, from the cafeteria to the faculty room, the formation of good character must be the central concern.
- *Principle 6: Curriculum.* The human community has a reservoir of moral wisdom, much of which exists in our great stories, works of art, literature, history, and biography. Teachers and students must together draw from this reservoir both within and beyond the academic curriculum.
- *Principle 7: Students.* Finally, young people need to realize that forging their own characters is an essential and demanding life task. And the sum of their school experiences—in successes and failures, academic and athletic, intellectual and social—provides much of the raw material for this personal undertaking.

This work is an example of the kinds of resources available to principals who are seeking to design or select curriculum to implement character education in their schools.

Policies and Procedures That Promote Ethical Behavior in Schools

The school principal is the most important person on the campus to promote and model ethical behavior and to implement policies that support an appropriate standard of conduct. As the principal goes, so goes the school. Principals can promote procedures that seek to enhance student learning by addressing the intellectual, emotional, and physical safety needs of students and staff. Principals can promote campus values in which all students receive a quality education that incorporates the teaching of respect for others and self, integrity, citizenship, and sense of commitment and obligation to the school and community—critical components for developing a safe and productive environment in which all students can learn and for contributing to the vitality of modern society. Principals and teachers should advance curricular activities that provide all students with an understanding of the necessity of ethical and legal conduct and a balancing of individual rights with the common good. It is first necessary for principals to work with teachers to advance moral and ethical leadership on the campus. "To be guides for the young in morality and ethics, teachers must understand the complex moral role that they occupy as ethical professionals and appreciate the significance of their own actions and decisions on the students in their care" (Campbell, 2008). It is important for the principal to ensure that all school personnel, board members, parents, students, and community agencies share a role in creating a safe and nurturing learning environment for all students and in helping to raise a generation of individuals who are respectful and responsible not only to themselves, but to others within their school and community.

Superintendents and School Boards. Principals can work with the superintendent and local school board in developing ethical policies and subsequent procedures that assist all teachers and administrators in creating a safe learning environment that addresses every child's needs and embodies the belief that schools are designed to educate all young people. Specifically, principals can promote certain concepts with the superintendent and school board. It is crucial for superintendents and school boards to value the school climate as a critical component of effective learning and to provide resources to establish supportive, healthy school climates. Superintendents and school boards, with the principal, can review all disciplinary policies to ensure that they encourage children to stay in school rather than exclude them from school. Principals must ask superintendents and school boards to provide appropriate resources for a broad array of after-school activities to maximize the number of students involved in constructive, adult-supervised activities. Superintendents and school boards, along with the principal, must ensure compliance with all health, safety, and equity standards pertaining to the school buildings, outdoor facilities, and curriculum so that every student has the maximum opportunity to learn in a healthy, safe, equitable, and nonhostile school environment.

School Actions. Schools can take action to promote and teach ethical behavior and work toward better citizenship and the common good of the society. Some of those activities include engaging students in clubs, leadership activities, service learning, and peer mentoring. Additionally, the campus staff should monitor and supervise all areas of the school (e.g., classrooms, hallways and stairwells, cafeterias, playgrounds, shop areas, lavatories, and locker rooms) to ensure the safety of all students at all times. All members of the school community must identify acts of name-calling, teasing, bullying, exclusion, and harassment and take immediate action, based on a previously developed intervention plan, to intervene in those situations that are detrimental to students and the learning environment.

Other actions that schools can take to support ethical behavior revolve around the components of family involvement, mentors, volunteers, and curriculum. Support families to identify and address their critical role of assisting the school in providing a safe and productive learning environment. Mentors or buddies can be assigned to ensure that all students share a caring relationship with at least one adult in the school, in which regular, ongoing interactions occur. Each adult, including volunteers (this means training of volunteers is necessary), must (a) send a clear and consistent message to students that each has a duty to behave responsibly and respectfully toward others, (b) model the positive behaviors they hope to instill in their students, and (c) consistently enforce rules and provide opportunities to develop and foster ethical reasoning, self-control, and a generalized respect for others. Schools can incorporate the examination of and reflection upon ethical issues into the curriculum; they can teach conflict resolution skills to provide students with the capacity and commitment to solve conflicts in fair, nonviolent ways (an example of this is to train students as conflict managers, so they can assist with conflicts that arise between students during the lunch period).

Parents and Families. Parents and families are a child's first and most important teacher; therefore, family involvement is crucial in developing a child's sense of personal responsibility to others, or ethical behavior. Principals can facilitate parent-family involvement programs that focus on working with families to instill a sense of responsibility and empathy in every student. Concepts taught in involvement programs include: (a) modeling and integrating ethical behavior into the everyday lives of the children; (b) providing consistent care and modeling pro-social behaviors; (c) setting strong examples; (d) correcting inappropriate actions (e.g., resolving conflicts peacefully, demonstrating tolerance and respect for individual differences, and encouraging lifelong learning); (e) becoming involved in school, community, and state events; and (f) taking an interest in national and global events.

Curriculum policies are also critical to the principal's ability to promote and ensure ethical behavior and decision making. When these policies are in place, principals have a foundation upon which to defend or enforce, if need be, the curriculum goals related to student respect and responsibility.

Curriculum. Principals must facilitate a curriculum that teaches students to take responsibility for observing state and national laws, campus and district policies and procedures, and school and classroom rules. It is critical to teach students to appreciate differences and to have respect for all other persons. Students, themselves, have a responsibility to contribute to a safe, productive school climate and to serve as positive role models in their school community as well as their local communities.

NATIONAL CODES OF ETHICS FOR PRINCIPALS

In this section we discuss three national ethical codes. Presented first is the American Association of School Administrators Code of Ethics; next are the national principal associations Code of Ethics, and finally, the general educator body, the National Education Association Code of Ethics.

American Association of School Administrators

In 1962, the American Association of School Administrators (AASA) created the AASA Code of Ethics to govern actions and behaviors of school administrators, revised in 2020. Although AASA is an organization composed primarily of school superintendents, the code was designated for all administrators, from the assistant principal to the superintendent. Of course, in joining AASA or one of its state affiliates, one is expected to up-hold the AASA Code of Ethics. The code states:

> Every member of a profession carries a responsibility to act in a manner becoming a professional person. This implies that each school administrator has an inescapable obligation to abide by the ethical standards of his profession. The behavior of each is the concern of all. The conduct of any administrator influences the attitude of the public toward the profession and education in general. (AASA, 2020, p. 16)

This AASA Code of Ethics was revised in 1976, in 1981, in 2007, 2000, and 2020 as follows:

> An educational administrator's professional behavior must conform to an ethical code. The code must be idealistic and at the same time practical so that it can apply reasonably to all educational administrators.
>
> The administrator acknowledges that the schools belong to the public they serve for the purpose of providing educational opportunities to all. However, the administrator assumes responsibility for providing professional leadership in the school and community. The responsibility requires the administrator to maintain standards of exemplary professional conduct. It must be recognized that the administrator's actions will be viewed and appraised by the community, professional associates, and students.
>
> To these ends, the administrator subscribes to the following statements of standards.
>
> The educational administrator:

1. Makes the well-being of students the fundamental value of all decision-making and actions.
2. Fulfills professional responsibilities with honesty and integrity.
3. Supports the principle of due process and protects the civil and human rights of all individuals.
4. Obeys local, state, and national laws and does not knowingly join or support organizations that advocate, directly or indirectly, the over-throw of the government.
5. Implements the governing board of education's policies and administrative rules and regulations.
6. Pursues appropriate measures to correct those laws, policies and regulations that are not consistent with sound educational goals.
7. Avoids using positions for personal gain through political, social, religious, economic or other influences.
8. Accepts academic degrees or professional certification only from duly accredited institutions.
9. Maintains the standards and seeks to improve the effectiveness of the profession through research and continuing professional development.
10. Honors all contracts until fulfillment, release or dissolution mutually agreed upon by all parties to contract.

(AASA, 2020)

National Association of Elementary School Principals and National Association of Secondary School Principals

The National Association of Elementary School Principals (NAESP) adopted the same Code of Ethics as did AASA in 1976. The National Association of Secondary School Principals (NASSP) also adheres to the same code; it was approved in 1973 and revised in 2001, and 2020. Revisions are slight with the body and meaning of the text remaining the same.

National Education Association

The National Education Association (NEA) adopted its Code of Ethics in 1975, revised in 2020. It mentions duty to the student and duty to the profession, in particular. The NEA code of Ethics (NEA 2020) follows:

> The educator, believing in the worth and dignity of each human being, recognizes the supreme importance of the pursuit of truth, devotion to excellence, and the nurture of the democratic principles. Essential to these goals is the protection of freedom to learn and to teach and the guarantee of equal educational opportunity for all. The educator accepts the responsibility to adhere to the highest ethical standards.

NEA's code includes two principles: (1) commitment to the student and (2) commitment to the profession.

STATE CODES OF ETHICS FOR PRINCIPALS

In this section, we present three state codes of ethics. The first two codes specify guidelines for principal actions; the third specifies enforceable violations of the ethical code of conduct.

New York State Code of Ethics for Educators

Although most states have a code of ethics for educators, the code may or may not be used in conjunction with disciplinary action toward educators. The case in New York is that the code cannot be used in any disciplinary action toward an employee. The New York code, adopted in 2002, is as follows:

> The Code of Ethics is a public statement by educators that sets clear expectations and principles to guide practice and inspire professional excellence. Educators believe a commonly held set of principles can assist in the individual exercise of professional judgment. This Code speaks to the core values of the profession. "Educator" as used throughout means all educators serving New York schools in positions requiring a certificate, including classroom teachers, school leaders and pupil personnel service providers. It maintains six principles.
>
> *Principle 1:* Educators nurture the intellectual, physical, emotional, social, and civic potential of each student.
> *Principle 2:* Educators create, support, and maintain challenging learning environments for all.
> *Principle 3:* Educators commit to their own learning in order to develop their practice.
> *Principle 4:* Educators collaborate with colleagues and other professionals in the interest of student learning.

Principle 5: Educators collaborate with parents and community, building trust and respecting confidentiality.

Principle 6: Educators advance the intellectual and ethical foundation of the learning community.

North Carolina Code of Ethics for Educators

The North Carolina State Board of Education adopted its Code of Ethics for educators in 1997. It has three principles related to responsibilities to the student, the school system, and the profession. The purpose of the North Carolina Code of Ethics is to define standards of professional conduct:

> The responsibility to teach and the freedom to learn, and the guarantee of equal opportunity for all are essential to the achievement of these principles. The professional educator acknowledges the worth and dignity of every person and demonstrates the pursuit of truth and devotion to excellence, acquires knowledge, and nurtures democratic citizenship. The educator exemplifies a commitment to the teaching and learning processes with accountability to the students, maintains professional growth, exercises professional judgment, and personifies integrity. The educator strives to maintain the respect and confidence of colleagues, students, parents and legal guardians, and the community, and to serve as an appropriate role model. To uphold these commitments, the educator must have (a) a commitment to the student, (b) a commitment to the School and School System, and (c) a commitment to the profession.

Texas Educator Code of Ethics

The Code of Ethics and Standard Practices for Texas Educators was rewritten in 2002 by the State Board for Educator Certification (SBEC), the entity responsible for enforcing the Code of Ethics. According to SBEC, it was difficult to enforce much of the old code because it was ambiguous. The new code endeavors to provide a more specific statement of the conduct that is expected from Texas educators.

Textbox 15.1 Enforceable Standard from Texas

Texas Code of Ethics: Enforceable Standards

I. Professional Ethical Conduct, Practices and Performance.

Standard 1.1. The educator shall not knowingly engage in deceptive practices regarding official policies of the school district or educational institution.

Standard 1.2. The educator shall not knowingly misappropriate, divert or use monies, personnel, property or equipment committed to his or her charge for personal gain or advantage.

Standard 1.3. The educator shall not submit fraudulent requests for reimbursement, expenses or pay.

Standard 1.4. The educator shall not use institutional or professional privileges for personal or partisan advantage.

Standard 1.5. The educator shall neither accept nor offer gratuities, gifts, or favors that impair professional judgment or to obtain special advantage. This standard shall not restrict the acceptance of gifts or tokens offered and accepted openly from students, parents, or other persons or organizations in recognition or appreciation of service.

Standard 1.6. The educator shall not falsify records, or direct or coerce others to do so.

Standard 1.7. The educator shall comply with state regulations, written local school board policies and other applicable state and federal laws.

Standard 1.8. The educators shall apply for, accept, offer, or assign a position or a responsibility on the basis of professional qualifications.

II. Ethical Conduct Toward Professional Colleagues.

Standard 2.1. The educator shall not reveal confidential health or personnel information concerning colleagues unless disclosure serves lawful professional purposes or is required by law.

Standard 2.2. The educator shall not harm others by knowingly making false statements about a colleague or the school system.

Standard 2.3. The educator shall adhere to written local school board policies and state and federal laws regarding the hiring, evaluation, and dismissal of personnel.

Standard 2.4. The educator shall no interfere with a colleague's exercise of political, professional or citizenship rights and responsibilities.

Standard 2.5. The educator shall not discriminate against or coerce a colleague on the basis of race, color, religion, national origin, age, sex, disability, or family status.

Standard 2.6. The educator shall not use coercive means or promise of special treatment in order to influence professional decisions or colleagues.

Standard 2.7. The educator shall not retaliate against any individual who has filed a complaint with the SBEC under this chapter.

III. Ethical Conduct Toward Students.

Standard 3.1. The educator shall not reveal confidential information concerning students unless disclosure serves lawful professional purposes or is required by law.

Standard 3.2. The educator shall not knowingly treat a student in a manner that adversely affects the student's learning, physical health, mental health or safety.

Standard 3.3. The educator shall not deliberately or knowingly misrepresent facts regarding a student.

Standard 3.4. The educator shall not exclude a student from participation in a program, deny benefits to a student, or grant an advantage to a student on the basis of race, color, sex, disability, national origin, religion, or family status.

Standard 3.5. The educator shall not engage in physical mistreatment of a student.

Standard 3.6. The educator shall not solicit or engage in sexual conduct or a romantic relationship with a student.

Standard 3.7. The educator shall not furnish alcohol or illegal/unauthorized drugs to any student or knowingly allow any student to consume alcohol or illegal/unauthorized drugs in the presence of the educator.

The revised Texas code, shown in textbox 15.1, outlines a comprehensive and enforceable set of ethical standards. (The statement of purpose, which is not enforceable, gives general ethical guidelines for educators.) The first two principles in the old code (principle 1, "professional ethical conduct," and principle 2, "professional practices and performance") have been merged into a new, broader principle, "professional ethical conduct, practices and performance." Additionally, old principle 5 ("ethical conduct toward parents and community") has been removed. The rationale for this was that the items in principle 5 did not properly and clearly identify the standards of conduct required of educators in an enforceable manner.

PSEL AND NELP STANDARDS

Policymakers and other constituents of PK–12 schools are holding school principals accountable for the academic success and well-being of every student in their care. School principals must provide clear evidence that all students are being better prepared for college, careers, and life. All principals are charged with the same fundamental challenge: support every student's learning and development.

Clear and consistent leadership standards can help principals understand these expectations (Canole & Young, 2013). The Council for Chief State School Officers (CCSSO) and the National Policy Board for Educational Administration (NPBEA) have led the effort to revise the national standards that guide the preparation programs and practice of school principals. The NELP campus-level standards are appropriate for graduate programs at the masters and doctoral levels that prepare principals. These standards provide a framework for understanding how to best prepare, support, and evaluate school principals in their efforts to help every child reach their full potential.

CCSSO crafted the first set of national standards for educational leaders known as the Interstate School Leaders Licensure Consortium (ISLLC) standards in 1996, followed by a modest update in 2008. Both versions provided frameworks for policy on education leadership at the state level for nearly twenty years.

Educators now have a better understanding of how and in what ways leadership contributes to student achievement. An expanding research base demonstrates that principals exert influence on student achievement by creating challenging and supportive conditions that are conducive to each student's learning. Given such knowledge, it is clear that principals needed new standards to guide their practice in directions that will be the most beneficial to students.

In November 2015, the Professional Standards for Educational Leaders (PSEL) were published by NPBEA. These standards, formerly known as the Interstate School Leaders Licensure Consortium (ISLLC) standards, articulate the knowledge and skills expected of school principals (Canole & Young, 2013; CCSSO, 1996; CCSSO, 2008). PSEL has "a stronger, clearer emphasis on students and student learning, outlining foundational principles of leadership to help ensure that each child is well-educated and prepared for the twenty-first century" (CCSSO, 2015, p. 2). "They are student-centric, outlining foundational principles of leadership to guide the practice of educational leaders so they can move the needle on student learning and achieve more equitable outcomes" (p. 1). The 2015 PSEL standards reflect the following leadership domains.

PSEL Standards.

1. Mission, Vision, and Improvement
2. Ethics and Professional Norms
3. Equity and Cultural Responsiveness
4. Curriculum, Instruction, and Assessment
5. Community of Care and Support for Students
6. Professional Capacity of School Personnel

7. Professional Community for Teachers and Staff
8. Meaningful Engagement of Families and Community
9. Operations and Management
10. School Improvement

Each of the standards emphasizes both academic success and student well-being. The PSEL standards have been adopted or adapted by many states to guide policies concerning the practice and improvement of school principals (e.g., licensure, evaluation, and professional learning policies).

In December 2015, a committee began developing a set of leadership preparation standards congruent to the PSEL. The preparation standards, formerly known as the Educational Leadership Constituent Council or ELCC standards, have been renamed the National Educational Leadership Preparation (NELP) standards and will be used to guide program design, accreditation review, and state program approval.

The NELP standards are aligned to the PSEL standards but serve a different purpose by providing greater specificity concerning performance expectations for principals. Whereas the PSEL standards define educational leadership broadly, the NELP standards specify what preparation program graduates should know and be able to do after completing a high-quality principal preparation program. Like the ELCC standards that preceded them, the NELP standards will be used to review principal preparation programs by the Council for the Accreditation of Educator Preparation (CAEP). There is one set of NELP standards for candidates preparing to become building principals and a second set of standards for candidates seeking to become district-level leaders. The National Policy Board for Educational Administration (NPBEA) published the NELP standards in 2018. The 2018 NELP standards reflect the following leadership domains.

NELP Standards.

1. Mission, Vision, and Improvement
2. Ethics and Professional Norms
3. Equity, Inclusiveness, and Cultural responsiveness
4. Learning and Instruction
5. Community and External Leadership
6. Operations and Management
7. Building Professional Capacity

The new NELP standards for building-level leaders reflect all of the elements of the 2011 ELCC standards for principals and the majority of elements from the PSEL standards. When compared to the 2011 ELCC standards for principals, there are several important additions. First, is the number of standards. The six content standards found in the 2011 ELCC standards have been expanded to seven in the NELP standards. The expansion enabled the NELP committee to develop standards that more closely reflect current understandings of school leadership, better align to the ten PSEL standards, and more clearly delineate several core leadership functions. For example, the 2011 ELCC standards addressed core values, professional norms, ethics, and equity within one standard (i.e., ELCC standard 6). The new NELP standards, like the 2015 PSEL standards, include one standard for ethics and professional norms (NELP standard 2) and one for equity, inclusiveness, and cultural responsiveness (NELP standard 3). These changes delineate expectations for educational leaders not present in the previous ELCC standards, such as developing the knowledge and "capacity to evaluate, communicate about, and advocate for ethical and legal decisions" (NELP standard 2, component 2) and the knowledge and "capacity to evaluate, cultivate, and advocate for equitable, inclusive, and culturally responsive instruction and behavior support practices among teachers and staff" (NELP standard 3, component 3). Although CAEP includes the notion of ethical practice in its CAEP unit standards and a focus on diversity among its core principles, it is essential that educational leadership preparation standards address ethics and diversity in ways that attend to the specific professional responsibilities of school principals. As such, they are included within the NELP leadership standards and stated in terms of appropriate educational leadership candidate professional actions.

Second, the NELP standards expand ELCC's concern for supporting "the success of every student" to promoting the "current and future success and well-being of each student and adult." The focus on each student and each adult reflects the focus on individual needs within the PSEL standards, which assert that when a leader meets the needs of each individual, no subgroup will be missed.

A third difference in the 2018 NELP standards is the addition of the building-level leaders' responsibility for the well-being of students and staff as well as their role in working with others to create a supportive and inclusive school culture. In addition to being included in each of the standard stem statements, this focus is found within components 2.1, 3.2, 4.3, and 7.2.

Fourth, the NELP standards articulate the principal's role in ensuring equitable access to educational resources and opportunities. Standard 3, which is a new standard with three components, focuses on gaining "the knowledge, skills, and commitments necessary to develop and maintain a supportive, equitable, culturally responsive, and inclusive school culture." In addition to standard 3, equity is also addressed in 4.2, 4.4, and 6.2.

A fifth difference between ELCC and NELP standards is the NELP standards' stronger focus on assessment. For example, standard 4, component 3 focuses on the leaders' role in evaluating, developing, and implementing formal and informal culturally responsive and accessible assessments that support instructional improvement and student learning and well-being. Additionally, standard 4, component 4 requires program completers to understand and demonstrate the capacity to collaboratively evaluate, develop, and implement the school's curriculum, instruction, and assessment practices in a coherent, equitable, and systematic manner.

Sixth, in contrast to ELCC, the 2018 NELP standards (component 6.3) require building-level leaders to "reflectively evaluate, communicate about, and implement laws, rights, policies, and regulations to promote student and adult success" but does not expect building-level leaders to act to influence those laws, rights, policies, and regulations.

A seventh difference between the 2018 NELP standards and the 2011 ELCC standards is the expanded focus of standard 7, component 1. This component expects building-level leaders to "develop the school's professional capacity through engagement in recruiting, selecting, and hiring staff." This expectation greatly expands upon the 2011 ELCC element 6.2, which only expected leaders to "understand and sustain a school culture and instructional program conducive to student learning."

514 ■ Chapter 15: The Principal and Ethics

Eighth, the NELP committee identified nine practices through which educational leaders achieve the expectations outlined in the standards. These nine key practices are consistently used throughout the NELP standards and their components. They include developing, implementing, evaluating, collaborating, communicating, modeling, reflecting, advocating, and cultivating. Importantly, several of these key practices (i.e., developing, implementing, evaluating) are essential for school improvement (Bryk et al., 2010).

SUMMARY

1. The ethical principal is one who, in the face of adversity, ambiguity, and challenge, will reflect on what is right by some set standard or code and will act in a rational and caring manner to resolve problems and conduct business.
2. Ethical principals must be able to enable followers to use many of their innate talents in pursuing the school goals and mission.
3. Ethical principals must be concerned with the following philosophical concepts: (a) rights, (b) freedom, (c) responsibility, (d) duty, (e) justice, (f) equity, (g) authority, (h) caring, (i) character, (j) commitment, (k) conflict of interest, (l) formality, (m) loyalty, and (n) prudence.
4. Ethical principals have a responsibility to respect the rights of others, as moral decision makers and as role models, but disagreement occurs about what rights should apply in a given situation or what constitutes violation of another person's rights.
5. The principal is responsible to all individuals on the campus to ensure the right of personal security.
6. Personal liberty is seen as an absolute right; however, in the case of schools it may become a prima facie right because it would be overridden if within the personal liberty there is potential harm or harassment to others or there is an endangerment of the equal rights of others.
7. Negative human rights are life, physical property, due process, privacy, autonomy, freedom of thought and expression; positive human rights include food, adequate housing, competent medical care, employment at a living wage, and education.
8. Particular rights are dependent upon specific circumstances; for example, a person who is promised a specific thing has the right to receive it.
9. Freedom is related closely to the exercise of rights and is aligned in Americans' minds with the notions of liberty, independence, and individuality.
10. Principals do not stand in a confidential relationship with others.
11. Authority is the power to influence the behavior of others.
12. Prima facie duties are (a) fidelity, (b) reparation, (c) gratitude, (d) justice, (e) beneficence, (f) self-improvement, and (g) non-maleficence. Other duties that may take precedence in the school arena over the prima facie duties are (a) duty to students, (b) duty to colleagues, (c) duty to discipline, (d) duty to the school team, (e) duty to the

profession, (f) duty to funding sources, (g) duty to parents, and (h) duty to community.

13. There are concerns for principals in dealing with justice; such concerns include the equal treatment of non-equals or the unequal treatment of equals. Equity is the bending of the rules to fit the situation. This definition implies treating equals equally and non-equals unequally to level the playing fields, but not to the point of being unfair.

14. Caring principals develop meaningful relationships and inspire others to excellence. Character is closely associated with caring; if a principal is perceived to have a good character, then they have exhibited behavior such as honesty, courage, dependability, and generosity, and acceptable motivations.

15. Commitment is related to character in that the principal must be committed to doing the right thing. Commitment is related to dependability.

16. A conflict of interests is a situation in which the principal would have a competing professional or personal interest that would make it difficult to fulfill his or her duties fairly.

17. Loyalty generally refers to faithfulness, devotion, and allegiance to a leader, person, group, ideal, cause, or duty.

18. Prudence refers to the exercise of good judgment, common sense, and even caution, especially in the conduct of practical matters. Principals must remember that their actions have influence on people.

19. The community looks to high school and junior high school principals to monitor the ethical behavior of the coaches and players on their campuses.

20. The *Character Education Manifesto* principles could serve as a guide or map for principals and teachers to develop a campus manifesto and curriculum on character education.

21. The school principal is the most important person on the campus to promote and model ethical behavior and to implement policies that support an appropriate standard of conduct. As the principal goes, so goes the school.

22. There are national and state codes of ethics. Most of these codes are unenforceable and serve as guides for ethical behavior by the principal.

23. In 2015, the Professional Standards for Educational Leaders (PSEL) were published. These standards, formerly known as the Interstate School Leaders Licensure Consortium (ISLLC) standards articulate the knowledge and skills expected of school principals.

24. In 2018, CAEP developed a set of leadership preparation standards congruent to the PSEL. The preparation standards, formerly known as the Educational Leadership Constituent Council (ELCC) standards, have been renamed the National Educational Leadership Preparation (NELP) standards and will be used to guide program design, accreditation review, and state program approval.

KEY TERMS

ethical principal
rights
freedom
responsibility
authority
duty
justice
procedural justice
substantive justice
retributive justice
remedial justice
distributive justice

equity
caring
character
commitment
formality
conflict of interest
loyalty
prudence
critique
profession
character education

FIELD-BASED ACTIVITIES

1. Look in back issues of the newspaper over the past several months, and find three examples of unethical or ethical behavior. Determine which principle or concept has been upheld or violated.
2. Review the curriculum at your school. Determine if character education is present and if the principles in the *Character Education Manifesto* are present. Design and conduct a study to determine if character education would be something that the community would support.
3. (a) Conduct a self-assessment; then have teachers on your team complete it. How do the ratings compare? Is your team compatible in relation to ethical thought? (b) Review your state ethical codes for principals or educators. Are there enforceable codes for your state?

SUGGESTED READINGS

Branson, C. M., & Gross, S. J. (2014). *Handbook of ethical leadership.* New York, NY: Routledge. The authors provide a rigorous yet practical approach to the difficult dilemmas that so often arise in school administration. Case studies are used to illustrate ethical issues.

Johnson, C. E. (2017). *Meeting the challenge of leadership: Casting light or shadow.* Thousand Oaks, CA: Sage. All principals assume ethical burdens and must make every effort to make informed ethical decisions and foster ethical behavior among followers.

Rebore, R. W. (2014). *The ethics of educational leadership.* Boston, MA: Pearson. The works of important philosophers provide the basis for development of the ethical principles presented in this book, including those dealing with gender equity, social justice, and educational administration policies.

Shapiro, J. P., & Stefkovich, J. A. (2016). *Ethical leadership and decision making in education: Applying theoretical perspectives to complex dilemmas.* New York, NY: Routledge. The authors aim at awakening educators to inequities in society and, in particular, in the schools. This ethic asks educators to deal with the questions regarding social class, race, gender, and other areas of difference, such as: Who makes the laws? Who benefits from the law, rule, or policy? Who has the power? Who are the silenced voices?

Starratt, R. J. (2004). *Ethical Leadership.* San Francisco, CA: Jossey-Bass. Starratt argues for much greater attention to ethical education and responds to skeptics who say that schools cannot be ethical in the face of a pluralistic, secular society that is badly fragmented over values. The author provides a conceptual foundation for ethical education broad enough for building consensus among teachers and parents, yet focused enough to provide guidance for highly specific learning activities. He presents a series of steps by which a school community might proceed in building an ethical school. The author shares exciting initiatives in ethical education.

Strike, K., Haller, E. J., & Soltis, J. F. (2005). *The ethics of school administration* (3rd ed.). New York: Teachers College Press. This book is designed to help teach a range of ethical concepts that are important to the practicing principal. It includes case studies and detailed analyses that include information and skills needed for a knowledgeable approach to thinking through the ethical problems encountered in schools.

16
Political and Policy Context

■ ■ ■

FOCUSING QUESTIONS

1. How does society affect policy and political occurrences in schools?
2. How is the principal's role impacted by the politics surrounding the creation and implementation of educational policies?
3. What is policy?
4. What is meant by politics?
5. What role does politics play in the relationship between the principal and the superintendent in the operation of a school district?

In this chapter, we respond to these questions concerning the principal's role in the political and policy context. We begin the chapter with a discussion of the connection between society and policy and political occurrences in schools. Then we examine more specifically the principal's role as it relates to politics and policy formulation and implementation. Next, we explore what is meant by policy. This is followed by a discussion of politics in general and the role of the principal in politics. Finally, we conclude the chapter with a discussion of politics within the school district, specifically the role that politics plays in principals' working relationship with their superintendents.

SOCIETY, POLICY, AND POLITICS

Because we address in this chapter both the encounters a principal may have with policy and politics within an ever-changing and diverse society and a framework for understanding policy and politics, we begin with a lengthy and relevant quote from John Dewey's *The School and Society* (1907). More than one hundred years ago, Dewey viewed a changing society as directly connected with the policy and political occurrences in schools. Dewey's observations related to the politics of his day and still linger today within surmounting national and world events that impact schools daily. The cyclical relationship between society's needs, social justice, and education exists today as it did so many years ago. Consider that Dewey's thoughts were published at the turn of the twentieth century and more than one hundred years later, the context in which we find ourselves is, again as Dewey noted, a social revolution affecting education.

Whenever we have in mind the discussion of a new movement in education, it is especially necessary to take the broader, or social view. Otherwise, changes in the school institution and tradition will be looked at as the arbitrary inventions of particular teachers—at the worst, transitory fads and, at the best, merely improvements in certain details—and this is the plane upon which it is too customary to consider school changes. The modification going on in the method and curriculum of education is as much a product of the changed social situation, and as much an effort to meet the needs of the new society that is forming, as are changes in modes of industry and commerce.

It is to this, then, that I especially ask your attention: the effort to conceive what roughly may be termed the "New Education" in the light of larger changes in society. Can we connect this "New Education" with the general march of events?

I make no apology for not dwelling at length upon the social changes in question. Those I shall mention are writ so large that he who runs may read. The change that comes first to mind, the one that overshadows and even controls all others, is the industrial one—the application of science resulting in the great inventions that have utilized the forces of nature on a vast and inexpensive scale: the growth of a worldwide market as the object of production, of vast manufacturing centers to supply this market, of cheap and rapid means of communication and distribution between all its parts. Even as to its feebler beginnings, this change is not much more than a century old; in many of its most important aspects it falls within the short span of those now living. One can hardly believe there has been a revolution in all history so rapid, so extensive, so complete. Through it the face of the earth is making over, even as to its physical forms; political boundaries are wiped out and moved about, as if they were indeed only lines on a paper map; population is hurriedly gathered into cities from the ends of the earth; habits of living are altered with startling abruptness and thoroughness; the search for the truths of nature is infinitely stimulated and facilitated and their application to life made not only practicable, but commercially necessary. Even our moral and religious ideas and interests, the most conservative because the deepest-lying things in our nature, are profoundly affected. That this revolution should not affect education in other than formal and superficial fashion is inconceivable. (Dewey, 1907, pp. 19–22)

To understand national, state, and local societal contexts as they relate to the politics of schooling, we believe that it is important for principals to consider an historical perspective first. Landmark events that have taken place in the latter part of the twentieth century mark changes that force leaders to take notice and work within a more diverse system than that of the 1940s and early 1950s. *Brown v. Board of Education of Topeka* is now more than a half-century old, and the marvel of it is that it forced schools to become the setting for change in the broader society related to civil rights. With the advent of Sputnik, the Soviet Union's Earth-orbiting satellite program, a new era was launched for the educational leader. Prior to Sputnik, leaders were not forced to consider *differentiation within the curriculum* for students who excelled in science or math.

In 1964, the Civil Rights Act was passed. For principals of today, this act still beckons them daily to consider *equity* in educational curricular and extracurricular activities related not only to race, but also to religion, national origin, color, and sex. In the mid-1960s the federal Elementary and Secondary Education Act forced principals to pay attention and address issues revolving around those who are *socioeconomically disadvantaged* and as a result may be *academically disadvantaged*. Even students performing above the mark received little attention in terms of political and educational reforms.

Sputnik and the legislative and judicial acts passed in subsequent years launched the 1972 Maryland definition of *gifted*—yet with minimal effect, as evidenced by the lack of federal legislation mandating a differentiated curriculum for gifted students. In the early 1970s, the Equal Rights Amendment was passed, but not ratified by all states until 1982; this legislation brought about more awareness related to another *equity* issue among leaders in education, who at that time were predominately male. Equity issues were added to the curricular and extracurricular issues related to *gender*. In the mid-1970s landmark legislation, Public Law 94-142 was passed; subsequent revisions have continued to develop. This law compelled leaders to adopt a different educational view of *children with disabilities* and to fully include these children in the public schools.

In the early 1980s, with the release of the landmark government report, *A Nation at Risk*, leaders were thrown into an age of *accountability and data-driven decision making* to an extent that had never before been experienced in schools. The 1990s brought about more change, with an influx of immigrants who spoke little or no English. The surge of immigrants affected principals in regard to curriculum, program choices, service delivery, and philosophical issues surrounding the *English language learner.*

The year 1999 and Columbine brought to the forefront school violence, jolting principals into strong consideration of safe school environments. September 11, 2001, followed soon after, and leaders tightened security to make schools even safer.

The enactment of No Child Left Behind (NCLB) of 2001 followed by Every Student Succeeds Act (ESSA) of 2015 placed education near the top of the national policy agenda. The federal law nationalized the discussion concerning the well-being of public schooling in America. At the time the reports were released and subsequently, there has been a concern with the achievement gap in America (Barton & Coley, 2010; Darling-Hammond, 2010; DuFour et al., 2010; Entwisle, Alexander, & Olson, 2010; Howard, 2020, Ladson-Billings, 2006; Lee & Bowen, 2006; Murphy, 2010; Nieto, 2002/2003; Ogbu, 2003; Paige, 2011; Rothstein, 2004; Singham, 2005; Sirin, 2003; Teranishi, Nguyen, & Curammeng, 2020; Wiggan, 2007) and our academic competitiveness with other nations, particularly in reading, mathematics, and science (US Department of Education, 2008). These achievement gaps and academic comparisons have led many people to conclude that the US public school system was underperforming. With recognition of an achievement gap and the rise of international educational comparisons, states began to focus their policy on standards, accountability, and the improvement of student academic achievement.

Political events and social issues affecting education today have been evolving for more than fifty years. These changes and events have created the more complex and politically charged school environments in which today's principals must lead.

Policy, Politics, and the Principal

Cooper, Cibulka, and Fusarelli (2015) state that principals must be knowledgeable and cognizant of the politics surrounding the creation and implementation of educational policies. They must be aware of the macro-level forces and actors; this means that principals must be very conscious of national, state, and even local events as their foundation and range. The scope of policymaking and politics is large, considering that it includes the federal government with new administrations in the White House potentially every four years, the federal and state courts, fifty state legislatures, and local school boards. This does not include the fifty state educational and certification agencies that develop procedures for the policies and, in doing so, sometimes make additional and layered policies.

In describing principals and their involvement in the macro politics and policy, we could begin with "once upon a time," because once upon a time, prior to the 1990s, the principal was basically isolated from politics and dealt only with policy. In the 1990s, things changed. School reforms began breaking up the isolation of principals within the four walls of their campuses. Principals became more connected, more involved. For example, under site-based decision making and management, a principal might find themselves dealing directly with the city council or the legislators (Fowler, 2013). Thus, enter policy and politics.

WHAT IS POLICY?

Simply put, **policy** is the outgrowth of governmental actions. It is courses of purposive action directed towards the accomplishment of some intended or desired set of goals (Bardoch & Patashnik, 2020). It is what governments choose to do or not to do, which could indicate that what governments do not do is of equal importance in making policy (Allen, Reupert, & Oades, 2021).

Cooper and colleagues (2015) provide a comprehensive definition of policy as "a political process where needs, goals, and intentions are translated into a set of objectives, laws, policies, and programs, which in turn affect resource allocations, actions, and outputs, which are the basis for evaluation, reforms, and new policies" (p. 3).

According to Duemer and Mendez-Morse (2002), "Once an individual or policy-making body sets a policy, there is no guarantee that it will be implemented in the same way it was originally intended. The difference between institutions and individuals is central to understanding how policy can change from development to implementation" (p. 1). These authors discussed the connection of policy to implementation of a specific policy based on the role of the individual. The principal's connection to policy is at the local campus level, the district level, the state level, and to some extent the national level. The principal's role is related to policy in the following ways: (a) orientation, (b) degree, (c) resources, (d) activity, (e) autonomy, (f) societal values, (g) institutional values, (h) rationale, and (i) power relationship.

Duemer and Mendez-Morse (2002) explain each of these nine areas in the form of questions that could be asked of the principal with respect to his involvement in developing and adopting policy. The questions imply an active role for the principal in policy development and adoption—a role that has not often been observed in the past. The following nine sections offer a summary of Deumer and Mendez-Morse's areas and questions.

Orientation
Orientation refers to one's position with respect to attitude, judgment, inclination, or interest. Was the principal supportive, oppositional, or neutral toward the policy in question? Did the principal voice her stance on the policy?

Degree

Degree is the scale of intensity or amount. To what degree did the principal support or oppose the policy? Did the principal share their opposition or support with others in the organization? What means of communication did they use to do this? To whom did they communicate the stance on the policy? If the principal opposed the policy, to what degree did they attempt to obstruct or alter its implementation?

Resources

Resources refer to action, money, influence, information, expertise, or measures that can be brought to bear in order to influence or use. What resources were available to the principal that could be used to help or hinder implementation? What types of resources did the principal expend on this policy? What resources were specifically used in communicating the policy?

Activity

Activity is the specific deed, action, or function; use of force, influence, or process. What communication actions did the principal take to support or obstruct policy? How much communication activity did the principal expend to support or obstruct policy? With whom did the principal interact during these communication activities?

Autonomy

Autonomy relates to the degree of independence; how closely one has to adhere to prescribed guidelines. A high degree of support or opposition will not have had much impact on expense of energy and resources if the principal had little autonomy to exert influence on policy. What level of autonomy does the principal have in their position? How does the principal's position influence the communication modes available to them?

Societal Values

Societal values are the ideals or customs for which people have an affective regard. How did societal values influence implementation? To what extent did the principal accept or reject specific societal values that influenced implementation? How did the principal's actions or decisions change the societal climate?

Institutional Values

Institutional values refer to professional ideals or customs for which members have an affective regard. How did institutional values influence implementation? How are the institutional values communicated to the principal? To what extent did the principal accept or reject specific institutional values that influenced implementation? How did the principal's actions or decisions change the institutional climate? How did the institutional climate change the principal's actions or decisions?

Rationale

Rationale means the fundamental, underlying reasons to account for something. What explanation does the principal provide for his orientation toward the policy? Does the principal have superseding interests, loyalties, or values that conflict with the policy? What ethical concerns does the principal have related to the policy?

Power Relationship

Power relationship is the degree of status relative to the principal's position. What type of communication, both informal and formal, occurred between same or different power levels?

Principals must use the previous questions to:

1. Establish a framework that is informative about their perspectives toward policy and policy implementation
2. Establish a relationship to policy implementation on individual terms
3. Recognize that the relationship between the principal and the organization is reciprocal rather than unidirectional
4. Include issues of both informal and formal means of communication
5. Take into account societal and institutional contexts through investigating communication lines that influence principals
6. Consider that principals change institutions through actions, decisions, and participation in both informal and formal means of communication.

(Duemer & Mendez-Morse, 2002)

THE EXAMINATION OF POLICY

Principals are obligated to analyze and understand policy. Cooper and colleagues (2015) suggest that examining policy through multiple lenses and frameworks could assist principals in discussing policy, planning it, and implementing it in practice. This type of examination also aids in understanding the impact that practice, growing from policy, might have on individuals in a school. We present seven theories by which principals can examine policy.

Systems Theory

The analysis of policy through systems theory provides a holistic look at the policy itself. It allows principals to analyze the "policy 'inputs' including demands, needs, and resources, the 'throughputs' that involve the key actors who implement policy, and policy 'outputs' such as educated, civic-minded students or improved economic productivity" (Cooper et al., 2015, p. 9). Principals can use **systems theory** to analyze policy and its impact on student achievement in relation to the entire school unit and community, and they can analyze that relationship with respect to the whole school district and state and federal rules and regulations. A model of systems theory analysis at the local district level is seen in figure 16.1.

Neopluralist Advocacy Coalition and Interest Group Theories

Neopluralist advocacy coalition theory and **interest group theory** are grounded in a political science perspective that seeks to answer "who gets what, when, and how" as key coalitions struggle to obtain from government the resources and support they believe necessary. These key actors (legislators, governors, mayors, superintendents, school boards, etc.) work out their interest group concerns in a variety of arenas, depending on the level in the federalist system (federal, state, county, city, school district, and individual schools). Bringing interest groups and their arenas together provides a useful means of understanding how laws are passed, shaped, implemented, and evaluated. (Cooper et al., 2015, p. 9)

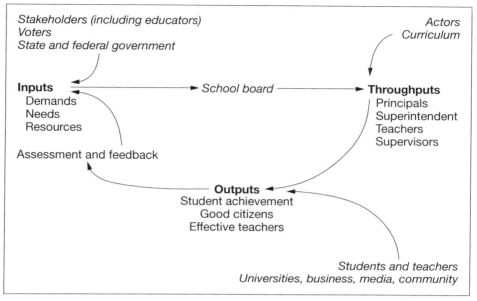

Figure 16.1 Model of System Theory Analysis of Policy

Neopluralist advocacy coalitions and interest groups are organizations or groups that seek to influence the development and application of policy (Harman, 2001); they communicate needs to decision makers, structure alternative policy choices, act as buffers between government and the wider community, check demands made by others, and compartmentalize access to decision makers (Froman, 1966). During the policy process as the issues emerge and agendas are set; during the review of options and policy development; during the policy decision, authorization, and implementation; and during policy review, termination, replacement, or redirection—the potential for interest group influence is not only at a single key decision point, but during each stage in the policy process (Harman, 2001).

Under analysis of policy herein, the principal must pay careful attention to advocacy groups and become savvy to how various coalitions are playing the political game to achieve their policy objectives. The principal will need to be able to read the political groups and the actors to determine the impact of that conflict as policy is developed upon the degree to which, and the time in which, campus goals and objectives can be accomplished.

Neoinstitutional Theory

Neoinstitutional theory indicates that the "structure of societal and political organizations exerts independent effects on policy" (Cooper et al., 2015, p. 9). "This theory emphasizes routines, imitation, unreflective responses, custom and normative practices, and convergence of organizational forms; it deemphasizes power and conflict" (Perrow, 2002, p. 19).

Neoinstitutional theory helps principals to understand why hegemonic practices may exist within the school or district. To understand policy, principals must understand the political institutions that enact and enforce the laws and regulations and the relationship to the schools and classrooms where the laws are carried out.

The principal can work with their state legislative representatives to determine what policies are being proposed or enacted. The principal may even assist the legislator to understand the impact the policy may have at the local school level.

The principal needs to anticipate the change associated with new legislation, whether at the state or national level, but understand that, under this theory, the legislative body, the school board, or the district officials may not determine that alternatives to education are legitimate and may conform to customary organizational or societal norms and practices. At times, when the principal is up against this situation and at the same time is seeking to offer alternative inputs for new policy based on analysis and feedback of the learners, they may not have any fruition of their ideas. It may be a time when the principal's norms are not in line with that of the policymaking body, and it may be a time for the principal to seek employment in a district that is aligned with their own values. Therefore, this theory analysis has a byproduct in that principals can determine their fit within the organization by understanding this theory within the framework of their school's policy development and adoption.

Critical Theory

Critical theory "questions the existing economic, political, and social purposes of schooling and examines policy through the lens of oppressed groups, with a normative orientation toward freeing disenfranchised groups from conditions of domination and subjugation" (Cooper et al., 2015, p. 9). This theory is concerned with equity and social justice analyses of policy. It tries to discover the "hidden uses of power through which policy is transformed into practice" (p. 9). The principal can work to shape policy based on equitable power structures related to class, culture, ethnicity, and language; analyze policies related to the social structure of his campus; and engage in understanding how the policy reflects inclusion or exclusion.

Feminist Theory

"**Feminist theory** is concerned primarily with the often unequal effects of education policies on issues relating to gender and sexual difference, including how education policies are translated through institutional processes that serve to reinforce or encourage gender inequity" (Cooper et al., 2015, p. 9). The principal must seek to analyze policies and outgrowths of practice from the policies in relation to gender equities or inequities. Such analyses may include an examination of such issues as (a) salaries for male and female teachers, administrators, and coaches; (b) job opportunities for both genders; and (c) sports equity for boys and girls with regard to facilities, spending, and opportunities.

Postmodernism

Postmodernism "argues that policy is contextually defined by those in authority and has little validity when separated from its setting" (Cooper et al., 2015, p. 9). This theory suggests that the scientific posturing in policy analysis only serves to perpetuate the highly racist, sexist, and class nature of most policies. Furthermore, it implies that schools do not progress due to the policies in place that support the privileged to maintain the status quo; this translates to keeping the upper-class, White, male leadership in power at the expense of the poor, women, people of color, and recent immigrants.

Skrla and Scheurich (2003) provide direction for principals. They ask questions that can be asked and investigated by principals. By what process did a particular problem emerge, or better, how did a particular problem come to be seen as a problem? What makes the emergence of a particular problem possible? Why do some "problems" become identified as social problems while other "problems" do not achieve that level of identification? They focused principals on prior conditions of the policy—the politics of the policy.

Ideological Theories of Policymaking

Ideological theories "place policy into a partisan, politically value-laden structure, hoping to gain insight into the econo-political context surrounding key policies" (Cooper et al., 2015, p. 10). This theory seeks to determine if a policy is associated with the liberal left or the conservative right. Political parties and federal judges have used "ideological theories (rather than upon legitimate considerations of the quality of education) to justify racial assignments and the deprivation of true equal opportunity for all students, including the gifted students who have such great potential to enrich American life" (Hardaway, 1995, p. 149).

For this kind of analysis, the principal need only look at the political party platforms and those in power for national trends in policy. Lyndon Johnson promoted liberal policies, including compensatory education, equity, and help for disadvantaged, at-risk students; Reagan promoted the legislating of choice, markets, higher standards, and vouchers (Cooper et al., 2015). Locally, then, the principal should become familiar with the superintendent's and the school board members' agenda to anticipate potential policy changes and their impact on the campus.

CONCEPTUAL FRAMEWORK FOR UNDERSTANDING POLICY

The previously discussed theories for examining policy help principals analyze their place and the school's place within policy, as well as to analyze the specific aspects of policies. To understand policies, principals can review the conceptual framework of four dimensions: (1) normative dimension, (2) structural dimension, (3) constituentive dimension, and (4) technical dimension (Cooper et al., 2015).

Normative Dimension

The **normative dimension** includes beliefs, values, and ideologies that drive societies to seek improvement and change. Diesing (1965) indicated there are four general criteria for judging the effect of a policy decision within a normative dimension: (1) the ability of the policy to reconcile or harmonize conflicting factors that blocked decision making; (2) the ability of the policy decision to increase toleration between various groups and their respective beliefs and values; (3) the decision's ability to establish balance between differing groups; and (4) the decision's ability itself to reject, repress, or otherwise exclude the threatening factors from the policy. Policies that are the expressed ideals of the society are considered to be normative in nature. Postmodernism and ideological theories are included in this dimension.

Structural Dimension

The **structural dimension** includes the "governmental arrangements, institutional structure, systems, and processes that promulgate and support policies in education"

(Cooper et al., 2015, p. 43). The structural dimension reflects the motivation, needs, and objectives expressed by political ideas and ideologies. Principals can attempt to define and promote ideas and influence structures; the community and groups can encourage or reply to ideas and confirm or reject structures through their participation—especially, but hardly exclusively, in the context of political democracy (Cyr, 1997, p. 10). The roles and effects of local, state, and federal governmental structures definitely influence the way educational policy is created. Neoinstitutional theory enlightens research in the structural dimension.

Constituentive Dimension

The **constituentive dimension** includes

> theories of networks, elites, masses, interest groups, ethnic/gender groups, providers and "end users," and beneficiaries who influence, participate in, and benefit from the policymaking process. Issues needing to be addressed in this dimension include who has access to power, how these interest groups make their needs felt, and the degree to which competing interests can work out a compromise solution or have their needs met. (Cooper et al., 2015, pp. 43–44)

In this dimension, the constituent groups either favor or oppose the policies developed. Neopluralist advocacy coalitions and interest group models, as well as critical and feminist theories, are the focus of this dimension.

Technical Dimension

The **technical dimension** "includes educational planning, practice, implementation, and evaluation—the nuts and bolts of policymaking. Systems theory is useful to understand developments in this dimension as we trace the technical and instrumental effects of policies" (Cooper et al., 2015, p. 44).

Figure 16.2 depicts how policy is formulated from an issue through these four dimensions to adoption, to implementation, and finally to evaluation.

Cooper and colleagues (2015) made a point that the framework must be concerned with ethics and social justice. Considerations of injustice and equity must be reviewed by the principal in observing how policies are made as well as how policies

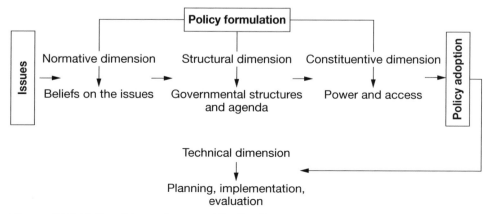

Figure 16.2 Policy Dimensions and Policy Process

affect the students they serve. Principals must consider a policy in regard to its context, impact, and future implications. What is the policy likely to yield for those in our society who are most needy and vulnerable? This is but one of the questions principals must ask themselves as they develop and review and evaluate, for example, policies related to funding, student achievement, teacher quality, technology, special programs, and/or curriculum.

Just as ethics and social justice enter into a principal's evaluation of policy, so does the concept of moral purpose as described by Fullan (2003). He indicates that leaders (principals) contribute for the better or worse to moral purpose in the schools and in society as a whole. Because, as Fullan suggests, moral purpose is about how humans evolve over time, especially regarding how they relate to each other, the evaluation of policy as it affects others is critical for a higher moral purpose.

Following are several examples of how social justice must enter into the evaluation of policy. In textbox 16.1, we share first an excerpt from Berliner and Biddle (1995) as they discuss the concept of intelligence and gifted education. The principal must consider the social justice or inequities brought out in the excerpt.

An example of ethics and justice related to policy recently occurred in a suburban school district and is still unresolved or unnoticed. A parent related to the authors that her daughter was participating in the high school band. They stated that there were numerous expenses incurred by this participation, in excess of $1,000. That was just the initial start-up fund for participation; there would be additional costs throughout the year, in addition to fund-raisers in which the child would be involved. So, what is the problem with ethics and justice in this school policy? The principal should be concerned with equity and justice under this policy. The parent who talked with them has the means to provide the extracurricular activity for her daughter; however, children who are, unfortunately, born into lesser financial conditions do not have this opportunity. The question becomes: Are there children from low-income families who are extremely talented and who would have their future in the musical field diminished via a public school policy that promotes and support a public school program giving benefits only to those with wealth who can afford it? The next question would be: What is the principal's role in promoting equal access to the band program for children of all financial circumstances? This policy, the way it currently is implemented, prohibits equal access and ultimately general access to future educational opportunities. This is similar to the arguments put forward by Berliner and Biddle (1995) in regard to gifted education and intelligence.

Another issue that mainly is identified by the time of adolescence is the issue of policy equity in counseling students. Both school policy and the students' own personal hindrances might prevent, for example, LGBTQ+ youth and rape or incest victims from being counseled. Traditionally, schools and communities are reluctant to broach such topics, admit such students' presence, or provide services for them. This presents a problem for the principals in that equitable services are negated by sheer neglect. Without the authority of explicit policy or law, individual school or social service personnel may fail to act because of moral or religious beliefs, fear of controversy, or being labeled "different" themselves (Lipkin, 1999). These types of controversial circumstances apply not only to policy but also to politics because the principal is, in each case, under the watchful eyes of the community in her implementation or interpretation of policy to her students, teachers, parents, and community constituents.

Textbox 16.1 Excerpt on Policy Implications for Gifted Education

Intelligence, Schooling, and Wealth. The implications of this revelation are disturbing. Consider, for example, the effects of wealth on intelligence. Rich parents in America often provide early experiences for their children that will make them smarter. Wealth allows those parents to purchase high-quality day care and to enroll their children in private preschools. It also permits them to purchase instructional toys, encyclopedias, computers, and first-rate health care—all of which are likely to improve a child's measured intelligence. This means that the sons and daughters of wealthy parents are likely to enter school with higher measured intelligence than that of the children of poor parents. This sounds bad if we believe in the ideal of equal opportunity for children, but there is worse. Since good schooling also leads to gains in intelligence, it follows that those children who attend "the best" schools will also gain the most. But since the quality of schools also varies greatly across the land, the growth of intelligence is not equal in America's schools. And in our country, children from rich families are much more likely than are children from poor families to attend "the best" schools—either because rich children are sent to private academies or because they attend well-funded public schools in affluent suburbs—and this means they will gain more in intelligence than will the sons and daughters of middle- or working-class families. (Such inequities in school funding appear less often in other Western countries, where private schools are fewer and public schools more often receive equal funding based on student enrollment.) Thus, in America we also allow the rich to "buy" intelligence-test points for their children through unequal school funding.

What Are the Implications for Educational Policy? In recent years, for example, the Bush and Clinton administrations both urged the states to adopt programs that would provide enriched educational experiences for students who are "truly gifted," and various states have obliged by passing laws setting up such programs. But intelligence tests are widely used to select students who are "truly gifted," and this means that children of the rich are far more likely to participate in such programs than are children of the poor. Many children from poor families could also profit from enrichment programs, but they cannot enter those programs because of the mistake they made at birth—they "chose" to be born to parents who were not wealthy! This is a problem for our democracy because we continue to preach that all people should have equal opportunities to rise through public schooling. Unfortunately, rising-through-schooling is probably happening less frequently in the present decade, in part because so many states have now instituted programs for the "truly gifted." The tests used to select students for these programs measure intelligence or other traits that reflect advantages that only wealthy parents can buy for their children. Such programs are inherently unfair. Other scholars have also made this point, of course, and we will have more to say later about special programs for "gifted" children. Here, we merely repeat that when high scores on intelligence tests are used to select students for enrichment programs, in the United States those programs always confer an unfair advantage on wealthy children. Our reasoning about wealth and intelligence also suggests that as the number of children living in poverty grows, as it did in the 1980s, the continuous rise in intelligence-test scores in this country is likely to stop. The cause for this will not be found in schools but in a society that imposes poverty on growing numbers of its young people. We would be willing to bet, however, that some critics will try to blame public schools for the coming IQ decline.

Summary. What, then, can we conclude from these studies of measured intelligence? First, today's children are smarter, not dumber, than their parents. Furthermore, the parents of today's children were also more intelligent than were their own parents, the grandparents of today's youth. Second, intelligence is affected not only by inheritance and early childhood experiences; schooling also affects IQ test performance. More and better schooling in the US and in other industrialized nations is the most likely reason for those nations' increases in IQ scores. High-quality instructional environments for toddlers, primary-school children, teenagers, and college students all seem to raise scores on IQ tests. Third, if wealthy people have better access than do poor people to high-quality education, as is the case so often in this country, then some children will do poorly and some will do well on IQ tests because of their parents' wealth rather than because of their genetic makeup or home environment.

Source: From *The manufactured crisis: Myths, fraud, and the attack on America's public schools* (pp. 49–50), by D. C. Berliner & B. Biddle, 1995, New York: Addison-Wesley.

WHAT IS MEANT BY *POLITICS*?

Politics and public education are inseparable. Since the mid-twentieth century, public education has been the setting for battles over race, class, and privilege. In *Webster's Dictionary*, the definitions of **politics** range from "the art and science of government" to "factional scheming for power." Elmore (2004) describes politics as occurring in an arena of conflict, where competing interest groups with different resources and capacities vie for influence to shape policy in their own image. Education is an arena of conflicting priorities and interests where politics manifests itself.

Most definitions of politics are rooted in a system of governance. If governance is the system of directing affairs or political administration, politics is a byproduct of that system. Our government is the structure, or machine, that we, the people, construct. The operation of the machine—the attempts to control the direction, speed, and function of the machine—is determined through politics. The not-so-favorable interpretations of politics arise from the fact that many differing factions would like to control the machine of governance, and there are an infinite number of interpretations of how it can and should be driven (Learning Points Associates, n.d.).

Added to this, societal conditions and demands are ever-changing. Because politics is an integral part of the operation of public education and the school campus, it is important for principals to understand the political milieu in which they work—not just in the obvious ways like election of school board members or, in some districts, local school councils, but in more integral, day-to-day ways.

As principals work within that political landscape, they might find Apple's (2018) work instructive. He suggests there are hegemonic groups in society who have been influential in setting public educational policy. Those groups he classifies as follows: (a) **neoliberals** who are relating schools to dollars and even marketing schools with voucher plans and tax credits; (b) **neoconservatives** who are deeply committed to establishing tighter mechanisms of control over knowledge, morals, and values through national or state curricula and national- or state-mandated reductive testing; (c) **authoritarian populists** who believe in a pedagogy that is based on traditional relations to authority where the teacher and the adults are always in control (they also believe that biblical authority should always supersede public policy); and (d) an upwardly mobile professional and managerial new middle class that thrives on **managerialism** and imposes policies of "steering at a distance" through national and state testing with tighter control through the use of industrial models, through cost/benefit analysis, and so on (this group is caught up in high-stakes testing). The bottom line is that these groups set agendas that establish connections between schools and the economy.

However, Apple (2018) also shares that there is another group, which he calls **"thick-visioned democrats"** (not the political party). He indicated they are concerned with issues involving the power of collective local decision making of the curriculum that is at the grass roots and that responds to the local needs, histories, and cultures of oppressed people, people of color, and economically disadvantaged people. This group advances a socially responsive pedagogy.

Schools and Politics

Moe and Chubb (2009) found that the most effective schools were characterized by a high level of professional autonomy at the individual building level, a condition that seldom exists in a highly politicized environment. In reality, the school is confronted with issues inextricably connected to their own political contexts. Too often, educational reform policy overlooks these connections, and educational innovations fail due to a lack of attention to the political context. The political context is often interference in policy implementation by the school board—or, more specifically, by individual members of the school board. For example, a principal in a rural district was attempting to do her job and was effectively having children succeed on benchmark tests for the state exam. They did something that individual members of the school board did not like. Consequently, they were contacted by two individual members who suggested strongly that they resign. The board president contacted the principal and told her to disregard the two previous contacts because, of course, they were in violation of the law. However, this brief example points out the political context in which the school resides; and in this case, the resulting interruption of consistent, effective leadership during the time of this event.

Politics or Policy?

It is difficult at times to distinguish between policy and politics. For example, the No Child Left Behind Act (NCLB) and its successor, Every Student Succeeds Act (ESSA), places teacher quality front and center for districts, campuses, and universities. Was it the politics or the policy? Whether teacher quality was an out-growth of politics or not, there is no doubt that teacher quality is the single most important factor influencing student achievement (Darling-Hammond & Oakes, 2019; Denicolo & Kompf, 2005; Reimers & Chung, 2021); therefore, the policy now dictates to principals that each classroom must house a highly qualified teacher. For the principal, the teaching community, and scholars, an imperative outgrowth of this policy is to determine what constitutes a highly qualified teacher. NCLB and ESSA indicates that a highly qualified teacher is simply one who has a degree in the subject area and certification as defined by her respective state.

We now enter politics again with policy talk. Cuban (2020) noted that there is a continual breach between *policy talk* and the world of daily school decisions. The author argued that most reforms exist mainly in the realm of **policy talk**—which amounts to visionary and authoritative statements about how schools should be different; is carried on among scholars and policymakers; and usually involves callous conclusions about students, teachers, superintendents, and principals. However, according to Elmore (2004), *policy talk* can be influential in shaping public perceptions of the quality of schooling and what should be done about it; yet, policy talk hardly ever influences the deep-seated and enduring structures and practices of schooling, which he called the school's "instructional core."

TYPES OF EDUCATIONAL POLITICS

Bryk et al. (1998) and Bryk (2020) indicate that, in the past, local school politics may have been limited largely to face-to-face relations between a principal and individual teachers. Today, however, local school politics involve entirely new groups with very different interests. The following perspectives on school politics might be beneficial for principals to understand within their own political, school contexts: (a) pluralist maintenance politics, (b) adversarial politics, (c) strong democratic politics, (d) consolidated principal power, and (e) unitary politics.

Pluralist Maintenance Politics

The pluralist perspective on educational politics has several aspects: (a) group or individual interests are viewed as fixed and static, (b) pluralist bargaining often takes place in one-on-one negotiations, and (c) pluralist politics rarely brings about systemic change—which is why the authors call it "maintenance politics." Maintenance politics may be appropriate for "good" schools where little needs to change. However, in situations where deep change is needed, pluralist politics is not likely to bring about this kind of change (Bryk et al., 1998, p. 47).

Adversarial Politics

Bryk and colleagues (1998) and Bryk (2020) recognize a form of community organizing that is adversarial by design. Some characteristics of this type of politics are as follows: (a) **adversarial politics** often focuses on short-term goals; (b) adversarial politics exacerbates tensions between opposing groups; (c) adversarial groups tend to "personalize" the evils of an unfair system (e.g., in a particular principal rather than in the entire system); and (d) adversarial politics often seeks to organize and define one group against other groups. Adversarial politics is likely to foster resentment among groups. The authors state that deep, lasting reform is a long-term effort that requires trust, respect, collaboration, and a common commitment to goals; adversarial politics is not likely to provide the potential for reform.

Democratic Politics

There are four main characteristics of strong **democratic politics**: (1) strong democratic politics fosters *sustained citizen participation* in the decision-making process and does not relegate decisions to representatives or "experts"; (2) there is an emphasis on *self-government and consensual politics*, in which the goal is to have citizens hammer out a common set of interests rather than merely try to accommodate or appease conflicting individual interests; (3) *public concern*, rather than individual interests, is the primary motivating force; and (4) core values and ideas are identified through *ongoing public debate*. Voting is less important than public talk that seeks to find common ground (Bryk et al., 1998).

The authors state that democratic politics could serve as a lever for deep structural change by challenging entrenched, narrowly defined interests. Citizens who have a stake in schools, but have never really had a voice, can now hold educational professionals accountable. The authors also indicate that this kind of politics is probably a transitional state. Day-to-day school operations would get bogged down if strong democratic politics were the norm for every decision. In describing the role of principals within this political milieu, the authors say:

> Principals in schools with strong democracy display a distinctive leadership style. They support broad participation of both parents and faculty in the decision-making process and spend time promoting this involvement. They encourage a searching for new ideas that might help the school, and are also willing to challenge the status quo to implement them. (Bryk et al., 1998, p. 66)

Consolidated Principal Power

Bryk and colleagues (1998) identify two principal leadership styles for maneuvering through school politics: (1) **autocratic**—the principal brings order through fear, intimidation, or threats of reprisals, and control of the school originates with and is sustained by the principal; and (2) **paternal/maternal**—the principal treats school personnel as family. It is their job to take care of the family, and the principal fosters dependence on himself. The authors note that a principal's ability to bring order to a chaotic situation often brings a loyal following and allows them to hold onto their power despite reform legislation. This type of political context is much of what is observed prior to reform efforts. It is a more compliant form of politics in which the principal will engage.

Unitary Politics

Bryk and colleagues (1998) observe the following in **unitary politics**: (a) a shared set of principles that provide a guiding framework for day-to-day operations; (b) a strong relational ethic, characterized by respect and trust; (c) small, stable communities where people have a common history, share a common vision of the future, and have ample opportunity to work together and get to know each other well (opportunities for substantive talk and collective planning are also critical); and (d) organizations that recruit like-minded individuals, or who aggressively socialize new members into group norms. The authors say that this form of politics is probably the norm in stable, high-performing schools. Unitary politics is more stable and efficient than strong democratic politics.

According to Kennedy (2000), educators have been told that they should stay out of political affairs, and that school people do not need to express opinions about such things in public. Kennedy indicates that such behavior is silent submission; the educators' reasoning is that while they are taking care of school, at another level, lawmakers are taking care of passing laws in educators' own interests and in the children's interests. Kennedy shares her own story as a young teacher. Her superintendent had warned her and other teachers that no teacher or principal was to get involved in the upcoming board of education election. They were not to donate money or make any visible show of support for a candidate. The superintendent admitted that even though she had an opinion about who should be elected to the board, she shared it with no one.

Kennedy (2000) points out that the voices of educators or principals can be heard in the hubbub of the political scene. For example, in 1999, an attempt to pass a collective bargaining bill in Missouri failed because of a concerted, organized opposition from elementary and secondary school principals. Kennedy indicates that the myriad of contacts received by lawmakers convinced them to defeat this bill despite support from the governor and house leadership. Kennedy provides another example from Michigan, where an amendment stating that every principal in the state would be an "at-will" employee generated more than one thousand calls from principals and convinced legislators to defeat that amendment.

Kennedy (2000) makes the following suggestions for principals as they become involved in making a difference through politics:

1. Use the resources of state and national principal-administrator associations. They have information about proposed legislation. For example, visit http://www.principals.org/s_nassp/sec_abstracts.asp?CID=28&DID=28.
2. Be sure you have correct information—don't contact a member of the House if the critical vote is in the Senate.
3. Be concise and accurate, and include a story in your message. You may use personal interest stories and leave students' names out, but tell the story. Talk about the effect the proposal will have on your students and your school.
4. Be alert. Follow the proposal as it moves through the process. Continue to push your issue between sessions of the legislature.
5. Get to know your senator and representative. Make frequent contacts.
6. Be sure to acknowledge those lawmakers who did support your issue. They appreciate a pat on the back.
7. Don't send a duplicated message. State and national lawmakers generally discount them.
8. Don't procrastinate.

Fowler (2013) adds the following:

1. Identify and monitor your competitors.
2. Study the timing of elections and the concerns within the elections.
3. Look for windows of opportunity to impact policy when both politicians and the public support an issue.
4. Network and build coalitions.
5. Build relationships with educational professionals.
6. Build relationships with other governmental agencies.

POLITICS IN THE DISTRICT: WORKING WITH THE SUPERINTENDENT AND OTHER EXTERNAL FORCES

Davis and Hensley (1999) put forth the notion that certainly politics plays a part in principals working with their superintendents. In particular, politics enters in during a principal's evaluation. The principal's job is multifaceted, with many demands from all directions—not just from above and below, but from outside—and this makes evaluation even more problematic (Brown & Irby, 2001). Davis and Hensley (1999) also observe that politics adds another important dimension to the issues of principal evaluation.

According to the *Synergistic Leadership Theory* (Irby et al., 2002), a leader's perceived effectiveness is formed by factors beyond their leadership ability alone. Those factors include (a) the organizational structure; (b) the values, beliefs, and attitudes of the leader and of those with whom they work in the organization; and (c) in the case of politics, external forces. For the principal to be perceived as effective, all three of the factors would have to be aligned with the factor leadership behavior, and the factors would need to be harmonious most of the time. It is recognized that there will be bumps in the road; however, for the principal, it is important to be able analyze synergistically all factors and get over the bump as quickly as possible. Principals displaying this ability ensure that the perception of their role remains positive both inside and outside of the organization.

As Davis (1999) points out, most principals are faced with an increasingly contentious and diverse array of pressures from what Irby and colleagues (2003) call external forces—those within the school, the community, the district office, the judicial system, and society at large. Davis (1999) suggests that only rarely do the constantly shifting values, preferences, and needs of school constituents find themselves in perfect alignment. For example, he states that, in most districts, the principal fits at midway in the management bureaucracy; at the same time, the principal is superordinate to teachers, staff, and students and subordinate to district office administrators. This situation may create incongruence among the factors of leadership behavior and external forces, as outlined in the synergistic leadership theory (Irby et al., 2002).

Davis (1998) found that poor interpersonal relationships and a lack of political acuity were far more likely to work toward the demise of a principal than was a lack of management skills or techniques. Principals who were weak in the areas of interpersonal relationships and political acuity failed to build confidence, trust, and support among constituent groups, or to effectively manage complex political influences. Davis's findings support the notion that many principals work within turbulent political environments that require skillful nurturing of interpersonal relationships and effective judgment about when and how to apply supportive leadership behaviors.

It appears that the balance between leadership behavior and external forces presents the most problems for principals; in Davis's (1998) research, the three critical areas cited by superintendents as highly related to a principal's performance failure were poor people skills, poor decision-making skills, and poor political skills. At the same time, most principals indicated particular concern about covert superintendent and/or board member agendas and perceptions. The principals believed that these factors, in concert with a few vocal or influential parents and teachers, could result in a negative evaluation. Principals also expressed concern about the increased number of parents and teachers who take their complaints directly to the superintendent or board members. Each of the principals complained that superintendents almost always over-reacted to parent and/or teacher complaints about the principal or school. Another external force, unions, was a serious concern for principals, who thought the teachers' union had them under their influence and felt that principals, along with superintendents, were powerless to challenge the union.

Davis (1998) has suggested the following strategies for principals when working within the political system and with their superintendents (we have integrated our strategies with his):

1. Focus on maintaining positive interpersonal relationships with parents, teachers, students, and supervisors. Project yourself as open, approachable, and caring. Be patient, listen well, and manage your anger (or frustration) when dealing with difficult circumstances. Learn to talk with, and not at, people. Distribute your attentions evenly and fairly among teachers, parents, the community, and students. Work on bringing people together in pursuit of common values and a clear vision for the school.

2. Maintain a sense of perspective relative to your status as principal. The days of principals acting like paternal or maternal authority figures are long gone. To survive, you need to know how to share power, empower others, and establish collaborative decision-making processes.

3. Know how others perceive you. Find out how teachers feel about you, and how parents and students perceive you. Without this feedback, you will never be certain how well you are doing in regard to maintaining positive relationships with others.

4. Know yourself. Assess your leadership style, your personality, and the way you interact with the world around you. Effective administrators tend to be self-reflective people who are honest about their shortcomings as well as their strengths; they are not afraid to seek assistance from others when confronted with complex problems or tasks. We suggest an analysis of your situation based upon the synergistic leadership theory, because it can assist you in understanding where there is misalignment.

5. Have a flexible leadership style. Develop the ability to apply different leadership styles as needed to address specific situations. Be willing and able to adapt to changing workplace conditions and environmental influences. Understand when to apply rational and logical perspectives to school issues and problems, when to focus on meeting individual needs, when to balance the competing interests of groups and individuals, and when to lead through the application of symbols and rituals.

6. Establish coalitions and partnerships with outside agencies; also establish professional relationships with statewide and national education associations.

7. Be proactive. Ask your superintendent to act as a mediator or broker between you and the community, to regularly communicate with the board about your school issues and outcomes, to redirect teacher and parent complaints to you, and to provide assistance or remediation if you are at risk early in your career.

8. As recommended by Brown and Irby (2001), complete an evaluation portfolio to critically analyze beliefs, experiences, understandings, and actions in the context of the school and district and to determine the impact of those actions upon student growth and the organization. As a tool for reflection, the portfolio can enhance the principal's ability to be cognizant of his or her place within the political context and the school.

As principals decide to move into the world of politics, probably the easiest route is through their superintendent. Principals and superintendents can influence board policy at the local level. First, the principal must become aware of local board policies and develop an understanding of "what is." Most board policies are divided into the following or similar sections: (a) basic district foundations, (b) local governance, (c) business and support services, (d) personnel, (e) instruction, (f) students, and (g) community and governmental relations. Principals, working with their superintendents, can influence the policies within each section at the board level, most particularly the policies dealing with personnel, instruction, and students.

Barbara Polnick, a curriculum expert in Texas (personal communication, September 5, 2020), related the following incident about a school administrator in Bellville Independent School District. Based on the curriculum management audit work of Frase and English (1995), the school administrator learned how to conduct curriculum audits and how to lead audit and alignment efforts. His work within the political context of his small district led to the development of a model local curriculum board policy that was presented to the board and subsequently adopted. For excerpts from that policy, see textbox 16.2.

Textbox 16.2 Excerpts from Bellville Independent School District's Local Curriculum Policy (a political action by a school administrator)

BELLVILLE INDEPENDENT SCHOOL DISTRICT LOCAL

Board Policy: Curriculum

Purpose. The Board recognizes the need and value of a systematic, on-going program of curriculum review and development. The Board shall encourage and support the professional staff in its efforts to investigate new curricular ideas, develop and improve programs, and evaluate results. In order to ensure quality control of the curriculum and be responsive to the school community and state requirements.

    Definition. Curriculum is defined as the knowledge, skills, attitudes, and processes to be taught and learned at the appropriate levels/areas or in courses in the District schools.

    Curriculum Philosophy. The curriculum of the District shall be developed by teachers and administrators in cooperation with community, business, and District educators to be responsive to the demand of the real-world workplace. Students shall possess competencies and skills to enable them to be viable contenders in a global society. Through equitable and quality authentic learning experiences, all students shall demonstrate high academic skills. The curriculum shall emphasize the core knowledge and skills that are necessary for profitably pursuing further education in college, technical/vocational education, and productive and responsible community membership. It shall be an objective of the curriculum to enable each student to obtain an education appropriate to his or her diverse interests, ambitions, and abilities. The Board seeks to ensure that each student receives the necessary instruction to progress successfully through the system. The Board requires that each student achieve basic standards for satisfactory advancement, particularly in progressing from elementary to junior high school, and from junior high school to senior high school. However, since initiative and flexibility in instructional techniques are encouraged, teaching methods may vary from campus to campus or from class to class.

    Alignment. The design and implementation of the curriculum shall be aligned with the planned and written curriculum as presented in the curriculum guide, the taught curriculum as presented to students by the teacher, and the tested curriculum as determined by student assessments. The teacher-made tests and standardized tests shall be congruent with the written and taught curriculum.

    Board Adoption. The Board shall officially adopt the curriculum that encompasses local goals and objectives, skills that are identified by state and federal guidelines, and mandates where applicable.

Accountability. The Superintendent shall be responsible for the implementation of the curriculum policy and shall serve as the primary mover of the curriculum management system. . . .

Principals. The building principal shall monitor the implementation of the curriculum, translating its importance to staff members on an on-going basis. The principal shall observe classes, monitor lessons, and evaluate teacher-made tests, using, as a minimum, the following strategies to monitor curriculum: (1) Classroom observations, (2) Interviews and conferences, (3) Confirmation of lesson plan alignment with curriculum.

Teachers. Teachers shall adhere to the curriculum philosophy of the District. They shall be responsible for teaching to the planned curriculum, testing their teaching, and accurately reporting results to parents.

Long-Range Planning. The curriculum process shall be aligned with the District Long-Range Plan.

Curriculum Direction. Subject-area written curriculum guides shall be developed locally for all grade levels or interdisciplinary subjects in the District. They shall be revised and readopted by the Board at least every five years. The guides shall contain or be based on the following: District mission statement; District philosophy of education; District curriculum philosophy; Belief statements related to the subject area and linked to appropriate exit expectations; Program goals and objectives for each subject area; Instructional focus for the elementary and secondary levels; Correlation of objectives and activities to the state essential knowledge and skills and statewide assessments; A scope and sequence chart for use in designing instruction at the appropriate level of difficulty for all learners; Correlation and integration of activities to and/or with instructional resources, adopted texts, and supplemental material; Real-world activities derived from the program goals and objectives for all subject areas; Relevant modifications and enrichment activities; and a statement of the means of evaluation of each of the content areas, skills, and attitudes to be taught. In formatting curriculum, the Superintendent shall make appropriate use of a wide range of resources, including professional staff; lay members of the community; experience of other systems; programs of schools, colleges, and universities; and information prepared by the schools of education, research institutions, educational foundations, and state and federal governments. Copies of the curriculum guides in complete sets shall be available for all teachers and the public in each principal's office and in the public libraries of the community for parental review and reference. The Superintendent shall take steps to conduct a major review of one curriculum area per year. A report/presentation shall be organized for the Board, demonstrating how this policy has been implemented, and making recommendations necessary for the improvement of pupil growth. The areas of review shall be: Mathematics; Language arts; Science; Social Studies (including geography, patriotism, government, and history); Health/safety; Fine arts; Vocational education; Special programs; Other languages; Technology; and Physical education. Other elective courses. The review process shall include a statement of instructional goals by grade level; assessment or testing trend data, as may be relevant; important new trends that are to be incorporated into the curriculum; recommended textbooks in the curriculum; and input from the teaching staff. The Superintendent shall employ one or more externally identified content area curriculum experts to critique the proposed or existing curriculum in light of available knowledge regarding appropriate curriculum in the areas being reviewed. Reports/critiques made by such experts shall be included in the report to the Board.

Review Committee. District-wide revisions in curriculum shall be considered by a District ad hoc committee in which a majority of the members have appropriate expertise to deal with the curriculum under consideration. The committee shall be composed of at least 50 percent teachers. The purpose of the committee shall be to provide the Superintendent and Board with additional campus-level input regarding curriculum changes. The scope of the committee's work shall be limited to reviewing the following: Determination of adequate training and preparation of teachers and administrators for implementation of the proposed program; Determination of adequate funding for personnel and materials; and Determination of adequate lead time for implementation of the proposed curriculum change.

Curriculum Changes. Curriculum changes that do not alter course offerings or course objectives may be approved by the Superintendent after consideration by the curriculum review committee; the administration shall then direct the staff to implement such changes. Curriculum changes that may involve the addition or deletion of courses shall be made only after Board approval.

Resource Allocation. The Board shall adopt a budget annually that provides the monetary resources to fund the curriculum training, materials and resources, and testing necessary to implement effectively the aligned curriculum. The budget development process shall ensure that goals and priorities are considered in the preparation of budget proposals and that any decision related to reduction or increase in funding levels can be addressed in those terms.

SUMMARY

1. Principals must be knowledgeable and cognizant of the politics surrounding the creation and implementation of educational policies.
2. Policy is the outgrowth of governmental actions.
3. Once policy is set, there is no guarantee that it will be implemented in the same way it was originally intended.
4. The principal could be related to policy in the following ways: (a) orientation, (b) degree, (c) resources, (d) activity, (e) autonomy, (f) societal values, (g) institutional values, (h) rationale, and (i) power relationship.
5. Principals can use theory to analyze policy. The analysis of policy through systems theory provides a holistic look at the policy itself. It allows principals to analyze the "policy 'inputs' including demands, needs, and resources, the 'throughputs' that involve the key actors who implement policy, and policy 'outputs' such as educated, civic-minded students or improved economic productivity."
6. Neopluralist advocacy coalition and interest group theories are grounded in a political science perspective that seeks to answer "who gets what, when, and how" as key coalitions struggle to obtain from government the resources and support they believe necessary.
7. Neoinstitutional theory indicates that the structure of societal and political organizations exerts independent effects on policy.
8. Critical theory questions the exiting economic, political, and social purposes of schooling and examines policy through the lens of oppressed groups, with a normative orientation toward freeing disenfranchised groups from conditions of domination and subjugation.
9. Feminist theory is concerned primarily with the often unequal effects of education policies on issues relating to gender and sexual difference, including how education policies are translated through institutional processes that serve to reinforce or encourage gender inequity.

10. Postmodernism argues that policy is contextually defined by those in authority and has little validity when separated from its setting.
11. Ideological theories place policy into a partisan, politically value-laden structure, hoping to gain insight into the econo-political context surrounding key policies.
12. To understand policies, principals can review the conceptual framework of four dimensions: (a) normative dimension (beliefs and values), (b) structural dimension (organizational and governmental structures), (c) constituentive dimension (networks, interest groups, and end users), and (d) technical dimension (educational planning, implementation, and evaluation).
13. Just as ethics and social justice enter into a principal's evaluation of policy, so does the concept of moral purpose.
14. Politics and public education are inseparable. At times it is difficult to distinguish between policy and politics.
15. Most definitions of politics are rooted in a system of governance. If governance is the system of directing affairs or political administration, politics is a by-product of that system.
16. Five perspectives on school politics are beneficial for principals to understand within their own political, school contexts: (a) pluralist maintenance politics, (b) adversarial politics, (c) strong democratic politics, (d) consolidated principal power, and (e) unitary politics.
17. Politics plays a part in principal evaluation due to the multifaceted and complex nature of the job.
18. Principals should work with their superintendents to alter policy within the school district's political context.

KEY TERMS

policy
orientation
degree
resources
activity
autonomy
societal values
institutional values
rationale
power relationship
systems theory
neopluralist advocacy coalition
    theory
interest group theory
neoinstitutional theory
critical theory
feminist theory
postmodernism

ideological theories
normative dimension
structural dimension
constituentive dimension
technical dimension
politics
neoliberals
neoconservatives
authoritarian populists
managerialism
"thick-visioned democrats"
policy talk
adversarial politics
democratic politics
autocratic
paternal/maternal
unitary politics

FIELD-BASED ACTIVITIES

1. Discuss with the superintendent how policy is established within your school district. Ask how principals are involved in policy development. Try to ascertain how the policy development, adoption, and implementation fit within the models presented in the chapter.
2. Review practices at your school campus. Can you identify any insidious policies that are in opposition to ethics and social justice? Talk with your principal about these policies, and determine a plan of action to remedy them.
3. Review the school board policies. (a) To what extent do the policies for curriculum adhere to the model policy presented? (b) Are policies inclusive of instruction? Personnel? Students? (c) Are the policies presented just?

SUGGESTED READINGS

Allen, K. A., Reupert, A, & Oades, L. (2021). *Building better schools with evidence-based policy: Adaptable policy for teachers and school leaders.* New York, NY: Routledge. The authors provide a broad range of popular topics for schools that are not readily accessible, and each policy is built on theory, driven by research, and created by experts.

Bardoch, E., & Patashnik, E. M. (2020). *A practical guide for policy analysis: The eightfold path to more effective problem solving* (6th ed.). Thousand Oaks, CA: Sage. The authors provide an eight-step process for political analysis: define the problem; assemble some evidence; construct the alternatives; select the criteria; project the outcomes; confront the trade-offs; stop, focus, narrow, deepen, decide; and tell your story.

Bryk, A. S., Sebring, P. B., Kerbow, D., Rollow, S., & Easton, J. Q. (1998). *Charting Chicago school reform: Democratic localism as a lever for change.* Boulder, CO: Westview. In 1989, Chicago began an experiment with radical decentralization of power and authority. This book tells the story of what happened to Chicago's elementary schools in the first four years of this reform.

Cooper, B. S., Cibulka, J. G., & Fusarelli, L. D. (Eds.). (2015). *Handbook of educational politics and policy* (2nd ed.). New York, NY: Routledge. This is the most comprehensive book on educational policy. The authors weave together literature from numerous subfields to provide a unifying four-dimensional framework for approaching educational issues. They use the latest research on the policy-making process and theory and apply this information to key policy areas. Policy areas examined in the text include governance, curriculum and standards, accountability, labor relations, finance, and school choice. The authors examine these policy areas in a framework consisting of normative, structural, constituent, and technical dimensions.

Fowler, F. C. (2013). *Policy studies for educational leaders: An introduction* (2nd ed.). Boston, MA: Pearson. This comprehensive book encourages future educational leaders to be proactive rather than reactive, and arms them with an understanding of educational policy and the important political theories upon which it is based. Coverage addresses theory, analysis, development, and implementation of educational policy, with the knowledge base of the typical reader in mind. Fowler explores the reasons for change in educational policy, the ways to track its evolution, and the techniques for influencing its ultimate destination. The text includes updated statistics drawn from the 2000 census and explores economic changes expected from the business cycle downturn and the effect of war. Fowler includes news stories for analysis—related to chapter content as well as key current issues, including the most recent legislation; new case studies on the teaching of Darwinian evolution and on parent revolts against state testing programs; and an entire chapter devoted to policy values and ideology. There is extensive coverage on educational policy at the state level.

Horsford, S. D., Scott, J. T., & Anderson, G. L. (2019). *The politics of education policy in an era of inequality: Possibilities for democratic schools*. New York, NY: Routledge. The growing problem of racial and social inequalities in the US has taken center stage in the policy arena. Record levels of economic inequality and reduced social mobility amid widening and deepening class divides present tremendous challenges for campus, school district leaders, and education advocates committed to ensuring equality of equal opportunity for all students. The rising economic inequality continues to be fueled by resource and opportunity gaps and troubling segregation of schools by race and class.

17

Legal Issues

■ ■ ■

FOCUSING QUESTIONS

1. What is the legal framework for education under which school principals operate?
2. How is the American judicial system of federal and state courts organized?
3. What are the major legal issues pertaining to schools and the state concerning compulsory school attendance, church-state relations, school fees, the curriculum, and state-mandated testing?
4. What are the major legal issues pertaining to students concerning freedom of expression, student appearance, extracurricular activities, student discipline, and students with disabilities?
5. What are the major legal issues pertaining to the school staff concerning certification, contracts, termination of employment, discrimination in employment, and tort liability?

In this chapter, we address these questions concerning legal issues pertaining to the school principal's role in maintaining a safe and orderly environment for learning. We begin our discussion by examining the legal framework for public education. Then we discuss the American judicial system of federal and state courts. Next, we examine schools and the state pertaining to compulsory school attendance, church-state relations, school fees, the school curriculum, and state-mandated testing. This is followed by a discussion of legal issues pertaining to students, including freedom of expression, student appearance, extracurricular activities, student discipline, and students with disabilities. We conclude the chapter with a discussion of legal issues pertaining to school staff, including certification, contracts, termination of employment, discrimination in employment, and tort liability.

LEGAL FRAMEWORK FOR PUBLIC EDUCATION

Those involved in administering schools, particularly superintendents and principals, should ensure that their actions are lawful. Educational decisions may not be enforced arbitrarily or capriciously but must be based on appropriate legal principles. Laws affecting schools cover a wide range of legal subject matter, including the basic areas of contracts, property, torts, constitutional law, and other matters of law that directly impact the operation of public elementary and secondary schools. Due to the breadth of the subject matter involved, it is necessary for the school principal to be versed in certain fundamental concepts of the law and to be able to apply this knowledge to situations that daily affect school operation.

SOURCES OF LAW

A beginning point for ensuring lawful administrative conduct in the operation of schools is a systematic study of the sources of law under which school principals operate. Such a study follows and is designed to analyze sources of law that emanate from each level of government: federal, state, and local. This overview establishes a context for subsequent topics in which we more fully discuss legal principles as they apply to specific school situations.

Federal Level

At the federal level, the US Constitution, federal statutes, federal administrative agencies, and case law all constitute sources of law under which school principals operate. We discuss each source in turn.

US Constitution. Although education is not specifically mentioned in the US Constitution, the federal government has had a significant involvement in education. In fact, programs under various federal statutes regarding PK–12 education in recent years have constituted more than 8 percent of the total expenditures for public elementary and secondary education (Digest of Education Statistics, 2019). Of greater significance has been the pervasive force of the federal government in influencing educational policy. The federal judiciary has addressed education issues such as racial segregation in schools, equitable state financing of public schools, due process of students and teachers, church-state relations, search and seizure, and freedom of expression of students and teachers.

Particularly significant are the General Welfare Clause of the US Constitution and the federal judiciary's interpretation of the Fourteenth Amendment to the Constitution. A brief examination of these precepts may be helpful to the school principal, based on their impact on the national well-being and the requirements for due process and equal protection of the law as they pertain to educational matters.

Under Article I, Section 8 of the Constitution, Congress has the power "to lay and collect taxes, duties, imposts and excises, to pay the debts and provide for the common defense and general welfare of the United States" (U.S. CONST. art. I, § 8). The **general welfare clause** has provided substantial federal support for research and instructional programs in the areas of reading, mathematics, science, special education, vocational education, career education, and bilingual education. Congress also has enacted legislation providing financial assistance for the school lunch program and for services to meet the needs of special groups of students, such as the educationally and culturally disadvantaged. Furthermore, Congress passed legislation pertaining to national health and safety concerns with the Asbestos School Hazard Detection and Control Act of 1980 and the Indoor Radon Abatement Act of 1988, which require the inspection of school buildings and, when necessary, corrective action to assure the safety of students and employees. Moreover, in an attempt to protect minor children's access to indecent material made available to them through the Internet, Congress passed the Children's Internet Protection Act of 2002; see

H.R. 5666 § 1721; U.S.C., § 9134 (f) (2002); 47 U.S.C., § 254 (h) (5) (2002). School principals need to abide by these provisions when operating their schools.

The Fourteenth Amendment is the most widely invoked constitutional provision in school litigation, because it specifically addresses state action. The US Supreme Court has interpreted Fourteenth Amendment liberties as incorporating the personal freedoms contained in the Bill of Rights (*Cantwell v. Connecticut*, 310 U.S. 296, 303, 1940; *Gutlow v. New York*, 268 U.S. 652, 666, 1925). Consequently, the first ten amendments, originally directed toward the federal government, have been applied to state action as well. In part, the Fourteenth Amendment stipulates, "No state shall . . . deprive any person of life, liberty, or property without due process of law; nor deny to any person within its jurisdiction the equal protection of the laws."

The **due process clause** of the Fourteenth Amendment, which prohibits states from depriving citizens of life, liberty, or property without due process of law, has been significant in school cases. Compulsory school attendance laws confer on students a legitimate property right to attend school. The granting of tenure gives teachers a property right to continued employment. Liberty rights include interests in one's reputation and fundamental rights related to marriage, family, and personal privacy. The **equal protection clause**, which prohibits states from denying to any person within its jurisdiction the equal protection of the laws, has played an important role in school litigation involving discrimination based on race, gender, ethnicity, and disabilities, as well as litigation calling for the equitable financing of schools.

Federal Statutes.   Congress has enacted many statutes that provide school principals with sources of law. The legal basis for this congressional involvement derives from the General Welfare Clause of the US Constitution. Federal statutes enacted by Congress are designed to provide financial assistance to public schools and to clarify the scope of individual's civil rights.

Much of the federal legislation enacted has provided funds to assist school districts in attaining equity goals and other national priorities, including national defense (National Defense Education Act of 1958); vocational education (Vocational Education Act of 1963); elementary and secondary education (Elementary and Secondary Education Act of 1965); bilingual education (Bilingual Education Act of 1968); and children with disabilities (Education for All Handicapped Children Act of 1975, renamed the Individuals with Disabilities Act of 1990 and the Individuals with Disabilities Act of 1997).

The most comprehensive law offering financial assistance to schools was the Elementary and Secondary Education Act of 1965 (ESEA). In part, it supplied funds for compensatory education programs for economically disadvantaged students. In 2015, President Barak Obama signed into law Every Student Succeeds Act (ESSA) (Pub. L. No. 114-95 Stat. 1177, 2015). The focus of the law is to improve the performance of public schools. The law pledges that all children, regardless of race, income, background, or address will make of their lives whatever they wish. Specifically, the law requires that states develop both content standards in reading, mathematics, and science and tests linked to the standards for grades three through twelve. States must identify adequate yearly progress (AYP) objectives and disaggregate test results for all students and subgroups of students based on socioeconomic status, race and ethnicity, English language proficiency, and disability. Moreover, the law mandates that 100 percent of students must score at the proficient level on state tests. Furthermore,

ESSA requires states to participate every other year in the National Assessment of Educational Progress (NAEP) in reading and mathematics.

Federal legislation designed to clarify the scope of an individual's civil rights include the Civil Rights Act of 1964 (prohibits employment discrimination on the basis of race, color, sex, religion, or national origin); the Age Discrimination in Employment Act of 1967 (protects employees over forty against age-based employment discrimination); Title IX of the Educational Amendments of 1972 (prohibits gender discrimination of participants in education programs); the Rehabilitation Act of 1973 (prohibits discrimination against otherwise qualified persons with disabilities); the Age Discrimination Act of 1975 (prohibits age-based discrimination in federally assisted programs); the Civil Rights Act of 1991 (prohibits race or ethnicity discrimination in making and enforcing contracts); and 42 U.S.C., § 1983, 2002 (provides the right of individuals to bring suit against any person who, acting under the authority of state law, impairs rights secured by the US Constitution and federal legislation).

Federal Administrative Agencies.   At the federal level, federal administrative agencies conduct the regulatory activities and structural details to implement broad legislative mandates. Originally established in 1867, the Office of Education became part of the Department of Health, Education, and Welfare in 1953. In 1980, the Department of Education was created. Its secretary is appointed by the president with the approval of the Senate and serves as a member of the president's cabinet.

The primary function of the Department of Education is to coordinate federal involvement in education. Regulations created by the Department of Education to implement federal legislation have had a significant impact on public elementary and secondary schools. The Department of Education administers regulations for more than one hundred different programs. Other federal administrative agencies—including the Department of Agriculture, the Department of Defense, the Department of Health and Human Services, the Department of Justice, and the Department of Labor—administer the remaining educational programs. The Office of Civil Rights and the Equal Employment Opportunity Commission, through their regulatory activities, review claims of discrimination in public schools and initiate suits against school districts for noncompliance with civil rights laws. The Environmental Protection Agency regulates compliance with national health and safety concerns designed to assure the safety of students and employees.

Case Law.   A fourth source of law is case law. **Case law** refers to principles of law established by the courts, as distinguished from the written law of constitutions, statutes, and administrative agencies. Case law frequently relies on earlier court decisions, which are called *precedents*. This practice is derived from the *doctrine of stare decisis*, meaning "let the decision stand." Under the doctrine of stare decisis, a court may stand by precedent and thereby not disturb an already settled point of law. Although courts generally rely on precedent, they are not bound by it in reaching a decision. A court may decide that the factual circumstances in the case being decided are not sufficiently similar to those of the precedent-setting case. Furthermore, the legal rationale used in reaching the precedent-setting case may not be applicable to the particular case under review.

Federal courts have contributed a significant body of case law, which has influenced educational policies governing the operation of public schools. Federal courts have addressed issues such as racial segregation, equitable methods of financing schools, separation of church and state, due process and equal protection concerns of students and teachers, freedom of expression of students and teachers, and dress and grooming standards of students and teachers. Precedents established by the federal courts regarding these issues provide school principals with an important source of law.

Case law is not always well settled, because occasionally federal district courts and courts of appeals render conflicting rulings within their jurisdictions. Consequently, school principals must follow case law rendered for their particular jurisdiction. The US Supreme Court is the single court whose decisions affect the administration and operation of public schools across the nation. A decision of the US Supreme Court may be modified only by another High Court decision or by an amendment to the constitution. Unfortunately, Supreme Court decisions have not always been followed by local school principals. Desegregation decisions and those dealing with Bible reading and reciting prayers during school hours are examples. It is vital for school principals to have a thorough understanding of well-settled case law and to enforce compliance with those decisions in operating their schools.

State Level

State-level sources of law include the state's constitution, state statutes, state administrative agencies, and case law. We discuss each source in turn.

State Constitutions. The Tenth Amendment to the US Constitution stipulates that "the powers not delegated to the United States by the Constitution, nor prohibited by it to the states, are reserved to the states respectively, or to the people." Because education is not mentioned in the Tenth Amendment to the US Constitution, it is left to the states to control. Therefore, state constitutions represent the basic source of law for individual states and generally require legislative bodies to make provision for a system of free public schools. Such provisions range from very specific educational provisions to broad mandates that direct the legislature of the state to provide funds for the support of a public school system. State constitutions also restrict the powers that legislative bodies may exercise.

State constitutions frequently address the same subject matter found in the federal Constitution, such as due process and/or equal protection of the law requirements, as well as separation of church and state. As a result, state courts are often asked to interpret these issues in an educational context. State constitutions may not contravene the federal Constitution.

State Statutes. The public schools of the United States are governed by state statutes enacted by state legislatures. State statutes represent an important source of law for school principals. The specificity of state statutes governing the operation of public schools varies from state to state and from subject to subject. Typically, however, state legislatures can raise revenue and distribute educational funds; prescribe curricular offerings; establish length of school day and year; mandate school attendance; establish pupil performance standards; set rules regarding suspension and expulsion of students; control teacher certification; establish procedures for tenure, retirement, collective bargaining, and fair dismissal procedures; create, alter, and abolish school districts and school boards; remove incumbent school board members and abolish their offices; set admission policies for local schools; impose penalties for noncompliance with state regulations; and regulate other specific aspects of public school operations, including state-funded charter schools and homeschooling.

State Administrative Agencies.   State-level agencies typically include a State Board of Education, a Chief State School Officer, and a State Department of Education. Specific functions of these state administrative agencies vary considerably among the states. Nevertheless, these agencies individually and collectively provide an important source of law for school principals.

The primary function of state boards of education is to develop policies and regulations to implement legislation and constitutional requirements. One regulatory method used by state boards of education to compel local school districts to abide by their directives is accreditation. The most common accreditation models typically include the establishment of minimum standards in areas such as curriculum, instructional materials, teacher qualifications, and facilities. State funds may be withheld from school districts for noncompliance with accreditation requirements. Other areas dealt with by state boards of education include school district organization, school closings, reductions in professional staff, and state-level review of appeals from local school boards.

The chief state school officer (CSSO), variously designated as state superintendent or commissioner of education, often acts as the executive head of the state's Department of Education. Typically, the CSSO's duties have been regulatory in nature; but they often include other activities such as research, long-range planning, and adjudicating educational controversies.

Each state also has established a state Department of Education, which may contain divisions for specialized services such as administration, finance, instruction, and research. State department personnel often collect data from local school districts to ensure that legislative requirements and State Board of Education policies are implemented; they also engage in activities to improve educational practices within the state.

Case Law.   State court decisions provide another source of law for school principals, where there is no policy direction from the state constitution, state statutes, or state administrative agencies. A decision of one state's highest court is not binding in another state. However, such a decision does provide school principals with the rationale of another state's highest court in an area of concern. And it should be noted that unless a federal issue is involved, there is no appeal of a decision of a state's highest court.

Courts have the final say on the meaning and effect of questioned laws. The power of individual courts to create law is illustrated in the cases appearing in later sections of this chapter. For example, among other things, courts determine issues involving whether a school principal lawfully exercised his or her authority or unlawfully abused administrative discretion.

Local Level

There are approximately 15,000 local school districts nationwide, ranging from a few students to several hundred thousand. Some states, particularly those with large numbers of school districts, like Texas, have created intermediate or regional service centers that perform regulatory or service functions for several school districts within a designated geographic area. School districts, acting through their local school boards, administer the public schools.

Local school board policies provide another source of law for school principals, as well as their individual school's rules or regulations. School board policies have the full force of the law as long as they do not contravene federal and state constitutions, federal and state statutes, or case law. Once these legal requirements are met, the school board as the delegated government at the local level may not violate its own policies. In many cases, school principals rely on this authority in dealing with such issues as administering corporal punishment, suspending or expelling a student, searching a student's locker or person, censorship of the school newspaper or yearbook, a student or teacher's refusal to participate in the Pledge of Allegiance or flag salute, use of the school building by the community, and dress and grooming standards of students and teachers.

State laws generally require that a school board can make official decisions only as a single corporate body, that is, as a whole at a duly convened official school board meeting (*Dugan v. Ballman*, 502 P. 2d 308, Fla. 1976; *Konovalchik v. Sch. Comm. of Salem*, 226 N.E. 2d 222, Mass. 1967; *State v. Consol. Sch. Dist.*, 281 S.W. 2d 511, Mo. 1955; *Whalen v. Minn. Spec. Sch. Dist.*, 2445 N.W. 2d 440, Minn. 1976). The school board meeting must be pursuant to proper public notification, attended by a quorum of board members, and open to the public (*Rathman v. Bd. of Dir. of Davenport Comm. Sch. Dist.*, 580 N.W. 2d 777, Ia. 1998). "Open meeting" or "sunshine" laws generally provide exceptions to open meeting requirements for school boards to meet in executive session to discuss the following issues:

1. Matters that threaten public safety or pending or current litigation (*Davis v. Churchill Cty. Sch. Brd.*, 616 F. Supp. 1310, D. Nev. 1985; *Hanten v. Sch. Dist. of Riverview Gardens*, 13 F. Supp. 2d 971, E.D. Mo. 1998; *Racine Union Sch. Dist. v. Thompson*, 321 N.W. 2d 334, Wis. 1982)
2. Labor negotiations (*Bassett v. Braddock*, 262 So. 2d 425, Fla. 1972)
3. Potential land purchase (*Collinsville Comm. Unit Sch. Dist. No. 10 v. White*, 283 N.E. 2d 718, Ill. 1972)
4. Personnel matters (*McCown v. Patagonia Union Sch. Dist.*, 629 P2d 94 Ariz. 1981; *Sch. Dist. of the City of Royal Oak v. Schulman*, 243 N.W. 2d 673, Mich. 1976) Although discussion of these matters may take place in closed meetings, state statutes usually require that formal action must take place in open meetings (*Connelly v. Sch. Comm.*, 565 N.E. 2d 449, Mass. 1991)

AMERICAN JUDICIAL SYSTEM

The United States judicial system consists of federal and state courts. The federal court system has its basis in the US Constitution. State court systems have their basis in state constitutions or statutory laws. The federal courts have primary jurisdiction on federal law questions, whereas state courts have primary jurisdiction on laws of each respective state. Most school actions involve nonfederal questions and are decided by state courts. However, in the last several decades, federal courts have litigated an increasing number of school cases.

Federal Courts

In part, Article III, Section 1 of the US Constitution provides that "The judicial power of the United States, shall be vested in one supreme court, and in such inferior courts as the Congress may from time to time ordain and establish" (U.S. CONST. art. III, § 1). Pursuant to this provision, Congress has created a network of courts. Presently,

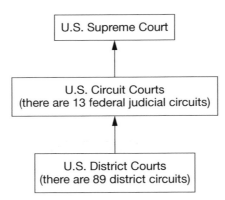

Figure 17.1 The Federal Court System

the federal court system in the United States includes district courts, circuit courts of appeal, and the Supreme Court (see figure 17.1).

District Courts. At the lowest court level, district courts hear and decide lawsuits arising within their territorial jurisdictions. There is at least one district court in each state; many states have two or three; and California, New York, and Texas each have four. Cases adjudicated before district courts are usually presided over by one judge. Decisions of district courts may be appealed to federal circuit courts of appeal.

Circuit Courts of Appeal. Courts of appeal represent the intermediate appellate level of the federal court system. The primary function of the appellate court is to review appeals from district courts within the circuit to determine if errors of law were committed, such as procedural irregularities, constitutional misinterpretations, or inappropriate application of rules of evidence. Federal circuit courts have from three to fifteen judges. Most circuit court decisions are rendered by a panel of the court, but in some instances the entire court will rehear a case. A federal circuit court decision is binding only in the states within that circuit, but such decisions often influence other appellate courts dealing with similar questions of law. The nation is divided into thirteen federal circuit courts of appeal, comprising eleven regions and the District of Columbia Circuit and Federal Circuit (see figure 17.2).

Supreme Court. The Supreme Court is the highest-level court in the federal court system, beyond which there is no appeal. It has been firmly established that the Supreme Court has the ultimate authority in interpreting federal constitutional provisions (*Marbury v. Madison,* 5 U.S. (1 Cranch) 137, 1803). If the constitutionality of a federal statute is contrary to legislative intent, such irregularities can be overturned only by an amendment to the Constitution or by subsequent ruling by the Supreme Court. Congress has done so with a number of civil rights laws in response to Supreme Court rulings (*Grove City Coll. v. Bell,* 465 U.S. 555, 1984). Nine justices, including one chief justice, constitute the Supreme Court. The appointments of Supreme Court justices are for life.

State Courts

State constitutions prescribe the powers and jurisdiction of state courts. The structure of judicial systems varies among the fifty states, but all states have at least three or four levels of courts: courts of limited jurisdiction, courts of general jurisdiction, intermediate appellate courts, and courts of last resort (see figure 17.3).

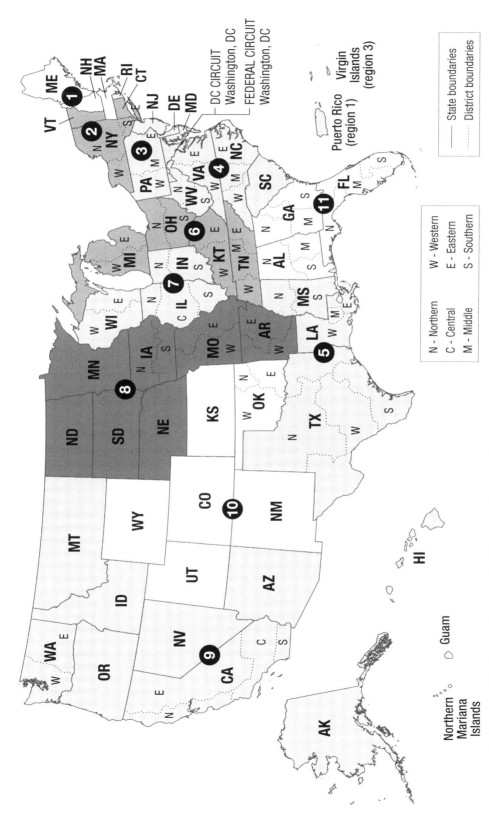

Figure 17.2 Geographical Boundaries of US Courts of Appeals and US District Courts

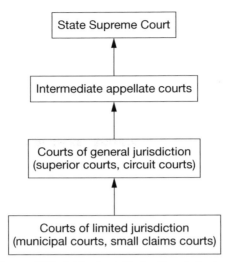

Figure 17.3 A Typical State Court System

Courts of Limited Jurisdiction.   Most states have trial courts, called courts of limited jurisdiction, that hear only certain types of cases (e.g., those concerning probate or criminal matters). These courts are referred to by a variety of names, including municipal, justices of the peace, probate, small claims, and traffic courts.

Courts of General Jurisdiction.   Courts of general jurisdiction are often referred to as circuit, chancery, district, superior, or juvenile courts.

Their jurisdiction covers all cases except those reserved for courts of limited jurisdiction. Decisions may be appealed from courts of general jurisdiction to intermediate appellate courts or, in some cases, to the court of last resort.

Intermediate Appellate Courts.   Most states have intermediate appellate courts. These courts have been established to hear appeals from trial courts or certain state agencies. The primary role of the intermediate appellate courts is to review proceedings from trial courts to determine if substantive or procedural errors occurred in applying the law. The purposes of the intermediate appellate courts and the courts of last resort are similar in this regard. The primary difference between the two courts is discretion. The intermediate appellate court has less discretion in accepting cases than does the court of last resort.

Court of Last Resort.   All states have a court of last resort. In most states, the court of last resort is called the supreme court. The primary function of this court is to review lower court decisions on appeal. Nonfederal matters may not be appealed beyond a state's supreme court. However, if a federal question is involved, an appeal may be forwarded to the federal courts or the US Supreme Court.

SCHOOLS AND THE STATE

Education is a state function. In this section we focus on the extent of state and local authority involving such issues as compulsory school attendance, church-state relations, school fees, the curriculum, and state-mandated testing. A school principal needs to be knowledgeable about these issues in order to avoid lawsuits against the school district or administrative staff. Due to their lack of knowledge as regards the following important issues, many school principals have caused lawsuits of sufficient severity to reach the Supreme Court.

Compulsory School Attendance

Every state has some form of compulsory school attendance law. These laws generally compel children between specified ages to attend school. Compulsory school attendance laws may be enforced in the following ways:

1. By criminal prosecution of parents for child neglect
2. By judicially ordering children to return to school; see *In re J.B.*, 58 S.W. 3d 575 (Mo. Ct. App. 2001); *In re C.S.*, 382 N.W. 2d 381 (N.D. 1986); *State ex. rel. Estes v. Egnor*, 443 S.E. 2d 193 (W.Va. 1994)
3. By court removal of a child from a parent's custody; see *Scoma v. Ill.*, 391 F. Supp. 452 (N.D. Ill. 1974); *Matter of McMillan*, 226 S.E. 2d 693 (N.C. 1976)
4. By placing truants in custodial schools, see *In re T.V.P.*, 414 N.E. 2d 209 (Ill. 1974)

In *Pierce v. Society of Sisters*, 268 U.S. 510 (1925), the US Supreme Court affirmed the mandate of compulsory school attendance. It also established the role of parochial and private schools in satisfying the state's requirement that children receive schooling. In essence, this landmark Supreme Court decision affirmed that parents do not have the right to determine *whether* their children are educated, but they do have the right to determine *where* such education takes place.

Most state statutes authorize home instruction programs that meet state standards; see *Deconte v. State*, 329 S.E. 2d 636 (N.C. 1985); *In re D.B.*, 767 P. 2d 801 (Col. Ct. App. 1988); *Tex. Educ. Agency v. Leeper*, 893 S.W. 2d 432 (Tex. 1994). However, courts do not agree that homeschooling must be equivalent to public school instruction; see *Minnesota v. Newstrom*, 371 N.W. 2d 525 (Minn. 1985); *Mazanec v. N. Judson—San Pierre Sch. Corp.*, 798 F. 2d 230 (7th Cir. 1986); *Jeffrey v. O'Donnell*, 702 F. Supp. 516 (M.D. Pa. 1988); *Blackwelder v. Safnauer*, 866 F. 2d 548 (2d Cir. 1989). Since 1980, many states have changed their laws to ease restrictions on home instruction, and no state has strengthened such regulations (Hail, 2003; Klicka, 1996). However, most states require students educated at home to be subjected to state-prescribed tests to ensure that students are mastering basic skills; see *Murphy v. State of Arkansas*, 852 F. 2d 1039 (8th Cir. 1988).

Exemptions. State laws typically exempt from compulsory school attendance certain classes of children, such as emancipated youngsters (married or self-supporting students), children who must work to provide essential family support, and children with severe disabilities. In addition to statutory exemptions from compulsory school attendance laws, the Supreme Court, in *Wisconsin v. Yoder*, 406 U.S. 205 (1972), granted an exemption of First Amendment religious grounds to Amish children who have successfully completed eighth grade. However, the courts have denied most other religious exemption claims.

Residency Requirements. Each state constitution places an obligation on its legislature to provide for free public schooling, thus creating a state entitlement (property right) for all children to be educated at public expense. This state entitlement encompasses all school-age children, usually between the ages of six and sixteen, who are bona fide residents in that they live in the attendance district with their parents or legal guardians; are emancipated minors (married or self-supporting beyond a certain age); or are adult students who live independently from their parents. Furthermore, the US Supreme Court, in *Plyer v. Doe*, 457 U.S. 202 (1982), held that school districts could not deny a free public education to resident children whose parents were illegal aliens.

Homeless children and state inter- and intra- district open enrollment plans may be subject to special rules. The federal Homeless Assistance Act of 1987 defines a homeless person as one who lacks a permanent nighttime residence or one whose residence is a temporary living arrangement. The law directs each state to adopt a plan for educating homeless children, including transportation and other school services; see 42 U.S.C.A., § 11302 (1987); *Harrison v. Sobel*, 705 F. Supp. 870 (S.D. N.Y. 1988); *G. Cooper Access to Education by Homeless Children*, 53 Ed. Law Rep. 757 (1989). Some states have enacted inter-district open enrollment plans, which allow students to apply for transfers to any public school district within the state. Transfer requests usually are subject to certain restrictions specified in the law, and participation by local districts may be optional under some plans. Most states now allow for some type of intra- or inter-district open enrollment plan; see *McMorrow v. Benson*, 617 N.W. 2d 247 (Wis. Ct. App. 2000). However, courts have rejected parents' claims that assignment to inadequate resident school districts was detrimental to their children's educational welfare; see *Ramsdell v. N. River Sch. Dist. No. 200*, 704 P. 2d 606 (Wash. 1985). Such claims may be more successful in the future in view of the federal No Child Left Behind Act of 2001. Under this federal legislation, students assigned to residence schools who have not met annual progress goals for two consecutive years must be provided other educational options, including transportation and all other school services; see 20 U.S.C., § 6316 (b) (2002).

Church-State Relations

The US Supreme Court and lower federal courts have consistently declared that school-sponsored prayer during regular school hours and Bible reading for sectarian purposes are unconstitutional. These issues have provided a plethora of litigation focusing on church-state relations.

The First Amendment stipulates, in part, that "Congress shall make no law respecting an *establishment of religion*, or prohibiting the *free exercise thereof*" (US CONST. Amendment I; emphasis added). The religious liberties of the First Amendment not only provide protection against actions by the Congress but also, when applied through the Fourteenth Amendment, protect the individual from arbitrary acts of the states (*Cantwell v. Connecticut*, 310 U.S., 296, 1940). Based on the Establishment and Free Exercise clauses of the First Amendment, courts must determine the constitutionality of such questions as allowing prayer and Bible reading in the public schools during normal school hours, prayer at graduations or football games, permitting religious clubs to meet on school grounds, disseminating religious materials, and observing religious holidays.

Prayer and Bible Reading. Two US Supreme Court decisions in the 1960s established case law regarding prayer and Bible reading in the public schools. In *Engel v. Vitale*, 370 U.S. 421 (1962), the Court held that daily recitation of a New York State Board of Regents prayer in the presence of a teacher was unconstitutional and in violation of the Establishment Clause. In *Sch. Dist. of Abington Township v. Schempp*, 374 U.S. 203 (1963), the Court held that reading the Bible for sectarian reasons and reciting the Lord's Prayer in public schools during normal school hours were unconstitutional. The result of *Engel* and *Schempp* was that religious exercises in the public schools are clearly unconstitutional. Neither state, nor school, nor teacher can hold religious services of any type in the public schools. The Court did assert, however, that Bible study as part of a secular program of education for its literary and historic values would not be unconstitutional.

Silent Prayer. Since *Engel* and *Schempp*, the courts have decided a number of school prayer cases. Many state constitutions, statutes, and school board policies were changed, thereby permitting voluntary prayer in the public schools. Teachers and students both have maintained that the Free Exercise Clause of the First Amendment permits them to conduct prayers in the classroom. This issue was settled by the US Supreme Court in *Wallace v. Jaffree*, 472 U.S. 38 (1985). The Court held that a period of silence for meditation or voluntary prayer in the public schools is unconstitutional. The Court ruled that the purpose of the 1981 Alabama silent prayer law was not secular and therefore violated the Establishment Clause. Courts have rejected most recent challenges to silent meditation or prayer.

Prayer at Graduation and Extracurricular Activities. Courts have been asked to render a decision on the constitutionality of prayers at graduation exercises and at other school-sponsored activities outside the classroom such as football games, team practices, and band concerts. The US Supreme Court, in *Lee v. Weisman*, 505 U.S. 577 (1992), held that prayers organized by school officials at graduation exercises were unconstitutional. The Court opined that while some common ground of moral and ethical behavior is highly desirable for any society, for the state to advance a Judeo-Christian religious doctrine is "coercive" and can create great discomfort for students who do not believe in the particular religious precept that is being visited upon them. And in *Sante Fe Independent School District v. Doe*, 530 U.S. 290 (2000), the US Supreme Court held that student-led, student-initiated prayer at football games violated the Establishment Clause. Thus *Santa Fe* joins a consistent array of precedents that enforce the secularization of public schools.

Equal Access Act. In 1984, Congress passed the Equal Access Act (EAA), which has since been amended in an attempt to clarify the unsettled area of law where students' free-speech rights compete with the rights of public schools to control access to the school as a forum for public discourse. The EAA, 20 U.S.C., § 4071 (1988), as amended, states in part:

It shall be unlawful for any public secondary school which received federal financial assistance and which has a limited open forum to deny equal access or a fair opportunity to, or discriminate against, any students who wish to conduct a meeting within that limited open forum on the basis of the religious, political, philosophical, or other con tent of the speech at such meetings.

A school has complied with the *fair opportunity* requirement if the meetings (a) are voluntary and student-initiated; (b) involve no school or government sponsorship; (c) allow the presence of school employees only in a nonparticipatory capacity; (d) do not materially and substantially interfere with the orderly conduct of educational activities within the school; and (e) are not directed, controlled, or regularly attended by nonschool persons; and the school cannot limit these groups to a specified size.

The US Supreme Court, in *Bd. of Educ. of the Westside Community Schools v. Mergens*, 496 U.S. 226 (1990), upheld the constitutionality of the Equal Access Act. The Court ruled that if a school allows any noncurricular groups to meet, then a limited open forum is created, and any student-initiated group has the right to assemble. These groups would be allowed to convene during noninstructional times when other groups meet.

Released Time for Religious Instruction. The practice of releasing public school children during regular school hours for religious instruction first began in the United States at the beginning of the twentieth century. Since then, two significant US Supreme Court cases have addressed the issue of releasing public school students to receive religious instruction. In *McCollum v. Bd. of Educ. of School District No. 71*, 333 U.S. 203 (1948), the Court struck down a plan in which pupils were released to attend religious instruction in the classrooms of public school buildings. The Court asserted that the use of tax-supported property for religious instruction, the close cooperation between school officials and religious authorities, and the use of the state's compulsory education system all tended to promote religious education and, therefore, violated the First Amendment. In a second decision, *Zorach v. Clauson*, 343 U.S. 306 (1952), the Court upheld a plan whereby students were released during public school hours to attend religious instruction off the school grounds. The Court found that the plan did not violate the First Amendment. The Court reasoned that whereas the Constitution forbids the government to finance religious groups and promote religious instruction, the First Amendment does not require the state to be hostile to religion. From the *Zorach* decision, it is clear that the Supreme Court does not prohibit some cooperation between public schools and churches; but the nature and degree of the cooperation are important in determining the constitutionality of the activity in question.

State Aid to Private Schools

Approximately 15 percent of all K–12 students in the United States attend private schools or home instruction (National Center for Education Statistics, 2020). Despite state constitutional provisions to the contrary, several states provide state aid to private school students, including those enrolled in parochial schools. The primary types of aid provided are for transportation, the loan of textbooks, state-mandated testing programs, special education, and counseling services. Because the use of public funds for private, primarily sectarian education has raised serious questions about the proper separation of church and state under the First Amendment, their constitutionality has been examined by the US Supreme Court.

Public funds to support religious schools dates back to 1930 when the US Supreme Court, in *Cochran v. Louisiana State Bd. of Educ.*, 281 U.S. 370 (1930), held that a state plan to provide textbooks to parochial school students does not violate the Fourteenth Amendment. The decision in *Cochran* was rendered ten years before the Supreme Court recognized in *Cantwell v. Connecticut*, 310 U.S. 296 (1940), that the fundamental concept of "liberty" embodied in the Fourteenth Amendment incorporates First Amendment guarantees and safeguards them against state interference. Since then, supreme courts have adopted the "child benefit" doctrine in many instances to defend the appropriation of public funds for private and parochial school use.

The US Supreme Court, in *Everson v. Bd. of Educ.*, 330 U.S. 1 (1947), held that the use of public funds for transportation of parochial school-children does not violate the First Amendment. The Court adopted the "child benefit" doctrine and reasoned that the funds were expended for the benefit of the individual child and not for religious purpose. Forty-one years later, the US Supreme Court, in *Bd. of Educ. v. Allen*, 392 U.S. 236 (1968), applied the reasoning of the *Cochran* and *Everson* cases in ruling that the loan of textbooks to parochial school students does not violate the Establishment Clause of the First Amendment. The Court reasoned that because there was no indication the textbooks were being used to teach religion, and because private schools serve a public purpose and perform a secular as well as sectarian function, such an expenditure of public funds is not unconstitutional.

The Supreme Court's decision in *Allen* created many questions in the minds of public and parochial school administrators throughout the nation. The Court used the public purpose theory in the *Allen* case "that parochial schools are performing, in addition to their sectarian function, the task of secular education." Thus, the Court reasoned that the state could give assistance to religious schools as long as the aid was provided only for secular services in the operation of parochial schools.

Many parochial school administrators interpreted this statement to mean that a state could provide funds to parochial schools for such things as teachers' salaries, operations, buildings, and so forth, as long as the parochial schools used the funds only for "public secular purposes." A plethora of bills flooded state legislatures to provide state support of parochial schools. Some were passed; others failed.

At around this time, the US Supreme Court, in *Lemon v. Kurtzman*, 403 U.S. 602 (1971), was asked to rule on the constitutionality of two such statutes, one from Pennsylvania and another from Rhode Island. The Court invalidated both statutes. The Pennsylvania statute provided financial support to nonpublic schools by reimbursing the cost of teachers' salaries, textbooks, and instructional materials. The Rhode Island statute provided a salary supplement to be paid to teachers dealing with secular subjects in nonpublic schools. The Court found that "secular purpose" standard to be inadequate and then added another standard of "excessive entanglement between government and religion." In *Lemon v. Kurtzman*, the Supreme Court first applied a three-part test to assess whether a state statute is constitutional under the Establishment Clause of the First Amendment. To withstand scrutiny under this test, often referred to as the Lemon test, governmental action must (a) have a secular purpose, (b) have a primary effect that neither advances nor impedes religion, and (c) avoid excessive government entanglement with religion.

In 1973 the Supreme Court delivered three opinions regarding financial aid to private schools after *Lemon*. The US Supreme Court, in *Levitt v. Committee for Public Education and Religious Liberty*, 413 U.S. 472 (1973), invalidated a New York statute stipulating that nonpublic schools would be reimbursed for expenses incurred in administering, grading, compiling, and reporting test results; maintaining pupil attendance and health records, recording qualifications and characteristics of personnel; and preparing and submitting various reports to the state. The Court stated that such aid would have the primary purpose and effect of advancing religion or religious education and that it would lead to excessive entanglement between church and state. The US Supreme Court, in *Committee for Public Education and Religious Liberty v. Nyquist*, 413 U.S. 756 (1973), struck down a New York statute that provided for the maintenance and repair of nonpublic school facilities, tuition reimbursement for parents of nonpublic school students, and tax relief for those not qualifying for tuition reimbursement. And the US Supreme Court, in *Sloan v. Lemon*, 413 U.S. 825 (1973), invalidated a Pennsylvania statute that provided for parent reimbursement for nonpublic school students. The Court reasoned there was no constitutionally significant difference between Pennsylvania's tuition-granting plan and New York's tuition-reimbursement scheme, which was held to violate the Establishment Clause in *Nyquist*.

The tripartite *Lemon* test was used consistently in Establishment Clause cases involving church-state relations issues until around 1992. A majority of the current justices, who are Reagan-Bush appointees to the US Supreme Court, have voiced dissatisfaction with the test, and reliance on *Lemon* has been noticeably absent in the Supreme Court's recent Establishment Clause rulings. Support for church-state separation seems to be crumbling.

The Supreme Court has allowed increasing government support for parochial school students beginning in the 1980s. In 1980, the US Supreme Court, in *Committee for Public Education and Religious Liberty v. Regan*, 444 U.S. 646 (1980), upheld government support for state-mandated testing programs in private schools. A few years earlier, the Supreme Court ruled, in *Levitt* and later in *Meek v. Pittenger*, 421 U.S. 349 (1975), that using state funds to develop and administer state-mandated as well as teacher-made tests was in violation of the Establishment Clause, because such tests could be used to advance sectarian purposes. In 1983, the US Supreme Court, in *Mueller v. Allen*, 463 U.S. 388 (1983), upheld a state tax benefit for educational expenses to parents of parochial school students. Ten years later, the Supreme Court, in *Zobrest v. Catalina Foothills Sch. Dist.*, 509 U.S. 1 (1993), held that providing state aid to sign-language interpreters in parochial schools is not a violation of the First Amendment. This decision represented a paradigm shift toward the use of public school personnel in sectarian schools.

The US Supreme Court, in *Agostini v. Felton*, 521 U.S. 203 (1997), held that using federal education funds under Title I of the Elementary and Secondary Education Act (ESEA) of 1965 to pay public school teachers who taught in programs aimed at helping low-income, educationally deprived students within parochial schools was allowed. This decision overruled two earlier Supreme Court decisions announced twelve years earlier, which had not allowed the practice; see *Aguilar v. Felton*, 423 U.S. 402 (1985) and *Grand Rapids School District v. Ball*, 473 U.S. 373 (1985). ESEA, which has gone through a number of reauthorizations since being enacted in 1965, requires that comparable services be provided for eligible students attending nonpublic schools. The most recent reauthorization of ESEA is P.L. 107-110, the No Child Left Behind Act of 2001, 20 U.S.C., § 6301 (2002). The Court in *Agostini*, for the first time, held that comparability can be achieved by permitting public school personnel to provide instructional services in sectarian schools. The Court further recognized that in *Zobrest* it abandoned its previous assumption that public school teachers in parochial schools would inevitably inculcate religion to their students or that their presence constituted a symbolic union between government and religion.

The US Supreme Court, in *Mitchell v. Helms*, 530 U.S. 793 (2000), held that using federal aid to purchase instructional materials and equipment for student use in sectarian schools did not violate the Establishment Clause. Specifically, the decision permits the use of public funds for computers, software, and library books in religious schools under Title II of the ESEA federal aid program. The Court reasoned that the aid was allocated based on neutral, secular criteria that neither favored nor disfavored religion; was made available to both religious and secular beneficiaries on a nondiscriminatory basis; and flows to religious schools simply because of the private choices of parents. *Mitchell* overruled decisions in *Meek v. Pittenger*, 421 U.S. 349 (1975), and *Wolman v. Walter*, 433 U.S. 229 (1977), which barred state aid from providing maps, charts, overhead projectors, and other instructional materials to sectarian schools.

School Fees

In public schools there is a growing practice of charging "user fees" for select services and materials such as transportation, textbooks, course materials, and extracurricular activities. This practice has raised objections that charging fees violates a student's right to a free public education under state law. Whether or not fees may be charged depends partly on the wording in state statutes and partly on judicial interpretations as to which school activities should be considered part of a free public education.

Transportation. The law is clear that public schools cannot charge tuition to resident students who attend regular school year classes but may charge tuition to parents or legal guardians of nonresident students for such attendance. Some courts have distinguished between tuition charges and transportation charges, reasoning that transportation is not an essential part of students' property right to a free public education (*Kadrmas v. Dickinson Pub. Schs.*, 487 U.S. 450, 1988; *Salazar v. Eastin*, 890 P.2d 43, Cal. 1995). School board policies that have distinguished between resident and nonresident students pertaining to transportation fees have been upheld by the courts in *Fenster v. Schneider*, 636 F. 2d 765 (D.D. Cir. 1980), and courts have upheld policies that allow school districts to charge fees for summer school transportation (*Crim v. McWharter*, 252 S.E. 2d 421, Ga. 1979).

In *Kadrmas v. Dickinson Public Schools*, 487 U.S. 450 (1988), the US Supreme Court held that a North Dakota statute allowing selected school districts to charge a transportation fee, not to exceed the school district's estimated cost of providing the service, does not violate a student's right to a free public education. The Court stated that unless mandated by state law, local school districts may refuse to provide school transportation services; thus, such services need not be free.

Whether or not reasonable school transportation fees can be imposed varies from state to state, depending on each state's classification of contested charges falling within or beyond the scope of that state's "free" public education. However, states do not have discretion regarding transportation for children with disabilities. Under federal and state laws, transportation is a related service that must be provided for free if necessary for a child with disabilities to participate in the educational program.

Textbooks, Courses, and Supplies. Some courts have upheld fees for textbooks, school supplies, and courses. Others have not. The US Supreme Court has not invalidated textbook or other fees under federal equal protection guarantees; therefore, the legality of such fees depends on interpretations of state statutes and constitutions.

The Montana Supreme Court, in *Granger v. Cascade County Sch. Dist. No. 1*, 159 Mont. 516, 499 P.2d 780 (1972), applied a principle or test to determine whether a school district can or should charge fees for textbooks, courses, or supplies. The Montana Supreme Court interpreted "tuition-free" in their constitution to mean "free" as far as required courses were concerned and did not prohibit fees and charges for optional extracurricular or elective courses or activities. The Montana Supreme Court offered the following principle or test:

> We believe that the controlling principle or test should be stated in this manner: Is a given course or activity reasonably related to a recognized academic and educational goal or a particular school system? If it is, it constitutes part of the free, public school system commanded by Art. XI, § 1 of the Montana Constitution and additional fees or charges cannot be levied, directly or indirectly, against the student or his parents. If it is not, reasonable fees or charges may be imposed.

The courts have consistently construed the language "without payment of tuition" or "tuition-free" or other such language to mean that a school district is prohibited from charging a fee for a pupil attending school. This language has also been construed as not prohibiting the charging of fees for textbooks or other educational materials. However, when state constitutions contain language such as "free public schools," "free common schools," or similar language, the courts have generally held, with few exceptions, that this language contemplates furnishing textbooks and other educational materials free of charge, at least to the elementary schools.

An issue receiving increased attention in the public schools is that of charging fees for participation in extracurricular activities. The following court decisions will shed some light on this issue. School principals and other school officials should consult their state statutes.

Extracurricular Activities.   Several courts have ruled that public schools can charge students fees for participation in extracurricular activities. In *Paulson v. Minidoka County School District No. 331*, 463 P.2d 935, 938 (Idaho 1970), the Supreme Court of Idaho upheld a school district's policy that required students to pay for participation in extracurricular activities. The court reasoned that such activities are not necessary elements of a high school career. In *Bd. of Educ. v. Sinclair*, 222 N.W. 2d 143 (Wis. 1974) and in *Granger v. Cascade County Sch. Dist. No. 1*, 499 P.2d 780 (Mont. 1972), the Wisconsin and Montana Supreme Courts reached conclusions similar to that of Idaho. The courts ruled that school districts can charge fees for activities that are optional or elective. In *Attorney General v. E. Jackson Public Schools*, 372 N.W. 2d 638 (Mich. Ct. Appl. 1985), a Michigan appeals court upheld fees for playing on interscholastic teams. The court reasoned that interscholastic athletics are not considered an integral, fundamental part of the educational program, which would require providing them free to resident students. The Michigan court also noted the confidential waiver process available for students who could not afford to pay the fees. The court recognized that no students had been denied participation because of inability to pay the fees. Earlier, an Indiana federal district court, in *Carder v. Michigan City School Corporation*, 552 F. Supp. 869 (N.D. Ind. 1982), ruled that the state student disciplinary code and federal equal protection guarantees precluded school boards from suspending students for parents' failure to pay fees assessed for educational materials. The Ninth Circuit Court, in *Canton v. Spokane Sch. Dist. No. 81*, 498 F. 2d 840 (9th Cir. 1974), held that students have a constitutional right not to be subjected to embarrassment, humiliation, or other penalties for failure to pay fees for instructional materials. The Supreme Court of West Virginia, in *Vandevender v. Cassell*, 208 S.E. 2d 436 (W.Va. 1974), upheld waivers for students who could not afford to pay the assessed fees. And later, the US Supreme Court, in *Kadrmas v. Dickinson Public Schools*, 487 U.S. 450 (1988), held that under the law, school districts have the discretion to waive any fee for families financially unable to pay fees assessed, and benefits such as diplomas and grades are not to be affected by nonpayment of fees. However, one year later, in *Association for Defense v. Kiger*, 537 N.E. 1292 (Ohio 1989), the Supreme Court of Ohio upheld state law that authorized school districts to withhold grades or credit if students failed to pay fees for educational materials.

Individual state laws may prohibit assessing students for participation in extracurricular activities. The Supreme Court of California, in *Hartzell v. Connell*, 679 P.2d 35, 44 (Cal. 1984), held that its state constitution prohibited charging students fees for participation in any extracurricular activities. The court stated that extracurricular activities are an integral part of the educational program and thus encompassed a guarantee of a free public education. The court further held that the fee violated the state administrative code, which stipulated that students shall not be required to pay any fees. Nevertheless, eight years later the same court, in *Arcadia Unified Sch. Dist. v. State Department of Education*, 825 P.2d 438 (Cal. 1992), held that school transportation fees were permissible under California law.

Given the fiscal constraints faced by school districts across the nation, an increasing number of school boards are likely to charge user fees for transportation, textbooks and other instructional materials, and extracurricular activities.

The School Curriculum

In view of the state's plenary power over education, the school curriculum is controlled primarily by states and local school boards. The federal government does influence the school curriculum through funds it provides for particular initiatives like "Reading First." States can apply for federal funds to strengthen reading instruction in the early grades; see (Reading First), 20 U.S.C., § 6362 (2002).

In all states, the local school district must offer a curriculum that state legislatures prescribe. In about half of the states, the local school district must offer the curriculum prescribed by state law. Even in those states where school districts retain some discretion, courses of study must be approved by the state board of education. Although states vary as to the specificity of course offerings, most states require instruction in American history and government, English, mathematics, drug education, health, and physical education. In addition, some state statutes specify the number, content, or quality of course offerings and what subjects will be taught at which grade levels. Many states have detailed legislation pertaining to vocational education, bilingual education, and special education.

Although states have substantial discretion in curricular matters, occasionally curriculum decisions by state legislatures have violated federal constitutional provisions. The US Supreme Court, in *Epperson v. Arkansas*, 393 U.S. 97 (1968), held that preventing public school teaching of evolution simply because it conflicts with certain religious views is a violation of the First Amendment. Nearly two decades later, the US Supreme Court, in *Edwards v. Aguillard*, 482 U.S. 578 (1987), struck down a Louisiana law requiring the teaching of creationism whenever evolution was introduced in the curriculum. The Court concluded that the law was a violation of the First Amendment because it unconstitutionally advanced religion.

The courts have generally enforced the view that the public schools should deal with secular matters and remain apart from sectarian affairs. The legal controversies that typically arise in this area generally involve some particular group seeking to impose particular religious and philosophical beliefs by restricting the school curriculum or demanding that certain books or courses be excluded from the instructional program. In response, the courts have traditionally upheld the "expansion of knowledge standard."

In *Board of Education v. Pico*, 457 U.S. 853 (1982), the US Supreme Court reinforced the expansion of knowledge rule by prohibiting the removal of books by the local school board, which was responding to political pressure from a local school group of conservative parents. The Court reasoned that expansion of knowledge was an objective of education policy and stated that "the right to receive ideas is a necessary predicate to the recipient's meaningful exercise of his own right of speech, press, and political freedom." This general precedent, that the expansion of knowledge is paramount, was set in an earlier Supreme Court case in *Sweeney v. New Hampshire*, 354 U.S. 234 (1957). The Court said, "Teachers and students must always remain free to inquire, to study and then evaluate. . . . [The state cannot] chill that free play of the spirit which all teachers ought especially to cultivate and practice."

More recently, however, a new judicial pattern has emerged that may suggest a possible retreat from the "expansion of knowledge" rule. The present US Supreme Court (Reagan-Bush appointees) has indicated its willingness to allow the final decision regarding the curriculum and the availability of books and materials to reside fully within the prerogative of the local school board, even though the result may be a contraction of the flow of information and a possible diminution of knowledge. This position was implied by the landmark 1988 Supreme Court decision involving students' free speech rights in *Hazelwood School District v. Kuhlmeier*, 484 U.S. 260 (1988). The Court declared that public school authorities can censor student expression in school-related activities, in this case the excision of two pages from a student newspaper, as long as it is "reasonably related to legitimate pedagogical concerns." Such a "reasonableness" standard is less definitive and gives local school authorities greater flexibility in determining whether to restrict or expand the curriculum. In this case, the Court further justified restriction of curriculum content by concluding that "a school must be able to take into account the emotional maturity of the intended audience."

In following this precedent of greater latitude to local school boards in controlling curriculum, books, films, and materials, a Wisconsin court upheld a school district's ban on showing R-rated films in *Barger v. Bisciglia*, 888 F. Supp. 97 (E.D. Wis. 1995); an Eleventh Circuit Court upheld a Florida school board's decision to ban a humanities book in *Virgil v. School Board*, 862 F. 2d 1517 (11th Cir. 1989); and a California appeals court upheld a school board's censor of instructional materials in *McCarthy v. Fletcher*, 254 Cal. Rptr. 714 (Ct. App. 1989), but the court noted in this case that school board authority does have limits and prohibited the banning of materials purely for religious reasons.

State-Mandated Performance Testing

The state has the authority to establish standards for promotion and graduation. In recent years, states have begun to rely heavily on the standardized test as a criterion to determine students' proficiency in core subject areas. For example, in the mid-1970s, only a few states had enacted testing legislation pertaining to students' academic proficiency. Now all states have laws or administrative regulations regarding statewide performance testing, and most states require passage of a test as a condition of graduation. As long as such measures of academic attainment are reasonable and nondiscriminatory, the courts will not interfere. Courts have traditionally given teachers and administrators wide latitude in deciding on appropriate academic requirements. The courts adopted this position of nonintervention as early as 1913 in *Bernard v. Inhabitants of Shelburne*, 216 Mass. 19, 102 N.E. 1095 (1913). The court said, "So long as the school committee acts in good faith, their conduct in formulating and applying standards and making decisions touching this matter is not subject to review by any other tribunal." The US Supreme Court reiterated this precedent in *Board. Of Curators v. Horowitz*, 435 U.S. 78 S. Ct. 948 (1978), when it said that "Courts are particularly ill-equipped to evaluate academic performance."

The federal government strongly supports statewide performance testing. Every Student Succeeds Act of 2015 requires annual testing in grades three through twelve in reading, mathematics, and science. The act also ties federal assistance and sanctions for schools to student test scores. High-stakes testing shapes the instructional program, and states increasingly are evaluating teachers' and principals' performance based on their students' test scores. A number of professional organizations (e.g., American Educational Research Association, American Evaluation Association, International Reading Association, National Council for Teachers of English, National Council for Teachers of Mathematics, National Council for the Social Studies, and National Education Association) oppose the inappropriate use of tests to make high-stakes decisions. And claims have been made that teachers are limiting the curriculum to material covered on the tests (Berliner, 2011; McNeil, 2000; Nichols, 2007).

The major source of litigation regarding statewide performance testing stems from the movement of many states to competency tests as minimal criteria for awarding a high school diploma. The high school diploma represents a measure of attainment and is thus of special interest to the student. The diploma, therefore, meets the criteria for a property interest under the Due Process Clause of the Fourteenth Amendment, enunciated by the US Supreme Court in *Bd. of Regents v. Roth*, 408 U.S. 564 (1972). The Court stated that "to have a **property interest** is a benefit, a person clearly must have more than an abstract need or desire for it. He must, instead, have a legitimate claim of entitlement to it." A high school diploma is a benefit that everyone needs, and when a student progresses academically for twelve years, one may assume that the diploma will be expected, contingent on the student's normal academic progress.

Litigation may occur when the competency tests used cause a risk of nonreceipt of the diploma and are the result of tests that do not measure the content they are supposed to measure. If tests do not measure the content they are supposed to measure, then the tests lack validity. Another important test concept is reliability, which requires that the test must yield consistent results.

These issues of due process and validity and reliability became the foci of the court in *Debra P. v. Turlington*, 644 F. 2d 397 (5th Cir. 1981), a case still widely cited as establishing the legal precedent pertaining to student proficiency tests. The court held that the property interest in receipt of a diploma necessitated sufficient notice of conditions attached to high school graduation and that an opportunity to satisfy the standards before a diploma can be withheld were not met (due process). Furthermore, the court held that the state may have administered an unfair test in that the test content did not match the material taught in the schools (validity). The state was enjoined from using the test as a diploma prerequisite for four years to provide time for the effects of prior school desegregation to be removed and to ensure that all minority students subjected to the test requirement started first grade under desegregated conditions. On remand, *Debra P. v. Turlington*, 564 F. Supp. 177 (M.D. Fla. 1983), affirmed 730 F. 2d 1405 (11th Cir. 1984), the district court ruled to lift the injunction, and the appeals court affirmed this decision. The state presented substantial evidence to the judiciary that the test was valid. Data also showed significant improvement among African American students during the six years the test had been administered. Thus the testing program could help remedy the effects of past racial discrimination.

Other courts have relied on *Debra P.* as precedent. A Texas federal district court, in *GI Forum v. Texas Education Agency*, 87 F. Supp. 2d 667 (W.D. Tex. 2000), struck down challenges to the Texas Assessment of Academic Skills (TAAS) test that has been administered to all Texas students since 1990. The court held that the test was valid in that the content of the test was congruent with the material taught in the schools, and students received adequate notice of the test requirement. The court noted that there was evidence of higher minority failure rates; but the passing-rate gap was narrowing, and the testing and remediation programs were addressing the effects of prior discrimination.

Two Texas federal district courts ruled differently with regard to students being allowed to participate in graduation exercises contingent on their passing the statewide proficiency test. In *Williams v. Austin Independent Sch. Dist.*, 796 F. Supp. 251 (W.D. Tex. 1992), the court ruled that students who failed the state's proficiency test have no constitutional right to participate in the graduation ceremony, because they had been given adequate notice of the test and were provided with the required courses to prepare for the test. In *Crump v. Gilmer Independent Sch. Dist.*, 797 F. Supp. 552 (E.D. Tex. 1992), the court struck down a school district's attempt to prevent students who had failed the state's proficiency test—but satisfied other graduation requirements—from participating in the graduation ceremony. The court reasoned that allowing students to graduate would provide no possible harm to the district from their participation, because their diplomas would be withheld until students passed the proficiency test. In another Texas federal district court case, *Hubbard v. Buffalo Independent Sch. Dist.*, 20 F. Supp. 2d 1012 (W.D. Tex. 1998), the court upheld a school district's requirement that all students who transfer from nonaccredited schools must take the state's proficiency test at their own expense.

Students with mental disabilities may be given a waiver from taking a proficiency test if the individualized education program (IEP) team agrees that the child is not likely to master the material covered on the test. And students with disabilities may be entitled to special accommodations in the administration of tests to ensure that their knowledge, rather than their disability, is being tested.

The specific nature of the accommodations remains controversial. Given mandatory testing provisions in ESSA, statewide performance testing is likely to continue. Statewide proficiency testing programs will likely generate additional litigation in federal and state courts. School principals can take steps to minimize legal challenges by ensuring that (a) the proficiency tests are aligned with both curriculum and instruction, (b) students are advised upon entrance into high school that passage of the proficiency test is a prerequisite to receipt of a diploma, (c) tests are not intentionally discriminatory and do not perpetuate the vestiges of past school segregation, (d) students who fail the proficiency test are provided remediation and opportunities to retake the test, and (e) students with disabilities are provided with appropriate accommodations (McCarthy, Eckes, & Decker, 2019).

STUDENTS AND THE LAW

Principals are given broad powers to adopt rules and regulations governing student conduct in the public schools. These powers are not absolute, and school authorities must implement rules and regulations within the scope of *reasonableness*. Generally, rules are thought to be reasonable in a school setting if they are necessary to maintain an orderly and safe environment conducive to learning. To protect the constitutional rights of students, courts have been diligent in determining the reasonableness and fairness of rules and regulations governing student conduct.

Court decisions in recent years pertaining to students' rights indicate that courts must often balance students' constitutional rights against the duty of school principals to maintain a safe and orderly environment for learning. To reduce legal confrontations pertaining to students' rights as well as to facilitate efficient and effective school operations, school principals should ensure that (a) the adoption of policies, rules, and regulations governing student conduct is legally and educationally sound; (b) the policies, rules, and regulations are clearly written; (c) the policies are adequately communicated to students and their parents; and (d) the policies are enforced in a fair and reasonable manner.

Freedom of Expression

Prior to the 1970s, courts generally upheld school principals' actions governing student conduct that simply satisfied the reasonableness standard. Public schools were perceived as possessing ***in loco parentis*** (in place of the parent) prerogatives (*State ex. rel. Burpee v. Burton*, 45 Wis. 150, 30 Am. Re. 706, 1878). Further, it was uncertain whether constitutional rights extended to students in school. However, in *Tinker v. Des Moines Independent Community Sch. Dist.*, 393 U.S. 503 (1969), the US Supreme Court stated that students do not "shed their constitutional rights to freedom of speech or expression at the schoolhouse gate." Freedom of expression is derived from the First Amendment to the US Constitution, which stipulates, in part, "Congress shall make no laws . . . abridging the freedom of speech, or of press or of the rights of peoples to peacefully assemble." The *Tinker* case confirmed that students are entitled to all First Amendment rights, subject only to the provision in which the exercise of these rights creates material and substantial disruption in the school. An excerpt from *Tinker* will help clarify the legal principles of the Court:

> School officials do not possess absolute authority over their students. Students in school as well as out of school are "persons" under our Constitution. They possess fundamental rights which the State must respect. . . . In the absence of a specific showing of constitutionally valid reasons to regulate their speech, students are entitled to freedom of expression of their views. (*Tinker v. Des Moines Independent Sch. Dist.*, 393 U. S. 503, 511, 1969)

The Court's decision in *Tinker* sent a clear message to the public school community that a student has the constitutional right of freedom of expression in school.

Subsequently, in *Goss v. Lopez*, 419 U. S. 565 (1975), the US Supreme Court ruled that public school students possess liberty and property interests in their education, and therefore that constitutional principles of due process apply to school officials in dealing with regulations governing student conduct and other school-related activities. Due process of law is derived from the Fourteenth Amendment to the US Constitution, which stipulates, in part, that "no state shall . . . deprive any person of life, liberty or property, without due process of law." Basically, due process is a procedure of legal proceedings following established rules that assure enforcement and protection of individual rights. The guarantees of due process require that every person be entitled to the protection of a fair hearing and a fair judgment. Following *Goss*, several significant federal laws also emerged in the early 1970s and extended through the early 1980s, further expanding the scope of students' rights. During this period, the courts often upheld students' legal challenges of school policies, rules, and regulations; many school principals perceived such rulings as an erosion of their authority.

By the mid-1980s, there was a noticeable shift in courts' tendency to uphold students' challenges. Two significant landmark Supreme Court decisions increased the public school principals' authority pertaining to students' freedom of expression and other issues concerning regulations that govern student conduct. In *Bethel School District No. 403 v. Fraser*, 478 U.S. 675 (1986), the US Supreme Court stated that "the constitutional rights of students in public school are not automatically coextensive with the rights of adults in other settings" and may be limited by reasonable policies designed to take into account the special circumstances of the educational environment. The Court further noted that school principals have broad discretion to curtail lewd and vulgar student expression in school. In *Hazelwood Sch. Dist. v. Kuhlmeier*, 484 U.S. 260 (1988), the Supreme Court held that school principals can censor student expression in school newspapers and other school-related activities as long as the censorship decisions are based on legitimate pedagogical concerns.

Students have challenged local school policies or state statutes requiring their participation in patriotic exercises. In *Sherman v. Community Consolidated Sch. Dist. 21*, 980 F. 2d 437 (7th Cir. 1992) cert. denied, 508 U.S. 950 (1993), the court upheld a student's position not to participate in reciting the Pledge of Allegiance to the American flag. The Seventh Circuit Court's decision follows the rationale of other courts that have litigated this issue. Sensitive constitutional issues are being raised, following terrorist attacks on September 11, 2001, pertaining to reciting the Pledge of Allegiance and other patriotic exercises, such as displaying "God Bless America" and "In God We Trust" banners in schools. These school activities will likely result in new challenges to First Amendment rights to refrain from participation in patriotic exercises, to criticize school policies, or to raise church-state relations questions in connection with these patriotic observances and displays in public schools.

Unprotected Expression.   Courts have recognized that defamatory, obscene, and inflammatory communications are not protected by the First Amendment. Nor are these forms of expression protected in the public school setting.

Defamatory Expression.   Defamation includes slander (verbal) and libel (written) statements that are false, expose another to ridicule, and are communicated to others. Courts have upheld school principals in banning libelous content from school publications and in sanctioning students for slanderous speech.

Unlike defamatory expression, comments about the actions of public figures that are neither false nor malicious are constitutionally protected. One example of the constitutionally protected speech of a public figure that received much media attention in the mid-1980s was litigated by the US Supreme Court in *Hustler Magazine v. Falwell*, 485 U.S. 46 (1988). In the public school setting, school board members and superintendents are generally considered public figures for defamation purposes.

Obscene or Vulgar Expression. Courts have held that individuals are not protected by First Amendment rights for speaking or publishing obscene or vulgar language. This was confirmed in *Bethel School District v. Fraser* (1986), in which the Supreme Court granted the school principal considerable latitude in censoring obscene and vulgar student expression. The Supreme Court declared that speech protected by the First Amendment for adults is not necessarily protected for children, reasoning that the sexual innuendos contained in a student's speech during a student government assembly were offensive to students and inappropriate in the public school context. Other courts have struck down similar cases involving student expressions of obscene and vulgar language in the public schools.

Inflammatory Expression. Threats and fighting words made by students toward classmates or school personnel are not protected by the First Amendment. In determining whether a legitimate threat has been made, courts generally use a four-part test: (1) reaction of the recipient of the threat and other witnesses, (2) whether the person making the threat had made similar statements to the recipient in the past, (3) if the statement was conditional or communicated directly to the recipient, and (4) whether the recipient had reason to believe that the person making the threat would actually engage in violence (*Shoemaker v. State of Arkansas*, 343 Ark. 727, 2001; *United States v. Dinwiddie*, 76 f. 3d 193, 8th Cir. 1996). The courts as well as school principals are taking all threats seriously since the terrorist attacks on September 11, 2001.

Student Appearance

Despite continuing controversy over the years surrounding the issue of dress and grooming and the courts' frequent involvement, the US Supreme Court has consistently declined to address the issue. Student dress and grooming as a form of freedom of expression are not viewed as significant as most other forms of free expression are. There is, however, a First Amendment constitutional right associated with them. School principals, however, may within reason prescribe rules governing student dress and grooming using the standard of reasonableness. The standard of reasonableness centers around well-established facts that (a) students have protected First Amendment constitutional rights, and (b) students' rights must be balanced against the legit mate right of school officials to maintain a safe and disruption-free learning environment. The courts now require school authorities to demonstrate the reasonableness of their rules before the courts will decide if the constitutional rights of students have been violated.

Dress and grooming generally are viewed as a form of self-expression, and a student must be afforded opportunities for self-expression. Therefore, restrictions on student dress and grooming are justified when there is evidence of substantial disruption of the educational process. Justifiable reasons to restrict certain types of dress and grooming include violation of health and safety standards, gang-related dress, and controversial slogans.

The following restrictions have been upheld by the courts regarding dress and grooming (Essex, 2015):

1. School regulations necessary to protect the safety of students (e.g., wearing long hair or jewelry around shop and laboratories)
2. School regulations necessary to protect the health of students (e.g., requiring students to keep hair clean and free of parasites)
3. School regulations prohibiting dress and grooming that do not meet standards of community decorum (e.g., dressing in a manner that calls undue attention to one's anatomy)
4. Dress and grooming that result in material and substantial disruption of the maintenance of a safe and orderly environment for learning (e.g., wearing T-shirts containing vulgar, obscene, or defamatory language based on race, color, gender, national origin, or religion)

Health and Safety Standards. School officials may regulate certain types of dress and grooming that pose a threat to students' safety and health. For example, excessively long hair worn by students in shop classes, laboratories, or around dangerous equipment may pose a threat to their safety. School principals may take appropriate steps to regulate hair length in these situations. Students wearing fancy jewelry in shop classes, in laboratories, around dangerous equipment, and in physical education classes may pose a safety threat. School principals may take measures to regulate the type of jewelry worn in these situations.

School principals may require students to wash long hair for hygiene purposes. Similarly, school principals may take measures to address other hygiene problems related to dress. Efforts should always be made in these situations to ensure that the individual's dignity and rights are protected. The establishment of reasonable dress codes that are communicated to students and parents can curtail litigation regarding these issues.

Gang-Related Dress. In recent years, school principals have witnessed an increase in the prevalence of gangs and hate groups in public schools. Gangs and hate groups pose serious problems for school authorities because the presence of such groups on a campus may contribute to substantial disruption of the educational process and threats to the safety of students. Members of such groups often wear clothing or symbols signifying their group membership. Such dress may be in violation of a school's dress and grooming codes but may be litigated to include violations of the First Amendment, gender discrimination, and racial discrimination. Examples of controversial student expression that may involve First Amendment protection include T-shirts depicting violence, drugs (e.g., marijuana leaves), or racial epithets; ripped, baggy, or sagging pants or jeans; colored bandanas, Confederate flag jackets, baseball or other hats; words shaved into the hair, brightly colored hair, distinctive haircuts or hairstyles, ponytails, and earrings for males; exposed underwear; Malcolm X symbols; Walkmans, cellular phones, or beepers; backpacks and baggy coats; tattoos, unusual-colored lipsticks, pierced noses, lips, and tongues; and decorative dental caps. Courts generally rule that such "expression" does not have constitutional protection under the First Amendment when there is evidence of gang activity in the school and community. Due to close scrutiny by parents, law enforcement officers, and school authorities, gangs will often change their appearances to become less recognizable. Today, many gang members wear professional sports team jackets, caps, and neutral T-shirts, making it difficult to detect them. School principals may take reasonable steps to minimize gang presence in school.

Controversial Slogans.   Slogans worn on T-shirts, caps, and other items of clothing that contain vulgar, lewd, or obscene pictures may be regulated by school principals. Suggestive clothing that draws undue attention to one's body may also be regulated. Banning controversial slogans and inappropriate attire generally has been upheld when there is evidence of disruption, when there is community sentiment regarding dress standards, and when the message is offensive to others based on race, gender, color, religion, or national origin (*Pyle v. South Hadley School Committee*, 861 F. Supp. 157, Mass. 1994).

School Uniforms.   The wearing of uniforms is gaining popularity in large city school districts, including Baltimore, Chicago, Cincinnati, Detroit, Houston, Los Angeles, Miami, New Orleans, New York, and Philadelphia (National Association of Elementary School Principals, 1998). Advocates assert that student uniforms provide easy identification of students, eliminate gang-related dress, promote discipline, reduce violence and socioeconomic distinctions, prevent unauthorized visitors from intruding on campus, and foster a positive learning environment. Typically, when school uniform dress codes are adopted, they apply to students in elementary and middle schools and may be either voluntary or mandatory. Many private and parochial schools have required uniforms for years.

Extracurricular Activities

It is clear that students have a property interest in their education and cannot be denied attendance without due process of law (*Goss v. Lopez*, 419 U.S. 565, 1975). But this property right does not extend to extracurricular activities. Courts generally hold that conditions can be attached to extracurricular participation, because such participation is a privilege rather than a right. The reasoning of the courts is that extracurricular activities, as the name implies, are usually conducted outside the classroom before or after regular school hours, usually carry no credit, are generally supervised by school officials or others, are academically nonremedial, and are of a voluntary nature for participants.

For these reasons, the courts have upheld the conditions typically attached to extracurricular participation. School principals may not be required by the Fourteenth Amendment to provide due process when denying students extracurricular participation, unless the school board has established policies for suspending or expelling students from extracurricular activities. Courts have upheld the suspension of students from interscholastic athletics for violating regulations prohibiting smoking and drinking, including off-campus and off-season conduct, providing the regulations so stipulate. Members of athletic teams and other extracurricular groups (drama, band, debate, cheerleading, and clubs) often are selected through a competitive process, and students have no property right to be chosen. Most state athletic associations prohibit students from involvement in interscholastic competition for one year after a change in a student's school without a change in the parent's address. Courts generally uphold age restrictions on extracurricular participation in an effort to equalize competitive conditions. Courts usually endorse rules limiting athletic eligibility to eight consecutive semesters, or four years after eighth grade. Several states have adopted "no pass, no play" provisions, which require students to maintain a 2.0 grade point average to participate in athletics (Hambrick, 2001). And the US Supreme Court, in *Vernonia School District 4-7J v. Acton*, 515 U.S. 646 (1995), and in *Bd. of Educ. v. Earls*, 122 S. Ct. 2559 (2002), upheld school board policies requiring student athletes and those participating in other extracurricular activities to submit to random urinalysis as a condition of participation.

Student Discipline

School principals have not only the authority but the responsibility to maintain discipline in public schools. Although policies, rules, and regulations made at any level (e.g., classroom, building, school board) cannot contravene federal and state laws, school principals and teachers are granted wide latitude in establishing and enforcing conduct codes that are necessary to maintain a safe and orderly environment for learning. In this section, we examine educators' prerogatives and students' rights in connection with suspensions and expulsions, corporal punishment, and search and seizure.

Suspensions and Expulsions. Students may be excluded from school for violating school or district policy. Suspensions generally involve exclusion of a student from school for a brief, definite period of time, usually not exceeding ten days. Courts have held that because students have a property interest in attending school, they must be provided due process before being excluded from school. Prior to 1975, procedural due process accorded to suspended students was poorly defined. Lower courts differed widely in their interpretation of the Fourteenth Amendment guarantees in suspension cases. In 1975, in *Goss v. Lopez*, 419 U.S. 565 (1975), the US Supreme Court prescribed the minimum constitutional requirement in cases involving student suspensions of ten days or less. The Court concluded that oral notice to the student of the reason for short suspensions, followed by an immediate, informal hearing by a local school official, would fulfill the due process requirement in brief suspensions. The Court specifically rejected the usual trial-type format including the involvement of attorneys and the presentation and cross-examination of adverse witnesses typical in criminal cases.

Somewhat related to suspensions are *disciplinary transfers* of students to a so-called alternative school. Generally, such transfers do not involve denial of public education, because students do not have an inherent right to attend a given school. Nevertheless, such transfers might implicate protected liberty or property interests due to the involuntary nature of the transfer for disciplinary reasons. Therefore, pupils facing involuntary disciplinary transfers are entitled to minimal due process, including (a) written notice to both the student and his or her parents; (b) a meeting involving school officials, parents, and the student during which the transfer may be discussed; and (c) a meeting during which evidence may be presented and witnesses examined.

From a practical standpoint, expulsion is the exclusion of a student from school for a period of time exceeding ten days or more. Under common law, expulsion is vested exclusively in the board of education. Professional personnel may not expel students unless authorized by state statute.

Generally, courts have held that expulsion of students from school jeopardizes a student's property interests in an education. Thus students are guaranteed at least minimum due process under the Fourteenth Amendment. The following list enumerates suggested elements of recommended procedural due process in such cases:

1. A speedy and full notification of the charges should be given to the accused.
2. The accused should be provided an opportunity to answer the charges and to prepare an adequate defense.
3. The hearing should be conducted by an impartial tribunal.
4. The accused should be given the names of adverse witnesses, access to adverse evidence, and the right to introduce evidence.
5. The decision must be based on the evidence adduced at the hearing.
6. A prompt finding, giving the reasons for the decision and the evidence supporting it, should be delivered at the conclusion of the hearing.
7. The accused (or her counsel) should have the right to cross-examine adverse witnesses and introduce witnesses in her defense.
8. The accused has a right to representation by legal counsel.
9. A written record of the proceedings should be maintained.
10. The accused should have the right to appeal an adverse decision.

The Rehabilitation Act (Section 504), the Individuals with Disabilities Education Act (IDEA), and the Americans with Disabilities Act (ADA) provide special safeguards in the suspension and expulsion of children with disabilities. IDEA, in particular, assures all children with disabilities a free appropriate public education in the least restrictive environment. The Supreme Court in *Honig v. Doe*, 484 U.S. 305 (1988), has regarded expulsion and long-term suspension as a change in placement when children with disabilities are involved.

A crucial issue when suspending or expelling a disabled child is whether the misbehavior is related to the disability. Disabled students may be suspended for ten days or less without inquiry into whether the student's misbehavior was caused by the disability (*Bd. of Educ. of Peoria v. Ill. State Bd. of Educ.*, 531 F. Supp. 148, C.D. Ill. 1982). Courts reasoned that short-term suspension is not a change of placement and therefore does not trigger the procedures of IDEA. Expulsions and suspensions of more than ten days are changes of placement. They may not be used if there is a relationship between the misbehavior and the child's disability; see *S-1 v. Turlington*, 635 F. 2d 342 (5th Cir. 1891), *cert. denied*, 454 U.S. 1030 (1981). In these cases, transferring the child to a more restrictive environment is an option, after following change-of-placement procedures. If the misbehavior is not related to the disability, then expulsion and long-term suspension are permissible; but all educational services cannot be terminated. These special safeguards for the disciplining of disabled children do not apply to pupils who use illegal drugs or alcohol as stipulated in the ADA (29 U.S.C.A., § 706 (8) (West Supp., 1992).

Corporal Punishment. Although several states allow corporal punishment to be used as a means of student discipline, twenty-seven states have now banned corporal punishment, and legislation is under way in many more (US Department of Education, 2000). The American Academy of Pediatrics (2000) has recommended that corporal punishment be abolished in all states because of its detrimental effect on students' self-image and achievement as well as possible contribution to disruptive and violent behavior.

In the landmark Supreme Court decision *Ingraham v. Wright*, 430 U.S. 651 (1977), the Court held that corporal punishment of students does not violate the Eighth Amendment or the due process guarantees of the Fourteenth Amendment. The Court said that the Eighth Amendment's prohibition of cruel and unusual punishment applies to criminals only and is not applicable to the disciplining of students in public schools. The Court noted that "at common law a single principle has governed the use of corporal punishment since before the American Revolution: Teachers may impose reasonable but not excessive force to discipline a child." Regarding due process, the Court held that a student is not entitled to notice and a hearing prior to the imposition of corporal punishment.

Although the Supreme Court has held that the federal Constitution does not prohibit corporal punishment in schools, its use may conflict with state constitutions, state statutes, or local school board policies. Teachers can be disciplined or discharged for violating these state and local policies regulating corporal punishment.

Search and Seizure.   The Fourth Amendment provides that "the right of people to be secure in their persons, houses, papers, and effects, against unreasonable searches and seizures shall not be violated, and no warrants shall issue, but upon probable cause." The clause has been involved in numerous criminal cases. Evidence obtained in violation of the amendment is inadmissible in court.

The introduction of drugs and other contraband in schools has placed school officials in the position of searching students' person or lockers, and students claim that such acts are a violation of their Fourth Amendment guarantees. A student's right to the Fourth Amendment's protection from unreasonable search and seizure must be balanced against the need for school officials to maintain discipline and to provide a safe environment conducive to learning. State and federal courts generally have relied on the doctrine of in loco parentis, reasoning that school officials stand in the place of a parent and are not subject to the constraints of the Fourth Amendment. In *New Jersey v. T.L.O.*, 469 U.S. 325 (1985), the U.S. Supreme Court held that searches by school officials in schools come within the constraints of the Fourteenth Amendment. The Court concluded that the special needs of the school environment justified easing the warrant and probable cause requirement imposed in criminal cases, provided that school searches are based on "reasonable suspicion."

In 1995, the U.S. Supreme Court rendered its decision in *Vernonia Sch. Dist. 4-7J v. Acton*, 515 U.S. 646 (1995), holding that a school district's random suspicionless drug testing of student athletes as a condition for participation in interscholastic athletics did not violate the Fourth Amendment's prohibition against unreasonable searches and seizures. In this particular case, however, the Court noted specific features including student athletes' decreased expectations of privacy, the relative unobtrusiveness of the search procedures, and the seriousness of the need met by this search. Regardless of the procedures, however, this case clearly lowered schools' previous legal search standard of reasonable suspicion as set forth by *New Jersey v. T.L.O.* in 1985.

The Supreme Court ruled on the issue of random suspicionless drug testing of students with its decision in *Bd. of Educ. v. Earls*, 122 S. Ct. 2559 (2002), a 10th Circuit case from Oklahoma in which drug testing of students in any extracurricular activities was determined to be unconstitutional. In a 5–4 decision, the Supreme Court upheld the school district's policy of random suspicionless drug testing of all students who participated in any extracurricular activities, not just athletics. Using

Vernonia as a guideline, the 10th Circuit in *Earls* held that "before imposing a suspicionless drug testing program a school must demonstrate some identifiable drug abuse problem among a sufficient number of those to be tested, such that testing that group will actually redress its drug problem." In overturning the 10th Circuit's decision, the Supreme Court's majority in *Earls* stated that "a demonstrated drug abuse problem is not always necessary to the validity of a testing regime." Furthermore, the Court defends this stance by adding that "the need to prevent and deter the substantial harm of childhood drug use provides the necessary immediacy for a school testing policy." Thus, based on the *Earls* decision, random suspicionless drug testing of students does not violate the Fourth Amendment's protection from unreasonable searches and seizures.

Students with Disabilities

Historically, the prevailing attitude concerning the education of disabled students was that learning disabled, emotionally disturbed, deaf, blind, or otherwise disabled children were not the responsibility of the public schools. Consequently, many disabled children were exempted from compulsory school attendance laws either by parental choice or by school district design. Nationally, services for the disabled were either nonexistent or nonextensive. Very few school districts provided services; where such services existed, they were inadequate to meet even the minimal needs of this vulnerable minority group.

In recent years, substantial changes in attitude toward the disabled have occurred. Although disabled students do not comprise any "protected group" (such as race or gender) that is entitled to constitutional guarantees, federal statutes and state special education statutes were enacted to satisfy their constitutional rights. Lower court decisions and federal and state legislative enactments of the past three decades have mandated that all children, including the disabled, are entitled to admission to a school and placement in a program that meets their special needs. As summarized in the landmark Supreme Court school desegregation case, *Brown v. Bd. of Educ. of Topeka*, 347 U.S. 483 (1954), "education . . . is a right which must be made available to all on equal terms." Although the *Brown* decision dealt with the constitutional protections afforded minority children, its consent agreement implied a mandate that all students of legal age must be provided with appropriate school and classroom placement.

Two key court decisions outlined the legal framework for the constitutional protections of disabled children. In *Pennsylvania Association for Retarded Children (PARC) v. Commonwealth*, 334 F. Supp. 279 (E.D. Pa. 1977), a federal district court held that retarded children in Pennsylvania were entitled to a free public education and that, whenever possible, disabled children must be educated in regular classrooms and not segregated from other students. In *Mills v. Bd. of Educ. of the District of Columbia*, 348 F. Supp. 866 D.D.C. (1972), another federal district court expanded the *PARC* decision to include all school-age disabled children.

Subsequent to the *PARC* and *Mills* decisions, Congress passed two landmark pieces of legislation that led to the rapid development of comprehensive, nationwide educational programs for the disabled. Section 504 of the Rehabilitation Act of 1973 is a broad-based federal law that addresses discrimination against the disabled both in the workplace and in schools. The statute, as amended, stipulates: "No otherwise qualified individual with handicaps . . . shall solely by reason of her or his handicap, be excluded from participation in, be denied the benefits of, or be subjected to discrimination under any programs or activity receiving Federal financial assistance" (29 U.S.C., § 794 (a), 1988). Thus Section 504 would cut off all federal funds from schools that discriminate against the disabled. The statute also provides that all newly constructed public facilities be equipped to allow free access by disabled individuals.

The Education for All Handicapped Children Act (EAHCA) of 1975, and currently the Individuals with Disabilities Education Act (IDEA), provide federal funds to school districts that comply with its requirements. The major thrust of the acts, however, was to ensure the right of all disabled children to a public education. Major provisions of the law include a free appropriate public education, an individualized education program, special education services, related services, due process procedures, and the least restrictive learning environment; see 20 U.S.C.A., § 1400 (a) (West Supp. 1992).

According to IDEA, all disabled children have the right to a "free appropriate public education." An appropriate education for the disabled is defined as special education and related services. Special education refers to specially designed instruction at public expense, including a variety of opportunities on a spectrum from regular classroom instruction and special classes to placement in a private facility. Related services include transportation, physical and occupational therapy, recreation, and counseling and medical diagnosis. A written **individualized education program** (IEP) is another key element in a free appropriate public education. An IEP includes an assessment of the child's needs, specification of annual goals, strategies (methods, materials, interventions) to achieve the goals, and periodic evaluations of the child's progress. And finally, a disabled child must be educated in the least restrictive environment. That is, the placement must be tailored to the disabled student's special needs. In combination with related state laws, these federal statutes provide the guidelines for the education of the disabled.

In addition to the Rehabilitation Act, the disabled are now protected by the Americans with Disabilities Act of 1990 (ADA); see 42 U.S.C.A., § 12101–2213 (1990 & West Supp. 1992). This law prohibits discrimination in employment (and other situations) against any "qualified individual with a disability." Essentially it amplifies and extends prohibitions of Section 504 of the Rehabilitation Act of 1973. Coverage is not dependent on involvement of federal funds. A "reasonable accommodation" that would permit a qualified individual with a disability to perform the "essential functions" of a position (or other activity) must be provided.

The definition of a disabled person under ADA is somewhat different from that given in the Rehabilitation Act. Under the newer law, a "qualified individual with a disability" means "an individual with a disability who with or without reasonable modifications . . . meets the essential eligibility requirements for the receipt of services or the participation in programs or activities provided by a public entity"; see 42 U.S.C.A. § 12131 (2) (West Supp. 1992). To prevent conflict between the Rehabilitation Act and ADA, legislation requires that ADA be interpreted consistently with the older law. Thus court decisions interpreting Section 504 are not affected by the later law. Furthermore, the Rehabilitation Act looks to the terms of IDEA for resolution of most disputes concerning the education of the disabled; and compliance with IDEA will usually meet the requirements of ADA.

Of these three laws, IDEA has had the most significant impact on public schools. The IDEA legislation can be grouped into the following major statutory provisions:

- free appropriate public education
- individualized education programs
- attention deficit hyperactivity disorder
- least-restrictive environment
- placement in private schools
- related services
- due process protections
- discipline
- compensatory education
- attorney's fees and liability for reimbursement to parents
- IDEA and AIDS

Each one will be discussed briefly in turn.

Free Appropriate Public Education. To qualify for federal funds under IDEA, each state must adopt a policy "that assures all handicapped children the right to a free appropriate public education (FAPE)." IDEA defines a FAPE as special education and related services that (a) have been provided at public expense, under public supervision and without charge, (b) meet the standards of the state education agency, (c) include an appropriate preschool, elementary, or secondary education in the state involved, and (d) are provided in conformity with the individualized education program (IEP) required under Section 1414 (a) (5) of this title (20 U.S.C., § 1401, 18). A free appropriate public education must be specifically designed to meet the unique needs of the child.

Congress did not define specifically what constitutes a free appropriate public education delegating to local public schools to make the determination in accordance with the law. In *Board of Education of Hendrick Hudson Central School District v. Rowley*, 458 U.S. 176 (1982) the US Supreme Court noted that the free appropriate public education clause of the EAHCA does not require a state to maximize the potential of each special needs child.

Individualized Education Programs. The individualized education program (IEP) is the centerpiece of the statute's education delivery system for disabled children:

The term "individualized education program" means a written statement for each child with a disability developed in any meeting by a representative of the local educational agency or an intermediate educational unit who shall be qualified to provide, or supervise the provision of, specially designed instruction to meet the unique needs of children with disabilities (20 U.S.C., § 1414, d, 1, A). The requirements for the child's IEP statement include the following:

1. The child's present level of performance must be stated, requiring the school district to specifically indicate "how the child's disability affects the child's involvement and progress in the general curriculum."
2. The annual goals must be "measurable," and the child must "progress in the general curriculum."
3. Program modifications must be provided that will enable the child to "advance appropriately" toward attaining annual goals.
4. Provision must be made for the child to participate in state or school district student achievement assessments.

5. Evaluation procedures must relate to IEP objectives and measure the child's progress toward annual goals.
6. Parents must receive periodic report cards indicating the child's progress and the extent to which the progress is sufficient to achieve annual goals (*Schaffer v. Weast*, 546 U.S. 49, 2005).

IEPs must be developed by teams. IEPs must enable the child to receive educational benefits. However, the IDEA does not require states to provide special needs children with a potential-maximizing education. In *Schaffer v. Weast*, 546 U.S. 49 (2005), the U.S. Supreme Court determined that, under IDEA, the burden of proof in an administrative hearing is placed upon the student.

Attention Deficit Hyperactivity Disorder. A disability not specifically listed under the IDEA is attention deficit hyperactivity disorder (ADHD). It is most commonly defined by the criteria of inattention, hyperactivity, and marked impulsiveness (C.F.R., § 300.7, a, 1). Focus cannot be kept on any one topic long enough for a detailed assessment.

Although not specified, ADHD children may be covered under the IDEA, Section 504 of the Rehabilitation Act of 1973, and the Americans with Disabilities Act of 1990 (ADA). An ADHD child may be eligible for IDEA services under one of three categories: (1) other health impaired, (2) specific learning disability, and (3) seriously emotionally disturbed (*Alvin Independent School District v. A. D.*, ex. Rel, 503 F.3d 378, 5th Cir., 2007).

According to IDEA, there needs to be an established causal link between the characteristics of the child's disability and the child's educational difficulties. For example, a student's behavioral problems derived from attention deficit hyperactivity disorder (ADHD) from related occurrences may not qualify the student as a "Child with a Disability" under IDEA. In *Alvin Independent School District v. A. D.*, ex. Rel, 503 F.3d 378 (5th Cir. 2007), the Fifth Circuit Court of Appeals determined that the appellee did not qualify as a "Child with a Disability" under IDEA.

Least-Restrictive Environment. The IDEA advances the general philosophy that children with disabilities should be educated with typically developing children in the normal educational setting whenever possible. What precisely the "least-restrictive environment" requirement means operationally has been fertile ground for speculation. Terms commonly used to define least-restrictive environment are "inclusion," "full inclusion," and "integrated services."

Neither of these terms is found in Public Law 94-142 (EAHCA, 1975), Public Law 101-476 (IDEA, 1990), or their implementing regulations. The inclusion movement came out of the US Department of Education in the early 1980s under the "regular education initiative." Other terms include "least-restrictive environment" and "mainstreaming." Integrating children with disabilities in regular classrooms is commonly known as "mainstreaming" or "inclusion" (*J.P. ex rel. Peterson v. County School Board of Hanover County, Va.*, 516 F.3d 245, 4th Cir. 2008; *C.G. ex rel. A.S. v. Five Town Community School District*, 513 F.3d 279, 1st Cir., 2008)

What meets the least-restrictive environment provision? The IDEA's goal is full inclusion. However, not all students with disabilities must be placed in regular education classes (*Clyde K. v. Puyallup School District No. 3*, 35 F.3d 1396, 9th Cir., 1994; *Capistrano Unified School District v. Wartenberg*, 59 F.3d 884, 9th Cir., 1995).

Courts have approved more restrictive placements where students were not able to function in regular classes. In *Beth v. Van Clay*, 282 F.3d 493 (2002), the Seventh Circuit Court of Appeals determined that school district placement of a student with a severe disability in special education with reverse mainstreaming opportunities meets the least-restrictive environment opportunities.

Placement in Private Schools. The IDEA 2004 amendments stipulate congressional intent to fund special education programs in private schools. The public school district must provide services for children with disabilities who are currently attending private schools and allocate a pro rata share of federal money for such services (20 U.S.C.A, § 1413, a, 4). The state must ensure the following: "That, to the extent consistent with the number and location of children with disabilities in the state who are enrolled in private elementary and secondary schools, provision is made for participation of such children in the program assisted or carried out under this subchapter by providing for such children special education and related services (20 U.S.C.A, § 1413, a, 4).

These services are provided and paid for from federal funds whether or not the actual educational process takes place in private, religious, or public school facilities. The constitutional justification for public funding of special education services is found in *Zobrest v. Catalina Foothills School District*, 509 U.S. 1, 113 (1993), in which case the US Supreme Court held that providing public funding for a sign-language interpreter for a student attending a Catholic high school did not violate the Establishment Clause of the First Amendment.

In *Florence County School District v. Carter*, 510 U.S. 7 (1993), the US Supreme Court concluded that if a court determines that the educational placement of a special needs student is inappropriate, then the public school can be ordered to reimburse the parents for costs, even if the parents unilaterally placed the child in a private school.

Related Services. Under Public Law 94-142, related services that enable special-needs children to benefit from special education must be made available without cost to the parents. The term "related services" means transportation, and such developmental, corrective, and other supportive services (including speech-language pathology and audiology services, psychological services, physical and occupational therapy, recreation, including therapeutic recreation, social work services, counseling services, including rehabilitation counseling, orientation and mobility services, and medical services, except that such medical services shall be for diagnostic and evaluation purpose only) as may be required to assist a child with a disability to benefit from special education, and includes the early identification and assessment of disabling conditions in children (20 U.S.C., § 1401, 17). This list of related services is illustrative not exhaustive.

Questions arise as to which medical services fall within the IDEA parameters. In *Irving Independent School District v. Tatro*, 468 U.S. 883 (1984), the US Supreme Court determined that catheterization falls within the definition of "Related Services." Furthermore, in *Cedar Rapids Community School District v. Garrett F.*, 526 U.S. 66 (1999), the US Supreme Court determined that continuous nursing services are "related services" that school districts must provide under IDEA.

Due Process Protections. The IDEA provides significant due process protections. The procedural safeguards in IDEA include the following:

1. An opportunity for the parents of a child with a disability to examine all records relating to such child and to participate in meetings with respect to the identification, evaluation, and educational placement of the child, and the provision of a free appropriate public education to such child, and to obtain an independent educational evaluation of the child;
2. Procedures to protect the rights of the child whenever the parents of the child are not known . . . ;
3. Written prior notice to the parents of the child whenever such agency—

   a. proposes to initiate or change; or
   b. refuses to initiate or change; the identification, evaluation, or educational placement of the child . . . or the provision of a free appropriate public education to the child.

4. procedures designed to ensure that the notice required . . . is in the native language of the parents, unless it clearly is not feasible to do so;
5. an opportunity for mediation;
6. an opportunity to present complaints with respect to any matter relating to the identification, evaluation, or educational placement of the child, or the provision of a free appropriate public education to such child.

(20 U.S.C.A., § 1415)

The written prior notice referred to in Section 1415 of the IDEA must include:

1. a description of the action proposed or refused by the agency;
2. an explanation of why the agency proposes or refused to take the action;
3. a description of any other options that the agency considered and the reasons why those options were rejected;
4. a description of each evaluation procedure, test, record, or report the agency used as a basis for the proposed or refused action;
5. a description of any other factors that are relevant to the agency's proposal or refusal;
6. a statement that the parents of a child with a disability have protection under the procedural safeguards of this part and, if this is not an initial referral for evaluation, the means by which a copy of a description of the procedural safeguards can be obtained; and
7. sources for parents to contact to obtain assistance in understanding the provisions of the part (20 U.S.C.A., § 1415).

A document describing these procedural safeguards must be given to parents on initial referral, on notification of an IEP meeting, and on registration of any complaint by a parent. The IDEA requires that this document must contain a full explanation of the rights of students with disabilities related to:

A. independent educational evaluation
B. prior written notice
C. parental consent
D. access to educational records
E. opportunity to present complaints

F.   the child's placement during the pendency of due process proceedings
G.   procedures for students who are subject to placement in an interim alternative educational setting
H.   requirements for unilateral placement by parents of children in private schools at public expense
I.   mediation
J.   due process hearings, including requirements for disclosure of consultation results and recommendations
K.   State-level appeals (if applicable in that State)
L.   civil actions; and
M.   attorneys' fees

(20 U.S.C.A., § 1415)

One of the most significant procedural due process protections in the reauthorized IDEA is the right to an impartial due process hearing. Under the IDEA, any party to a hearing shall be given:

1. the right to be accompanied and advised by counsel and by individuals with special knowledge or training with respect to the problem of children with disabilities;
2. the right to present evidence and confront, cross-examine, and compel the attendance of witnesses;
3. the right to a written, or, at the option of the parents, electronic verbatim record of such hearing; and
4. the right to written, or, at the option of the parents, electronic findings of fact and decisions.

(20 U.S.C.A., § 1415)

Discipline.   All students are guaranteed due process of law, including notice and hearing prior to significant infringements of their property rights and liberty interests. However, special concerns exist in disciplining children with disabilities. When school officials seek to suspend or expel children with disabilities, the IDEA imposes significant legal protections for these children, including a "stay-put" provision to protect them from being removed from their current placements. The United States Supreme Court addressed the issue of removing children with disabilities for disciplinary reasons and the effect of the "stay-put" provision in *Honig v. Doe*, 484 U.S. 305 (1988).

The Court held that the language of the stay-put provision states that during the pendency of any proceedings initiated under IDEA, unless the state or local educational agency and the parents or guardian of a disabled child agree, "the child shall remain in the current educational placement" (*Honig v. Doe*). The Court did recognize a "dangerousness" exception to the stay-out provision by stating "while the child's placement may not be changed during any complaint proceeding, this does not preclude the agency from using its normal procedures for dealing with children who are endangering themselves and others," (*Honig v. Doe*) including the use of study carrels, timeouts, detention, or restriction of privileges. More drastic measures may be taken, where a student poses an immediate threat to the safety of others. In such situations, school officials may temporarily suspend the disabled student for up to ten school days.

With recent concerns over school violence and drug use, the revised IDEA provides school principals with additional authority to change the placement of special education students who carry weapons; sell or use drugs, or are a danger to themselves or others. The IDEA amendments state:

> School personnel under this section may order a change in the placement of a child with a disability—
>
> i. to an appropriate educational setting, another setting, or suspension, for not more than ten school days (to the extent such alternatives would be applied to children without disabilities); and
> ii. to an appropriate interim alternative educational setting for the same amount of time that a child without a disability would be subject to discipline, but for not more than 45 days—
> iii. the child carries a weapon to school or to a school function . . .
> iv. the child knowingly possesses or uses illegal drugs or sells or solicits the sale of a controlled substance while at school or a school function
>
> (20 U.S.C.A, § 1415, k).

If students with disabilities present a serious danger to themselves and others, school authorities may request a disciplinary transfer of the student to an alternative setting. The reauthorized IDEA provides that:

> A hearing officer . . . may order a change in the placement of a child with a disability to an appropriate interim alternative educational setting for not more than forty-five days if the hearing officer—
>
> a. determines that the public agency has demonstrated by substantial evidence that maintaining the current placement of such child is substantially likely to result in injury to the child or to others
> b. considers the appropriateness of the child's current placement
> c. considers whether the public agency has made reasonable efforts to minimize the risk of harm in the child's current placement, including the use of supplementary aids and services; and
> d. determines that the interim alternative education setting meets [other requirements of the IDEA]
>
> (20 U.S.C. A., § 1415, k)

School officials, however, must establish by "substantial" evidence that maintaining the current placement of the student will likely result in injury.

Attorney's Fees and Liability for Reimbursements to Parents. Attorney's fees were permitted by a 1986 amendment to the Education for All Handicapped Children Act of 1975. This amendment was considered necessary because Congress observed that the burden of heavy attorney's fees could conceivably make parents reluctant to raise valid complaints challenging school district actions. Furthermore, the Supreme Court in *Florence County School District v. Carter*, 510 U.S. 7 (1993) affirmed that local school districts may be liable for reimbursement to parents for tuition associated with alternative placement in private schools. However, in *Arlington Central School District v. Murphy*, 548 U.S. 291 (2006), the US Supreme Court determined that non-attorney expert's fees are not reimbursable to parents from the state.

IDEA and Aids. Are children with AIDS covered by the IDEA? The IDEA defines "handicapped children" as mentally retarded, hard of hearing, deaf, speech or language impaired, visually handicapped, seriously emotionally disturbed, orthopedically impaired, or *other health impaired children*, or children with specific learning disabilities who by reason thereof *require special education and related services* (20 U.S.C.A., § 1401, a, 1).

In the case of Aids students, the category that would most closely fit is "other health impaired children." This phrase is defined as "[l]imited strength, vitality or alertness due to chronic or acute health problems such as heart condition, tuberculosis, rheumatic fever, nephritis, asthma, sickle-cell anemia, *hemophilia*, epilepsy. Lead poisoning, leukemia, or diabetes, which adversely affects a child's educational performance" (34 C.F.R., § 300.5 b, 7).

AIDS is not listed as an example of an acute or chronic health problem by the IDEA. In October 1984, the Department of Education addressed the applicability of the IDEA to AIDS victims. The Department stated that an AIDS child is not considered to be "handicapped" as defined in IDEA unless the child needs special education. The policy states:

> Children with AIDS could be eligible for special education programs under the category of "other health-impaired," if they have chronic or acute health problems which adversely affect their educational performance (*Doe v. Bellville Public School District No. 118*, 672 F. Supp. 342 [S.D. Ill. 1987]). The question courts will ask: Is a child with AIDS a significant risk, and if so, could the child be reasonably accommodated?

TEACHERS AND THE LAW

A primary function of the state is to provide for an efficient system of public schools. The operation of public schools is governed by state statutory and regulatory policy. However, the actual administration of public school systems is delegated to state boards of education, state departments of education, and local school boards. These agencies adopt and enforce reasonable rules and regulations pursuant to state statutes for the operation of public school systems.

Although state statutes and regulatory policy are prominent in defining the employment conditions of public school personnel, they cannot be viewed independently of state and federal constitutional provisions, civil rights laws, and agreements between school boards and employee unions. These provisions may restrict or modify options stipulated in the state school code. In this section, we discuss licensure and certification, contracts, termination of employment, discrimination in employment, collective bargaining, and tort liability.

Licensure and Certification

The schools employ several categories of professional personnel: superintendents, principals, curriculum specialists, business managers, school psychologists, social workers, counselors, classroom teachers, and the like. To be eligible for employment in a professional position, the individual should possess a valid license or certificate issued according to statutory provisions of a given state. These statutes, varying from state to state, concern requirements and procedures for obtaining the different certificates. Generally, the legislature delegates the legal authority to issue and process certification to state boards and departments of education. In some states, however, the legislature delegates that authority to a local school district, as is the case in New York City and more recently in Chicago.

The preparation standards for each type of certificate are similar from state to state, with only a few exceptions. For example, every state requires applicants to have a college degree with a minimum number of credit hours in a prescribed curriculum. Besides educational requirements, other prerequisites may include evidence of good moral character, a minimum age, US citizenship, and satisfactory performance on a state-administered examination.

The initial certification is usually issued for a specified period of time, including various designations such as temporary, emergency, conditional, standard, life, or permanent. It is the certificate holder's responsibility to keep it renewed. This may require evidence of additional coursework, professional experience in a public school, or passage of a standardized examination such as the National Teachers Examination (NTE). The US Supreme Court, in *United States v. South Carolina*, 445 F. Supp. 1094 (D.S.C. 1977), *aff'd sub nom. National Education Association v. South Carolina*, 434 U.S. 1026 (1978), has upheld its use, even though the exam has been shown to disproportionately disqualify minority candidates. The Supreme Court of Texas, in *State v. Project Principle*, 724 S.W. 2d 387 (Tex. 1987), held that teachers possessing life certificates may be required to pass a state examination as a condition of continued employment. Certificates also include specific endorsements (e.g., superintendent, principal, counselor, teacher), subject areas (e.g., English, social studies, mathematics, sciences), and grade levels (e.g., elementary, middle or junior high school, high school). A school board's failure to assign professional personnel to positions for which they are certified can result in loss of state accreditation and federal funding (McCarthy, Eckes, & Decker, 2019).

The state also has the power to revoke certification. Certification revocation is different from dismissal from employment by a local board of education. A local school board can legally dismiss a superintendent, principal, teacher, or other professional employee; but the state is generally the only government body that can revoke a certificate. Moreover, state statutes usually specify the grounds and procedures for certification revocation. For example, under the Kentucky statute, it is provided that "any certification . . . may be revoked by the Education Professional Standards Board for immorality, misconduct in office, in-competency or willful neglect of duty. . . . Before the certification is revoked defendant shall be given a copy of the charges against him and given an opportunity, upon not less than twenty (20) days' notice, to be heard in person or by counsel" (Kentucky Revised Statutes, Ch. 161.120, 2018).

Contracts

A certificate renders the holder eligible for employment in a state; it does not guarantee employment. Statutory law provides that local boards of education have the legal authority to enter into contracts with professional personnel. The relationship between a school board and its professional employees is contractual. The general legal principles governing contracts—offer and acceptance, competent parties, consideration, legal subject matter, and proper form—apply to this contractual relationship.

Offer and acceptance pertains to the job description, compensation level, and time of performance to which both parties have agreed. In most states, because only the board of education has the power to employ personnel, it must exercise that function itself. It cannot delegate the employment duty to the superintendent of schools or to individual members of the school board. Further, a local board of education is considered to be a legal body only as a corporate unit; therefore, for a board to enter into a valid contract with a teacher or other professional personnel, there must be a meeting of the board.

Competent parties means that, for a valid contract to exist, the parties must be authorized by law to enter into a contractual relationship. By law the school board possesses the legal authority to enter into contracts. A teacher or other professional employee is legally competent to contract, providing they possess the necessary certification and meets other state requirements. An application of this element of contracts is found in a Kentucky case. A teacher lacked a certificate when they began teaching and was ineligible for one because they were under the state's minimum-age requirement for certification. Consequently, the contract between the parties was void, and the teacher was not entitled to receive a salary for the work they performed while a minor (*Floyd County Bd. of Educ. v. Slone*, 307 S.W. 23d. 912, Ky. 1957).

Consideration pertains to the promises bargained for and exchanged between the parties. Consideration is something of value—usually money or the equivalent. Promises to perform services gratuitously are not contracts, because they are not supported by consideration. To have valid consideration, each party must give up something of value. In the case of an employment contract, consideration consists of the exchange of promises between the employee and the school district. The employee promises to perform specified services, and the school board promises to pay a specified salary.

Legal subject matter refers to mutual assurance between the parties that the job and its performance would not be a violation of the law. Finally, *proper form* means that all legal requirements, as stipulated in the state's statutes, must be followed in order for a contract to be valid. The precise form for contracts may vary from one state to another, but in most states, the statute requires that contracts with professional personnel be written (*Jones v. Houston Independent School District*, 805 F. Supp. 476, S.D. Tex. 1991, *aff'd*, 979 F. 2d 1004, 1992).

The policies and procedures of the local board of education, provisions of the state constitution and its statutes, and the collective bargaining agreement, if there is one, are considered part of the contract between the school district and the teacher or other professional employee. It is recommended therefore that the aforementioned inclusions to an employee's contract be referenced either in the body or on the face of the contract; they then become expressly part of the individual employment contract.

Termination of Employment

Local boards of education possess the legal authority to terminate the employment of school personnel. The US Supreme Court bestowed on school boards this authority when it held that "school authorities have the right and the duty to screen the officials, teachers, and employees as to their fitness to maintain the integrity of the schools as part of ordered society" (*Adler v. Bd. of Educ.*, 342 U.S. 485, 1952). How-ever, despite the legal authority of a board of education to terminate the employ-ment, it cannot arbitrarily discharge personnel at any time.

Tenure Law. **Tenure** statutes protect teachers (and other school district personnel specifically enumerated in state statutes) from arbitrary actions by local boards of education. The courts have sustained the constitutionality of such statutes. Teachers' Tenure Act cases (*Teachers' Tenure Act Cases*, 329 Pa. 214, 197 A. 344, 1938) have concluded that tenure exists to protect competent teachers and other members of the teaching profession against unlawful and arbitrary board actions and to provide orderly procedures for the dismissal of unsatisfactory teachers and other profes-sional personnel.

Tenure is attained by complying with specific provisions prescribed by state stat-utes. The nature of these provisions varies from state to state, but certain conditions are included in most legislation. Nearly all statutes require that teachers serve a pro-bationary period before tenure becomes effective. Generally, the probationary period ranges from three to five years, during which time a teacher is employed on a term contract. On completion of the probation period, personnel acquire tenure either automatically or by school board action. Texas law is an exception and permits the local school board to choose between adopting continuing contracts and remaining under term contracts, in which case teachers do not have tenure (*White v. South Park Ind. Sch. Dist.*, 693 F. 2d 1163, 5th Cir. 1983).

Which positions are to be covered under tenure law is within the prerogative of state legislatures. In some jurisdictions, tenure legislation extends to selected administrative positions, but rarely to superintendents. Others afford tenure only to teachers. For example, in South Carolina, South Dakota, and Missouri, a school administrator possessing a teacher's certificate is a "teacher" within the meaning of tenure laws (*Snipes v. McAndrew*, 313 S.E. 2d 294, S.C. 1984; *Waltz v. Bd. of Educ.*, 329 N.W. 2d 131, S.D. 1983; *Fuller v. N. Kansas City Sch. Dist.*, 629 S.W. 2d 404, Mo. 1982). In Kentucky, "(t)he term 'administrator' for the purpose of [tenure] shall mean a certified employee, below the rank of superintendent" (*Ky. Rev. Stat.*, Ch. 161.720, § 8, 2018).

Although principals and certain other supervisory personnel can acquire tenure either as teachers or as principals in states having tenure laws, superintendents are not generally covered by tenure in that position unless the statute specifically indi-cates such inclusions. For example, the Illinois Supreme Court ruled that because they are district employees who require certification, superintendents are covered by the tenure law, but that the tenure protection extended only to a teaching position and not to an administrative one (*Lester v. Bd. of Educ. of Sch. Dist. No. 119*, 230 N.E. 2d 893, Ill. 1967). On the other hand, tenure can be acquired by superinten-dents in New Jersey (*N.J. Stat. Ann.*, § 18A:28–5(4), 2018).

In discussions of the termination of employment of teachers and supervisory personnel, the terms *nonrenewal* and *dismissal* are often used interchangeably. There is a substantial difference, however, in the manner in which the termination operates in each case. If not protected by tenure, a school employee may be nonrenewed for no reason or for any reason whatsoever, providing it does not violate an employee's substantive constitutional rights (e.g., free speech, protection against racial discrimi-nation). Courts have reasoned in these cases that the contract has simply terminated and there is no "expectancy of continued employment." Dismissal, on the other hand, whether under tenure status or during an unexpired contract, is permissible only "for cause." Consequently, a tenured employee or a non-tenured professional who is dismissed during a contract year is entitled to a due process hearing embodying all the statutory and constitutional safeguards.

Dismissal Procedures.   Most tenure laws provide specific procedures for dismissing tenured employees. The procedure typically includes three elements: notice by a specific date, specification of charges against the employee, and a hearing at which the charges are discussed. When state law describes a specific procedure for dismissal, it must be followed exactly to make the action legal.

Besides the procedures required under state law, tenure rights qualify for constitutional procedural protections encompassed within the concepts of *property interests* and *liberty interests* under the Due Process Clause of the Fourteenth Amendment. The holding of a teaching position qualifies as a **property right** if the employee has an unexpired contract or has acquired tenure. The aforementioned protections of the Fourteenth Amendment do not normally extend to nontenured employees. The Supreme Court in *Board of Regents v. Roth*, 408 U.S. 564 (1972), has affirmed the view of the courts that nontenured employees have no property or liberty interests in continued employment. In exceptional situations, courts have recognized "de facto tenure" where there was no tenure law, but tenure was acquired by custom and precedent (*Perry v. Sinderman*, 408 U.S. 593, 1972). However, de facto tenure is not possible where there is a well-established statewide system.

A **liberty interest** would be an issue in dismissal, and due process required, when evidence exists that a charge has been made that places a stigma on an employee's reputation, thus foreclosing future employment opportunities or seriously damaging his standing in the community (*Roth*). A liberty interest would not be a constitutional safeguard when school board members and school administrators refrain from making public statements or releasing information that is derogatory to the employee. Even when statements are made, if they simply describe unsatisfactory performance in general, normally they do not constitute a violation of the employee's Fourteenth Amendment rights.

Examples of charges against employees not involving stigma include ineffective teaching methods, inability to maintain classroom discipline, and inability to get along with administrators and colleagues. Failure to award tenure does not automatically create a stigma. Examples of stigmas that qualify for constitutional due process protection include the following charges: manifest racism, immoral conduct, serious mental disorder, a drinking or drug problem, willful neglect of duty, and responsibility for the deterioration of a school (Russo, 2015).

Causes for dismissal are generally specified in state statutes and differ from one state to another; however, there are similarities. For example, in Kentucky tenured employees can be dismissed for insubordination; immoral character or conduct; physical or mental disability; or inefficiency, incompetency, or neglect of duty (*Ky. Rev. Stat.*, Ch. 161.790, 2018). In Illinois cause for dismissal is specified as incompetency, cruelty, negligence, immorality or other sufficient cause, and whenever in the board's opinion a teacher is not qualified to teach or the best interests of the school require it (*Ill. Ann. Stat.*, Ch. 122, § 10–22.4, 2018). In Connecticut cause is enumerated as inefficiency, incompetency, insubordination, moral misconduct, disability as shown by competent medical evidence, elimination of position, or for other due and sufficient cause (*Conn. Gen. Stat. Ann.*, Tit. 5A, § 10–151, 2018).

Discrimination in Employment

Recent federal laws intended to remove discrimination in employment have had a direct impact on school board employment practices. Such legislation includes Title VII of the Civil Rights Act of 1964, Title IX of the Education Amendments of 1972, the Rehabilitation Act of 1973, the Equal Pay Act of 1963, the Age Discrimination Act of 1986, the Pregnancy Discrimination Act of 1978, and the Americans with Disabilities Act of 1990 (ADA). In addition, guidelines and policies from such federal agencies as the Equal Employment Opportunities Commission (EEOC), the Office of Economic Opportunity (OEO), and 42 U.S.C., § 1983, in particular, have been applied in claims of employment discrimination. In this section we briefly discuss race and gender discrimination; sexual harassment; discrimination based on disabilities; and age, religious, and pregnancy discrimination.

Race and Gender Discrimination.   Beginning in the early 1970s, the federal courts heard several cases challenging discrimination. In 1971 the US Supreme Court, in *Griggs v. Duke Power Company*, 401 U.S. 424 (1971), determined that Title VII of the Civil Rights Act of 1964 (pertaining to hiring, promotion, salary, and retention) covered not only overt discrimination but also practices that are discriminatory in operation. The Court held that an employment practice is prohibited if the exclusion of minorities cannot be shown to be related to job performance. The case involved requiring job applicants to possess a high school diploma and make a satisfactory score on a general intelligence test as criteria for employment. The practice was shown to discriminate against Black applicants. During the same year, the Court, in *Phillips v. Martin Marietta Corporation*, 400 U.S. 542 (1971), handed down a decision relative to the disparate treatment of the sexes in the workplace. The Court ruled that discriminatory treatment of the sexes, by employment practices not necessary to the efficient and purposeful operation of an organization, is prohibited by the same federal legislation.

The effect of these two landmark decisions was to force employers to remove "artificial, arbitrary, and unnecessary" barriers to employment that discriminate on the basis of race and gender classification. In 1972, coverage of these provisions of Title VII, which previously had applied only to private employment, was extended to discriminatory employment practices in educational institutions. Subsequent to *Griggs* and *Phillips*, lower courts have applied these same legal standards to Fourteenth Amendment, Section 1983, and Title VII equal protection cases.

To establish a constitutional violation of equal protection, aggrieved individuals must prove that they have been victims of discrimination. In 1981, the Supreme Court, in *Texas Department of Community Affairs v. Burdine*, 450 U.S. 248 (1981), set forth the procedural steps to file a Title VII suit. The plaintiff has the initial burden of establishing a prima facie case of discrimination by showing the existence of five factors: (1) member in a protected group (e.g., minorities, women, aged, handicapped), (2) application for the position, (3) qualification for the position, (4) rejection for the position, and (5) employer's continued pursuit of applicants with the plaintiff's qualifications for the position. These factors constitute an initial, or prima facie, case of discrimination in any type of personnel decision. Once a prima facie case of discrimination is established, the defendant (employer) must articulate a nondiscriminatory reason for the action. If this is accomplished, the plaintiff (employee or applicant) then must prove that the explanation is a pretext for discrimination, the real reason for the personnel decision being based on the consideration of "impermissible factors" in employment (*McDonnell Douglas Corp. v. Green*, 411 U.S. 792, 1973). In 1993, the Supreme Court, in *St. Mary's Honor Center v. Hicks*, 509 U.S. (1993), reiterated that the ultimate burden of proof in a discrimination suit lies with the plaintiff. The legal standards emanating from *Griggs*, *Phillips*, and *Hicks* in claims of discriminatory employment practices under Title VII have been applied also under civil rights legislation barring discrimination based on age. Title VII does not cover discrimination based on disabilities. Employees with disabilities in public schools must look to the Rehabilitation Act of 1973 (Section 504) and the Americans with Disabilities Act of 1990 (ADA).

Sexual Harassment. Charges of sexual harassment in the workplace have been litigated under Title VII of the Civil Rights Act of 1964 and Title IX of the Education Amendments of 1972. The regulations implementing Title VII define sexual harassment as follows:

> Unwelcome sexual advances, requests for sexual favors, and other verbal or physical conduct of a sexual nature constitute sexual harassment when (i) submission to such conduct is made either explicitly or implicitly a term or condition of an individual's employment, (ii) submission to or rejection of such conduct by an individual is used as the basis for employment decisions affecting such individual, or (iii) such conduct has the purpose or effect of unreasonably interfering with an individual's work performance or creating an intimidating, hostile, or offensive working environment. (29 C.F.R., § 1604.11(a), 1991)

In *Meritor Savings Bank v. Vinson*, 477 U.S. 57 (1986), the Supreme Court initiated this definition by identifying two different forms of sexual harassment: quid pro quo harassment and hostile environment harassment. **Quid pro quo sexual harassment** involves conditioning tangible employment benefits (e.g., promotion, demotion, termination) on sexual favors. **Hostile environment sexual harassment** involves a pattern of unwelcome and offensive conduct that unreasonably interferes with an individual's work performance or creates an intimidating or offensive work environment. The Court warned that "for sexual harassment to be actionable, it must be sufficiently severe or pervasive to alter the conditions of (the victim's) employment and create an abusive working environment." The Supreme Court, in *Harris v. Forklift Systems, Inc.*, 114 S. Ct. 367, 126 L. ed. 2d 295 (1993), elaborated further on the concept of the hostile environment form of sexual harassment, which creates a more difficult task for the courts to interpret than quid pro quo. In reaffirming the standard set in *Meritor*, the Court said that for sexual harassment to be actionable the conduct must cause "tangible psychological injury" rather than conduct that is "merely offensive." Courts determine this by examining such factors as frequency of the conduct, severity of the conduct, whether it is physically threatening or humiliating, and whether it unreasonably interferes with the employee's work performance.

Five kinds of sexual harassment include sexual bribery, sexual imposition, gender harassment, sexual coercion, and sexual behavior (Lunenburg, 2010k).

1. *Sexual bribery.* **Sexual bribery** is solicitation of sexual activity or other sex-linked behaviors by promise of rewards; the proposition may be either overt or subtle.
2. *Sexual imposition.* Examples of gross **sexual imposition** are forceful touching, feeling, grabbing, or sexual assault.

3. *Gender harassment*. **Gender harassment** means generalized sexist statements and behaviors that convey insulting or degrading attitudes about women. Examples include insulting remarks, offensive graffiti, obscene jokes, or humor about sex or women in general.
4. *Sexual coercion*. **Sexual coercion** means coercion of sexual activity or other sex-linked behavior by threat of punishment; examples include negative performance evaluations, withholding of promotions, threat of termination.
5. *Sexual behavior*. **Sexual behavior** means unwanted, inappropriate, and offensive sexual advances. Examples include repeated unwanted sexual invitations; insistent requests for dinner, drinks, or dates; persistent letters, phone calls, and other invitations.

School principals are strictly liable for quid pro quo sexual harassment under both Title VII of the Civil Rights Act of 1964 and Title IX of the Education Amendment of 1972. Therefore, school leaders need to take positive steps to prevent sexual harassment in the workplace.

School principals can take several positive approaches to preventing sexual harassment and maintaining a positive work environment.

- *Establish a no-tolerance policy*. Declare that the employer will not stand for sexual harassment, discrimination, or retaliation in the workplace. Under the law, the employer has the affirmative duty to rid the workplace of sexual harassment and discrimination. All employees should know their employer's policy that forbids sexual harassment, discrimination, and retaliation.
- *Widely disseminate the policy*. Everyone should have the policy readily available. This is important for both employer and employee.
- *Make it easy for employees to file complaints*. Employees should be able to complain to some-one other than their immediate superior. Someone outside the employee's chain of command, such as a human resource staff member, should be available to hear the complaint.
- *Investigate complaints promptly and objectively*. Promptness and objectivity should be the standard response. If management has knowledge of discrimination or sexual harassment occurring, an investigation should be conducted. Prompt and objective investigation says to everyone that the complaint is serious.
- *Take appropriate remedial action to prevent a reoccurrence*. Actions might include informal resolution between parties and disciplinary action against harassers. Offer the victim free counseling, if appropriate. Most important, provide training to all employees periodically.

Discrimination Based on Disabilities. The primary federal statutes that affect persons with disabilities are Section 504 of the Rehabilitation Act of 1973, 29 U.S.C., § 794 (2002), and the Americans with Disabilities Act of 1990 (ADA), 42 U.S.C., § 12101 *et seq.* (2003). These statutes prohibit discrimination based on disabilities against persons who are "otherwise qualified" for employment. These laws extend to all stages of employment, from recruiting and screening to hiring, promotion, and dismissal.

Section 504 and the ADA define a disabled person as one who has a physical or mental impairment that substantially limits one or more of such person's major life activities, has a record of such impairment, or is regarded as having such impairment. The ADA and Section 504, as recently amended, specifically exclude from the coverage of either law persons currently using illegal drugs and alcoholics whose use of alcohol interferes with job performance. But those in drug rehabilitation programs or who have successfully completed a program may be considered disabled.

The statutory definitions of a disabled person seem to include those with communicable diseases who are qualified to perform the job and whose condition does not threaten the health and safety of others. For example, the Supreme Court has ruled that the definition of a disabled person includes those with an infectious disease such as tuberculosis (*Sch. Bd. of Nassau Cty. Fla. v. Arline*, 480 U.S. 273, 1987). A lower court has extended coverage to teachers with AIDS (*Chalk v. U.S. District Court*, 840 F. 2d 701, 9th Cir., Cal. 1988).

The Supreme Court has said that an otherwise qualified disabled person is one who can meet all essential requirements of a job despite the disability. In determining whether a person with a disability is qualified to do a job, the central factors to consider are the nature of the disability in relation to the demands of the job. However, when a disabled person cannot meet all of the requirements of a job, an employer must provide "reasonable accommodation" that permits a qualified individual with a disability to perform the "essential functions" of a position. Furthermore, courts have ruled that Section 504 and the ADA protect otherwise qualified disabled individuals but do not require accommodations for persons who are not qualified for the positions sought (*Southeastern Community College v. Davis*, 442 U.S. 397, 1979; *Beck v. James*, 793 S.W. 2d 416, Mo. Ct. App. 1990; *DeVargas v. Mason & Hanger-Silas Mason Co.*, 911 F.2d 1377, 10th Circ. 1990, *cert. denied*, 111 S. Ct. 799, 1991).

Age Discrimination. The Age Discrimination in Employment Act (ADEA), 29 U.S.C., § 621 *et seq.* (2002) was enacted to promote employment of older persons based on their ability and to prohibit arbitrary age discrimination in the terms and conditions of employment. The law covers public employees, including teachers and school administrators. Thus, mandatory retirement for teachers is prohibited by law.

The act parallels Title VII in its application and operation. Litigation under ADEA thus follows the disparate treatment standard used for race and gender discrimination cases. A school district charged with age discrimination may defend itself by articulating nondiscriminatory reasons for the adverse employment decision, such as inferior qualifications or poor performance rather than age.

Religious Discrimination. Citizens' free exercise of religion is protected under the religion clauses of the First Amendment and the Equal Protection Clause of the Fourteenth Amendment. These clauses prohibit discrimination against any public school employee on the basis of religious beliefs. In addition to constitutional safeguards, public school employees are protected from religious discrimination under Title VII. In Title VII, as amended, Congress requires accommodation of "all aspects of religious observances and practices as well as belief, unless an employer demonstrates that he is unable to accommodate an employee's or prospective employee's religious observance or practice without undue hardship on the conduct of the employer's business" (U.S.C., § 2000e [j], 2002). The Equal Employment Opportunity

Commission (EEOC) has developed guidelines with suggested accommodations for religious observance, such as assignment exchanges, flexible scheduling, job assignment changes, and using voluntary substitutes.

Pregnancy Discrimination. According to the Pregnancy Discrimination Act (PDA), 42 U.S.C., § 2000e (k), (2002) which is an amendment to Title VII enacted in 1978, employers may not discriminate based on pregnancy, childbirth, or related medical conditions. Mandatory maternity leave policies have been the subject of litigation. In *Cleveland Board of Educ. v. LaFleur*, the Supreme Court held that a school board policy which required all pregnant teachers regardless of circumstances to take mandatory maternity leave for specified periods before and after childbirth was unconstitutional. The Court stated that it had long recognized that freedom of personal choice in matters of marriage and family choice liberties were protected under the Due Process Clause of the Fourteenth Amendment: "By acting to penalize the pregnant teacher for deciding to bear a child . . . can constitute a heavy burden on the exercise of these protected freedoms."

The US Constitution still permits school boards to implement maternity leave policies that are not arbitrary and fulfill a legitimate goal of maintaining continuity of instruction in a school system. For example, a mandatory maternity leave beginning date for teachers set at the beginning of the ninth month of pregnancy was upheld on "business necessity" grounds by the Court of Appeals, Ninth Circuit (*deLaurier v. San Diego Unified Sch. Dist.*, 588 F 2d 674, 9 Cir. 1978). A New Jersey court has sustained a period of child-bearing disability of four weeks before expected birth and four weeks following the actual date of birth for purposes of sick leave benefits (*Hynes v. Bd. of Educ. of Twp. of Bloomfield, Essex County,* 1190 N.J. Super. 36, 461 A. 2d 1184, 1983). A court found a male teacher not entitled to paid maternity leave for the purpose of caring for his disabled pregnant wife (*Ackerman v. Bd. of Educ.*, 287 F. Supp. 76, S.D. N.Y. 1974). However, child-rearing leave must not be made available only to females. Such a provision in a collective bargaining agreement was declared to violate Title VII (*Shafer v. Bd. of Educ. of Sch. Dist. of Pittsburgh, PA*, 903 F. 2d 2443, 3d Cir. 1990).

A federal law, the Family and Medical Leave Act of 1993 (FMLA), P.L. 103-3, requires state and local government employers to provide up to twelve work weeks of unpaid leave during any twelve-month period for the birth or adoption of a child. Upon return from FMLA leave, an employee must be restored to his or her original job, or to an equivalent job with equivalent pay and benefits. Other provisions of the act are requirements to provide 30 days' notice of leave, medical certifications supporting the need for leave, and reports regarding the employee's intention to return to work. Employees can bring civil action for employer violations of FMLA provisions.

Tort Liability

A **tort** is a civil wrong, not including contracts, for which a court will award damages. The three major categories of torts are intentional interference, strict liability, and negligence. Instances of intentional interference and strict liability in school-related injuries are rare and will not be pursued in this section. Accordingly, we examine the elements of negligence and the defenses against liability. We also address liability under Section 1983 of the Civil Rights Act.

Elements of Negligence. To establish a legal cause for action in tort, four essential elements must exist: The individual has a duty to protect others against unreasonable risks; the individual failed to exercise an appropriate standard of care; the negligent act is the proximate cause of the injury; and there is a physical or mental injury, resulting in actual loss or damage to the person (Alexander & Alexander, 2019; McCarthy, et al, 2019; Russo, 2015).

Duty. School employees have a **duty** to protect students entrusted to their care from being injured. Specifically, these duties include adequate supervision and instruction, maintenance of premises and equipment, and foreseeability. The test of foreseeability is whether under all circumstances the possibility of injury should have been reasonably foreseen and that supervision likely would have prevented the injury. For example, a teacher was found guilty of negligence when an eighth-grade pupil was injured from pebble throwing during a morning recess (*Sheehan v. St. Peter's Catholic School*, 291 Minn. 1, 188 N.W. 2d 868, 1971). Similarly, in a New Jersey suit, an elementary school principal was held liable for injuries suffered when a pupil was struck by paper clips shot from a rubber band by another child before the classrooms opened. The court found the principal had acted improperly by announcing no rules on the conduct of students before entering classrooms, by not assigning teachers to assist him in supervising the pupils before school, and by engaging in activities other than overseeing the pupils' activities (*Titus v. Lindberg*, 49 N.J. 66, A. 2d 65, 1967).

Standard of care. Failure of a school employee to act in a manner that conforms to an appropriate **standard of care** can render said employee negligent. The standard of care is that which a reasonable and prudent person would have exercised under similar circumstances. For example, the Oregon Supreme Court said "Negligence . . . is . . . the doing of that thing which a reasonably prudent person would not have done, in like or similar circumstances" (*Biddle v. Mazzocco*, 284 P. 2d 364, Ore. 1955). The model for the reasonable and prudent person has been described as one who possesses "(1) the physical attributes of the defendant himself, (2) normal intelligence, (3) normal perception and memory with a minimum level of information and experience common to the community, and (4) such superior skill and knowledge as the actor has or holds himself out to the public as having" (Alexander & Alexander, 2019, p. 502).

The standard of care required would depend on such circumstances as the age, maturity, and experience of students; the type of activity; the environment; and the potential for danger. The amount of care owed to children increases with their immaturity. A higher standard of care is required in shop, physical education, and laboratory classes and in situations and environments that pose a greater threat of danger (e.g., school field trips).

Proximate cause. There must be a connection between the action of school personnel and the resultant injury sustained by the student. Courts will ask, "Was the failure to exercise a reasonable standard of care the **proximate cause** of the injury?" The cause of the injury first must be established. Then it must be shown that there was some connection between the injury and the employee's failure to exercise a reasonable standard of care.

As in determining whether an appropriate standard of care has been exercised, the test of foreseeability is used in establishing proximate cause. For proximate cause to be established, it is not necessary to have foreseen a particular injury. If reasonable precautions are taken and an intervening injury not foreseen occurs, no negligence exists. Such was the case when a student returned to his desk and sat on a sharpened pencil placed there by another student. School authorities were not held liable for the injury (*Swaitkowski v. Bd. of Educ. of City of Buffalo*, 36 A.D. 2d 685, N.Y. 1971).

Injury. There must be proof of actual loss or damage to the plaintiff resulting from the **injury**. If the injury suffered is caused by more than one individual, damages will be apportioned among the defendants (McCarthy et al., 2019). A school district may be required to compensate an injured party for negligent conduct of an officer, agent, or employee of the district. Individual school board members or employees (superintendents, principals, teachers) may also be liable personally for torts that they commit in the course of their duties.

Defenses Against Negligence. Several defenses can be invoked by a defendant (school board, superintendent, principal, teacher) in a tort action. These defenses include contributory negligence, assumption of risk, comparative negligence, and government immunity.

Contributory negligence. If it is shown that a student's own negligence contributed to the injury, the law in many states would charge the student with **contributory negligence**. However, a student cannot be charged with contributory negligence if he is too immature to recognize the risks: A standard of care that is adequate when dealing with adults generally will not be adequate when dealing with children. For example, in about a dozen states, courts have ruled that students under seven years of age cannot be prohibited from recovery of damages because of negligence. In other states, the age has been set at four, five, or six years. And for older children up to the age of fourteen, there is a "rebuttable presumption" that they are incapable of contributory negligence (Fischer et al., 2003).

Assumption of risk. Another commonly used defense in tort actions is the doctrine of **assumption of risk**. It is based on the theory that one who knowingly and willingly exposes oneself to a known danger may be denied tort recovery for injury sustained. Requisite to invoking a defense of assumption of risk is that there be knowledge and appreciation of the danger. Thus it was held that a child who was cut by submerged broken glass while playing in a high school sandpit did not assume the risk of injury because he did not know the glass was in the sandpit (*Brown v. Oakland*, 124 P. 2d 369, Cal. 1942). On the other hand, the Oregon Supreme Court found an assumption of risk in the injury of a high school football player when he was injured in a scheduled football game (*Vandrell v. Sch. Dist. No. 26C, Malheur Cty.*, 233 Ore. 1, 376 P. 2d 406, 1962). As with contributory negligence cases, courts will consider the age and maturity level of students when assessing a defense of assumption of risk in tort.

Comparative negligence. Where the common-law rule of contributory negligence and assumption of risk is followed, plaintiffs whose own negligence contributed to an injury are barred completely from recovery. This harsh rule has been modified. Some states have adopted the doctrine of **comparative negligence**. Under the comparative negligence doctrine, a plaintiff can obtain a proportionate recovery for injury depending on the amount of negligence they contributed to the injury. Specific statutory provisions vary from state to state (Alexander & Alexander, 2019).

Government immunity. The origin of the doctrine of **government immunity** from tort liability can be traced to two early cases, one in England in 1788 and the other in Massachusetts in 1812 (*Russell v. Men of Devon*, 100 Eng. Rep. 359, 2 T.R. 667, 1788; *Mower v. Leicester*, 9 Mass. 237, 1812). The courts held that the government could not be sued for negligence; thus, the precedent of the immunity of school districts from tort liability was established and remained in effect until the passage of the Federal Tort Claims Act of 1946. Subsequently, the doctrine of state immunity in tort has been abrogated or modified by state legislatures. However, tort law does extend certain immunity to teachers and administrators in the scope and performance of their duties. One example is administering corporal punishment in schools (*Ingraham v. Wright*, 430 U.S. 651, 1977).

School board members also have some degree of immunity in the scope and performance of their duties. However, Section 1983 of the Civil Rights Act, rooted in 1871, changed the status of the immunity of school board members regarding their activities. This section provides that every person who subjects any citizen of the United States to the deprivation of any rights secured by the US Constitution be liable to the (injured) party in an action at law (42 U.S.C., § 1983, 1871). A plethora of court cases have been litigated under the act, primarily dealing with First and Fourteenth Amendment rights. The tort liability of school board members was further extended under Section 1983 to students by the Supreme Court decision in *Wood v. Strickland*, 420 U.S. 308 (1975). The Court held that school board members could be sued individually by students whose constitutional rights were denied. The case involved a denial of due process of students in a suspension hearing.

SUMMARY

1. All three levels of government—federal, state, and local—exercise some degree of authority and control over public education.
2. At the federal level, the US Constitution, federal statutes, federal administrative agencies, and case law all constitute sources of law under which school principals operate.
3. State-level sources of law under which school principals operate include the state's constitution, state statutes, state administrative agencies, and case law.
4. At the local level, local school board policies provide another source of law for school principals, as well as their individual school's rules and regulations.
5. The American judicial system consists of federal and state courts. The federal court system has its basis in the US Constitution. State court systems have their basis in state constitutions or statutory laws. The federal courts have primary jurisdiction on federal law questions, while state courts have primary jurisdiction on laws of each respective state.
6. Litigation has reached both federal and state courts in the areas of compulsory school attendance, church-state relations, school fees, the curriculum, and state-mandated testing.
7. US Supreme Court decisions have been prevalent in such student-related issues as freedom of expression, corporal punishment, search and seizure, suspensions and expulsions, and students with disabilities.

8. US Supreme Court decisions have been prevalent also in such staff-related issues as certification and licensure, contracts, termination of employment, discrimination in employment, sexual harassment, and tort liability.

KEY TERMS

general welfare clause
due process clause
equal protection clause
case law
property interest
in loco parentis
individualized education program
   (IEP)
tenure
property right
liberty interest
quid pro quo sexual harassment
hostile environment sexual
   harassment

sexual bribery
sexual imposition
gender harassment
sexual coercion
sexual behavior
tort
duty
standard of care
proximate cause
injury
contributory negligence
assumption of risk
comparative negligence
government immunity

FIELD-BASED ACTIVITIES

1. Litigation has reached both federal and state courts in the areas of compulsory school attendance, church-state relations, school fees, the curriculum, and state-mandated testing. Consult school board policies in your district and interview your building principal, and your school district's attorney, concerning each of the issues just listed. Record your responses in your journal.
2. US Supreme Court decisions have been prevalent in such student-related issues as freedom of expression, corporal punishment, search and seizure, suspensions and expulsions, and students with disabilities. Consult school board policies in your district and interview your building principal, and your school district's attorney, concerning each of the student-related issues. Record your responses in your journal.
3. US Supreme Court decisions have been prevalent also in such staff-related issues as certification and licensure, contracts, termination of employment, discrimination in employment, sexual harassment, and tort liability. Consult school board policies in your district and interview your building principal, and your school district's attorney, concerning each of the staff-related issues. Record your responses in your journal.

SUGGESTED READINGS

Alexander, K., & Alexander, M. D. (2019). *American public school law* (9th ed.). St. Paul, MN: West Academic. This book is intended for graduate students studying education or students in law schools who desire a comprehensive view of the law that governs the public school system of America. The legal precedents presented and discussed herein deal with the multitude of issues occurring in a country that has developed an extraordinary reliance on the public schools as a mechanism for social and economic justice and improvement.

Essex, N. L. (2015). *School law and the public schools: A practical guide for educational leaders* (6th ed.). Boston, MA: Pearson. This book was written to provide practical knowledge to practicing and prospective educational leaders, students of educational leadership, and policymakers at all educational levels. The author thoroughly yet succinctly covers legal issues of constitutional, statutory, and case law.

Imber, M., & von Geel, T. (2018). *Education law* (6th ed.). New York, NY: Routledge. In this sixth edition, the authors of *Education Law* provide a comprehensive survey of the legal problems and issues that confront school administrators and policymakers. The greater the likelihood of litigation or error in a particular area of professional practice, the more extensive the discussion. Landmark cases and cases that best illustrate major principles of education law have been retained and surrounded by expanded discussion and analysis.

McCarthy, M. M., Eckes, S. E., & Decker, J. R. (2019). *Public school law: Teachers' and students' rights* (8th ed.). Boston, MA: Pearson. The text addresses legal principles applicable to practitioners in a succinct but comprehensive manner. It blends a detailed treatment of landmark cases with a thorough discussion of the legal context, trends, and generalizations to guide all school personnel in their daily activities. Information in this text will help alleviate concerns voiced by educators who either don't know the legal concepts that govern schools or feel that the scales of justice have been tipped against them.

Russo, C. J. (2015). *The law of public education* (9th ed.). St. Paul, MN: West Academic. This ninth edition of *The Law of Public Education* is designed to provide basic knowledge of the laws affecting public education in the United States. The text covers principles and patterns of law applied to various aspects of public education. Citations now include references to West's *Education Law Reporter*, thereby making it easier for instructors and students to locate cases.

Part IV Case Study

A Case for the Attorney

■ ■ ■

Setting: Knowland High School is the second high school in the Eisenhower School District. Knowland lies across town from Dover High School and is known as the "country" high school because of its location at the edge of the city. Many of the students attending this school reside in several very small communities that recently have been incorporated by the city. When Knowland is compared to Dover High School, the most glaring difference is the larger number of disadvantaged students.

Scenario: As he comes down the hall to his office at Knowland, Principal Gary Jones hears his secretary say, "If you would only wait for a few minutes, Ms. Freer, I am sure that Mr. Jones will see you about this urgent matter."

Mr. Jones rounds the corner to the waiting room and greets Ms. Freer, saying, "Good morning, Ms. Freer. How are you today?"

"You wouldn't ask if you knew what I was going to say, Mr. Jones. I need to see you right away, and privately." She looks pointedly at the secretary, who immediately resumes processing the daily mail.

After getting Ms. Freer settled in his office, Mr. Jones inquires, "What is your urgent concern, Ms. Freer?"

"Well," she huffs, "I believe I saw Coach White having a beer with one of our students in a café in the neighboring town. I went in to see about a carryout meal, and there they were big as life, just sitting at the bar looking into each other's eyes. Each of them had a mug of beer in one hand. They were so engrossed with each other, they didn't even see me."

"Are you sure you saw Coach White? And what was the name of the student you saw?"

"I am sure the man was Coach White. He was still in his coaching shirt and shorts with our school colors. Can you imagine that? Bringing such disgrace on our high school! I have no idea who the girl was. She was mighty pretty and so was the gold jewelry she was wearing! Now what are you going to do about such a scene?"

"I'll look into the situation and take the appropriate action, Ms. Freer. Please trust me to handle this in an appropriate way."

As soon as Ms. Freer leaves the office, Mr. Jones calls the athletic director, Steve Hill, and asks him to come to his office. He tells Director Hill what has been reported and asks if he has seen or heard anything about Coach White dating one of the high school students.

"No, but I will tell you that I have heard rumors about him being associated with some gold jewelry disappearing in the locker room. I never could get anyone, students or staff, to tell me anymore, so I let it go. I figured that if someone had valuable jewelry stolen, they would report it and then we could investigate. Oh, and one more thing, one of the girls seemed pretty upset last week. She was crying and wanted to talk to Coach White, but I never could get her to tell me anything. It seems to me that at one time she was Coach White's student trainer when he was coaching the girls' basketball team. Maybe you could talk to her and find out more."

"What is her name, Steve?"

"Clara Garcia is her name, and she is a junior."

When Clara comes into Mr. Jones's office, she is visibly upset. Mr. Jones starts the conversation by asking about her activities and her work as a student trainer. She shares that she had enjoyed working with Coach White.

"Why, then, were you so upset last week?" asks Mr. Jones.

At first Clara denies being upset; but after learning that the athletic director has seen her crying, she admits that she is in turmoil. She has lost her gold necklace and her gold bracelet. Her father gave both items to her when she turned sixteen.

"Where do you think you lost your jewelry?" asks Mr. Jones.

Clara's answer surprises the principal. "I gave my jewelry to Coach White for safekeeping, and he says he lost it."

Mr. Jones tells Clara that he will check for her missing jewelry and asks her to bring him a detailed description. He also tells her that she should keep alert to rumors and possible sightings of her jewelry.

About two weeks later, Steve Hill, the athletic director, visits Mr. Jones in the office and says, "I think I know who the current girlfriend is. I think I also know who Coach White's ex-girlfriend is—Clara Garcia." He continues, saying that he overheard a couple of the boys talking about Clara and how stuck up she was now that she had had an affair with Coach White. "The new girl is a senior, seventeen years old, going on twenty-five in looks. Her name is Sara Blitz."

Just then Mr. Jones's secretary buzzes him to let him know that Clara Garcia is outside wanting to see him right away. He asks Director Hill to leave via the back door to his office and invites Clara to come in and sit down. Immediately Clara blurts out, "I saw it, Mr. Jones. Sara Blitz is wearing my jewelry. Please help me get my jewelry back. My dad will kill me if he finds out that I lost it!" Mr. Jones calms Clara and sends her on her way, assuring her that action will be taken.

He calls in Sara Blitz, who is indeed wearing a beautiful gold necklace and bracelet. He asks her where she got them and she says, "They are gifts from my boyfriend."

"Who is your boyfriend?"

"Someone you don't know."

"May I have a closer look at the jewelry? It is beautiful."

After noting the make and marks, Mr. Jones knows that this jewelry belongs to Clara Garcia and presses Sara to tell him more. She resists at first, but eventually confesses that Coach White is her boyfriend. With that confession, Mr. Jones takes her into the counselor's office and tells her to remain there until he comes for her.

Mr. Jones takes a few minutes to call Dr. Petrovsky, superintendent, to inform him of the facts. He promises to visit personally to brief Dr. Petrovsky about all the details as soon as the current crisis is addressed.

Now Mr. Jones knows that he must confront Coach White about sexual abuse and sexual harassment of Clara Garcia and Sara Blitz. He must also confront Coach White about what appears to be a clear case of theft of Clara's jewelry. He knows that he must give due process to Coach White, but at the moment he is so angry that he can hardly think straight. He needs time to organize his thoughts, but he knows that both Sara and Clara are waiting. He also knows that he must ask both students about the extent of their involvement with Coach White, and he must report all of this to the parents of the students.

Upon questioning each girl independently, first Sara and then Clara, Mr. Jones learns that both girls have been intimate with Coach White. He also learns that neither set of parents has a clue about what has been an ongoing set of affairs with Coach White. He understands better than ever before in his tenure as principal that being knowledgeable about the law is critical to any administrative role.

Questions

1. What laws have been violated? What school board policies have been violated? What "good causes" for termination of Coach White will most likely be pursued?
2. What due process must the district provide?
3. What are the students' legal rights in a situation such as this?
4. What court or courts could possibly end up hearing the case?
5. What kind of liability does Mr. Jones possibly have in this case? Steve Hill, the athletic director? The school district?

References

■ ■ ■

20 U.S.C.A, § 1400

20 U.S.C.A., § 1401(a)(1)

20 U.S.C.A., § 1412(a)(10)(i)(l)

20 U.S.C.A., § 1415

20 U.S.C., § 1401 (17)

20 U.S.C., § 1401 (18)

20 U.S.C., § 1414 (d)(1)(A)

20 U.S.C., § 1413 (a)(4)

20 U.S.C., § 1415(k)

20 U.S.C. § 2000 e (j)

29 C.F.R., § 1604.11(a)

34 C.F.R., § 300.5(b)(7)

34 C.F.R., § 300.7(a)(1)

Abbott, M. G., & Caracheo, F. (1988). Power, authority, and bureaucracy. In N. J. Boyan (Ed.), *Handbook of research on educational* administration (pp. 239–257). New York, NY: Longman.

Abdul-Hamid, H., Saraogi, N., & Mintz, S. (2017). *Lessons learned from World Bank education management information system operations: Portfolio review, 1998–2014*. World Bank Publications.

Abramson, P. (2010). Fifteenth annual school construction report. *School planning and management*. Dayton, OH: Peter Li Education Group, p. 2.

Ackerman v. Board of Education, 287 F. Supp. 36, N.Y. (1974).

Adair, J. (2019). *Decision Making and Problem Solving*. London, GBR: Kogan Page.

Adams, S. (2018). *Win bigly persuasion in a world where facts don't matter*. New York, NY: Penguin.

Addams, J. (1910). *Twenty years at Hull House: With autobiographical notes*. New York, NY: Macmillan.

Addonizio, M. F., & Phelps, J. L. (2000). Class size and student performance: A framework for policy analysis. *Journal of Education Finance, 26*, 135–156.

Adler, M. (1961). *Great ideas from the great books*. New York, NY: Simon & Schuster.

Adler, M. (1982). *The Paideia Proposal,* New York, NY: Macmillan.

Adler v. Board. of Education, 342 U.S. 485 (1952).

Agarwal-Rangnath, R. (2020). *Planting the seeds of equity: Ethnic studies and social justice in the k–12 classroom*. New York, NY: Teachers College Press.

Age Discrimination Employment Act (ADEA), 29 U.S.C., § 621 et seq (2002).

Agor, W. H. (1989). *Intuition in organizations*. Newbury Park, CA: Sage.

Agostini v. Felton, 521 U.S. 223 (1997).

Agran, M., Blanchard, C., Wehmeyer, M., & Hughes, C. (2001). Teaching to self-regulate their behavior: The differential effects of student versus teacher-delivered reinforcement. *Research in Developmental Disabilities, 22*(4), 319–332.

Aguilar, E. (2013). *The art of coaching: Effective strategies for school transformation*. San Francisco, CA: Jossey-Bass.

Aguilar v. Felton, 423 U.S. 402 (1985).

Aken, V., & Berends, H. (2018). *Problem solving in organizations*. New York, NY: Cambridge University Press.

Albanese, R., & Van Fleet, D. D. (1985). Rational behavior in groups: The free-riding tendency. *Academy of management Review, 10*(2), 244–255.

Alberto, P. A., & Troutman, A. C. (2009). *Applied behavioral analysis for teachers* (8th ed.). Boston, MA: Pearson.

Alexander, K., & Alexander, M. D. (2019). *American public school law*. St. Paul, MN: West Academic Publishing.

Alexander, N. A. (2013). *Policy analysis for educational leaders: A step-by-step approach*. Boston, MA: Pearson.

Alford, B. J., & Sampson, P. M. (2016). Transcending the contexts of a rural school in Texas and an urban school in California: A cross-case comparison of principal leadership and student success. *Journal of Educational Leadership, Policy, and Practice, 31*(1/2), 195–205.

Algozzine, B., Daunic, A. P., & Smith, S. W. (2010). *Preventing problem behaviors: Schoolwide programs and classroom practices* (2nd ed.). Thousand Oaks, CA: Corwin Press.

Algozzine, B., & White, R. (2002). Preventing problem behaviors using schoolwide discipline. In B. Algozzine & P. Kay (Eds.), *Preventing problem behaviors: A handbook of successful prevention strategies* (pp. 85–103). Thousand Oaks, CA: Corwin Press.

Allen, D. (1995a). *Resources for teacher-constructed curriculum*. Unpublished manuscript, ATLAS Seminar, Providence, RI: Coalition of Essential Schools, Brown University.

Allen, D. (1995b). *The tuning protocol: A process for reflection* (Studies on Exhibitions Monograph No. 15). Providence, RI: Coalition of Essential Schools, Brown University.

Allen, D. (2015). *Getting things done: The art of stress-free productivity*. New York, NY: Penguin Random House.

Allen, K. A., Reupert, A., & Oades, L. (2021). *Building better schools with evidence-based policy: Adaptable policy for teachers and school leaders*. New York, NY: Routledge.

Allen, J., Weissberg, R., & Hawkins, J. (1989). The relation between values and social competence in early adolescence. *Developmental Psychology, 25*, 458–464.

Allen, M. (2013). What was Web 2.0? Versions as the dominant mode of Internet history. *New Media & Society, 15*(2), 260–275.

Allen, R. F., & Pilnick, S. (1973). Confronting the shadow organization: How to select and defeat negative norms. *Organizational Dynamics, 1*(4), 3–18.

Allender, J. S., & Allender, D. S. (2008). *The humanistic teacher: First the child, then curriculum*. Boulder, CO: Paradigm Publishers.

Alvin Independent School District v. A.D. ex. Rel, 503 F. 3d 378 (5th Cir. 2007).

Amabile, T. M. (1997). Motivating creativity in organizations: On doing what you love and loving what you do. *California Management Review, 40*(1), 39–58.

Amabile, T. M. (1988). A model of creativity and innovation in organizations. In B. M. Shaw and L. L. Cummings (Eds.). *Research in organizational behavior*, vol. 10 (pp. 128–138). Greenwich, CT: JAI Press.

Amabile, T. M. (2004). Leader behaviors and the work environment for creativity: Perceived leader support. *Leadership Quarterly, 15*(1), 5–32.

Ambrose, S. A., Bridges, M. W., DiPietro, M., Lovett, M. C., & Norman, M. K. (2010). *How learning works: 7 research-based principles for smart teaching*. San Francisco, CA: Jossey-Bass.

American Academy of Pediatrics. (2000, August). Corporal punishment in schools. *Pediatrics, 106*, 343.

American Arbitration Association. (2022). *Arbitration and the law*. Huntington, NY: Juris Publishing.

American Association of Collegiate Registrars and Admissions Officers (AACROA) (2019). *Student records management: Retention, disposal, and archive of student records*. Washington, DC: American Association of Collegiate Registrars and Admissions Officers (AACROA).

American Association of School Administrators (AASA) (2020). *Code of ethics for school leaders*. Alexandria, VA: AASA.

American Educational Research Association (AERA) (2014). *Standards for educational and psychological testing*. The American Educational Research Association, the American Psychological Association, and the National Council on Measurement in Education.

American Institute of Certified Public Accountants (2022). *Understanding audits and the auditor's report: A guide for financial statement users*. Jersey City, NJ: American Institute of Certified Public Accountants.

American Institutes for Research (2019). *National center of family homelessness*. Project Web page. https://www.air.org/center/national-center-family-homelessness.

American Management Association (2022). *Present-day administrative and financial controls*. New York, NY: American Management Association.

American School Counselor Association (2022). *The ASCA national model: A framework for school counseling programs* (4th ed). Alexandria, VA: American School Counselor Association.

American Society of Civil Engineers. (2017). Infrastructure Report Card. ASCE Foundation. https://www.infrastructurereportcard.org/cat-item/schools/.

Amstuz, L. S., & Mullet, J. H. (2014). *The little book of restorative discipline for schools: Teaching responsibility and creating caring climates*. New York, NY: Good Books.

Anderman, E. M., & Anderman, L. H. (2014). *Classroom motivation* (2nd ed.). Boston, MA: Pearson.

Anderman, E. M., & Leake, V. S. (2007). The interface of school and family in meeting the belonging needs of young adolescents. In S. B. Mertens, V. A. Anfara, & M. M. Caskey (Eds.). *The young adolescent and the missile school* (pp. 163–182). Charlotte, NC: Information Age Publishing.

Andersen, J. A. (2000). Intuition in managers: Are intuitive managers more effective? *Journal of Managerial Psychology, 15*(1–2), 46–63.

Anderson, C. A. (2017). Screen violence and youth behavior. *Pediatrics, 140*(2), 1–10.

Anderson, C. A., Berkowitz, L., Donnerstein, E., Huesman, L. R., Johnson, J., Linz, D., Malamuth, N., & Wartella, E. (2003). The influence of media violence on youth. *Psychological Science in the Public Interest, 4*(1), 81–110.

Anderson, C. A., Bushman, B. J. (2001). Effects of violent video games on aggressive behavior, aggressive cognition, aggressive affect, psychological arousal, and prosocial behavior: A meta-analytic review of the scientific literature. *Psychological Science, 12*(5), 353–359.

Anderson, D. L. (2018). *Organization design: Creating strategic and agile organizations*. Thousand Oaks, CA: Sage.

Anderson, L. W., & Krathwohl, D. R. (2001). *A taxonomy for learning, teaching, and assessing: A revision of Bloom's taxonomy of educational objectives*. New York, NY: Longman.

Andler, N. (2019). *Tools for coaching, leadership, and change management*. New York, NY: Wiley.

Angstadt v. Midd-West School District, 182 F. Supp.2d 435 (M.D. Pa. 2002).

Apple, M. W. (2018). *The struggle for democracy in education: Lessons from social realities*. New York, NY: Routledge.

Arcadia Unified Sch. Dist. v. state department of Education, 825 P.2d 438 (Cal. 1992).

Argyris, C. (2007). *Reasons and rationalizations: The limits to organizational knowledge*. New York, NY: Oxford University Press.

Argyris, C. (2009). *Learning in organizations*. Alexandria, VA: American Society for Training and Development.

Aritzeta, A., Swailes, S., & Senior, B. (2007). Belbin's team role model: Development, validity, and applications for team building. *Journal of Management Studies*, *44*(1), 96–118.

Arlington Central School District v. Murphy, 548 U.S. 291 (2006).

Arnette, R. C., Harden Fritz, J. M., & Bell, L. M. (Eds.). (2009). *Communication ethics literacy: Dialogue and difference*. Thousand Oaks, CA: Sage.

Arthur, D. (2019). *Recruiting, interviewing, selecting, and orienting new employees*. New York, NY: Harper Collins.

Association for Defense v. Kiger, 537 N.E. 1292 (Ohio 1989).

Astor, R.A., & Benbenishty, R. (2017). *Mapping and monitoring bullying and violence: Building a safe school climate*. New York, NY: Oxford University Press.

Atay, A., & Toyosaki, S. (Eds.) (2018). *Critical intercultural communication pedagogy*. Lanham, MD: Lexington Books/Rowman & Littlefield.

Attorney General v. E. Jackson Public Schools, 372 N.W.2d 638 (Mich. Ct. App. 1985).

Au, W. (2007). High-stakes testing and curricular control: A qualitative metasynthesis. *Educational Researcher*, *36*(5), 258–267.

Ausubel, D. (2000). *The acquisition and retention of knowledge: A cognitive view*. New York, NY: Springer.

Avard v. Dupuis, 376 F. Supp. 479 (D.N.H. 1974).

Avison, W. R., & Gotlib, I. H. (2013). *Stress and mental health: Contemporary issues and prospects for the future*. New York, NY: Springer.

Ayers, W. (2011). *To teach*. New York, NY: Teachers College Press.

Bacon v. Bradley-Bourbonnais High School District, 707 F. Supp. 1005 (Ill. 1989).

Bailey, G. D., & Littrell, J. H. (1981). The blueprint for curriculum development: Establishing a systemic design. *NASSP Bulletin*, *65*, 22–28.

Baker, B. D. (2018). *Educational inequality and school finance: Why money matters for America's students*. Cambridge, MA: Harvard Education Press.

Baker, B. D., Green, P., & Richards, C. E. *Financing education systems*. Upper Saddle River, NJ: Pearson/Merrill Prentice Hall. 2008

Bakshi, A. V. (2009). *Electromagnetic field theory*. New York, NY: Technical Publications.

Bales, R. F. (1950). *Interaction process analysis*. Cambridge, MA: Addison Wesley.

Ball v. Board of Trustees Retirement Fund, 58 Atl. 111 (N.J. 1904).

Banasiewicz, A. (2019). *Evidence-Based decision making*. New York, NY: Routledge.

Bandura, A. (1986). *Social foundations of thought and action*. Upper Saddle River, NJ: Prentice Hall.

Bandura, A. (1994). Social cognitive theory of mass communication. In J. Bryant & D. Zillman (Eds.), *Media effects: Advances in the theory of behavioral change* (pp. 61–90). Hillsdale, NJ: Erlbaum.

Bandura, A. (1997). *Self-efficacy: The exercise of control*. New York, NY: Freeman.

Bandura, A., Ross, D., & Ross, S. A. (1961). Transmission of aggression through imitation of aggressive models. *Journal of Abnormal & Social Psychology*, *63*, 575–582.

Bandura, A., Ross, D., & Ross, S. A. (1963). Imitation of film-mediated aggressive models. *Journal of Abnormal & Social Psychology*, *66*, 3–11.

Banks, J. A. (2009). *Teaching strategies for ethnic studies* (8th ed.). Boston, MA: Pearson.

Banks v. Board of Public Instruction of Dade County, 314 F.Supp. 285(S.D. Fla. 1970), aff'd, 450 F.2d 1103 (5th Cir. 1971).

Barbian, E., Gonzales, G. C., & Mejia, P. (Eds.). (2017). *Rethinking bilingual education: Welcoming home languages in our classrooms*. New York, NY: Taylor & Francis.

Bardoch, E., & Patashnik, E. M. (2020). *A practical guide for policy analysis: The eight-fold path to more effective problem solving* (6th ed.). Thousand Oaks, CA: Sage.

Barger v. Bisciglia, 888 F. Supp. 97 (E.D. Wis. 1995).

Barnard, C. (1964). Functions and pathology of status systems in formal organizations. In W. F. Whyte (Ed.), *Industry and society* (pp. 46–83). New York, NY: McGraw-Hill.

Barnard, C. I. (1938). *The functions of the executive.* Cambridge, MA: Harvard University Press.

Barrett, J., & Barrett, T. (2018). *Ultimate aptitude tests: Over 1000 practice questions for abstract, visual, numerical, verbal, physical.* London, GBR: Kogan Page.

Barron, F., & Harrington, D. M. (1981). Creativity, intelligence, and personality. *Annual Review of Psychology, 32*, 439–476.

Barton, P. E., & Coley, R. J. (2009). *Parsing the achievement gap II: Policy information report.* Princeton, NJ: Educational Testing Service. http://www.ets.org/research/pic/parsing.pdf. ERIC: ED 505163.

Barton, P. E., & Coley, R. J. (2010). *The black-white achievement gap: When progress stopped.* Princeton, NJ: Educational Testing Service. http://www.ets.org/research/policy_research_reports/publications/report/2010/igxu.

Bas, E. (2004). *Indoor air quality: A guide for facility managers* (2nd ed.). Lilburn, GA: Fairmont Press.

Basham, V., & Lunenburg, F. C. (1989). Strategic planning, student achievement, and school district financial and demographic factors. *Planning and Changing, 20*, 158–171.

Basken, P. (2008, July 11). Spellings term fought over emphasizing liberal arts. *Chronicle of Higher Education*, 1–12.

Bassett v. Braddock, 262 So.2d 425 (Fla. 1972)

Battles v. Anne Arundel County Board of Education, 904 F. Supp. 471 (D. Md. 1995).

Baume, D., & Kahn, P. (2016). *A guide to staff and educational development.* New York, NY: Routledge.

Bazerman, M. H., & Moore, D. A. (2013). *Judgment in Managerial Decision Making.* New York, NY: Wiley.

Beal, D. J., Cohen, R. R., Burke, M. J., & McLendon, C. L. (2003). Cohesion and performance in groups: A meta-analytic clarification of construct relations. *Journal of Applied Psychology, 88*(6), 989–1004.

Bear, G. G. (2009). The positive in positive models of discipline. In R. Gilman, E.S. Huebner, & M. J. Furlong (Eds.), *Handbook of positive psychology in schools* (pp. 305–321). New York, NY: Routledge.

Beauchamp, G. A. (1981). *Curriculum theory* (4th ed.). Itasca, IL: F. E. Peacock.

Beck v. Board of Education of Harlem Consolidated School District No. 122, 344 N.E.2d 440 (Ill. 1976).

Beck v. James, 793 S.W.2d 416 (Mo. Ct. App. 1990).

Beck, L., & Murphy, J. (1994). *Ethics in educational leadership programs: An expanding role.* Thousand Oaks, CA: Corwin Press.

Beckner, W. (2004). *Ethics for educational leaders.* Boston, MA: Pearson.

Begley, P. J., & Johansson, O. (2003). *The ethical dimensions of leadership.* New York, NY: Springer.

Behling, O., & Eckel, N. L. (1991). Making sense out of intuition. *Academy of Management Executive, 5*(1), 46–54.

Beilan v. Board of Education, 357 U.S. 399 (1958).

Bell, L., & Stevenson, R. (2006). *Education policy: Process, themes, and impact.* New York, NY: Routledge.

Belvel, P. S. (2010). *Rethinking classroom management: Strategies for prevention, intervention, and problem solving.* Thousand Oaks, CA: Corwin Press.

Benner, A. D., & Mistry, R. S. (2007). Congruence of mother and teacher educational expectations and low-income youth's academic competence. *Journal of Educational Psychology, 99*(1), 140–153.

Bennett, C. I. (2011). *Comprehensive multicultural education: Theory and practice* (7th ed.). Boston, MA: Pearson.

Bennett, W. (1993). *The book of virtues: A treasury of great moral stories.* New York, NY: Simon & Schuster.

Bennett, W. (1995). *The moral compass: A companion to the book of virtues.* New York, NY: Simon & Schuster.

Bennett, W., Finn, C., & Cribb, J. T. E. (1999). *The educated child: A parent's guide for pre-school through eighth grade*. New York, NY: Simon & Schuster.

Bennis, W. G. (1966). *Changing Organizations*. New York, NY: McGraw-Hill.

Bennis, W. G. (1987). Managing the Dream: Leadership in the 21st Century. *Journal of Organizational Change Management*, 2, 7.

Bennis, W. G. (1990). *Why leaders can't lead: The unconscious conspiracy continues*. San Francisco, CA: Jossey-Bass.

Bennis, W. G. (2006). *Reinventing leadership: Strategies to empower the organization*. New York: HarperCollins.

Bennis, W., & Nanus, B. (1985). *Leaders: The strategies for taking charge*. New York, NY: Harper & Row.

Benson, T. A., & Fiarman, S. E. (2020). *Unconscious bias in schools: A developmental approach to exploring race and racism*. Cambridge, MA: Harvard Education Press.

Berchick, E. R., & Mykyta, L. (2019). Children's public health insurance coverage lower than in 2017. https://www.census.gov/library/stories/2019/09/uninsured-rate-for-children-in-2018.html.

Berg v. Glen Cove City School District, 853 F. Supp. 651 (E.D. N.Y. 1994).

Berg, J. H., Connolly, C., Lee, A., & Fairley, E. (2018). A matter of trust: Leading the energized school. *Educational Leadership*, *75*(6), 56–61.

Berger v. Rensselaer Central School Corporation, 982 F.2d 1160 (7th Cir. 1993).

Berkelman v. San Francisco Unified School District, U.S.D., 501 F.2d 1264 (9 Cir. 1974).

Berkowitz, L. E., & Walster, E. E. (1976). *Advances in experimental social psychology*, Vol. 9, *Equity theory: Toward a general theory of social interaction*. New York, NY: Academic Press.

Berliner, D. (2011). Rational responses to high-stakes testing: The case of curriculum narrowing. *Cambridge Journal of Education*, *41*(3), 287–302.

Berliner, D. C., & Biddle, B. (1995). *The manufactured crisis: Myths, frauds, and the attack on America's public schools*. New York, NY: Addison-Wesley.

Berliner, D. C., & Glass, G. V. (2014). *50 myths and lies that threaten America's public schools: The real crisis in education*. New York, NY: Teachers College Press.

Bermúdez, A. B., & Marquez, J. A. (1996). An examination of four-way collaborative to increase parent involvement in the schools. *The Journal of Educational Issues of Language Minority Students, Special Issue*, *16*, 1–16.

Bermúdez, A. B., & Padron, Y. M. (1988). University-school collaboration that increases minority parent involvement. *Educational Horizons*, *66*(2), 83–86.

Bernard v. Inhabitants of Shelburne, 216 Mass. 19, 102 N.E. 1095 (1913).

Bernhardt, V. L. (1999). *The school portfolio: A comprehensive framework for school improvement* (2nd ed.). Larchmount, NY: Eye on Education.

Bernhardt, V. L. (2013). *Using data to improve student learning in school districts*. New York, NY: Routledge.

Beth v. Van Clay, 282 F. 3d 493 (2002).

Bethel School District No. 403 v. Fraser, 478 U.S. 675 (1986).

Beveridge, M., & Jerrams, A. (1981). Parental involvement in language development: An evaluation of a school-based parental assistance plan. *British Journal of Educational Psychology*, *51*, 259–269.

Beyer, J. M., & Trice, H. M. (1979). A reexamination of the relations between size and various components of organizational complexity. *Administrative Science Quarterly*, *24*(1), 48–64.

Beyer, J. M., & Trice, H. M. (1984). A field study of the use and perceived effects of discipline in controlling work performance. *Academy of Management Journal*, *27*(4), 743–764.

Biddle, D. (2017). *Adverse impact and test validation: A practitioners guide to valid and defensible employment testing*. New York, NY: Routledge.

Biddle v. Mazzocco, 284 P. 2d 364 (Ore. 1955).

Bidwell, C. E. (1965). The school as a formal organization. In J. G. March (Ed.), *Handbook of organizations* (pp. 972–1022). Chicago, IL: Rand McNally.

Birdwhistell, R. L. (2013). *Kinesics and context*. Philadelphia, PA: University of Pennsylvania Press.

Birkeland, S., & Feiman-Nemser, S. (2012). Helping school leaders help new teachers: A tool for transforming school-based induction. *The New Educator*, *8*(2), 109–138.

Blackstone, W. (1941). *Blackstone's commentaries on the laws of England (1765–1769)*, edited by B. C. Gavit. Washington, DC: Washington Law Book Co.

Blackwelder v. Safnauer, 866 F. 2d (2nd Cir. (1989).

Blake, R., & Mouton, J. S, (1994). *The managerial grid: Leadership styles for Achieving production through people*. Houston, TX: Gulf.

Blanchfield, K., & Ladd, P. (2013). *Leadership, violence, and school climate*. Lanham, MD: Rowman & Littlefield.

Blau v. Fort Thomas Public School District, 401 F.3d 381, 395–96 (2005).

Bloom, A. (1987). *The closing of the American mind*. New York, NY: Simon & Schuster.

Bloom, B. S. (Ed.). (1956). *Taxonomy of educational objectives: Handbook I. Cognitive domain*. New York, NY: McKay.

Bloomquist, M. L., & Schnell, S. V. (2002). *Helping children with aggression and conduct problems: Best practices for intervention*. New York, NY: Guilford Press.

Bluestein, J. (2001). *Creating emotionally safe schools: A guide for educators and Parents*. Dearfield Beach, FL: Health Communications, Inc.

Blumenson, E., & Nilsen, E. S. (May, 2002). How to construct an underclass, or how the war on drugs became a war on education. *The Journal of Gender, Race, & Justice*, 65–89.

Board of Curators v. Horowitz, 435 U.S. 78. 89–90 (1978).

Board of Education, Island Trees Union Free School District v. Pico, 457 U.S. 853, 857 (1982).

Board of Education v. Allen, 392 U.S. 236 (1968).

Board of Education v. Earls, 122 S. Ct. 2559 (2002).

Board of Education v. Pico, 457 U.S. 853 (1982).

Board of Education v. Sinclair, 222 N.W.2d 143 (Wis. 1974).

Board of Education of Hendrick Hudson Central School District v. Rowley, 458 U.S. 176 (1982).

Board of Education of Independent School District No. 92 of Pottawatomie v. Earls, 536 U.S. 822 (2002).

Board of Education of Mountain Lakes v. Maas, 152 A.2d 394 (N.J. Super Ct. App. Div. 1959).

Board of Education of Peoria v. Ill. State Board of Education, 531 F. Supp. 148, C.D. (Ill. 1982).

Board of Education of Westside Community Schools v. Mergens, 496 U.S. 226 (1990)

Board of Regents v. Roth, 408 U.S. 564 (1972).

Bodilly, S. J. (2011). *Continuing challenges and potential for collaborative approaches to education reform*. Santa Monica, CA: The RAND Corporation.

Bolling v. Sharpe, 347 U.S. 497 (1954).

Bolman, L. G., & Deal, T. E. (2017). *Reframing organizations: Artistry, choice, and leadership* (6th ed.). San Francisco: Jossey-Bass.

Bond v. Public Schools of Ann Arbor School District, 178 N.W.2d 484 (Mich. 1970).

Bonito, J. (2019). *Interaction and influence in small group decision making*. New York, NY: Routledge.

Bonstingl, J. J. (2001). *Schools of quality*. Thousand Oaks, CA: Corwin Press.

Boone v. Boozman, 217 F. Supp.2d 938 (E.D. Ark. 2002).

Borich, G. D. (2011). *Effective teaching methods: Research-based practice* (7th ed.). Boston, MA: Pearson/Allyn & Bacon.

Born, C. (2020). *Making sense of school finance: A practical state-by-state approach*. Lanham, MD: Rowman & Littlefield.

Bowden, M. (2011). *Winning body language: Control the conversation. command attention, and convey the right message without saying a word*. New York, NY: McGraw-Hill.

Bowers, A. J., Shoho, A. R., & Barnett, B. G. (2016). *Using data in schools to inform leadership and decision making*. Charlotte, NC: Information Age Publishing.

Bowers, D. G., & Franklin, J. L. (1977). *Survey-guided development: Data-based organizational change*. La Jolla, CA: University Associates.

Boyle, B., & Charles, M. (2016). *Curriculum development: A guide for educators*. Thousand Oaks, CA: Sage.

Bracken, A., Drahan, J., Durkin, C., & Flood, N. (Eds.). (2015). *Emerging issues in K–12 campus security: Leading lawyers and school security experts on creating an emergency response plan, training staff, and observing warning signs (inside the minds)*. Aspatore.

Bradley, T. P., Allen, J. M., Hamilton, S., & Filgo, S. K. (2006). Leadership perception: Analysis of 360-degree feedback. *Performance Improvement Quarterly, 19*(1), 7–24.

Bradstreet v. Soboal, 650 N.Y.S.2d 402 (N.Y. App. Div. 1996).

Bragg, S. M. (2016). *Accounting best practices* (7th ed.). New York, NY: Wiley.

Bransford, J. D., Brown, A. L., & Cocking, R. R. (Eds.) (2021). *How people learn: Brain, mind, experience, and school* (Expanded Edition). Washington, DC: National Academy Press.

Branson, C. M., Gross, S. J. (2014). *Handbook of ethical leadership*. New York, NY: Routledge.

Bray v. Lee, 337 F. Supp. 934 (Mass. 1972).

Breidenstein, A., Glickman, C.D., Fahey, K., & Hensley, F. (2012). *Leading for powerful learning: A guide for instructional leaders*. New York, NY: Teachers College Press.

Brenden v. Independent School District, 477 F.2d 1292 (8 Cir. 1973).

Brewer, E. C., & Westerman, J. (2017). *Organizational communication: Today's life in context*. New York, NY: Oxford University Press.

Bricker, M. A., Harkins, S. G., & Ostrom, T. M. (1986). Effects of personal involvement: Thought-provoking implications for social loafing. *Journal of Personality and Social Psychology, 51*(4), 763–769.

Brigman, G., Villares, E., & Webb, L. (2017). *Evidence-based school counseling: A student success approach*. New York, NY: Routledge.

Brimley, V., Verstegen, D. A., & Garfield, R. R. (2020). *Financing education in a climate of change* (13th ed.). Boston, MA: Pearson.

Bringing the Constitution to life; now is a good time to teach the hows and whys of liberty. (2003, March 24). *The Washington Times*, p. A23.

Brock, S. E., Sandoval, J., & Lewis, S. (2001). *Preparing for crisis in the schools: A manual for building school crisis response teams* (2nd ed.). New York, NY: Wiley.

Brookfield, S. D. (2013). *Powerful techniques for teaching adults*. San Francisco, CA: Jossey-Bass.

Brookhart, S. (2010). *How to assess higher order thinking skills in your classroom*. Alexandria, VA: ASCD.

Brookhart, S. (2011). *Grading and learning practices that support student achievement*. Bloomington, IN: Solution Tree.

Brookhart, S., & McMillan, J. H. (2019). *Classroom assessment and educational measurement: Applications of educational measurement and assessment*. New York, NY: Routledge.

Brookhart, S., & Nitko, A. (2008). *Assessment and grading in classrooms*. Upper Saddle River, NJ: Allyn & Bacon.

Brookmeyer, K. A., Fanti, K., & Henrich, C. C. (2006). Schools, parents, and youth violence: A multilevel, ecological analysis. *Journal of Clinical and Adolescent Psychology, 35*(4), 504–514.

Brooks, J. G., & Brooks, M. G. (2021). *Schools reimagined: Unifying the science of learning with the art of teaching*. New York, NY: Teachers College Press.

Brophy, J. E. (2011). *Motivating students to learn*. New York, NY: Taylor & Francis.

Broudy, H. S., Smith, B. O., & Bunnett, J. R. (1964). *Democracy and excellence in American secondary education*. Chicago, IL: Rand McNally.

Browder, L. H. (2001). Coping with children on their own. In T. Kowalski & G. Perreault (Eds.). *21st century challenges for school administrators*. Lanham, MD: Scarecrow Press.

Brown, G., & Irby, B. J. (2000). *The career advancement portfolio*. Thousand Oaks, CA: Corwin Press.

Brown, G., & Irby, B.J. (2001). *The principal portfolio*. Thousand Oaks, CA: Corwin Press.

Brown, G., & Irby, B.J. (2002). Documenting continuing professional education requirements using the professional development portfolio. *Texas Study, 11*(2), 13–16.

Brown, G., Irby, B. J., & Fisher, A. (2001). The leadership framework: Facilitating reflection for 21st century leaders. In T. Kowalski & G. Perreault (Eds.). *21st century challenges for school administrators*. Lanham, MD: Scarecrow Press.

Brown, P. C. (1989). Involving parents in the education of their children. *ERIC Digest*. ERIC Document Reproduction Service No. ED308988.

Brown, J. L., Roderick, T., Lantieri, L., & Aber, J. (2004). The resolving conflict creatively program: A school-based social and emotional learning program. In J. E. Zins, R. P. Weissberg, M. C. Wang, & H. J. Walberg (Eds.). *Building academic succeson social and emotional learning: what does the research say?* New York, NY: Teachers College Press.

Brown, S., & Race, P. (2003). *Lecturing: A practical guide*. London, UK; Kogan Page.

Brown v. Board of Education of Topeka, 347 U.S. 483 (1954).

Brown v. Oakland, 124 P.2d 369 (Cal. 1942).

Brown v. Stine, 378 So.2d 218 (Miss. 1979).

Brown, W. B., & Moberg, D. J. (2015). *Organizational theory and management* (8th ed.). New York, NY: Wiley.

Brownell, J. (2017). *Listening: Attitudes, principles, and skills* (6th ed.). Boston, MA: Pearson.

Brownlie, F. (2000). *Learning in safe schools: Creating classrooms where all students belong*. Portland, ME: Stenhouse Publishers.

Bruce, K., Lara-alecio, R., Parker, R., Hasbrouck, J. E., Weaver, L., & Irby, B. (1997). Inside transitional bilingual classrooms: Accurately describing the language learning process. *Bilingual Research Journal, 21*(1–2), 123–145.

Bruner, J. (1960). *The process of education*. Cambridge, MA: Harvard University Press.

Bruner, J. (1966). *Toward a theory of instruction*. Cambridge, MA: Harvard University Press.

Bruning, R. H., Schraw, G. J., & Norby, M. M. (2011). *Cognitive psychology and instruction* (5th ed.). Boston, MA: Pearson.

Brush, T., & Saye, J. (2001). The use of embedded scaffolds with hypermedia-supported student-centered learning. *Journal of Educational Multimedia and Hypermedia, 10*(4), 333–356.

Brutus, S., & Derayeh, M. (2002). Multisource assessment programs in organizations: An insider's perspective. *Human Resource Development Quarterly, 13*(2), 187–202.

Bryk, A. S. (2010). Organizing Schools for Improvement. *Phi Delta Kappan, 91*, 23–30.

Bryk, A. S. (2020). *Improvement in action: advancing quality in America's schools*. Cambridge, MA: Harvard Education Press.

Bryk, A. S., Sebring, P. B., Kerbow, D., Rollow, S., & Easton, J. Q. (1998). *Charting Chicago school reform: Democratic localism as a lever for change*. Boulder, CO: Westview.

Bryon, M. (2018). *Ultimate psychometric tests: Over 1,000 verbal, numerical, diagrammatic, and IQ practice tests*. Milford, CT: Kogan Page.

Bubnicki, Z. (2003). *Analysis and decision making in uncertain systems*. New York: Springer.

Bulach, C., & Lunenburg, F. C. (2008). *Creating a culture for high-performing schools: A comprehensive approach to school reform and dropout prevention*. Lanham, MD: Rowman & Littlefield.

Bulach, C., & Lunenburg, F. C. (2011). *Creating a culture for high-performing schools: A comprehensive approach to school reform, dropout prevention, and bullying behavior* (2nd ed.). Lanham, MD: Rowman & Littlefield.

Bulach, C., & Lunenburg, F. C. (2016a). *School culture vis-à-vis student learning: Keys to collaborative problem solving and responsibility*. Lanham, MD: Rowman & Littlefield.

Bulach, C., & Lunenburg, F. C. (2016b). *Enhancing a school's culture and climate: New insights for improving schools*. Lanham, MD: Rowman & Littlefield.

Bullough, R. V. (2012). Mentoring and new teacher induction in the United States: A review and analysis of current practices. *Mentoring & Tutoring: Partnership in Learning, 20*(1), 57–74.

Burgoon, J. K., Guerrero, L. K., & Floyd, K. (2010). *Nonverbal communication*. Upper Saddle River, NJ: Allyn & Bacon.

Burke, L. A., & Miller, M. K. (1999). Taking the mystery out of intuitive decision making. *Academy of Management Executive, 13*(4), 91–99.

Burke, N. J., Hellman, J. L., Scott, B. G., Weems, C. F., & Carrion, V. G. (2011). The impact of adverse childhood experiences on an urban pediatric population. *Child Abuse & Neglect, 35*(6), 408–413.

Burns, T., & Stalker, G. M. (1961). The management of innovation. London, UK: Tavistock.

Burroughs, H. E., & Hansen, S. J. (2004). *Managing indoor air quality*. Lilburn, GA: Fairmont Press.

Bushe, G., & Coetzer, G. (2007). Group development and team effectiveness. *Journal of Applied Behavioral Science, 43*(1), 184–212.

Butler, S. M, & McMunn, N. D. (2006). *A teacher's guide to classroom assessment: Understanding and using assessment to improve student learning*. San Francisco, CA: Jossey-Bass.

C. G. ex rel. A.S. v. Five Town Community School District, 513 F.3d 279 (1st Cir., 2008).

Callahan, K., & Sadeghi, L. (2014). TEACHJ: An evaluation of two years of implementation. *US-China Education Review A, 4*(10). http://www.davidpublisher.org/.

Campbell, D. (2012). *Business strategy: An introduction*. New York, NY: Palgrave Macmillan.

Campbell, E. (2008). The ethics of teaching as a moral profession. *Curriculum Inquiry, 38*(4), 357–385.

Campbell, J. P., & Dunnette, M. D. (1968). Effectiveness of T-group experience in managerial training and development. *Psychological Bulletin, 70*, 73–104.

Campbell, J. R., Hombo, C. M., & Mazzeo, J. (2000). *NAEP trends in academic progress: three decades of student performance*. Washington, DC: National Center for Education Statistics (NCES No. 2000–469).

Campion, M. A., Palmer, D. K., & Campion, J. E. (1997). A review of structure in the selection interview. *Personnel Psychology, 50*, 655–702.

Canole, M., & Young, M. D. (2013). *Standards for educational leaders: An analysis*. Washington, DC: Council of Chief State School Officers (CCSSO).

Canton v. Spokane School District No. 81, 498 F.2d 840 (9th Cir. 1974).

Cantwell v. State of Connecticut, 310 U.S. 296 (1940).

Capistrano Unified School District v. Wartenberg, 59 F.3d 884 (9th Cir. 1995).

Capper, C. A. (1996). We're not housed in an institution; we're housed in a community: Possibilities and consequences of neighborhood-based interagency celebration. In J. Cibulka & W. J. Kritek (Eds.), *Coordination among schools, families, and communities: Prospects for educational reform* (pp. 299–312). Albany: State University of New York Press.

Card, D., & Giuliano, L. (2015). *Can universal screening increase the representation of low-income minority students in gifted education?* National Bureau of Economic Research (NBER) working paper no. 21519, Cambridge, MA, September 2015. http://www.nber.org/papers/w21519.

Carder v. Michigan City School Corp., 552 F. Supp. 869 (N.D. Ind. 1982).

Cardiff v. Bismarck Public School District, 263 N.W.2d 105 (N.D. 1978).

Carlson, J. F., Geisinger, K. F., & Jonson, J. L. (2021). *The twenty-first mental measurements yearbook*. Lincoln, NB: Buros Institute of Mental Measurements.

Carlson, R. V., & Awkerman, G. (1991). *Educational planning: Concepts, strategies, and practices*. New York, NY: Longman.

Carmichael, D. R. (2011). *PPC's guide to audits of financial institutions*. Fort Worth, TX: Practitioners.

Carpio v. Tucson High School District No. 1 of Pima County, 524 P.2d 948 (Ariz. 1974), cert. denied, 420 U.S. 982 (1975).

Carrell, M. R. (2007). *Negotiating essentials: Theory, skills, and practices*. Boston, MA: Pearson.

Carrell, M. R. (2010). *Labor relations and collective bargaining*. Boston, MA: Pearson.

Carter, C., Bishop, J., & Kravits, S. (2014). *Keys to effective learning: Developing powerful habits of mind* (6th ed.). Boston, MA: Pearson.

Caruth, D. L. (2009). *Staffing the contemporary organization: A guide to planning, recruiting, and selecting for human resource professionals*. Westport, CT: Greenwood.

Castillo, C. L. (2008). *Children with complex medical issues in schools: Neuropsychological descriptions and interventions*. New York, NY: Springer.

Castleman, B. (2005). *Asbestos: Medical and legal aspects*. New York, NY: Aspen Publishers.

Castro Garces, A.Y., & Granada, L. (2016). The role of collaborative action research in teachers' professional development. *Profile: Issues in Teachers' Professional Development*, *18*(10, 39–54.

Cavanaugh, M. A., Boswell, W. R., Roehling, M. V., & Boudreau, J. W. (2000). An empirical examination of self-reported work stress among U.S. managers. *Journal of Applied Psychology*, *85*(1), 65–74.

Cedar Rapids Community School District v. Garrett F., 526 U.S. 66 (1999).

Ceniceros v. Board of Trustees of the San Diego Unified School District, 106 F.3d 878 (9th Cir. 1997).

Center for Immigration Services. (2019). *67.3 million in US spoke a foreign language at home in 2018*. https://cis.org/Report/673-million-United-States-Spoke-Foreign-Language-Home-2018.

Center for the Advancement of Ethics and Character Education (2003). *Character education manifesto*. Boston University. https://www.bu.edu/ccsr/about-us/partnerships/character-education-manifesto/.

Center on Education Policy (2008, November). *Lessons from the classroom level: Federal and state accountability in Rhode Island*. http://www.cep-dc.org.

Center on Education Policy (2012, January). *Year two of implementing the common core state standards: States' progress and challenges*. http://www.cep-dc.org/displayDocument.cfm?DocumentID=391.

Centers for Disease Control and Prevention (CDC) (2010). *Strategic plan for the elimination of lead poisoning* (rev. ed.). Washington, DC: US Government Printing Office. smoking. Accessed December 26, 2014, from http://www.cdc.gov/tobacco/data_statistics/fact_sheets/health_effects/effects_cig_smoking/.

Centers for Disease Control and Prevention (CDC) (2021). National Center for Injury Prevention and Control. *Web-based injury statistics query and reporting system (WISQARS) 2021*. www.cdc.gov/injury.

Chalk v. U.S. District Court, 840 F.2d 701 (9 Cir., Cal. 1988).

Chall, J. (1996). *Stages of reading development* (2nd ed.). Fort Worth, TX: Harcourt Brace.

Chance, P. (2014). *Learning and behavior* (7th ed.). Belmont, CA: Cengage Learning.

Chandler, A. D. (1962). *Strategy and structure*. Cambridge, MA: MIT Press.

Chandler, A.D. (2003). *Strategy and structure: Chapters in the history of the American industrial enterprise*. Frederick, MD: Beard Books.

Charmot, A. U., & Stewner-Manzaneres, C. (1985). *A summary of current literature on English as a second language* (Part C: Research agenda). Rosslyn, VA: InterAmerica research Associates, 1985. ERIC Documemt Reproduction Service No. ED261539.

Charters, W. W. (1967). Stability and change in the communication structure of school facilities. *Educational Administration Quarterly, 3*, 15–38.

Chavkin, N. F., & Williams, D. L. (1989). Low-income parents' attitudes toward parents' involvement in education. *Journal of Sociology & Social Welfare, 16*, 17–28.

Cherkowski, S., Walker, K. D., & Kutsyruba, R. (2015). Principals moral agency and ethical decision making: Toward a transformational ethics. *International Journal of education policy and leadership, 10*(5), 1–17.

Cheung. D., Clemente, B., Pechman, E. (2000). *Protecting the privacy of student records: Guidelines for education agencies*. New York, NY: DIANE.

Child Evangelism Fellowship of N.J. v. Stafford Township School District, 386 F.3d 514 (3d. Cir. 2004).

Child Evangelism Fellowship v. Montgomery County Public Schools, 457 F.3d 376 (4th Cir. 1989).

Chitpin, S., & Evers, C. W. (2015). *Decision making in educational leadership*. New York, NY: Routledge.

Chowdhury, A., & Kirkpatrick, C. (1994). *Developmental policy and planning: An introduction to models and techniques*. New York, NY: Routledge.

Christian, D. (19940. *Two-way bilingual education: Students learning through two languages*. Santa Cruz, CA: National Center for Research on Cultural Diversity and Second Language Learning.

Church, A., & Vogelsong, J. (2018). *Organizational development in action*. New York, NY: Palgrave Macmillan.

Ciadini, R. B. (2001, October). Harnessing the science of persuasion. *Harvard Business Review, 1*(9), 72–79.

Circle School v. Phillips, 270 F. Supp. 2d 616 (2003).

Ciulla, J. B. (2014). *Ethics: The heart of leadership* (3rd ed.). Santa Barbara, CA: Praeger.

Claessens, B. J. C., Van Eerde, W., Rutte, C. G., & Roe, R. (2004). Planning behavior and perceived control of time at work. *Journal of Organizational Behavior, 25*(8), 937–950.

Clark, R. M. (1988). Parents as providers of linguistic and social capital. *Educational Horizons, 6*(2), 93–95.

Clotfelter, C. T., Ladd, H. F., & Vigdor, J. L. (2010). Teacher credentials and student achievement in high school; a cross-subject analysis with student fixed effects. *Journal of Human Resources, 45*(3), 655–681.

Cleveland Board of Education v. LaFleur, 414 U.S. 632 (1974).

Clonlara, Inc. v. State Board of Education, 501 N.W.2d 88 (Mich. 1993).

Clyde K. v. Puyallup School District No. 3, 35 F.3d 1396 (9th Cir. 1994).

Coakley, J. J. (2021). *Sports in society: Issues and controversies* (13th ed.). New York, NY: McGraw-Hill.

Cochran v. Louisiana state Board of Education, 281 U.S. 370 (1930).

Coffin, S., & Cooper, B. S. (2017). *Sound school finance for educational excellence*. Lanham, MD: Rowman & Littlefield.

Cogan, M. (1961). *Supervision at the Harvard-Newton summer school*. Cambridge, MA: Harvard Graduate School of Education.

Cogan, M. (1973). *Clinical supervision*. Boston, MA: Houghton Mifflin.

Cohen, P. (2016, February 21). A rising call to promote STEM education and cut liberal arts funding. *New York Times*, B1.

Cohen, D. M., March, J. G., & Olsen, J. D. (1972). A garbage can model of organizational choice. *Administrative Science Quarterly, 17*, 1–25.

Cohen, D. S. (2011). *The talent search: A behavioral approach to hiring, developing, and keeping top performers*. New York, NY: Wiley.

Cohen, J., & Espelage, D. L. (Eds.). (2020). *Feeling safe in school: Bullying and violence prevention around the world*. Cambridge, MA: Harvard Education Publishing Group.

Cohen, R. J., & Swerdlik, M. E. (2018). *Psychological testing and assessment: An intro-duction to tests and measurement* (9th ed.). New York, NY: McGraw-Hill.

Cohen, R. K., Opatosky, D. K., Savage, J., Stevens, S. O., & Darrah, E. P. (2021). *The meta-cognitive student: How to teach academic, social, and emotional intelligence in every content area*. Indianapolis, IN: Solution Tree Press.

Colby, A., Kohlberg, L. & DeVries, R. (1987). *The measurement of moral judgment* (2 vols.). New York, NY: Cambridge University Press.

Cole, C. (2010). *Videoconferencing for k–12 classrooms: A program development guide*. Eugene, OR: International Society for Technology in Education.

Collins, J. C., & Porras, J. (1998, July). Purpose, mission, and vision. *Stanford Business School Magazine*.

Collinsville Community Unit School District v. White, 283 N.E.2d 718 (Ill. 1972)

Combs, A. W. (1965). *The professional education of teachers*. Boston, MA: Allyn & Bacon.

Combs v. Homer-Center School District, 540 F.3d 231 (3d Cir. 2008).

Comer, D. R. (1995). A model of social loafing in real work groups. *Human Relations, 48*(6), 647–667.

Comer, J. (1980). *School power: Implications for an intervention project*. New York, NY: Free Press.

Comer, J. P. (1986). Parent participation in the schools. *Phi Delta Kappan, 67*, 442–446.

Comer, J. P. (1999). *Child by child*. New York, NY: Teachers College Press.

Comer, J. P., Joyner, E. T., & Ben-Avie, M. (2004). *Six pathways to healthy child devel-opment and academic success*. Thousand Oaks, CA: Corwin Press.

Commission on the Reorganization of Secondary Education. (1918). *Cardinal principles of secondary education* (Bulletin No. 35). Washington, DC: US Government Printing Office.

Committee for Public Education and Religious Liberty v. Nyquist, 413 U.S. 756 (1973).

Committee for Public Education and Religious Liberty v. Regan, 442 U.S. 928 (1980).

Common Core State Standards Initiative (2012). *Implementing the common core state standards*. http://www.corestandards.org/.

Commonwealth v. Kerstetter, 94 A.3d 991 (Pa. 2014).

Conchas, G., Gottfried, M., Hinga, B., & Oseguera, L. (2018). *Educational policy goes to school: Case on the limitations and possibilities of educational innovation*. New York, NY: Routledge.

Congreve, R. (2015). Using dialogic lesson observations and participatory action research to support teacher development. *Education Today, 65*(3), 16–20.

Conlon, E. J., & Short, L. O. (1984). Survey feedback as a large-scale change device: An empirical examination. *Group and Organization Studies, 9*, 399–416.

Conn. General. Statutes Annotated, Title 5A, § 10–151 (2018).

Conn, J. H., & Foshee, D. (1993). Artificial turf injuries, economics, emotion, and eth-ics. In P. J. Graham (Ed.), *Sports business: Operational and theoretical aspects* (pp. 132–142). Dubuque, IA: W. C. Brown.

Conn, J. H., & Gerdes, D. A. (1998, Fall). Ethical decision making: Issues and applications to American sport. *Physical Educator, 55*(3), 121–126.

Connelly v. School Community, 565 N.E.2d 449 (Mass. 1991).

Conrad, C. D. (2011). *The handbook of stress: Neuropsychological effects on the brain*. New York, NY: Wiley-Blackwell.

Contrada, R. J., & Baum, A. (Eds.) (2011). *The handbook of stress science: Biology, psy-chology, and health*. New York, NY: Springer.

Conway, J. M., Jako, R. A., & Goodman, D. F. (1995). A meta-analysis of interrater and internal consistency reliability of selection interviews. *Journal of Applied Psychol-ogy, 80*, 565–579.

Conway, M. (2015, March 16). The problem with history classes. *The Atlantic*.

Coombs, T. W. (2018). *Strategic communication, social media, and democracy*. New York, NY: Routledge.

Cooper, B. S., Cibulka, J. G., & Fusarelli, L. D. (2015). *Handbook of educational politics and policy* (2nd ed.). New York, NY: Routledge.

Cooper, C. L., Dewe, P. J., & O'Driscoll, M. P. (2002*). Organizational stress: A review and critique of theory, research, and application.* Thousand Oaks, CA: Sage.

Cooperrider, D. L., & Godwin, L. (2019). *Positive organizational development: Beyond intervention, toward the design of strength-based innovation.* New York, NY: Wiley.

Corey, G., Callanan, P., & Russell, J. M. (2015). *Group techniques* (4th ed.). Belmont, CA: Cengage Learning.

Cornelius-White, J. (2007). Learner-centered teacher-student relationships are effective: A meta-analysis. *Review of educational Research, 77*(1), 113–143.

Cornue, J. (2017). *Changing the grade: A step-by-step guide to grading for student growth.* Alexandria, VA: ASCD.

Corwin, E. S. (1978). *The constitution* (rev.). H. W. Chose & C.R. Ducet. Princeton, NJ: Princeton University Press, pp. 139–144.

Costa, A. L., Garmston, R. J., & Zimmerman, D. P. (2014). *Cognitive capital: Investing in teacher quality.* New York, NY: Teachers College Press.

Costa, A. L., Garmston, R. J., Hayes, C., & Ellison, J. (2015). *Cognitive coaching: Developing self-directed leaders and learners.* Lanham, MD: Rowman & Littlefield.

Couch, H. M. (2019). *The school counselor's guide to surviving the first year: Internship through professional development.* New York, NY: Routledge.

Council for the Accreditation for Educator Preparation (CAEP) (2017). *Guidelines on program review with national recognition using Specialized Professional Association (SPA) standards.* Washington, DC: CAEP.

Council of Chief State School Officers (CCSSO). (1996). *Interstate School Leaders Licensure Consortium standards (ISLLC) standards.* Washington, DC: CCSSO.

Council of Chief State School Officers (CCSSO). (2008). *Interstate School Leaders Licensure Consortium standards (ISLLC) standards.* Washington, DC: CCSSO.

Council of Chief State School Officers (CCSSO). (2015). *Professional standards for Educational Leaders (PSEL).* Washington, DC: CCSSO.

Cowan, K. (2010). New teachers and the culture gap. *Harvard Education Letter, 26*(5), 1–4.

Craig, S, Chi, M., & VanLehn, K. (2009). Improving classroom learning by collaboratively observing human tutoring videos while problem solving. *Journal of Educational Psychology, 101*(4), 779–789.

Craighead, J. E., & Gibbs, A. R. (2008). *Asbestos and its diseases.* New York, NY: Oxford University Press.

Crampton, F. E., & Thompson, D. E. (2008). *Building minds, minding buildings: School infrastructure funding need.* Washington, DC: American Federation of Teachers.

Cranston, J. (2011). Relational trust: The glue that binds a professional learning community. *Alberta Journal of Educational Research, 57*(1), 59–72.

Crawford, G. B. (2004). *Managing the adolescent classroom: Lessons from outstanding teachers.* Thousand Oaks, CA: Corwin Press.

Crawford, J. (1997). The campaign against proposition 227: A post mortem. *Bilingual Research Journal, 21*(1), 1–29.

Cremin, L. A. (1961). *The transformation of school.* New York, NY: Random House.

Crim v. McWharter, 252 S.E.2d 421 (Ga. 1979).

Crowder, Z. (2014). From the editorial board: The politization of the common core. *High School Journal, 98*(1), 1–4.

Crozier, M., & Friedberg, E. (2010). *The bureaucratic phenomenon.* Edison, NJ: Transaction Publications.

Cruickshank, D. R. (2008). *The act of teaching.* New York, NY: McGraw-Hill.

Cruikshank, J. L. (2005). *The apple way.* New York, NY: McGraw-Hill.

Crump v. Gilmer Independent School District (E.D. Tex. 1992).

Cuban, L. (2020). *Chasing success and confronting failure in America's public schools.* Cambridge, MA: Harvard Education Press.

Cuban, L., & Usdan, M. (Eds.). *Powerful reforms with shallow roots: Improving America's urban schools*. New York, NY: Teachers College Press.

Culbertson v. Oakridge School District, 258 F.3d 1061 (9th Cir. 2001).

Cunningham, D. (2011). *Improving teaching with collaborative action research*. Alexandria, VA: Association for Supervision and Curriculum Development.

Currie, B. M. (2015). *All hands on deck: Tools for connecting educators, parents, and communities*. Thousand Oaks, CA: Corwin Press.

Cushman, K. (2003). *Fires from the bathroom: Advice for teachers from high school students*. New York, NY: the New Press.

Cushman, K., & Rogers, L. (2008). *Fires in the middle school bathroom: Advice for teachers from middle schoolers*. New York, NY: the New Press.

Cushway, B. (2018). *The Employer's Handbook: An Essential Guide to Employment Law: Personnel Policies and Procedures*. Milford, CT: Kogan Page.

Cypress-Fairbanks Independent School District (2018). *Student code of conduct: 2018–2019*. Houston, TX: Cypress-Fairbanks Independent School District.

Cyr, A. (1997). *After the Cold War: American foreign policy, Europe, and Asia American foreign policy*. Basingstoke, UK: Macmillan.

Daft, R. L. (2016). *Organization theory and design* (12th ed.). Belmont, CA; Cengage Learning.

Daft, R. L., & Lengel, R. H. (1984). Information richness: A new approach to managerial behavior and organization design. *Research in Organizational Behavior, 6*, 191–233.

Dai, D. Y. (2012). *Design research on learning and thinking in educational settings*. New York, NY: Routledge.

Dale v. Board of Education, Lemmon Independent School District 52–2, 316 N.W.2d 108 (S.D. 1982).

Daly, S. E. (2018). *Everyday school violence: An educator's guide to safer schools*. Lanham, MD: Rowman & Littlefield.

Dane, E., & Pratt, M. G. (2007). Exploring intuition and its role in managerial decision making, *Academy of Management Review, 32*(1), 33–54.

Danielson, C. (2006). *Teacher leadership that strengthens professional practice*. Alexandria, VA: ASCD.

Danielson, C. (2010–2011). Evaluations that help teachers learn. *Educational Leadership, 68*(4), 35–39.

Danielson, C. (2016). *Talk about teaching! Leading professional conversations*. Corwin Press.

Dans, K. *Human behavior at work*. New York: McGraw-Hill.

Darling-Hammond, L. (2008). *Powerful learning: What we know about teaching for understanding*. New York, NY: Wiley.

Darling-Hammond, L. (2010). *The flat world and education: How America's commitment to equity will determine our future*. New York, NY: Teachers College Press.

Darling-Hammond, L. (2017). *Empowered educators: How high-performing systems shape teaching quality around the world*. San Francisco, CA: Jossey-Bass.

Darling-Hammond, L., & Adamson, R. (2014). *Beyond the bubble test: How performance assessments support 21st century learning*. San Francisco, CA: Jossey-Bass.

Darling-Hammond, L., & Baratz-Snowden, J. (2009). *A good teacher in every classroom: Preparing highly qualified teachers our children deserve*. San Francisco, CA; Jossey-Bass.

Darling-Hammond, L., & Bransford, J. (Eds.) (2007). *Preparing teachers for a changing world: What teachers should learn and be able to do*. San Francisco, CA: Jossey-Bass.

Darling-Hammond, L., Cook-Harvey, C. M., Flook, L., Gardner, M., & Melnick, H. (2019). *With the whole child in mind: Insights from the Comer school development program*. Alexandria, VA: ASCD.

Darling-Hammond, L., & McLaughlin, M. W. (2011). Policies that support professional development in an era of reform. *Phi delta Kappan, 92*(6), 81–92. http://www.pdkintl.org/publications/kappan/.

Darling-Hammond, L., & Oakes, J. (2019). *Preparing teachers for deep learning*. Cambridge, MA: Harvard Education Press.

Darling-Hammond, L., Ramos-Beban, N., Altamirano, R. P., & Hyler, M. E. (2015). *Be the change: Reinventing school for student success*. New York, NY: Teachers College Press.

Datnow, A., & Park, V. (2015). *Data-driven leadership*. New York, NY: Wiley.

Daugherty v. Vanguard Charter School Academy, 116 F. Supp.2d 897 (W.D. Mich. 2000).

David-Ferdon, C., Vivola-Kantor, M., Dahlberg, L. L., Marshal, K. J., Rainford, N., & Hall, J. E. (2018). *A comprehensive technical package for the prevention of youth violence and associated risk behaviors*. Atlanta, GA: National Center for Injury Prevention and Control, Centers for Disease Control and Prevention https://www.cdc.gov/violenceprevention/pdfyvtechnicalpackage.pdf.

Davidson, J. E. et al. (2003). *The psychology of problem solving*. New York, NY: Cambridge University Press.

Davidson, M., Khmelkov, V., & Lickona, T. (2010). The power of character: Needed for, and developed from teaching and learning. In T. Lovat, R. Toomey, & N. Clement (Eds.). *International research handbook on values education and student wellbeing* (pp. 427–454). New York, NY: Springer.

Davidson-Taylor, C. M. (2002). Is instruction working? *Principal Leadership*, *3*(2), 30–35.

Davis, S. H. (1998, November). Why do principals get fired? *Principal*, *78*(2), 34–39.

Davis, S. H., & Davis, P.B. (2003). *The intuitive dimensions of administrative decision making*. Lanham, MD: Rowman & Littlefield.

Davis, S. H., & Hensley, P. A. (1999, September). The politics of principal evaluation. *Thrust for Educational Leadership*, *29*(1), 22–26.

Davis v. Churchhill County School Board, 616 F.Supp. 1310 D. Nev. (1985).

Davis v. Monroe County Board of Education, 526 U.S. 629 (1999).

Dawes, L. (2011). *Creating a speaking and listening classroom*. New York, NY: Taylor and Francis.

Deal, T. E., & Kennedy, A. A. (1984). *Corporate cultures: The rites and rituals of corporate life*. Reading, MA: Addison-Wesley.

Deal, T. E., & Peterson, K. D. (2016). *Shaping school culture: Pitfalls, paradoxes, and promises* (3rd ed.). San Francisco, CA: Jossey-Bass.

deBiasi, K. (2018). *Solving the change paradox by means of trust: Leveraging the power to trust to provide continuity in times of organizational change*. New York, NY: Springer.

Deblieux, M. (2003). *Performance appraisal source book: A collection of practical samples*. Alpharetta, GA: Society for Human Resource Management.

de Bono, E, (1970). *Lateral thinking: creativity step-by-step*. New York, NY: Harper & Row.

de Bono, E. (1985). *Six thinking hats*. Boston, MA: Little, Brown.

de Bono, E. (2008). *Creativity workout: 62 exercises to unlock your most creative ideas*. Berkeley, CA: Ulysses Press.

Debra P. v. Turlington, 644 F.2d 397reh'g denied, 654 F.2d 1097 (5th Cir. 1981).

Debra P. v. Turlington, 564 F. Supp. (M.D. Fla. 1983), affirmed 730 F.2d 1405 (11th Cir. 1984).

Deconte v. State, 329 S.E.2d 636 (N.C. 1985).

De Corte, E. (2003). Transfer as the productive use of acquired knowledge, skills, and motivations. *Current Directions in Psychological Science*, *12*(4), 142–146.

Dee, T. S. (2004). Teachers, race, and student achievement in a randomized experiment. *Review of economics and statistics*, *86*(1), 195–210.

deLaurier v. San Diego Unified School District, 588 F.2d 674 (9 Cir.1978).

Deming, W. E. (2000). *Out of the Crisis*. Cambridge, MA: MIT Press.

DeMitchell, T. A. (2020). *Teachers and their unions: Labor relations in uncertain times*. Lanham, MD: Rowman & Littlefield.

Dempsey v. Alston, 966 A.2d 1.8 (N.J. Super. Ct. Att. Div. 2009).

DeNavas-Walt, C., & Proctor, B. D. (2015). US Census Bureau. Current population reports, P60–252, *Income and poverty in the United States: 2014*. Washington, DC: U.S. Government Printing Office.

Denicolo, P., & Kempf, M. (2005). *Connecting policy and practice: Challenges for teaching and learning in schools*. New York, NY: Routledge.

Dennick, R. (2010). *Giving a lecture: From presenting to teaching*. New York, NY: Routledge.

Dennis v. United States, 341 U.S. 494 (1951).

Deutsch, N. L. (2017). *After-school programs to promote positive youth development*. New York, NY: Springer.

DeVargas v. Mason & Hanger-Silas Mason Co., 911 F.2d 1377 (10 Cir., 1990, cert. denied, 111 S. Ct. 799 (1991).

DeVito, J. A. (2014). *The nonverbal communication book*. New York, NY: McGraw-Hill.

Dewey, J. (1907). The school and social progress. In *The school and society* (pp. 19–44). Chicago, IL: University of Chicago Press.

Dewey, J. (1966). *Democracy and education*. New York, NY: Macmillan/Free Press (originally published in 1916).

Dewey, J. (1933). *How we think: A restatement of the relation of reflective thinking to the educative process* (rev. ed.). Boston. MA: Heath.

Dewey, J. (1938). *Experience and education*. New York, NY: Collier Books.

Dewey, J. (1959). *Dewey on education*. New York, NY: Simon & Schuster.

Dharmarajan, K. (2007). *Eightstorm: Eight step brainstorming for innovative managers*. Las Vegas, NV: Book Surge Publishing.

Dias de Figueiredo, A. (1995, July). What are the big challenges of education for the XXI century: Proposals for action. Invited contribution for the preparation of the White Book on Education and Training for the XXI Century, Eurydice, The Education Information Network in the European Unit, Department of Informatics Engineering University of Coimbra, Portugal. http://eden.dei.uc.pt/~adf/whitebk.htm.

Diesing, P. (1965). Bargaining strategy and union-management relationships. In J. D. Singer (Ed.). *Human behavior and instructional politics*. Chicago, IL: Rand McNally.

Digest of Education Statistics (2019). Washington, DC: US Government Printing Office.

Dijkstra, P., Kuyper, H., van der Werf, G., Buunk, A. P., & van der Zee, Y. G. (2008). Social comparisons in the classroom. *Review of Educational Research, 78*(4), 828–879.

Dimmitt, C., Carey, J. C., & Hatch, T. (Eds.). (2007). *Evidence-based school counseling: Making a difference with data-driven practices*. Thousand Oaks, CA: Corwin Press.

Dishion, T., and D. Andrews. (1995). Preventing escalation of problem-behavior with high-risk young adolescents: immediate and 1-year outcomes. *Journal of Consulting and Clinical Psychology, 643*, 538–548.

Dishion, T. J., McCord, J., & Poulin, F. (1999). When interventions harm: peer groups and problem behavior. *American Psychologist, 54*, 755–764.

Dismuke, D. P. (2018). *Terms and conditions of employment in collective bargaining agreements*. Naperville, IL: Apollo Publications.

Doe v. Acton-Boxborough Regional school District, 8 N.E.3d 737 (Mass. 2014).

Doe v. Belleville Public School District No. 118, 672 F. Supp. 342 (S.D. Ill. 1987).

Doe v. Dolton Elementary School District, 694 F. Supp. 440 (N.D. Ill. 1988).

Doe v. Duncanville Independent School District, 70 F.3d 402 (5th Cir. 1995).

Doh, J. C. (1971). *The planning-programming-budgeting systems in three Federal agencies*. Manchester, NH: Irvington.

Doll, R. C. (1996). *Curriculum improvement: Decision making and process* (9th ed.). Needham Heights, MA: Allyn & Bacon.

Donahue, P. L., Voelkl, K. E., Campbell, J. R., & Mazzeo, J. (1999). *The NEAP 1998 reading report card for the nation and the states*. Washington, DC: National Center for Education Statistics (NCES No. 1999–500).

Donovan ex. rel. Donovan v. Punxsutawney Area School Board, 336 F.3d 211 (3d Cir. 2003).

Dornbusch, S. M, & Ritter, P. L. (1988). Parents of high school students: A neglected resource. *Educational Horizons, 66*(2), 75–77.

Doud, J. L. (1989a). The k-8 principal in 1988. *Principal, 68*, 6–12.

Doud, J. L. (1989b). The k-12 principal in 1988. *Principal, 68*, 6–12.

Dougherty, T. W., Turban, D. B., & Callender, J. C. (1994). Confirming first impressions in the employment interview: A field study of interviewer behavior. *Journal of Applied Psychology, 79*, 659–665.

Doyle, W. (1985). Effective teaching and the concept of master teacher. *Elementary School Journal, 86*, 30.

Doyle, W. (1992). Curriculum and pedagogy. In P. W. Jackson (Ed.), *Handbook of research on curriculum* (pp. 486–516). New York, NY: Macmillan.

Drucker, P. F. (1993). *Managing for results*. New York, NY: HarperCollins.

Dryfoos, J. (2002). Partnering—full service community schools: Creating new institutions. *Phi Delta Kappan, 83*(5), 393.

DuBrin, A. (2018). *Fundamentals of organizational behavior*. Solon, OH: Academic Media Solutions.

Duemer, L. S., & Mendez-Morse, S. (2002, September). Recovering policy implementation: Understanding implementation through informal communication. *Education Policy Analysis Archives, 10*(39). http://epaa.asuedu/epaa/v10n39.html.

Duffett, A., Farkas, S., Rotherdam, A. J., & Silva, E. (2008). *Waiting to be won over: Teachers speak on the profession, unions, and reform*. Washington, DC: Education Sector.

DuFour, R. (1997). Make the words of mission statements come to life. *Journal of Staff Development, 18*(3), 54–55.

DuFour, R., DuFour, R., & Eaker, R. (2006). Professional learning communities at work: Plan book. Bloomington, IN; Solution Tree.

DuFour, R., DuFour, R., & Eaker, R. (2008). Revisiting Professional learning communities at work: New insights for improving schools. Bloomington, IN: Solution Tree.

DuFour, R., DuFour, R., & Eaker, R., & Karhanek, G. (2004). *Whatever it takes: How professional learning communities respond when kids don't learn*. Bloomington, IN: Solution Tree.

DuFour, R., DuFour, R., Eaker, R., & Karhanek, G. (2010). *Raising the bar and closing the gap: Whatever it takes*. Bloomington, IN: Solution Tree.

DuFour, R., DuFour, R., & Eaker, R., Many, T. (2006). *Learning by doing: A handbook of professional learning communities at work*. Bloomington, IN: Solution Tree.

DuFour, R., DuFour, R., & Eaker, R., Many, T., & Mattos, M. (2016). *Learning by doing: A handbook of professional learning communities at work*. Bloomington, IN: Solution Tree.

DuFour, R., DuFour, R., Eaker, R., Mattos, M., & Muhammed, A. (2021). *Revisiting professional learning communities at work* (2nd ed.). Indianapolis, IN: Solution Tree Press.

DuFour, R., & Eaker, R. (1998). *Professional learning communities at work: Best practices for enhancing student achievement*. Bloomington, IN: Solution Tree.

DuFour, R., & Eaker, R. (2009). *Professional learning communities at work: Best practices for enhancing student achievement* (2nd ed.). Bloomington, IN: Solution Tree.

Dugan v. Ballman, 502 P.2d 308 (Fla. 1976).

Dulye, L. (2006, July). Get out of your office. *HR Magazine*, 99.

Dunlap, E. S. (Ed.) (2013). *The comprehensive handbook of school safety*. New York, Taylor & Francis.

Dunn, R., & Dunn, K. (1992). *Teaching Students Through Their Individual Learning Styles*, 2 vols.: *Practical Approaches for Grades 3–12*. Needham Heights, MA: Allyn & Bacon.

Dunn, R., Dunn, K., & Perrin, J. (1994). *Teaching young children through their individual learning styles: Practical approaches for grades k–2*. Needham Heights, MA: Allyn and Bacon.

Durkin, M. C. (1993). *Thinking through class discussion: The Hilda Taba approach*. Lancaster, PA: Technomic.

Duro v. District Attorney, Second Judicial District of North Carolina, 368 N.W.2d 74 (4th Cir. 1983).

Dyer, K. M. (2001). The power of 360-degree feedback. *Educational Leadership*, *58*(5), 35–38.

Dyer, W. G. (1994). *Team building: Issues and alternatives*. Reading, MA: Addison-Wesley.

Eaker, R., DuFour, R., & DuFour, R. (2002). *Getting started: Reculturing schools to become professional learning communities*. Bloomington, IN: Solution Tree.

Eaker, R., DuFour, R., & DuFour, R. (2007). *A leader's companion: Inspiration for professional learning communities at work*. Bloomington, IN: Solution Tree.

Eaker, R., Hagadone, M., Keating, J., & Rhoades, M. (2021). *Leading professional learning communities (PLCs) at work districtwide: From boardroom to classroom*. Indianapolis, IN: Solution Tree Press.

Earl, L. M. (2013). *Assessment as learning: Using classroom assessment to maximize student learning* (2nd ed.). Thousand Oaks, CA: Corwin Press.

Earthman, G. I. (personal communication, April 9, 2010).

Earley, P. C. (1993). East meets West meets Mideast: Further explanations of collectivistic and individualistic work groups. *Academy of Management Journal*, *36*(1), 319–348.

Eby, J. W., Herrell, A. L., & Jordan, M. (2010). *Teaching in k–12 schools: A reflective action approach*. Upper Saddle River, NJ: Pearson/Prentice Hall.

Echevarria, J., Vogt, M. E., & Short, D. (2017). *Making content comprehensible for English learners: The SIOP model* (5th ed.). Boston, MA: Pearson.

Eckert, J. (2018). *Leading together: Teachers and administrators improving student outcomes*. Thousand Oaks, CA: Corwin Press.

Education for All Handicapped Children Act (Public Law 94–142) in 1975 [29 U.S.C.A. § 794 (a)].

Educational Policies Commission. (1940). *Learning the ways of democracy*. Washington, DC: National Education Association.

Edwards, P. A. (2019). *New ways to engage parents: Strategies and tools for teachers and leaders, k–12*. New York, NY: Teachers College Press.

Edwards, P. A., Spiro, R. J., Domke, L. M., Castle, A. M., Peltier, M. R., Donohue, T. H., & White, K. L. (2019). *Partnering with families for student success: 24 scenarios for problem solving with parents*. New York, NY: Teachers College Press.

Edwards v. Aguillard, 482 U.S. 578 (1987).

Egalite, A. J., Kisida, B., Winters, M. A. (2015). Representation in the classroom: The effect of own-race teachers on student achievement. *Economics of Education Review*, *45*, 44–52.

Ehrgott, M. (2011). *Trends in multiple criteria decision analysis*. New York, NY: Springer.

Ehrhart, M. G., & Nauman, S. E. (2004). Organizational citizenship behavior in work groups: A group norms approach. *Journal of Applied Psychology*, *89*(6), 960–974.

Eisner, E. W. (1991). Should America have a national curriculum? *Educational Leadership*, *49*, 76–81.

Eisner, E. W. (2002). *The educational imagination* (3rd ed.). Columbus, OH: Merrill.

Elkgrove School District v. Newdow, 542 U.S. 1 (2004), reh'g denied, 542 U.S. 961 (2004).

Ellemers, N., Spears, R., & Doosie, B. (2002). Self and social identity. *Annual Review of Psychology*, *53*(1), 161–186.

Elliott, D. S., Hamburg, B. A., &Williams, K. R. (Eds.). (1998). *Violence in American schools*. New York, NY: Cambridge University Press.

Elmore, R. F. (2004). *School reform from the inside out: Policy, practice, and performance*. Cambridge, MA: Harvard Education Publishing Group.

Elson, M., & Ferguson, C. J. (2014). Twenty-five years of research on violence in digital games and aggression: Empirical evidence, perspective, and debate gone astray. *European Psychologist*, *9*(1), 33–46.

Emery, J. (2019). *Leading for organizational change: Building purpose, motivation, and belonging*. New York: Wiley.

Emmer, E. T., & Evertson, C. M. (2017). *Classroom management for middle and high school teachers* (10th ed.). Boston, MA: Pearson.

Emmer, E. T., & Stough, L. M. (2001). Classroom management: A critical part of educational psychology, with implications for teacher education. *Educational Psychologist, 36*(2), 103–112.

Engel v. Vitale, 370 U.S. 421 (1962).

English, F., & Steffy, B. (2001). *Deep curriculum alignment: Creating a level playing field for all children on high-stakes tests of educational accountability*. Lanham, MD: Scarecrow Press.

English, F. W. (2011). *Deciding what to teach and test: Developing, aligning, and leading the curriculum*. Thousand Oaks, CA: Corwin Press.

English, F.W. (2015). *The Sage guide to educational leadership and management*. Thousand Oaks, CA: Sage.

Entwisle, D. R., Alexander, K. L., & Olson, L. S. (2010). Socioeconomic status: Its broad sweep and long reach in education. In J. L. Meece & J. S. Eccles (Eds.). *Handbook of research on schools, schooling, and human development* (pp. 237–255). New York, NY: Routledge.

Epperson v. Arkansas, 393 U.S. 97 (1968).

Eppley, K. (2015). Seven traps of the Common Core standards. *Journal of Adolescent and Adult Literacy, 59*(2), 207–216.

Epstein, J. L. (2018). *School, family, and community partnerships: Preparing educators and improving schools*. Boulder, CO: Westview Press.

Epstein, J. L., Sanders, M. G., Sheldon, S. B., Simon, B. S., Salinas, K. C., Jansorn, N. R., Van Voorhis, F. L., et al. (2018). *School, family and community partnership* (4th ed.). Thousand Oaks, CA: Corwin Press.

Erdogan, I., & Campbell, T. (2008). Teacher questioning and interaction patterns in classrooms facilitated with differing levels of constructivist teaching practices. *International Journal of Science Education, 30*(4), 1891–1914.

Erez, M., & Somech (1996). Is group productivity less the rule or the exception? Effects of culture and group-based motivation. *Academy of Management Journal, 39*(6), 1513–1537.

Erford, B. T., (2018a). *Orientation to the counseling profession: Advocacy, ethics, and essential professional foundations*. Boston, MA: Pearson.

Erford, B. T., (Ed.). (2018b). *Group work: Processes and applications*. New York, NY: Routledge.

Erford, B. T., (2019a). *45 techniques every counselor should know* (3rd ed.). New York, Ny: Merrill.

Erford, B. T., (2019b). *Transforming the school counseling profession* (5th ed.). Boston, MA: Pearson.

Erford, B. T., (2020). *Assessment of counselors: Research and evaluation in counseling, school counseling, and stress management*. Boston, MA: Pearson.

Erford, B. T., Byrd, R. T., & Byrd, R. B. (2013). *Applying techniques to common encounters in school counseling: A case-based approach*. New York, NY: Merrill.

ERIC Digest (2003). Class size reduction and urban students. *ERIC Clearinghouse on Urban Education, 182*, 1–26.

Essex, N. L. (2016). *School law and the public schools: A practical guide for educational leaders*. Boston, MA: Allyn & Bacon.

Ettinger, A. S., Bornschein, R. L., Farfel, M., Campbell, c., Ragan, N. B., Rhoads, G. G., Brophy, M., Wilkins, S., & Dockery, D. W. (2002). Assessment of cleaning to control lead dusting homes of children with moderate lead poisoning: Treatment of lead-exposed children trial. *Environmental Health Perspectives, 110*(12), 773–779.

Etzioni, A. (1975). *A comparative analysis of complex organizations*. New York, NY: Free Press.

Etzioni-Halevy, E. (2010). *Bureaucracy and democracy*. New York, NY: Routledge.

Evans, G. W., & Schamberg, M. A. (2009). Childhood poverty, chronic stress, and adult working memory. *Proceedings of the National Academy of Sciences of the United States of America*, *106*(16), 6545–6549.

Evans, R. W. (2011). *The tragedy of American school reform: How curriculum politics, and entrenched dilemmas have diverted us from democracy*. New York, NY: Palgrave Macmillan.

Everson v. Board of Education of the Township of Ewing, 330 U.S. 1 (1947).

Evertson, C. M., & Emmer, E. T. (2017). *Classroom management for elementary teachers* (10th ed.). Boston, MA: Pearson.

Every Student Succeeds Act of 2015, Pub. L. No. 114–95 Stat. 1177 (2015).

Ewy, R. (2010). *Stakeholder-driven strategic planning in education: A practical guide for developing and deploying successful long-range plans*. Milwaukee, WI: ASQ Press.

Eysenck, H. (2018a). *Intelligence: A new look*. New York, NY: Routledge.

Eysenck, H. (2018b). *The structure and measurement of intelligence*. New York, NY: Routledge.

Fahey, K., Breidenstein, A., Ippolito, J., & Hensley, F. (2019). *An uncommon theory of school change: Leadership for reinventing schools*. New York, NY: Teachers College Press.

Falk, B. (2009). *Teaching the way children learn*. New York, NY: Teachers College Press.

Falkheimer, J., & Heide, M. (2018). *Strategic communication: An introduction*. New York, NY: Routledge.

Farina v. Board of Education, 116 F.2d 503 (E.D.N.Y. 2000).

Farr, J. L., & Tippins, N. T. (Eds.) (2017). *Handbook of employee selection* (2nd ed.). New York, NY: Routledge.

Farrell, A. D., and A. L. Meyer (1997). "The Effectiveness of a school-based curriculum for reducing violence among urban sixth-grade students." *American Journal of Public Health*, 87, 979–988.

Fawcett, G., Brobeck, D., Andrews, S., & Walker, L. (2001). Principals and belief-driven change. *Phi Delta Kappan*, *82*, 404–410.

Federal Bureau of Investigation (2019). *Crime in the United States: 2018*. Washington, DC: US Department of Justice.

Fehr, E., & Fischbacher, U. (2004). Social norms and human cooperation. *Trends in Cognitive Sciences*, *8*(4), 185–190.

Feinstein, J. S. (2009). *The nature of creative development*. Stanford, CA: Stanford University Press.

Feist, G. J. (1999). The influence of personality on artistic and scientific creativity. In R. J. Sternberg (Ed.). *Handbook of creativity* (pp. 273–296). New York, NY: Cambridge University Press.

Feldman, D. C. (1984). The development and enforcement of group norms. *Academy of Management Review*, *9*(1), 47–53.

Fennelly, L. J., & Perry, M. A. (2014). *The handbook for school safety and security*. Waltham, MA: Elsevier.

Fenner, D. S., & Snyder, S. (2017). *Unlocking learners' potential: strategies for making content accessible*. Thousand Oaks, CA: Corwin Press.

Fenster v. Schneider, 636 F.2d 765 (D.D. Cir. 1980).

Ferguson, C. J. (2016). Social media, societal changes, and mental health: You can live online wholesale. In C. Marky (Ed.). *Encyclopedia of mental health* (2nd ed.). Oxford, UK: Elsevier.

Ferrandino, V. (2001). Challenges for the 21st century elementary school principals. *Phi Delta Kappan*, *82*, 440–442.

Fink, D. (2000). *Good schools/real schools: Why school reform doesn't last*. San Francisco, CA: Jossey-Bass.

Fink, E., & Resnik, L. B. (2001). Developing principals as instructional leaders. *Phi Delta Kappan*, *82*(8), 598–600.

Finn, C., & Petrilli, M. J. (2020). *How to educate an American: The conservative vision*. New York, NY: Simon & Schuster.

Finn, C., & Sousa, R. (2014). *What lies ahead for America's children and their schools*. Stanford, CA: Hoover Institute Press.

Fiore, D. J. (2022). *School-community relations*. New York, NY: Routledge.

Firestone, W. A., & Herriott, R. E. (1981). Images of organization and the promotion of change. In R. G. Corwin (Ed.), *Research in sociology of education and socialization*, vol. 2 (pp. 221–260). Greenwich, CT: JAI Press.

Fisher, D., Frey, N., Pumpian, I. (2019). *How to create a culture of achievement in your school and classroom*. Alexandria, VA: ASCD.

Flanagan, D. P., McDonaugh, E. M., & Kaufman, A. S. (2018). *Contemporary intellectual assessment; Theories, tests, and issues* (4th ed.). New York, NY: Guilford.

Flaxman, E., & Inger, M. (1991). Parents and schooling in the 1990s. *ERIC Review, 1*(3), 2–6.

Flora, S. R. (2004). *The power of reinforcement*. Albany, NY: State University of New York Press.

Florence County School District v. Carter, 510 U.S. 7 (1993).

Florida Department of Education. (1999). *Impact of staff development (Issue brief)*. Tallahassee, FL: Florida Department of Education.

Florida Department of Health v. Curry, 722 So.2d 874 (Fla. Ct. App. 1998).

Florey v. Sioux Falls School District, 619 F.2d 1311 (8th Cir. 1980).

Florio, J. J. (1988). Asbestos in the schools: New requirements take effect. *PTA Today, 14*, 31–32.

Floyd County Board. of Education v. Slone, 307 S.W. 23d. 912 (Ky. 1957).

Foote, N., Matson, E., Weiss, L., & Wenger, E. (2002). Leveraging group knowledge for high-performance decision-making. *Organizational Dynamics, 31*(2), 280–295.

Ford, D. (2014). Why education must by multicultural. *Gifted Child Today, 37*(1), 59–62.

Ford, D., & Thomas, A. (1997, June). *Under-achievement among gifted minority students: Problems and promises*. ERIC EC Digest. (ERIC Document Reproduction Service No. E544).

Forsyth, P. B., & Hoy, W. K. (1978). Isolation and alienation in educational organizations, *Educational Administration Quarterly, 14*, 80–96.

Fossum, J. (2014). *Labor relations: Development, structure, and process*. New York: McGraw-Hill.

Foster, C. R. (2017). *Extra-curricular activities in the high school*. Andesite Press.

Fowler, F. (2013). *Policy studies for school leaders: An introduction* (4th ed.). Boston, MA: Pearson.

Frank, A. D. (1984). Trends in communication: Who talks to whom?" *Personnel, 62*(2), 41–47.

Franklin v. Gwinnett County Public Schools, 503 U.S. 60 (1992).

Franzke, M., Kintsch, E., Caccmise, D., Johnson, N., & Dooley, S. (2005). Summary street computer support for comprehension and writing. *Journal of Educational Computing Research, 33*(1), 53–80.

Frase, L. (2003). *School management by wandering around*. Lanham, MD: Scarecrow Education.

Frase, L. E., & English, F. W. (1995). *The curriculum management audit: Improving school quality*. Lancaster, PA: Technomic.

Frazier v. Alexandre, 434 F. Supp.2d 1350 (S.D. Fla. 2006).

Freeman, J. (2012). *The tyranny of e-mail: The four-thousand-year journey to your inbox*. New York: Simon & Schuster.

Freedman, J. L. (2002). *Media violence and its effect on aggression: Assessing the scientific evidence*. Toronto, Canada: University of Toronto Press.

Freiler v. Tangipahoa Parish Board of Education, 185 F.3d 337 (5th Cir.), reh'g en blanc 105 denied, 201 F.3d 602 (5th Cir.), cert. denied 530 U.S. 1251 (2000).

Fretwell, E. K. (2018). *Extra-curricular activities in secondary schools: Scholar select*. Franklin Classics.

Friedman, M, & Rosenman, R. H. (1974). *Type A behavior and your heart*. Greenwich, CT: Fawcett Publications.

Fried, R. L. (2001). *The passionate teacher: A practical guide*. Boston, MA: Beacon Press.

Froman, L. A. (1966). Some effects of interest group strength in state politics. *American Political Science Review*, 60(4), 952–962.

Frost Elementary (2019). Home page. Allegany County Public Schools https://www.acpsmd.org/Domain/43.

Fry, R. W. (2011). *Ask the right questions: Hire the best people*. Pompton Plains, NJ: Career Press.

Fullan, M. (1993). *Change forces: Probing the depths of educational reform*. London, UK: Falmer Press.

Fullan, M. (2003). *The moral imperative of school leaders*. Thousand Oaks, CA: Corwin Press.

Fullan, M. (2010). *The moral imperative realized*. Thousand Oaks, CA: Corwin Press.

Fullan, M. (2014). *The principal: Three keys to maximizing impact*. San Francisco, CA: Jossey-Bass.

Fullan, M. (2015). *The new meaning of educational change*. New York, NY: Teachers College Press.

Fullan, M. (2018). *Surreal change: The real life of transforming public education*. New York, NY: Routledge.

Fullan, M., & Gallagher, M. J. (2020). *The devil is in the details: System solutions for equity, excellence, and student well-being*. Thousand Oaks, CA: Corwin Press.

Fullan, M., & Hargreaves, A. (2012). *Professional capital: Transforming teaching in every school*. New York, NY: Teachers College Press.

Fullan, M., & St. Germain, C. (2006). *Learning places: A field guide for improving the context of schooling*. Thousand Oaks CA: Corwin Press.

Fuller, A., & Fuller, L. (2021). *Neurodevelopmental differentiation: Optimizing brain systems to maximize learning*. Indianapolis, IN: Solution Tree Press.

Fuller v. N. Kansas City School District, 629 S.W.2d. 404 (Mo. 1982).

Furman, G. (2003). Moral leadership and the ethic community. *Values and Ethics in Educational Administration*, 2(1), 1–8.

Furnham, A. (2011). *Body language in business: Decoding the signals*. New York, NY: Palgrave Macmillan.

Furr, R. M. (2018). *Psychometrics: An introduction* (3rd ed.). Thousand Oaks, CA: Sage.

Fusco, E. (2012). *Effective questioning strategies in the classroom: A step-by-step approach to engaged thinking and learning, k–8*. New York, NY: Teachers College Press.

G. Cooper Access to Education by Homeless Children, 53 Ed. Law Rep. 757 (1989).

GI Forum v. Texas Education Agency, 87 F. Supp.2d 667 (W.D. Tex. 2000).

G.N. v. State, 833 N.E.2d 107 (Ind. Ct. App. 2005).

Gaethy, G. J., & Shanteau, J. (1984). Reducing the influence of irrelevant information on experienced decision makers. *Organizational Behavior and Human Performance*, 33(2), 187–203.

Gage, N. L. (1981). *The scientific basis of the art of teaching*. New York, NY: Teachers College Press.

Gage, N. L. (2010). *A conception of teaching*. New York, NY: Springer.

Gagne, R. (1985). *The conditions of learning* (4th ed.). New York: Holt, Rinehart & Winston.

Galanes, G. J., & Adams, K. (2019). *Effective group discussion: Theory and practice* (15th ed.). New York, NY: McGraw-Hill.

Gall, M. D., & Acheson, K. A. (2010). *Clinical supervision and teacher development: Preservice and inservice applications* (6th ed.). New York, NY: Wiley.

Gallagher, M.J., & Fullan, M. (2020). The devil is in the details: System solutions for equity, excellence, and student well-being. Thousand Oaks, CA: Corwin Press.

Gambino v. Fairfax County School Board, 564 F.2d 157 (4th Cir. 1977).

Gammage, K. L., Carron, A. V., & Estabrooke, P. A. (2001). Team cohesion and individual productivity: The influence of the norm for productivity and identifiability of individual effort. *Small Group Research*, *32*(1), 3–18.

Ganske, K. (2017). Lesson closure: An important piece of the learning puzzle. *The Reading Teacher*, *71*(1), 95–100.

Garcia, O., Johnson, S. I., & Seltzer, K. (2016). *The translanguaging classroom: Leveraging student bilingualism for learning*. Caslon Publishing.

Garcia, O., & Kleifgen, J. A. (2018). *Educating emergent bilinguals: Policies, programs, and practices for English learners* (2nd ed.). New York, NY: Teachers College Press.

Gardner, D. (2007). Confronting the achievement gap. *Phi Delta Kappan*, *88*(7), 542–546.

Gardner, H. (1994). *Frames of Mind* (rev. ed.). New York: Basic Books.

Gardner, H. (1999). *Intelligence reframed: Multiple intelligences for the 21st century*. New York, NY: Basic Books.

Gardner, H. (2005). *Frames of mind: The theory of multiple intelligences*. New York: Basic Books.

Gardner, H. (2007). *Multiple intelligences: New horizons*. New York. NY: Basic Books.

Garguilo, R. M., & Metcalf, D. (2017). *Teaching in today's inclusive classrooms: A universal design for learning approach* (3rd ed.). Boston, MA: Cengage Learning.

Garnett v. Renton School District No. 403, 21 F.3d 1113 (9th Cir. 1994), on remand, 1994 WL 555397 (W.D. Wash. 1994)

Garrett, R. (personal communication, April 18, 1990).

Gatchel v. Gatchel, 824 N.E.2d 576 (2005).

Gay, G. (2018). *Culturally responsive teaching: Theory, research, and practice* (3rd ed.). New York, NY: Teachers College Press.

Gebser v. Lago Vista Independent School District, 524 U.S. 274 (1998).

Genus, A. (2018). *Decisions, technology, and organizations*. New York, NY: Routledge.

George, J. M. (1992). Extrinsic and intrinsic origins of perceived social loafing in organizations. *Academy of Management Journal, 35*(1), 191–202.

George, J. M., & Bettenhausen, K. (1990). Understanding prosocial behavior, sales performance, and turnover: A group-level analysis in a service context. *Journal of Applied Psychology*, *75*(6), 698–709.

George, J. M., & Jones, G. R. (2012). *Understanding and managing organizational behavior*. Boston, MA: Pearson.

George, J. M., & Zhou, J. (2001). When openness to experience and conscientiousness are related to creative behavior: An interactional approach. *Journal of Applied Psychology*, *86*(3), 513–524.

Gershon, W. S. (2017). *Curriculum and students in classrooms: Everyday urban education in an era of standardization*. Lanham, MD: Lexington Books/Rowman & Littlefield.

Gersick, C. J. G. (1988). Time and transition in work teams: Toward a new model of group development. *Academy of Management Journal*, *31*(1), 9–41.

Gersick, C. J. G. (1989). Marking time: Predictable transitions in task groups. *Academy of Management Journal*, *32*(2), 274–309.

Gersten, R. (1999). The changing face of bilingual education. *Educational Leadership*, *56*(7), 41–45.

Getgood, S. (2011). *Professional blogging*. New York: Wiley.

Gibbons v. Ogden, 22 U.S. 9Wheat) 1 (1924).

Ghayer, K., & Churchill, D. D. (2013). *Career success: Navigating the new work environment* (2nd ed.). Charlottesville, VA: CFA Institute.

Gilligan, C. (1982). *In a different voice: Psychological theory and women's development*. Cambridge, MA: Harvard University Press.

Gilligan, C. (1988). Exit-voice dilemmas in adolescent development. In C. Gilligan, J. Ward, J. Taylor, & B. Bardige (Eds.). *Mapping the moral domain: A contribution of women's thinking to psychological theory and education.* Cambridge, MA: Harvard University Press.

Gilio ex. rel. J.G. v. School Board of Hillsborough County, 905 F. Supp.2d 1262 (M.D. Fla. 2012).

Gilovich, T., Griffin, D., & Kahneman, D. (2002). *Heuristics and biases: The psychology of intuitive judgment.* New York, NY: Cambridge University Press.

Gitlow v. New York, 268 U.S. 652 (1925).

Gitomer, D. H., Bell, C. A. (Eds.). (2016). *Handbook of research on teaching* (5th ed.). Washington, DC: AERA.

Gladwell, M. (2005). *Blink: The power of thinking without thinking.* New York, NY: Little, Brown.

Glandel, M., & Vranek, J. (2001). Standards: Here today, here tomorrow. *Educational Leadership, 59,* 7–13.

Glass, B. (1980). *The timely and timeless.* New York, NY: Basic Books.

Glatthorn, A. A., Boschee, F., Whitehead, B. M., & Boschee, B. F. (2018). *Curriculum leadership: Strategies for development and implementation* (5th ed.). Thousand Oaks, CA: Sage.

Glanz, J. (2006). *What every principal should know about ethical and spiritual leadership.* Thousand Oaks, CA: Corwin Press.

Glasser, W. (1969). *Schools without failure.* New York, NY: Harper & Row.

Glasser, W. (1990). *The quality school.* New York, NY: HarperCollins.

Glatthorn, A. A., Boschee, F. A., Whitehead, B. A., & Boschee, B. F. (2018). *Curriculum leadership: Strategies for development and implementation* (5th ed.). Thousand Oaks, CA: Sage.

Glatthorn, A. A., Jailall, J. M. S., Jailall, J. K. (2017). *The principal as curriculum leader: Shaping what is taught and tested.* Thousand Oaks, CA: Corwin Press.

Glickman, C. D. (2006). *Leadership for learning: How to help teachers succeed.* Alexandria, VA: Association for Supervision and Curriculum Development, 2006).

Glickman, C. D., & Burns, R. W. (2020). *Leadership for learning: How to bring out the best in every teacher* (2nd ed.). Alexandria, VA: ASCD.

Glickman, C. D., Gordon, S. P., & Ross-Gordon, J. M. (2018). *Supervision and instructional leadership: A developmental approach.* Boston, MA: Pearson.

Glickman, C., & Mette, I. M. (2020). *The essential renewal of America's schools: A leadership guide for democratizing schools from the inside out.* New York, NY: Teachers College Press.

Global Partnerships in Education (2019). *Education data highlights.* https://www.globalpartnership.org.results/education-data-highlights.

Goetz v. Ansell, 477 F.2d 636 (2d Cir. 1973).

Golann, J. W. (2015). The paradox of success at a no excuses school. *Sociology of Education, 88*(2), 103–119.

Gold, M. E. (2018). *An introduction to labor and employment law.* Geneseo, NY: SUNY College at Geneseo Press.

Goldhaber, D., & Hansen, M. (2010). Race, gender, and teacher testing: How informative a tool a teacher licensure testing? *American Educational Research Journal, 47*(1), 218–251.

Goldhammer, R. (1969). *Clinical supervision: Special methods for the supervision of teachers.* New York, NY: Holt, Rinehart, and Winston.

Goldhammer, R., Anderson, R. H., & Krajewski, R. (1993). *Clinical supervision: Special methods for the supervision of teachers* (3rd ed.). Fort Worth, TX: Harcourt Brace Jovanivich.

Goldring, E. B. (1990). Elementary school principals as boundary spanners: Their engagement with parents. *Journal of Educational Administration, 28*(1), 53–62.

Goldring, E., Grissom, J., Neumerski, C., Blissett, R., Murphy, J., & Porter, A. (2019). Increasing principals time on instructional leadership. *Journal of Educational Administration*, *58*(1). 19–37.

Goldstein, S. E., Young, A., & Boyd, C. (2008). Relational aggression at school: Associations with school safety and social climate. *Journal of Youth & Adolescence*, *37*, 641–654.

Good News Club v. Milford Central School, 533 U.S. 98 (2001).

Good, T. L. (1987). Two decades of research on teacher expectations: Findings and future directions. *Journal of Teacher Education*, *38*(4), 32–47.

Good, T. L. (2009). *21st century education: A reference handbook*. Thousand Oaks, CA: Sage.

Good, T. L., & Brophy, J. E. (1986). Teacher behavior and student achievement. In M. C. Whitrock (Ed.). (1986). *Handbook of research on teaching* (3rd ed.). New York, NY: Macmillan.

Good, T. L., & Lavigne, A. L. (2018). *Looking in classrooms* (11th ed.). New York, NY: Routledge.

Good, T. L., & Nichols, S. L. (2001). Expectancy effects in the classroom: A special focus on improving the reading performance of minority students in first-grade classrooms. *Educational Psychologist*, *36*(2), 113–126.

Gooding, R. Z., & Wagner, J. A. (1985). A meta-analytic review of the relationship between size and performance: The productivity and efficiency of organizations and their subunits. *Administrative Science Quarterly*, *30*(4), 462–481.

Goodlad, J. I. (1963). *Planning and organizing for teaching*. Washington, DC: National Education Association.

Goodman-Scott, E., Betters-Bubon, J., & Donohue, P. (2019). *The school counselor's guide to multi-tiered systems of support*. New York, NY: Routledge.

Goodstein, L. (2011). *Strategic planning: A leadership imperative*. Alexandria, VA: American Society for Training and Development.

Gordon, J. (2002). A perspective on team building. *Journal of the American Academy of Business*, *2*(1), 185–189.

Gorski, P. C. (2018). *Reaching and teaching students in poverty: Strategies for erasing the opportunity gap* (2nd ed.). New York, NY: Teachers College Press.

Goss v. Lopez, 416 U.S. 565 (1975).

Gottfredson, D. C. (1987). An evaluation of an organization development approach to reducing school disorder. *Evaluation Review*, *11*, 739–763.

Gottlieb, M. (2016). *Assessing English language learners: Bridges to educational equity equals connecting academic language proficiency to student achievement* (2nd ed.). Thousand Oaks, CA: Corwin Press.

Goulart v. Meadows, 345 F.3d 239 (4th Cir. 2003).

Graenewagan, P., Ferguson, J. E., Moser, C., & Borgatti, S. P. (2017). *Structure, content, and meaning of organizational networks: Extending network thinking*. Bingley, GBR: Emerald Publishing Group, Ltd.

Graham, A. T., Renaud, G. A., & Rose, M. M. (2020). *Developing effective special educators: Building bridges across the profession*. New York, NY: Teachers College Press.

Graham, S., & Hudley, C. (2005). Race and ethnicity in the study of motivation and competence. In A. J. Elliott & C. W. Dweck (Eds.). *Handbook of competence and motivation* (pp. 392–413). New York, NY: Guilford Press.

Grand Rapids School District v. Ball, 473 U.S. 373 (1985).

Granger v. Cascade County School District No. 1, 499 P.2d 780 (Mont. 1972).

Granger v. Cascade County Sch. Dist. No. 1, 159 Mont. 516, 499 P.2d 780 (1972).

Grath-Marnat, G., & Wright, A. J. (2016). *Handbook of psychological assessment*. New York, NY: Wiley.

Greenberg, J. (2014). *Organizational behavior* (11th ed.). Upper Saddle River, NJ: Prentice Hall.

Greene, J. A. (2017). *Self-regulation in learning*. New York, NY: Routledge.

Greene, M. (2008). *The public school and the private vision: A search for America in education and literature*. New York, NY: The New Press.

Greenfield, W. D. (1988). Moral imagination, interpersonal competence, and the work of school administrators. In D. Griggiths, R. T. Stout, & P. B. Forsyth (Eds.), *Leaders for America's schools* (pp. 207–232). Berkeley, CA: McCutchan.

Greenwald, E. A., Persky, H. R., Campbell, J. R., & Mazzeo, J. (1999). *The NAEP 1998 writing report card for the nation and states*. Washington, DC: National Center for Education Statistics (NCES No. 1999–462).

Gregory, A., & Weinstein, R. S. (2004). Connection and regulation at home and at school: Predicting growth in achievement for adolescents. *Journal of Adolescent Research, 4*, 405–427.

Griggs v. Duke Power Company, 401 U.S. 424 (1971).

Grigg v. Virginia, 297 S.E.2d 799 (Va. 1982)

Gregorio, T. v. Wilson, 59 F.3d 1002 (9th Cir. 1995).

Gregory, A., Cornell, D., & Fan, X. (2011). The relationship of school structure and support to suspension rates for black and white high school students. *American Educational Research Journal, 48*(4), 904–934.

Gregory, A., Skiba, R. J., & Noguera, P. A. (2010). The achievement gap and the discipline gap: Two sides of the same coin? *Educational Researcher, 39*, 59–68.

Greiner, L. E. (1967, May–June). Patterns of organization change. *Harvard Business Review*, 126.

Griffin, R. W., Phillips, J. M., & Gully, S. M. (2019). *Organizational behavior: Managing people and organizations*. Belmont, CA: Cengage Learning.

Groenewegan, P., Ferguson, J. E., Moser, C, & Borgatti, S. P. (2017). *Structure, cantent, and meaning of organizational networks: Extending network thinking*. Bingley, GBR: Emerald Publishing Ltd.

Grogan, M., & Shakeshaft, C. (2011). *Women in educational leadership*. San Francisco, CA: Jossey-Bass.

Gross, S., & Shapiro, J. (2004). Using multiple ethical paradigms and turbulence theory in response to administrative dilemmas. *International Studies in Educational Administration, 32*(2), 47–62.

Grossman, R. (2018). *Systematic organizational development*. Charlotte, NC; Information Age Publishing.

Grove City College v. Bell, 465 U.S. 555 (1984).

Grove v. Mead School District No. 354, 753 F.2d 1528 (9th Cir. 1985), cert. denied 474 U.S. 826.

Gruenert, S., & Whitaker, T. (2019). *School culture recharged strategies to energize your staff and culture*. Alexandria, VA. ASCD.

Guerin, L., & Barreiro, S. (2018). *The essential guide to federal employment law*. Berkeley, CA: NOLO.

Guerra, N. G., Leidy, M. S. (2008). Lessons learned: recent advances in understanding and preventing childhood aggression. In R. V. Kail (Ed.). *Advances in child development and behavior* (pp. 287–330). San Diego, CA: Academic Press.

Guilford, J. P. (1967). *The nature of human intelligence*. New York, NY: McGraw-Hill.

Guindon, M. H., & Lane, J. J. (2019). *A counseling primer: An orientation to the profession*. New York, NY: Routledge.

Gujarati, J. (2012). A comprehensive induction system: A key to the retention of highly qualified teachers. *Educational Forum, 76*(2), 218–223.

Gunnthorsdottir, A., & Rapapot, A. (2006). Embedding social dilemmas in intergroup competition reduces free-riding. *Organizational Behavior and Human Decision Processes, 101*(1), 184–199.

Gunzelmann, B. (2015). *Developing safer schools and communities for our children: The interdisciplinary responsibility of our time*. Lanham. MD: Rowman & Littlefield.

Gurian, M. (2011). *Boys and girls learn differently: A guide for teachers and parents.* New York, NY: Wiley.

Guru, B. S., & Hiziroglu, H. R. (2004). *Electromagnetic field theory fundamentals.* New York, NY: Cambridge University Press.

Guskey, T. R. (2015). *On your mark: Challenging the conventions of grading and reporting.* Indianapolis, IN: Solution Tree.

Guskey, T. R., & Brookhart, S. (2019). *What we know about grading: What works, what doesn't, and what's next.* Alexandria, VA: ASCD.

Guthrie, J. W., Hart, C. C., Ray, J. R., Candoli, I. C., & Hack, W. G. (2008). *Modern school business administration.* Boston, MA: Pearson/Allyn & Bacon.

Gutlow v. New York, 268, U.S. 652, 666 (1925).

Guyer v. School Board of Alachua County, 634 So.2d 806 (Fla. Dist. Ct. App. 1994).

Hackman, J. R. (1992). Group influences on individuals. In M. D. Dunnette & L. M. Hough (Eds.), *Handbook of industrial & organizational psychology* (2nd ed., vol. 3; pp. 235–250). Palo Alto, CA: Consulting Psychologists Press.

Hackman, J. R, & Oldham, G. R. (1975). Development of the job diagnostic survey. *Journal of Applied Psychology, 60,* 159–170.

Hackman, J. R., & Oldham, G. R. (1980). *Work redesign.* Reading, MA: Addison-Wesley.

Hage, J. (1965). An axiomatic theory of organizations," *Administrative Science Quarterly, 10,* 289–320.

Hail, D. W. (2003). *The impact of state regulation upon the homeschooling movement as measured by specific descriptive factors.* Doctoral Dissertation. Huntsville, TX: Sam Houston State University.

Hakonsson, D. P., Burton, R. M., & Obel, B. (2020). *Organizational design: A step-by-step approach.* New York, NY: Cambridge University Press.

Hall, E. T. (1966). *The hidden dimension.* Garden City, NY: Doubleday.

Hall, E. T. (1983). Proxemics. In A. M. Katz & V. T. Katz (Eds.), *Foundations of nonverbal communication.* Carbondale, IL: Southern Illinois University Press.

Hall, G. E., & Hord, S. M. (2010). *Implementing change: Patterns, principles, and potholes.* Boston, MA: Pearson/Allyn & Bacon.

Hall, R. H. (2002). *Organizations: Structures, processes, and outcomes* (8th ed.). Upper Saddle River, NJ: Prentice Hall.

Hambrick, J. G. (2001). *Principals' perceptions of the influence of extracurricular activities on selected student academic performance factors: The impact of the no pass-no play rule.* Unpublished doctoral dissertation, Sam Houston State University, Huntsville, Texas.

Hamby, S., & Grych, J. (2013). *The web of violence; Exploring connections among different forms of interpersonal violence and abuse.* New York, NY: Springer.

Hamer v. Board of Education of School District No. 109, 264 N.E.2d 616 9Ill. 1970).

Hammond, J. S., Keeney, R. L., & Raiffa, H. (2006). The Hidden Traps in Decision Making. *Harvard Business Review,* 118–126.

Hammond, T. H., & Knott, J. H. (1980). *Zero-based look at zero-based budgeting.* New Brunswick, NJ: Transaction.

Han, K. T., & Laughter, J. (2019). *Critical race theory in teacher education.* New York, NY: Teachers College Press.

Han, S., Pfizenmaier, D. H., Garcia, E., Eguez, M. L., Ling, M., Kemp, F. W., & Bogden, J. D. (2000). Effects of lead exposure before pregnancy and dietary calcium during pregnancy on fetal development and lead accumulation. *Environmental Health Perspectives, 108*(6), 527–531.

Hannaway, J., & Rotherham, A. J. (2006). *Collective bargaining in education: Negotiating change in today's schools.* Cambridge, MA: Harvard Education Press.

Hanten v. School District of Riverview Gardens, 13 F.Supp.2d 971, E.D. (Mo. 1998).

Hanzel v. Arter, 625 F. Supp. 1259 (S.D. Ohio 1985)

Harasim, L. (2011). *Learning theory: Design and educational technology.* New York, NY: Routledge.

Hardaway, R. M. (1995). *America goes to school: Law, reform, and crisis in public education*. Westport, CT: Praeger.

Hargreaves, A., & Fullan, M. (2012). *Professional capitol: Transforming teaching in every school*. New York, NY: Teachers College Press.

Harman, G. (20010. The politics of quality assurance =: The Australian quality assurance program for higher education, 1993–1995. *Australian Journal of Education*, *45*(2), 168+.

Harper, M. C., Estreicher, S., & Griffith, K. (2019). *Labor law: Selected statutes, forms, and agreements*. New York, NY: Walters Kluwer Law and Business.

Harrigan, J. (2009). *New handbook of methods of nonverbal behavior research*. New York, NY: Oxford University Press.

Harris, A., & Jones, M. (2010). Professional learning communities and system improvement. *Improving Schools*, *13*(2), 172–181.

Harris, A., Jones, M., & Huffman, J. B. (Eds.) (2018). *Teachers leading educational reform: Teacher quality and school development*. New York, NY: Rutledge.

Harris, B. M. (1975). *Supervisory behavior in education* (2nd ed.). Englewood Cliffs, NJ: Prentice Hall.

Harris T. E., & Nelson, M. D. (2018). *Applied organizational communication: Theory and practice in a global environment*. New York, NY: Routledge.

Harris v. Forklift Systems, Inc., 510 U.S. 17 (1993).

Harrison v. Sobel, 705 F. Supp. 870 (S.D. N.Y. 1988).

Harrow, A. J. (1972). *A taxonomy of the psychomotor domain*. New York: Longman.

Harry, B., & Ocio-Stoutenburg, L. (2020). *Meeting families where they are: Building equity through advocacy with diverse schools and communities*. New York, NY: Teachers College Press.

Hart, H. (1954). The relations between state and federal law. *Columbia Law Review*, *54*, 419.

Hartley, D. E. (2004). Pick up your PDA, training and development, 58(2), 22–25.

Hartsock, N. (1987). *Foucault on power: A theory for women*. In L. J. Nicholson (Ed.), *Feminism/postmodernism*. New York, NY: Longman.

Hartzell v. Connell, 679 P.2d 35, 44 (Cal. 1984).

Harvey, S., & Light, R. L. (2015). Questioning for learning in game-based approaches to teaching and coaching. *Asia-Pacific Journal of Health, Sport, and Physical Education*, *6*(2), 175–190.

Hassberger v. Board of Education, No. 00 C 7873 (N.D. Ill. 2003).

Hatch, T. (2006). *Into the classroom: Developing the scholarship of teaching and learning*. New York, NY: Wiley.

Hatch, T. (2013). *The use of data in school counseling; Hatching results for students, programs, and the profession*. Thousand Oaks, CA: Corwin Press.

Hatch, T., Duarte, D., & DeGregorio, L. K. (2018). *Hatching results for elementary school counselors: Implementing core curriculum and other tier one activities*. Thousand Oaks, CA: Corwin Press.

Hatch, T., Duarte, D., Triplett, W., & Gomez, V. (2019). *Hatching results for secondary school counseling: Implementing core curriculum, individual student planning, and other tier one activities*. Thousand Oaks, CA: Corwin Press.

Hatch v. Goerke, 502 F.2d 1189 (10th Cir. 1974).

Hativa, N. (2009). *Lecturing for effective learning*. Sterling, VA: Stylus Publishing.

Hawkins, D. J., Farrington, D. P., & Catalano, R. F. (1998). Reducing violence through the schools. In D. S. Elliott, B. A. Hamburg, and K. R. Williams (Eds.), *Violence in American schools*. New York: Cambridge University Press.

Hay, P. (2017). *The Law of the United States: An Introduction* (New York, NY: Routledge, pp. 113–124.

Hayes, D., & Apple, M. W. (2007). *Teachers and schooling making a difference: Productive pedagogies, assessment, and performance*. New South Wales, Australia: Allen & Unwin.

Haynes, F. (2014). Teaching children to think for themselves: From questioning to dialogue. *Journal of Philosophy in Schools, 1*(1), 131–146.

Haynes, M., Maddock, A., & Goldrick, L. (2014). *On the path to equity: Improving the effectiveness of beginning teachers.* Washington, DC: Alliance for excellent Education. http://www.pathwaylibrary.org/ViewBiblio.aspx?aid=22637.

Hazelwood School District v. Kuhlmeier, 484 U.S. 260 (1988).

Heath, C. (1996). Do people prefer to pass along good news or bad news? Valence and reverence of news as predictors of transmission propensity. *Organizational Behavior and Human Decision Processes, 68*, 79–94.

Heath, R. L., & Winni, J. (2018). *Encyclopedia of strategic communication.* New York, NY: Wiley.

Heidegger, M. (2011). *Phenomenology of intuition and expression.* New York, NY: Continuum International Publishing Group.

Heineke, A. J., McTighe, J. (2018). *Using understanding by design in the culturally and linguistically diverse classroom.* Arlington, VA: ASCD.

Hellriegel, F. D., & Slocum, J. W. (2015). *Organizational behavior* (15th ed.). Mason, OH: South-Western/Cengage Learning.

Hemry v. School Board of Colorado Springs School District No. 11, 760 F. Supp. 856 (D. Colo. 1991).

Henderson, T., & Boje, D. M. (2018). *Organizational development and change theory.* New York, NY: Routledge.

Hennessey, B. A., & Amabile, T. M. (1998). Reward, intrinsic motivation, and creativity. *American Psychologist, 53*(6), 674–675.

Henrich, C., J. Brown, J. L, & Aber, L. (1999). Evaluating the effectiveness of developmental approaches. *Social Policy Report, 13*(1–4), 1–98.

Herbert, B. (2010, January). Invitation to Disaster. *New York Times*, p. A19.

Herrera, S. (2020). *Biography-driven culturally responsive teaching.* New York, NY: Teachers College Press.

Herrera, S. G., Porter, L., & Barko-Alva, K. (2020). *Equity in school-parent partnerships.* New York, NY: Teachers College Press.

Hertel, P., Geiser, S., & Konradt, U. (2005). Managing virtual teams: A review of current empirical research. *Human Resource Management Review, 15*, 69–95.

Herzberg, F. (2009). *One more time: How do you motivate employees?* Cambridge, MA: Harvard Business School Press.

Hess, F. M., & Noguera, P. A. (2021). *A search for common ground: Conversations about the toughest questions in K–12 education.* New York, NY: Teachers College Press.

Hess, G. A. (1995). *Restructuring urban schools: A Chicago perspective.* New York, NY: Teachers College Press.

Hewitt, D. (2008). *Understanding effective learning: Strategies for the classroom.* New York: McGraw-Hill.

Hickson, M. (2011). *Nonverbal communication: Studies and applications.* New York, NY: Oxford University Press.

Highhouse, S. (2002, December). A history of the T-group and its early application in management development. *Group Dynamics: Theory, Research, and Practice, 6*(4), 277–290.

Highhouse, S., Doverspike, D., & Guion, R. M. (2015). Essentials of personnel assessment and selection. New York, NY: Routledge.

Hillebrand, F. F. (2011). *Short Message Service (SMS): The Creation of Personal Global Text Messaging.* New York: Wiley.

Hills v. Scottsdale Unified School District, 329 F.3d 1044 (9th Cir. 2003), cert. denied, 540 U.S. 1149 (2004).

Hinduja, S., & Patchin, J. W. (2013). *Bullying beyond the schoolyard: Preventing and responding to cyberbullying.* Thousand Oaks, CA: Corwin.

Hinnant, J. B., O'Brien, M., & Ghazarian, S. R. (2009). The longitudinal relations of teacher expectations to achievement in the early school years. *Journal of Educational Psychology, 101*(3), 662–670.

Hipp, K. K., Huffman, J. J., Pankake, A. M. & Olivier, D. F. (2008). Sustaining professional learning communities: Case studies. *Journal of Educational Change, 9*, 173–195.

Hirsch, E. D. (1987). *Cultural literacy: What every American needs to know* (rev. ed.). Boston, MA: Houghton Mifflin.

Hirsch, E.D. (2006). *The knowledge deficit*. Boston, MA: Houghton Mifflin.

Hirschhorn, L. N. (1983). Managing rumors. In L. Hirschhorn (Ed.), *Cutting back* (pp. 54–56). San Francisco, CA: Jossey-Bass.

Hitt, M. A., Miller, C. C., & Colella, A. (2018). *Organizational behavior*. New York, NY: Wiley.

Hobson v. Hansen, 269 F. Supp. 401 D.C.C. 1967), aff. Smack v. Hobson, 408 F.2d 175 (D.C.C. (1969).

Hodges, J. (2018). *Employee engagement for organizational change*. New York, NY: Routledge.

Hodges, J. (2019). *Managing and leading people through organizational change: The theory and practice of sustaining change through people*. New York, NY: Routledge.

Hoigaard, R., Safvenbom, R., & Tonnessen, F. E. (2006). The relationship between group cohesion, group norms, and perceived social loafing in soccer teams. *Small Group Research, 37*(2), 217–232.

Holden v. Board of Education, Elizabeth, N.J., 216 A.2d 387 (N.J. 1966).

Holt, L. C., & Kysilka, M. (2006). *Instructional patterns*. Thousand Oaks, CA: Sage.

Honig v. Doe, 484 U.S. 305 (1988).

Hooks, K. L. (2011). *Auditing and assurance services: Understanding the integrated audit*. New York, NY: Wiley.

Hoppe, M. (2007). *Active listening: Improve your ability to listen and lead*. Greensboro, NC: Center for Creative Leadership.

Hord, S. M. (2004). *Learning together. Leading together: Changing schools through professional learning communities*. New York, NY: Teachers College Press.

Hord, S. M., & Sommers, W. A. (2008). *Leading professional learning communities*. Thousand Oaks, CA: Corwin Press.

Horowitz, M. J. (1997) *Stress response syndromes: PTSD, grief, and adjustment disorders* (3rd ed.). Washington, DC: APA.

Horowitz, M., & Bollinger, D. M. (2015). *Cyberbullying in social media within educational institutions*. Lanham, MD: Rowman & Littlefield.

Horsford, S. D., Scott, J. T., & Anderson, G. L. (2019). *The politics of education policy in an era of inequality: Possibilities for democratic schooling*. New York, NY: Routledge.

Horton, H. D., Martin, L. L., & Fasching-Varner, K. J. (2017). *Race, population studies, and America's public schools: A critical demography perspectives*. Lanham, MD: Lexington Books/Rowman & Littlefield.

Hosoda, M., Stone-Romero, E. F., Coats, G. (2003). The effects of physical attractiveness on job-related outcomes: A meta-analysis of experimental studies. *Personnel Psychology, 56*(2), 431–462.

Houston, P. D., Blankenstein, A.M., Cole, R.W. (2008). *Spirituality in educational leadership*. Thousand Oaks: Corwin Press.

Hovell, J. P., & Dorfman, P. W. (1986). Leadership and substitutes for leadership among professional and nonprofessional workers. *Journal of Applied Behavioral Science, 22*, 29–46.

Howard, T. G. (2020). *Why race and culture matter in schools: Closing the achievement gap in America's classrooms* (2nd ed.). New York: Teachers College Press.

Howell, J. B., & Saye, J. W. (2016). Using lesson study to develop a shared professional teaching knowledge culture among 4th grade social studies teachers. *Journal of Social Studies Research, 40*(1), 25–37.

Howlett, M., Ramesh, M., Perl, A. (2020). *Studying public policy: Principles and processes*. New York, NY: Oxford University Press.

Hoy, A. W., & Hoy, W. K. (2013). *Instructional leadership: A research-based guide to learning in schools*. Boston, MA: Allyn & Bacon.

Hoy, W. K., & Miskel, C. G. (2013). *Educational administration: Theory, research, and practice* (9th ed.). New York, NY: McGraw-Hill.

Hoy, W. K., & Sweetland, S. R. (2000). School bureaucracies that work: Enabling, not coercive. *Journal of School Leadership, 10*(6), 525–541.

Hoy, W. K., & Sweetland, S. R. (2001). Designing better schools: The meaning and nature of enabling school structure. *Educational Administration Quarterly, 37*, 296–321.

Hruska, D. (2016). Radical decision making: Leading strategic change in complex organizations. New York, NY: Palgrave Macmillan. http://www.cec.sped.org/pp/IDEA_129204.pdf.

Hsu v. Roslyn Union Free School District, 85 F.2d 839 (2d Cir. 1996), cert. denied, 519 U.S. 1040 (1996).

Hubbard v. Buffalo Independent School District, 20 F. Supp2d 1012 (W.D. Tex. 1998).

Hudley, C., Graham, S., & Taylor, A. (2007). Reducing aggressive behavior and increasing motivation in school: The evolution of an intervention to strengthen school adjustment. *Educational Psychologist, 42*(4), 251–260.

Huffcutt, A. I., & Woehr, D. J. (1999). Further analysis of employment interview validity: A quantitative evaluation of interviewer-related structuring methods. *Journal of Organizational Behavior, 50*, 549–560.

Huffman, J. B., & Hipp, K. K. (2003). *Reculturing schools as professional learning communities*. Lanham, MD: Scarecrow Press.

Huffman, J. B., & Jacobson, A. L. (2003). Perceptions of professional learning communities. *International Journal of Leadership in Education, 6*(3), 239–250.

Hughes, L. W. (Ed.) (2005). *Current issues in school leadership*. New York, NY: Routledge.

Hughes, M. (2018). *Managing and leading organizational change*. New York, NY: Routledge.

Humphrey, S. E., Morgeson, F. P., & Mannor, M. J. (2009). Developing a theory of the strategic core of teams: A role composition model of team performance. *Journal of Applied Psychology, 94*(1), 48–61.

Hunt-Sartori, M. A. (2007). *Intervention strategies, sense of belongingness, quality of school life, and student achievement*. ProQuest LLC. EdD Dissertation, Sam Houston State University. Ann Arbor, MI.

Hunter, M. (1984). *Mastery teaching* (4th ed.). Needham Heights, MA: Allyn & Bacon.

Hunter, R. (2004). *Madeline Hunter's mastery teaching*. Thousand Oaks, CA: Corwin Press.

Hussar, B., Zhang, J., Hein, S., Wang, K., Roberts, A., Cui, J., Smith, M., Bulloch Mann, F., Barmer, A., & Dilig, R. (2020). *The condition of education 2020* (NCES 2020–144). Washington, DC: US Department of Education, National Center for Education Statistics. https://nces.ed.gov/pubs2020/2020144.pdf.

Hustler Magazine v. Falwell, 485 U.S. 46 (1988).

Hutchins, R. M. (1954). *Great books: The foundation of a liberal education*. New York, NY: Simon & Schuster.

Hynes v. Board of Education of Township of Bloomfield, Essex County, 1190 N.J. Super. 36, 461 A.2d 1184 (1983).

Iacocca, L. (1999). *Iacocca: An autobiography*. Darby, PA: DIANA Publishing Company.

IDEA 2004 (Public Law 108–446) http://www.cec.sped.org/pp/IDEA _129204.pdf

Ihlen, O., & Heath, R. L. (2018). *The handbook of organizational rhetoric and communication*. New York, NY: Wiley.

Ill. Ann. Stat., Ch. 122, sec. 10 – 22.4 (2018).

Indiana State Board of Education v. Brownsburg Community School Corporation, 865 N.E.2d 660 (Ind. Ct. App. 2007).

Inger, M. (1992). Increasing the school involvement of Hispanic parents. *ERIC Digest, No. 80*. Washington, DC: clearinghouse on Urban Education.

Ingraham v. Wright, 430 U.S. 651 (1977).

In re C.S., 382 N.W.2d 381 (N.D. 1986).

In re D.B., 767 P.2d 801 (Col. Ct. App. 1988).

In re J.B., 58 S.W.3d 575 (Mo. Ct. App. 2001).

In re LePage, 18 P.3d 1177 (Wyo. 2001).

In re T.V.P., 414 N.E.2d 209 (Ill. 1974).

Internet Society. (2017). Internet access and education: Key considerations for policy makers. *Public Policy*. Reston, VA: Internet Society. https://www.internetsociety.org/resources/doc/2017/internet-access-and-education/.

Irby, B. J., & Brown, G. (1996, October). *Administrative portfolio evaluation system training*. Paper presented at Judson Independent School District, San Antonio, TX.

Irby, B. J., & Brown, G. (1998). *Women leaders: Structuring success*. Dubuque, IA: Kendall/Hunt.

Irby, B. J., & Brown, G. (2000). *The career advancement portfolio*. Thousand Oaks, CA: Corwin Press.

Irby, B. J., & Brown, G., Duffy, J. A., & Trautman, D. (2002). The synergistic leadership theory. *Journal of Educational Administration, 40*(4), 304–322.

Irby, B. J., Brown, G., & Lara-Alecio, R. (2013). The synergistic leadership theory. In B. Irby, G. Brown, & R. Lara-Alecio (Eds.), *The handbook of educational theories* (pp. 985–996). Charlotte, NC: Information Age Publishing.

Irby, B. J., Brown, G., & Yang, L. L. (2009). The synergistic leadership theory: A 21st century leadership theory. In C. M. Achilles, B. J. Irby, B. Alford, & G. Perreault (Eds.), *Remember our mission: Making education and schools better for students* (pp. 95–105). Lancaster, PA: Pro-Active.

Irby, B. J., & Lara-Alecio, R. (2001). Educational policy and gifted/talented, linguistically diverse students. In J. A. Castellano & E. Diaz (Eds.), *Reaching new horizons: Gifted and talented education for culturally and linguistically diverse students* (pp. 265–281). Boston, MA: Pearson.

Irby, B. J., & Lunenburg, F. C., (2006). Curriculum development and implementation. In F. C. Lunenburg & B. J. Irby (2006). *The principalship: Vision to action* (pp. 63–66). Belmont, CA: Thomson Wadsworth.

Irby, B. J., & Lunenburg, F. C. (2014). Promoting ethical behavior for school administrators. *Journal of Ethical Educational Leadership, 1*(4), 1–28.

Irving Independent School District v. Tatro, 468 U.S. 883 (1984).

Isenberg, D. J. (1984). How senior managers think. *Harvard Business Review, 62*, 81–90.

Ishimaru, A. M. (2020). *Just schools: Building equitable collaborations with families and communities*. New York, NY: Teachers College Press.

Israel, P. (1999). *Edison: A life of invention*. New York, NY: Wiley.

Ivancevich, J. M., Konopaske, R., & Matteson, M. T. (2017). *Organizational behavior and management*. New York, NY: McGraw-Hill.

Jabri, M. (2018). *Rethinking organizational change*. New York, NY: Routledge.

Jackson-Cherry, L. R., & Erford, B. J. (2018). *Crisis assessment, intervention, and prevention*. Boston, MA: Pearson.

Jackson, R. R. (2011). *How to motivate reluctant learners*. Alexandria, VA: ASCD.

Jackson, S. A., & Lunenburg, F. C. (2010). School performance indicators, accountability ratings, and student achievement. *American Secondary Education, 39*(1), 27–44.

Jacobi, J. (2009). *How to say it with your voice*. Upper Saddle River, NJ: Prentice Hall.

Jacobson, S., McCarthy, M., & Pounder, D. (2015). What makes a leadership preparation program exemplary? *Journal of Research on Leadership Education, 10*(1), 63–76.

Jacobsen v. Commonwealth of Massachusetts, 197 U.S. 11 (1905)

Janis, I. L. (1982). *Groupthink: Psychological Studies of Policy Decisions and Fiascoes* (2nd ed.). Boston, MA: Houghton Mifflin.

Jarvis, P. (2006). *The theory and practice of teaching*. New York: Routledge.

Jassawalla, A., Sashittal, H., & Malshe, A. (2009). Students' perception of social loafing: Its antecedents and consequences in undergraduate business classroom teams. *Academy of Management Learning and Education, 8*(1), 42–54.

Jaumont, F. (2017). *The bilingual revolution: The future of education is two languages.* Brooklyn, NY: TBR Books.

Jeffrey v. O'Donnell, 702 F. Supp. 516 (M.D. Pa. 1988).

Jennings, J., & Rentner, D. S. (2006). *Ten big effects of the No Child Left Behind Act on public schools. Phi Delta Kappan, 88*(2), 110–113.

Johnson, C. E. (2017). *Meeting the challenge of leadership: Casting light or shadow* (6th ed.). Thousand Oaks, CA: Sage.

Johnson, C. S., & Thomas, A. T. (2009). Caring as a classroom practice. *Social Studies and the Young Learner. 22*(1), 8–11.

Johnson, D. J. (2018). *Teams and their leaders: A communication network perspective.* Toronto, Ontario: Peter Lang.

Johnson, D. W., & Johnson, R. T. (2009). Energizing learning: The instructional power of conflict. *Educational Researcher, 38*(1), 37–51.

Johnson, J. F. (1998, October). Improving public schools in Texas, *43*(2). http://www.c-b-e.org/articles/texas.htm.

Johnson, R. B., & Christensen, L. (2020). *Educational research: Quantitative, qualitative, and mixed approaches* (7th ed.). Thousand Oaks, CA: Sage.

Johnson v. Charles City Community Schools, 368 N.W.2d 74 (Iowa 1985).

Johnson v. New York State Education Department, 449 F.2d 871 (1972), per curium, 409 U.S. 75, 76 (1972), certiorari, 409 U.S. 916 (1972).

Johnson v. Prince William County School Board, 404 S.E.2d 209 (Va. 1991).

Johnson v. Town of Deerfield, 25 F. Supp. 918 (D. Mass. 1939), aff'd 306 U.S. 621 (1939), reh'g denied, 307 U.S. 650 (1039).

Johnston, L. D., Miech, R. A., O'Malley, P. M., Bachman, J. G., Schulenberg, J. E., & Patrick, M. E. (2019). *Monitoring the future national survey results on drug use 1975–2018: Overview, key findings on adolescent drug use.* Ann Arbor, Institute for Social Research, University of Michigan. http://www.monitoringthefuture.oeg//pubs/monographs/mtf-overview2018.pdf.

Johnston-Loehner v. O'Brien, 859 F. Supp. 575 [94 educ. rep. 167] (M.D. Fla. 1994).

Joki v. Board of Education, 745 F. Supp. 823 (N.D. N.Y. 1990).

Jones, B. D. (2007). The unintended outcomes of high-stakes testing. *Journal of Applied School Psychology, 23*(2), 65–86.

Jones, B., Wells, L., Peters, R., & Johnson, D. (1988). *Guide to effective coaching principles and practices.* Newton, MA: Allyn & Bacon.

Jones, G. R. (1984). Task visibility, free riding, and shirking: Explaining the effect of structure and technology on employee behavior. *Academy of Management Review, 9*(4), 684–695.

Jones, G. R. (2013). *Organizational theory, design, and change* (7th ed.). Upper Saddle River, NJ: Pearson/Prentice Hall.

Jones v. Clear Lake Independent School District, 977 F.2d 963 (5th Cir.), reh'g denied, 983 F.2d 234 (5th Cir. 1992), cert. denied, 508 U.S. 967 (1993).

Jones v. Houston Independent School District, 805 F. Supp. 476, S.D. (Tex. 1991), affirmed, 979 F.2d 1004 (1992).

Jones v. West Virginia State Board of Education, 622 S.E.2d 289 (W.Va. 2005).

Joo, Y-J., Bong, M., & Choi, H.-J. (2000). Self-efficacy for self-regulated learning, academic self-efficacy, and Internet self-efficacy in Web-based instruction. *Educational Technology Research and Development, 48*(2), 5–17.

Joyce, B., & Calhoun, E. (2010). *Models of Professional Development.* Thousand Oaks, CA: Corwin Press.

Joyce, B., & Calhoun, E. (2019). Peer coaching in education: From partners to faculties and districts. In S. J. Zepeda & J. A. Ponticell (eds.). *The Wiley handbook of educational supervision* (pp. 307–328). New York, NY: Wiley.

Joyce, B., Calhoun, E., & Weil, M. (2018). *Models of teaching.* Boston, MA: Pearson.

Joyce, B., & Showers, B. (2002). *Student achievement through staff development.* Alexandria, VA: ASCD.

J. P. ex rel. Peterson v. County School Board of Hanover County, Va., 516 F.3d 254 (4th Cir. 2008).

Kadrmas v. Dickinson Public Schools, 487 U.S. 450 (1988).

K. A. ex rel. Ayers v. Pocono Mountain School District, 710 F.3d 446 (3d Cir. 2013).

Kafka, J. (2012). *The history of zero tolerance in American public schools*. New York, NY: Palgrave Macmillan.

Kann, L., McManus, T., & Harris, W. A. (2018). *Youth risk behavior surveillance—US morbidity and mortality weekly report—surveillance summaries*. 67(SS08): 1–479. https://www.cdc.gov/healthyyouth/data/yrbs/pdf/2017/ss6708.pdf.

Kaplan, L. S., & Owings, W. A. (2015). *Introduction to the principalship: Theory to practice*. New York, NY: Routledge.

Kaplan, R. M., & Saccuzzo, D. P. (2017). *Psychological testing: Principles, applications, and issues*. Belmont, CA: Cengage Learning.

Karakowsky, L., & McBey, K. (2001). Do my contributions matter? The influence of imputed expertise on member involvement and self-evaluations in the work group. *Group & Organization Management, 26*(1), 70–92.

Karau, S. J., & Williams, K. D. (1993). Social loafing: A meta-analytic review and theoretical integration. *Journal of Personality and Social Psychology, 65*(4), 681–706.

Karelitz, T. M., & Busescu, D. V. (2004). You say "probable" and I say "likely": Improving interpersonal communication with verbal probability phrases. *Journal of Experimental Psychology: Applied, 10*, 25–41.

Kariya, T., & Rappleye, J. (2020). *Education, equality, and meritocracy in a global age: The Japanese approach*. New York, NY: Teachers College Press.

Karr v. Schmidt, 401 U.S. 1201 (1972).

Katz, R. L. (1974). Skills of an effective administrator. *Harvard Business Review, 52*, 90–102.

Kauchak, D. P., & Eggen, P. D. (2006). *Learning and teaching: Research-based methods*. Boston, MA: Allyn & Bacon.

Kearney, S. (2014). Understanding beginning teacher induction: A contextualized examination of best practice. *Cogent Education, 1*(1), Article 967477.

Keith, K. D. (2011). *Cross-cultural psychology: Contemporary themes and perspectives*. New York, NY: Wiley.

Kelleher, J. (2003, June). A model for assessment-driven professional development. *Phi Delta Kappan*, 751–756.

Kember, D., & Kwan, K-P. (2000). Lecturers' approaches to teaching and their relationship to conceptions of good teaching. *Instructional Science, 28*, 469–490.

Kemmis, S., Heikkinen, H., Frensson, G., Aspfors, J., & Edwards-Groves, C. (2014). Mentoring of new teachers as a contested practice: Supervision, support, and collaborative self-development. *Teaching and Teacher Education, 43*, 154–164. http://www.sciencedirect.com/science/article/pii/SO742051X14000778.

Kena, G., Musu-Gillette, L., Robinson, J., Wang, X., Rathbun, A., Zhang, J., & Wilkinson-Flicker, S. (2013, May). *The condition of education 2013* (NCES 2013–037). US Department of Education, National Center for Education Statistics, Washington, DC.

Kennedy, C. (2000). Principal: Too quiet, too long. *High School Magazine, 7*(6), 20–23.

Kennedy-Phillips, L. C., Baldasare, A., & Christakis, M. N. (2015). *Measuring cocurricular learning: the role of IR office, New directions for institutional research*, vol. 164. San Francisco, CA: Josset-Bass.

Kentucky Revised Statutes, Ch. 161.593 (2018).

Kepner, C. H., & Tregoe, B. B. (2004). *The new rational manager* (rev. ed.). New York, NY: Kepner-Tregoe.

Kern, D. (2014). Common core-less?: A critical review of the Common Core State Standards research. *Review of Research in the Classroom, 50*(1), 75–77.

Kerr, N. L., & Bruun, S. E. (1981). Ringelmann revisited: Alternative explanations for the social loafing effect. *Personality and Social Psychology Bulletin, 7*(2), 224–231.

Kerr, S., & Jermier, J. M. (1978). Substitutes for leadership: The meaning and measurement. *Organizational Behavior and Human Performance, 22*(3), 375–403.

Kettler, T. (2016). *Modern curriculum for gifted and advanced academic students*. Waco, TX: Prufrock Press.

Khatri, N., & Ng, H. A. (2000). The role of intuition in strategic decision making. *Human Relations, 53*(1), 57–86.

Kim, Y. K., Losen, D. J., & Hewitt, D. T. (2010). *The school-to-prison pipeline: restructuring legal reform*. New York, NY: New York University Press.

Kirschner, P. A., Sweller, J., & Clark, R. E. (2006). Why minimal guidance during instruction does not work: An analysis of the failure of constructivist, discovery, problem-based, experiential, and inquiry-based teaching. *Educational Psychologist, 41*, 75–86.

Kishi, H., Koji, I., Sugiura, S., & Kinoshita, R. (2012). A study of Maslow's hierarchy of needs and decision making. In J. Watada, T. Watanabe, G. Phillips-Wren, R. J. Howlett, & L. C. Jain (Eds.). *Intelligent decision technologies*. Berlin Heidelberg, Germany: Springer-Verlag.

Kitzmiller v. Dover Area School District, 400 F. Supp. 2d 707 (M.D. Pa. 2005).

Klein, D. A. (2014). *The strategic management of intellectual capital*. New York, NY: Routledge.

Klein, G. (2005). *The power of intuition: How to use your gut feelings to make better decisions at work*. New York: Knopf Doubleday.

Klein, K. J., Lim, B., Saltz, J. L., & Mayer, D. M. (2004). How do they get there? An examination of the antecedents of centrality in team networks. *Academy of Management Journal, 47*(6), 952–963.

Klenowski, V., & Wyatt-Smith, R. (2014). *Assessment for education: Standards, judgments, and moderation*. Thousand Oaks, CA: Sage.

Klicka, C. (1996). *Home Schooling in the United States: A Legal analysis*. Paconian Springs, VA; Home School Legal defense Association.

Kline, P. (2016). *Personality: Measurement and theory*. New York, NY: Routledge.

Klinge, C. M. (2015). A conceptual framework for mentoring in a learning organization. *Adult Learning, 26*(4), 160–164.

Klinger, A., & Klinger, A. (2018). *Keeping students safe every day: how to prepare for and respond to school violence, natural disasters, and other hazards*. Alexandria, VA: Association for Supervision and Curriculum Development.

Kmetz, J. T., & Willower, D. J. (1982). Elementary school principals work behavior. *Educational Administration Quarterly, 18*, 62–78.

Knapp, M. L., & Hall, J. (2010). *Nonverbal communication in human interaction*. Belmont, CA: Wadsworth/Cengage Learning.

Kneen, J. (2011). *Essential skills: Essential speaking and listening skills*. New York, NY: Oxford University Press.

Knoester, M., & Parkinson, P. (2015). Where is citizenship education in an age of common core state standards. *Critical Education, 6*, 220. https://ojs.library.ubc.ca/index.php/criticaled/article/view/185901.

Knowles, M. S., Holton, E. F., & Swanson, R. A. (2011). *The adult learner: The definitive classic in adult education and human research development* (7th ed.). Portsmouth, NH: Butterworth-Heineman.

Knox v. O'Brien, 72 A.2d 389 (N.J. Cnty Ct. 1950).

Koger, S. M., & Du Nann, D. (2010). *The psychology of environmental problems: Psychology for sustainability* (3rd ed.). New York, NY: Psychology Press.

Kohlberg, L. (1969). Moral stages and moralization: The cognitive-developmental approach to socialization. In D. A. Goslin (Ed.), *Handbook of socialization theory and research*. Chicago, IL: Rand McNally.

Kohlberg, L. (1976). Moral stages and moralization: The cognitive-developmental approach. In T. Lickona (Ed.), *Moral development and behavior: theory, research, and social issues*. New York, NY: Holt, Rinehart & Winston.

Kohlberg, L. (1978). Revisions in the theory and practice of moral development. In W. Damon (Ed.). *New directions for child development: Moral development* (no. 2). San Francisco, CA: Jossey-Bass.

Kohn, A. (2005). Unconditional teaching. *Educational Leadership, 63*, 20–24.

Kolbert, J. B., Williams, R. L., Morgan, L. M., Crothers, L. M., & Hughes, T. L. (2016). *Introduction to professional school counseling: Advocacy, leadership, and intervention.* New York, NY: Routledge.

Kominiak. T. (2017, March 14). America's school building are failing. *TrustedEd.* https://www.k12insight.com/trusted/americas-school-buildings-infrastructure/.

Konovalchik v. School Community of Salem, 226 N.E.2d 222 9Mass. (1976).

Koppell v. Levine, 347 F.Supp. 456 E.D. NY 1972.

Kotter, J. P. (1996). *Leading change.* Boston, MA: Harvard Business School Press.

Kouzes, J. M., & Posner, B. Z. (2017). *The leadership challenge: How to make extraordinary things happen in organizations.* New York, NY: Wiley.

Kowalski, T. J., Dolph, D. A. (2015). Principal dispositions regarding the Ohio teacher evaluation system. *AASA Journal of Scholarship and Practice, 11*(4), 1–20.

Kozlowski, S. W. J., & Bell, B. S. (2003). Work groups and teams in organization. In W. C. Borman, D. R. Ilgen, & R. J. Klimoski (Eds.). *Comprehensive handbook of psychology* (vol. 12; pp. 333–375). New York, NY: Wiley.

Kraft, M. A. (2010). From ringmaster to conductor: 10 simple techniques can turn an unruly class into a productive one. *Phi Delta Kappa, 91*(7), 44–47.

Kramarski, B., & Zeichner, O. (2001). Using technology to enhance mathematical reasoning: Effects of feedback and self-regulation learning. *Educational Media International, 38*(2/3), 77–82.

Kramen, A. (2013). *Guide for preventing and responding to school violence.* New York, NY: DIANE Publishing Company.

Kramer, R. (1988). *Maria Montessori: A biography.* Reading, MA: Perseus Books.

Kramer, S.V. (Ed.). (2021a). *Charting a course for collaborative teams: Lessons from priority schools in a PLC at work.* Indianapolis, IN: Solution Tree Press.

Kramer, S.v V. (Ed.). (2021b). *Charting the course for leaders: Lessons from priority schools in a PLC at work.* Indianapolis, IN: Solution Tree Press.

Krathwohl, D. R., Bloom, B. S., & Masia, B. B. (1964). *Taxonomy of educational objectives: Handbook II. Affective domain.* New York, NY: Longman.

Kravitz, D. A., & Martin, B. (1986). Ringelmann rediscovered: The original article. *Journal of Personality and Social Psychology, 50*(5), 936–941.

Kreitner, R., Kinicki, A. (2016). *Organizational behavior* (11th ed.). New York, NY: McGraw-Hill.

Kreitner, R., & Luthans, F. (1984). A social learning approach to behavioral management: Radical behaviorists' mellowing out. *Organizational Dynamics, 13*, 47–65.

Kreps, G. L. (2019). *Communicating and organizing: Blending theory and practice.* New York, NY: Routledge.

Krestan v. Deer Valley Unified School District No. 57 of Maricopa County, 561 F. Supp.2d 1078 (D. Ariz. 2008).

Kroll, L. R. (2012). *Self-study and inquiry into practice: Learning to teach for equity and social justice in the classroom.* New York, NY: Routledge.

Kruger, J., Epley, N., Parker, J., & Ng, Z. (2008). Egocentrism over e-mail: Can people communicate as well as they think. *Journal of Personality and Social Psychology, 89*, 925–936.

Kryza, K., Duncan, A., & Stephens, S. J. (2010). *Differentiation for real classrooms.* Thousand Oaks, CA: Corwin Press.

Kubiszyn, T., & Borish, G. (2015). *Educational tests and measurement: Classroom application and practice* (11th ed.). New York, NY: Wiley.

Kuklinski, M. R., & Weinstein, R. S. (2001). Classroom and developmental differences in a path model of teacher expectancy effects. *Child Development, 72*, 1554–1578.

Kumkale, G. T., & Albarracin, D. (2004). The sleeper effect in persuasion: A meta-analytic review. *Psychological Bulletin, 130*, 143–1772.

Kundu, A. (2020). *The power of student agency: Looking beyond grit to close the opportunity gap*. New York, NY: Teachers College Press.

Kurz, D. W. (2000). *Policies and procedures manual for accounting and financial control*. Englewood Cliffs, NJ: Prentice Hall.

L.A. v. Superior Ct. ex. rel. County of San Diego, 147 Cal. Rptr.3d 431 (Cal. Ct. App. 2012).

Labby, S., Lunenburg, F. C., & Slate, J. R. (2014). Principal characteristics and their emotional intelligence skills. In R.V. Nata (Ed.), *Progress in education*, vol. 31 (pp. 105–116). New York, NY: Nova Science Publishers, Inc.

Ladson-Billings, G. (2002). But that's just good teaching! The case for culturally relevant pedagogy. In S. J. Denbo & L. M. Beaulieu (Eds.). *Improving schools for African American students* (pp. 95–102). Springfield, IL: Charles C. Thomas.

Ladson-Billings, G. (2006). From the achievement gap to the education debt: Understanding achievement in US schools. *Educational Researcher, 35*(10), 3- 12.

Lalor, A. D. (2017). *Ensuring high-quality curriculum: How to design, revise, or adopt curriculum aligned to student success*. Arlington, CA: ASCD.

Lambert, L. (2004). *Leadership capacity for lasting school improvement*. Alexandria, VA: Association for Supervision and Curriculum Development.

Lamb's Chapel v. Center Moriches Union Free School District, 77 F. Supp. 91 (E.D. N.Y. 1991), aff'd, 959 F.2d 381 (2d Cir. 1992).

Lampkin v. District of Columbia, 886 F. Supp. 56 (D.D.C. 1995).

Landau, B. M., & Gathercoal, P. (2000). Creating peaceful classrooms: Judicious discipline and class meetings. *Phi Delta Kappan, 8*(6), 450–452, 454.

Landrigan, P. J., Schechter, C. B., Lipton, J. M., Fahs,M. C., & Schwartz, J. (2002). Environmental pollutants and disease in America's children: Estimates of morbidity, mortality, and costs for lead poisoning, asthma, cancer, and developmental disabilities. *Environmental Health Perspectives, 110*(7), 721- 728.

Langfred, C. (1998). Is group cohesiveness a double-edged sword? An investigation of the effects of cohesiveness on performance. *Small Group Research, 29*(1), 124–143.

Lanphear, B. P. (2001, April 30). *Blood levels below acceptable value linked with IQ deficits*. Paper presented at the Pediatric Academic Societies, Cincinnati, OH.

Lantieri, L. (1995). Waging peace in our schools: Beginning with the children. *Phi Delta Kappan, 76*(5), 386–388.

Laosa, L. M. (1977). Socialization, education, and community: The importance of the sociocultural context. *Young Children, 32*(5), 21–27.

Laosa, L. M. (1978). Maternal teaching strategies in Chicano families of varied educational and socioeconomic levels. *Child Development, 49*(4), 1129–1135.

Laosa, L. M. (1982). School, occupation, culture, and family: The impact of parental schooling on the parent-child relationship. *Journal of Educational Psychology, 74*(6), 791–827.

Lara-Alecio, R., & Parker, R. (1994). A pedagogical model for transitional English bilingual classrooms. *Bilingual Research Journal, 18*(3–4), 119–133.

Lara-Alecio, R., Bass, J., & Irby, B. J. (2001). Science of the Maya: Teaching ethnoscience in the classroom. *Science Teacher, 68*(3), 48–51.

Lara-Alecio, R., Galloway, M., Mahadevan, L., Mason, B., Irby, B. J., Brown, G., & Gomez, L. (2004). *Texas dual language cost analysis*. College Station, TX: Language Diversity Network. http://Ldn.tamu.edu/Archives/CBARReport.pdf/.

Lara-Alecio, R., Irby, B. J., & Ebener, R. (1997). Developing academically supportive behaviors among Hispanic parents: What elementary school teachers and parents can do. *Preventing School Failure, 42*, 27–32.

Lasonde, C. A., Israel, S. E., & Almasi, J. F. (2009*). Teacher collaboration for professional learning: Facilitating study, research, and inquiry communities*. New York, NY: Routledge.

Lassiter, W. L., & Perry, D. C. (2013). *Preventing violence and crime in America's schools from put-downs to lock-downs*. Lanham, MD: Scarecrow Press.

Latane, B. (1986). Responsibility and effort in organizations. In P. S. Goodman (Ed.). *Designing effective work groups* (pp. 227–245). San Francisco, CA: Jossey-Bass.

Latane, B., & Nida, S. (1980). Social impact theory and group influence: A social engineering perspective. In P. B. Paulus (Ed.), *Psychology of group influence* (pp. 3–34). Hillsdale, NJ: Erlbaum.

Latane, B., Williams, K., & Harkins, S. (1979). Many hands make light the work: The causes and consequences of social loafing. *Journal of Personality and Social Psychology, 37*(6), 822–832.

Latham, G. P. (2009). Motivate employee performance through goal setting. In E. A. Locke (Ed.), *Handbook of principles of organizational behavior* (pp. 161–178). New York, NY: Wiley.

Lathan, G. P., & Locke, E. A. (2006). Enhancing the benefits and overcoming the pitfalls of goal setting. *Organizational Dynamics, 35*(4), 332–340.

Lathe, T. R. (2018). *The working-class student in higher education: Addressing a class-based understanding*. Lanham, MD: Lexington Books/Rowman & Littlefield.

Laurea, A. (1989). *Home advantage: Social class and parental intervention in elementary education*. Philadelphia, PA: Falmer Press.

Lawler, E. E. (2001). *Organizing for high performance*. San Francisco, CA: Jossey-Bass.

Lawrence-Ell, G. (2002). *The invisible clock: A practical revolution in finding time for everyone and everything*. Seaside Park, NJ: Kingsland Hall.

Lazarus, R. S. (1999). *Stress and emotion: A new synthesis*. New York, NY: Springer.

League of United Latin American Citizens v. Wilson, 908 F. Supp. 755 (C.D. Cal. 1995).

League of United Latin American Citizens v. Wilson, 997 F. Supp. 1244 (C.D. Cal. 1997).

Learning Points Associates (n.d.). *Implementing the No Child Left Behind Act: Implications for rural schools and districts*. North Central Regional Educational Laboratory. http://www.ncrel.org/policy/pubs/html/implicate/intro.htm.

Lee, F. (1993). Being polite and keeping MUM: How bad news is communicated in organizational hierarchies. *Journal of Applied Social Psychology, 23*, 1124–1149.

Lee, H. (2005). Behavioral strategies for dealing with flaming in an online forum. *The Sociological Quarterly, 46*(2), 385–403.

Lee, J.-S., & Bowen, N. K. (2006). Parent involvement, cultural capital, and the achievement gap among elementary school children. *American Educational Research Journal, 43*(2), 193–218.

Lee, V. E., & Smith, J. B. (1999). Social support and achievement for young adolescents in Chicago.: the role of school academic press. *American Education Research Journal, 36*, 907–945.

Lee v. Weisman, 505 U.S. 577 (1992).

Leithwood, K. (2018). *Leadership development on a large scale: Lessons for long-term success*. Thousand Oaks, CA: Corwin Press.

Leithwood, K., & Louis, K. S. (2012). *Linking leadership to student learning: Empirical insights*. New York, NY: Wiley.

Leithwood, K., Sun, J., & Pollock, K. (Eds.). (2017). *How school leaders contribute to student success*. New York, NY: Springer.

Lemaine, P., Levernier, E., & Richardson, M. D. (2018). *Strategic planning for school leaders*. San Diego, CA: Cognella.

Lemon v. Kurtzman, 403 U.S. 602 (19710.

Lengel, R. H., & Daft, R. L. (1988). The selection of communication media as an executive skill. *Academy of Management Executive, 2*, 225–232.

Leonard, D., & Swap, W. (1999). *When sparks fly: Igniting creativity in groups*. Boston, MA: Harvard Business School Press.

LePine, J. A., Colquitt, J. A., Erez, A. (2000). Adaptability to changing task contexts: Effects of general cognitive ability, conscientiousness, and openness to experience. *Personnel Psychology, 53*(3), 563–595.

Lepsinger, R., & Lucia, A. (2009). *The art and science of 360-degree feedback*. New York, NY: Wiley.

Lester v. Board of Education of School District No. 119, 230 N.E.2d 893 (Ill. 1967).

Leung, A. K., Maddux, W.W., Galinsky, A. D., & Chiu, C. (2008). Multicultural experience enhances creativity. *American Psychologist, 63*(3), 169–180.

LeVake v. Independent School District No. 656, 625 N.W.2d 502 (Minn. Ct. App. 2001).

Levine, D. U., & Lezotte, L. W. (1990). *Unusually effective schools: A review and analysis of research and practice*. Madison, WI: National Center for Effective Schools Research and Development, University of Wisconsin-Madison.

Levin, H. M. (1987). *Accelerated schools for at-risk students* (CPRHE research report RR-010). New Brunswick, NJ: Rutgers University, Center for Policy Research in Education.

Levin, J., & Nolan, J. F. (2010). *Principles of classroom management: A professional decision-making model* (6th ed.). Boston, MA: Pearson.

Levine, M. J. (2007). *Pesticides: A toxic time bomb in our midst*. Westport, CN: Praeger.

Levine, S. R. (2007, January). Make meetings less dreaded. *HR Magazine*, 107–109.

Levinson, M., & Fay, J. (2016). *Dilemmas of educational ethics: Cases and commentaries*. Cambridge, MA: Harvard Education Press.

Levitt v. Committee for Public Education and Religious Liberty. 413 U.S. 472 (1973).

Lewin, K. (1951). *Field theory in social science*. New York, NY: Harper & Row.

Lewin, L. (2010). *Teaching comprehension with questioning strategies that motivate middle school readers*. New York, NY: Scholastic.

Lewis, A. (1989). *Wolves at the Schoolhouse Door*. Washington, DC: Education Writers Association.

Lewis, A. (2011). *The art of lecturing*. West Roxbury, MA: B & R Samizdat Express.

Lewis, H. (2007). *Excellence without soul*. New York, NY: Public Affairs.

Lewis, L. (2019). *Organizational change: Creating change through strategic communication* (2nd ed.). New York, NY: Wiley.

LexisNexis (2020). *Texas school law bulletin*. New York, NY: LexisNexis.

Lezotte, L. W., & Snyder, K. M. (2010). *What effective schools do: Re-envisioning the correlates*. Bloomington, IN: Solution Tree.

Licata, J. W., & Hack, W. G. (1980). School administrator grapevine structure. *Educational Administration Quarterly, 16*, 82–99.

Licata, J. W., & Harper, G. W. (2001, February). Organizational health and robust school vision. *Educational Administration Quarterly, 37*(1), 5–26.

Licata, J. W., Teddlie, C. B., & Greenfield, W. B. (1999). Principal vision, teacher sense of autonomy, and environmental robustness. *Journal of Educational Research, 84*(2). 93–99.

Lickona, T. (2010). *Character matters: How to help our children develop good judgement, integrity, and other essential virtues*. New York, NY: Simon & Schuster.

Lickona, T., & Davidson, M. (2005). *Smart and good high schools: Integrating excellence and ethics for success in school, work, and beyond*. Cortland, NY: Center for the 4th and 5th Rs (respect and Responsibility) / Washington, DC: Character Education Partnership. www.cortland.edu/character/high school/.

Liden, R. C., Wayne, R. A., Jaworski, R. A., & Bennett, N. (2004). Social loafing; A field investigation. *Journal of Management, 30*(2), 285–304.

Lieberman, A., & Darling-Hammond, L. (2011). *High quality teaching and learning: International perspectives on teacher education*. New York, NY: Taylor & Francis.

Liebowitz v. Dinkins, 575 N.Y.s.2d 827 (App. Div. 1991).

Lightfoot, S. L. (1978). *Worlds apart: Relationships between families and schools*. New York, NY: Basic Books.

Likert, R. (1961). *New patterns of management*. New York, NY: McGraw-Hill.

Likert, R. (1967). *The human organization: Its management and value*. New York, NY: McGraw-Hill.

Likert, R. (1979). From production and employee-centeredness to systems 1–4. *Journal of Management, 5*, 147–156.

Likert, R. (1987). *New patterns of management.* New York, NY: Garland.

Lindberg, J. A., & Swick, A. M. (2006). *Commonsense classroom management for elementary school teachers* (2nd ed.). Thousand Oaks, CA: Corwin Press.

Lindblom, C. E. (1993). *The science of "muddling through."* New York, NY: Irvington.

Lindquist, A. K., & Metzger, E. G. (2004). *Teacher recruitment consortium.* Washington, DC: National School Boards Association.

Lindsay, C. A., & Hart, C. M. (2017). Exposure to same race teachers and student disciplinary outcomes for black students in North Carolina. *Educational Evaluation and Policy Analysis, 39*(3), 485–510.

Lindsey, D. B., Lindsey, R. B., Hord, S. M., & von Frank, V. (2016). *Reach the highest standard of professional learning outcomes.* Thousand Oaks, CA: Corwin Press.

Ling, R. (2011). *New technology, new ties: How mobile communication is reshaping social cohesion.* Cambridge, MA: MIT Press.

Linzmeyer, O., & Linzmeyer, O. W. (2004). *Apple confidential 2.0: The history of the world's most colorful company.* San Francisco, CA: No Starch Press.

Lipari, R. N., Van Horn, S. L. (2017). *Children living with parents who have a substance use disorder. The CBSHSQ report: August 24, 2017.* Center for Behavioral Health Statistics and Quality, Substance Abuse and Mental Health services Administration, Rockville, MD.

Lipkin, A. (1999). *Understanding homosexuality, changing schools: A text for teachers, counselors, and administrators.* Boulder, CO: Westview.

Little, M. E., & Houston, D. (2003). Research into practice through professional development. *Remedial and Special education, 95*(10), 3–10.

Little, T., & Ellison, K. (2015). *Loving learning: How progressive education can save America's schools.* New York, NY: W.W. Norton

Liu, C., Spector, P. E., & Shi, L. (2007). Cross-national job stress: A quantitative and qualitative study. *Journal of Organizational Behavior, 28*(2), 209–239.

Locke, E. A., & Latham, G. P. (2002). Building a practically useful theory of goal setting and task motivation: A 35-year odyssey. *American Psychologist, 57*(9), 705–717.

Locke, E. A., & Latham, G. P. (2006). New directions in goal-setting theory. *Current Directions in Psychological Science, 15*(5), 265–268.

Lockwood, A. L. (2014). *The case for character education: A developmental approach.* New York, NY: Teachers College Press.

Long, M. (2012). *The psychology of education: The evidence base for teaching and learning.* New York, NY: Routledge.

Losen, D. J. (2015). *Closing the school discipline gap: Equitable remedies for excessive exclusion.* New York, NY: Teachers College Press.

Losen, D. L. (2011). *Discipline policies, successful schools, and racial justice.* Boulder, CO: National Education Policy. http://nepc.colorado.edu/publication,discipline-policies.

Losen, D. L., & Skiba, R. (2010). *Suspended education: Urban middle schools in crisis.* Montgomery, AL: Southern Poverty Law Center. http://www.splcenter.org/get-informed/publication/suspended-education.

Loucks-Horsley, S., Stiles, K. E., Mundry, S., Love, N., & Hewson, P. W. (2010). *Designing professional development for teachers of science and mathematics* (3rd ed.). Thousand Oaks, CA: Corwin Press.

Loughead, T. (2018). *Critical university: Moving higher education forward.* Lanham, MD: Lexington Books/Rowman & Littlefield.

Louis, K. S. (2012). Learning communities in learning schools: Developing social capacity for change. In C. Day (Ed.), *International handbook of teacher and student development* (pp. 477–492). New York, NY: Routledge.

Louis, K. S. (2013). Collective responsibility: A way forward to real reform. In F. Whalen (Ed.), *Collective responsibility for student learning* (pp. 227–245). Rotterdam, Holland: Sense Publishers.

Louis, K. S., & Marks, H. M. (1998). Does professional learning community affect classroom teachers' work and student experience in restructured schools. *American Journal of Education, 106*(4), 532–575.

Louis, K. S., & Murphy, J. (2016). Trust, caring, and organizational learning: The leader's role. *Journal of Educational Administration, 55*(1), 1–24.

Louis, K. S., Murphy, J., & Smylie, M. (2016). Caring leadership in schools: Findings from exploratory analysis. *Educational Administration Quarterly, 52*(2), 310–348.

Louwers, T. (2014). *Auditing and assurance services.* New York, NY: McGraw- Hill.

Lovallo, W. R. (2005). *Stress and health: Biological and psychological interactions* (2nd ed.). Thousand Oaks, CA: Sage.

Lowry, R., Sleet, D., Duncan, C., Powell, K., & Kolbe, L. (1995). Adolescents at risk for violence. *Educational Psychology Review, 7*(1), 7–39.

Luiten, J., Ames, W., & Ackerson, G. (1980). A meta-analysis of the effects of advance organizers on learning and retention. *American Educational Research Journal, 17,* 211–218.

Lunenburg, F. C. (1983a). *Conceptualizing school climate: Measures, research, and effects.* Berkeley, CA: McCutchan.

Lunenburg, F. C. (1983b). Pupil control ideology and self-concept as a learner. *Educational Research Quarterly, 8,* 33–39.

Lunenburg, F. C. (1984). Custodial teachers: Negative effects on schools. *The Clearing House, 58*(3), 112–116.

Lunenburg, F. C. (1991). Educators' pupil control ideology as a predictor of educators' reactions to pupil disruptive behavior. *High School Journal, 72*(2), 81–87.

Lunenburg, F. C. (1999). Helping dreams survive: Dropout interventions *Contemporary Education, 71*(1), 9–14.

Lunenburg, F. C. (2000a). Collective bargaining in the public schools: Issues, tactics, and new strategies. *Journal of Collective Negotiations, 29*(4), 259–272.

Lunenburg, F. C. (2000b). America's hope: Making schools work for all children. *Journal of Instructional Psychology, 37*(1), 39–47.

Lunenburg, F. C. (2000c). Early childhood education programs can make a difference in academic, economic, and social arenas. *Education, 120*(3), 519–528.

Lunenburg, F. C. (2002). Improving student achievement: Some structural incompatibilities. In G. Perreault & F. C. Lunenburg (eds.), *The changing world of school administration* (pp. 5–27). Lanham, MD: Scarecrow Press.

Lunenburg, F. C. (2003). The post-behavioral science era: Excellence, democracy, and justice. In F.C. Lunenburg and C.S. Carr (Eds.), *Shaping the future: Policy, partnerships, and emerging perspectives* (pp. 36–55). Lanham, MD: Rowman & Littlefield.

Lunenburg, F. C. (2005). Accountability, educational equity, and district-wide effective schools processes: The transformation of one state. *Journal of Effective Schools, 4*(1), 65–87.

Lunenburg, F. C. (2006). Heuristics in decision making. In F. English (Ed.), *Encyclopedia of educational leadership and administration* (pp. 455–457). Thousand Oaks, CA: Sage.

Lunenburg, F. C. (2007). The management function of organization. In F. L. Dembowski (Ed.). *Educational administration: The roles of leadership and management* (pp. 142–166). Houston, TX: NCPEA Press/Rice University.

Lunenburg, F. C. (2010a). Substitutes for leadership theory. *Focus on Colleges, Universities, and Schools, 4*(1), 1–5.

Lunenburg, F. C. (2010b). Developing a culture: Learning for all. *Schooling, 1*(1), 1–7.

Lunenburg, F. C. (2010c). Schools as open systems. *Schooling, 1*(2), 1–5.

Lunenburg, F. C. (2010d). Sexual harassment: An abuse of power. *International Journal of Management, Business, and Administration, 13*(1), 1–7.

Lunenburg, F. C. (2010e). The interview as a selection device: Problems and possibilities. *International Journal of Management, Business, and Administration, 13*(2), 1–7.

Lunenburg, F. C. (2010f). Communication: The process, barriers, and improving effectiveness. *Schooling*, *1*(3), 1–12.

Lunenburg, F. C. (2010g). The demise of bureaucracy and emergent models of organizational structure. *Schooling*, *1*(4), 1–12.

Lunenburg, F. C. (2010h). Total quality management applied to schools. *Schooling*, *1*(5), 1–7.

Lunenburg, F. C. (2010i). The power of intuition: How to use your gut feeling to make better leadership decisions. *International Journal of Management, Business, and Administration*, *13*(3), 1–6.

Lunenburg, F. C. (2010j). School violence in America's schools. *Focus on Colleges, Universities, and Schools*, *4*(2), 1–8.

Lunenburg, F. C. (2010k). Sexual harassment: An abuse of power. *International Journal of Management, Business, and Administration*, *13*(4), 1–7.

Lunenburg, F. C. (2011). Advances in information technology: Influences on the quantity and quality of communication in the workplace. *International Journal of Scholarly Intellectual Diversity*, *14*(1), 1–7.

Lunenburg, F. C. (2011a). Why school improvement efforts have failed: School reform needs to be based on a set of core principles. *International Journal of Scholarly Intellectual Diversity*, *13*(1), 1–6.

Lunenburg, F. C. (2011b). Mechanistic-organic organizations—an axiomatic theory: Authority based on bureaucracy or professional norms. *International Journal of Management, Business, and Administration*, *15*(1), 1–8.

Lunenburg, F. C. (2011c). Organizational structure: Mintzberg's framework. *International Journal of Scholarly, Academic, Intellectual Diversity*, *14*(2), 1–9.

Lunenburg, F. C. (2011d1). Professional development: A vehicle to reform schools. *Schooling*, *2*(1), 1–8.

Lunenburg, F. C. (2011d2). Collective bargaining: Legislation, issues, and process. *Focus on Colleges, Universities, and Schools*, *6*(1), 1–8.

Lunenburg, F. C. (2011e). Performance appraisal: Methods and rating Errors. *International Journal of Scholarly Academic Intellectual Diversity*, *14*(3), 1–11.

Lunenburg, F. C. (2011f). Goal-setting theory of motivation. *International Journal of Management, Business, and Administration,* *15*(2), 1–8.

Lunenburg, F. C. (2011g). Early childhood education: Implications for school readiness. *Schooling*, *2*(2), 1–9.

Lunenburg, F. C. (2011h). Can schools regulate student dress and grooming in school? *Focus on Colleges, Universities, and Schools*, *5*(1), 1–5.

Lunenburg, F. C. (2011i). The art and science of personnel selection: the use of tests and performance simulations. *International Journal of Management, Business, and administration*, *15*(3), 1–7.

Lunenburg, F. C. (2012a). Power and leadership: An influence process. *International Journal of Management, Business, and Administration*, *15*(4), 1–10.

Lunenburg, F. C. (2012b). Selection practices: The interview as an integral determinant in the hiring decision. *Focus on Colleges, Universities, and Schools*, *6*(1), 1–8.

Lunenburg, F. C. (2012c). Racial disparities in school discipline: A matter of social justice. In G. Perreault, L. Zellner, J. Ballinger, B. Thornton, & S. Harris (Eds.), *Social justice, competition and quality: 21st century leadership challenges* (pp. 101–114). Blacksburg, VA: NCPEA Publications.

Lunenburg, F. C. (2013a). America's obsession with student testing: Costs in money and lost instructional time. *International Journal of Scholarly Intellectual Diversity*, *15*(1), 1–4.

Lunenburg, F. C. (2013b). The challenge of equal opportunity for all: The road to excellence and equity in America's schools. *Journal of Education and Social Justice*, *1*(1), 102–118.

Lunenburg, F. C. (2013c). Reclaiming public education: Enabling all children to learn. *Schooling*, *4*(1), 1–6.

Lunenburg, F. C. (2015). Chapter 18: A free public education for all: Rediscovering the promise. In F. W. English (Ed.), *Sage guide to educational leadership and management* (pp. 273–286). Thousand Oaks, CA: Sage.

Lunenburg, F. C. (2016). Forms of power. In A. Farazmand (Ed.). *Global encyclopedia of public administration, public policy, and government* (pp. F1–11). New York, NY: Springer.

Lunenburg, F. C. (2017). Organizational structure and design. *Journal of Educational Leadership and Policy Studies, 1*(1), 21–43.

Lunenburg, F. C. (2019). National policy/standards: Changes in instructional supervision since the implementation of recent federal legislation. In S. J. Zepeda and J. A. Ponticell (Eds.). *The Wiley-Blackwell handbook of instructional supervision* (pp. 381–406). New York, NY: Wiley-Blackwell.

Lunenburg. F. C., & Columba, L. (1992). The 16PF as a predictor of principal performance: An integration of quantitative and qualitative research methods. *Education, 113*, 68–73.

Lunenburg, F. C., & Irby, B. J. (2000). *High expectations: An action plan for implementing goals 2000*. Thousand Oaks, CA: Sage.

Lunenburg, F. C., & Irby, B. J. (2008). *Writing a successful thesis or dissertation: Tips and strategies for students in the social and behavioral sciences*. Thousand Oaks, CA: Corwin Press.

Lunenburg, F. C., & Irby, B. J. (2011, October–December). Instructional strategies to facilitate learning. *International Journal of Educational Leadership Preparation, 6*(4). http://cnx.org/content/m41144/latest/.

Lunenburg, F. C., & Lunenburg, M. R. (2015). Developing high-performance teams: Long standing principles that work. *International Journal of Organizational Behavior, 3*(1), 1–17.

Lunenburg, F. C., & Lunenburg, M. R. (forthcoming). *The fat-burning phenomenon: Exercise, nutrition, and the brain*. New York, NY: Harmony Books.

Lunenburg, F. C., & O'Reilly, R. R. (1974). Personal and organizational influence on pupil control ideology. *Journal of Experimental Education, 42*, 31–35.

Lunenburg, F. C., & Ornstein, A. O. (2022). *Educational administration: Concepts and practices* (7th ed.). Thousand Oaks, CA: Sage.

Lunenburg, F. C., & Schmidt, L. J. (1989). Pupil control ideology, pupil control behavior, and the quality of school life. *Journal of Research and Development in Education, 22*(4), 36–44.

Luthans, F., & Kreitner, R. (1985). *Organizational behavior modification and beyond: An operant and social learning approach*. Glenview, IL: Scott, Foresman.

Luthans, F., Luthans, B. C., & Luthans, K. W. (2015). *Organizational behavior: An evidence-based approach*. Charlotte, NC: Information Age Publishing.

Luxen, M. F., & van de Vijver, F. J. R. (2006). Facial attractiveness, sexual selection, and personnel selection: When evolved preferences matter. *Journal of Organizational Behavior, 27* (2), 241–255.

Lyons, J. E. (1990). Managing stress in the principalship. *NASSP Bulletin, 74*, 42–49.

Maag, J. W. (2001). Rewarded by punishment: Reflections on the disuse of positive reinforcement in schools. https://doi.org/10.1177/001440290106700203.

Macdonald, D. (2015). Teachers-as-knowledge-broker in a futures-oriented health and physical education. *Sport, Education, and Society, 20*(1), 27–41, DOI: 10.1080/13573322.2014.735320.

MacKinnon, C. (1987). Sexual harassment of working women: A hidden issue. In D.G. Schneider. Sexual harassment and higher education. *Texas School Law Review, 65*(25), 46.

Madfis, E. (2014). *The risk of school rampage: Assessing and preventing threats of school violence*. New York, NY: Palgrave Macmillan.

Mahwinny, T. S., & Sagan, L. L. (2007). The power of personal relationships. *Phi Delta Kappan, 88*(6), 460–464.

Manning, T, Parker, R., & Pogson, G. (2006). A revised model of team roles and some research findings. *Industrial and Commercial Training*, *38*(6), 287–296.

Mannix, E., Neale, M. A., & Blount-Lyon, S. (2004). *Time in groups*. St. Louis, MO: Elsevier.

Marbury v. Madison, 5 U.S. (1 Cranch) 137 (1803).

March, J. G. (2010). *Primer on decision making: How decisions happen*. New York, NY: Simon & Schuster.

March, J. K., & Peters, K. H. (20020. Effective schools—Curriculum development and instructional design in the effective schools process. *Phi Delta Kappan, 85*(5), 379.

Marietta, G., d'Entremont, C., & Kaur, E. M. (2017). *Improving education together: A guide to labor management community collaboration*. Cambridge, MA: Harvard Education Publishing Group.

Markham, S. E., Dansereau, F., & Alutto, J. A. (1982). Group size and absenteeism rates: A longitudinal analysis. *Academy of Management Journal*, *25*(4), 921–927.

Markowitz, G., & Rosner, D. (2013). *Lead wars: The politics of science and the fate of America's children*. Oakland, CA: University of California Press.

Marland, S. P. (1971). *Education of gifted and talented* (2 vols.). Washington, DC: Government Printing Office.

Marshall, C., & Gerstl-Pepin, C. I. (2005). *Re-framing educational politics for social justice*. Boston, MA: Pearson.

Marshall, C., Gerstl-Pepin, C., & Johnson, M. (2020). *Educational politics for social justice*. New York, NY: Teachers College Press.

Marshall, K. (2006). The why's and how's of teacher evaluation rubrics. *Edge: The Latest Information for the Education Practitioner*, *2*(1), 2–19.

Marshall, T. (2021). *Reclaiming the principalship: Instructional leadership strategies to engage your school community and focus on learning*. Portsmouth, NH: Heinemann.

Marshall v. School District RE No. 3 Morgan County, 553 P.2d 784 (Colo. 1976).

Martin, C., & Ruitenberg, C. W. (2018). *Ethics in professional education*. New York, NY: Routledge.

Martin, L. E., Kragler, S., Quatroche, D. J., & Bauserman, K. L. (Eds.). (2014). *Handbook of professional development in education: Successful models and practices, pre-k–12*. New York, NY: The Guilford Press.

Martin, W. J., & Willower, D. J. (1981). The managerial behavior of high school principals. *Educational Administration Quarterly*, *17*, 69–90.

Martinez v. Bynum, 461 U.S. 321 (1983).

Martinez v. School Board of Hillsborough County, 861 F.2d 1502, 1506 (11th Cir. 1988), on remand, 711 F. Supp. 1066 (M.D. Fla. 1989).

Marzano, R. (2006). *Classroom assessment and grading that works*. Alexandria, VA: ASCD.

Marzano, R. (2012). The two purposes of teacher evaluation. *Educational leadership: Department of Supervision and Curriculum Development, NEA*, *70*(3), 14–19.

Marzano, R. J. (2017). *The new art and science of teaching: More than fifty new instructional strategies for academic success*. Indianapolis, IN: Solution Tree Press.

Marzano, R. J. (2018). *The handbook for the new art and science of teaching*. Alexandria, VA: ASCD.

Marzano, R., Pickering, D., & Pollack, J. (2001). *Classroom instruction that works: research-based practices for increasing student achievement*. Alexandria, VA: Association for Supervision and Curriculum Development.

Maslow, A. (1968). *Toward a psychology of being* (2nd ed.). Princeton, NJ: Van Nostrand.

Maslow, A. H. (1987). *Motivation and personality* (3rd ed.). New York, NY: Harper & Row.

Maslow, A. H. (1998). *Maslow on management*. New York, NY: Wiley.

Maslow, V. J., & Kelley, C. J. (2012). Does evaluation advance practice? The effects of performance evaluation on teaching quality and system change in large school districts. *Journal of School Improvement*, *22*, 600–632.

Mason v. General Brown Central School District, 851 F.2d 47 (2d Cir. 1988).

Mathur, S., Gehrke, R., & Kim, S. (2013). Impact of teacher mentorship program on mentors' and mentees' perceptions of classroom practices and the mentoring experience. *Assessment for Effective Intervention, 38*(3), 154–162.

Matter of McMillan, 226 S.E.2d 693 (N.C. 1976).

Matthews, G. (2006). *Pesticides: Health, safety, and the environment*. New York, NY: Wiley.

Matthews, L. J., & Crow, G. M. (2010). *The principalship: New roles in a professional learning community*, Boston, MA: Pearson.

Mathis v. Gordy, 47 S.E. 171 (Ga. 1904).

Mathur, S. R., Gehrke, R., & Kim, S. H. (2013). Impact of teacher mentorship program on mentors' and mentees' perceptions of classroom practices and mentoring experience. *Assessment for effective intervention, 38*(3), 154–162.

Mayer, R. E. (2011). *Handbook of research on learning and instruction*. New York, NY: Routledge

Mazenec v. N. Judson—San Pierre School Corp., 798 F.2d 230 (7th Cir. 1987).

Mazur, J. E. (2013). *Learning and behavior* (7th ed.). Boston, MA: Pearson.

M.B. ex rel. Martin v. Liverpool Central School District, 487 F. Supp. 2d 117 (N.D. N.Y. 2007).

McAuliff Elementary School (2003). *Parent student handbook*. Accessed December 3, 2003, http://www.mcauliff.cps.k12.il.us/mcauliffevision.htm,

McCabe, C. (2017). *The fearless school leader: Making the right decisions*. New York, NY: Routledge.

McCarthy v. Boozman, 212 F. Supp.2d 945 (W.D. Ark. 2002).

McCarthy, M., Eckes, S. E., & Decker, J. R. (1019). *Legal rights of school leaders, teachers, and students* (8th ed.). Boston, MA: Pearson.

McCarthy, M. M. (2006). Instruction about the Origin of Humanity; Legal Controversies Evolve," *Education Law Reporter, 203*, 453–467.

McCarthy v. Boozman, 212 F. Supp.2d 945 (W.D. Ark. 2002).

McCarthy v. Fletcher, 254 Cal. Rptr. 714 (Ct. App. 1989).

McCarthy v. Ozark School District, 359 F.3d 1029 (8th Cir. 2004).

McCartney v. Austin, 298 N.Y.S.2d 26 (N.Y. App. Div. 1969).

McChesney, C., Covey, S., Huling, J., Thele, S., & Walker, B. (2021). *The 4 disciplines of execution: Achieving your wildly important goals* (rev. ed). New York, NY: Simon & Schuster.

McCollum v. Board of Education of School District No. 71, 333 U.S. 203 (1948).

McCombs, B. L. (2006). *Learner-centered classroom practices and assessments: Maximizing student motivation, learning, and achievement*. Thousand Oaks, CA: Corwin.

McCown, R., Driscoll, M., & Roop, P. (1996). *Educational psychology: A learning-centered approach to classroom practice* (2nd ed.). Boston, MA: Allyn & Bacon.

McCown v. Patagonia Union School District, 629 P.2d 94 (Ariz. 1981)

McCreary County, Kentucky v. American Civil Liberties Union of Kentucky, 354 F.3d 438 (2005).

McDaniel, M. A., Whetzel, D. L., Schmidt, F. L., & Maurer, S. D. (1994). The validity of employment interviews: A comprehensive review and meta-analysis. *Journal of Applied Psychology, 79*, 599–616.

McDonald, D. (2015). Teacher-as-knowledge-broker in a futures-oriented health and physical education. *Sport, Education and Society, 20*(1), 27–41.

McDonnell Douglas Corp. v. Green, 411 U.S. 792 (1973).

McHugh, M. (1997). The stress factor: Another item for the change management agenda. *Journal of Organizational Change Management, 10*, 345–362.

McKeon, D. (1987). Different types of ESL programs. *ERIC Digest*. Washington, DC: ERIC Clearinghouse on Languages and Linguistics. (ERIC Document reproduction service No. ED289360).

McKinney-Vento Homeless Assistance Act (2007) [42 U.S.C.A., § 11431 (1)].

McKown, C., Gregory, A., & Weinstein, R. S. (2010). Expectations, stereotypes, and self-fulfilling propheciesin classroom and school life. In J. L. Meece & J. S. Eccles (Eds.), *Handbook of research on schools, schooling, and human development* (pp. 256–274). New York, NY: Routledge.

McLaughlin, M. W., & Shields, P. M. (1987). Involving low-income parents in the schools: A role for policy. *Phi Delta Kappan, 69*, 156–160.

McLean v. Arkansas Board of Education, 529 F. Supp. 1255 (E.D. Ark. 1982).

McMorrow v. Benson, 617 N.W. 2d 247 (Wis. Ct. App. 2000).

McMullen, J. G. (2002). Behind closed doors: Should states regulate homeschooling? *South Carolina Law Review, 54*, 75–109.

McMullen, R. (2019). *The law and unfair dismissal*. New York, NY: Oxford University Press.

McMurrer, J. (2007, July). Choices, change, and challenges: Curriculum and instruction in the NCLB era. *Center on Education Policy*. http://www.cep-dc.org.

McNeil, L. M. (2000). *Contradictions of school reform: Educational costs of standardized testing*. New York, NY: Routledge.

McShane, S. L., & Von Glinow, M. A. (2018). *Organizational behavior*. New York, NY: McGraw-Hill/Irwin.

McTighe, J., & Ferrara, S. (2021). *Assessing student learning by design: Principles and practices for teachers and school leaders*. New York, NY: Teachers College Press.

Meece, J. L., & Kurtz-Costes, B. (2001). Introduction: The schooling of ethnic minority children and youth. *Educational Psychologist, 36*, 1–7.

Meek v. Pittenger, 421 U.S. 348 (1975).

Meier, D. (2006). As though they owned the place: Small schools as membership communities. *Phi Delta Kappan, 87*, 657–662.

Mendel, J. (2011). *Perceptual computing: Aiding people in making subjective decisions*. New York, NY: Wiley.

Mercer v. Michigan State Board of Education, 379 F. Supp. 580 (E.D. Mich. 1974), aff"d, 419 U.S. 1081 (1974).

Meritor Savings Bank v. Vinson, 477 U.S. 57 (1986).

Merriam, S. B., & Baumgartner, L. M. (2020). *Learning in adulthood: A comprehensive guide* (4th ed.). San Francisco, CA: Jossey-Bass.

Merriam, S. B., & Bierema, L. L. (2014). *Adult learning; Linking theory and practice*. San Francisco, CA: Jossey-Bass.

Merriam School (2003). *Merriam's mission and vision statements*. http://merriam.ab.mec.edu/igeneral.html.

Merriman, J, & Hill, J. (1992). Ethics, law, and sport. *Journal of Legal Aspect of Sport, 2*(2), 56–63.

Meyer, J. W., & Rowan, B. (1977). Institutionalized organizations: formal structure as myth and ceremony. *American Journal of Sociology, 83*, 440–463.

Meyer, N. D. (2017). *Principle-based organizational structure: A handbook to help you engineer entrepreneurial thinking and teamwork into organizations*. NDMA Publishing.

Meyer v. Nebraska, 262 U.S. 390 (1923).

Midgley, C. (2014). *Goals, goal structures, and patterns of adaptive learning*. New York, NY: Routledge.

Millenium Development Goals (2003, September). *Education*. http://www.developmentgoals.org/Education.htm,

Millenium Development Goals: A compact among nations to end human poverty. (2003). *The Millennium development goals report 2015*. New York, NY: United Nations. http://www.undp.org/hdr2003/pdf/hdr03_overview.pdf

Miller, C. C., & Ireland, R. D. (2005). Intuition in strategic decision making: Friend or foe in the fast-paced 21st century. *Academy of Management Executive, 19*(1), 19–30.

Miller, D., Miller, M., Linn, R., & Gronlund, N. (2012). *Measurement and assessment in teaching* (11th ed.). Boston, MA: Pearson.

Miller, P. M. (2008). Examining the work of boundary spanning leaders in community contexts. *International Journal of Leadership in Education*, *11*(4), 353–377.

Miller, S. J. (2019). *About gender identity justice in schools and communities*. New York, NY: Teachers College Press.

Miller v. California, 413 U.S. 15 (1973).

Mills v. Board of Education of the District of Columbia, 348 F. Supp. 866 D.D.C. (1972).

Millward, R., & Gerlach, G. (1991). *Pre-teacher assessment: An innovative concept in pre-teacher evaluation*. Indiana, PA: Indiana University of Pennsylvania.

Miner, J. B. (2015). *Organizational behavior 4: From theory to practice*. New York, NY: Taylor & Francis.

Minersville School District v. Gobitis, 310 U.S. 586 (1940).

Minnesota v. Newstrom, 371 N.W. 2d 525 (Minn. 1985).

Mintzberg, H. (1992). *Structure in fives: Designing effective organizations* (2nd ed.). Upper Saddle River, NJ: Prentice Hall.

Mintzberg, H. (1998). *The nature of managerial work*. Reading, MA: Addison-Wesley.

Mintzberg, H. (2009). *Tracking strategies: Toward a general theory of strategy formation*. New York: Oxford University Press.

Mintzberg, H. (2013). *Simply Managing: What managers do—and can do better*. San Francisco, CA: Berrett-Koehler.

Miranda, M. L., Dolinoy, D. C., & Overstreet, M. A. (2002). Mapping for prevention: GIS models for directing childhood lead poisoning prevention programs. *Environmental Health Perspectives*, *110*(9), 947–953.

Mishra, J. (1990). Managing the grapevine," *Public Personnel Management*, *19*(2), 213–228.

Mississippi University for Women v. Hogan, 458 U.S. 718 (1982).

Mitchell v. Helms, 530 U.S. 793 (2000).

Moe, T. M., & Chubb, J. E. (2009). *Liberating learning: Technology, politics, and the future of American education*. San Francisco, CA: Jossey-Bass.

Moede, W. (1927). Die Richtlinien der leistungs-psychologie. *Industrielle Psychotechnik*, *4*, 193–207.

Moeller v. Schrenko, 554 S.E.2d 198 (Ga. Ct. App. 2001).

Molsching, R., & Ryback, D. (2018). *Transforming communication in leadership and teamwork: Person-centered innovation*. New York, NY: Springer.

Moon, R. E. (2008). *The power of pedagogy*. Norwood, MA: Christopher-Gordon.

Moore, E. H, Bagin, D. H., & Gallagher, D. R. (2020). *The school and community relations* (12th ed.). Boston, MA: Pearson.

Moore, L., & Rudd, R. (2002). Using Socratic questioning in the classroom. *The Agricultural Education Magazine*, *75*(3), 24–25.

Moos, D. C., & Azevedo, R. (2009). Learning with computer-based learning environments: A literature review of computer self-efficacy. *Review of Educational Research*, *79*(2), 576–600.

Mora, J. K., Wink, J., & Wink, D. (2001). Dueling models of dual language instruction: A critical review of the literature and program implementation guide, *Bilingual Research Journal*, *25*(4), 435–460.

Moran, C. (19930. Content area instruction for students acquiring English. In J. Villareal & A. Ada (Eds.), *The power of two languages*. New York, NY: McGraw-Hill.

Moreno, J. L. (1953). *Who shall survive?* (rev. ed.). (New York NY: Beacon House.

Morgan, G. (1988). *Riding the waves of change*. San Francisco, CA: Jossey-Bass.

Morgan, G. (2007). *Images of organization*. Thousand Oaks, CA: Sage.

Morgan v. Plano Independent School District, 724 F.3d 579 (5th Cir. 2013).

Morgan v. Swanson, 755 F.3d 757 (5th Cir. 2014).

Morrison, J. Q., & Jones, K. M. (2007). The effects of positive peer reporting as a class-wide positive behavior support. *Journal of Behavioral Education*, *16*(2), 111–124.

Moscoso, S., & Salgado, J. F. (2002). Psychometric properties of a structured behavioral interview to hire private security personnel. *Journal of Business & Psychology*, *16*(1), 51–59.

Moskaw, M. H. (2017). *Teachers and unions: The applicability of collective bargaining in public education*. Philadelphia, PA: University of Pennsylvania Press.

Moustakas, C. E. (1990). *Heuristic research: Design, methodology, and application*. Thousand Oaks, CA: Sage.

Mower v. Leicester, 9 Mass. 237 (1812).

Mueller v. Allen, 463 U.S. 388 (1983).

Mullen, B., & Copper, C. (1994). The relation between group cohesiveness and performance: An integration. *Psychological Bulletin*, *115*(2), 210–227.

Muller v. Jefferson Lighthouse School, 98 F.3d 1530 (7th Cir. 1996), cert. denied, 520 U.S. 1156 (1997).

Mulvey, P. W., Bowes-Sperry, L., & Klein, H. J. (1998). The effect of perceived loafing and defensive impression management on group effectiveness. *Small Group Research*, *29*(3), 394–415.

Mulvey, P. W., & Klein, H. J. (1998). The impact of perceived loafing and collective efficacy on group goal processes and group performance. *Organizational Behavior and Human Decision Processes*, *74*(1), 62–87.

Mumby, D. K. (2019). *Organizational communication: A critical approach*. Thousand Oaks, CA: Sage.

Mumford, M. D., & Gustafson, S. B. (1988). Creativity syndrome: Integration, application, and innovation. *Psychological Bulletin*, *103*(1), 27–43

Murphy, A., & Torff, B. (2016). Growing pains: The effect of common core state standards on perceived teacher effectiveness. *The Educational Forum*, *80*(1), 21–33.

Murphy, J. (1990). Principal instructional leadership. In P. W. Thurston & L. S. Lotto (Eds.), *Advances in educational administration*, vol. 1B (pp. 162–200). Greenwich, CT: JAI Press.

Murphy, J. (1998). What's ahead for tomorrow's principals. *Principal*, *78*, 13–16.

Murphy, J. (2002). Reculturing the profession of educational leadership: New blueprints. *Educational Administration Quarterly*, *39*(2), 176–191.

Murphy, J. (2010). *The educator's handbook for understanding and closing achievement gaps*. Thousand Oaks, CA: Corwin Press.

Murphy, J. (2013). *The architecture of school improvement: Lessons learned*. Thousand Oaks, CA: Corwin Press.

Murphy, J. (2016a). *Leading school improvement: A framework for action*. West Palm Beach, FL: Learning Sciences International.

Murphy, J. (2016b). *Creating instructional capacity*. Thousand Oaks, CA: Corwin Press.

Murphy, J. (2016c). *Understanding schooling through the eyes of students*. Thousand Oaks, CA: Corwin Press.

Murphy, J. (2020). *Bottling fog: Essential lessons in leadership*. New York, NY: Teachers College Press.

Murphy, J., & Bleiberg, J. (2019). *School turnaround policies and practices: Learning from failed reform*. Dordrecht, The Netherlands: Springer.

Murphy, J. & Louis, K. S. (2018). *Positive school leadership*. New York, NY: Teachers College Press.

Murphy, J., Torre, D. (2014). *Creating productive cultures in schools: For students, teachers, and parents*. Thousand Oaks, CA: Corwin Press.

Murphy, S. M., Wayne, S. J., Liden, R. C., & Erdogan, B. (2004). Understanding social loafing: The role of justice perceptions and exchange relationships. *Human Relations*, *56*(1), 61–84.

Murphy v. Alexander, 852 F.2d 1039 (8th Cir. 1988).

Murphy v. State of Arkansas, 852 F.2d 1039 (1988).

Myers, D. (2002). *Intuition: Its power and perils*. New Haven, CT: Yale University Press.

Myers v. Loudoun County School Board, 500 F. Supp.2d 539 (E.D. Va. 2007).

Nagy v. Evansville-Vanderburgh School Corporation, 844 N.E.2d 481, 484 (Ind. 2006).

Napier, N. K., & Nilsson, M. (2008). *The creative discipline: Mastering the art and science of innovation*. Santa Barbara, CA: Praeger.

Narayanan, M. P. (2004). *Finance for strategic decision making: What non-financial managers need to know*. New York, NY: Wiley.

Narayanan, M. P., & Nanda, V. K. (2004). *Finance for strategic decision making*. New York, NY: Wiley.

National Alliance for Safe Schools. (2020). *Safe schools—better schools*. Eastbound, WA: National Alliance for Safe Schools.

National Assessment of Educational Progress (NAEP) Report Card: 2019 NAEP Mathematics Assessment.

National Assessment of Educational Progress (NAEP) Report Card: 2019 NAEP Reading Assessment.

National Association of Elementary School Principals. (1998). *Backgrounder on public school uniforms*. Alexandria, VA: National Association of Elementary School Principals.

National Association of Elementary School Principals. (2020). Code of ethics for elementary school principals. Alexandria, VA: National Association of Elementary School Principals

National Association of Secondary School Principals. (n.d.). *Leaders for the future: Assessment and development programs*. Reston, VA: National Association of Secondary School Principals.

National Association of Secondary School Principals. (2020). Code of ethics for secondary school principals. Reston, VA: National Association of Secondary School Principals.

National Association of State Directors of Education Plant Services (2008). *Projection of population by states, 2009–2019*. Washington DC: Institute of Education Sciences.

National Center for Children in Poverty. (2019). *Basic facts about low-income children*. http://www.nccp.org/publications/pub_1170.html.

National Center for Education Statistics. (1999). *Digest of education statistics* http://nces.ed.gov/pubs2000/digest99/d99to53.asp.

National Center for Education Statistics. (2003). *Status and trends in the education of Hispanics*. http://nces.ed.gov/pubs2003/hispanics/.

National Center for Education Statistics. (2004). *Digest of education statistics*. Washington, DC: US Department of Education.

National Center for Education Statistics. (2017). *Digest of education statistics*. Washington, DC: US Government Printing Office, Table 214.20.

National Center for Education Statistics, (2018a). Public school enrollment.. *The condition of education*. Department of Education. Institute of Education Sciences https://nces.ed.gov/programs/coe/indicator_cga.asp.

National Center for Education Statistics (2018b). Characteristics of public elementary and secondary school teachers in the United States: Research from the 2015–2016 national teacher and principal survey first look (NCES 2017–072 rev.). Washington, DC: US Department of Education, NCES. https://nces.ed.gov/pubs2017/2017072rev.pdf.

National Center for Education Statistics (2019). *NAEP 2019 for children in poverty: Basic facts about low-income children*. http://www.nccp.org/publications/pub_1170.html.

National Center for Education Statistics (2019). Indicator 6: Elementary and secondary enrollment. *Status and trends in the education of racial and ethnic groups*. https://nces.ed.gov/programs/raceindicators/indicator_rbb.asp.

National Center for Education Statistics (2019). Teacher characteristics and trends. *Fast facts*. https://nces.ed.gov/fastfacts/display.asp?id=28.

National Center for Effective Schools Research and Development. (2000). *The triumph of effective schools: A review and analysis of research and practice.* Madison,

WI: Wisconsin Center for Education Research, University of Wisconsin, the National Center for Effective Schools Research and Development.

National Children's Alliance (2015). *2015 CAC statistics*. National Children's Alliance Web site http://www.nationalchildrenalliance.org/cac-statistics.

National Commission on Excellence in Education (1983, April). A nation at risk: The imperative for educational reform. Washington, DC: US Department of Education. https://www2.ed.gov/pubs/NatAtRisk/index.html.

National Conference of State Legislators. (2000). *Legislative guidance for comprehensive state groundwater protection program*. Denver, CO: National Conference of State Legislators.

National Conference of State Legislators (2003). *Legislative requirements under the clean act amendments* (rev. ed.). Denver, CO: National Conference of State Legislators.

National Education Association (1975). *Code of ethics for educators*. Washington, DC: National Education Association

National Federation of State High School Associations (NFHS). (2022). *Coaches code of ethics*. NFHS. https://www.nfhs.org/nfhs-for-you/coaches/coaches-code-of-ethics/.

National School Boards Association (n.d.). *National education policy reference manual*. Alexandria, VA: National School Boards Association.

National School Public Relations Association. (n.d.). *Getting a public relations program started*. Rockville, MD: National School Public Relations Association. http://www.nspra.org.

National Staff Development Council. (2020). *Code of ethics*. Washington, DC: National Staff Development Council. http://www.nsdc.org.

Navarro, J. (2011). *Louder than words: Take your career from average to exceptional with the hidden power of nonverbal intelligence*. New York, NY: HarperCollins.

Neal, R. G. (1982). *Bargaining tactics: A reference manual for public sector labor negotiations*. Manassas, VA: Richard Neal Associates.

Neck, C. P., Houghton, J., & Murray, E. L. (2019). *Organizational behavior: A skill building approach*. Thousand Oaks, CA; Sage.

Nehring, J. (2010). *The practice of school reform: Lessons from two centuries*. Albany, NY: State University of New York Press.

Nelson, D., & Quick, J. (2019). *Organizational behavior*. Mason, OH: Cengage South-Western.

Nelson, J. (2004). *The art of focused conversation for schools: Over 100 ways to guide clear thinking and promote learning*. Gabriola Island, BC: New Society.

Newdow v. Rio Linda Union School District, 597 F.3d 1007 (9th Cir. 2010).

Newdow v. U.S. congress, 292 F.3d 597 (9th Cir. 2002), 328 F.3d 466 (9th Cir. 2003), cert. granted sub nom. Elk Grove Unified School District v. Newdow, 540 U.S. 945 (2003).

Newdow v. U.S. Congress, 383 F. Supp.2d 1229 (E.D. Cal. 2005).

New Jersey Statutes Annotated, § 18A:28–5(4) (2018).

New Jersey v. T.L.O., 469 U.S. 325 (1985).

New York State Board of Education (2002). *New York state code of ethics for educators*. Albany, NY: New York State Board of Education.

Newmann, F., Carmichael, D. I., & King, M. B. (2015). *Authentic intellectual work: Improving teaching for rigorous learning*. Thousand Oaks, CA: Corwin Press.

Newmann, R. (2008). American democracy at risk. *Phi Delta Kappan, 89*, 328–339.

Newstrom, J. W. (2016). *Organizational behavior: Human behavior at work*. New York, NY: McGraw-Hill.

Newton, P., & Burgess, D. (2017). *The best available evidence: Decision making for educational improvement*. Boston, MA: Brill.

Nichols, S. (2007). High-stakes testing: Does it increase achievement? *Journal of Applied School Psychology, 23*(2), 47–64.

Nichols, S. L., & Berliner, D. C. (2007). *Collateral damage: How high-stakes testing corrupts America's schools*. Cambridge, MA: Harvard Education Press.

Nicolau, S., & Ramos, C. L. (1990). *Together is better: Building strong relationships between schools and Hispanic parents*. Washington, DC: Hispanic Policy Development Project.

Nielsen, H. (2011). *Bounded rationality in decision making*. Dobbs Ferry, NY: Manchester University Press.

Nieto, S. (2002/2003). Profoundly multicultural questions. *Educational Leadership*, *60*(4), 6–10.

Nieto, S. (2010). *Language, culture, and teaching: Critical perspectives for a new century*. New York, NY: Routledge.

Nieto, S. (2011). *The light in their eyes: Creating multicultural learning communities*. New York, NY: Teachers College Press.

Nieto, S. (2012). *Affirming diversity: The sociopolitical context of multicultural education* (6th ed.). Boston, MA: Pearson.

No Child Left Behind Act of 2001, Pub. L. No. 107–110, § 115, Stat. 1425.

Noddings, N. (1984/2003). *Caring: a feminine approach to ethics and moral education* (2nd ed.). Berkeley, CA: University of California Press.

Noddings, N. (2002). *Educating moral people*. New York, NY: Teachers College Press.

Noddings, N. (2003). *Happiness and education*. Cambridge, England: Cambridge University Press.

Noddings, N. (2005a). *The challenge to care in schools* (2nd ed.). New York, NY: Teachers College Press.

Noddings, N. (2005b). What does it mean to educate the whole child? *Educational Leadership, 63*, 8–13.

Noddings, N. (2007). *When school reform goes wrong*. New York, NY: Teachers College Press.

Noddings, N. (2008). Caring and moral education. In L. P. Nucci & D. Narvaez (Eds.), *Handbook of moral and character education* (pp. 161–174). New York, NY: Routledge.

Noddings, N. (2010). Moral education in an age of globalization. *Educational Philosophy and Theory, 42*(4), 390–396.

Noddings, N. (2015). *Education and democracy in the 21st century*. New York, NY: Teachers College Press.

Noguera, P. A., & Syeed, E. (2020). *City schools and the American dream 2. The enduring promise of public education* (2nd ed.). New York, NY: Teachers College Press.

Nolet, V., & McLaughlin, M. J. (2005). *Assessing the general curriculum: Including students with disabilities in standards-based reform* (2nd ed.). Thousand Oaks, CA: Corwin Press.

Noltemeyer, A., McLaughlin, C. L., McGowan, M. R. (2017). Family responses to school and community mass violence. In C. A. Price, K. R. Bush, & S. J. Price (Eds.), *Families and change: Coping with stressful events and transitions* (pp. 269–289). Thousand Oaks, CA: Sage.

Nordstrom, R., Lorenzi, P., & Hall, R. V. (1990). A review of public posting of performance feedback in work settings. *Journal of Organizational Behavior Management*, *11*(2), 101–123.

Norlin, J. M. (2009). *Human behavior and the social environment: Social systems theory*. Upper Saddle River, NY: Prentice Hall.

North Carolina State Board of Education (1997). *North Carolina code of ethics for educators*. North Carolina State Board of Education.

Northouse, G. (2018). *Leadership: Theory and practice* (8th ed.). Thousand Oaks, CA: Sage.

Norton, M. S. (2014). *The principal as human resources leader: A guide to exemplary practices for personnel administration*. New York, NY: Routledge.

Noumair, D. A., & Shani, A. B. (2018). *Research in organizational change and development*. Bingley, UK: Emerald Publishing.

Nye, R. D. (1992). *The legacy of B. F. Skinner*. Pacific Grove, CA: Brooks/Cole.

Oakes, J. (2005). *Keeping track* (2nd ed.). New Haven, CT: Yale University Press.

Obasi, C. (2019). Application of logistic differential equation to investigate the extent of emphasizing stimulus variation in mathematics instruction (STME) *Supremum Journal of Mathematics Education, 3*(1), 11–17.

O'Connor, K. (2009). *How to grade for learning: K–12* (3rd ed.). Thousand Oaks, CA: Corwin Press.

Odden, A. R., & Picus, L. O. (2020). *School finance: A policy perspective* (6th ed.). New York, NY: McGraw-Hill.

Office of Juvenile Justice and Delinquency Prevention. (2022). *Creating safe and drug-free schools: An action plan*. Office of Juvenile Justice and Delinquency Prevention, US Department of Justice.

Ogbu, J. U. (2003). *Black American students in an affluent suburb*. Mahwah, NJ: Erlbaum Associates.

O'Leary,L. I. (2018). *Microsoft powerpoint 2017: A case approach, complete*. New York, NY: McGraw-Hill.

Oliva, P. F., & Gordon, W. R. (2013). *Developing the curriculum* (8th ed.). Upper Saddle River, NJ: Pearson Education.

Olpin, M. (2016). *Stress management for life* (4th ed.). Belmont, CA: Cengage Learning.

Olweus, D. (1994). Bullying at school: Basic facts and effects of a school-based intervention program. *Journal of Child Psychology and Psychiatry and Allied Disciplines, 35*, 1171–1190.

O'Malley, & Waggoner, D. (1984). Public school teacher preparation and the teaching of ESL. *TESOL Newsletter, 18*(1). 18–22.

O'Neill, J. (2000, February). SMART goals, SMART schools. *Educational Leadership, 57*(5), 46–50.

Opinion of the Justices to the Senate, 373 Mass. 883, 366 N.E. 2d 733 (1977).

Ornstein, A. C. (1986). How do educators meet the needs of society? How are education's aims determined? *NASSP Bulletin, 70*, 36–47.

Ornstein, A. C. (2004). Curriculum planning and development. In F. C. Lunenburg and A. C. Ornstein, *Educational administration: Concepts and practices* (4th ed.) (p. 493). Belmont, CA: Wadsworth.

Ornstein, A. C. (2012). *Wealth vs. Work: How 1% victimize 99%*. Bloomington, IN: AuthorHouse.

Ornstein, A. O. (2016). *Excellence vs. equality: Can society achieve both goals?* New York, NY: Routledge.

Ornstein, A. O., & Hunkins, F. P. (2017). *Curriculum: Foundations, principles, and Issues* (7th ed.). Boston, MA: Pearson.

Ornstein, A. O., Pajak, E., & Ornstein, S. B. (2015). *Contemporary issues in curriculum* (6th ed.). Boston, MA: Pearson.

Orozco ex. rel. Arroyo v. Sobol, 703 F. Supp. 1113 (S.D.N.Y. 1989).

Osborn, A. F. (1957). *Applied imagination*. New York, NY: Scribner.

Osterman, K. F. (2000). Students' need for belonging in the school community. *Review of Educational Research, 70*(3), 323–367.

Ovando, C. J., & Collier, V. P. (1998). *Bilingual education and ESL classrooms* (2nd ed.). Boston, MA: McGraw-Hill.

Owings, W., & Kaplan, L. (2020). *American public school finance* (3rd ed.). New York, NY: Routledge.

OXFAM. (2019). Billionaire fortunes grew by $2.5 billion a day last year as poorest saw their wealth fall. https://www.oxfam.org/en/press-releases/billionaire-fortunes-grew-25-billion-day-last-year-poorest-saw-their-wealth-fall.

Paige, R. (2011). *The black-white achievement gap: Why closing it is the greatest civil rights issue of our time*. New York, NY: Amacom.

Pajak, E. (2008). *Supervising instruction: Differentiating for teacher success*. Norwood, MA: Christopher-Gordon.

Palestini, R. (2013). *Feminist theory and educational leadership: Much ado about something*! Lanham, MD: Rowman & Littlefield.

Palmour, J. (1986). *On moral character: a practical guide to Aristotle's virtues and vices.* Washington, DC: Archon Institute for Leadership development.

Pankake, A., & Abrego, J. (2017). *Lead with me: A principal's guide to teacher leadership.* New York, NY: Routledge.

Paradis, T. (2002). Message to Wall Street: Save e-mail. *Wall Street Journal*, p. C5.

Pardo, E. B., & Tinajero, J. V. (1993). *Literacy instruction through Spanish: Linguistic, cultural and pedagogical considerations.* In J. Villareal & A. Ada (Eds.). *The power of two languages.* New York, NY: McGraw-Hill.

Parents of Child, Code No. 87091w v. Coker, 676 F. Supp. 1072 (E.D. Ok. 1987).

Paris, D., & Alim, H. S. (2017). *Culturally sustaining pedagogies: Teaching and learning for justice in a changing world.* New York, NY: Teachers College Press.

Paris, S. G., & Paris, A. H. (2001). Classroom applications of research on self-regulated learning. *Educational Psychologist, 36*(2), 89–101.

Parker, R., Lara-Alecio, R., Ochoa, S., Bigger, M., Hasbrouck, J., & Parker, W. (1996). School improvement ideas; guidance from parents and students from three ethnic groups. *Journal of Educational Issues of Language Minority Students, 16*, 149–178.

Parker, S., Gulson, K. N., Trevor, G. (Eds.) (2017). *Policy and inequality in education.* New York, NY: Springer.

Parnes, S. J. (1992). *Source book for creative problem solving.* Buffalo, NY: Creative Foundation Press.

Parrini-Alemanno, S., & Benoit, D. (2019). *Trust and communication.* New York, NY: Wiley.

Pascale, R. T. (1985). The paradox of corporate culture: Reconciling ourselves to socialization. *California Management Review, 27*, 26–41.

Pascarella, S. A., & Lunenburg, F. C. (1988). A field test of Hersey and Blanchard's situational leadership theory in a school setting. *College Student Journal, 21*, 33–37.

Pasmore, W. (2011). *Research in organizational change and development.* Bingley, UK: Emerald Publishing Group.

Pasmore, W. A., Barnes, M. A., & Gipson, A. N. (2018). *The Palgrave handbook of organizational change.* New York, NY: Palgrave Macmillan.

Patrick, H., Ryan, A.m., & Kaplan, A. (2007). Early adolescents' perceptions of the classroom social environment, motivational beliefs, and engagement. *Journal of Educational Psychology, 99*(1), 83.

Paulson v. Minidoka County School District No. 331, 463 P.2d 935 (Idaho, 1970).

PDK Poll (2020). *The 52nd annual PDK poll of the public's attitudes toward public schools.* Arlington, VA: Phi Delta Kappa Poll, September, 2020.

Peck v. Upsur County Board of Education, 155 F.3d 274 (4th Cir. 1998).

Pellerin, L. A. (2005). Student engagement and the socialization styles of high schools. *Social Forces, 84*, 1161–1179.

Pelletier v. Maine Principals Association, 261 F. Supp.2d 10(D. Me. 2003).

Peloza v. Capistrano Unified School District, 37 F.3d 517 (9th Cir. 1994).

Pennsylvania Association for Retarded Children (PARC) v. Commonwealth, 334 F. Supp. 279 (E.D. Pa. 1972).

Penson, P. E. (2012). Lecturing: a lost art. *Currents in pharmacy teaching and learning, 4*(1), 72–76.

People v. Bennett, 501 N.W.2d 106 (Mich. 1993)

Perlman, L. (2011). *Facebook.* New York, NY: Wiley.

Perrone, V. (1998). *Teacher with a heart.* New York, NY: Teachers College Press.

Perrow, C. (1972). *Complex organizations: A critical essay.* New York: McGraw-Hill.

Perrow, C. (1986). *Complex organizations: A critical essay* (3rd ed.). Glencoew, IL: Scott, Foresman.

Perrow, C. (2002). *Organizing America: Wealth, power, and the origins of corporate capitalism.* Princeton, NJ: Princeton University Press.

Perry Education Association v. Perry Local Educators' Association, 460 U.S. 37 (1983).

Perry-Smith, J. E., & Shalley, C. E. (2003). The social side of creativity: A static and dynamic social network perspective. *Academy of management Review*, *28*(1), 89–106.

Perry v. Sinderman, 408 U.S. 593 (1972).

Peterson, R. S., & Behfar, J. (2003). The dynamic relationship between performance feedback, trust, and conflict in groups: A longitudinal study. *Organizational Behavior and Human Decision Processes*, *92*(1–2), 102–112.

Peters, T. J., & Waterman, R. H. (1982). *In Search of* Excellence. *New* York, NY: Warner Books.

Peters, T. J., & Waterman, R. H. (2006). *In Search of Excellence* (rev. ed.). New York, NY: Warner Books.

Pfeffer, J., & Sutton, R. (2000). *The knowing-doing gap: How smart companies turn knowledge into action*. Cambridge, MA: Harvard Business School Press.

Phenix, P. (1962). The use of the disciplines as curriculum content. *Educational Forum*, *26*(3), 273–280.

Phenix, P. (1964). *Realms of meaning*. New York, NY: McGraw-Hill.

Phillips v. Martin Marietta Corporation, 400 U.S. 542 (1971).

Phinney, A. (2004, September). *Preparedness in America's schools: A comprehensive look at terrorism preparedness in America's twenty largest school districts*. America Prepared Campaign. http://www.americaprepared.org/pdf/SchoolsAssessment _0904.pdf.

Phipps v. Saddleback Valley Unified School District, 251 Cal. Reptr. 720 (Cal. Ct. App. 1988).

Piaget, J. (1950). *The psychology of intelligence*. New York, NY: Harcourt.

Piaget, J. (1983). Piaget's theory. In P. Mussen & W. Kessen (Eds.). *Handbook of child psychology*, vol. 1, *History, theory, and methods* (4th ed.) (pp. 103–128). New York, NY: Wiley.

Pianta, R. C., Belsky, J., Houts, R., Morrison, F., & National Institute of Child Health and Human Development Early Child Care Research Network (2007, March). Teaching: Opportunities to learn in America's elementary classrooms. *Science*, *315*(5820), 1795–1796.

Piccadilly (2018). *The big book of personality tests*. Del Mar, CA: Piccadilly Enterprises, Inc.

Pierce v. Society of Sisters of the Holy Names of Jesus and Mary, 268 U.S. 510.

Pink, D. H. (2011). *Drive: The surprising truth about what motivates us*. New York, NY: Riverhead Books.

Pirtle, S. S., & Tobia, E. (2014). Implementing effective professional learning communities. *SEDL Insights*, 2(3), 1–8.

Pitts v. State, 748 So.2d 426 (Ga. 2013).

Plucker, J. A., & Callahan, C. M. (2020). *Critical issues and practices in gifted education: A survey of current research on giftedness and talent development* (3rd ed.). Waco, TX: Prufrock Press.

Plyer v. Doe, 457 U.S. 202 (1982).

Podsakoff, N. P., LePine, J. A., & LePine, M. A. (2007). Differential challenge-hindrance stressor relationships with job attitudes, turnover intentions, turnover, and withdrawal behavior: A meta-analysis. *Journal of Applied Psychology*, *92*(2), 438–454.

Podsakoff, P. M., MacKenzie, S. B., & Ahearne, M. (1997). Moderating effects of goal acceptance on the relationship between group cohesiveness and productivity. *Journal of Applied Psychology*, *82*(6), 974–983.

Poekert, P. (2012). Teacher leadership and professional development: Examining links between two concepts central to school improvement. *Professional Development in Education*, *38*(2), 169–188.

Police Department of the City of Chicago v. Mosley, 408 U.S. 96 (1972).

Poling v. Murphy, 872 F.2d 757 (6th Cir. 1989), cert. denied, 493 U.S. 1021 (1990).

Pollock, J. E. (2007). *Improving student learning one teacher at a time*. Alexandria, VA: ASCD.

Popham, W. J. (2003). *Test better, teach better: The instructional role of assessment*. Alexandria, VA: ASCD.

Popham, W. J. (2010). *Everything school leaders need to know about assessment*. Thousand Oaks, CA: Corwin Press.

Popham, W. J. (2011). *Transform assessment in action: An inside look at applying the process*. Alexandria, VA: ASCD.

Popham, W. J. (2020). *Classroom assessment: What teachers need to know* (9th ed.). Boston, MA: Pearson.

Porter, A., McMaken, J., Hwang, J., & Yang, R. (2011). Common Core standards: The new US intended curriculum. *Educational Researcher, 40*(3), 103–116.

Posthuma, R. A., Moregeson, F. P., & Campion, M. A. (2002). Beyond employment interview validity: A comprehensive narrative review of recent research and trends over time. *Personnel Psychology, 55*, 1–12.

Postrel, S. (2009). Multitasking teams with variable complementarity: Challenges for capability management. *Academy of Management Review, 34*(2), 273–296.

Pounds v. Katy Independent School District, 517 F. Supp.2d 901 (S.D. Tex. 2007).

Pounds v. Katy Independent School District, 730 F. Supp.2d 636 (S.D. Tex. 2010).

Poverty USA (2019). *The population of poverty USA*. https://www.povertyusa.org/facts.

Poze, T. (1983). Analogical connections: The essence of creativity. *Journal of Creative Behavior, 17*(4), 38–46.

Prashnig, B. (2006). *Learning styles and personalized teaching*. London, UK: Continuum International Publishing Group.

Pregnancy Discrimination Act (PDA), 42 U.S.C., § 2000 e (j), 2002.

Preiss, R. W., Gayle, B. A., Burrell, N., Allen, M., & Bryant, J. (2007). *Mass media effects research: Advances through meta-analysis*. New York, NY: Routledge.

Presidents Counsel, District 25 v. Community School Board No. 25, 457 F.2d 289 (2d Cir. 1972).

Pressley, M., & Hilden, K. (2006). Cognitive strategies. In D. Kuhn & R. Siegler (Eds.), *Handbook of child psychology: Cognition, perception, and language* (vol. 2, pp. 511–556). New York, NY: Wiley.

Preuss, P. (2017). *Data-Driven Decision Making and Dynamic Planning: A School Leader's Guide*. New York, NY: Routledge.

Price, K. H. (1987). Decision responsibility, task responsibility, identifiability, and social loafing. *Organizational Behavior and Human Development Processes, 40*(1), 330–345.

Prince v. Jacoby, 303 F.3d 1074 (9th Cir. 2002), cert. denied, 540 U.S. 813 (2003).

Prosser, W. L., & Keeton, P. W. (1984). *The law of torts* (5th ed.). St. Paul, MN: West.

Prosser, W. L., Wade, J., & Schwartz, V. (2010). *Cases on torts* (10th ed.). St. Paul, MN: West.

Pugh, K. J., & Bergin, D. (2005). The effect of schooling on students' out-of-school experience. *Educational Researcher, 34*(9), 15–23.

Purkey, W. W., & Novak, J. M. (1996). *Inviting school success: A self-concept approach to teaching, learning, and democratic practice* (3rd ed.). Belmont, CA: Wadsworth.

Pyle v. South Hadley School Committee, 861 F. Supp. 157 (Mass. 1994).

Osborn, A. F. (1957). *Applied imagination* (rev. ed.). New York, NY: Scribner.

Queen, J. A. (2002). *Student transitions from middle school to high school: Improving achievement and creating a safer school environment*. New York, NY: Routledge.

Quick, J. C., Cooper, C. L., Gavin, J. H., & Quick, J. D. (2008). *Managing executive health*. New York, NY: Cambridge University Press.

Quick, J. C., Wright, T. A., Adkins, J. A., Nelson, D. L., & Quick, J. D. (2014). *Preventive stress management in organizations* (2nd ed.). Washington, DC: American Psychological Association.

Quinn, C. (2018). *Motivation-based interviewing: A revolutionary approach to hiring the best.* Alexandria, VA: Society for Human Resource Management.

Racine Union School District v. Thompson, 321 N.W. 2d 334 (Wis. 1982).

Raftery, D. (2011). *Gender balance and gender bias in education: International perspectives.* New York, NY: Taylor & Francis.

Raina, R. (2018). *Change management and organizational development.* Thousand Oaks, CA: Sage.

Raine, A. (2013). *The anatomy of violence: The biological roots of crime.* New York, NY: Knopf Doubleday Publishing Group.

Rallis, S. F., Rossman, G. B., Cobb, C. D., Reagan, T. G., & Kuntz, A. (2008). *Leading dynamic schools: How to create and implement ethical policies.* Thousand Oaks, CA: Corwin Press.

Ramirez, J. D. (1992). Executive summary. *Bilingual Research Journal, 16*(1–2), 1–62.

Ramsdel v. N. River Sch. Dist. No. 200, 704 P.2d 606 (Wash. 1985).

Ramsey, R. D. (2007). Ten things that never change for supervisors. *SuperVision, 64*(3), 16–18.

Randell, G., & Toplis, J. (2014). *Towards organizational fitness: A guide to diagnosis and treatment.* New York, NY: Routledge.

Randolf County Board of Education v. Adams, 467 S.E.2d 150 (W. Va. 1995).

Rathman v. Board of Directors of Davenport Community School District, 580 N.W.2d 777 (Ia. 1998).

Ravitch, D. (1995). *National standards in American education.* Washington, DC: Brookings Institute press.

Ravitch, D. (2013). *Reign of terror: The hoax of the privatization movement and the danger of America's public schools.* New York, NY: Alfred A. Knopf.

Ravitch, D. (2016). *The death and life of the great American school system.* New York, NY: Basic Books.

Ravitch, D. (2020). *Slaying goliath: The passionate resistance to privatization and the fight to save America's public schools.* New York, NY: Alfred A. Knopf.

Rawalle, S., Paatsch, L., Campbell, C., Wells, M., & Tytler, R. (2016). *Improving schools: Productive tensions between the local, the systemic, and the global.* New York, NY: Springer.

Ray, B. D. (2005). *Worldwide guide to homeschooling.* Salem, OR: National Home Education Research Institute.

Raylor, A. C. (2011). *Videoconferencing: Technology, Impact, and applications.* Hauppauge, NY: Nova Science Publishers.

Raynor, S., & Cools, E. (Eds.). (2011). *Style differences in cognition, learning, and management: Theory, research, and practice.* New York, NY: Routledge.

Ready, D. D., & Wright, D. L. (2011). Accuracy and inaccuracy in teachers' perceptions of young children's cognitive abilities: The role of child background and classroom context. *American Educational Research Journal, 48*(2), 335–360.

Reardon, S. F., Weathers, E. S., Fahle, E. M., Jang, H., & Kalogrides, D. (2019). Is separation still unequal? New evidence on school segregation and racial academic achievement gaps (CPEA working paper No. 19–06). Stanford Center for Education Policy Analysis. http://cpea.stanford.edu/wp19–06.

Rebore, R. W. (2014). *Human resources administration.* Boston, MA: Pearson.

Rebore, R. W. (2014). *The ethics of educational leadership.* Boston, MA: Pearson.

Reese, T. (2014). Road tested/lesson closure: Stick the landing. *ASCD Education Update, 56*(6), 1–2.

Reeves, D. (2016). *Elements of grading: A guide to effective practice.* Indianapolis, IN: Solution Tree Press.

Reeves, D. (2021). *Deep change leadership: A model for renewing and strengthening schools and districts.* Indianapolis, IN: Solution Tree Press.

Reid v. Kenowa Hills Public Schools, 680 N.W.2d 62 (Mich. Ct. App. 2004).

Reimers, F. M., & Chung, C. K. (2021). *Teaching and learning for the twenty-first century: Educational goals, policies, and curricula from six nations*. Cambridge, MA: Harvard Education Press.

Reinke, W. M., Lewis-Palmer, T., & Merrell, K. (2008). The classroom checkup: A class wide teacher consultation model for increasing praise and decreasing disruptive behavior. *School Psychology Review*, *37*(3), 315–332.

Remesh, A. (2013). Microteaching: An efficient technique for learning effective teaching. *Journal of Research in Medical Science*, *18*(2), 158–163.

Rennie, J. (1993). *ESL and bilingual program models*. Washington, DC: Clearinghouse on Language and Linguistics. (ERIC Document Reproduction Service No. Ed 362–072).

Renzulli, J. (1985). *The schoolwide enrichment model*. Mansfield Centre, CT: Creative Learning Press.

Renzulli, J., S., & Reis, S. S. (1986). Systems and models for developing programs for the gifted and talented. In J. S. Renzulli, (Ed.) *The schoolwide enrichment model*. Mansfield Centre, CT: Creative Learning Press.

Research and Markets. (2019). Artificial intelligence market in the US education sector, 2018–2022. https://www.researchmarkets.com/reports/4613290/artificial-intellegence-market-in-the-us.

Research Points (2003). *Class size: Counting students can count*. Washington, DC: American Educational Research Association. www.aera.net/pubs/rp/RPFall03ClassSize-PDF2.pdf.

Rettig, P. (2017). *Reframing decision making in education: Democratic empowerment of teachers and parents*. Lanham, MD: Rowman & Littlefield.

Reynolds v. United States, 98 U.S. (8 Otto) 145 (1879).

Rice, P. L. (1998). *Stress and health* (3rd ed.). Belmont, CA: Cengage Learning.

Rice, R. E. (1992). Task analyzability, use of new media, and effectiveness: A multi-site exploration of media richness. *Organization Science*, *3*, 475–500.

Richardson, J. W. (2005). *The cost of being poor: Poverty, lead poisoning, and political implementation*. New York, NY: Praeger.

Richey, R. C. (2011). *The instructional design knowledge base: Theory, research, and practice*. New York, NY: Routledge.

Richman, L. S. (1988, June 6). Why throw money at asbestos? *Fortune*, 155–170.

Riggs, E., & Gholar, C. (2009). *Strategies that promote student engagement.: Unleashing the desire to learn* (2nd ed.). Thousand Oaks, CA: Corwin Press.

Ring v. Grand Forks School District No. 1, 483 F. Supp. 272 (N.D. 1980).

Rivera-McCutchen, R. L. (2021). *Radical care: Leading for justice in urban schools*. New York, NY: Teachers College Press.

Rivera v. East Otero School District R-1, 721 F. Supp. 1189 (D. Colo. 1989).

Roark v. South Iron R-1 School District, 573 F.3d 556 (8th Cir. 2009).

Robbins, S. P., & Judge, T. A. (2019). *Organizational behavior* (18th ed.). New York, NY: Pearson Prentice Hall.

Roberts, J. L., Inman, T. F., & Robins, J. H. (Eds.). (2018). *Introduction to gifted education*. Waco, TX: Prufrock Press.

Roberts, S. M., & Pruitt, E. Z. (2003). *Schools as professional learning communities*. Thousand Oaks, CA: Corwin Press.

Robins, J., Jolly, J. L., Karnes, F. A., & Bean, S. M. (Eds.). (2020). *Methods and materials for teaching the gifted* (5th ed.). Waco, TX: Prufrock Press.

Robins, K. N., Lindsey, R. B., Lindsey, D. B., & Terrell, R. D. (2012). *Culturally proficient instruction* (3rd ed.). Thousand Oaks, CA: Corwin Press.

Rock, M. (2019). *The e coaching continuum for educators: Using technology to enrich professional development and improve student outcomes*. Alexandria, VA: ASCD.

Rogers, C., & Farson, R. F. (n.d.). *Active listening*. Chicago, IL: Industrial Relations Center, University of Chicago.

Rogers, C. R. (1942). *Counseling and psychotherapy*. Boston, MA: Houghton Mifflin.

Rogers, C. R. (1961). *On becoming a person*. Boston, MA: Houghton Mifflin.

Rogers, C. R. (1983). Freedom to learn (2nd ed.). *Freedom to learn*. Columbus, OH: Merrill.

Rogers, C. R., & Freiberg, H. J. (1994). *Freedom to learn* (3rd ed.). New York, NY: Merrill.

Rogers, E. M., & Rogers, R. A. (1976). *Communication in organizations*. New York: Free Press.

Romanelli, E., & Tushman, M. L. (1994). Organizational transformation as punctuated equilibrium: An empirical test. *Academy of Management Journal, 37*(5), 1141–1166.

Roorda, D. L., Koomen, H. M. Y., Spilt, J. L., & Oort, F. J. (2011). The influence of affective teacher-student relationships on students' school engagement and achievement: A meta-analytic approach. *Review of Educational Research, 81*(4), 493–529.

Rosenberg v. Board of Education of City of New York, 92 N.Y.S.2d 344 (N.Y. 1949).

Rosenfeld, R. (2013). *Economics and youth violence: Crime, disadvantage, and community*. New York, NY: New York University Press.

Rosenshine, B. V. (1979). Content, time, and direct instruction. In P. L. Peterson & H. J. Walberg (Eds.), *Research on teaching: Concepts, findings, and implications* (pp. 28–56). Berkeley, CA: McCutchen.

Rosenshine, B. V., & Furst, N. F. (1971). Research in teacher performance criteria. In

Rosenshine, B. V., & Furst, N. F. (1973). The use of direct observation to study teaching. In R. M. Travers (Ed.). *Second handbook of research on teaching* (pp. 122–183). Chicago, IL: Rand McNally.

Rosenthal, R. (2002). The Pygmalion effect and its mediating mechanisms. In J. Aronson (Ed.), *Improving academic achievement* (pp. 26–36). San Diego, CA: Academic Press.

Rosnow, R. L., & Fine, G. A. (1976). *Rumor and gossip: The social psychology of hearsay*. New York: Elsevier.

Ross, D. D., Bondy, E., Gallingane, C., & Hambacher, E. (2008). Promoting academic engagement through insistence: Being a warm demander. *Childhood Education, 84*(3), 142–146.

Rothstein, Children with AIDS, 12 *Nova L. Rev.* 1259 (1988).

Rothstein, R. (2004). A wider lens on the black-white achievement gap. *Phi Delta Kappan, 86*(2), 104–110.

Rothstein, R. (2004). *Class and schools: Using social, economic, and educational reform to close the black-white achievement gap*. New York, NY: Teachers College Press.

Rowan, B. (1990). Commitment and control: Alternative strategies for the organizational design of school. *Review of Research in Education, 16*, 353–389.

Rowan, B. (1998). The task characteristics of teaching: Implications for the organizational design of schools. In R. Bernhardt, C. Hedley, G. Cattari, & V. Svolopoulos (Eds.), *Curriculum leadership: Rethinking schools for the 21st century* (pp. 37–54). Creskill, NJ: Hampton Press.

Rowan, B., Raudenbush, S. W., & Cheong, Y. E. (1993). Teaching as a nonroutine task: Implications for the management of schools. *Educational Administrative Quarterly, 29*, 479–499.

Rowan, R. (1986). *The intuitive manager*. New York, NY: Little, Brown, & Company.

Rowe, A. J., & Mason, R. O. (1987). *Managing with style: A guide to understanding, assessing, and improving decision making*. San Francisco, CA: Jossey-Bass.

Rubin, R., Baldwin, T., & Bommer, B. (2019). *Managing organizational behavior: What great leaders know and do*. New York, NY: McGraw-Hill.

Ruelas, B. (2011). *Psychology of intuition*. New York: Nova Science Publishers.

Ruggiero, V. R. (2012). *The art of thinking: A guide to critical and creative thought* (10th ed.). Boston, MA: Pearson.

Rupp, A. A., & Leighton, J. P. (2017). *The Wiley handbook of cognition and assessment: Frameworks, methodologies, and applications*. New York, NY: Wiley.

Rush, J. A. (1999). *Stress and emotional health: Applications of clinical anthropology*. Westport, CT: Greenwood.

Rusk v. Crestview Local School District, 379 F.3d 418 96th Cir. 2004).

Russell v. Men of Devon, 100 Eng. Rep. 359, 2 T.R. 667 (1788).

Russo, C. J. (2015). *The law of public education* (9th ed.). St. Paul, MN: West Academic Press.

Ryan, A. M., & Patrick, H. (2001). The classroom social environment and changes in adolescents' motivation and engagement during middle school. *American Educational Research Journal, 38*(2), 437–460.

S-1 v. Turlington, 635 F.2d 342 (5th Cir. 1981).

Sadler-Smith, E., & Shefy, E. (2004). The intuitive executive: Understanding and applying gut feel in decision making. *Academy of Management Executive, 18*(4), 76–91.

Salazar v. Eastin, 890 P.2d 43 (Cal. 1995).

Samples, F., & Aber, L. (1998). Evaluations of school-based violence prevention programs. In D. S. Elliott, B. A. Hamburg, and K. R. Williams (Eds.), *Violence in American schools*. New York: Cambridge University Press.

Santa Fe Independent School District v. Doe, 530 U.S. 290 (2000).

Saranow, J., & Ali, J. (2006, October). GPS: The next generation of navigation devices with new tools hits the market. *The Wall Street Journal*, p. D1.

Sarason, S. B. (1996). *Revisiting the culture of the school and the problem of change*. New York, NY: Teachers College Press.

Sarason, S. B. (2004). *And what do you mean by learning*? Portsmith, NH: Heinemann.

Sashkin, M., & Huddle, G. (1987). *A synthesis of job analysis research on the job of the school principal*. Washington, DC: Office of Educational Research and Improvement, US Department of Education.

Saunders, C. C., Robey, D., & Vavarek, K. A. (1994). The persistence of status differentials in computer conferencing. *Human Communications Research, 20*, 443–472.

Saylor, J. G., Alexander, W. M., & Lewis, A. J. (1981). *Curriculum planning for better teaching and learning*. New York, NY: Holt, Rinehart, & Winston.

Schadler, T. (2009). *The state of the workforce technology adoption: US benchmark*. http://www.forrester.com/rb/research/state_of_workforce_technology-adoption_us-benchmark/qid/55367/t/2.

Schaffer v. Weast, 546 U.S. 49 (2005).

Schargel, F. P. (2014). *Creating safe schools: A guide for school leaders, teachers, counselors, and parents*. New York, NY: Routledge.

Schein, E. H., & Schein, P. (2016). *Organizational culture and leadership* (5th ed.). New York, NY: Wiley.

Schein, E. H., & Schein, P. A. (2018). *Humble leadership: The power of relationships, openness, and trust*. Oakland, CA: Berrett-Kohler.

Scheiter, K., & Gerjets, P. (2007). Learner control in hypermedia environments. *Educational Psychology Review, 19*(3), 285–307.

Scherz, J. M., & Scherz, D. (2014). *Catastrophic school violence: A new approach to prevention*. Lanham, MD: Rowman & Littlefield.

Scheurich, J., & Skrla, L. (2003). *Leadership for equity and excellence: Creating high-achievement classrooms, schools, and districts*. Thousand Oaks, CA: Corwin Press.

Schiller, P., Clements, D., & Lara-Alecio, R. (2003). *Home connections resource guide*. New York, NY: McGraw-Hill.

Schilling, C. A., & Tomal, D. R. (2019). *School finance and business management: Optimizing fiscal, facility, and human resources* (2nd ed.). Lanham, MD: Rowman & Littlefield.

Schimmer, T. (2016). *Grading from the inside out: Bringing accuracy to student assessment through a standards-based mindset*. Indianapolis, IN: Solution Tree.

Schlechty, P. C. (2011). *Leading for learning: How to transform schools into learning organizations*. New York, NY: Wiley.

Schmidt, F. L., & Hunter, J. E. (1998). The validity and utility of selection methods in personnel psychology: Practical and theoretical implications of 85 years of research findings. *Psychological Bulletin, 124*(2), 262–274.

Schmidt, W. H., Burroughs, N. A., Zoido, P., & Houang, R. T. (2015). The role of schooling in perpetuating educational inequality: An international perspective. *Educational Researcher*, *44*(7), 371–386.

Schneider, K. (1993, March 24). Battling radon: Changing targets. *New York Times*, C19.

Schneider, M. K. (2016). *School choice: The end of public education?* New York, NY: Teachers College Press.

School Board of Nassau County, Fla. v. Arline, 480 U.S. 273 (1987).

School District of Abington Township v. Schempp, Murray v. Curlett, 374 U.S. 203 (1963).

School District of the City of Royal Oak v. Schulman, 243 N.W.2d 673 (Mich. 1976).

Schulz, P. J. (2011). *Communication Theory*. Thousand Oaks, CA: Sage.

Schumaker, M. (2018). *Focus: elevating the essentials to radically improve student learning* (2nd ed.). Alexandria, VA: ASCD.

Schunk, D. H., & Greene, J. A. (2018). *Handbook of self-regulation of learning and performance*. New York, NY: Routledge

Schwab, J. J., & Harper, W. R. (1970). *The practical language for curriculum*. Washington, DC: National Education Association.

Schwan v. Board of Education of Lansing School District, 183 N.W.2d 594 (Mich. Ct. App. 1970).

Sclafani, S. (2001). Using an aligned system to make real progress in Texas students. *Education and Urban Society*, *33*(3), 305–312.

Scoma v. Ill., 391 452 (N.D. Ill. 1974).

Scopes v. State, Tenn., 289 S.W. 363, 364 (Tenn. 1927).

Scott, R. W. (2007). *Organizations and organizing: Rational, natural, and open systems perspectives*. Upper Saddle River, NJ: Prentice Hall.

Seaward, B. (2011). *Managing stress: Principles and strategies for health and well-being*. Burlington, MA: Jones & Bartlett Learning.

Section 504 of the Rehabilitation Act of 1973 (29 U.S.C.A., § 794, a)

Sedlak, A. J., Mettenburg, J., Basena, M., Petta, I., McPherson, K., Greene, A., & Li, S. (2010). *Fourth national incidence study of child abuse and neglect (NIS-4): Report to Congress*. Washington, DC: US Department of Human Services, Administration for Children and Families.

Seif, E. (2021). *Teaching for lifelong learning: How to prepare students for a changing world*. Indianapolis, IN: Solution Tree Press.

Selfridge, J. (2004). The resolving conflict creativity program: How we know it works. *Theory into Practice*, *43*(1), 59–67.

Senge, P. (1990). *The fifth discipline: The art and practice of the learning organization*. New York, NY: Doubleday Currency.

Senge, P. (1996). Leading learning organizations. In F. Hesselbein, M. Goldsmith, & R. Beckhard (Eds.), *The leader of the future* (pp. 41–58). San Francisco, CA: Jossey-Bass.

Senge, P. (2006). *The fifth discipline: The art and practice of the learning organization* (rev. ed.). New York, NY: Currency/Doubleday.

Senge, P., Cambron-McCabe, N., Lucas, T., Smith, B., Dutton, J., & Kleine, A. (2012). *Schools that learn: A fifth discipline field book for educators, parents, and everyone who cares about education*. New York, NY: Doubleday/Currency.

Sergiovanni, T. J. (1992). *Moral leadership: Getting to the heart of school improvement*. San Francisco, CA: Jossey-Bass.

Sergiovanni, T. J., & Green, R. (2016). *The principalship: A reflective practice approach*. Boston, MA: Pearson.

Sergiovanni, T. J., & Starratt, R. J., & Cho, V. (2013). *Supervision: A redefinition* (9th ed.). New York, NY: McGraw-Hill.

Servage, L. (2008). Critical and transformative practices in professional learning communities. *Teacher Education Quarterly*, *35*(1), 63–77.

Seyforth, J. (2008). *Human resource leadership for effective schools*. Richmond, VA: Pearson.

Shadowitz, A. (2010). *The electromagnetic fields*. Mineola, NY: Dover Books.

Shafer v. Board. of Education of School District. of Pittsburgh, PA, 903 F.2d 2443 (3d Cir. 1990).

Shafritz, J. (2011). *Classics of organization theory*. Belmont, CA: Wadsworth/Cengage Learning.

Shani, A. B., Chandler, D., Coget, J. F., & Lau, J. B. (2014). *Behavior in organizations: An experiential approach* (10th ed.). New York, NY: McGraw-Hill.

Shanley v. Northeast Independent School District, 462 F.2d 960 (5th Cir. 1972).

Shapira, I., & Jackman, T. (2007, April 17). Gunman kills 32 at Virginia Tech in deadliest shooting in US history. *Washington Post*, A1.

Shapiro, B. B. (2014). Engaging novice teachers in semiotic inquiry: Considering the environmental messages of school learning settings. *Cultural Studies of Science Education, 9*(4), 809–824.

Shapiro, J. P., & Stefkovich, J. A. (2016). *Ethical leadership and decision making in education: Applying theoretical perspectives to complex dilemmas*. New York, NY: Routledge.

Sharan, Y., & Sharan, S. (1999). Group investigation in the cooperative classroom. In S. Sharan (Ed.), *Handbook of cooperative learning methods* (pp. 97–114). Westport, CT: Greenwood Press.

Sharp, W. L. (2012). *Winning in collective bargaining: Strategies everyone can live wit*h. Lanham, MD: Rowman & Littlefield.

Sharp, W. L., & Walter, J. K. (2003). *The principal as school manager* (2nd ed.). Lanham, MD: Scarecrow Press.

Shaw, P. (2006). *The four Vs of leadership: Vision, values, value added, and vitality*. New York, NY: Wiley.

Shea, T. M., & Bauer, A. M. (2011). *Behavior management: A practical approach for educators* (10th ed.). Boston, MA: Pearson.

Sheehan v. St. Peter's Catholic School, 291 Minn. 1, 188 N.W.2d 868 (1971).

Sheldon, K. M., & Bettencourt, B. A. (2002). Psychological need satisfaction and subjective well-being within social groups. *British Journal of Social Psychology, 41*(1), 25–38.

Sheppard, J.A. (1993). Productivity loss in performance groups: A motivational analysis. *Psychological Bulletin, 113*(1), 67–81.

Sherman Community Consolidated School District, 8 F.3d 1160 (7th Cir. 1993), cert. denied, 511 U.S. 536, 1110 (1994).

Sherman v. Community Consolidated School District 21 of Wheeling Township (1992).

Sherry, J. L. (2001). The effects of violent video games on aggression: A meta- analysis. *Human Communication Research, 27*(3), 409–431.

Shih, C. (2011). *The Facebook era: Tapping online social networks to market, sell, and innovate on the Web*. Upper Saddle River, NJ: Prentice Hall.

Shinn, S. (2008). Leadership in the round. *BizEd, 7*(2), 32–38.

Shoemaker v. State of Arkansas, 343 Ark. 727 (2001).

Short, P. (2018). *Information Collect: The key to data-based decision making*. New York, NY: Routledge.

Shouse, R. C. (1996). Academic press and sense of community: Conflict and congruence in American high schools. *Research in Sociology of Education, 11*, 173–202.

Shulman, L. S. (2005). *The wisdom of practice: Essays on teaching, learning, and learning to teach*. New York, NY: Wiley.

Silver, H. F. (2007). *The strategic teacher: Selecting the right research-based strategy for every lesson*. Alexandria, VA: Association of Supervision and Curriculum Development.

Silver, H. F., & Perini, M. J. (2010). *The interactive lecture: How to engage students, build memory, and deepen comprehension*. Alexandria, VA: Association for Supervision and Curriculum Development.

Simon, H. A. (1982). *Models of bounded rationality*. Cambridge, MA: MIT Press.

Simon, H. A. (1997). *Models of bounded rationality: Empirically grounded economic reason.* Cambridge, MA: MIT Press.

Simon, H. A. (2009). *Economics, bounded rationality and the cognitive revolution.* Northampton, MA: Edward Elgar Publishing.

Simonsen, B., Fairbanks, S., Briesch, A., Meyers, D., & Sugai, G. (2008). Evidence-based practices in classroom management: Considerations for research to practice. *Education and Treatment of Children, 31*(3), 351–380.

Sims, R. R. (2002). *Managing organizational behavior.* Westport, CT: Quorum Books.

Sindelar, N. W. (2015). *Assessment powered teaching.* Thousand Oaks, CA: Corwin Press.

Singham, M. (2003). The achievement gap: Myth and reality. *Phi Delta Kappan, 84*(8), 586–591.

Sinofsky, S., & Iansiti, M. (2016). *One strategy: Organizing, planning, and decision making.* New York, NY: Wiley.

Sirin, S. R. (2005). Socioeconomic status and academic achievement: A meta-analytic review of research. *Review of Educational Research, 75*(3), 417–453.

Sizer, T. (1984). *Horace's compromise: The dilemma of the American high school.* Boston, MA: Houghton Mifflin.

Sizer, T. (1992). *Horace's school: Redesigning the American high school.* New York, NY: Houghton Mifflin.

Skiba, R., & Horner, R. H. (2010). *Race is not neutral: A national investigation of African American and Latino disproportionality in school discipline.* Washington, DC: US Department of Education, Office of Civil Rights.

Skinner, B. F. (1968). *The technology of teaching.* New York, NY: Appleton-Century-Crofts.

Skinner, B. F. (1974). *About behaviorism,* New York: Knopf.

Skinner, B. F. (1991). *The behavior of organisms.* Acton, MA: Copley.

Sklar, B., & Harris, F. J. (2019). *Digital communications: Fundamentals and applications.* Boston, MA: Pearson.

Sklare, G. B. (2014). *Brief counseling that works: A solution-focused approach for school counselors.* Thousand Oaks, CA: Corwin Press.

Skrla, L., & Scheurich, J. (2003). *Educational equity and accountability: Paradigms, policies, and politics.* New York, NY: Routledge.

Slavin, R. E. (2011). Instruction based on cooperative learning. In R. E. Mayer & P. A. Alexander (Eds.), *Handbook of research on learning and instruction* (pp. 344–360). New York, NY; Routledge.

Slavin, R. E., & Madden, N. A. (Eds.). (2001). *One million children: Success for all.* Mahwah, NJ: Erlbaum.

Sleeter, C. E. (2002). State curriculum standards and the shaping of student consciousness. *Social Justice, 29*(4), 8–25.

Sleeter, C. E., & Zavala, M. (2020). *Transformative ethnic studies in schools: Curriculum, pedagogy, and research.* New York, NY: Teachers College Press.

Sloan v. Lemon, 413 U.S. 825 (1973).

Smith, A., & Bondy, E. (2007). "No I Won't!" Understanding and responding to student defiance. *Childhood Education, 83*(3), 151–157.

Smith, B. O. (Ed.), *Research on teacher education.* Englewood Cliffs, NJ: Prentice Hall.

Smith, R. (2013). *Human Resources administration: A school-based perspective.* New York, NY: Taylor & Francis.

Smither, J. W., London, M., Reilly, R. R., & Millsap, R. E. (1995, Spring). An examination of an upward feedback program over time. *Personnel Psychology*, 1–34.

Smylie, M., Murphy, J., & Louis, K. S. (2016). Caring school leadership: A multidisciplinary, cross-occupational model. *American Journal of Education, 123*, 1–35.

Smylie, M., Murphy, J., & Louis, K. S. (2020a). *Caring school leadership.* Thousand Oaks, CA: Corwin Press.

Smylie, M., Murphy, J., & Louis, K. S. (2020b). *Stories of caring principals*. Thousand Oaks, CA: Corwin Press.

Sneed v. Greensboro City Board of Education, 264 S.E.2d 106 (N.C. 1980)

Snipes v. McAndrew, 313 S.E.2d 294 (S.C. 1984).

Snowman, J., & McCown, R. (2015). *Psychology applied to teaching* (14th ed.). Stamford, CT: Cengage Learning.

Snyder, K. J., Krieger, R., & McCormick, R. (1984). School improvement goal-setting: A collaborative model. *NASSP Bulletin, 68*, 60–65.

Somekh, B., & Zeichner, R. (2009). Action research for educational reform: Remodeling action research theories and practices in local contexts. *Educational Action Research, 17*(1), 5–21.

Sorenson, R. D., & Goldsmith, L. M. (2018). *The principal's guide to school budgeting* (3rd ed.). Thousand Oaks, CA: Sage.

Southeastern Community College v. Davis, 442 U.S. 397 (1979).

Spengler, J. D., Samet, J. M., & McCarthy, J. (2001). *Indoor air quality handbook*. New York, NY: McGraw-Hill.

Spielman, K. (2018). *The logic of intelligence analysis*. New York, NY: Routledge.

Spillane, J. P., & Lowenhaupt, R. (2019). *Navigating the principalship; Key insights for new and aspiring school leaders*. Alexandria, VA: ASCD.

Spiller, J., & Power, K. (2019). *Leading with intention: 8 areas for reflection and planning in your PLC*. Indianapolis, IN: Solution Tree Press.

Spitz, H. H. (1999). Beleaguered pygmalion: A history of the controversy over claims that teacher expectancy raises intelligence. *Intelligence, 27*(3), 199–234.

Stajkovic, A. D., & Luthans, F. (1997). A meta-analysis of the effects of organizational behavior modification on task performance, 1975–1995 *Academy of Management Journal, 40*, 1122–1149.

Stajkovic, A. D., Luthans, F. (2003). Behavioral management and task performance in organizations: Conceptual background, meta-analysis, and test of alternative models. *Personnel Psychology, 56*(1), 155–194.

Stark, A. (2001, August/September). Pizza Hut, Domino's, and the public schools. *Policy Review Online*, 108. http://www.policyreview.org/AUG01/stark.html.

Stark, E. M., Shaw, J. D., & Duffy, M. K. (2007). Preference for group work, winning orientation, and social loafing behavior in groups. *Group and Organization Management, 32*(6), 699–723.

Starratt, R. J. (2004). *Ethical leadership*. San Francisco, CA: Jossey-Bass.

State ex. rel. Andrews v. Webber, 8 N.E. 708 (Ind. 1886).

State ex. rel. Burpee v. Burton, 45 Wis. 150, 30 Am. Re. 706 (1878).

State ex. rel. Estes v. Egnor (W.Va. 1994).

State ex. rel. Massie v. Gahanna-Jefferson Public Schools Board of Education, 669 N.E.2d 839 (Ohio 1996).

State v. Anderson, 427 N.W.2d 316 (N.D. 1988), cert. denied, 488 U.S. 965 (1988).

State v. Consolidated School District, 281 S.W.2d511 (Mo. 1955).

State v. Lundquest, 278 A.2d 263 (Md. 1971).

State v. Massa, 231 A.2d 252 (N.J. Cnty Ct. 1967).

State v. Newstrom, 371 N.W.2d 525 (Minn. 1985).

State v. Project Principle, Inc., 724 5. W.2d 387 (Tex. 1987).

State v. Trucke, 410 N.W.2d 242 (1987)

State v. Rivera, 497 N.W.2d 878 (Iowa, 1990), reh'g denied (1993).

State Tax Commission v. Board of Education of Holton, 73 P.2d 49 (Kan. 1937).

Stefkovich, J. A. (2006). *Best interests of the students: Applying ethical constructs to legal cases in education*. Mahwah, NJ: Erlbaum.

Stefkovich, J., & Begley, P.T. (2007, Apr.). Ethical school leadership: Defining the best interests of students. *Educational Management Administration and Leadership*. https://doi.org/10.1177/1741143207075389.

Stephans, K., Karnes, F. A. (Eds.). (2015). *Introduction to curriculum design in gifted education*. Waco, TX: Prufrock Press.

Sternberg, R. J. (1985). *Beyond IQ: A triarchic theory of human intelligence*. New York, NY: Cambridge University Press.

Sternberg, R. J. (1994). Allowing for thinking styles. *Educational Leadership, 52*(3), 36–40.

Sternberg, R.J. (2013). *Thinking and problem solving: Handbook of perception and cognition*. New York, NY: Academic Press.

Sternberg, R.J. (2021). *Adaptive intelligence: Surviving in times of uncertainty*. New York, NY: Cambridge University Press.

Stephens v. Bongart, 189 A.131 (N.J. Juv. and Dom. Rel. Ct. (1937).

Sterrett, W. (2016). *Igniting teacher leadership*. Alexandria, VA: ASCD.

Stevenson, I., & Weiner, J. M. (2020). *The strategy playbook for educational leaders*. New York, NY: Routledge.

Stewart, G. L. (2006). A meta-analytic review of relationships between team design features and team performance. *Journal of Management, 32*(1), 29–54.

Stewart, M. A. (2017). *Understanding adolescent immigrants: Moving toward an extraordinary discourse for extraordinary youth*. Lanham, MD: Lexington Books/Rowman & Littlefield.

Stiggins, R. (2017). *The perfect assessment system*. Alexandria, VA: ASCD.

St. Mary's Honor Center v. Hicks, 509 U.S. 502 (1993).

Stobaugh v. Wallace, 757 F. Supp. 653 (W.D. Pa. 1999).

Stoll, L., Bolan, R., McMahon, A., Wallace, M., & Thomas, S. (2006). Professional learning communities: A review of the literature. *Journal of Educational Change, 7*(4), 221–258.

Stoll, L., & Louis, K. S. (2007). *Professional learning communities*. New York, NY: Open University.

Stone, R. (2010a). *More best practices for elementary school classrooms: What award-winning teachers do*. Thousand Oaks, CA: Corwin Press.

Stone, R. (2010b). *More best practices for middle school classrooms: What award-winning teachers do*. Thousand Oaks, CA: Corwin Press.

Stone, R. (2010c). *More best practices for high school classrooms: What award-winning teachers do*. Thousand Oaks, CA: Corwin Press.

Stone v. Graham, 599 S.W.2d 157 (1980).

Stoner, J. A. (1968). Risky and cautious shifts in group decisions: the influence of widely held values. *Journal of Experimental Social Psychology, 4*, 442–459.

Strauss, V. (2017, October 18). Why we still need to study the humanities in a STEM world. *Washington Post*.

Strike, K. A. (2007). *Ethical leadership in schools: Creating community in an environment of accountability*. Thousand Oaks, CA: Corwin Press.

Strike, K., Haller, E. J., & Soltis, J. F. (2005). *The ethics of school administration* (3rd ed.). New York, NY: Teachers College Press.

Stronge, J. H. (2018). *Qualities of effective teachers* (3rd ed.). Alexandria, VA: ASCD.

Stuart v. School District No. 1 of Village of Kalamazoo, 30 Mich. 69 (Mich. 1874).

Suárez-Orozco, C., & Suárez-Orozco, M. M. (2010). *Learning a new land: Immigrant students in American society*. Cambridge, MA: Harvard University Press.

Sullivan, S., & Glanz, J. (2013). *Supervision that improves teaching: Strategies and techniques* (4th ed.). Thousand Oaks, CA: Corwin Press.

Suskie, L. (2018). *Assessing student learning: A common sense guide* (3rd ed.). New York, NY: Wiley.

Sutton v. Cadillac Area Public Schools, 323 N.W.2d 582 (Mich. Ct. App. 1982).

Swaitkowski v. Board of Education of City of Buffalo, 36 A.D.2d 685 (N.Y. 1971).

Swanson v. Guthrie, 345 F.3d 239 (4th Cir. 2003).

Sweeney v. New Hampshire, 354 U.S. 234 (1957).

Sypnieski, K. H., & Ferlazzo, L. (2018). *The ELL teacher's toolbox: Hundreds of practical ideas to support your students*. San Francisco, CA: Jossey-Bass.

Syska v. Montgomery County Board of Education, 415 A.2d 301 (Md. Ct. Spec. App. Div.1980), cert. denied, 288 Md. 744 (Md. 1980, appeal dismissed, 450 U.S. 961 (1981).

Taba, H. (1962). *Curriculum development: Theory and practice*. New York, NY: Harcourt, Brace.

Taba, H. (1971). *Teacher's handbook for elementary social studies*. Reading, MA: Addison-Wesley.

Tahtah, A. (2021). *School violence, school safety: help keep schools safe*. Self-published.

Tam, A. C. F. (2015). The role of professional learning community in teacher change: A perspective from beliefs and practice. *Teachers and Teaching, 21*(1), 22–43.

Tannen, D. (1995, September/October). The power of talk: Who gets heard and why. *Harvard Business Review*, 138–148.

Tannen, D. (1998, February 2). How you speak shows where you rank. *Fortune*, 156.

Tannen, D. (2000, April). Proven strategies for gaining cooperation. *Manager's Edge*, 4.

Tannenbaum, R., & Schmidt, W. (1973). How to choose a leadership pattern. *Harvard Business Review, 51*, 162–180.

Taylor, H., Fieldman, G., & Altman, Y. (2008). E-mail at work: A cause for concern? The implications of the new communication technologies for health, wellbeing, and productivity at work. *Journal of Organizational Transformation and Change, 5*, 159–173.

Taylor, J. C., & Bowers, D. G. (1972). *Survey of organizations: A machine scored standardized questionnaire instrument*. Ann Arbor: Institute for Social Research, University of Michigan.

Teachers' Tenure Act Cases, 329 Pa. 214, 197 A. 344 (1938).

Teller, E. (2001). *Memoirs: A twentieth-century journey in science and politics*. Cambridge, MA: Perseus Press

Tenenbaum, H. R., & Ruck, M. D. (2007). Are teachers' expectations different for racial minority than for European American students? A meta-analysis. *Journal of Educational Psychology, 99*(2), 253–273.

ten Have, S., & ten Have, W. (2018). *The social psychology of change management*. New York, NY; Routledge.

Teranishi, R. T., Nguyen, B. M. D., Alcantar, C. M., & Curammeng, E. R. (2020). *Measuring race: Why disaggregating data matters for addressing educational inequality*. New York, NY: Teachers College Press.

Tesser, A., & Rosen, S. (1975). The reluctance to transmit bad news. In L. Berkowitz (Ed.). *Advances in experimental social psychology* (vol. 8, pp. 192–132). New York, NY: Academic Press.

Texas Department of Community Affairs v. Burdine, 450 U.S. 248 (1981).

Texas Education Agency (2018). *Texas school law bulletin*. Eagan, MN: West Law/ Thomson Reuters.

Texas Education Agency v. Leeper, 893 S.W.2d 432 (Tex. 1994).

Texas State plan for the education of limited English proficient students, ESC sec. 19, Austin, TX, Texas Education Agency, April, 2019.

Theobald, D. (2015). *Before and after school activities: Managing your before and after programs*. Atlanta, GA: Humanistics Learning.

Theobald, P. (2006). Urban and Rural Schools: Lingering Obstacles. *Phi Delta Kappan, 67*, 116–122.

Thomas, M., Barab, S., & Tuzun, H. (2009). Developing critical implementations of technology-rich innovations: A cross-case study of the implementation of Quest Atlantis. *Journal of Educational Computing Research, 41*(2), 125–153.

Thomas, W. P., & Collier, V. P. (1997). *School effectiveness for language minority students*. Washington, DC: National Clearinghouse for Bilingual Education.

Thomas, W. P., & Collier, V. P. (1999). Accelerated schooling for English language learners. *Educational Leadership, 56*(7), 46–49.

Thompson, L. (2003). Improving the creativity of organizational work groups. *Academy of Management Executive, 17*(1), 96–109.

Thompson, L. L. (2000). *Making the team.* Upper Saddle River, NJ: Prentice Hall.

Thompson, R. (2012). *Professional school counseling: Best practices for working in the schools* (3rd ed.). New York, NY: Routledge.

Thompson, V. (1961). *Modern organization.* New York: Knopf.

Thompson v. Waynesboro Area School District, 673 F. Supp. 1379 (M.D. Pa. 1987).

Thornton, G. C., Mueller-Hanson, R. A., & Rupp, D. E. (2017). *Developing organizational simulations: A guide for practitioners and researchers.* New York, NY: Routledge.

Timar, T. B., Maxwell-Jolly, J. (2012). *Narrowing the achievement gap: Perspectives and strategies for changing times.* Cambridge, MA: Harvard Education Press.

Tingstrom, D. H., Sterling-Turner, H. E., & Wilczynski, S. M. (2006). The good behavior game: 1969–2002. *Behavior Modification, 30*(2), 225–253.

Tinker v. Des Moines Independent Community School District, 393 U.S. 503 (1969).

Titus v. Lindberg, 49 N.J. 66, A.2d 65 (1967).

Tizard, J., Schofield, W.N., & Hewison, J. (1982). Collaboration between teachers and parents in assisting children's reading. *British Journal of Educational Psychology, 52,* 1–15.

Toch, T., & Rothman, R. (2008, January). *Rush to judgment: Teacher evaluation in public education.* Washington, DC: Education Sector Reports.

Toffler, A. (1984a). *Future shock.* New York, NY: Bantam.

Toffler, A. (1984b). *The third wave.* New York, NY: Bantam.

Tomal, D. R., & Schilling, C. A. (2018). *Human resource management: Optimizing organizational performance.* Lanham, MD: Rowman & Littlefield.

Tomlinson, C. A. (2002). Invitations to learn. *Educational Leadership, 60*(1), 6–10.

Tomlinson, C. A., & Murphy, M. (2015). *Leading for differentiation: Growing teachers who grow kids.* Alexandria, VA: ASCD.

Toogood, G. (2011). *The articulate executive: Look, act, and sound like a leader.* New York, NY: McGraw-Hill.

Torff, B. (2011). Teacher beliefs shape learning for students. *Phi Delta Kappan, 93*(3), 21–23.

Tough, P. (2012). *How children succeed: Grit, curiosity, and the hidden power of character.* New York, NY: Houghton Mifflin Harcourt.

Tourish, D. (2010). *Auditing organizational communication: A handbook of research, theory and practice.* New York: Routledge.

Towers Perrin HR Services. www.towersperrin.com/hrservices/global/default.htm.

Townsend, M. A. R., & Clarihew, A. (1989). Facilitating children's comprehension through the use of advance organizers. *Journal of Literacy Research, 21*(1), 15–35.

Tracy, B. (2004). *Time power.* New York, NY: AMACOM.

Tsang, E. W. (2004). Toward a scientific inquiry into superstitious decision-making. *Organization Studies, 25,* 923–946.

Tschannen-Moran, M., & Tschannen-Moran, B. (2020). *Evocative coaching: Transforming schools one conversation at a time* (2nd ed.). Thousand Oaks, CA: Corwin Press.

Tuckman, B. W. (1965). Development sequence in small groups. *Psychological Bulletin, 63*(6), 384–399.

Tuckman, B. W. (2008). *Learning and motivation strategies: Your guide to success.* Upper Saddle River, NJ: Prentice Hall.

Tuckman, B. W., & Jensen, M. A. (1977). Stages of small group development revisited. *Group & Organization Studies, 2*(3), 419–427.

Tudor v. Board of Education of Borough of Rutherford, 100 A.2d 857 (N.J. 1953)

Turner, L. H., & West, R. (2018). *An introduction to communication.* New York, NY: Cambridge University Press.

Turner v. Liverpool Central School District, 186 F. Supp.2d 187 (N.D.N.Y. 2002).

Tversky, A., & Kahneman, D. (1974). Judgment under certainty: Heuristics and Biases. *Science, 185,* 1124–1131.

Tyack, D., & Cuban, L. (1995). *Tinkering toward utopia: A century of public school reform*. Cambridge, MA: Harvard University Press.

Tyler, R. W. (1949). *Basic principles of curriculum and instruction*. Chicago, IL: University of Chicago Press.

Tziner, A. (1982). Differential effects of group cohesiveness types: A clarifying overview. *Social Behavior and Personality, 10*(2), 227–239.

Ubben, G., Hughes, L. W., & Norris, C. J. (2017). *The principal: Creative leadership for excellence in schools* (8th ed.). Boston, MA: Pearson.

Uhl-Bien, M., Schermerhorn, J. R., & Osborn, R. N. (2016). *Organizational behavior* (13th ed.). New York, NY: Wiley.

Ukpokodu, O. (2010). How a sustainable campus-wide diversity curriculum fosters academic success. *Multicultural Education, 17*(2), 27–36.

UNICEF (2019). *Disparities in primary education*. https://data.unicef.org.topic/education/primary-education/.

United States v. Dinwiddie, 76 F.3d 193 (8th Cir. 1996).

United States v. South Carolina, 445 F. Supp. 1094, *affirmed*, 434 U.S. 98 S. Ct. 756 (1978).

USA Today (2008, December 11). Students choke as EPA sighs, 10A.

US Agency for Toxic Substances (2010). *Lead poisoning in the nation's children: Academic and neurobehavioral problems in school*. Washington, DC: US Government Printing Office.

US Census Bureau (2015). *Population of the United States by age, sex, race, and Hispanic origin*. Washington, DC: Government Printing Office.

U.S. Census Bureau (2018). Quick facts United States. https://www.census.gov/quick facts/fact/table/US#.

US Constitution, Articles I, II, II, ratified 1789.

US Constitution, Article I, § 8, cl. 1.

US Constitution, Article I, § 8, cl. 3.

US Constitution, Article I, § 10.

US Department of Education (2000). *1998 Elementary and secondary school civil rights compliance report no. 614/221–8829*. Washington, DC: US Government Printing Office.

US Department of Education (2008). *The condition of education*. Washington, DC: US Government Printing Office.

US Department of Education (2014). *Condition of America's public school facilities, 2012–2013*. Washington, DC: US Department of Education.

US Department of Education (2015). *Teacher shortage areas (TSA) nationwide listing 1990–1916*. Washington, DC: US Government Printing Office.

US Department of Education, National Center for Education Statistics (2018). *Teacher Shortage Areas (TSA) Nationwide Listing 1990–2019*. Washington, DC: US Government Printing Office.

US Department of Homeland Security (2015, September) *2014 yearbook of immigration statistics* Washington, DC: US Department of Homeland Security, Office of Immigration Statistics. http://dhs.gov/yearbook-immigration-statistics.

US Department of Labor, Bureau of Labor Statistics (2022). *Handbook for job analysis*. Washington, DC: US Government Printing Office.

US Environmental Protection Agency (2010a). *The cost of asbestos removal in the nation's schools*. Washington, DC: US Government Printing Office.

US Environmental Protection Agency (2010b). High levels of radon gas found in 54% of 130 randomly selected public schools. http://www.epa.gov/radon/pubs/physic .html#HealthRisk.

US Environmental Protection Agency (2010c). *High levels of radon gas found in randomly selected public schools*. Washington, DC: U.S. Government Printing Office. http://www.epa.gov/ne/children/pgfs/healthy-schools.pdf.

US Government Accountability Office (2013a). *Auditing and financial management.* Memphis, TN: General Books, LLC.

US Government Accountability Office (2013b). *School finance: State and federal efforts to target poor students.* Memphis, TN: General Books LLC.

US Office of Civil Rights, US Department of Education (2016). *Corporal punishment in US public schools: Social policy report,* vol. 30, nos. 1, 2. Washington, DC: Office of Civil Rights, US Department of Education.

Valcik, N. A. (2017). *Strategic planning and decision making for public and non-profit organizations.* New York, NY: Routledge.

Van Aken, J., & Berends, H. (2018). Problem solving in organizations. New York, NY: Cambridge University Press.

Van Bladel, J. G. (2007). *Electromagnetic fields* (2nd ed.). New York, NY: Wiley.

Van der Molen, H. T., & Gramsbergen-Hoogland, Y. (2018). *Communication in organizations: Basic skills and conversation.* New York, NY: Routledge.

Van Klaveren, C. (2011). Lecturing style teaching and student performance. *Economics of Education Review, 30*(4), 729–739.

Van Soelen, T. M. (2021). *Meeting goals: Protocols for leading effective, purpose-driven discussions in schools.* Indianapolis, IN: Solution Tree Press.

Vandevender v. Cassell, 208 S.E2d 436 (W. Va. 1974).

Vandiver v. Hardin, 925 F.2d 927 (6th Cir. 1991).

Vandrell v. School District No. 26c Malheur County, 233 Ore. 1, 376 P.2d 406 (1962).

VanTassel-Baska, J., & Little, C.A. (2017). *Content-based curriculum for high-ability learners* (3rd ed.). Waco, TX: Prufrock Press.

Vatteratt, C. (2015). *Rethinking grading: Meaningful assessment for standards-based learning.* Alexandria, VA: ASCD.

Vernonia School district 47 v. Acton, 515 U.S. 646 (1995).

Vescio, V., Ross, D., Adams, A. (2008). A review of research on the impact of professional learning communities on teaching practice and student learning. *Teaching and Teacher Education, 24,* 80–91.

Vespa, J., Armstrong, D. M., & Medina, L. (2018). *Demographic turning points for United States: Population projections for 2020 to 2060, current population reports* (P25–1144). Washington, DC: US Census Bureau. https://www.census.gov/content/dam/Census/library/publications/2018/demo/P25_1144.pdf.

Victory Through Jesus Sports Ministry Foundation v. Lee's Summit R-7 School District, 640 F.3d 329 (8th Cir. 2011).

Virgil v. School Board, 862 F.2d 1517 (11th Cir. 1989).

Von Krogh, G., Ichijo, K., & Nonaka, I. (2000). *Enabling knowledge creation: How to unlock the mystery of tacit knowledge and release the power of innovation.* New York, NY: Oxford University Press.

Vorchheimer v. School District of Philadelphia, 532 F.2d 880 (3 Cir. 1976, aff 430 U.S. 703 (1977).

Vroom, V. H. (1994). *Work and motivation.* San Francisco, CA: Jossey-Bass.

Vroom, V., Yetton, P., & Yago, A. (1998). *The new leadership: managing participation in organizations.* Englewood Cliffs, NJ: Pearson/Prentice Hall.

Vygotsky, L. S. (1986 [1934]). *Thought and language* (trans. A. Kozulin). Cambridge, MA: MIT Press.

Wagner, P. A., & Simpson, D. J. (2009). *Ethical decision making in school administration: Leadership as moral architecture.* Thousand Oaks, CA: SAGE Publications.

Wake Cares v. Wake County Board of Education, 675 S.E.2d 345 (N.C. 2009).

Walberg, H. J. (2011). *Advancing youth accomplishments and learning.* Stanford, CA: Hoover Institution Press.

Wald, P. J., & Castleberry, M. S. (2000). *Educators as learners: Creating a professional learning community in your school.* Alexandria, VA: Association for Supervision and Curriculum Development.

Walker, R. (2019). Culturally relevant pedagogy, identity, presence, and intentionality: A brief review of the literature. *Journal of Research Initiatives, 4*(3), 1–13.

Wallace, J. C., Edwards, B. D., Arnold, T., Frazier, M. L., & Finch, D. M. (2009). Work stressors, role-based performance, and moderating influence of organizational support. *Journal of Applied Psychology, 94*(1), 254–262

Wallace, J. D., & Becker, D. (2018). *The handbook of communication training: A framework for assessing and developing competence*. New York, NY: Routledge.

Wallace v. Jaffree, 472 U.S. 38 (1985).

Wallas, G. (1926). *The art of thought*. New York, NY: Harcourt Brace.

Walters, S. B. (2011). *Principles of kinesic interview and interrogation*. Boca Raton, FL: CRC Press.

Walters, S. B. (2019). *Principles of kinesic interview and interrogation*. New York, NY: Taylor & Francis.

Walz v. Egg Harbor Township Board of Education, 342 F.3d 271 (3d Cir. 2003).

Wang, K., Chen, Y., Zhang, J., & Oudekerk, B. A. (2020). *Indicators of school crime and safety: 2019* (NCES 2020–063/NCJ 254484). National Center for Education Statistics, US Department of Education, and Bureau of Justice Statistics, Office of Justice Programs, US Department of Justice, Washington, DC. http://nces.ed.govorhttps:bjs.gov.

Wangsness, R. K. (1986). *Electromagnetic fields* (2nd ed.). New York, NY: Wiley.

Wang, T. (2019, May 21). United States educational building construction costs by select city 2018. *Statista*. https://www.stastista.com/statistics/830447/construction-costs-of-educational-buildings-in-us-cities/.

Wang, T (2020, February 4). United States projected value of new construction 2018–2023. *Statista*. https://www.statista.co/statistics/961990/projected-value-of-total-usoffice-construction/.

Wankel, C., Wankel, L. A. (2016). *Integrating curricular and co-curricular endeavors to enhance student outcomes*. Emerald Group Publishing.

Washagesic v. Bloomingdale Public Schools, 33 F.3d 697 (6th Cir. 1994).

Wasley, P, Hampel, R., & Clark, R. (1996). *The puzzle of the whole school change*. Providence, RI: Coalition of Essential Schools, Brown University.

Watson v. City of Cambridge, 32 N.E. 864 (Mass. 1893).

Weatherspoon, F. D. (2018). *Equal employment opportunity and affirmative action*. New York, NY: Routledge.

Weber, M. (1947). *The theory of social and economic organization* (trans. T. Parsons). New York, NY: Oxford University Press.

Webster v. New Lenox School District No. 122, 917 F.2d 1004 (7th Cir. 1990).

Weick, K. E. (1976). Educational organizations as loosely coupled systems. *Administrative Science Quarterly, 21*, 1–19.

Weiner, I. B., & Greene, R. L. (2017). *Handbook of personality assessment*. New York, NY: Wiley.

Weisberg, D., Sexton, S., Mulhern, J., & Keeling, D. (2009). The widget effect: Our national failure to acknowledge and act on differences in teacher effectiveness. Brooklyn, NY: The New Teacher Project.

Weisberg, R. W. (1999). Creativity and knowledge: A challenge to theories. In R. J. Sternberg (Ed.), *Handbook of creativity* (pp. 226–250). New York, NY: Cambridge University Press.

Weinstein, C. S., Romano, M. E., & Mignano, A. J. (2011). Elementary classroom management: Lessons from research and practice (5th ed.). New York, NY: McGraw-Hill.

Welling v. Board of Education of Livonia School District, 171 N.W.2d 545 (Mich. 1969).

Wellman, C. (2019). *The proliferation of rights: Moral progress or empty rhetoric*? New York, NY: Routledge.

Wentzel, K. R., (2010). Students' relationships with teachers. In J. L. Meece & J. S. Eccles (Eds.). *Handbook of research on schools, schooling, and human development* (pp. 75–91). New York, NY: Routledge.

Wesson, M. J., LePine, T. A., & Colquitt, J. (2016). *Organizational behavior: Improving performance and behavior in the workplace* (5th ed.). New York, NY: McGraw-Hill.

West, B. J., Patera, J. L., & Carsten, M. K. (2009). Team level positivity: Investigating positive psychological capacities and team level outcomes. *Journal of Organizational Behavior, 30*(2), 249–267.

West, P. E., Lunenburg, F. C., & Hines, M. T. (2014). Teacher quality variables and efficacy for teaching minority students. *Education Leadership Review of Doctoral Research, 1*(1), 40–58.

Westfield High School L.F.F.E. Club v. City of Westfield, 249 F. Supp. 2d 98 (D. Mass. 2003).

Westley, K. E. (2011). *Teacher quality and student achievement.* New York, NY: Nova Science Publishers.

Whalen v. Minnesota special school District, 2445 N.W.2d 440 (Minn. 1976).

Wheatley, M. J. (1994). *Leadership and the new science.* San Francisco, CA: Barrett-Koehler Publishers.

Wheeler v. Barrera, 417 U.S. 402 (1974), *modified,* 422 U.S. 1004 (1975).

White v. South Park Independent School District, 693 F.2d 1163 (5th Cir. 1983).

White, R., Algozzine, B., Audette, R., Marr, M. B., & Ellis, E. D. (2001). Unified discipline: A schoolwide approach for managing problem behavior. *Intervention in School and Clinic, 37*(1), 3–8.

Widmar v. Vincent, 454 U.S. 263 (1981).

Wigg v. Sioux Falls School District 49–5, 382 F.2d 807 (8th Cir. 2004), reh'g and reh'g en blanc denied (2004).

Wiggan, G. (2007). Race, school achievement, and educational inequality: Toward a student-based inquiry perspective. *Review of Educational Research, 77*(3), 310–333.

Wiggins, G., & McTighe, T. (2008). *Schooling by design: Mission, action, and achievement.* Alexandria, VA: Association for Supervision and Curriculum Development.

Wilen, W. W. (Ed.). (1987). *Questions, questioning techniques, and effective teaching.* Washington, DC: National Education Association.

Wilk, S. L., & Cappelli, P. (2003). Understanding the determinants of employer use of selection methods. *Personnel Psychology, 56*, 111–118.

Williams, K., Harkins, S., & Latane, B. (1981). Identifiability as a deterrent to social loafing: Two cheering experiments. *Journal of Personality and Social Psychology, 40*(2), 303–311.

Williams, K. J. (2018). *School, family, and community partnerships*: 4th ed.). Thousand Oaks, CA: Corwin Press.

Williams v. Austin Independent School District, 796 F. Supp. 251 (W.D. 1992).

Williams v. Board of education of County of Kanawha, 388 F. Supp. 93 (S.D. W.Va. 1975), aff"d, 530 F.2d 972 (4th Cir. 1975).

Williamson, C., & Williams, L. (2018). *Master the art of interview success with hundreds of typical questions and answers.* London, GBR: Kogan Page.

Williamson, R., & Blackburn, B. R. (2016). *The principalship from a to z* (2nd ed.). New York, NY: Routledge.

Willis, J. (2021). *Thinking protocols for learning.* Indianapolis, IN: Solution Tree Press.

Wilson, C. E. (2007). Brainstorming pitfalls and best practices. *Interactions, 8*(5), 50–53.

Windschitl, M. (2002). Framing constructivism in practice as the negotiation of dilemmas: An analysis of the conceptual, pedagogical, cultural, and political challenges facing teachers. *Review of Educational Research, 72*, 131–175.

Winston, S., & Parekh, G. (2019). *Critical perspectives on education policy and schools, families, and communities.* Charlotte, NC: Information Age Publishing.

Winter, M. (2001a). The brain on lead: Animal models are helping researchers understand the effects of lead exposure in children. *Human Ecology, 29*(4), 1- 17.

Winter, M. (2001b). Heavy metal: It doesn't take as much lead as the center for Disease Control thought to lower a child's IQ. *Human Ecology, 29*(4), 18–33.

Wisconsin v. Yoder, 406 U.S. 205 (1972).

Wolman v. Walter, 433 U.S. 229 (1977).

Wood v. Strickland, 420 U.S. 308 (1975).

Woodman, R. W., Sawyer, J. E., & Griffin, R. W. (1993). Toward a theory of organizational creativity. *Academy of Management Review*, *18*(1), 293–321.

Woodward, N. H. (2006, December). Doing town hall meetings better. *HR Magazine*, 70.

Woolfolk, A. E. (2019). *Educational psychology* (14th ed.). Boston, MA: Pearson.

Woolfolk, A. H., & Weinstein, C. S. (2006). Student and teacher perspectives on classroom management. In C. M. Evertson & C. S. Weinstein (Eds.), *Handbook of classroom management: Research, practice, and contemporary issues* (pp. 181–219). Mahwah, NJ: Lawrence Erlbaum.

Wootton, S., & Horne, T. (2021). *Strategic thinking: A step-by-step approach to strategy and leadership* (3rd ed.). London, UK: Kogan Page.

Workman v. Mingo County Board of Education, 419 Fed. Appx. 348 (4th Cir. 2011).

World Food Programmes (2019). *2019—The state of food security and nutrition in the world (SOFI): Safeguarding against economic slowdowns and downturns*. https://www.wfp.org/.

World Health Organization (2019). *Children: Reducing mortality*. World Health Organization Web site. https://www.Who.int/news-room/fact-sheets/detail/children-reducing-mortality.

World Health Organization (2019). *Drinking-water*. World Health Organization Web site. https://www.who.int/news-room/factsheets/detail/drinking-water.

World History Encyclopedia. (2004). "Conflict of interest." http://www.worldhistory.com/wiki/c/conflict-of-interest.htm.

Wormeli, R. (2018). *Fair isn't always equal: Assessing and grading in the differentiated classroom*. Stenhouse.

Worren, N. (2018). *Organization design: Simplifying complex systems* (2nd ed.). New York, NY: Routledge.

Wright v. Houston Independent School District, 146 F.2d 137 (5th Cir. 1973).

Wright ex. rel. A.W. Pulaski County Special School District, 803 F. Supp. 2d 980 (E.D. Ark. 2011).

Wyckoff, W. L. (2015). The effect of stimulus variation on learning. *Journal of Experimental Education*, *41*(3), 85–90.

Yank, J. L. (2006). The power of number 4.6. *Fortune*, *153*(11), 122.

Yeh, S. S. (2001). Tests worth teaching to: Constructing state mandated tests that emphasize critical thinking. *Educational Researcher*, *30*, 12–17.

Yeh, S. S. (2006). *Raising student achievement through test reform*. New York, NY: Teachers College Press.

Young, K. S. (2008). *Communicating nonverbally: A practical guide to presenting yourself more effectively*. Long Grove, IL: Waveland Press.

Yu, M-C. (2009). Employees' perception of organizational change: The mediating effects of stress management strategies. *Public Personnel Management*, *38*(1), 121–132.

Yukl, G. (2019). *Leadership in organizations* (9th ed.). Boston, MA: Pearson.

Zacarian, D., & Silverstone, M. (2020). *Teaching to empower: Taking action to foster student agency, self-confidence, and collaboration*. Alexandria, VA: ASCD.

Zander, A. (1982). *Making groups effective*. San Francisco, CA: Jossey-Bass.

Zeer, D. (2004). *Office feng shui: Creating harmony in your work space*. San Francisco, CA: Chronicle Books.

Zeidner, R. (2007, July). Keeping e-mail in check. *HR Magazine*, 4.

Zepeda, S. J. (2004). *Instructional leadership for school improvement*. Larchmont, NY: Eye of Education.

Zepeda, S. J. (2013). *The principal as instructional leader: A handbook for supervisors* (3rd ed.). New York, NY; Routledge.

Zepeda, S. J. (2015). *Job-embedded professional development: Support, collaboration, and learning in schools*. New York, NY: Routledge.

Zepeda, S. J. (2016). *The leader's guide to working with underperforming teachers: Overcoming marginal teaching and getting results*. New York, NY: Routledge.

Zepeda, S. J. (2017). *Instructional supervision: Applying tools and concepts* (4th ed.). New York, NY: Routledge.

Zepeda, S. J. (2018). *The job-embedded nature of coaching: Lessons and insights for school leaders at all levels*. Lanham, MD: Rowman & Littlefield.

Zepeda, S. J. (2019). *Professional development: What works* (2nd ed.). New York, NY: Routledge.

Zepeda, S. J., Goff, L. R., & Steele, S. W. (2019). *C.R.A.F.T. conversations for teacher growth: How to build bridges to cultivate expertise*. Alexandria, VA: ASCD.

Zhang, L., & Sternberg, R. J. (2006). *The nature of intellectual styles*. Mahwah, NJ: Erlbaum.

Zhang, Y. (2004). *Indoor air quality engineering*. Boca Raton, FL: CRC Press.

Zhao, Y., & Qiu, W. (2009). How good are the Asians? Refuting four myths about Asian-American academic achievement. *Phi Delta Kappan, 990*(5), 338–344.

Zhao, Y., Emler, T. E., Snethen, A., & Yin, D. (2020). *An education crisis is a terrible thing to waste: How radical changes can spark student excitement and success*. New York, NY: Teachers College Press.

Zielinski, A. E., & Hoy, W. K. (1983). Isolation and alienation in elementary schools. *Educational Administration Quarterly, 19*, 27–45.

Zimmerman, B. J., & Kitsantas, A. (2005). The hidden dimension of personal competence: Self-regulated learning and practice. In A. J. Elliott & C. S. Dweck (Eds.), *Handbook of competence and motivation* (pp. 509–526). New York, NY: Guilford Press.

Zobrest v. Catalina Foothills School District, 509 U.S. 1 (1993).

Zopounidis, C. (2011). *Multiple criteria decision aiding* (New York, NY: Nova Science Publishers.

Zorach v. Clauson, 343 U.S. 306 (1952).

Zucht v. King, 260 U.S. 174 (1922).

Name Index

■ ■ ■

Subject Index

■ ■ ■

Italicized page references indicate illustrations.

oral, employment assessments of, *449*
as organizing skill, 224
with parents/families, 170–72, 473–74
persuasive, 333–34
process of, 298–300
process problems in, as source of change, 342
public relations, 475–83, *479–80*
of strategic plans, 363
teacher-parent, 473
training for, 305
for violence prevention, 430
vision articulation, 38
See also communication flow; networks and networking
communication flow
downward, 304–6, *305*
grapevine, 311–12
horizontal, *305*, 309–11
rumors, 312–14
upward, *305*, 306–9
See also networks and networking
Community Consolidated Sch. Dist. 21, Sherman v., 568
community involvement, 468–69
community relations
curriculum development and, 87
family involvement, 471–72
field-based activities addressing, 484
goal setting, 45
natural disaster response, 469–70
overview, 467
principals' roles within, 467–68
public relations, 475–83, *479–80*
services as expenditure, 385
violence and, 413
violence prevention partnerships, 413, 414, 426
volunteerism and coordinated services, 468–69
community schools, 469
comparative negligence, 594
compensatory justice, 498
competent parties, 585
competitions, 185
competitiveness, 303, 311, 312, 369
complaining, 303
complexity (specialization), 233–34, 235, *235*
compotential intelligence, 186
comprehensive partnerships, 471
Comprehensive technical package for the prevention of youth violence and associated risk behaviors, A (David-Ferdon, Vivola-Kantor, Marshal, Rainford and Hall, J. E.), 438
compromise modeling, 432

computers, 70–71, 319–24, 404
conceptual decision-making style, 263–64
conceptual skills, *226*, 226–27, 263–64, 452
concrete operational stage, 115–16
concurrent enrollment, *185*
conditioning, 328
confidence, 286
conflict resolution, 427, 432, 506
conflicts of interest, 499–500
conformity, 274, 282–83, 297
Connecticut, Cantwell v., 547, 556, 558
Connell, Hartzell v., 563
Connelly v. Sch. Comm., 551
conscience orientation, 117
consequences, behavioral, *356, 357*. *See also* student discipline
consideration, as contract principle, 585
consistency, 96
consolidated principal power, 534
constituentive dimension, 528
construction, new school, 396–98
content
as curriculum component, 58
educational objectives relationship to, 65–66
learning experiences balanced with, 61–62
of moral knowledge, 74
selection criteria, 58–59
technology and, 71
content, input, process, and product (CIPP) evaluations, 206
Content-Based ESL Programs, 198
contents of thinking, *113*, 113–15
contextual intelligence, 186
contextual rationality, 259
contingencies of reinforcement, 357–58
continuous improvement, 5–6
Contract Activity Packages (CAPS), 120
contracts, teaching, 145, 221, 309, 344–45, 458–64, 584–85
contractual-legalistic orientations, 117
contributory negligence, 594
conventional thinking, 269–70
convergent thinking, 113, *113*, 114
convocations, *185*
cooks, 309
cooperation, 174, 303, 311
co-optation, 346
coordination, 296, 309–10
copy machines, 402, 404
corporal punishment, 573–74
Corporate Cultures (Deal and Kennedy, A.), 13
corrective feedback, 332
cost, as organization variable, 234, 235, *235*, 236

as gifted education service, *185*
for interviewee training, 445
as professional development method, 133,
136, 151
Wright, Ingraham v., 574, 595
written communication
barriers of, 327
as communication type, 299, 320
e-mails, 226, 319–21, *325*, 411, 412
employment assessments of, *449*
instant messaging, 321, *325*
numerical documents, 325, *325*
readibility suggestions, 299–300

Y
yearbooks, 173, 551
Y networks, 315, *315*
Yoder, Wisconsin v., 555
Youth Risk Behavior Survey, 409

Z
zero-based budgeting (ZBB), 390–91
zero-tolerance policies, 41, 221, 414–16, 429
zipper clauses, 460
Zobrest v. Catalina Foothills School District,
560, 579
Zorach v. Clauson, 558

About the Authors

■ ■ ■

Frederick C. Lunenburg is Jimmy N. Merchant Professor of Education at Sam Houston State University. Previously, he was on the faculty of educational administration at the University of Louisville, Loyola University Chicago, and Southern Utah University, where he also served as Dean of the College of Education. In addition, he has held public school positions as high school English teacher and reading specialist, high school principal, and superintendent of schools. Dr. Lunenburg's scholarship includes forty-eight books, twenty-three book chapters, and more than two hundred articles published in both practitioner and academic/research journals.

Beverly J. Irby is Associate Dean for Academic Affairs, Regents Professor, and Marilyn Kent Byrne Endowed Chair for Student Success at Texas A&M University, College Station, Texas. In addition, she serves as Director of the Educational Leadership Research Center at Texas A&M University. She is editor of the following research journals: *Mentoring and Tutoring*, *Advancing Women in Leadership*, *Dual Language and Practice*, and *Education Policy Briefs*. She is Principal Investigator: SEED Grant (APLUS) and OELA Grants (PAL and MOOPIL). Dr. Irby has written numerous books, research reports, and articles, many of which have been presented at regional, national, and international meetings.